D0915926

Roosevelt and the Isolationists

Roosevelt
& the
Isolationists

1932-45

Wayne S. Cole

University of Nebraska Press
Lincoln and London

Publication of this book was aided by a grant
from the Andrew W. Mellon Foundation.

The paper in this book meets the guidelines for
permanence and durability of the Committee on
Production Guidelines for Book Longevity of the
Council on Library Resources.

Library of Congress Cataloging in Publication Data

Cole, Wayne S.
Roosevelt and the Isolationists, 1932-45

Bibliography: p.
Includes index
1. United States - Foreign relations—1933-1945.
2. United States - Neutrality.   3. Roosevelt,
Franklin D. (Franklin Delano), 1882-1945.   I. Title.
E806.C594 1983   327.73   82-8624
ISBN 0-8032-1410-3   AACR2

They were my students;
they became my teachers;
they are my friends:

Joan M. Lee
Jolyon P. Girard
Charles J. Errico
J. Samuel Walker
Edward C. Mishler
Steven M. Mark
Stephen J. Sniegoski
David R. Kepley

Contents

Preface

For more than 140 years after the Declaration of Independence in 1776, no United States military forces fought in Europe. Similarly, for nearly a century and one-half after its alliance with France ended at the beginning of the nineteenth century, the United States avoided what Thomas Jefferson called "entangling alliances." The terms "isolationism" and "isolationist" did not gain wide acceptance until the twentieth century, and even then they were largely pejorative labels used by critics to discredit the policies and their spokesmen. Nonetheless, isolationism—that is, nonintervention in Europe and unilateralism—prevailed in the conduct of American foreign affairs. It won nearly universal support from the American people and their leaders, whatever their political affiliations. The United States expanded across the North American continent and built an overseas empire in the Caribbean and the Pacific without departing from those traditional policies. It waged the War of 1812, the Mexican War, and the Spanish-American War all without entering alliances and without sending troops to fight in Europe. Even in World War I the United States fought as an associate power rather than as a full ally. And when that war ended, the United States rejected membership in the League of Nations.

All that changed during the middle decades of the twentieth century. American armed forces played massive roles in helping defeat Fascist Italy, Nazi Germany, and militarist Japan in World War II. The United States has maintained a continuous military presence in Europe from that time until this. It helped form the United Nations after World War II and has been a leading member throughout the history of that world organization. Through the North Atlantic Treaty Organization, the Organization of American States, and various bilateral and multilateral pacts, the United States has maintained military alliances with dozens of countries all over the world.

That shift from traditional isolationism to massive multilateral involvement in world affairs constituted a major watershed in the history of American foreign policies. Countless individuals and developments, at home and abroad, played roles in accomplishing that shift. But key changes occurred while President Franklin D. Roosevelt led and directed American policies at home and abroad: he orchestrated the transition. One can gain understanding of that tremendously important transition by examining Roosevelt's policies and actions toward isolationists from the time of his election to the presidency in 1932 until his death in 1945 near the close of World War II and by studying the attitudes and actions of isolationists toward Roosevelt, his administration, and his policies. Those are the subjects of this book. It is a colorful, exciting, and controversial story. Its consequences have affected the lives of hundreds of millions of people in the United States and all over the world; they will continue to affect many millions in the foreseeable future.

This subject has become very nearly a lifetime project for me and has provided its full measure of intellectual and professional challenge and adventure. Though I was never an active participant in the events I describe, I was a school boy, a young college student, and an Army Air Force flight instructor during the years covered by this book. I took my first research notes on the isolationists and on Roosevelt in June, 1947, when I began graduate studies under the direction of Professor Fred Harvey Harrington at the University of Wisconsin. That was slightly more than two years after the death of Roosevelt.

During the next thirty years I traveled many thousands of miles to research manuscripts and records in libraries and archives scattered all over the United States and abroad—from California to Connecticut; from North Dakota to North Carolina; from the Franklin D. Roosevelt Library in Hyde Park, New York, to the Herbert Hoover Presidential Library in West Branch, Iowa; from the National Archives, the Library of Congress, and the Federal Bureau of Investigation in Washington, D.C., to state historical societies in Wisconsin, Minnesota, and Kansas; to many places in between; from New York City to the Public Record Office in London, England. Altogether I researched more than one hundred manuscript and archival collections. Most of the leading participants in the story are no longer living. While they lived, however, I benefited from opportunities to interview and visit informally with many of them. And I corresponded with others involved in the story.

Along the way, I wrote books on America First, Gerald P. Nye, and Charles A. Lindbergh, and articles on Key Pittman and Henrik Shipstead. Those publications were, in effect, preludes to or byproducts of my much larger project on Roosevelt and the isolationists. It has been by far the largest, most complex, most difficult, and (I believe) the most important scholarly project I have ever undertaken.

I have based this book largely on primary sources—manuscript, printed, and oral. Over the years I have tried to keep up with the burgeoning published scholarly work produced by research historians. For the convenience of readers I have cited many of the more valuable of those secondary accounts in the notes. I have also drawn at times, in revised forms, from my earlier publications when it seemed to me that I had already treated aspects of the subject as well as I could. For the most part, however, I have done this book from scratch, basing it on my reading and understanding of the original primary materials. In most cases I did my research in the original manuscripts. Many of those manuscripts have since been printed in published volumes. When those published versions were accurate, I have generally cited the published form rather than the original manuscripts, to make it easier for readers to check my citations.

A grant from the University of Wisconsin made possible my research in the America First papers. A summer grant from the American Philosophical Society in 1958 enabled me to begin my research in Roosevelt Library. A summer grant from the Social Science Research Council supported my research on Senator Nye. Summer grants from the General Research Board of the University of Maryland enabled me to press ahead with my research on Roosevelt and the isolationists, as did a sabbatical leave in 1971. And a sabbatical leave from the University of Maryland combined with a fellowship from the National Endowment for the Humanities allowed me to devote a full year without interruption in 1978–79 to writing much of this book. I am grateful for their support.

Countless archivists, librarians, and library aides, the unsung heroes and heroines of historical research, shared their knowledge of their materials with me, facilitated my access to those materials, and made my task more enjoyable. I am deeply grateful to each of them. Among those of special importance for my work were four heads of the Franklin D. Roosevelt Library (the late Herman Kahn, Elizabeth

B. Drewry, William J. Stewart, and William R. Emerson) and their staffs, whom I thank for their unfailing help and encouragement. Thomas T. Thalken, director of the Herbert Hoover Presidential Library, and his staff were similarly helpful. I am grateful to R. Douglas Stuart, Jr., the late Robert E. Wood, the late Gerald P. Nye, the late Charles A. Lindbergh, and Mrs. Ruth Sarles Benedict for allowing me to do research in their personal papers, for sharing their recollections with me in extended interviews and conversations, and for honoring my intellectual freedom and independence in the use of their papers. My many research trips were intellectually exciting, but they could also be lonely. I am grateful to the many people who extended thoughtful kindnesses to me on those trips. My friend and colleague, Horace Samuel Merrill of the University of Maryland, carefully read several of the chapters and helped me revise and shorten the original manuscript. To all of those and many others I am grateful.

Over the years my sister, Bonnie Lewis, has helped buoy my spirits through the pride and confidence she expressed in me. Most important is my wife, Virginia Rae Miller Cole. She and our son, Thomas Roy Cole, have never known me when I was not deeply involved in historical research and writing. She helped me type research notes in the Roosevelt and Nye papers. She read proof. But more precious, she provided a comfortable and tranquil home setting, she did more than her share in rearing our son, and she provided unfailing support and encouragement. My gratitude and love for her know no bounds.

Chapter 1

A Great Divide

At 8:45 on the evening of January 30, 1882, on the second floor of the big house overlooking the Hudson River far below, a husky, healthy, ten-pound son was born to James and Sara Roosevelt. Christened Franklin Delano Roosevelt, the infant was to become one of the greatest of America's presidents. Serving from 1933 until his death in 1945, longer than any other president, Roosevelt guided the United States through enduring changes at home and abroad. Among those was the transition from America's traditional isolationism into a powerful role as an active leader in world affairs. That transition affected the lives of hundreds of millions of people in the United States and on every continent of the earth from that time onward.

The United States that winter night in 1882 had as many ties with the past as with the future. The horseless carriage had not yet made its first appearance in the tranquil village of Hyde Park, New York, that was home to the boy and his parents. Even as little Franklin took his first steps, frontiersmen, prospectors, cattlemen, farmers, and entrepreneurs were still struggling westward to fill the lands and exploit the resources that lay on the frontier within the boundaries of the young nation. Nearly seven of every ten Americans lived and worked either on farms or in small towns. The magic of radio developed only slowly while Franklin was a teenager and young adult. And the tall, handsome young man had celebrated his twenty-first birthday before Orville and Wilbur Wright accomplished the first powered airplane flight.

When projected into foreign affairs, the United States of 1882 was as much in the horse-and-buggy era as it was at home. It had not had an alliance with any foreign state since it had ended its alliance with France at the beginning of the nineteenth century. Secure behind the oceans, the British fleet, and the balance of power, the United States maintained only minuscule military forces. No United States army had ever been sent into battle on the European continent. The United States made itself felt in the Western Hemisphere, but it was not a world power, and most Americans at that time saw no useful purpose to be served in trying to become one.

A century later the United States that honored the centennial of Roosevelt's birth was so different that it was almost as though one were viewing a foreign country. The population was 230 million, more than four times the number when Roosevelt was born that winter evening in 1882. The geographic frontier in the lower forty- eight was gone. Two-thirds of all Americans lived in cities or suburbs, small towns had faded, and the farm population had dwindled to less than 3 percent of the total. A century after Roosevelt's birth the super-metropolis replaced the small town and farm as the symbol of the American way of life.

The United States had become the leading industrial, financial, and agricultural economy in the world. American business and financial organizations became huge and complex, with greater wealth and power than many independent governments. Gigantic American-dominated multinational corporations functioned very nearly as sovereign entities. That incredibly productive economy transcended national boundaries. American-manufactured products, food and fiber, and loans and investments went to every continent, to nearly all countries and to countless millions of individual homes and businesses. Jet airliners regularly traveled all over the world. Europe, which had been days or even weeks away, was a few hours by jet (minutes by missile). Television and satellite communication quickly brought developments abroad and nationally into the living rooms of most Americans.

Those revolutionary domestic changes projected into a radically changed role for the United States in world affairs. The North American state had become the leading world power. The continental emphasis of 1882 had given way to a worldwide perspective. The traditional "no entangling alliances" policy was abandoned as the United States maintained alliances with dozens of governments and played leading roles in major international organizations. Nothing of any importance happened in international affairs that was outside the concern of the United States. Any action (or inaction) by the United States could affect people and governments anywhere in the world.

That tremendous power included awesome military might. President Roosevelt had set in motion the Manhattan Project that perfected atomic bombs that ended World War II and inaugurated the nuclear age. During FDR's lifetime American armed forces fought abroad in World Wars I and II. After his death they fought in Korea, Vietnam, and elsewhere. With the centennial of Roosevelt's birth American armed forces were equipped with the most incredibly powerful and potentially destructive array of weapons ever known, with a capacity to destroy any enemy—and all humanity with it. But that power and America's internationalist role had also helped prevent a third world war during the generation following the death of Roosevelt.

Franklin D. Roosevelt did not cause or control most of the changes during the past century. While he was president, however, he helped guide the United States and the world in new directions. He played a central role in the transition of American foreign policy from its traditional isolationism toward its present formidable leadership role in world affairs.

Roosevelt's relations with American isolationists from 1932 to 1945 had enduring significance for the history of American foreign policy. Those relations with isolationists extended into domestic matters as well as foreign affairs; they included personal and political relations and varied concerns with the New Deal and Great Depression. In the foreign policy contest, President Roosevelt decisively triumphed over the isolationists. His victory over them marked a watershed in the history of American foreign policy.[1]

Certain aspects of Franklin D. Roosevelt's background, experiences, and character had particular significance for his dealings with isolationists.[2] First, his eastern, wealthy, almost aristocratic family background encouraged an outward-looking world view. He was proud of the maritime activities of his ancestors. That background encouraged his interest in China and the Pacific. He visited Europe several times as a boy and teenager. He had more personal exposure to Europe than he had to America's heartland. That family background and those childhood experiences helped give him a cosmopolitan perspective; they were not conducive to continentalism.

Second, Roosevelt's political experiences in New York State provided a microcosm of his political dealings later with isolationists and internationalists on the national scene. He began his political career as a progressive Democrat in upriver New York in Dutchess County. In his campaigns for election to the state senate he sympathized with the problems of farmers, small businessmen, and debtors in opposition to big business, financiers, and city political machines. Those patterns were similar to his appeals to the West and South nationally when he sought nomination and election to the presidency in 1932. But if he hoped for bigger things politically in New York, he had to make his peace with the city, with Tammany—and he did. Similarly, as president, if he hoped to prevail in the increasingly urban America, and if he hoped to build a political base for a larger role for the United States in world affairs, he had to win the support of the great cities—and he did. Roosevelt's early political experiences in the state of New York provided splendid training for his later roles as president and for his dealings nationally with American isolationists and internationalists.

Third, Roosevelt's experiences as assistant secretary of navy under President Woodrow Wilson from 1913 to 1920 affected his later dealings with isolationists. From childhood onward, Roosevelt had loved ships and the seas. He embraced the big-navy views of Captain Alfred Thayer Mahan. He was convinced of the importance of military preparedness in general and naval preparedness in particular. There was no position in the new Wilson administration that he preferred in 1913 over the one he got as assistant secretary of navy. Roosevelt's experiences in that post before, during, and after World War I further strengthened his convictions on the importance of sea power. They enhanced his alertness to the role of power in foreign affairs. They reinforced his world view.

Fourth, there were his experiences in 1920 as the vice-presidential candidate on the Democratic ticket, along with James M. Cox. Under President Wilson's watchful eye, Roosevelt campaigned for approval of the Versailles treaty and for American membership in the League of Nations.

Fifth, Roosevelt's subsequent career was affected by his crippling attack of poliomyelitis in 1921. He never fully regained effective use of his legs. But the illness and his struggle to overcome its physical effects influenced his character. With help and encouragement from his wife, Eleanor, and from Louis M. Howe, Roosevelt fought back and rejected the invalid role. The ordeal increased his emotional strength, toughness, persistence, and patience.

And finally, one must underscore Roosevelt's undoctrinaire style. Roosevelt was the despair of the doctrinaire, the structured, the systems-makers, the ideologues. They tried to make him conform to rigid formulas—and he would not conform. At least he would not do so consistently. He had values, and he battled to implement them. He was a progressive and a liberal; he was neither a socialist nor a radical. He was a country gentleman with certain rural values, but he adjusted to American urbanization. He accepted constitutional constraints on presidential powers, but his was a decidely loose constructionist view of the Constitution. He believed the president of the United States had the responsibility and authority to lead. He believed in democracy, in representative government, in constitutional processes; he abhorred dictatorship and totalitarianism. But his democracy included a strong admixture of paternalism and noblesse oblige.

In foreign affairs Roosevelt hated war and pressed for disarmament. But he was not a pacifist. He thrilled to the challenge of war and delighted in his role as commander in chief. He was an internationalist who was also a patriot and a nationalist. He criticized imperialism and embraced the right of self-determination, but he led the United States in directions that vastly expanded American power and influence over much of the world. His sympathies for Great Britain were more fundamental than his friendship and admiration for Winston Churchill; his anti-German biases were deeper than his abhorrence of Hitler's Nazi dictatorship and military aggression. He traced his sympathies for China back to ancestors who had been active in the China trade, though his knowledge of China never got much beyond superficial. President Roosevelt earnestly wanted to prevent war in Europe and Asia, he hoped the United States could stay out of war, and he did not expect America's military presence in Europe to last long after the war ended. For all of that, however, Roosevelt was not an isolationist.

A multitude of variables often blurred those patterns and values. Roosevelt was intuitive rather than systematic, artful rather than scientific, and innovative rather than doctrinaire. He was highly flexible and shied away from rigid formulas or systems. He liked to play with ideas, to explore alternative approaches, without irrevocably committing himself to any single policy or approach. He was not troubled by inconsistencies. He had the emotional self-confidence and political realism that allowed him to abandon policies that did not work or methods that proved ineffective. He kept his options open.

Roosevelt liked people, enjoyed being with them, and disliked personal controversy. He could reduce highly complex problems to remarkably clear analyses of the essentials at issue. He could and did dispute with others, but he preferred to avoid abrasive confrontations. He used personal charm, warm good humor, and the prestige of his office to soften or avoid direct clashes. Sometimes he played to his audience so effectively that he said (or others believed he said) what they wanted to hear, rather than what he may have believed. It could be difficult to nail him down in conversations or press conferences.

Philip La Follette of Wisconsin noted that in conversations Roosevelt had a habit of saying "Yep, yep" as others spoke to him. He may have intended his *yeps* as indications that he was listening and understanding, but those who spoke to him could interpret them as meaning, yes, he agreed with them. Many left White House conferences confident that Roosevelt shared their views—even when he really did not.[3] Roosevelt drew on ideas and phrases of others and could be affected by the last person with whom he talked. In 1940, after serving in the cabinet for nearly seven years, Secretary of Agriculture Henry A. Wallace wrote in his diary that it was "always interesting in conversation with the President to note the extent to which he repeats a conversation with the person who has been in to see him recently or a speech which he has recently made. He is a continuous and vivid mirror of that which has been happening in the immediate past."[4] Individuals could sometimes get to him, only to have someone else get to him in a different way later.

Roosevelt was keenly alert to the political implications, possibilities, and limitations of any policy or action at home or abroad. But politics did not always control his course; friendships, sentiment, patriotism, personal values, constitutional considerations, and conceptions of national interest played their role as well.

All of that was complicated by the many-faceted situations that confronted the president. Most who conferred with him did so on just one or a few matters; he had responsibility for a wide range of complex matters difficult or impossible to reconcile. His responsibilities extended to the entire United States—not just to one state, section, class, group, or interest. He had responsibility for both domestic and foreign policies. Those with narrower interests often found it difficult to understand his broader responsibilities or to sympathize with his failure to give their particular concerns priority. Those and other parts of Roosevelt's background, experiences, and character affected his dealings with isolationists from 1932 to 1945.

The terms "isolationism" and "isolationist" have had emotional and pejorative connotations.[5] If defined literally, they are misleading. Isolationists did not wish to cut the United States off from the rest of the world. They did not want to sever trade and credit relations with other parts of the world. Isolationists were not pacifists—though they sometimes cooperated with pacifists on particular issues. Leading isolationists were not apathetic or uninterested in foreign affairs. In the 1930s most leading isolationists were not conservatives; many were to the left of Roosevelt and his New Deal. Furthermore, most isolationists were not unpatriotic; most were not pro-Nazi, pro-fascist, or pro-Axis.

Turning from what they were not to what they were, isolationists were opposed to American intervention in European wars. Those noninterventionist views generally extended to Asia and Latin America as well (many were critical of American imperialism in Latin America). But not necessarily. It was possible (though uncommon) for an individual to be an isolationist with regard to European wars and still favor military involvement in Asia, the Pacific, or Latin America. Isolationists were also unilateralists; they opposed American involvement in "entangling alliances," collective security commitments, or international organizations such as the League of Nations. In that regard, they tenaciously guarded American sovereignty and freedom of action. They did not oppose all American activity abroad, but they wanted to leave Americans free to determine for themselves when, where, how, and whether the United States should involve itself abroad. They did not want to be bound by prior commitments in alliances or international organizations.

Isolationists favored building and maintaining military forces for the defense of the United States. But they saw a relationship between military preparations and foreign policies. They opposed military preparations that seemed designed for involvement in foreign wars—particularly in Europe; they supported preparations that seemed suited for continental defense in the Western Hemisphere. Generally they were critical of large naval appropriations, fearing a big navy would be used to support intervention abroad. They tended to give priority to Army appropriations, especially air power preparations. They believed the United States could successfully defend itself in the Western Hemisphere.

American isolationists had faith in the power of example. They believed the United States could more effectively lead the world to the good life by building and sustaining democracy, freedom, and prosperity at home than it could through military involvement in foreign wars. They opposed any American efforts to police the world or to rebuild the world in an American image. Many feared that involvement in foreign wars would shatter domestic reform programs at home and could destroy the very freedoms, democracy, and prosperity they were supposed to defend. They favored full and open discussion of foreign policy issues. They urged legislation restraining the president, the military, big business, and financiers as they operated in foreign affairs.

In terms of sources of support for isolationism,[6] in the 1930s most Americans were isolationists, and one could find them in all sections and all groups. There were, however, variations in different segments of the population. Isolationists were most numerous in the Middle West, and least numerous in the South. They were relatively stronger in the Republican party than in the Democratic party. In economic terms isolationists were relatively numerous among farmers outside the South (especially cattle-wheat farmers on the Great Plains and corn-hog farmers in the Middle West), small businessmen, retailers, light-goods manufacturers, and in service industries. In social origins, isolationists were relatively more numerous in rural and small-town America than in the great cities. In ethnic terms they were relatively numerous among Irish-Americans, German-Americans, Italian-Americans, and, perhaps, Scandinavian-Americans. In religious terms they were relatively numerous among Roman Catholics and Lutherans —though those patterns were due more to the ethnic composition of those religious organizations than to theology. They were slightly more numerous among women than among men. Though one could encounter highly educated isolationists, they tended to be relatively more numerous among those with less formal education than among those with more. Those were only tendencies, however, and there were exceptions to every generalization.

Millions of Americans were isolationists during the Roosevelt years, and thousands of them played active roles in the foreign policy debates. But among the more prominent and influential isolationist leaders were Senator William E. Borah, progressive Republican from Idaho; Senator Hiram Johnson, progressive Republican from California; Senator Burton K. Wheeler, progressive Democrat from Montana; Senator George W. Norris, progressive from Nebraska; Senator Arthur Capper, progressive Republican from Kansas; Senator Gerald P. Nye, progressive Republican from North Dakota; Henrik Shipstead, Farmer-Labor senator from Minnesota; Senator Robert M. La Follette, Jr., and Governor Philip La Follette, progressives from Wisconsin; Democratic Senator Bennett Champ Clark of Missouri; Republican Senator Arthur H. Vandenberg from Michigan; Republican Senator Robert A. Taft of Ohio; and Republican Congressman Hamilton Fish of FDR's home district in New York. Most famous and controversial of the isolationists was the aviator Colonel Charles A. Lindbergh.

Specific patterns in relations between Franklin D. Roosevelt and leading isolationists varied continually. For purposes of analysis, however, the relations can be divided into three fairly distinct chronological periods roughly corresponding to Roosevelt's presidential terms. The first was "An Uneasy Alliance" extending from the conventions and elections of 1932 through Roosevelt's first term in the White House to 1937. The second was "A Parting of the Ways" from 1937 through Roosevelt's second term to 1941. The third and final period could be called "Victor and Vanquished," and included Roosevelt's third term begining in 1941 and continued to his death on April 12, 1945, early in his fourth term.

American isolationism approached a high tide during Roosevelt's first term as president with the adoption of the Johnson Act of 1934, Senate rejection of the World Court in 1935, the Nye investigation of the munitions industries in 1934–36, and enactment of neutrality laws beginning in 1935. Isolationist strength inhibited the president's conduct of foreign affairs. For the most part, however, domestic issues dominated in the early relations between Roosevelt and the isolationists. The key word then was "progressive"—not "isolation." From 1932 to 1937, Roosevelt actively solicited political support from progressives in his election campaigns and for enactment of his New Deal program.[7] His appeals to them generally did not focus on foreign affairs, but most western progressives were isolationists. Western progressive isolationists were concerned with ending the depression, restoring prosperity, and implementing their progressive goals for the United States. They were uneasy about whether Roosevelt was sufficiently firm in his commitment to progressivism. In planning his legislative moves, the president consulted closely with such progressive senators as Norris, Wheeler, Johnson, and La Follette—isolationists all. Though isolationist Senators Borah and Nye criticized Roosevelt's National Recovery Administration for being too favorable to big business, much of the early New Deal was consistent with the economic nationalism they favored. By the time Roosevelt ran for a second term in 1936, leading isolationists felt no overwhelming need to make an issue of the president's performance on foreign affairs. There had been differences during that first term, and one could identify issues that would divide them sharply later. But most isolationists supported Roosevelt for reelection, and foreign affairs played no significant role in the outcome. The "Uneasy Alliance" prevailed.

Roosevelt's second term as president from 1937 to 1941 saw a "Parting of the Ways" in his relations with isolationists. Again the patterns were set initially by domestic rather than foreign affairs. The first major wedge driven between Roosevelt and the isolationists during his second term was his court-packing proposal early in 1937. Senator Wheeler led the opposition, and most Senate isolationists voted with him to kill the president's proposal. The economic recession of 1937–38, Democratic reverses in the election of 1938, and growing opposition in Congress alerted the president to the political dangers if he pressed ahead with his New Deal program.

At the very moment when he faced growing opposition on domestic issues, however, alarming international developments in other parts of the world increasingly demanded the attention of the American people and the energies of President Roosevelt. In 1935–36, Mussolini's Fascist Italy conquered Abyssinia in Africa. In 1936, Nazi Germany under Adolf Hitler remilitarized the Rhineland. Germany and Italy provided men and equipment to help Franco's fascists triumph in the Spanish civil war from 1936 to 1939. The Sino-Japanese war in Asia erupted in July, 1937. Hitler's Nazi Germany took over Austria in March, 1938. In October, after the Chamberlain-Daladier appeasement of Hitler at Munich, Germany seized the Sudetenland of Czechoslovakia. In November, the Nazis violently stepped up their persecution of German Jews. Early in 1939, Hitler dismembered the rest of Czechoslovakia in violation of his promises at Munich. The Russo-German nonaggression pact of August, 1939, opened the door for Hitler's invasion of Poland on September 1. Determined to appease no more, Britain and France declared war on Germany, and World War II formally began in Europe. The Russo-Finnish war won the headlines during the winter of 1939–40, but in April, 1940, Hitler once again unleashed his blitzkrieg. German forces quickly overran Denmark, Norway, and the Low Countries. They drove the British into the sea at Dunkirk, and (with help from Mussolini's Italy) forced the surrender of France in June, 1940. Under its new prime minister, Winston Churchill, Britain braced for the expected assault on its home islands. In "Their finest hour" Britain's Royal Air Force fighters and Royal Navy checked the Germans in the Battle of Britain during the autumn of 1940. But as Americans conducted their presidential conventions and elections and as Roosevelt's second term neared its close, Britain's capacity to survive in its contest with Nazi Germany was by no means certain. And its ability to defeat the Axis powers in Europe, Africa, and Asia was very much in doubt.

Franklin D. Roosevelt did not want war abroad, and he did not want the United States to enter that war. But there was an unintended, unplanned, but politically happy coincidence that at the very moment Roosevelt's domestic policies were floundering, developments abroad provided new political energies to keep Roosevelt and his administration moving on successfully. He was going with the political currents when he shifted from domestic affairs to foreign affairs during his second term. That refocus required a break between Roosevelt and the isolationists, however, and helped assure his triumph over them.

In October, 1937, Roosevelt's Quarantine Address troubled isolationists. In January, 1938, his intervention to help block consideration of the Ludlow amendment in the House of Representatives increased isolationist fears concerning his intentions in foreign affairs. As the president slowly shaped and began to implement his efforts to aid Axis victims with methods short of war, isolationists were more alarmed than Axis leaders were. From 1937 onward in episode after episode foreign crises drove the wedge deeper between Roosevelt and the isolationists. Individual isolationists broke with the president, and, one by one, others turned from their earlier cautiously cooperative tone to varied degrees of alienation, distrust, and even hatred of the president. Senator Norris was unique among leading isolationists in continuing to follow on most issues as Roosevelt shifted to more active involvement abroad.

Americans overwhelmingly sympathized with Britain, France, and China in their struggles against the Axis powers. Until the middle of 1940, however, the majority believed it was more important for the United States to stay out of the European war than to assure defeat of the Axis. With Dunkirk, the fall of France, and the Battle of Britain, however, those patterns changed. Most Americans continued to oppose a declaration of war against the Axis, but from the autumn of 1940 onward a majority believed it was more important for the United States to assure a British victory over the Axis than to stay out of the European war. The president's moves to aid Britain short of war won majority approval. In that sense Roosevelt had already won his battle against the isolationists; from then on isolationists were a minority. There were to be many more skirmishes and battles between Roosevelt and the isolationists, but by the end of 1940 Roosevelt had the upper hand.[8]

Isolationists were still strong enough in the summer of 1940 to get noninterventionist planks in the platforms of both the Democratic and Republican parties. But both parties rejected isolationist contenders for their presidential nominations. Roosevelt decided to seek a third term. And the Republican party turned to Wall Street's Wendell Willkie, who shared the president's general foreign policy views. Roosevelt and Willkie both appeased isolationist strength in campaign speeches, but the isolationists would not control the presidency, whichever candidate won the election in 1940.

Roosevelt's reelection to an unprecedented third term in November prepared the way politically for the last phase of his dealings with the isolationists. During his third and fourth terms from 1941 to 1945, President Roosevelt presided over the final defeat of the isolationists. Extreme interventionists thought the president was too timid and cautious and urged him to lead more boldly and candidly. They thought he exaggerated the strength of isolationists and underestimated his own powers of leadership. Nonetheless, from 1941 to 1945, Roosevelt skillfully and almost ruthlessly demolished the isolationists and isolationism. The White House actively helped the interventionist Committee to Defend America by Aiding the Allies and, later, the Fight for Freedom Committee that were contesting against the isolationist America First Committee. The Office of Civilian Defense that the president created under Fiorello La Guardia had responsibility to build national morale and unity, partly by downing the isolationists.

At a time when 80 percent of the American people continued to oppose a declaration of war, President Roosevelt's aid-short-of-war tactics provided the maximum involvement that Congress and the public seemed willing to approve before Pearl Harbor. The isolationists were unable to defeat any administration aid-short-of-war proposal actually put to a vote in Congress at any time after the European war began in September, 1939. The patrol system and shoot-on-sight policy in the Atlantic and the steadily increasing economic squeeze on Japan in the Pacific in effect encouraged the possibility that developments abroad might cause Congress and the American people to abandon their opposition to a declaration of war (as they did after the Japanese attack on Pearl Harbor).

Though he did not invent the approach, Roosevelt and his top advisors used the guilt-by-association method to discredit isolationists. That is, they helped build the impression that the isolationists were serving the Nazi cause. Even before Pearl Harbor, when presumably free discussion and debate were both rights and duties for citizens and legislators alike, patriotic isolationist opponents of Roosevelt's policies were seen as little better than Nazis. The president authorized wiretaps and FBI probes in contending with opposition. Shortly before Pearl Harbor he suggested that the attorney general initiate a grand jury investigation of the America First Committee. Isolationists continued their opposition to the president's foreign policies down to the very moment that the Japanese attacked Pearl Harbor on December 7, 1941. Leading isolationists were thoroughly beaten and discredited, however, even before that attack provided the coup de grâce.

With the attack on Pearl Harbor, Senate and House isolationists (save only Republican Jeannette Rankin of Montana) joined with their colleagues in voting for war against Japan, and then against Germany and Italy. They ceased their noninterventionist activities and pledged support for the war effort.

In 1943, the Fulbright Resolution in the House and the Connally Resolution in the Senate won overwhelming approval; they were designed to proclaim that Congress would not block American membership in the world organization to be created at the close of World War II as it had done after World War I. Secretary of State Cordell Hull skillfully laid the groundwork to assure bipartisan support for the United Nations organization. President Roosevelt was less utopian than Hull in his view of a postwar world organization, but he urged it partly as a way of making certain that the United States did not return to isolationism as it had done after World War I.

One by one isolationists in Congress faded from the scene. Borah died early in 1940, and Hiram Johnson died the day the United States dropped its atomic bomb on Hiroshima. Isolationists fared surprisingly well in the elections of 1942, but in 1944 and 1946 most of them went down to defeat. Nye, Clark, and Fish were ousted by the voters in 1944, and Wheeler, La Follette, Shipstead, and others were turned out in 1946.

Franklin D. Roosevelt died on April 12, 1945, while serving in his fourth term. Italy had already surrendered, and the end was in sight for Germany and Japan. Figuratively, Roosevelt's death had been preceded by the death of American isolationism as a dominant force in American foreign policy. Roosevelt had won his battle against the isolationists just as surely as the United States under his leadership was successfully sharing in accomplishing the military triumph over the Axis powers in World War II.

One could contend that American isolationism succumbed to changing impersonal circumstances abroad and at home, circumstances that Roosevelt did not create and did not really control. In other parts of the world the declining power of Britain and France, the challenges from the Axis powers and later from the Soviet Union, and the terrifying destructive capabilities made possible by the impact of scientific and technological developments on modern warfare forced the United States to play a larger role in world affairs. At the same time, within the United States, urbanization, the decline of rural and small town America, and the spectacular growth of American industrial capacities and capital accumulations compelled the United States to seek broader horizons and play larger roles in world affairs. Those changing circumstances at home and abroad might have crushed the isolationists sooner or later with or without Roosevelt. Nonetheless, President Franklin D. Roosevelt provided leadership for the destruction of American isolationism. With his triumph over the isolationists there was no turning back either for America or the world.

Part I: An Uneasy Alliance

Chapter 2

Choosing a New President

Neither Franklin D. Roosevelt nor the isolationists gave center stage to foreign policy issues in the election of 1932. Most leading isolationists were agrarian progressives on domestic issues. Their progressive perspectives determined their attitudes toward Roosevelt and other possible candidates.

Most isolationist leaders opposed the reelection of Herbert Hoover to a second term. They wanted the Republicans to nominate a progressive rather than Hoover, but that was politically impossible. Some toyed with the possibility of an independent or third-party progressive candidate, but they saw no chance for election success through that procedure. That left them with the Democratic party.

If Hoover were the Republican nominee, and if the Democrats nominated a conservative or an urban-oriented Tammany candidate, leading isolationists might feel compelled either to go fishing on election day or to turn to a third-party candidate with the realization that he would be defeated. Consequently, before the Democratic convention in 1932, most western progressives saw FDR as an attractive possibility. They had reservations about him, but they preferred Roosevelt to Hoover and to other contenders. Among isolationists who actively supported Roosevelt before the national convention were Burton K. Wheeler, George W. Norris, Joseph P. Kennedy, Raymond Moley, and George N. Peek.

The youngest of ten children of a Quaker shoemaker, Burton K. Wheeler was born in Hudson, Massachusetts in 1882. He supported William Jennings Bryan and free silver in his first public debate in high school. The tall, lean towhead worked his way through the University of Michigan, where he received his law degree in 1905. He went west and began his legal career in Butte, Montana. He became a successful trial lawyer and made his political mark by challenging

Anaconda Copper Mining Company's hold on the state government. In 1913, President Wilson appointed him district attorney for Montana. Though he supported Wilson's foreign policies, he refused to go along with what he considered wartime hysteria against German-Americans, pacifists, and radicals. Wheeler welcomed political support from the Nonpartisan League in Montana as he battled for the farmer, worker, and small businessman against "the Company," corruption, and party bosses. He won election to the United States Senate as a Democrat from Montana in 1922, and served four terms before going down to defeat in 1946. Wheeler was Fighting Bob La Follette's vice-presidential running mate on the National Independent Progressive party ticket in 1924. He battled shoulder to shoulder along with other western progressives on behalf of the common man and against the special interests and corruption in government. Tenaciously independent, Wheeler was a rugged, aggressive political warrior; he enjoyed a good fight. By 1932, Wheeler was not yet prominently identified with isolationism, but he became a leading opponent of Roosevelt's foreign policies before Pearl Harbor.[1]

Wheeler first saw Roosevelt in 1928, when the New York politician nominated Governor Al Smith for president at the Democratic National Convention. While campaigning with Smith in the West later that year, the Montana Democrat urged Smith to have FDR run for governor in New York. Early in 1930, Roosevelt and Wheeler met and conferred in Washington, but the two men were not close.[2]

In April, 1930, more than two years before the Democratic convention in Chicago, Senator Wheeler publicly endorsed Roosevelt for president—the first prominent Democrat to do so. He gave that endorsement in an address before a Jefferson Day dinner meeting of the National Democratic Club in New York City. In his speech Wheeler said: "As I look around for a general to lead the Democratic Party on these two issues, the tariff and control of power and public utilities, I ask to whom can we go? I say that, if the Democratic Party of New York will elect Franklin D. Roosevelt governor, the West will demand his nomination for President and the whole country will elect him."[3]

Wheeler endorsed Roosevelt because the New Yorker was a progressive, because the senator thought FDR could win the election, and because he wanted to head off the renomination of Al Smith. Wheeler had admired Smith, but he found his Roman Catholic religion to be a major political liability in Montana. He thought Roosevelt was the Democratic party's "best bet" and feared that if it did not nominate FDR, it might turn to "some ultra conservative."[4]

Governor Roosevelt wrote to Wheeler thanking him for his endorsement and praising the senator's progressive leadership. But he waited six weeks to do so. Even then he equivocated on whether he would really seek the nomination. FDR invited Wheeler to visit him in Albany and wanted the Montana senator to keep him "in touch with the general thought in the Mountain States on the power question."[5]

In January, 1932, Oswald Garrison Villard of the *Nation* complained to Wheeler that FDR was not the man to lead in the economic emergency. Senator Wheeler responded: "I am not intimately acquainted with Governor Roosevelt, but I have watched his career for sometime, and I am convinced that among the candidates who have been mentioned as possibilities on the democratic ticket that he is by far the most progressive. He probably would not go as far as I would go, but we cannot always get as candidates, people who entirely agree with our views." He did not see another liberal Democrat on whom the party could agree. Wheeler was encouraged by the thought "that all of the Power Interests, and practically all of the big banking interests in New York City, and men like Hague and Raskob desire to beat him."[6] Wheeler later claimed credit for winning the support of both Senator Huey Long of Louisiana and financier Joseph P. Kennedy of Massachusetts for Roosevelt.[7]

Wheeler had known Joseph Kennedy since 1924. Democratic Senator David I. Walsh of Massachusetts gave a dinner for Wheeler early in 1932 and invited Kennedy. According to Wheeler's recollections many years later, Kennedy asked him that evening whom he favored for president. When Wheeler responded, "Roosevelt," Kennedy then asked whether John J. Raskob, chairman of the Democratic National Committee, favored Roosevelt—and he did not. Kennedy then told Wheeler that "if that so-and-so Raskob is against Roosevelt, I'll be for him." Later in the spring, the senator guided Frank C. Walker to Kennedy in money-raising efforts for Roosevelt.[8] Kennedy, Walsh, and Wheeler were all isolationists before Pearl Harbor, and all were Democrats.

More typical of progressive isolationists in 1932 was Senator George W. Norris of the Great Plains state of Nebraska. An independent Republican, Norris had impecable credentials both as an isolationist and as a progressive. Born on a farm in Sandusky County, Ohio in 1861, the eleventh of twelve children, Norris knew both poverty and hard work while still no more than a child. He worked his way through Indiana Normal College, taught school, read law, and was admitted to the bar in 1883. Two years later he moved west to

Nebraska just in time to witness the droughts, hard times, and restiveness that led to the Populist movement under his fellow Nebraskan, William Jennings Bryan. Active in state politics, Norris was fully as critical of the old guard in his own Republican party as he was of the Democrats. He served five terms in the House of Representatives from 1903 to 1913 during the Progressive Era and helped break the power of Speaker of the House Joe Cannon. He then won election to the United States Senate and served five terms from 1913 to 1943. During those years he earned a reputation as the most effective and respected western progressive legislator. Through most of his career Norris was fully as isolationist as the rest of the western progressives—and on the same grounds. He denounced the influence of special interests, big business, and eastern financiers on American foreign affairs, and blamed them for what he deemed excessive naval armaments and imperialism. He was one of only six senators who voted against the American declaration of war on Germany in 1917, and he never regretted his vote. As an irreconcilable he vigorously opposed the Versailles treaty and American membership in the League of Nations.[9]

Many progressive Republicans urged their party to reject Hoover at the 1932 convention and nominate a progressive. Among those mentioned for the nomination were Senators Norris of Nebraska, Borah of Idaho, and Johnson of California. All were progressives, and all were isolationists. Except for Johnson, however, all came from states with few electoral votes. And all were considered to be too old. Norris was over seventy, and Johnson and Borah were both past sixty-five. Norris was convinced that it would be impossible for him or any other progressive to win the GOP presidential nomination. He opposed renomination of Hoover, but thought there was no way to prevent it. He flatly refused to be a candidate for the Republican presidential nomination.[10]

At the same time, Norris saw no real hope for the progressive cause through an independent or third-party candidate. He successfully won elections running as an independent, but the electoral college system blocked success for that tactic in a presidential race. If the Republicans renominated Hoover and if the Democrats chose a conservative, Norris might have supported a progressive third-party cadidate. But he would have done so with the realization that it would be a futile effort. And for progressives to turn to a third party before the national conventions would deprive them of any influence they might have on platforms and nominees in the major parties. In 1932, his hopes rested with the Democratic party and with Franklin D. Roosevelt.[11]

Governor Roosevelt actively courted the old senator's support, using his endorsement of public power projects as his main appeal. The senator might have preferred someone else. "He would not be my first choice, if I were picking a President." But Norris became convinced that it was Roosevelt or nothing so far as progressives were concerned. In May, 1932, the Nebraska senator announced that he would support FDR if the Democratic party nominated him and that he would not support Hoover.[12]

The Reverend John Haynes Holmes wrote to Norris complaining that, as governor, Roosevelt had failed the reform interests of New York. He urged Norris to support Socialist Norman Thomas instead. The old senator responded by emphasizing "the absolute impossibility" of electing Thomas. He also reminded Holmes that he was a progressive, not a socialist. "As I look at it," Norris wrote, "the country is going to be presented with the opportunity of reelecting President Hoover or of electing the candidate for President who will be nominated by the Democrats in the coming National Democratic Convention. If they nominate another man like President Hoover, we will be practically helpless and there will be no opportunity to save the country from another four years of Hoover regime. I have been perfectly sincere in my belief," Norris continued, "that Roosevelt was the one man who came the nearest to representing Progressive ideas of all those who stand any show of being nominated at the National Democratic Convention. I have, therefore, been anxious to see him nominated."[13]

Republican Senators Hiram W. Johnson of California and William E. Borah of Idaho also had impressive credentials as progressives and isolationists. Both were stubbornly independent. Neither was so artful as Norris in getting legislation passed. Though they generally found themselves on the same side on both domestic and foreign policy issues, they did not like each other personally. Perhaps each was too much of a prima donna to appreciate the posturing of the other. But on foreign affairs they had acquired more power and prestige than had Norris. They were ranking members of the Senate Foreign Relations Committee, and Borah was chairman of that powerful committee from 1924 until 1933.

By 1932, both Johnson and Borah opposed President Hoover. Each toyed with the possibility of seeking the Republican presidential nomination, partly to block Hoover and the conservatives. But both realized the odds against them in such efforts. And both played their cards close to their vests. In January, 1932, Senator Johnson wrote his sons that if he were to enter state primaries seeking the presidential nomination, he could "see nothing ahead after a long and killing contest, but the prevention of the renomination of Hoover, and the nomination of somebody almost as bad, who would be selected by the present masters of the Republican Party." He told his sons that if he "were younger and richer," he "would have a bully time." But "being old and broke," he would amuse himself as long as he could "by looking wise and mysterious."[14]

Johnson felt a growing sympathy for Roosevelt. In May, Johnson wrote: "The one thing that draws to Roosevelt those of us who believe in real democracy is the character of the opposition to him. This opposition embraces all of those who believe in the right to exploit government for their own selfish advantage. Smith has become the mouth piece of these people." As he explained to his sons, "This campaign is going to present quite a problem to the old man. I can't support Hoover. I would not want to support a Democrat, who represented exactly what Hoover represents, and I can see the possibility of being a hard working lawyer during the campaign."[15]

Republican Gerald P. Nye of North Dakota had not yet completed his first full term in the United States Senate and was absorbed in his own campaigns to win renomination and reelection in 1932. Though he shared the agrarian progressivism and isolationism of Senators Norris, Borah, and Johnson, Nye was still a young man. He would not have his fortieth birthday until after the election. He had yet to win much national prominence as an isolationist. But he too turned away from President Hoover and found favorable things to say about Governor Roosevelt. More than a year before the national conventions, young Nye praised Roosevelt for his support of the Saint Lawrence power project and for giving attention to economic problems. He thought "Roosevelt would make a very strong candidate"— much stronger than Al Smith. Vigorous campaigning against his conservative opponent in the Republican primary won renomination for Nye in the June primaries. He did not formally endorse any presidential contender and was comparatively free of party constraints as the national conventions drew near.[16]

Governor Roosevelt's most spectacular and controversial foreign policy statement before the Democratic convention, and at any time during the election year, related directly to American isolationism.

Leading isolationists could not entirely ignore the fact that as the Democratic vice-presidential candidate in 1920 Roosevelt had campaigned aggressively for American membership in the League of Nations. Similarly, Roosevelt's big-navy views and his service as President Wilson's assistant secretary of navy made him suspect to western isolationists.

Publisher William Randolph Hearst was particularly uneasy about Roosevelt's internationalism and support for the league. His newspapers had large circulation in many parts of the country. When Hearst's inquiries through James A. Farley produced only private oral assurances that FDR no longer favored American membership in the League of Nations, he was not satisfied. Hearst wrote: "I must say frankly that if Mr. Roosevelt is not willing to make public declaration of his change of heart, and wants only to make his statement to me privately, I would not believe him."[17]

Consequently, in an address before a meeting of the New York State Grange on February 2, 1932, Governor Roosevelt made the statement that Hearst called for. Roosevelt said the League of Nations had often been "a mere meeting place for the political discussion of strictly European political national difficulties. In these the United States should have no part." He concluded that "American participation in the League would not serve the highest purpose of the prevention of war and a settlement of international difficulties in accordance with fundamental American ideals." Therefore, he did "not favor American participation."[18] That statement partly appeased Hearst and made progressive isolationists feel more comfortable in supporting him. But it displeased internationalists.[19] And even Hearst continued to support Garner before the convention.

Both major parties held their national conventions in Chicago—the Republicans in mid-June, and the Democrats at the end of the month. As expected, the Republicans renominated Hoover for president and Charles Curtis for vice-president. The platform defended the domestic and foreign policies of the Republican years and the Hoover administration. At the Democratic convention two weeks later, Roosevelt won nomination on the fourth ballot. It was a victory for the South and West over the urban Northeast, and for progressives over conservatives.

A. Mitchell Palmer, President Wilson's former attorney general, drafted most of the short Democratic platform. But he had help from Senator Cordell Hull of Tennessee, who was to serve as Roosevelt's secretary of state. President Hoover's Secretary of State Henry L.

Stimson of New York drafted most of the Republican foreign policy plank. Though Hull and Stimson differed in backgrounds and styles, neither was an isolationist. And neither Hull's South nor Stimson's urban Northeast was an isolationist stronghold. Years later Hull wrote in his memoirs that he and Palmer had "inserted as many basic peace and international cooperation objectives in the foreign policy plank" as they thought the convention would accept. The Democratic platform called for "settlement of international disputes by arbitration" and urged making the Pact of Paris effective "by consultation and conference in case of violation of treaties." Both platforms endorsed joining the World Court. But neither urged membership in the League of Nations, and neither favored canceling war debts. The Republican platform rejected "alliances or foreign partnerships." The platforms did not cause isolationists to believe that the Democrats would be more active, expansionist, or internationalist in foreign affairs than the Republicans. The foreign policy planks did not give isolationists cause for alarm.[20] Leading isolationists bemoaned the renomination of Hoover and were pleased with the nomination of Roosevelt. But foreign affairs played little direct role in determining those attitudes.

Great Britain's ambassador to the United States, Sir Ronald Lindsay, correctly wrote that "foreign affairs do not promise to become an issue" in the campaign. The ambassador provided the British Foreign Office with a thumbnail sketch of Roosevelt's characteristics: "He is a gentleman in every sense of the word, well meaning and very ambitious. He has antennae and political sense to his very finger-tips. Instinctively he knows what the feeling of the moment is and what is politically possible. His intellectual endowment is not conspicuously great, and when confronted with an unfamiliar problem his first movement is to send for the man who can best advise him; but as he has no intellectual pride, if things go wrong he will not hesitate to send for someone else."[21]

Both Hoover, the Republican candidate, and Norman Thomas, the Socialist, were active noninterventionist opponents of President Roosevelt's foreign policies before the United States entered World War II in 1941. But in 1932 neither Hoover nor Thomas won much support from major isolationist leaders. Many who voted for Thomas would later oppose American entry into World War II, but they would do so more as pacifists than as isolationists. Senators Arthur Capper of Kansas and Arthur Vandenberg of Michigan both endorsed Hoover. Colonel Charles A. Lindbergh voted for Hoover, but did so with little enthusiasm and no publicity.[22] Some leading isolationists maintained a discreet neutrality or silence in the 1932 presidential race. Others opposed Hoover without endorsing Roosevelt.

Busy with his own campaign in North Dakota, young Senator Nye criticized Hoover but withheld endorsement of Roosevelt. Fearing that voters tended to vote straight tickets, he thought it would be "foolish" for a Republican nominee in North Dakota to announce for Roosevelt, a Democrat. Early in November he told an audience, "I have had too much trouble making up my own mind who to vote for for president to seek now to inflict my choice upon the people of North Dakota." Many years later Nye said he had voted for Hoover in 1932—but he said that long after he had broken with Roosevelt and after he had been voted out of the Senate. Senator Henrik Shipstead of Minnesota, like Nye, criticized Hoover but did not endorse Roosevelt. Without endorsing FDR, Republican Senator James Couzens of Michigan probably was correct when he wrote in September, 1932: "There is one thing I am quite certain of and that is, if Roosevelt is elected, it will not be because they love Roosevelt the more, but Hoover the less. It will certainly be a protest vote." Senator Borah of Idaho maintained a sphinxlike silence on the presidential contest. Privately he criticized Hoover and his policies, but he did not bolt the Republican party and did not endorse Roosevelt.[23]

If leading isolationists had been forced to line up on one side or the other before election day, however, most would have been with Roosevelt in opposition to Hoover. Among the more active in their support for Roosevelt were Senators Norris and Wheeler. More cautious or belated in their endorsements of FDR were Senator Johnson of California, Senator Robert M. La Follette, Jr., of Wisconsin, and Governor Philip La Follette of Wisconsin. In September, 1932, Senator Norris became chairman of the national committee of the National Progressive League for Franklin D. Roosevelt. It was nonpartisan, independent of the Republican party, and drew support from progressive Republicans, Democrats, and independents. Norris was not just a figurehead; he campaigned vigorously in the West for Roosevelt. In mid-October, Senator La Follette announced his support for the election of Roosevelt. And late in October, when the old Nebraska senator fell ill, Governor La Follette filled in on short notice at a speaking engagement in Illinois on behalf of the election of Roosevelt.[24]

Senator Johnson publicly commended Roosevelt for promptly traveling to Chicago to make his acceptance speech at the Democratic convention. In early October when FDR campaigned in California, he and Johnson conferred. Each made laudatory public comments about the other. When representatives of seventy newspapers in southern California urged Johnson to support the Republican ticket, the old senator snapped back vigorously. He identified himself as a progressive Republican and saw Hoover as "ultra-conservative." He did not mention Roosevelt, but insisted, "I cannot and I will not support Mr. Hoover." To Senator Bronson Cutting of New Mexico, Johnson wrote: "I shall do what I can in behalf of Roosevelt. It is the only hope, in my opinion, of Progressivism." He concentrated his activity for Roosevelt mainly in his home state of California.[25]

Amos R. E. Pinchot, later prominent in the isolationist movement, privately wrote during the campaign that most of the liberals he knew were supporting Franklin Roosevelt. Pinchot publicly endorsed FDR through the National Progressive League for Franklin D. Roosevelt. He described Roosevelt as "by all odds the best man nominated by either party since Woodrow Wilson." He conceded that "Roosevelt does not go as far as I would like him to go along certain lines. But I long ago gave up hope of being able to vote for a presidential candidate cut precisely to my pattern."[26]

Roosevelt generally avoided foreign affairs during his campaign. That did not trouble most of his isolationist supporters, but internationalists were disappointed. Professor William E. Dodd of the University of Chicago was a doctrinaire Wilsonian internationalist. He supported FDR for president, but was disappointed that he did not come out for the League of Nations. In the midst of the campaign Dodd wrote Daniel C. Roper proposing to include an endorsement of the league in an article supporting Roosevelt for president. Roper forwarded Dodd's letter to Roosevelt. In response, Louis Howe, the governor's political adviser, called Roper to urge Dodd "not to refer to Roosevelt's attitude with regard to the League of Nations at this time." Roper wrote Dodd: "You and I know his ideas with regard to the League of Nations, but they do not wish it to be emphasized that he feels one way and speaks another."[27]

Francis B. Sayre, President Wilson's son-in-law, told Roosevelt that "many quite influential people" said they were going to vote for Hoover because Roosevelt had "failed" to declare himself "in a progressive spirit on the problem of foreign relations and because of their feeling that the foreign problems are some of the most vital which America will have to face during the coming four years." Those "influential people" were troubled by FDR's speech in February rejecting membership in the league. Sayre thought those ideas "should be corrected" with "a ringing declaration" showing Roosevelt's "true slant" that "would win the support of a large number of influential leaders and mean a great many votes."[28] Roosevelt preferred, however, to refer to foreign affairs piecemeal along with other topics rather than have a major address summarizing his foreign policy views.

The British Embassy, in reporting to London on the presidential campaign, concluded that "with a good Secretary of State I see no reason why Mr. Roosevelt should not be just as satisfactory, from our point of view, as Mr. Hoover."[29] But that embassy official was giving more direct attention to foreign policy considerations of the campaign than either Roosevelt or leading isolationists gave in the summer and fall of 1932.

Franklin D. Roosevelt and the Democrats decisively defeated Herbert Hoover and the Republicans in the election on November 8, 1932. Most leading isolationists shared in opposing the reelection of Hoover; many of them actively supported Roosevelt. Roosevelt and his party were careful to say nothing on foreign affairs during the campaign that might lose the support of isolationists on election day. But it was the Great Depression—not foreign affairs—that determined the outcome of the election. Most Americans blamed the Hoover administration for the depression, its intensity, and its duration. Though voters were unsure just what Roosevelt and the Democrats might do to restore prosperity, they preferred to risk the uncertainties offered by Roosevelt's dynamic optimism than to suffer more of the failures that they identified with Hoover. Most isolationists shared those general attitudes. They identified Hoover with conservatism and special privilege; they saw hope for progressivism in Roosevelt. Except that Roosevelt carefully avoided making statements on foreign affairs that might have alienated isolationists, foreign policy issues played little direct role in shaping the attitudes and actions of isolationists toward Roosevelt in the campaign and election of 1932.

Chapter 3

Interregnum

The four months between Franklin D. Roosevelt's election on November 8, 1932, and his inauguration on March 4, 1933, were characterized by confusion and deepening economic crises. The banking system very nearly collapsed. Anxious worries about domestic violence and revolution were not entirely unjustified. Lame duck President Herbert Hoover painfully recognized the seriousness of the situation but was powerless to commit the government beyond March 4—and he lacked effective power to get action even for that interim. He sought the cooperation of President-elect Roosevelt. FDR expressed willingness to cooperate, but was not prepared to bind his new administration to Hoover's discredited policies. And Roosevelt had no legal authority to make governmental decisions until he was inaugurated. Courteous letters and formal conferences could not satisfactorily ease the transition.

Roosevelt also had the usual responsibilities of any newly elected president for appointing his cabinet members and filling other top positions in his administration. He determined to call a special session of Congress to meet when he took office, and that session would require his positive leadership. Roosevelt thrived on challenges and seemed almost to delight as he moved to meet them. As Hiram Johnson observed, "He has, apparently, no nervous system, or he could not stand up in the fashion that he does."[1]

In the chaos and confusion during the winter of 1932–33, neither the word nor the idea of isolationism presented itself conspicuously. Leading isolationists were part of the political scene, but at that time most of them were garbed as progressives rather more than as isolationists. Their political situation as progressives was more promising than it had been for a decade and a half, but it had elements of uncertainty. Though most of them had opposed the reelection of Hoover and many had actively supported Roosevelt, most were not Democrats. Roosevelt's nomination and election owed much to those western progressive isolationists. He shared certain progressive (and possibly foreign policy) values with them. They were a part of his political thinking and planning before inauguration, and they gave much thought to their relations with the new Democratic administration under his leadership.

The president-elect determined to include one or more progressive Republicans in his cabinet, and rumors abounded on whom he might name. George Norris was a good possibility for secretary of agriculture, and he could have had a position if he had made himself available. But Norris made it clear from the beginning that he would not accept a cabinet post if one were offered; he preferred to remain in the Senate.[2]

Rumors circulated that Hiram Johnson might be named to the cabinet. The old California senator shared his thoughts on the possibility in a letter to his sons: "I have lived so long in absolute independence that it is a very difficult thing for me to see myself a member of any group where I would discipline myself to the views of any one, or any few men. . . . I have never been able to take my politics or my government policies from others. And this is why, perhaps I have been in rebellion and opposition so much." He knew that he could not change, and "would not want to change."[3]

During the afternoon and evening of Thursday, January 19, 1933, Governor Roosevelt moved decisively to bring progressives into his cabinet. On arriving from New York at the Mayflower Hotel in Washington, Roosevelt's first appointment at 3:45 P.M. was with Senator Johnson. In their twenty-minute meeting alone, FDR offered Johnson the position of secretary of interior. Johnson graciously but firmly declined. The president-elect pressed his offer, but the senator could not be moved.

Though he refused the appointment, Johnson came away from the meeting favorably impressed by Roosevelt: "I liked him, and I liked his manner. He is genial, kindly, and sympathetic. . . . he is just a human being." Johnson thought Roosevelt had not clearly "thought out a fixed, definite program for national relief," but did not criticize him for that "because no one else" had either. Johnson (who had been Theodore Roosevelt's vice-presidential running mate on the Progressive ticket twenty years before) concluded that FDR presented "as fair a hope for us as during my political career has been presented by any man."[4]

Early in the evening on that same Thursday, Governor Roosevelt in a brief interview offered the Interior Department, which Johnson had rejected, to Republican Senator Bronson M. Cutting of New Mexico. Cutting's background was much like Roosevelt's. The son of a wealthy businessman, Cutting was born on Long Island, reared in New England, and educated at Groton and Harvard, where he was a Phi Beta Kappa. Tall, handsome, and well built, he never lost his Harvard accent. Afflicted with tuberculosis, in 1910 he fled west to New Mexico for his health. He immersed himself and his future in that state, becoming owner and publisher of the *Santa Fe New Mexican*. Already fluent in French, German, and Italian, he learned Spanish and became active on behalf of New Mexico's Spanish-speaking population. He supported Theodore Roosevelt's Bull Moose Progressive party in 1912. During World War I he served as America's assistant military attaché in London, rising to the rank of captain. In the 1920s he became powerful in the American Legion and other organizations in New Mexico. In 1928, the state governor appointed him to the United States Senate to fill the vacancy left by the death of the incumbent. As a progressive Republican, Cutting actively campaigned for Roosevelt in 1932.[5]

Though Cutting was not an isolationist, he was fully a part of the western progressive group, most of whom were isolationists. He commanded the unqualified respect, confidence, and friendship of Senators Norris, Johnson, Wheeler, and Borah. He was particularly close to Bob and Phil La Follette. His appointment to Roosevelt's cabinet would have pleased all of them. When their brief session ended early in the evening on January 19, Cutting promised Roosevelt that he would give careful consideration to the proffered position as secretary of interior.[6]

Building on the family tradition and political groundwork laid by their father, Philip and his older brother Young Bob La Follette led the progressive movement and later the Progressive party in Wisconsin. Bob had filled the elder La Follette's seat in the United States Senate since the father had died in 1925. Phil had won election as a progressive Republican governor of Wisconsin in 1930, but had been defeated in his bid for a second term in the republican primary of 1932. Both had campaigned for Roosevelt in 1932.

Young Bob and Phil shared the La Follette family pride. They shared in their devotion to progressive principles—and to isolationism in foreign affairs. Both had impressive talent and courage in politics. They were devoted to each other and consulted closely on family and political matters. But the brothers also had distinctive individual qualities; their styles and temperaments were different. Phil was brighter, more energetic, bolder, more ambitious, more aggressive, less discreet—and in the final analysis the less successful and less respected of the two. Bob was more introspective, less comfortable in the rough-and-tumble of politics, more preoccupied with his own illness (real or imagined), more reflective, more cautious, less impulsive, and over the years more effective in accomplishing political goals and more respected on the national scene by friend and foe alike.[7]

Defeated in the Wisconsin Republican gubernatorial primary in September, 1932, Phil and his wife sailed for Europe on January 5, 1933, just after his term as governor formally ended. By coincidence, they were in Europe when Adolf Hitler first became chancellor in Germany. They toured England, Germany, the Soviet Union, Austria, Italy, and other countries and conferred with high officials on developments in Europe and America. Their stay in Europe was cut short in March by word that President Roosevelt wanted to consult Phil about a position in his new administration.[8]

Senator Robert M. La Follette, Jr., was scheduled to meet with Governor Roosevelt in the Mayflower Hotel in Washington on Thursday evening, January 19—the same day that Roosevelt had offered the interior post first to Johnson and then to Cutting. When La Follette was ushered in to see the governor, he was in the midst of a conference with Democratic Senator Burton K. Wheeler. Brain truster Raymond Moley also joined them. At the beginning of the session Roosevelt told La Follette: "I want Phil in my official family. I do not know just where yet, but he must come in." The conversation then turned to other matters. With a steady stream of people and interruptions, La Follette did not get the opportunity for the private discussion he had hoped to have with FDR. When he and Wheeler took their leave, La Follette told Roosevelt: "If you are to give any further and more serious consideration to the suggestion which you threw out shortly after I came into the room, I think it important that we should have an opportunity to talk the situation out more frankly." Roosevelt suggested that they handle it either by telephone or by a visit at Warm Springs, Georgia.[9]

The La Follettes (and progressives in general) were guarded in considering their possible relations with and roles in the new Roosevelt administration. They were not completely confident that FDR actually would pursue progressive policies. They carefully considered the effects their participation might have on progressivism in the future as well as on their individual political futures. If the appointment of progressives was just a ploy to disarm them politically without giving them effective power to guide the administration in progressive directions, they would have none of it. The appointment of just one progressive Republican to the cabinet could, in effect, be little more than tokenism. It would be more encouraging if two were included to give strength to the progressive cause in the new administration—or so Cutting and the La Follette brothers reasoned.

In his brief session with Roosevelt, Cutting got the impression that FDR was considering either Felix Frankfurter or Philip La Follette for attorney general. Cutting's decision on his appointment as secretary of interior would be influenced by (and in fact was determined by) the place Phil might have in the new administration. On Friday, January 20, just before Roosevelt left for the South from Washington, he told Senator Cutting that he had offered the attorney general appointment to the old Irish-Catholic Democratic senator from Montana, Thomas J. Walsh. Though they had questions about his age and health, progressives did not object to the possibility of Walsh as attorney general. But that appointment would not leave a cabinet opening for Philip La Follette, and in that event Cutting might not be willing to enter the cabinet either. Roosevelt told Cutting, however, that Walsh might not accept the offer, and he suggested that Senators Cutting and La Follette confer with him on the matter at Warm Springs.[10]

La Follette and Cutting arrived in Warm Springs late in the afternoon on Sunday, January 22. Roosevelt discoursed at length on the policies he had under consideration for his administration (he did most of the talking). La Follette found Roosevelt's expressed attitudes on domestic economic policies to be "in substantial accord with the progressive position." La Follette was also "impressed" by Roosevelt's knowledge of the Democratic leadership in the Senate. Roosevelt spoke highly of Philip La Follette and said that if Walsh declined, he intended to offer the position of attorney general to him. If Walsh accepted, Roosevelt wanted Bob to find out what position outside the cabinet the former Wisconsin governor would consider accepting. According to La Follette and Cutting, FDR said he must have Phil's help in the crisis. He urged Cutting to accept the position as secretary of interior. The New Mexico Republican made it clear that his decision would be influenced by developments relating to Philip La Follette.

Senator La Follette assured Roosevelt that he would support the new administration so long as it pursued progressive policies. He pointed out that the progressive program Roosevelt had outlined that evening would inevitably force a split in the Democratic party and that

FDR was being "presented with an opportunity to make the Democratic party the instrumentality of progressive thought in the future." Roosevelt responded that he realized that his program would divide the Democratic party and that that was one of the reasons he wanted the help of people such as Cutting and the La Follettes. While preserving his own independence, Senator La Follette determined that he would support Roosevelt's policies when they were "in conformity with progressive principles" and that he would do all he could to make the administration a success so long as Roosevelt pursued "genuine progressive policies." He followed that same course so far as Roosevelt's foreign policies were concerned as well.[11]

Cutting decided that he would accept the position as secretary of interior only if Walsh declined the appointment to head the Justice Department and if that cabinet post then went to Philip La Follette. When Walsh accepted the appointment as attorney general in mid-February, there was no cabinet position for Phil. And though Roosevelt seriously explored other important assignments for Phil outside the cabinet, that did not suffice. Cutting turned down the proffered position of secretary of interior. On February 21, Bob cabled Phil in London, explaining the developments and asking whether he would "consider chairmanship Power or appointment Trade Commission." Bob advised Phil not to accept appointment to those positions, but urged him to return promptly to confer directly with the president. Phil did as his brother advised.[12]

The two brothers spent an hour with the new president at the White House at mid-day on March 20, 1933. Roosevelt discussed his relief policies and queried Phil on the European situation. Phil warned of "the imminent danger of war" in Europe and blamed that "war psychology" on "the economic process that was going on in every country." He thought "Russia was the key to the peace of Europe" and advised recognizing the Soviet Union "promptly and without a lot of preliminaries." He favored recognition "as a part of the program to dispose of our agricultural surplus," believing that the needs of the large Russian population were "sufficiently great at the present time to absorb about the entire surplus in our warehouses."

Then President Roosevelt said he was eager to have Phil join his administration and asked what position might interest him. Roosevelt suggested the possibility of apointments in the Power Commission, the transportation system, the Federal Trade Commission, or in public works and relief. But Phil responded that he thought "for the present" he "could be of greater service" helping "to formulate public opinion on the firing line" in Wisconsin and the Middle West.

Roosevelt acquiesced, but told Phil, "If you see anything that you think you want, I wish you would let me know." And he urged the former Wisconsin governor to keep in close touch with him. "Come and see me often." Phil responded: "All you have to do is to let me know and if I have the railroad fare I will come." With that they shook hands and departed in a warm and friendly spirit. From time to time later, Roosevelt offered Phil positions in his administration, but the Wisconsin progressive never accepted.[13]

As inauguration day on March 4, 1933, had drawn near, for one reason or another the progressive Republicans George W. Norris of Nebraska, Hiram W. Johnson of California, Bronson Cutting of New Mexico, and Philip F. La Follette of Wisconsin were out of the picture so far as the new president's cabinet was concerned. In no case were foreign policy considerations directly involved in keeping them from the cabinet. With the exception of Cutting, all were isolationists.

At the last minute Roosevelt did get a progressive Republican to serve as secretary of interior in his Cabinet. The position went to Harold L. Ickes of Chicago, who was to be one of only two persons to serve in the cabinet the entire time that Roosevelt was president. Ickes was a bona fide progressive Republican, and a former Bull Mooser. He had vigorously supported Roosevelt in 1932, and he eagerly sought an appointment in the new administration. He was a close friend of Hiram Johnson and was known to the other western progressives. Johnson thought Ickes might prove to be "as good a secretary of the Interior as we have ever had."[14] During Roosevelt's first term, one might have seen Ickes as both a progressive and an isolationist. But with the outbreak of war in Asia and Europe, long before the Japanese attack on Pearl Harbor, Ickes became one of the more extreme interventionists in the president's cabinet. From 1938 onward he broke sharply on foreign affairs with western progressive isolationists.

Because of circumstances unrelated to foreign affairs, none of the leading isolationists was included in Roosevelt's cabinet. But they were much interested in FDR's top cabinet appointment, that of secretary of state. And they voiced their opinions on the position to Roosevelt and his closest advisors. Directly reflecting their agrarian progressive values, those major isolationists wanted to make certain that the new secretary of state was not identified with Wall Street, with the House of Morgan banking interests, or with one of the prestigious New York international law firms.

Again, Senator Johnson expressed the attitudes of leading isolationists clearly and effectively. During his meeting with Roosevelt on

January 19, Johnson told FDR that "the most important position he had to fill was that of Secretary of State." The California senator said: "Since 1920 the personnel of the State Department had been drawn from three sources, and always visaed by one. It came either from [Charles Evans] Hughes office, or [Elihu] Root's office, or the Morgan House in New York City, and had to be approved by Morgan and Company. During these past twelve years, our foreign affairs have been manipulated, operated, managed, directed and controlled by Morgan and Company and until the fourth of March this would be the undoubted fact." Johnson urged Roosevelt to "have his own man in charge of our foreign affairs, not Morgan's man, not a man of the international bankers, not a member of the present regime, nor one who had been representing Mr. Hoover ostensibly for the past year in Europe [i.e., Norman H. Davis], but his own man with an American viewpoint." Roosevelt told Johnson that he agreed with him and that he "had just such a man, free from any of the influences" that Johnson had mentioned. Roosevelt did not, however, tell Johnson at that time who he had in mind.[15]

The appointment of Senator Cordell Hull of Tennessee to be secretary of state generally was consistent with Johnson's advice. Hull was not an isolationist. He was a doctrinaire Wilsonian internationalist whose magnificent obsession was trade reciprocity. But he was not identified with Wall Street, with the House of Morgan, or with any of the New York international law firms. His appointment did not greatly impress isolationists—but neither did it displease them initially. Hiram Johnson, who knew Hull fairly well, wrote that he had "the good-will and the praise of all the press." Personally, Johnson found Hull "a pleasant, kindly disposed individual, utterly colorless, wholly without position in the [Senate] body at all." The California senator considered Hull "a nice man, and perhaps in the position he now has, he may develop into a great man," but he did not expect that to happen. Johnson thought that Roosevelt made his appointments "in the most casual fashion."[16] Leading isolationists in Congress did not play large roles in controlling or influencing patronage in the Roosevelt administration.

Progressive isolationists also had to determine their role in the two houses of Congress, where Democrats controlled substantial majorities. What would be the status in Senate and House committees of those progressive isolationist Republicans who had campaigned actively for Roosevelt? Old-line conservative Republicans had never trusted those "Sons of the Wild Jackasses" from the West, and their performances in the 1932 elections did nothing to enhance their status in Republican leadership circles. To clear away any uncertainty so far as he was concerned, after the election Senator Norris wrote Joseph T. Robinson of Arkansas, Democratic leader in the Senate, that he did not expect or, under the circumstances, even want to retain his chairmanship of the Senate Judiciary Committee.[17] In practice, none of the other progressive Republicans who had supported Roosevelt either expected or received treatment as Democrats in the matter of committee assignments or chairmanships.

Despite his enthusiasm for Roosevelt, Senator Norris preferred to lay aside his burdens as chairman of the National Progressive League for Franklin D. Roosevelt. With encouragement from La Follette, Cutting, and others, however, Norris called a meeting of some progressive senators in his office for Saturday, January 28, 1933. Senator Johnson did not attend. He berated the "political and intellectual bankruptcy of the Old Guard," but considered the "insurgent group" to be "hopeless from the standpoint of real action." Johnson's attitude illustrated in caricature a central political difficulty that inhibited the effectiveness of the western progressive isolationists. Always a minority in Congress, they needed all the unity and cooperation they could get on both domestic and foreign affairs. But their proud independence made it difficult for them to work effectively with each other; those "outside the faith" found those progressives to be difficult and unreliable political partners. Nonetheless, Senators Norris, Wheeler, La Follette, Cutting, Shipstead, Nye, Lynn J. Frazier of North Dakota, Edward P. Costigan of Colorado, and John J. Blaine of Wisconsin did attend the meeting in Norris's office, as did Basil Manly and David Niles. All favored continuing a permanent progressive organization. Senators Cutting, Wheeler, and La Follette were named as a subcommittee to consider the form, functions, and financing of the organization in the future.[18]

By the time Franklin D. Roosevelt stood to take the oath of office as president of the United States on March 4, 1933, the ever-changing relations between FDR and the progressive isolationists were becoming fixed. Those patterns included Roosevelt's warm efforts to assure support for his administration from progressives; they included guarded hope on both sides that the new president and the western progressive isolationists could work together effectively to accomplish progressive goals. Only occasionally, in passing references, had either the isolationists or FDR explored the place of foreign policy in that relationship.

Chapter 4

The Hundred Days

The economic crisis enveloping the United States by the time Franklin
D. Roosevelt took the oath of office on March 4, 1933, was the worst
in American history. Faith in old gods was being shattered. The American people, the Congress, businessmen, workers, and farmers alike
shared in an almost desperate eagerness to follow a leader who might
restore prosperity. Many worried about the possibilities of violence
and revolution. Traditional American faith in the future, in the in-
evitability of progress, was severely shaken. And that anxiety extended to the hearts and emotions of most Americans—whatever their
opinions of the handsome man who solemnly and confidently took the
oath of office—and who then told them that "the only thing we have
to fear is fear itself."

Deeply concerned western progressive isolationists were cautiously
hopeful about the new leader. Senators Norris, Johnson, Wheeler, La
Follette, Borah, Nye, Shipstead, Capper, and others differed among
themselves on details. But they shared certain values and a generalized
image of what constituted the good life, the good society, good
government, a good economy, and a sound foreign policy. In general
they preferred an individualistic rural, small-town social structure,
with wide distribution of property and power. In a broad sense most
of them were Jeffersonians rather than Hamiltonians. They feared
and distrusted bigness of almost any sort—big business, big finance,
big military, big government, big unions, and big corporate farms.
Their sympathies were with debtors rather than creditors, with
farmers rather than city people, with small businessmen rather than
big business, with workers rather than employers, with producers
rather than financiers and distributors, with free competition within
the country rather than monopoly, with equality of opportunity rather
than special privilege, with limited constitutional government rather

than monarchy or dictatorship, with legislative authority rather than presidential power, with democracy rather than elitism, with faith in the common man rather than experts, with domestic progress rather than international expansion. Those isolationists tended to be biased against big cities, the East, big business, Wall Street, Europe in general, and England in particular. They conceded the necessity for a large role by the federal government in time of war and in the economic emergency of 1932–33. But they were not socialists, and they did not favor continuous massive involvement by the federal government in economic matters.

Their individual devotion to grass-roots democracy was long and consistent; their fears about the abuses of concentrated political, economic, or military power was genuine. But in that awful emergency some allowed themselves to speculate briefly about the needs for, and the dangers of, strong leadership, even of dictatorship, in that crisis. Commenting on midwestern farmers who violently blocked mortgage foreclosures and who prevented marketing of farm products at ruinously low prices, Senator Hiram Johnson wrote to his eldest son five weeks before inauguration day that "if these farmers with their love for law and order ever united with the disorderly and anti-government spirit of the cities, we can look for almost anything." Two weeks later Johnson wrote that they were "much closer to a sort of dictatorship in this country than we have been during any of our lives," and that they "may be closer to revolution than we have ever been in our lives." Two weeks before inauguration newsmen quoted young Senator Gerald P. Nye of North Dakota as saying that "the situation today is calling for a dictatorship so that the necessary economies can be brought about by President Roosevelt." Republican Senator Arthur H. Vandenberg of Michigan was a conservative, an isolationist, and had opposed FDR's election. Three days after Roosevelt's inauguration Vandenberg wrote in a personal letter: "I think we need a 'dictator' in this particular situation."[1]

That atmosphere of desperation might have moved the United States in any of several directions, depending on the performance of the new president. Franklin D. Roosevelt was determined and able to lead. But the major political parties had not chosen extremists as their presidential candidates; even in those desperate times the voters had not cast their ballots for extremists. Both FDR and leading isolationists, like most Americans, placed their hopes in moderate solutions within the limits set by America's traditional patterns of democracy, private enterprise, and constitutional government.

The leading Senate isolationists closest to Roosevelt during the Hundred Days and most directly involved in shaping legislative proposals and tactics were Hiram Johnson of California, George Norris of Nebraska, Robert La Follette of Wisconsin, and Burton Wheeler of Montana—all independent progressive Republicans except for Democrat Wheeler. All participated in long White House sessions with the president and his administrative advisors before and during the special session of Congress that lasted from Thursday, March 9, until Friday, June 16, 1933. All kept their fingers crossed as they shared and supported the new administration's rapid-fire initiatives. Legislative proposals on banking, economy, relief, Tennessee Valley Authority, agriculture, veterans affairs, and recovery tumbled out one after the other with confusing speed and complexity. With varied reservations, most leading isolationists wished success for the new administration in its efforts to restore prosperity.

Senator Johnson recorded his reactions at length in letters to his sons in California. In those letters his enthusiasms and hopes far overshadowed his reservations. He confessed that the inaugural ceremony on March 4, 1933, was the first he had ever attended. Johnson liked Roosevelt's inaugural address, particularly "his outspoken references to the money-changers, and how they had failed and fled." Johnson attended long White House sessions with the new president on Sunday, March 5, and again on Wednesday evening, March 8, the night before the special session began. He liked what he saw and heard at those meetings. He was awed by Roosevelt's energy, good humor, equanimity, and willingness to lead. Johnson, perhaps like Roosevelt himself, did not understand all that the administration was proposing, but he applauded FDR for boldly trying. Johnson assumed that some of the experiments would fail, but he welcomed the efforts nonetheless. "The remarkable thing about him to me was his readiness to assume responsibility and his taking that responsibility with a smile." At the Wednesday evening session Johnson dramatically advised Roosevelt to "kick" all the Wall Street bankers "into oblivion," and thought he saw the president nod his approval. Observing FDR's work pace, Johnson wrote: "I do not see how any living soul can last physically going the pace that he is going, and mentally any one of us would be a psychopathic case if we undertook to do what he is doing. And with it all, the amazing thing to me was there never was a note of impatience in all the hours we sat there Wednesday night, or the previous Sunday, and never anything but the utmost good nature." He thought FDR could not "resist long the flattery and the blandishments of great power and wealth.'' But he had "the first hope" he had had "in more than twenty years in this respect.'' Johnson believed Roosevelt's remedies were purely empirical. "They may aid a little, or much, or not at all.'' The old senator did not care whether Roosevelt "blunders or not in a particular measure or a specific policy, he has had the guts to go on and do as he thought he ought to do.'' Johnson was willing to support the president so long as it did not violate his own "fundamental ideas.''[2]

On April 1, Johnson wrote: "Roosevelt keeps up his astonishing efforts. He has an energy I little suspected, and a capacity for work I have never seen excelled. . . . I can not believe that any one human being can thoroughly digest all that he is undertaking, but the very undertaking is the delightful thing to witness.'' Johnson said he thought the United States was "nearer our philosophy of government than we have ever been in my lifetime in this nation.'' Two weeks later he thought congress was "fiddling along with more legislation than any one man or any legislative body can accurately digest,'' but the senator was "still in the mood of trying anything that may be suggested, and the country is still in the mood, in my opinion, of following Roosevelt in anything that he desires.'' Johnson believed FDR was likely "to come a cropper at any time,'' but he hoped not. Roosevelt was "attempting so much that all can not succeed.''[3]

As the special session neared its close early in June, Johnson noted that Roosevelt was "losing a little of his astounding poise'' and "a bit of his extreme good nature.'' Johnson also detected "a revolt in the air in the Congress.'' But Roosevelt, "clever as he is, senses that fact, and before there is an actual break, he wishes us out of the way.'' The day after the special session adjourned on June 16, 1933, Johnson wrote his sons: "The latter part of this session has been terrible. We're all tired and many are disgruntled.'' The California Senator's enthusiasm for FDR was more qualified than it had been earlier. But even in his weariness, Johnson concluded: "The great balance, however, in the Roosevelt administration is favorable, and perhaps we ought not only to discount, but to forget the other side of the ledger.''[4]

Senator George W. Norris of Nebraska had impressions of FDR that paralleled Johnson's. Differences in the reactions of the two progressives partly reflected their personalities and styles. Both Johnson and Norris were tough old warriors who wore their political scars as proud emblems of their long crusades for progressive causes. But the Nebraska senator was more mellow, more flexible, and less rigidly self-righteous in his political independence than was Johnson.

A month after the special session began, Senator Norris wrote: "I believe that Roosevelt is doing the very best he can to redeem his promises and to make good. The question confronting me, however, as to whether it is possible for him to do so. He is working day and night. I do not really see how he stands up under the terrible burden, but he seems to be cheerful and I feel confident that his heart is in the right place. He does not," Norris continued, "claim to be a super-man, thank God, and that is one reason why I feel that the country will still believe in him and trust him, even though some of his propositions fail. I fear some of them will fail."[5]

Norris was affected by the political leadership and support that Roosevelt gave to make the Tennessee Valley Authority. The Nebraska senator had waged a long and lonely battle after World War I to make the government-owned Muscle Shoals facility in Tennessee into a functioning showpiece for regional planning and public power. But his efforts had failed until FDR threw the might of his office behind the project. TVA was the first major reform measure enacted in Roosevelt's New Deal. With the president's strong backing, Congress moved quickly to make the old senator's dream into reality. With little debate, the necessary legislation won approval in the House on April 25, 1933, by a vote of 306 to 92. Republican Hamilton Fish of New York cast his vote against it. On May 3, the Senate adopted the resolution 63 to 20. The affirmative votes included all the progressive isolationists who voted. The negative votes included Republicans W. Warren Barbour of New Jersey, Arthur Vandenberg of Michigan, and Wallace H. White, Jr. of Maine—more conservative isolationists. The conference report won Senate approval on May 16, without record vote, and in the House the following day 258 to 112 (with Fish again in opposition). President Roosevelt signed it into law on May 18, 1933, with Senator Norris proudly watching over his shoulder and treasuring a pen the president used to affix his signature.[6] FDR did not buy Norris with TVA, but his essential support for that project helped convince Norris that Roosevelt was a true friend of progressivism. From time to time Norris would oppose Roosevelt on specific issues, but FDR's role in making TVA a reality helped lay groundwork for the personal and political friendship between the New York patrician in the White House and the aging Nebraska progressive that endured until the senator's political defeat and his death more than a decade later.

Other western progressives pressed for comparable regional programs elsewhere. Shipstead was interested in an Upper Mississippi Valley project. Nye wanted a Missouri River diversion project. Johnson pressed for a Central Valley project in California. They had potential for industrial growth, conservation, job opportunities, and prosperity for the people, states, and regions served by western progressive isolationist legislators. At the same time, however, success for such projects would have encouraged the industrial growth, including potentially defense-oriented growth, that could erode the older agrarian and small-town life in those regions, the socioeconomic bases for isolationist foreign policy projections of that life, and the political bases from which those isolationist legislators worked.

In comparison with other western progressives, Senator Robert M. La Follette, Jr., of Wisconsin was less rigidly tied to rural values and more flexibly adjusted to the needs of urban America, including urban labor. La Follette also was less pleased and had more doubts about FDR's early performance than either Johnson or Norris. He was less sympathetic than Johnson and Norris with Roosevelt's undoctrinaire experimental improvisation. In April, La Follette wrote: "I cannot yet make out what the President is driving at. My own impression is that he has no concerted plan and is prone to meet each situation as it arises in the way which seems best at the moment. With lots of luck this technique may prove effective. However, it is so contrary to my own way of thinking and my training that I find it difficult to be patient." He feared that "the policy of leaping and looking afterwards may very easily prove disastrous." Like other western progressives, young La Follete regretted the deflationary effects of the administration's banking policies and of its economy and veterans' legislation.[7]

Senator La Follette was instrumental in prodding the Roosevelt administration to action on relief and public works programs. In March, 1933, Congress quickly passed legislation creating the Civilian Conservation Corps. There was little debate and no record vote in either house. The Federal Emergency Relief Administration (FERA), created in May, 1933, under the direction of Harry Hopkins, authorized federal grants for relief to be administered by the states. All leading isolationists present were among the fifty-five voting for the Senate version of the resolution authorizing FERA. The Public Works Administration that Secretary of Interior Harold L. Ickes headed was created by Title II of the National Industrial Recovery Act of 1933. Though many progressives had misgivings about Title I that set up NRA, few objected to the public works part of the resolution.[8] La Follette approved of those actions, but saw them as temporary palliatives and attached greater importance to "making a drive for a fundamental and far-reaching attack on the causes of the depression." Unless the administration quickly produced "a large program for re-employment and synthetic recovery," La Follette feared "a sharp recession within the next two or three months which will create another crisis . . . more severe than any we have yet experienced."[9]

Controversies between prominent isolationists and the Roosevelt administration over the operation of the National Recovery Administration highlighted significant patterns in their relations. One of the more important parts of the early New Deal, Title I of the National Industrial Recovery Act of June, 1933, authorized the president through the National Recovery Administration to approve and enforce codes of fair competition in the various segments of American industry and business. Section 7(a) of the legislation was to extend benefits to workers. The arrangement envisaged cooperation between business, labor, and government to increase prices, profits, and wages. It called for economic planning to revive prosperity, with primary reliance on domestic markets. The legislation included authority to increase tariffs and restrict imports if necessary to prevent low-cost foreign products from undercutting prices, profits, and wages sought through NRA.

The government planning that NRA attempted was not necessarily in conflict with the domestic planning that such continentalists as Charles A. Beard, Norman Thomas, or Stuart Chase advocated. Senator Nye earlier had introduced legislation calling for codes of fair competition similar to those the National Industrial Recovery Act authorized.[10] Nonetheless, the most pointed and effective criticism of NRA came from isolationists Borah and Nye, and their attacks won approval from other western progressive isolationists in and out of Congress.

Borah was not drawn so deeply into White House deliberations as Senators Norris, Johnson, Wheeler, and La Follette. He attended White House sessions, but the president's charm and political artfulness had little impact on him. None surpassed Johnson's self-image as a loner. But in actual performance it was Borah who most tenaciously and successfully spurned Roosevelt's blandishments. The Idaho progressive insisted that he was never a president's man or anybody else's man—except his own. In May, 1933, Borah wrote that he had voted for some of Roosevelt's proposals and would vote for others. "But when I reach the conclusion that a measure is unconstitutional or, as I think, hurtful to the public interests, I know of nothing else to do than to record my views by my vote." He believed Congress had "granted powers to the President" that it had "no authority under the Consititution to grant.'' Like other western progressives, Borah feared concentrated economic power in monopolies and urged antitrust policies. Not surprisingly, therefore, he (and they) had serious misgivings about the National Industrial Recovery Act.[11]

The administration's recovery bill quickly passed the House that May. Borah, Wheeler, La Follette, Bennett Champ Clark of Missouri, Huey Long of Louisiana, and other progressives played conspicuous roles in the Senate deliberations. Most important was Borah's opposition to suspension of antitrust laws. With solid support from other western progressives and with unenthusiastic acquiescence from administration spokesmen, Borah won approval for an amendment providing that the codes of fair competition should "not permit combinations in restraint of trade, price fixing, or other monopolistic purposes." The conference committee named to work out differences between the Senate and House versions, however, watered down Borah's amendment. The formidable Idaho senator insisted that the conference report provided "no protection to the consumer and no protection to small or independent business." In the final Senate vote on the conference report, without the Borah amendment, most western progressives and isolationists voted against the NIRA. They feared it would permit the growth and dominance of big business and would hurt small businessmen, workers, farmers, and the political democracy for which those progressives had been crusading for so many years. With the bill signed into law by the president on June 16, 1933, western progressives watched skeptically to see how NRA functioned. They did not have long to wait.[12]

President Roosevelt named General Hugh S. Johnson to head the National Recovery Administration. A West Point graduate and career army officer, Johnson had great energy and aggressive courage. He had helped administer the selective service in World War I. Along with George N. Peek and others, he was drawn into the work of the War Industries Board under Bernard M. Baruch during the war, and he shared with Peek in a continuing devotion to Baruch in the years that followed. With Peek, Johnson became involved in operating the Moline Implement Company in the 1920s, before returning to service in Baruch's various corporate and financial activities. Like Peek, Johnson saw domestic markets as more essential to American prosperity than developments abroad. Like Peek, Johnson was from the Middle West; like Peek, Johnson was a nationalist. In 1932 he campaigned actively for and with Franklin D. Roosevelt. Peek and Johnson both played major roles in Roosevelt's early New Deal, both soon fell by the wayside, and both later opposed the increasingly internationalist orientation of Roosevelt's economic and diplomatic policies.[13] Before Pearl Harbor, both were to share with other isolationists in opposing President Roosevelt's foreign policies.

As Johnson moved quickly to prod business and labor to share in drafting the various codes, and as he provided government authority for those codes, the fears of progressives seemed to be realized. In November and December, 1933, Senators Nye and Borah provided major challenges to Johnson's administration of NRA. In a public letter to General Johnson on November 25, Nye charged that NRA was failing to protect small businesses against monopolistic practices. The North Dakota Republican promised that unless there was a "complete reversal of present NRA policies," he would "demand the most sweeping investigation ever made into a governmental activity."[14]

As a consequence of his letter, Nye was drawn into meetings with General Johnson, the president, and Borah. On December 29, Roosevelt told newsmen that in the meetings they were trying to provide "adequate protection of the little fellow against the big fellow" and to retain "the principles of the Sherman Anti-trust Law."[15]

Early in January, 1934, Borah introduced a resolution to repeal the portion of NIRA that had suspended antitrust laws, but it never won approval. In a major broadcast on January 26, Nye charged that "new-deal machinery" was "being captured by the old dealers." He saw "monopolists taking advantage of N.R.A. machinery and improving upon their chance to win a more complete concentration of industry, of wealth, and of the power that always goes with it."[16]

General Johnson conceded that mistakes had been made and insisted that he welcomed constructive criticism. But he denied that NRA promoted monopoly or reduced competition. He boasted that the codes helped workers get shorter hours and higher pay and charged that many of the small businesses that Nye and Borah eulogized undercut competition by exploiting workers with sweat shop wages and child labor. He berated the two senators for what he saw as politically inspired attacks.[17]

On March 7, 1934, President Roosevelt created a National Recovery Review Board chaired by the famed lawyer Clarence Darrow. Nye conceived the idea and, along with Borah, suggested some of the board's members. The president directed it to determine whether the codes were "designed to promote monopolies or to eliminate or oppress small enterprises or operate to discriminate against them.'' And he asked it to recommend changes to ''rectify or eliminate such results.''[18]

The board's report to the president early in May was a highly partisan attack on NRA from much the same perspective that Nye and Borah had used. General Johnson and Donald Richberg, general counsel for NRA, produced an equally partisan reply.[19] Roosevelt and Johnson found the Darrow reports unfair, but Nye and Borah said the reports confirmed what they had contended all along. Both stepped up their attacks on NRA in speeches, letters, and press interviews.[20]

Senator Borah summed up his perspective in a significant letter dated October 7, 1934: ''I look upon the fight for the preservation of the 'little man,' for the small, independent producer and manufacturer, as a fight for a sound, wholesome, economic national life. It is more than that. It is a fight for clean politics and for free government. When you have destroyed small business, you have destroyed our towns and our country life, and you have guaranteed and made permanent the concentration of economic power. When you have made permanent the concentration of economic power, you have made certain the concentration of political power. The concentration of wealth always leads, and always has led, to the concentration of political power. Monopoly and bureaucracy are twin whelps from the same kennel.

''With the destruction of small business, your merchant becomes your absentee landlord. He will care little about local government, about schools, or even the condition of the family. What is it that has made our thousands of towns and villages, kept our small communities intact—those small communities where are bred the strong, self-reliant, capable citizens? It is the small, independent businessman.

''I do not wish to see these great Western states come under the blighting influence of those who are in the states for the sole purpose of collecting what they can exact and transferring it to other parts of the country.''[21]

That Borah letter revealed more about the contest between Roosevelt and the isolationists than may appear on first reading. It was more than just an attack on a particular New Deal agency. It was a paean to a way of life—rural, small town, small business, with emphasis on individualism and local self-government. It was, in effect, an attack on urbanization, on big business, on centralized government planning. Tacitly it was a defense of foreign policy projections of that older way of life and an attack on foreign policy projections of the urbanized-industrialized-centralized Hamiltonian America. Borah's letter reveals roots of the contest between isolationists and interventionists in foreign affairs. In his first term as president, Roosevelt could identify with the kind of society that Borah and Nye were speaking for, but he had long since departed that path by the time he died in 1945.

The Roosevelt administration attempted reforms and reorganization of NRA, but none of the changes silenced critics. In July, Roosevelt sent the overwrought Johnson on vacation, and the general resigned as head of NRA in October, 1934. In February, 1935, Senators Nye and Patrick McCarran of Nevada introduced a scorching Senate resolution berating NRA and calling for an investigation of its operations. And the whole experiment came to an end in May, 1935, when the United States Supreme Court ruled it unconstitutional.[22]

The economic nationalism of NRA was consistent with American isolationism. And in some respects its first administrator, General Johnson, was an appropriate mentor. But its call for national planning, its favoring big business, its failure to benefit small businessmen and workers, and its partnership between federal bureaucracy and big business all alienated western progressives—most of whom were isolationists. As both Borah and Nye clearly recognized, it pointed to a kind of government, economy, and society that differed radically from what progressives envisaged for the good life. Its demise helped send the Roosevelt administration, its New Deal, and American foreign policies off in directions that would also be unacceptable to isolationists.

The Agricultural Adjustment Act of May, 1933, and related New Deal farm legislation, were supposed to do for farmers what the National Industrial Recovery Act tried to do for industry and labor. All isolationists in Congress endorsed efforts to help farmers, and most of them put the restoration of agricultural prosperity at or near the top of their priorities. The depression had been a serious reality for rural America a dozen years before Roosevelt took office. Huge mortgages, high interest rates, increasing taxes and fixed costs, overproduction, languishing foreign markets, and declining prices for farm products combined to make the so-called prosperity decade of the 1920s into a depression decade for farmers. The stock market crash of 1929 and the ensuing Great Depression made an already bad situation even worse for farmers. In the acute crises of 1933, the Agricultural Adjustment Act truly was emergency legislation. Action (of almost any sort) was both an economic and political necessity.

In that desperate situation the combined efforts of farm organizations, economic experts, administration leaders, and Congress produced a complex, confusing, even contradictory hodgepodge bill to authorize the administration to attempt a variety of solutions to restore farm prosperity. Neither in its original form nor as amended and signed into law on May 12, 1933, did the Agricultural Adjustment Act please everyone. California's Hiram Johnson called it "the most bizarre thing that was ever suggested to a set of sentient beings." He thought that if it were not for the president's influence, "it would not have a corporal's guard supporting it in the Senate." Missouri's Democratic Senator Bennett Champ Clark considered it "an exceedingly bad bill as it passed the Senate" and thought the conference report worked out between the House and Senate versions was "infinitely worse." Many had doubts about the constitutionality of the legislation and were fearful of the powers it delegated to the president and his secretary of agriculture. Most were unenthusiastic about trying to limit production through acreage controls. They were skeptical of parity efforts based on 1909–14 price levels. Like the old-fashioned agrarian radicals they were, western progressive isolationists had more confidence in inflation, credit and financial schemes, and debt moratoriums than in subsidies or acreage allotments. But they could all agree that something had to be done for farmers.[23]

Many progressives wanted price controls for farm products tied to a cost-of-production formula and supported an amendment to that effect introduced by Senator Norris. With all progressive isolationists voting for it, the Senate approved the Norris amendment to the farm bill.[24]

Progressive and silver-state senators also pushed to attach inflationary amendments to the farm bill. Despite the emergency atmosphere, the eagerness to follow Roosevelt's leadership, and the devotion of western progressives to the welfare of farmers, the administration's farm bill might have been rejected by the Senate if the president had not yielded to inflationary demands. Burton K. Wheeler of Montana, Huey Long of Louisiana, Elmer Thomas of Oklahoma, and Key Pittman of Nevada played central roles in pressing for adoption of inflationary amendments.

Wheeler later recalled that his "first rift with the new President was over the question of silver." Though his Montana was a silver-producing state, Wheeler insisted that his "interest in silver was to add it to our monetary system to offset the severe deflation that was continuing to depress the national economy and to inflict unwarranted hardship on all who owed money." He complained that the legislation so far adopted had all been deflationary. Wheeler told the Senate that the farm bill would "inevitably fail unless the consuming public is endowed with a greater purchasing power than it now enjoys." He introduced an amendment to accomplish inflation through remonetization of silver at sixteen to one.[25]

Borah agreed that there was "no divorcing the subject of farm relief and inflation." But he preferred to deal with the money question through international agreement; he was more hopeful than Wheeler was about the pending London Economic Conference. When he learned that Roosevelt opposed the silver amendment to the farm bill, Borah promised not to vote for the amendment. With the administration opposed, the Senate rejected the Wheeler silver amendment by a vote of forty-four to thirty-three. Borah, McNary, Vandenberg, Walsh, and White voted with the administration in opposition. But most progressive isolationists voted with the minority in favor of the silver amendment.[26]

Though the administration successfully blocked Wheeler's initial silver amendment, Roosevelt felt compelled to yield to inflationary pressures. With Wheeler's amendment defeated, the Senate turned to a broader amendment for controlled inflation introduced by Senator Elmer Thomas of Oklahoma. Senator Millard Tydings of Maryland charged that the Thomas inflation amendment would "compel us to assume a policy of isolation." It would be "a policy of America living unto herself" and would be saying "good-bye for all time to their export market." On April 28, with administration approval, the Senate voted sixty-four to twenty-one to approve the Thomas amendment to the farm bill. The affirmative votes included virtually all progressive isolationists.[27]

With the Norris cost-of-production amendment and the Thomas inflation amendment attached, the Senate on April 28 adopted the administration's emergency farm bill by a vote of sixty-four to twenty. Among leading isolationists only Clark and Vandenberg voted against it. The House of Representatives overwhelmingly accepted the Senate's inflation amendment, but was adamant in rejecting the cost-of-production amendment. Those House votes coincided with administration wishes. None of the progressives was happy with the loss of the Norris amendment—or with the final form of the farm bill. Without the Thomas inflation amendment most of them would have voted against it; the administration concession on inflation salvaged some of their votes. The Senate adopted the conference report (including the Thomas amendment but without the Norris amendment) by a vote of fifty-three to twenty-eight. Capper, Couzens, Johnson, La Follette, Long, McNary, Norbeck, Norris, and Shipstead were among those voting for the bill. But in the absence of the cost-of-production provision, the negative votes included those of Bone, Borah, Clark, Costigan, Frazier, McCarran, Nye, Vandenberg, Wheeler, and White. There was no doubt about the eagerness of leading isolationists to provide government help to farmers. But none was satisfied with what they adopted. Most of them found the inflation and debt provisions the only really hopeful parts of the legislation.[28]

Despite differences on specific issues, western progressive isolationists generally had supported President Roosevelt's New Deal legislative program during the special session of Congress. In September, 1933, the *Progressive,* a weekly published in La Follette's Wisconsin, tabulated Senate votes on ten public issues dealing with labor, agriculture, taxes, and veterans. By its standards only eight senators voted on the progressive side on all ten issues. The eight were Henrik Shipstead of Minnesota, Lynn Frazier and Gerald Nye of North Dakota, Robert La Follette of Wisconsin, Bronson Cutting of New Mexico, Burton Wheeler of Montana, Arthur Robinson of Indiana, and Huey Long of Louisiana. All eight with perfect records were from the West or South. Most were leading isolationists on foreign affairs.[29] Republican Senator Arthur Capper of Kansas had opposed the election of Roosevelt. But in May, 1933, he lauded the president's "quiet audacity" and his courage to "lead the way on untrod paths." He urged cooperation with Roosevelt's program, including his international policies. When the special session ended, Capper wrote that "so far as the farm belt is concerned, things are on the up-grade again."[30] Other western progressive isolationist leaders shared that hopeful view.

Chapter 5

The World Economic Conference

At the same time that the president, the Congress, and the American people grappled with the Great Depression at home, they faced equally demanding and intractable problems abroad. War debts and disarmament cried out for constructive and innovative actions. The acute economic emergency within the United States was part of a worldwide depression that called for (and frustrated) international efforts. In January, 1933, those formidable difficulties overshadowed even the rise of Adolf Hitler to power in Germany. Doctrinaire internationalists and isolationists made their voices heard as the new administration groped for America's proper role abroad. But the participation of the United States in those international strivings revealed the imprint of Franklin D. Roosevelt's values, temperament, and undoctrinaire style.

The World Economic Conference in London, England, from June 12 to July 27, 1933, dramatized the international scope of the Great Depression and the wide variety of conflicting national interests and policies. For each of the participating countries, the conference dramatized what Raymond Moley later called "the confluence of foreign and domestic policies." Because planning for the conference began while Hoover was president and continued into the early months of the Roosevelt administration, it dramatized the contrast between Hoover's emphasis on international solutions for the depression and Roosevelt's preference for domestic solutions. It dramatized the variety of domestic interests and influences on the Roosevelt administration, personified in such internationalists as Secretary of State Cordell Hull and in such isolationists, or nationalists, as Roosevelt's brains truster Assistant Secretary of State Raymond Moley. The conference highlighted the conflict between New Deal programs such as the NRA and the AAA, which Moley saw as pointing "unmistakably toward a more self-contained economy," and the reciprocal trade agreements program on which Secretary Hull placed his hopes.[1] It dramatized some of Roosevelt's political difficulties at home as he balanced everything from Johnson-type isolationists to Hull-type internationalists.

At the time, President Roosevelt's course was more consistent with American isolationism than with internationalism. Ironically, however, it was Cordell Hull, almost alone among the participants, who emerged with enhanced stature in the eyes of the president and the American people. And it was Raymond Moley and his program for "a considerable insulation of our national economy from the rest of the world" whose humiliation at the hands of the president was most complete and whose departure from the administration was speeded by the fiasco.[2]

Along with Roosevelt and Hull, Raymond Moley was prominent in America's participation in the World Economic Conference. With Rexford Tugwell and Adolf Berle, Moley was part of the brains trust that helped Roosevelt shape ideas for the New Deal program that carried the New York governor to the White House and through the early months of the new administration. A Columbia University professor of public law, Moley had been reared in small town Ohio. The imprint of the Populist-Progressive era revealed itself in his admiration for William Jennings Bryan, Cleveland's reform Mayor Tom Johnson, Henry George, and Woodrow Wilson. His doctoral studies at Columbia University exposed him to the powerful mind of historian Charles A. Beard. Moley climbed the academic ladder, but he preferred direct involvement in public affairs. Roosevelt's rising political fortunes provided the professor with his great opportunity. In his dignified, reserved, thoughtful style, Moley made a large imprint both on the New Deal and on Roosevelt's early conduct of foreign affairs. He rejected the isolationist label (as did most who were called isolationists then and later)—he preferred the term "intranationalism"—yet his values and priorities gave him some common ground with leading isolationists.[3]

Initial planning for the London conference began during the final months of the Hoover administration. That planning was consistent with Hoover's conviction that basic causes and solutions for the Great Depression lay on the world scene. The meetings (three in all) and communications between President Hoover and Governor Roosevelt during the four months from the election in November to the inauguration in March included consideration of the pending conference. Ironically, President Hoover (who later was seen as an isolationist opponent of Roosevelt's foreign policies before Pearl Harbor) played the role of internationalist in those exchanges of 1932–33, while Roosevelt (who as president was later to lead the United States away from isolationism) played the role of isolationist, or economic nationalist. Similarly, Hoover's Secretary of State Henry L. Stimson, Secretary of Treasury Ogden L. Mills, and Ambassador Norman H. Davis (a Democrat who served on diplomatic missions for both the Hoover and the Roosevelt administrations) struggled to move Roosevelt in internationalist directions. At the same time, Roosevelt's brains truster, Raymond Moley, was a force for economic nationalism.

President Hoover and his top advisers saw a close relationship between the war debts controversy, disarmament, and the problems to be treated at the London conference. Hoover insisted that he only wanted to facilitate transition from one administration to the other and to have the president-elect share in arranging orderly procedures for that transition. He denied that he was trying to commit Roosevelt to the policies of the outgoing administration, although he did hope the London conference would meet as early as possible.[4]

Governor Roosevelt and Moley, however, were wary of Hoover's intentions. They suspected him of trying to commit Roosevelt to policies that the voters had already rejected at the polls. Roosevelt, Moley, and Tugwell insisted that war debts and disarmament be excluded from deliberations at the London conference. They wanted the conference delayed as long as possible to give the new administration time to implement its domestic New Deal program. Furthermore, Governor Roosevelt emphasized that until he was inaugurated, he had no constitutional or legal authority to assume responsibility for government decisions, policies, or actions.[5]

At the same time, Moley and Tugwell became uneasy about the possible influence that Ambassador Davis and Secretary Stimson might be having on Roosevelt. Stimson and Davis were both dedicated internationalists; each had extended private discussions with the president-elect that winter, and Moley saw Roosevelt becoming a bit more internationalist under their persuasive influence. In January, Moley also was troubled by Roosevelt's decision to appoint Cordell Hull as secretary of state. He knew Hull's obsession on trade reciprocity; he knew that Hull did not share his views or priorities on the domestic New Deal program.[6]

Moley therefore had mixed feelings about Roosevelt's determination to appoint him assistant secretary of state. Nominally, that would place Moley under Hull in the State Department. As Roosevelt's close adviser, however, Moley would have easy direct access to him. Moley feared the unusual relationships and conflicting views would create difficulties between them. Roosevelt brushed aside Moley's misgivings. The president explicitly defined Moley's duties as assistant secretary of state to include handling war debts, the World Economic Conference, "and such additional duties as the President may direct in the general field of foreign and domestic government."[7]

Through Secretary Stimson, the president-elect invited British Ambassador Sir Ronald Lindsay to meet with him for informal conversations at Warm Springs on January 28, 1933. By inauguration day, Secretary of State Hull had received from Ambassador Lindsay a formal memorandum, "British Policy on Economic Problems." With unmistakable reference to American isolationism, that memorandum emphasized that the world depression could not "be effectively remedied by isolated action on the part of individual Governments," that the depression was "essentially international in its character," and that it required "international action on a very broad front." It suggested an exchange of views between President Roosevelt and the British before the conference convened. And it concluded that the war debts constituted "an insuperable barrier to economic and financial reconstruction" with "no prospect of the World Economic Conference making progress" if that barrier were not removed.[8]

Though Assistant Secretary Moley had primary responsibility within the State Department for handling conference matters, Norman Davis continued to serve abroad as the American representative on the organizing committee for the conference under President Roosevelt as he had earlier under Hoover. That was certain to complicate matters. Two days after the inauguration, Moley accidentally discovered Davis (with Hull's approval) busily drafting a reply to the British memorandum, despite Roosevelt's instructions that war debts and the conference were Moley's responsibility. Moley felt surrounded in the State Department by people who did not, in his opinion, understand or sympathize with Roosevelt's "domestic and foreign objectives sufficiently to be capable of directing the preparations for the foreign economic conversations." Furthermore, so far as Moley could determine, the president was not troubled by the apparent conflict between State Department policies and his domestic New Deal program. Moley quashed Davis's draft reply to the British, and the actual State Department response was consistent with Moley's views.[9]

Near the end of April, Britain's Prime Minister J. Ramsay Mac-Donald conferred in the United States with President Roosevelt on war debts, disarmament, and plans for the economic conference. On his heels came France's Edouard Herriot and representatives from other governments. Those conversations included the clear understanding that war debts and disarmament were to be excluded from consideration at the conference.[10]

In May, the president named the six members of the American delegation. Although Moley declined to serve, Roosevelt consulted him in choosing the delegates. It was a weak and divided group. None of the six had had previous diplomatic experience. They were selected for their political positions and ties, rather than for their negotiating skills or their expertise on international trade and finance. Not one of them was from the urban Northeast. Three were internationalists of varied degree, two were economic nationalists, and the sixth's views were not known to the president.

Roosevelt chose Secretary Hull to head the delegation, though he did not consult him in selecting the other delegates. For vice-chairman of the delegation he picked former Governor James M. Cox of Ohio who had been the Democratic party's presidential nominee in 1920 when Roosevelt had run for vice-president. He was a moderate internationalist. The president named men from both houses of Congress and from both parties. He included the chairman of the Senate Foreign Relations Committee, Democrat Key Pittman from Nevada, and the chairman of the House Foreign Affairs Committee, Democrat Samuel D. McReynolds of Tennessee. Pittman (like Moley) was an economic nationalist and a protectionist and disagreed with Hull's trade views. But his most notable characteristics were his passionate devotion to the silver interests of America's West, his anti-Japanese bias, his political shrewdness, and his heavy drinking. He was as obsessed with silver as Hull was with trade reciprocity. McReynolds shared Hull's general trade views, but without Hull's crusading fervor. A last minute choice was Ralph W. Morrison, a retired banker and cotton dealer from Texas who had been recommended by James A. Farley and Vice-President John Nance Garner of Texas.[11]

President Roosevelt also determined to include a western progressive. Burton K. Wheeler of Montana was suggested. But Wheeler (like Pittman) was both a Democrat and a silver senator. Roosevelt needed a Republican. Furthermore, to include two silver senators on the delegation would give that perspective greater weight than Roosevelt wanted. Roosevelt turned instead to California's Republican

Senator Hiram Johnson—progressive, nationalist, isolationist, and vigorously opposed to any cancellation or compromise on war debts. At the White House on May 21, the president asked Johnson to serve on the delegation. Both President Roosevelt and Mrs. Johnson turned to the senator's friend, Secretary of Interior Harold Ickes, to help them persuade the old progressive to accept.[12] Ever the man of independence, however, Johnson eventually declined and resisted all efforts to get him to reconsider. He believed that legislators should not accept diplomatic assignments; such appointments eroded the separation of powers and could undercut legislative restraints on the executive in foreign affairs. He did not share Hull's trade views and had no intention of abandoning his protectionist efforts on behalf of his California constituents. And he doubted that the conference would accomplish much, with or without him.[13]

Roosevelt then turned to another progressive isolationist, Senator Robert M. La Follette, Jr., of Wisconsin. But young La Follette too rejected the appointment—and for some of the same reasons.[14]

Finally Roosevelt appointed Michigan Republican Senator James Couzens to the slot. Canadian-born, wealthy, elderly, a onetime business associate of Henry Ford, moderately progressive, and independent, Couzens was also an isolationist. He served conscientiously in London, but his was not a strong appointment.[15]

On May 30, 1933, the day before they sailed for London from New York, President Roosevelt (along with Moley and Bernard Baruch) met with the delegation and its staff to give them their instructions. President Roosevelt instructed the delegates not to discuss war debts or disarmament. Similarly, the delegation had no authority to negotiate a currency stabilization agreement; that responsibility was assigned to Oliver M. W. Sprague of the Treasury Department and George L. Harrison of the New York Federal Reserve Bank. Though they conducted their discussions in London at the same time, they were not delegates to the World Economic Conference and were not subject to Hull's authority. The president's instructions authorized the delegation to consider the tariff truce instituted for the duration of the conference, general principles for coordinating monetary and fiscal policy, removal of foreign exchange restrictions, groundwork for an international monetary standard, a basic agreement for gradual removal of trade barriers, and basic agreements for control of production and distribution of certain commodities.[16]

If the objective of the Roosevelt administration was to accomplish

positive international agreement to end the world depression, those instructions were not likely to produce fruitful results. If the objective
was to procrastinate and delay on the world scene to give Roosevelt's
New Deal time to revive prosperity within the United States and to
build a stronger domestic base from which to negotiate international
agreements later, both the delegation and the instructions may have
been ideal. If that were the hope, the divided counsels within and
among the dozens of other countries represented at the London Economic Conference were certain to facilitate that end.

The president further limited the power of the delegation by undercutting Secretary Hull in the one area in which Hull had real hopes for
accomplishment—reciprocal trade agreements. Under Hull's careful
eye, the Department of State had drafted reciprocity legislation on
which he placed high hopes. But Congress was becoming restive and
rebellious; Roosevelt was eager to have it adjourn before it got out of
hand and before the economic conference got under way. Troubled by
rumors, Hull radioed the president on June 7 that he hoped reports
were "unfounded" that the president did not intend to submit the
reciprocal trade bill to Congress. But the rumors were correct. The
president radioed Hull that the situation in the closing days of the session was "so full of dynamite that immediate adjournment is
necessary. Otherwise bonus legislation, paper money inflation, etc.,
may be forced." He insisted that "tariff legislation seems not only
highly inadvisable, but impossible of achievement." Hull could, the
president advised, negotiate general reciprocal trade treaties subject to
Senate approval.[17]

President Roosevelt's response dismayed Secretary Hull. His
treasured project was being lightly set aside for another time. As Hull
saw it, the president's decision wiped out the slim possibility of accomplishing anything significant at the conference. William C. Bullitt
wrote that the president's response had completely unnerved Hull.
Cox and Bullitt sent the president an "ultra-confidential" message on
June 11, advising him of the seriousness of the situation. Roosevelt
immediately tried to assuage Hull—without really backing down. He
cabled Hull not to "worry about the situation here in regard to tariff
reduction and removal of trade obstacles. The eleventh-hour rows in
Congress over domestic problems made general tariff debate
dangerous to our whole program." The president assured Hull that he
was "squarely behind" him and the "nothing said or done" in
Washington would hamper Hull's efforts. All that did not solve Hull's

problems in London or give him the legislation he so much wanted in Washington. But he regained his composure and pressed on with his mission—not knowing that the worst was yet to come.[18]

A major address broadcast by Moley on May 20 before the delegation left for England and Secretary Hull's address to the conference on June 14 illustrated the clash of thought and theory within the administration. In his address (which Moley later contended the president had seen and approved earlier in the form of a draft article), Moley urged Americans and the world not to expect too much from the conference. He thought it would "be difficult to make extensive attacks upon trade barriers, however much this may be desired." In his view "a good part of the ills of each country is domestic," and "an international conference which attempted to bring about cures for these difficulties solely by concerted international measures would necessarily result in failure." As Moley explained it (and as the New Deal measures enacted during the Hundred Days implied): "In large part the cures for our difficulties lie within ourselves. Each nation must set its own house in order and a meeting of representatives of all the nations is useful in large part only to coordinate in some measure these national activities." Moley insisted that "world trade is, after all, only a small percentage of the entire trade of the United States. This means that our domestic policy is of paramount importance." He saw international cooperation as only a potentially helpful adjunct to the central task of building prosperity through domestic actions.[19]

Secretary Hull (who had not been consulted about the speech) sharply disagreed. He thought the speech impaired the standing of the American delegation and that "Moley deserved a severe call-down from the President" for making it. In his *Memoirs* later, Hull wrote that "the question of a conflict between the reduction of tariff and trade barriers at London and the high-tariff demands of the NRA and AAA" was not discussed until just before the American delegation prepared to depart for London.[20]

In his address to the conference on June 14 (an address that President Roosevelt in Washington had toned down considerably before Hull delivered it), the secretary of state spoke out boldly against the "cherished idea of the extreme type of isolationist that each nation singly can, by bootstrap methods, lift itself out of the troubles that surround it." He conceded that "each nation by itself can to a moderate extent restore conditions by suitable fiscal, financial and economic steps" like those undertaken during the first three months of the Roosevelt administration. But he emphasized the "necessity for

an equally important international economic program of remedies."
In his view "international cooperation" was "a fundamental necessity." Hull urged the conference to "proclaim that economic nationalism" was "a discredited policy," explaining that "many
measures indispensable to full and satisfactory business recovery are
beyond the powers of individual states." He concluded by urging the
conference to "proceed to the herculean task of promoting and establishing economic peace which is the fundamental basis of all peace."[21]

Hull did not rule out domestic efforts to assist recovery, and
Moley did not exclude all international efforts. But the emphases and
priorities of the two men were so different as to render effective
cooperation almost impossible. And in the context they symbolized
the contest between Moley's early New Deal isolationism, or "intranationalism," and Hull's reciprocal trade internationalism. It took a
Franklin D. Roosevelt to attempt to reconcile the irreconcilable within
his administration, within the international community, within the
United States, and possibly within his own mind as well.

From the beginning the conference proved to be an exercise in
futility characterized by confusion bordering on chaos. It might have
failed whatever role Roosevelt and the United States had played.
Countries were interested in different issues and in irreconcilable solutions to problems. Each country wanted a stabilization agreement that
would give it advantages over the others in international exchange.
And the American delegation had no authority to negotiate a
stabilization agreement at all. Weak, divided, without authority to
treat key matters, some members of the American delegation considered returning home. Key Pittman's heavy drinking rendered him
incapable of functioning at times. And silver was the only economic
subject of real interest to him at the conference anyway. Sprague and
Harrison (not part of the delegation or conference, but conducting
separate negotiations in London on stabilization at the same time)
allowed themselves to be moved by the British negotiators to consider
stabilization terms favorable to Britain and unacceptable to Roosevelt.[22] Observing the chaos about him, Senator Couzens became convinced the nations had "not yet suffered enough to be willing to meet
in complete humility." Like Moley and Hull, Couzens recognized the
conflict between the economic nationalism represented by America's
New Deal program and economic internationalism. He thought that
"sooner or later in the Conference we shall have to decide which pro-
gramme we are going to follow."[23]

In the midst of the confusion, when it seemed that the conference might collapse in failure, President Roosevelt decided to send Moley as his personal liaison to the American delegation and the conference. Things got out of hand. Announced at a time when the conference and negotiations were floundering, the move took on the appearance of vital importance. Moley was at least partly to blame for the sensation his mission created. Before his departure he made a dramatic air-sea trip to confer with the president, who was on a vacation cruise off the New England coast, relaxing from the strains of the now-adjourned special session of Congress. Encouraged by furtive meetings, massive press coverage, general uncertainty, and desperate hopes, many assumed that Moley was bringing some bold new proposal from the president that would bring order out of chaos, accomplish agreement in the midst of conflict, and restore world prosperity where there was panic and depression. The conference very nearly came to a standstill as it nervously awaited Moley's arrival. Despite modest statements playing down the importance of his mission, Moley clearly enjoyed the attention and did not convincingly disabuse others about the potential significance of his role. Many saw the Moley mission as evidence of the president's dissatisfaction both with the conference and with the American delegation. Moley arrived in England on June 27. Despite Moley's patronizing gestures, Cordell Hull was left ignored (even humiliated) in the shadows.[24]

Moley immediately became the central figure for flurries of conversations and negotiations variously relating to stabilization. The objective was to make a declaration strong enough to quiet financial panic on the Continent, where gold-standard countries feared "the United States would push their currencies off gold and into inflation." At the same time, Moley and the others tried to make the declaration innocuous enough to be acceptable to President Roosevelt, who had already rejected two stabilization agreements considered by Sprague and Harrison.

In Moley's view, the declaration finally proposed was little more than "a rephrasing of one of the 'instructions' given to our delegation by Roosevelt before the delegation sailed—a statement of policy that had been introduced into the Conference as a resolution on June 19th by Senator Pittman." It was not a monetary stabilization agreement—either temporary or permanent. Moley saw it as "completely harmless," but hoped it might "save the Conference from wreck." The proposed declaration would have asserted that it was "in the interests of all concerned that stability in the international monetary field be attained as quickly as practicable" and that "gold should be reestablished as the international measure of exchange value.'' But "the parity and time at which each of the countries now off gold [including the United States] could undertake to stabilize must be decided by the respective governments concerned.'' That was no "stabilization agreement.'' The declaration would have had the countries "use whatever means they consider appropriate to limit exchange speculation" and to ask their central banks to cooperate to that same end.[25]

The proposal that Moley and Sprague forwarded to Secretary of Treasury William Woodin and to President Roosevelt on June 30 arrived at an awkward time. Woodin was seriously ill at his home in New York, and Roosevelt was vacationing with Louis Howe and Henry Morgenthau, Jr., at Campobello, which had no telephone link with the mainland. After delays caused by communication difficulties and Woodin's illness, the proposed declaration won the endorsement of Secretary Woodin, Undersecretary of the Treasury Dean Acheson, and presidential adviser Bernard Baruch.[26]

Moley confidently assumed that Roosevelt would give his approval. But the president's response was slow in coming. As the hours slipped by, the suspense grew, and Moley's uneasiness increased. Finally, on Saturday afternoon, July 1, Moley received the president's response. Roosevelt rejected the proposed declaration. He chose to consider it the equivalent of a stabilization agreement. As Moley saw it, "The declaration was therefore rejected in terms that had no relation to what the declaration was about.''[27]

But that was not to be the end of Moley's humiliation at the hands of the president. On July 2, 1933, Roosevelt sent his famous Bombshell Message to Hull for release on Monday morning, July 3. In it the president insisted, "The sound internal economic system of a nation is a greater factor in its well being than the price of its currency in changing terms of the currencies of other nations.'' He concluded: "When the world works out concerted policies in the majority of nations to produce balanced budgets and living within their means, then we can properly discuss a better distribution of the world's gold and silver supply to act as a reserve base of national currencies.''[28] The ideas in both of the president's communications were consistent with Moley's "intranationalist" views earlier and later, but at that moment Roosevelt used them to undercut Moley in London.

The president's message shook Moley and very nearly provided the coup de grace for the already floundering World Economic Conference. The French and delegates from other gold standard countries were furious at the president. Britain's MacDonald was distraught and angered. He agreed with delegates from the gold countries that the conference should adjourn after placing responsibility for its failure on the shoulders of Roosevelt and the United States. Even Moley thought the conference should recess for two to ten weeks while the president formulated his ideas in specific form for later consideration by the delegates. Roosevelt opposed adjournment or recess, however, and suggested further conversations on monetary policies and tariffs.[29]

At that critical moment, when the conference was at the point of collapse and when the president was being blamed for the disaster, Secretary Hull, in his capacity as head of the American delegation, stepped out of the shadows where he had been thrust with Moley's arrival. Conducting himself with impressive dignity, poise, and skill, Hull successfully blocked immediate adjournment, turned back formal indictment of the president, and moved the conference to continue its futile efforts. The conference stumbled on three weeks longer. Except for a silver agreement that Senator Pittman managed to put together, it accomplished nothing positive.[30]

The future careers of Cordell Hull and Raymond Moley, and their subsequent relations with President Roosevelt, would not have led observers to suspect that the World Economic Conference had floundered on economic nationalism or that Roosevelt had been a party to that economic nationalism. It was Moley the nationalist who fell from power and from the president's grace; it was Hull the internationalist who gained in stature and presidential favor.

On July 4, 1933, the day after Roosevelt's Bombshell Message was made public, Moley summarized his reactions and recommendations in a telegram marked "CONFIDENTIAL SECRET FROM MOLEY TO PRESIDENT ALONE AND EXCLUSIVELY WITH NO DISTRIBUTION IN THE DEPARTMENT." But he made the mistake of having it sent through Ambassador Robert W. Bingham in State Department code; its contents quickly reached Hull and the others on the American delegation. In his secret telegram Moley told Roosevelt that Pittman was the "only member of delegation able intellectually and aggressively to present" the president's ideas to the conference. He advised that a "reconstituted delegation would be helpful." That language, of course, did not please any of the American delegates in London—except Pittman. Moley closed his telegram by calling the president's message "splendid" and "the only way to bring people to their senses."[31]

Moley helped Hull's efforts to prevent the conference from adjourning. He bade farewell to Hull and the other delegates in London on July 6. One of the messages Hull asked him to take back to the president (as Moley recalled in his memoirs later) was "not to give progressive Republicans too prominent a place in the administration, since they didn't seem capable of working with anybody." Hull had Senator Couzens in mind at that time, but he surely would have underscored that advice many times later in other contexts as the Roosevelt administration's contest with the isolationists ran its long and complicated course.[32]

Moley sailed from Southampton for the United States on Friday, July 7 and saw Roosevelt a week later on July 14. Their conversation was friendly and informal as Moley reported to the president. He made it clear that he thought Roosevelt should have accepted the proposed declaration. Roosevelt expressed regret that Moley had been seen as a "savior" at the conference. For all the amiable tone, however, it was clear that Moley's days as an intimate presidential advisor were numbered. Moley thought he deserved better from the president for his efforts. He considered resigning at that time, but hoped that by staying on he might disarm the charge that he had been repudiated by Roosevelt. But it was only a matter of when and how his departure from the administration would be accomplished.[33]

The process of easing him out came in the form of an announcement by the president on August 2 that Moley would undertake a special assignment to study Justice Department handling of kidnappings. With that study underway, Moley personally delivered his resignation to the president at Hyde Park on Sunday, August 27, to become effective on September 7. He resigned to edit a weekly news magazine, *Today,* which in 1937 merged with *Newsweek.* He continued to be welcome at the White House, but his official career in the Department of State and in the Roosevelt administration was ended.[34]

In striking contrast, Hull's standing with the president mounted. On July 6, Roosevelt telegraphed his congratulations to Hull for blocking adjournment. Hull vigorously defended the president in a blunt exchange of letters with Prime Minister MacDonald—copies of which he forwarded to Roosevelt. At the same time Hull sent a long cablegram to the president relating and berating Moley's performance in London. Just before the secretary of state departed London for his return to the United States, President Roosevelt sent a warm telegram telling Hull of his "affectionate regard for and confidence in" him. He invited Secretary and Mrs. Hull to come directly to Hyde Park for the night after they reached New York.[35]

President Roosevelt's early New Deal, its efforts to increase commodity prices, and its projection to the World Economic Conference in the form of the Bombshell Message were popular in the United States. The White House received thousands of telegrams and letters praising the message and lauding the president for sending it.[36]

But it was Secretary of State Cordell Hull, the doctrinaire internationalist, whose standing with Roosevelt and with the public was enhanced by the developments in London. As the years passed, Roosevelt was to turn more and more boldly toward variants of Hull's internationalism in his conduct of American foreign affairs. Those patterns were still mostly in the future when the president warmly received the secretary and his wife at his home at Hyde Park in early August, 1933. But in his first major disarmament initiatives, the president had already provided important indications of the directions his foreign policies were to take later.

Chapter 6

Disarmament

In the 1920s and 1930s millions of people blamed the military armaments race for the eruption of the Great War and for financial and political dislocations that followed. Many saw disarmament as a way to preserve peace and prevent the bloodbath of a second world war. In varied degree Franklin D. Roosevelt and leading isolationists shared those beliefs and hopes. Roosevelt and the isolationists were not pacifists, however, and were not sanguine about the practical possibilities for accomplishing disarmament. Their separate approaches on the issue conflicted and helped defeat efforts of both the administration and the isolationists. Given the impasse between the French and Germans on armaments in Europe, given the determinations of the Japanese in Asia, and given the world's record on disarmament, those armament limitation efforts conceivably could be seen as exercises in futility. But both responsible reason and desperate hopes led world leaders to try. They failed.

During President Roosevelt's first term the United States explored the possibilities (and suffered the frustrations) of two major disarmament conferences. The World Disarmament Conference in Geneva began its deliberations with dramatic fanfare early in 1932 and continued through much of Roosevelt's first term. The London Naval Conference undertook its briefer effort with little hope in December, 1935, and ended with none in March, 1936.

Under President Roosevelt and Secretary Hull, the key American negotiator was Norman H. Davis. Like Hull, Davis was born in Tennessee and had become a devoted Wilsonian internationalist. But while Hull followed the elective pathway through membership in the House and Senate to appointment as secretary of state, Davis took the path of business and finance to appointments under President Wilson in the Treasury and State departments and at Versailles. As a southern

Democrat, an Episcopalian, a Wilsonian, and a New York financier with ties to the House of Morgan, Norman Davis emerged from sectors of the United States that were to undergird Roosevelt's increasingly internationalist foreign policies later. Though he served in diplomatic positions under Republican Presidents Coolidge and Hoover, Davis was among those mentioned for appointment as Roosevelt's secretary of state. He had known Roosevelt since they had both served in the Wilson administration during and after World War I. His identification with J. P. Morgan and Company, however, made him anathema to western progressive isolationists whose support Roosevelt sought. Instead, Davis functioned as something of an ambassador-at-large as he flitted back and forth across the Atlantic and from one country and conference to another throughout Roosevelt's first term. He enjoyed the top level backstage maneuvering that that role entailed. The British were not so favorably impressed by him as Roosevelt and Hull believed. But he was a skilled, energetic, persistent, realistic, and cautiously optimistic negotiator. He was never an isolationist and never a pacifist.[1]

In a letter to Roosevelt in 1928, Davis had advised against "a policy of isolation" or "an independent role" for the United States. Instead, he had urged "a policy of cooperation." In his opinion, "If we are not going to cooperate, then we ought to arm to the hilt. . . . War can only be banished by mobilizing the positive moral forces to combat it, and that requires cooperation."[2] Roosevelt shared that general view, and it took on special significance in the context of European power and security perspectives.

In 1932, the German Weimar Republic under Chancellor Heinrich Brüning had wanted a disarmament agreement that would reduce Allied might and relax Versailles restrictions on Germany. If such an agreement were not accomplished, he feared the failure could play into the hands of Adolf Hitler and his Nazis. It wasn't, and it did.

France's overwhelming obsession was security against a revived Germany. France would consider substantial armament limitations only if Germany were kept weak and if France had firm assurances of effective military support to check any German challenge.

Great Britain shared some of the French views, but was more flexible. It wanted to keep Germany down, but was more willing to consider softening the Versailles settlement. It sided with France, but would not give the unequivocal assurances of support against Germany that France required as a prerequisite to disarmament. England had to balance its empire and commonwealth interests against European considerations. By the time Roosevelt became president in March, 1933, the World Disarmament Conference had been stumbling along ineffectively for more than a year. Some were prepared to admit failure, end the conference, go home, and prepare for war. But most were determined to continue to try.[3]

Roosevelt favored military preparedness. As president he kept close tabs on naval matters, and even used Public Works Administration funds for naval construction. Throughout his first term Roosevelt officially and actively supported disarmament efforts. But he was never naive or sanguine about those efforts, and in personal letters he expressed pessimism about European developments in general and disarmament in particular.

Roosevelt conferred at length with Davis in August, 1932 before the presidential election, and in December after election but before he took office. On March 9, 1933, shortly after he took office, Roosevelt asked Hull to have Davis arrange an appointment at the White House before returning to the deliberations at Geneva. In their extended discussions Roosevelt and Davis were each favorably impressed by the knowledge, understanding, and realism of the other on the prospects for disarmament.[4] In April, Britain's Prime Minister Ramsay Mac-Donald and France's Foreign Minister Edouard Herriot separately came to the United States to confer with Roosevelt and Hull on disarmament and on the economic crises. In mid-May, Germany's Chancellor Adolf Hitler was scheduled to deliver a major address that was expected to relate to proceedings at the World Disarmament Conference.

At that juncture in May, 1933, the Roosevelt administration made its major move to break the impasse at the conference in Geneva. That effort came in the midst of the acute economic crisis in the United States, while the one-hundred-day special session of Congress was rushing to enact legislation for Roosevelt's New Deal and as plans were being finalized for the upcoming World Economic Conference in London.

On May 16, 1933, the day before Hitler's scheduled speech and less than a month before the opening of the World Economic Conference, President Roosevelt cabled identical messages to the heads of fifty-four states represented at the conferences in Geneva and London. His appeal linked the Geneva efforts for political peace with the London strivings for economic peace. He endorsed the partial elimination of offensive weapons called for in Britain's MacDonald Plan. He saw that, however, as only preliminary to "complete elimination of all offensive weapons," such as bombers, heavy mobile artillery, tanks, and poison gas. Pending that accomplishment, the president urged no increase in "existing armaments over and above the limitations of treaty obligations." And he called on all states to enter "a solemn and definite pact of non-aggression" promising to "send no armed force of whatsoever nature across their frontiers."[5]

Official responses generally were favorable (even in Hitler's Reichstag speech the next day), but each government gave special emphases and qualifications appropriate to its own definition of national interest. Neither Britain nor France was particularly impressed by Roosevelt's specific proposals, but both hoped the move signaled a willingness by the president to lead the United States to larger security commitments in Europe.[6]

Less than a week later British and French hopes were further encouraged by a major policy statement on behalf of the United States by Norman Davis. That statement grew out of cabled inquiries from Davis in April, modified and approved by President Roosevelt and Secretary Hull, and drafted with meticulous care by Roosevelt, Hull, Davis, and top State Department and White House officials. On May 22, 1933, in Geneva, Davis restated President Roosevelt's disarmament proposals. He urged supervision of disarmament and indicated America's willingness to participate in that supervision. Davis told the assembled delegates that if the conference accomplished substantial general disarmament, the United States would be "willing to consult the other states in case of a threat to peace with a view to averting conflict." He said that if "the states, in conference, determine that a state has been guilty of a breach of the peace in violation of its international obligations and take measures against the violator, then, if we concur in the judgment rendered as to the responsible and guilty party, we will refrain from any action tending to defeat the collective effort which such state may make to restore peace."[7]

That cautious statement by Davis in Geneva was as far as President Roosevelt and Secretary Hull believed the United States dared go at that time in the direction of collective security to encourage disarmament and to preserve peace. Davis would have preferred to have the United States undertake those assurances in treaty form, but he recognized the "political problems" that such a treaty would encounter. Sensitive to the strength of America's tradition of avoiding entangling commitments in Europe, confronted with noninterventionist sentiment in Congress and public opinion, in degree sharing some of those feelings, absorbed with shaping and implementing the New

Deal program, and alert to political currents at home and abroad, Roosevelt did not risk the treaty route. He preferred a unilateral declaration rather than a binding treaty to be agreed upon by other states and requiring a two-thirds vote in the Senate.[8]

Roosevelt also kept the Davis statement as general as possible, avoiding details that might provoke controversy either among those who feared it would involve the United States too deeply in European affairs or among those who feared it would not represent a sufficiently muscular American role abroad. That pattern (general, flexible, undoctrinaire) was consistent with Roosevelt's style then and later. The key portion of the statement made no reference to the League of Nations, the Kellogg-Briand Pact, or disarmament conference organizational machinery. The United States (presumably the president) would decide the form and occasion for consultation, the United States would decide for itself whether the judgment of guilt of the state violating the peace was justified or not, and the statement did not promise any positive steps to help collective action against a guilty state—only that the United States would refrain from doing anything tending to defeat collective action.

Actually, neither the president's message nor the Davis statement accomplished practical results for disarmament. The president's proposals did not win approval at the World Disarmament Conference. Since the policies outlined by Davis in Geneva were conditional upon general disarmament, those policies never went into effect. The impasse between Hitler's ambitions, French security concerns, and British ambiguity probably would have doomed disarmament negotiations in the 1930s whatever the United States, President Roosevelt, and American isolationists might have done.

Nevertheless, isolationism and isolationists were part of the compound that helped frustrate those efforts. Isolationists shared in blaming armaments for insecurity and war. They railed at military expenditures and saber-rattling in Europe, Japan, and the United States. They urged disarmament. But they had little confidence in conference diplomacy, fearing that selfish national interests, military leaders and advisers, and munitions makers and financiers would undercut possibilities for armaments limitation agreement. They thought the United States should not speed up the armaments race through its own military buildup, and should restrict its preparations to the requirements of continental defense. Isolationist strength inhibited commitments the administration dared make on behalf of peace and disarmament in Europe. Traditional isolationism weakened British and French confidence in the role the United States was likely to play in European settlements and reduced the weight that Hitler may have attached to America. A more specific (but less important) role of isolationists in the failure of the administration's disarmanent initiatives in 1933 involved the Senate's performance on arms embargo and neutrality legislation.

In approving the Davis statement of May 22, the Roosevelt administration envisaged changes in American neutrality policies in the interests of disarmament and peace. Traditionally the United States had insisted on the right of Americans to trade with all belligerents, subject to the rules of international law. That meant the right to trade with all belligerents (subject to contraband and blockade regulations) without distinguishing between aggressors and victims of aggression. The United States had insisted upon neutrality, neutral rights, and equal treatment to and by belligerents under the law. In contrast, under the Davis statement in certain circumstances the United States would "refrain from any action tending to defeat the collective effort" to restore peace and would deny protection to American nationals aiding war-making states. Conceivably under certain circumstances the United States might ban sale of munitions to aggressors while permitting their sale to victims of aggression and to states aiding those victims.[9]

That was not a new idea. In 1929, Senator Arthur Capper of Kansas, a moderate agrarian isolationist, had introduced a resolution that would have authorized the president to prohibit sale of arms and munitions to states violating the Kellogg-Briand Pact of Paris. The Stimson Doctrine of 1932 directed against Japanese conquest of Manchuria moved Capper to renew efforts to win approval of his arms embargo resolution. He hoped it would give "a greater freedom of action for the Executive" to deal with the Manchurian crisis.[10]

Prodded by Secretary Stimson, on January 10, 1933, President Hoover sent a message to Congress recommending approval of the Traffic in Arms Convention of 1925 and adoption of legislation giving the president discretionary authority, in cooperation with other countries, to limit or prohibit shipment of arms and munitions to any state when he believed the shipment of such materials would encourage conflict abroad. President-elect Roosevelt promptly endorsed the general idea. Confronted with opposition in both houses of Congress, however, none of the arms embargo resolutions was enacted during the hectic closing days of the Hoover administration.[11]

In March, 1933, the new president and secretary of state, Roosevelt and Hull, were as persuaded of the wisdom of discretionary arms embargo legislation as Secretary Stimson had been, and more than Hoover had been. But in the frenzied economic and political pyrotechnics that marked the beginning of the new administration the embargo legislation did not have priority. Prodding to move the issue off dead center did not come from Roosevelt and Hull, but rather from the British, from American diplomats in Europe, and from second-level State Department officials. Of central importance was Norman H. Davis. He did not want to apply it to Japan, but looked primarily to Europe. He provided the initiatives that won approval from Roosevelt and Hull for communications to British and other missions indicating the administration's intention to press for enactment of legislation necessary for discretionary arms embargo authority. Senator Capper reintroduced his resolution and elicited sympathetic responses from the president and secretary of state. Hull, however, preferred the more elastic provisions in a resolution sponsored by McReynolds in the House.[12]

But the White House moved slowly and cautiously. At Hull's direction the State Department drafted a presidential message to Congress on the issue, but Roosevelt rejected it, fearing it might give an arms embargo undue emphasis. Instead, the president asked Secretary Hull to explain the administration's position in letters to Senator Key Pittman, chairman of the Foreign Relations Committee, and to Representative Sam McReynolds, chairman of the Foreign Affairs Committee. The letters were drafted, approved, signed, and sent on their way. But the president changed his mind that evening and asked Hull to withdraw them. Consequently, the next day Hull sent Undersecretary William Phillips scurrying to the Capitol to withdraw the letters and have all copies destroyed. Next they planned to have Undersecretary of State Phillips testify at a meeting of the House Foreign Affairs Committee scheduled to consider the arms embargo resolution on Tuesday morning, March 21. But Monday afternoon Phillips telephoned to cancel his appearance. Rather than a presidential message, formal letters to committee chairmen, or testimony by the number-two man in the State Department, the administration finally made its views known by sending Joseph C. Green of the Division of Western European Affairs of the State Department to testify. That pattern did not represent a policy change, but it provided a much lower emphasis on the issue at a time when the president was focusing his political strength (including that provided by western progressive isolationists) to win approval for New Deal legislation he sought from Congress.[13]

That equivocating gave Republican Congressmen Hamilton Fish of New York and George Tinkham of Massachusetts the opportunity in the House committee to organize and publicize opposition to the embargo resolution. They called opposition witnesses to testify. At the same time, Senator Borah, ranking minority member of the Foreign Relations Committee, publicly endorsed the House resolution, contending that it rested "upon a sound and wise policy." He insisted that the resolution did not violate the Constitution and could not be used "to foment war or make trouble unless there is a deliberate desire to do so. Any reasonable use of it would be in the interest of peace." On March 28, in a straight party vote of fifteen to six, the Foreign Affairs Committee reported the resolution favorably to the House of Representatives. After a brief debate, the House of Representatives passed the arms embargo resolution without amendment by more than a two-thirds margin on April 17, 1933.[14]

The resolution ran into difficulties in the Senate Foreign Relations Committee. The new chairman, Democrat Key Pittman of Nevada, did not speed action on the resolution. After the committee considered it at length on May 10, Pittman wrote to Hull outlining some of the objections. According to Pittman, members of the committee were troubled because it was "indefinite as to what governments the President shall cooperate with." It could hurt American producers. Authority to treat one set of belligerents differently from another "would have a strong tendency to involve the United States to such an extent that a condition of war might arise." And committee members feared that adoption of the resolution at that time "might be accepted by Japan as aimed at her." Certain amendments had been suggested to assuage misgivings, and Pittman asked Hull whether he would be willing to appear personally before the committee on the matter.[15]

The secretary declined, but he approved a detailed statement that Joseph Green presented to the committee in his stead on May 17. That statement assured the senators that there was "no intention of sacrificing the interests of American manufacturers to those of foreign manufacturers." The embargo would not include "foodstuffs, ordinary clothing and ordinary articles of peaceful commerce." The statement concluded: "It is not our policy to have this Government posing before the world as a leader in all the efforts to prevent or put an end to wars but on the other hand it is not our policy to lag behind the other nations of the world in their efforts to promote peace. The passage of this Resolution is necessary in order that this Government may keep pace with other Governments of the world in this movement.''[16]

Progressive Republican Hiram Johnson of California led the opposition in the Foreign Relations Committee, and he drew heavily on legal advice from John Bassett Moore. Initially Johnson assumed that the committee would report the resolution favorably and that he could accomplish little more than record his objections. But he won more support than he expected. Though Green presented the department's statement in executive session, Hearst newspapers the next day carried the substance of that part relating to Japan. According to Green, news of that leak elicited from the usually staid Cordell Hull "a stream of unprintable profanity imputing canine maternity to certain persons not designated by name.''[17]

On May 25, 1933, three days after Norman Davis's major policy statement at the Geneva Disarmament Conference, Senator Johnson formally proposed an amendment drafted by Moore that provided that any arms embargo must "apply impartially to all the parties in the dispute or conflict to which it refers." It would have prevented the administration from discriminating against aggressors in the application of the embargo.[18]

Senator Pittman conferred with President Roosevelt at the White House and told him that the strength of the opposition made it impossible to win committee approval for the resolution or adoption in the Senate without the Johnson amendment. Without consulting his secretary of state, the president agreed to Pittman's recommendation that the resolution, with the Johnson amendment attached, be reported to the Senate. Roosevelt wanted discretionary authority in the use of the embargo, and he did not like the Johnson amendment. But he was prepared to accept the amended version as the best he could get from Congress at that time. He had been president less than three months, the country was suffering from the most critical economic emergency in its history, he was in the midst of the pressure-packed and politically chaotic rush to win enactment of his early New Deal program, and Hiram Johnson was high among the western progressives whose political support and friendship he was assiduously and (with reservations) successfully cultivating at that time. The arms embargo resolution was important, but in that context Roosevelt faced many other matters that were important as well. With the president's go-ahead, on May 27, 1933, the Foreign Relations Committee voted unanimously to report the amended resolution favorably. And Congressmen McReynolds and Sol Bloom planned to have the House Foreign Affairs Committee concur in the Johnson amendment.[19]

Secretary of State Hull, however, was less willing to compromise. He promptly telephoned the president opposing the Johnson amendment. And in a memorandum to Roosevelt, Hull pointed out that the amendment was "directly in conflict with our position at Geneva as expressed by Norman Davis." Hull telephoned the president again on Monday, May 29, and Roosevelt deferred to Hull's wishes. The secretary of state got authority to state at his press conference that same day that the Johnson amendment did not represent the president's views or his. On May 30, the president decided to allow the resolution to die and not to have it brought to a vote. They might try again the next session. Johnson and his isolationist colleagues were unable to enact a mandatory arms embargo in 1933, but they successfully blocked the administration's more internationalist proposal.[20]

Though they did not like it, Americans closest to the disarmament negotiations at that time were not entirely convinced that the Johnson amendment directly conflicted with the Davis statement. United States Minister to Switzerland Hugh R. Wilson wrote from Geneva that, except for consultation, the Davis statement promised only "passive undertakings" and did not require any positive "cooperation in the collective action." He thought the administration should "not mislead these nations over here into thinking that the statement which Norman Davis made has any obligation to positive action." He contended that the arms embargo with the Johnson amendment would not "diminish the value of the declarations of the President and of Norman Davis." Joseph Green conceded that the Davis statement implied "a passive attitude rather than specific action on our part, whereas an embargo on the export of arms would be positive action." But he still saw the Johnson amendment as "contrary to our general policy in regard to neutrality as expressed in that telegram and that statement." In Green's view, the isolationists in the Senate "seized upon the Embargo Resolution and offered this amendment as an expression of their opposition to our recently announced policy in regard to neutrality." He thought that if the arms embargo resolution were revived during the next session of Congress, isolationists would use it as "the excuse for a pitched battle on the issue of strict isolation and international cooperation."[21]

In January, 1934, J. Pierrepont Moffat, of the Western European Division of the State Department, advised Secretary Hull not to press for enactment of the discretionary embargo in that session of Congress. He predicted that efforts to get it passed would lead to "a strenuous fight" that could interfere with "passage of legislation more vital to our foreign relations." And, like Wilson, Moffat contended that it was "but one phase, and a relatively small one, of a much larger picture."[22]

On January 25, 1934, Norman Davis sent a five-page memorandum to the president along similar lines. He wrote that Congress and the press had "misinterpreted" his Geneva statement "as indicating a willingness to abandon neutrality and as constituting a binding commitment as to future action." Davis reminded the president that the declaration did "not involve any attempt to predetermine the action of the United States," that "the obligation under the declaration is a negative one, involving no participation in collective or punitive action against a treaty violator," that the declaration did "not imply an abandonment of neutrality," and that the policy was "contingent upon the conclusion and ratification of a general disarmament agreement satisfactory to the United States."[23]

By the middle of February, 1934, President Roosevelt had decided not to press for legislative action on the embargo resolution that session. Secretary Hull passed that word along to Senator Pittman and Congressman McReynolds. It was allowed to die. Secretary Hull, Undersecretary Phillips, Davis, Moffatt, and Green, as well as the president, had discussed repeatedly and at length the relationship between the arms embargo resolution (with and without the amendment) and the Davis statement. They had concluded, according to Green, that "Mr. Davis's offer would have . . . full validity without the passage of the Embargo Resolution, but, on the other hand, its validity would be gravely impaired by the passage of the Resolution with the Johnson amendment."[24]

So far as the Geneva Disarmament Conference was concerned, all that was "academic." The states were unable to reach accord on general disarmament in any form; that failure made the Davis statement a dead letter. The conference dragged on into 1934 and 1935, but its hopes for real accomplishment had long since evaporated. In October, 1933, Germany under Hitler withdrew both from the conference and from the League of Nations and speeded its armaments program. The course of events relative to the arms embargo resolution had little effect on European diplomacy. But, as Green and others correctly believed, the embargo resolution was a tangible target at which isolationists could concentrate their attacks against the administration's internationalist inclinations. And the administration's cautious efforts to redefine neutrality policies in the interests of peace and disarmament served as a crack in the door through which isolationists could and did move to restructure American neutrality policies in the interests of noninvolvement in European conflicts.

The London Naval Conference of 1935–36 began its deliberations with even less hope for success than the World Disarmament Conference had known—and that pessimism proved justified. Whereas the Geneva conference had focused on Europe, the London conference looked largely to the Pacific and Asia. From an Anglo-American perspective Japan was to the London conference what Germany had been to Geneva. The London conference conducted its sessions after Japan had completed its conquest of Manchuria, while the undeclared Italian-Ethiopian war raged in Africa, while Nazi Germany was building its armaments in Europe, at a time when many congressmen and senators from both parties were returning from a junket to Hawaii, Japan, and the Philippines (where they had attended the inauguration of Manuel Quezon as the first president of the Philippine Commonwealth), and at a time when tensions continued to mount in relations between Japan and China. Again Norman H. Davis was chief delegate for the United States, both at the preparatory negotiations in 1934 and at the formal conference itself from December 9, 1935, to March 26, 1936.

Though President Roosevelt was a Europe-firster and saw Nazi Germany as the most dangerous threat to peace and security, he had greater personal interest in and knowledge of naval matters than land and air power. In the 1920s the United States had allowed its naval strength to fall below levels permitted by the five-power Treaty for the Limitation of Naval Armament of 1922, and the Roosevelt administration set about building toward authorized levels. Most Americans shared hard-line attitudes toward Japan in the Pacific and East Asia. Isolationists and pacifists generally opposed Roosevelt's naval preparations in the 1930s, fearing that they pointed toward military and diplomatic involvement abroad. With few exceptions, however, that opposition to the administration's naval program did not extend to sympathy for the Japanese during the London Naval Conference or in the armaments race that followed.

Roosevelt, Davis, and the British wanted to retain the five-five-three naval tonnage ratio for capital ships agreed to at the Washington conference of 1921–22. To the Japanese that seemed unfair and demeaning, but the British and Americans insisted that it provided equal relative security for the powers involved. In the preliminary negotiations for the London Naval Conference, President Roosevelt wanted naval reductions across the board (preferably 20 percent reductions). He would have accepted smaller reductions, but he flatly opposed any treaty giving Japan tonnage equality with the United States and Britain, and he firmly rejected increasing authorized tonnage.[25]

In sharp contrast, Japan was determined to gain naval equality with the United States and Britain. Japan wanted general naval levels to be reduced and offensive naval capabilities to be limited or abolished. The practical effect of Japan's proposals would have been to reduce relative British and American power in the Pacific and to leave Japan more free from British and American restraints. That pattern would have left Britain and the United States less able to defend their commerce, colonies, and interests in the western Pacific and East Asia. The diplomatic impasse left little room for maneuver or negotiation. Consequently, in December, 1934, Japan gave formal notice that it would terminate its commitment to the Washington five power naval agreement of 1922—effective two years later on December 31, 1936. With that diplomatic deadlock and the Japanese notice, there was virtually no hope that the London Naval Conference of 1935–36 could accomplish positive results. And it didn't.[26]

With the formal opening of the London Naval Conference on December 9, 1935, spokesmen for each government restated their position—which had already been found unacceptable by at least one of the others. Davis read Roosevelt's letter of instruction calling for across-the-board reductions while preserving the Washington treaty ratios, Britain proposed a qualitative naval limitations plan that included retention of the ratios, and Japan called for equality with Britain and the United States. The delegates halfheartedly explored qualitative proposals to delay briefly the inevitable impasse on the quota issue. On January 15, 1936, when the delegates rejected the plan for naval parity, Japan withdrew from the conference, determined to build beyond treaty limits when the treaties of 1922 and 1930 expired on December 31, 1936. Britain, the United States, and France signed a new naval treaty on March 25, 1936, but in the absence of the Japanese it was meaningless and futile. The London Naval Conference ended in failure, and with it another strand in the fragile fabric of peace snapped.[27] Japan, Britain, the United States, France, Germany, Italy, and other states plunged headlong into a naval armaments race that continued through World War II.

As with the World Disarmament Conference earlier, so with the

London Naval Conference the actions and inactions of American isolationists had little direct impact on the results of the negotiations. The conference would have failed at that time whatever the isolationists might or might not have done. Pacifists favored more flexible, conciliatory, and bolder disarmament proposals than Roosevelt and his advisers were prepared to endorse. But most isolationists were as distrustful of the Japanese as President Roosevelt was. Senator Johnson and others on the West Coast were particularly anti-Japanese, and so was Senator Pittman of Nevada. Early in 1935, Johnson told Davis that he thought the United States had taken the proper stand in the preliminary negotiations, but (according to Davis) the California Republican was skeptical of the ability of Britain and the United States combined "to avoid ultimate trouble with Japan because he feels that Japan can not be trusted to keep any agreement whatever."[28] Throughout the 1930s most western progressive isolationists opposed the administration's naval building programs, believing them not necessary for national defense and likely to involve the United States in distant conflicts. But even in their oppositon to large naval appropriations, most isolationists stopped short of expressing sympathy for the Japanese.

An exception to that pattern was progressive Republican Senator Gerald P. Nye of North Dakota. Though not a pacifist, he was closer to and cooperated more with pacifist leaders than did many isolationists. He shared with other noninterventionists in battling (always unsuccessfully) against the administration's ever-larger naval appropriation requests. In March, 1934, Senator Nye charged that disarmament conferences failed because they "are manipulated, are played with, are influenced, by lobbyists for the munition makers who do not want, above all things else, anything resembling disarmament."[29]

In a public address late in 1934, Nye endorsed Japanese claims for naval equality. That statement, and a similar one by Senator Borah, worried Secretary Hull. He encouraged Joseph Green to visit with Nye and tactfully explain the error of his ways. Green did so, and Nye listened. But the senator responded that "his chief fear was that if we did not accede to the Japanese demands, the big Navy advocates in Congress would succeed in initiating a naval race which could not be checked." The North Dakotan did not change his views. Early in 1935, a Japanese newspaper reported a trans-Pacific telephone interview in which Senator Nye was supposed to have said that "Japan has a right to feel secure, with a free hand in the Far East and the same degree of freedom from intervention from without that America enjoys in the western hemisphere. The United States ought to be fair enough to agree on naval equality with Japan.'' The newspaper reported Nye as saying that he hoped to prevent an armaments race ''by organizing public opinion against such folly'' and that permitting ''both America and Japan to float a navy big enough for defense but not big enough for offense. . . . is the only lasting solution of the naval problem.'' Less than a month after Japan withdrew from the London conference, Nye said that he thought America's navy at that time was ''adequate, and even more than adequate, to repulse any nation that is going to be so foolish as to attack us.''[30]

In May, 1936, in an address opposing the administration's naval appropriation bill, Nye told the Senate that on his trip to Japan a few months earlier representative citizens of Japan had told him ''that the military dominance in Japan would have died of its own weight long ago except for the fact that at least once a year the United States gives the Japanese military some ground or other upon which to stand when they say, 'We have to be better prepared for the trouble that the United States is getting ready to make for us.' . . . The race which is involved is one which certainly is not going to get us anywhere except into the very thing we are trying to prevent.''[31]

In April, 1936, after Norman Davis had returned to the United States from his latest unsuccessful effort to negotiate disarmament, he visited at length with Secretary of State Cordell Hull. As the two former Tennesseans talked over the developments, ''it became clearly manifest'' (as Hull explained in his memoirs later) ''that peace on the basis of disarmament was next to impossible.'' The question, then, was whether and to what extent the law-abiding nations could cooperate to curb the rapidly developing plans of military aggression. ''But our government, we knew, was obliged virtually to ignore this possible method of preserving peace for the patent reason that public opinion here was, in majority, militantly and almost violently against our entering any such joint undertakings.'' As Hull saw it, the ''only alternative remaining'' for the United States was to ''arm our nation without delay to the extent adequate for our security.''[32]

There was a touching but logical end to the tale. The diplomatic career of Norman H. Davis continued until after the Brussels conference failed in its efforts to end the Sino-Japanese war near the end of 1937. With that failure, President Roosevelt asked Davis to accept the position as head of the American Red Cross. Davis wrote at the time: "Having failed to accomplish anything very concrete in my efforts for disarmament and peace and the consequent prevention of human cruelty, misery and distress, I am somewhat intrigued by the new job I am taking on as Chairman of the American Red Cross, because I can thus at least help to alleviate human suffering which cannot be prevented."[33] Isolationists, however, still hoped to avert such suffering for Americans by preventing American involvement in European and Asiatic wars.

Chapter 7

War Debts and the Johnson Act

Henry L. Stimson, secretary of state under Hoover and later Roosevelt's secretary of war, favored canceling the war debts owed by European governments to the United States. He believed that President Roosevelt agreed with him.[1] Whether Stimson was correct about Roosevelt's personal views or not, the president never endorsed cancellation in his official dealings with debtor governments or in his public statements. Publicly and officially Roosevelt provided a reasonably clear position on the war debts issue that was consistent with the attitudes of isolationists and public opinion. The actual course of events, however, included repudiation of reparations by Germany, default on war debt payments by the European governments (except by Finland), and ultimately the financial burden for the debts falling on American taxpayers. That was essentially the course advocated all along (in strikingly different vocabulary, of course) by many internationalists in the United States (and by debtor governments in Europe—governments that were not entirely innocent of nationalistic sentiments of their own).

During and immediately after World War I the United States government had loaned over ten billion dollars to European governments. The largest loans went to Great Britain, France, and Italy.[2] In the 1920s the United States concluded refunding agreements with debtor governments. Those agreements did not change the principal due, but they substantially reduced the financial obligations by scaling down interest rates. Under those agreements European governments promised to pay the United States more than twenty-two billion dollars in principal and interest over a period of sixty-two years. Debtor governments in Europe, however, were short of both the money and the will to pay. They contended that the loans should be treated as part of America's contribution to the war effort of World

War I. They emphasized the economic relationship between reparations owed to the Allies by Germany and war debts owed to the United States by the Allies. They insisted that any reduction of reparations be matched by comparable reductions in war debts. The European governments did not have gold enough to pay the debts, and America's high tariffs made it extremely difficult for them to pay by exports. The stock market collapse of 1929, the Hawley-Smoot Tariff of 1930, and the worldwide depression of the 1930s made an already difficult situation almost impossibly worse.

American internationalists (including, among others, both urban liberals and conservative financiers) generally believed war debts should be scaled down and tariffs reduced. Some urged cancellation of the debts. Those views, however, never won the majority position in the United States in the 1920s and 1930s.

Americans generally (and isolationists in particular) favored a firm line on war debts. Neither the Democratic nor the Republican party platforms advocated cancellation of war debts, and no presidential administration between the two world wars endorsed cancellation. Both Republican and Democratic presidential administrations maintained that reparations and war debts were separate issues to be treated independently. Americans insisted that the loans were financial transactions and included both legal and moral obligation to repay. In the 1920s spokesmen for debtor farmers contended that if the United States scaled down or canceled debts owed by foreign governments, it should do the same for American farmers who had gone deeply into debt in their efforts to increase food production for the war effort in World War I. Progressive isolationists charged that efforts to reduce or cancel the war debts would give American financiers first access to European financial resources. They saw renegotiation, reduction, or cancellation as tactics for transferring the financial burden from Europeans to the American taxpayers (including farmers) to the advantage of American financiers and European militarists. They contended that if Europeans could afford to spend large sums for big navies and military forces, they could well afford to pay their debts to the United States. Some hoped that debt payments would keep those governments so short of money that they would have less available for military expenditures.

The war debts issue provided the immediate occasion for President Herbert Hoover's initiative that led to the first meeting between Hoover and Roosevelt on November 22, 1932, after the election. In the middle of 1932, representatives of European governments had met in Lausanne, Switzerland, to discuss reparations. The agreements concluded there would have drastically reduced German reparations. In an accompanying secret gentlemen's agreement, however, the Allied governments tied reparations to war debts by promising to withhold ratifications if comparable concessions were not made to them on war debts. The gentlemen's agreement made the reparations settlement conditional on war debt settlement with the United States, and it presented something of a united front in treating with the United States on war debts. President Hoover was more flexible on the issue than Roosevelt was to be, but both Hoover and Roosevelt opposed cancellation, and neither acknowledged a relationship between reparations and war debts. If either Hoover or Roosevelt had shown signs of wavering or weakening on the matter, the strong feelings in Congress and the American public might have been sufficient to keep either from backing down. Neither Hoover nor Roosevelt would treat with debtor governments on the terms worked out at Lausanne.

Immediately after the presidential election, the British, French, and other governments communicated to the State Department their wish to reopen consideration of the war debts and to suspend the debt payments due on December 15, pending negotiation of revised arrangements on the war debts—not excluding the possibility of cancellation. On November 12, Hoover wrote Governor Roosevelt of those communications and invited Roosevelt to confer with him on the matter. They did so at the White House on November 22, with Moley accompanying Roosevelt and Secretary of Treasury Mills attending with Hoover.

The president thoroughly briefed Roosevelt and Moley on the war debt situation and sought their cooperation in winning congressional authorization for reconstituting the joint congressional-administration World War Foreign Debt Commission. Hoover did not win the cooperation he sought from Roosevelt. The two men issued separate statements after their meeting. Both insisted that the European governments make the payments due on December 15, both held that the Europeans were obligated to pay, both indicated that the United States would treat debtor governments individually rather than as a bloc, both denied that war debts and reparations were related so far as the United States was concerned, and both asserted that the United States should take account of the ability of debtor governments to pay. Roosevelt also encouraged continued negotiation on the issue. Until March 4, 1933, however, presidential responsibility and authority continued to rest exclusively with Hoover, and Roosevelt declined to share with the president in efforts to persuade Congress to reconstitute the debt commission. Without his cooperation in winning Democratic votes, no congressional action was politically possible. Great Britain, Italy, and other governments made their debt payments due on December 15, 1932, but France and others defaulted.[3]

Moley worried about the influence of Stimson and Davis on Roosevelt. He was uneasy about Roosevelt's visit at Warm Springs with the British Ambassador Ronald Lindsay on January 29. Moley was convinced that Hoover and the British were attempting to commit the president-elect to link war debt negotiations with other economic issues to be considered at the World Economic Conference in London. In his account of their conversations, Lindsay contended that Roosevelt saw debt cancellation as the best (though politically impossible) solution. Roosevelt's relations with Stimson, Davis, and Lindsay were cozier than Moley would have preferred.[4]

Nonetheless, in practice Roosevelt held firm. A second exchange of communications between Hoover and Roosevelt later in December, 1932, a second meeting between them in Washington on January 20, 1933 (with Stimson, Mills, Davis, and Moley present), and continuing communications between Governor Roosevelt and Secretary Stimson did not draw from the president-elect assurances or commitments on the war debts issue that were satisfactory either to Hoover or to the British. Roosevelt refused to be drawn into responsibility for decision-making or advanced planning jointly with the outgoing Hoover administration on either war debts or the World Economic Conference.[5]

As preliminary planning for the conference progressed, as the economic crises worsened, and as the date for the beginning of the new administration drew closer, Britain's Prime Minister J. Ramsay MacDonald grew increasingly troubled by the war debt issue. In a personal letter on February 10, 1933, MacDonald urged Governor Roosevelt that "no settlement with any European nation can meet the present situation unless it is, in fact, one which will keep the Lausanne Agreement going and enable it to be ratified." That would have meant no reparations settlement without a war debt settlement. He advanced the thought that it might be necessary to postpone debt payments in June, 1933. The memorandum, "British Policy on Economic Problems," which Ambassador Lindsay handed to Secretary Hull on March 4, closed with the assertion that the war debts constituted "an insuperable barrier to economic and financial reconstruction" and to the success of the World Economic Conference. War debts were among the subjects discussed in the conversations that MacDonald,

Herriot, and others had in Washington with President Roosevelt, Hull, and other administration officials during the spring of 1933.[6]

The president and his administration stood firm and consistent on the war debts issue. The Department of State reply on March 24 to "British Policy on Economic Problems" showed Moley's dominant influence and was approved by Roosevelt and Hull. It made clear that the United States was "prepared to discuss the debt question at the same time as—but separately from—the range of questions" to be treated at the World Economic Conference. And it flatly rejected the idea "that a new settlement of the debt owed by the British Government be a precedent to a solution of the questions" to be considered at the London Conference. In his conversations with foreign statesmen and diplomats, President Roosevelt was careful to emphasize that war debts were to be excluded from the conference deliberations. His written and oral instructions to Hull and the other members of the American delegation to the London conference explicitly directed them not "to carry on, formally or informally, any discussion of either war debts or disarmament. These two problems will be handled by me in Washington." Hull and other Americans considered it a breach of prior assurances when Prime Minister MacDonald alluded to war debts and debt reduction in his opening address to the conference on June 12, 1933.[7]

President Roosevelt's official and public position on war debts was consistent throughout. He expressed those views repeatedly in his letters, his press conferences, in conversations reported by others, and in a formal message on the subject that he presented to Congress on June 1, 1934. The president was willing to receive proposals and representations from debtor governments concerning war debts and to give their proposals thoughtful consideration. But he emphasized repeatedly that he had no legal or constitutional authority to reduce or cancel war debts. He stressed that only Congress had authority to extend any moratorium on debt payments. In June, 1933, during the closing days of the special session, the press of domestic legislation, according to the president, made it impossible to win from Congress any moratorium on the debt payments due June 15. Congressional approval for debt reduction or cancellation was impossible in the hectic rush to adjourn (and probably would have been politically impossible even if unhurried deliberation were possible at some less traumatic time). He did not consider a partial payment as a default. But President Roosevelt did not at any time ask Congress to authorize postponement, reduction, or cancellation of war debt payments. And he consistently insisted that war debts were separate from reparations so far as the United States was concerned. Isolationists worried that Roosevelt might weaken on the issue. They were uneasy about the possible deleterious influence of Norman Davis and other internationalists. In practice, however, they had no cause to find fault with President Roosevelt's public and official position on war debts.[8]

Progressive Republican Senator Hiram Johnson of California played the largest active role in isolationist and congressional responses to the war debt controversy. A year younger than Borah, Johnson was born in Sacramento, California, in 1866. He attended the University of California at Berkeley, but left school in his junior year and never graduated. He read law in his father's office, was admitted to the bar in 1888, and practiced law in Sacramento and later in San Francisco. Active in Republican party politics, he opposed the party machine and supported progressive reforms. As governor of California from 1911 to 1917 he emerged as one of the nation's leading state reformers. He won the vice-presidential nomination as Theodore Roosevelt's running mate in the unsuccessful third party Bull Moose Progressive party effort in 1912. Elected to the United States Senate in 1916, Johnson was in his fifth term when he died in 1945. Johnson was second only to Borah in seniority among Republicans in the Senate Foreign Relations Committee during the years that Japan, Italy, and Germany mounted their alarming challenges to world peace and security in the 1930s. Fully as independent, chauvinistic, and isolationist as Borah, Johnson personally was more crusty, abrasive, and subjective. He resented Borah's good relations with the press and his talent for winning headlines. Even more than other western progressives, Johnson saw himself as fighting almost alone against the forces of evil. He could be a formidable political opponent, and he commanded impressive oratorical and legislative skills.[9]

In 1931–32, Johnson conducted a Senate Finance Committee investigation of American loans abroad. His probe and report touched on war debts, but it focused largely on private American loans to Latin American governments. As he probed deeper, Johnson became increasingly troubled by the role (almost the partnership) of the Department of State in the whole process. The State Department, according to Johnson, helped financiers arrange loans to Latin American governments, failed to alert small creditors to the questionable soundness of the bonds, and then through official secrecy helped cover their tracks (and those of the financiers). State Department officials withheld dispatches from Johnson's committee (documents that were available to financiers involved). He reached the conclusion that the United States had "a government of, for, and by international bankers, owned by those who have, and without the slightest concern for those who have not." Johnson's investigation in 1931–32 directed its fire against international bankers and the State Department much more than against European debtor governments.[10]

Nonetheless, the California senator had repeatedly criticized America's war debt policies. He opposed the Hoover moratorium on intergovernmental debts, and he vigorously objected to reducing or canceling the war debts. He actively supported Roosevelt before and after the election of 1932, but he worried that Roosevelt might weaken on the debts issue under pressure from eastern "cancellationists." On November 14, 1932, when he learned that President Hoover had invited the president-elect to meet at the White House to discuss war debts, the senator telegraphed Roosevelt through James A. Farley, advising him to "beware of Greeks bearing gifts." He thought Hoover was trying to trap him on the debts issue. In his telegram Johnson contended that the American people were overwhelmingly opposed to cancellation or reduction of the debts. He thought Congress generally reflected that sentiment. There would be time enough for Roosevelt to deal with debts after inauguration; it "would be folly" to participate or share in the consequences of Hoover's actions.[11]

Near the close of the Hoover administration, two of the giants among isolationists, Hiram Johnson of California and William E. Borah of Idaho, took the floor for a moving Senate debate on war debts. Though they disliked each other personally, Johnson and Borah generally took similar stands on public issues. On war debts, however, they disagreed enough to produce a memorable oratorical contest. With France and other countries expected to default on their payments due December 15, both Borah and Senator Pat Harrison of Mississippi had given notice of their intention to speak on the subject. But neither had acted. Hiram Johnson, ever suspicious of the motives of others, suspected that either the Hoover administration or the international bankers had silenced them and that there "was a policy thereafter of hush hushing upstairs." He grew increasingly impatient, and after the holiday adjournment he gave notice of his intention to speak. He took the floor on Wednesday, January 4, 1933.[12]

For more than two hours Senator Johnson held forth, speaking largely without notes. His was a dramatic, powerful oration restating arguments against the moratorium and against either reducing or canceling the debts. He provided factual background on the history of the debts, the original agreements, the renegotiations in the 1920s, and the moratorium. In moving terms he described the plight of American farmers and workers whose acute economic difficulties led to foreclosures and bankruptcies without benefit of compassion or help from either the United States government or big financiers. He reminded his listeners that those same Americans, in their capacities as taxpayers, would bear the financial burdens if the war debts were reduced or canceled. Highly critical of the debtor governments, particularly France, he insisted those governments were obligated to pay and were capable of paying. In his opinion, if European governments chose to violate their agreements to pay, they should bear the onus for defaulting; the United States should not relieve them of that opprobrium by transferring the burden to American taxpayers through moratorium, reduction, or cancellation of the debts.

Though he criticized the European governments, Johnson directed his most eloquent denunciations against American internationalists that he called "the American foreign legion." In that category he included international bankers, the internationalist press, intellectuals, and the Hoover administration. He wished his voice might extend across the ocean to give Europeans the message "that no administration can settle these debts, no international banker will be permitted to revise or reduce them, no international press can befog the issue and drive the American people into reducing them." That authority, he pointed out, rested solely with the Congress of the United States—and Congress would not do it. Senator Johnson was exhausted after his two-and-one-half hour performance. He wrote his sons later that it went over "very, very well." And indeed it had.[13]

Though the old California progressive left the chamber after his address, later that same afternoon Senator Borah continued the deliberations with a major address of his own. There were none in the Senate who surpassed Borah's reputation or talent for oratory. The Idaho progressive Republican conceded many of Johnson's points. He did not favor having the United States unilaterally reduce or cancel the war debts. He did not believe that canceling the debts would contribute significantly, by itself, to restoring prosperity or preserving peace. Borah did believe that there were other economic considerations more important than debts, however, and that the United States should be willing to use debt adjustments to gain world markets that could contribute to prosperity for the United States and the world.

In his address Borah claimed to be speaking "from the viewpoint of the farmer" and insisted that there could not be "a restoration of real and permanent prosperity in the United States without a restoration of prosperity to the American farmer.'' He cited statistics on the sharp drop in foreign trade during the depression and contended that without revived commerce there could not be ''any reasonable return of prosperity in the United States.'' He thought it would be impossible for farmers ''to prosper upon his local market.'' In a key statement Senator Borah said: ''If we could open the markets for the American farm, revive trade and commerce, reestablish our monetary systems upon a sound basis and drastically reduce the armaments of the world . . . it would be infinitely more valuable to the people of the United States than the payment of the debts.'' He wanted to use those debts to negotiate for more important economic advantages for the American people. He praised the Lausanne agreements of 1932 as ''a tremendous step in the right direction.'' He asked how the senators ''proposed to restore prosperity on the farm without markets? Without that all schemes fail. My remedy may be wrong, but in the name of a suffering people then tell me what is the remedy.''[14]

Senator Borah, as always, was magnificently impressive as he addressed the Senate that afternoon. Despite his concern for the farmer and farm markets, however, his language was more in tune with that of internationalists than with that of most of his fellow isolationists. On that subject, and in that address, Secretary of State Stimson was correct in grouping the Idaho senator with himself and with ''the bankers and economists.'' Johnson was, in a sense, justified in associating Borah's position with ''the New York bankers.''[15] But President Roosevelt did not pursue the course urged by Senator Borah. Whatever Roosevelt's personal views may have been, in practice he followed policies that were consistent with those that Hiram Johnson advocated so eloquently. And he conferred with Johnson on the issue both before and after inauguration.

Johnson was uneasy, however, about Roosevelt's position; he did not like the way the president-elect was ''monkeying around with our war debts.'' He disapproved of FDR's January meeting at Warm Springs with Britain's Ambassador Lindsay. In mid-February, he wrote that he was ''very deeply concerned over Roosevelt's attitude in respect to our foreign debts.''[16]

On March 22, 1933, at the beginning of the Roosevelt administration, Senator Johnson introduced a bill (S. 682) that would have prohibited private American loans to any foreign government that defaulted on its debts to the United States government or to private individuals and corporations in the United States. The Judiciary Committee reported it out favorably to the Senate. Initially it did not win legislative support from Roosevelt, and it was not passed by either house during the special session. Roosevelt gave priority to his domestic New Deal program during the One Hundred Days. He was evasive on the debts issue in his press conferences. Time grew short and tempers flared as the special session rushed to adjournment just as the June 15 war debt payments came due and just as the World Economic Conference got under way in London.[17]

Though the special session had not acted on his bill, neither Johnson nor Roosevelt was through with the matter. President Roosevelt, Secretary Hull, Assistant Secretary Moley, William C. Bullitt, and others consulted with Johnson on the bill. The Senate passed it without objection on January 11, 1934. Later that same day, however, Democratic Majority Leader Senator Joseph T. Robinson of Arkansas delayed matters when he moved for reconsideration. Robinson was in consultation with the White House and the State Department, and there were objections to the bill in its original form.[18]

Johnson believed the president "really favored the bill" and "would like it as a weapon in dealing with these European welchers," but "desired some amendments to protect him in what he was doing in South America, [and] with Russia." The administration wanted three major changes—and got its way on two of them. Roosevelt suggested that the bill be changed to give him discretionary authority to determine when there was a default, and thus when and whether the penalties against debtors should go into effect. Johnson objected to that proposed change and insisted that he "would not leave to any individual, however much I cared for him, the right to do as he pleased with these foreign debts." The president yielded to his wishes on that matter.[19]

Both the president and the State Department objected to the language in the original bill that would have applied it to those governments that had defaulted on debts to private American bondholders; they wanted it to apply only to governments that had defaulted on debts owed to the United States government. The change they urged would have made it applicable on the war debts issue, but would not have had it apply to Latin American defaults that affected small private bondholders whose plight had aroused Johnson's concern in the course of his 1931–32 investigation. In a letter to the president, Johnson complained that if that change were made, "we protect our *Government* and then deny the same protection to our people." He thought "there should be no distinction." But he reluctantly yielded to the president's wishes on that important change. And finally, Roosevelt and the State Department wanted it amended to prevent it from interfering with trade with the Soviet Union that they hoped would develop with help from the Export-Import Bank established for that purpose. Again Johnson yielded to the administration's wishes.[20]

On February 2, 1934, the Senate reconsidered Johnson's bill. With the Californian's assent, and with Johnson and Robinson handling the necessary legislative procedures, the Senate quickly approved the amendments desired by the administration. The amended bill promptly passed the Senate without debate, without dissent, and without record vote.[21]

It then went on to the House of Representatives. Johnson kept a watchful eye on its progress there.[22] On March 2 it was referred to the Foreign Affairs Committee. Chairman McReynolds arranged to have Senator Johnson testify on behalf of his bill. After consultation with Assistant Secretary of State R. Walton Moore, Johnson agreed "not to unnecessarily quote" the president in the course of his testimony. Johnson did his job effectively, and the committee reported the bill out favorably on March 14.[23]

On Wednesday afternoon, April 4, the House of Representatives considered Johnson's "little bill," under a suspension of the rules that limited debate and did not permit amendments. McReynolds, Democratic chairman of the Foreign Affairs Committee, and Hamilton Fish, New York Republican and ranking minority member of the committee, led the deliberations. All who participated in the one-hour debate approved the general purposes of the bill. Criticism came principally from those who thought it did not go far enough.

The most severe criticisms focused on that part designed to permit Export-Import Bank credits to the Soviet Union. The pertinent language was general, exempting from the application of the measure any public corporation created by Congress or any corporation controlled by the Unted States government. It did not explicitly mention the Soviet Union. Anticipating objections, McReynolds had obtained a formal resolution from the board involved that "no actual credit transactions with the Soviet Government shall be undertaken unless and until that government shall submit to the President of the United States an acceptable agreement respecting the payment of the Russian indebtedness to the Government of the United States and its nationals."

Isolationist Hamilton Fish was scathing in his comments on that provision. "Just why we should show any favoritism to the Communists is a matter for the 'brain trust' to explain, for I know of no reason for it unless we are verging toward a socialist dictatorship as many claim.'' Fish and others would have preferred changing the bill to prohibit loans or credits to the Soviet Union, but amendments were not permitted under the suspension of the rules. Fish said he had been assured by "a prominent official" of the State Department, however, that the government would "not lend any money to Soviet Russia until the debts she owes us have been settled . . . to the satisfaction of the President.'' With those assurances, Fish would vote for the bill. Despite objections to the provision permitting credits to the Soviet Union, the House after its brief debate gave two-thirds approval to the bill, with no roll call vote, and sent it on to the president.[24]

If he had been prepared to pay the political price, Roosevelt probably could have blocked action on Johnson's bill—but he did not do so. The president's New Deal legislative priorities helped account for the failure of the special session to consider Johnson's bill in the spring of 1933, but Roosevelt did not speak out against it either then or later. The president and the State Department had a hand in Robinson's move to reconsider the bill after the Senate first approved it in January, 1934. And the president and the State Department successfully compelled Johnson to accept amendments that the senator really did not want. Roosevelt did not publicly urge Congress to adopt the bill, but neither did he publicly oppose it. Spokesmen for the legislation (including Johnson) were careful not to quote the president or to state in Congress or in committee that he favored the bill. But Assistant Secretary of State R. Walton Moore (who played the largest State Department role in the legislative course of the bill) wrote Undersecretary William Phillips that it was "a fact that the President favors the legislation.'' And the British Ambassador Lindsay noted in a communication to his government that the Senate approval on February 2 was accomplished "without any opposition, with perfecting amendments proposed by the State Department, and with the Administration leaders of the Chamber standing by in favourable neutrality, all circumstances combining to indicate an absence of opposition by the White House.''[25]

Both internationalists in the United States and statesmen from debtor governments denounced the bill. But even if Roosevelt had agreed with them (and he provided no solid evidence that he did), he was not prepared to pay the political price required to quash it. He wanted and needed the political support of western progressive isolationists (including Johnson) who felt strongly on war debts in general and on this legislation in particular. Whatever his personal convictions (and he may have agreed with Johnson), he was not going to endanger his New Deal legislative program and his political standing in the country on an issue where feelings ran so high as they did on war debts. Secretary of State Cordell Hull offered "no objection to the form of the bill," and President Roosevelt signed it into law on April 13, 1934. He invited Senator and Mrs. Johnson to dinner at the White House soon after, and even sent an inscribed picture of himself to Mrs. Johnson.[26]

The Johnson Act of 1934 raised many legal uncertainties, and the White House and State Department conferred with the Californian in resolving those technicalities. The new law did not affect short-term credits involved in day-to-day operation of normal commercial dealings between countries. Before the adoption of the Johnson Act, the president had ruled that Britain and other countries that made partial payments were not in default. Under the Johnson Act, however, governments that made only partial payments would be in default. Johnson and administration leaders agreed that the new definition of default should not be retroactive, but it clearly applied when the next payments came due on June 15, 1934. In practice, neither Britain nor any other debtor governments (except Finland) made any further payments (token or otherwise) on their war debts to the United States after the adoption of the Johnson Act in 1934.[27]

In his address to Congress on January 3, 1934, Roosevelt had indicated that he would send a message to Congress on war debts, but he procrastinated. Finally, on June 1, 1934, after he had signed the Johnson Act, after the main legal questions involved had been worked out, and when it was clear that the act would be met by general default by the debtor governments, the president presented his debts message to Congress. It was largely a factual summary of the course of policies and developments on war debts from 1931 through the end of 1933.

In his message the president neither called for new legislation nor mentioned the Johnson Act. He repeated his earlier statements that the war debts had "no relation whatsoever to reparations payments" and that each debtor government was free to discuss its problem with the United States. He reminded the debtor governments of "the sacredness" of their obligations. He concluded his message by affirming that "the final power" on America's war debt policies lay "with the Congress" and promising to "keep the Congress informed from time to time and make such new recommendations as may later seem advisable.'' No such "new recommendations" were ever forthcoming from President Roosevelt.[28]

The Johnson Act was not exactly what the California progressive Republican had intended it to be. It did not apply to those governments that defaulted on obligations to small private bondholders in the United States—the matter that had first given rise to his concern. The Johnson Act did not ban loans by the United States government to those governments that had defaulted on debt payments. By defining default to include both nonpayment and partial payment, the act provided no incentive for Britain and other governments to continue making token payments. If it was designed to coerce debtor governments into paying their debts, it failed. Except for Finland, none of the European governments made any further payments after the Johnson Act went into effect in 1934. The law was more of an angry nationalistic slap at Europeans than any real effort to win further payments. It was a widely approved manifestation of America's disenchantment with Europe after World War I. For many (including Johnson) it was an expression of hostility against international bankers and big financiers. In its restrictions on private American financial ties with European governments, the Johnson Act was a precursor to the neutrality laws of the 1930s that were designed to prevent economic ties that might involve the United States in European wars.

There were no serious moves either by the administration or by Congress to repeal the Johnson Act during the years that Franklin D. Roosevelt was president of the United States. Not until the financial needs of Britain, France, China, and the Soviet Union in World War II became of growing concern did President Roosevelt publicly allude to the problem again. And he did so then only to take a fresh tack that might "eliminate the dollar sign" and avoid the "mistakes" that had so inflamed America's relations with Europe in the war debt controversies that had followed World War I.

Chapter 8

Reciprocal Trade
Agreements Program

Isolationist economic concerns extended to foreign trade, tariffs, and reciprocity. No leading isolationist wanted the United States to cut itself off economically from the rest of the world. Many actively sought foreign markets for American products—particularly agricultural and mineral products. In that connection, they urged construction of a Saint Lawrence seaway to give the Middle West direct access by oceangoing ships to markets and products of other parts of the world.

Nonetheless, isolationist views on trade, tariffs, and reciprocity differed from those of internationalists. Some in retail businesses, service industries, and protected manufacturing sold only on the domestic market and felt no direct need for foreign markets. Some parts of agriculture (truck farming, for example) sold largely in the domestic market. Farmers and miners produced surpluses that found their way into foreign markets, but they did not directly handle exports, shipping, and marketing abroad. Consequently, often they were not alert to the economic significance of foreign markets. In any event, they were primarily interested in agricultural and mineral products. Tariffs that protected industrial sectors of the economy and reciprocal trade agreements that seemed to encourage industrial exports in exchange for agricultural and mineral imports did not appeal to western progressive isolationists. They emphasized the right of farmers to the American market. They criticized legislative delegation of authority to the president to conclude reciprocal trade agreements.

Those considerations were personalized in the contest between Secretary of State Cordell Hull and Foreign Trade Adviser George N. Peek over trade policies. Even more decisively than in his earlier contest with Moley, Hull triumphed over Peek. Like Moley a few months

earlier, Peek fell from presidential grace and left the Roosevelt administration before the end of 1935.

President Roosevelt's role in the Hull-Peek confrontation was less
spectacular than it had been in the earlier Hull-Moley clash. But his
personal views on trade and reciprocity became more clearly sympathetic with Hull's side than they had been in the Hull-Moley clash.
In both the Hull-Peek episode and evolving trade policies, Roosevelt
increasingly identified with the reciprocal trade program for which
Secretary Hull crusaded so tenaciously. Hull's reciprocal trade agreements did not contribute so much to prosperity and peace as he had
predicted. But the developing patterns were part of the gradual
estrangement of isolationists in general and agrarian progressive isolationists in particular from the Roosevelt administration's conduct of
foreign relations.

Throughout his public career Frankin D. Roosevelt had favored
lowering tariff barriers and expanding foreign markets. But he was
never so rigidly doctrinaire as Hull was on reciprocal trade agreements. In 1932–33, Roosevelt was sufficiently artful in his choice of
words to satisfy those who wanted tariff protection for their particular
sectors of the economy (as well as those who favored mutual reductions through the hard tariff bargaining) and those who urged sweeping multilateral tariff reductions. In a letter to Hull in 1929, Governor
Roosevelt applauded the Tennessee congressman's tariff stand and
predicted that in 1932 the tariff issue would "be more to the front
than at any time since 1892." In his address to the New York State
Grange in February 1932 (the speech in which he said he no longer
favored American membership in the League of Nations), Governor
Roosevelt criticized the high Smoot-Hawley tariff of 1930. He blamed
it for provoking other countries to raise their tariff walls and so close
foreign markets to American products. Roosevelt pointed to the "simple fact that the farmers of America have been buying in a protected
market and selling in a market open to the competition of the whole
world." He urged "reciprocal methods" to negotiate mutually beneficial tariff reductions at a "trade conference with the other Nations
of the world."[1]

Before the Democratic convention in 1932, Hull got the impression
that Roosevelt "was entirely favorable in principle" to his reciprocal
trade agreement idea. Hull and A. Mitchell Palmer wrote the plank in
the Democratic platform that called for "a competitive tariff for
revenue with a fact-finding tariff commission free from executive
interference, reciprocal tariff agreements with other nations, and an

international economic conference designed to restore international trade and facilitate exchange." In his acceptance speech Roosevelt explicitly endorsed the tariff plank in the platform and urged "restoration of the trade of the world" by negotiating with other countries.[2]

The tariff views of Roosevelt's campaign advisers ranged from the reciprocity ideas of Hull and Charles W. Taussig to the economic nationalism and protectionism of Hugh Johnson, Raymond Moley, Key Pittman, and George N. Peek. Roosevelt's responses to their range of guidance provided insight into the man and his methods. Hull and Taussig drafted a tariff speech for him in accord with their reciprocal trade views; brains truster Hugh Johnson dictated a different draft calling for "old-fashioned Yankee horse-trades" in tough bilateral negotiations. Moley thought the two drafts differed so fundamentally that they were irreconcilable (Hull would have thought so too). After reading them both, however, Roosevelt casually asked Moley to "weave the two together." Moley considered it "an impossible assignment." But when the speech was ready for delivery before an Iowa audience, Roosevelt believed they had succeeded. He saw it as "a compromise between the free traders and the protectionists." In Moley's opinion, however, the speech ignored "the Hulls of the party" and threw them "a couple of sops" in the form of attacks on the Smoot-Hawley tariff.[3] Critics might consider Roosevelt's response an indication of his economic ignorance, his fuzzy thinking, his talent for obfuscation, or his lack of principle. But it might be just as accurate to suggest that Hull, Moley, and Peek wore doctrinal blinders, while Roosevelt demonstrated his political artfulness, his talent for keeping his options open, and his flexible undoctrinaire style. His position on tariffs during the campaign was not exactly what Hull wanted, but it was not what the Smoot-Hawley tariff provided either.

In a campaign address in Seattle on September 20, Governor Roosevelt denounced the "outrageous rates" in the Smoot-Hawley tariff for raising "havoc" with plans "to stimulate foreign markets." He urged "a tariff policy based in large part upon the simple principle of profitable exchange, arrived at through negotiated tariff, with benefit to each Nation." Speaking in Sioux City, Iowa, on September 29, Roosevelt again denounced the Smoot-Hawley tariff for increasing the prices of the industrial goods the farmer bought without at the same time increasing the prices the farmer received for his products. He charged that the high Republican tariff had "largely extinguished the export markets for our industrial and our farm surplus." He called for "a competitive tariff" that would "put the American producers on a market equality with their foreign competitors." In his opinion "international negotiation" was "the most desirable method" to accomplish that goal, using "good old-fashioned trading" and "successful barter." Roosevelt denied that the Democrats wanted free trade. He charged that the Republicans "would put the duties so high as to make them practically prohibitive" and promised that the Democrats "would put them as low as the preservation of the prosperity of American industry and American agriculture will permit." On October 25, in a speech in Baltimore, Roosevelt denied Republican charges that he would hurt farmers by reducing tariffs on farm products. Six days later he told an audience in Boston that he favored continued tariff protection "for American agriculture as well as American industry."[4]

In his inaugural address on March 4, 1933, President Roosevelt gave priority to his domestic program. "Our international trade relations, though vastly important, are in point of time and necessity secondary to the establishment of a sound national economy." He promised to "spare no effort to restore world trade by international economic readjustment, but the emergency at home cannot wait on that accomplishment." That tone and priority coincided with Moley's views, but could not have been entirely pleasing to the new president's secretary of state.[5]

Cordell Hull of Tennessee was a Wilsonian Democrat. He shared the South's traditional low tariff views and those of Woodrow Wilson (himself a product of the South). From the beginning of his long career in the House of Representatives, Hull had taken special interest in economic issues—particularly tax, tarriff, and trade matters. Long before he became secretary of state, Hull's obsession had become multilateral trade reciprocity, his central solution to the problems of the United States and the world. He was not a free-trader, but he favored legislation authorizing the president to negotiate bilateral reciprocal trade agreements. Hull firmly believed that mutually beneficial trade relations contributed to improved diplomatic relations between states and reduced international friction and hostility. He was persuaded that international peace and prosperity went hand in hand and that his trade program would contribute to both peace and prosperity for the United States and the world.[6]

Sophisticated critics ridiculed his single-minded preoccupation with reciprocity. Whether the reciprocal trade agreements program had the utopian results he expected from it may be doubted. But his persistent, determined, and skillful efforts were centrally responsible for its enactment and implementation during the Roosevelt administration. Hull, more than any other individual, guided President Roosevelt from his generalized sympathy for tariff reduction to positive action culminating in the enactment of the reciprocal trade agreements program in the middle of 1934.[7] And just as Roosevelt's early New Deal program and the president's role in the World Economic Conference were in tune with economic nationalism and isolationism, so Hull's reciprocal trade agreements program was in tune with the administration's slowly developing internationalism and its gradual estrangement from isolationism.

It may well be that fundamental circumstances at home and abroad were moving the United States in the internationalist directions that Secretary Hull's trade views pointed. But his success on the issue was not accomplished without overcoming difficulties and frustrations. Roosevelt's brains trusters (including Moley, Tugwell, Johnson, and Peek), western progressive isolationists, and the early New Deal's economic nationalism (including that of NRA and AAA) encouraged a modified self-containment that was fundamentally at odds with Hull's trade views and with internationalism.

As head of the American delegation to the World Economic Conference in June, 1933, Hull was acutely distraught when he learned en route to London that Roosevelt had decided not to press for enactment of trade agreements legislation. He seriously considered resigning. James M. Cox and William C. Bullitt dissuaded him, however, and prodded Roosevelt into sending a message reassuring Hull of his continued dedication to the enactment of reciprocity legislation—at an unspecified later date. Hull dried his tears, stiffened his back, squared his shoulders, and pressed on with his frustrating duties as head of the American delegation in London. He loyally defended his president and won Roosevelt's gratitude at the close of the fruitless conference. But Hull was to have more tribulations before his brainchild could become a reality. And part of his difficulties came in the person of George N. Peek.

Peek of Illinois (like Hugh S. Johnson) was a protégé of Bernard M. Baruch, having served under him on the War Industries Board of World War I. He had experience as a businessman in the manufacture of farm equipment before and after World War I. Priding himself on his business experience and on getting hard facts as bases for action, Peek took a dim view of academic theoreticians (and of Hull's lack of experience in the practical world of business). He was not an agrarian radical, and on many domestic issues he disagreed with western progressives. But he shared their devotion to agriculture—and to isolationism. Like western progressives, Peek gave priority to domestic considerations over foreign affairs and to the needs of farmers over those of urban sectors of the economy (though he denied that there was any fundamental conflict between rural and urban interests within the United States). He played a central role in developing the two-price system urged by agricultural reformers in the 1920s; he proposed to increase farm income by protecting the domestic market for American producers and by selling agricultural surpluses on the world market. He favored negotiating bilateral trade agreements with foreign governments, including barter agreements, but wanted them subject to Senate approval. He strongly opposed Hull's unconditional-most-favored-nation scheme.[8]

In 1932, Hugh Johnson drew Peek into the Roosevelt camp. In the new Roosevelt administration Peek helped draft the first Agricultural Adjustment Act and served as the first head of the Agricultural Adjustment Administration. He found himself at odds, however, with Secretary Henry A. Wallace, Rexford G. Tugwell, Jerome N. Frank, and others in the Department of Agriculture. He saw them as 'internationalists" and "collectivists" who were trying to make the AAA into "an instrument to regiment the farmer through acreage control." He opposed "planned scarcity." They, in turn, objected to Peek's plans to raise farm incomes by disposing of agricultural surpluses abroad through dumping, subsidized exports, and bilateral barter arrangements.[9]

Wallace and Tugwell would have been pleased if the president had simply fired Peek. But that was not Roosevelt's way. He eschewed personal unpleasantness and found it difficult to dismiss anyone. He was concerned about Peek's political following in the Middle West. The president solved the problem by easing it from the Department of Agriculture to the Department of State, from Secretary Wallace to Secretary Hull. And he did so while Hull was out of the country heading the American delegation to the Inter-American Conference at Montevideo, Uruguay. At a carefully staged White House meeting on December 11, 1933, the president arranged for Peek to resign as Agricultural Adjustment Administrator and then appointed him to head a temporary committee to recommend a permanent organization "to coordinate all government relations to American foreign trade." In advance of the White House meeting the president had confided to Undersecretary of State William Phillips that Peek's new assignment was "window dressing" to resolve the Peek-Wallace impasse and "to save the face of Peek." Insiders assumed that Peek was on his way out—but it proved to be a long slow process. He submitted his temporary committee's report to the president on December 30; early in February, 1934, Roosevelt named him to head the new Export-Import banks; and on March 23, 1934, he appointed Peek to be special adviser to the president on foreign trade. Hull later wrote that "if Mr. Roosevelt had hit me between the eyes with a sledge hammer he could not have stunned me more than by this appointment."[10]

Personally, Peek was likable enough. Some two years younger than Hull, he shared the secretary of state's single-minded devotion to a cause he considered vital; he shared Hull's doctrinaire rigidity and unshakable conviction that his own particular approach was right. To use religious terms for their secular ideologies, Peek and Hull were both true believers. But each worshiped a different god, and each was intolerant of those of different faiths. Both emerged from agricultural sectors of the society—but with a difference. Hull of Tennessee was a product of the South, long and consciously dependent on foreign markets for its cotton and on foreign suppliers for its industrial imports; Peek of Illinois was a product of the Middle West with its corn-hog agriculture, its protectionist tariff views, and its less acute awareness of the importance of foreign markets for agricultural prosperity.

From December, 1933, until November, 1935, Hull and Peek were locked in a continuing contest over control of trade policies. Both had direct access to the president. Each thought Roosevelt could have resolved the difficulty by unequivocally committing his administration to one trade policy or the other. That the president was agonizingly slow to do. Peek inundated Roosevelt with facts, figures, reports, and recommendations. Secretary Hull, Undersecretary Phillips, Assistant Secretary Francis B. Sayre (President Wilson's son-in-law), and others in the State Department alertly countered each of Peek's initiatives by persuading the president to dilute, block, or bury them. Roosevelt's personal views were closer to Hull's than to Peek's, but he insisted that the two were not so far apart as each believed. Peek persisted. And there were repeated scares in the State Department that he might slip through one or another of his schemes. Even the adoption of Hull's precious Reciprocal Trade Agreements Act in June, 1934, did not immediately end the contest or determine with certainty that Hull's trade views would prevail over Peek's in implementing the new law.

The reciprocal trade agreements bill (H.R. 8687) was the product of many minds—including those of both Hull and Peek. Leaders in both houses of Congress were consulted in the deliberations. President Roosevelt approved the draft legislation at a White House meeting on February 28, 1934, at which both Hull and Peek were present. On March 2, the president sent a message to Congress urging adoption of the reciprocity resolution. Roosevelt pointed out that "a full and permanent domestic recovery depends in part upon a revived and strengthened international trade and that American exports cannot be permanently increased without a corresponding increase in imports." Describing it as "an emergency program necessitated by the economic crisis," the president promised to "pay due heed to the requirements of other branches of our recovery program, such as the National Industrial Recovery Act."[11]

On March 16, Democratic Representative Robert L. Doughton of North Carolina, chairman of the House Ways and Means Committee, introduced the administration's resolution. His committee conducted hearings. Congressman Doughton opened the House debate on March 23 with a major address urging adoption. Republican Congressman Allen Treadway of Massachusetts led the opposition. Though agricultural representatives held forth against the bill, spokesmen for protected industries held center stage for the opposition. In the final vote on March 29, more than two-thirds of the legislators assured House approval, 274 for and 111 against.[12]

On April 2, the Senate Finance Committee, under Mississippi's Democratic Senator Pat Harrison, held extensive hearings at which Hull and others testified. During the extended and sometimes heated debate on the Senate floor, spokesmen for industry, labor, and agriculture shared in marshaling arguments against Hull's reciprocity proposal. But California's Hiram Johnson and other agrarian progressive isolationists dominated closing phases of the deliberations with their unsuccessful efforts to amend the bill to exclude agricultural products from reciprocity agreements to be concluded under the program. A few, including Arthur Capper of Kansas, voted for Johnson's amendment (though correctly anticipating its defeat), and then voted for the administration's bill even without the amendment (believing it would "give President Roosevelt an opportunity to open up foreign markets for our surplus, especially our farm products"). Johnson, Borah, Nye, and other western progressives objected to delegating authority to the president to conclude trade agreements ("treaties") that would not be subject to Senate approval. Johnson regretted that he had to oppose the president on the issue and feared the proposal would "destroy the entente cordiale which has, thus far, existed between the President and the Congress." He blamed Hull and Wallace (whom he called "internationalists" and "freetraders") for persuading the president to seek authority to make reciprocity agreements. Johnson thought Wallace wanted "to uplift the entire world," "cancel our foreign debts if he can," and "break down every tariff barrier here and abroad." He considered Hull "a nice old gentleman" who had "more delusions concerning the world in general than a dog has fleas." With his California constituents explicitly in mind, Johnson opposed putting Hull and Wallace "in command of the things that we raise from the soil, particularly upon which we have to compete with the Mediterranean and other countries." On April 15, Johnson wrote his son: "I am sorry to say that the Administration is internationally-minded. I really think I have had much to do in preventing open and public expression, of views by the Administration, thus far. This time, however, is doubtless at an end. A Californian can not be a free-trader like Wallace and Hull."[13]

The Senate voted minor clarifying amendments approved by the administration, but the efforts to exclude farm products from tariff-reducing agreements were defeated. The Senate voted its approval of the slightly amended resolution on June 4, 1934, with fifty-seven for and thirty-three against. Isolationists in general and western agrarian progressives in particular were nearly unanimous by 1940 in their opposition to extending the reciprocal trade agreements legislation, but they divided when the legislation was adopted initially in 1934. Senators Borah, Cutting, Frazier, Johnson, Long, McNary, Nye, Vandenberg, and White voted against the reciprocity bill in 1934. But Senators Capper, La Follette, McCarran, Norbeck, Norris, Pittman, Shipstead, and Wheeler voted for it.[14] Party considerations were involved. Loyalty to the president and to his varied efforts to restore prosperity moved some. But part of the split among isolationists on the issue may have grown out of the still-unresolved contest between Hull and Peek. Secretary Hull brimmed with joy as he watched the president sign the measure into law on the night of June 12, 1934.[15] But the future directions of that trade agreements program (and the attitudes of western progressive isolationists toward it) were still to be determined by the final outcome of the contest between Hull and Peek. That contest would have to be resolved by the president. And he was slow to act. Procrastination to give the difficulty time to disappear did not work, and neither did efforts to find a compromise.

The Reciprocal Trade Agreements Act was an amendment to the

Smoot-Hawley Tariff Act of 1930. It authorized the president to negotiate executive trade agreements, not subject to Senate approval, in which the United States could alter existing tariff rates by as much as 50 percent in return for comparable adjustments in the customs duties of other states. Each agreement was to include an unconditional-most-favored-nation clause that would extend the tariff reductions to all countries that did not discriminate against the United States in their trade policies. Under Hull that meant, in practice, generalizing those reductions to most countries except Nazi Germany. Peek opposed the unconditional-most-favored-nation clause. And he believed the language of the new law permitted exceptions abroad that could severely limit the generalizing of tariff reductions. He identified scores of trade agreements between other countries (including the 1932 Ottawa agreements providing preferential rates in trade between British Commonwealth states) that sufficiently discriminated against the United States to justify withholding tariff concessions from them. On November 19, 1934, Roosevelt in a "Private and Confidential" memorandum suggested that if Hull and Peek "could spend a couple of hours some evening together talking over this problem of the most-favored-nation clauses, it would be very helpful in many ways." The two men met and talked—but it was not "helpful" at all.[16]

Throughout 1934 and 1935, Hull and his department repeatedly clashed with Peek on the negotiation of trade agreements with specific countries. Two proposed agreements—one with Germany and the other with Canada—highlighted the issues and the outcome of the contest. They involved the clash of agricultural and industrial interests, the relative roles of domestic economic and foreign policy concerns, and evolving patterns that were to see the United States drawing closer to Britain and the Commonwealth in opposition to Germany and the Axis.

Late in 1934 Peek, in his dual capacities as foreign trade adviser and head of the Export-Import banks, negotiated a barter agreement with Germany. In effect it would have sent raw cotton to Germany in exchange for American dollars and cut-rate German products. On December 13, when Hull was in Tennessee away from his office, Undersecretary Phillips learned from the White House that the president was likely to approve Peek's cotton deal with Germany. Phillips strongly urged the White House to delay the decision until after Hull returned the next day. Phillips alerted Hull to the crisis and sent a subordinate to brief the secretary on the train back to Washington. On Friday, December 14, Assistant Secretary Sayre met with the president to argue against the barter deal, Hull and his advisers drafted a letter to the president opposing the agreement, and Hull presented his case against it at the cabinet meeting in the afternoon. They objected on the grounds that Germany was defaulting on debts to American creditors and followed discriminatory trade policies. Cut-rate German products could hurt American industries. And many would object to such an arrangement with the oppressive Nazi government. Peek, in turn, thought the agreement was sound economically and would benefit both countries. Though he considered Nazi persecutions "deplorable," on strictly economic and legal grounds Peek saw no reason why Germany should be "black listed" when other countries that discriminated against the United States through preferential trade agreements were not. The efforts by Secretary Hull and the State Department prevailed. The president yielded to their guidance. The proposed agreement with Germany was blocked. Peek lost the skirmish.[17]

Hull later described the episode as the end of "Peek's intention to negotiate similar deals with other countries" and wrote that the reciprocal trade agreements program "steadily weakened and broke down the Peek program." J. Pierrepont Moffat in the State Department wrote that the episode blocked "Peek's one accomplishment to date," but he noted "that politically the President wishes to keep Peek in the picture and to keep him reasonably contented." Peek was not "reasonably contented," but he persisted in his opposition to Hull's program—both with the president and the public.[18]

In February 1935, Phillips urged the president to resolve the matter —presumably by ousting Peek. But Roosevelt said that Peek had indicated he would not continue much longer; the president would not "take action one way or the other to relieve the situation." Early in May, after Peek again attacked Hull's policies publicly, Phillips wondered how the president could let the "controversy continue"; yet he understood that Roosevelt was still "perfectly willing to ride both horses." At its meeting on May 10, cabinet members discussed Peek and his place in the administration. According to Secretary of Interior Ickes, "Everyone seems to want to get rid of him, but the President is afraid that if he eases him out, Peek, who has a good deal of strength with certain farming elements, might proceed to organize against the Administration." Hull remonstrated with Roosevelt against Peek again on May 17.[19]

On July 16, 1935, Peek submitted his resignation to the president because he felt "increasingly out of sympathy with the foreign trade

policies now being pursued.''[20] Superficially Peek's proffered resignation gave Roosevelt an easy opportunity to resolve the difficulty to
the satisfaction of Hull and the State Department. But Congress was
in the midst of a whole range of legislative battles on major items in
Roosevelt's domestic New Deal program. He could not lightly risk
alienating congressmen and senators from western agricultural states
when their votes were so needed on key legislation during the hectic
closing weeks of the session. Roosevelt was concerned about the
strength of Peek's following in agricultural regions of the Middle
West. Peek was likely to depart the administration eventually. From
the perspective of Roosevelt's political dealings with Congress on New
Deal matters, however, that was not the right time.

Roosevelt asked Jesse Jones to "get hold of George and tell him he
is silly and stupid about the general Foreign Trade policy. The amount
involved in the special Trade agreements is so small in dollars and
cents and so small in relation to our total commerce that it is captious
of George Peek to try to make this an issue. . . . his position is so close
to that of the State Department that the difference is one of detail and
not of principle." Neither Peek nor Hull would have agreed with that
contention. On July 25, Roosevelt wrote Peek asking him to delay his
resignation and suggesting that though the two were not "entirely in
agreement," they were "probably not as far apart" as Peek believed.
Peek agreed to stay on "for the time being." But he reemphasized to
the president that he considered "the policies in question as unsound
economically and politically" and that he could not place himself in a
position "of endorsing them by remaining silent." He stayed on, but
both Roosevelt and Peek (and Hull) must have known that it could
not be for long.[21]

Peek's proposed agreement with Germany in 1934 would have sold
American agricultural products abroad. In contrast, Hull's reciprocal
trade agreement concluded with Canada a year later pointed to the export of American industrial products in exchange for the import of
Canadian farm and mineral products into the United States. That was
precisely the pattern that Peek and western agrarian and mining
spokesmen feared and opposed. Canada did not produce cotton or
rice that might have competed with southern agriculture, and its
manufacturers did not constitute any formidable challenge to American industry. But Canada did produce wheat, cattle, and minerals
that competed with products from America's West. And the unconditional-most-favored-nation clause extended those tariff reductions to

producers of those agricultural and mineral products in other countries as well.

Conservative New York Republicans such as Henry L. Stimson and Frederic R. Coudert could and did applaud the reciprocity agreement with Canada as "one of the best things effected by American policy in years." But spokesmen for western agricultural and mining interests had different perspectives. They had fought against Canadian reciprocity in 1911, and they did not find it any more acceptable in 1935. Peek wrote that "the plain intent of the agreement is to trade a share of the American farm market for industrial export trade." Though Senator Norris of Nebraska defended the Canadian agreement, most western legislators shared Peek's general reaction. But it went into effect nonetheless.[22] And it coincided with the final break between Roosevelt and Peek.

On Armistice Day, November 11, 1935, four days before the signing of the Canadian agreement, Peek delivered a major address, "America's Choice—Which Shall It Be?," before the War Industries Board Association in New York. In that address he contrasted an eight-point "Policy for Internationalists" with what he called "A Policy for America" and urged his listeners to "choose America." The "Policy for Internationalists" that he rejected included relaxing immigration laws, reducing tariffs under unconditional-most-favored-nation arrangements, international monetary stabilization, free export of capital and resumption of foreign loans, international naval limitation agreement, dependence on foreign shipping and communications, submitting disputes to the World Court, and "automatic intervention in European or Asiatic political disputes" through the Kellogg-Briand Pact, Stimson Doctrine, or League of Nations. The "Policy for America" that Peek endorsed called for tightening of immigration laws (partly to "reduce alien influence in our domestic affairs"), "preservation of the American market, American price levels and American employment" through "selective imports and exports" and "tariff reductions only for specific advantages in individual foreign countries," and "stabilization of American dollar at American price level." That "Policy for America" also called for control of export capital, a navy designed for American requirements (including Panama and the Pacific coast), development of American shipping and communications systems, settlement of disputes by arbitration arrangements subject to Senate approval, and "in the case of wars in Europe or Asia, strict neutrality and avoidance of 'moral' judgments on belligerents." That final point also called for cash-and-carry in trade with belligerents and for the Monroe Doctrine and Good Neighbor policy in the Western Hemisphere. The speech was reported widely in the press. Hearst newspapers gave it major play on their editorial pages as a vehicle for attacking the Roosevelt administration's foreign policies, which they identified with "A Policy for Internationalists."[23]

Peek met with Roosevelt on November 19, two days after the Canadian agreement was made public. He left with the president a two-page memorandum drawn from his Armistice Day speech, including the two-column contrast of "A Policy for Internationalists" and "A Policy for America."[24]

Three days later while in Warm Springs, Roosevelt wrote Peek a biting letter excoriating the memorandum Peek had left with him. In his letter Roosevelt contended that he did not know who wrote the memo, but that it was "rather silly" and sounded "like a Hearst paper." The president commented on each of the eight points and denied that either the government or the public advocated any of those policies as listed in the "Internationalist" column. He concluded that the memo was "nothing more than the setting up deliberately of straw men . . . and then making a great show of knocking them over."[25]

That did it. Peek responded with a letter identifying himself as the author of the memo and resigning from the administration effective immediately. He denied that his memorandum was designed as an attack on the administration. But he insisted that the issue between the two policy patterns was real and that he had tried to present them fairly. "In the face of so fundamental a difference of opinion as to policy," he saw no other course but to resign. Roosevelt drafted a reply contending that he "honestly had no idea" that Peek had written the memo, but he decided not to send it.[26] Another isolationist had fallen from the administration. Hull and his internationalist reciprocal trade program prevailed.

In 1936, George N. Peek moved back to Republican ranks and supported Kansas's Alf M. Landon against Roosevelt for president. And in 1941, Peek served on the national committee of the isolationist America First Committee actively opposing the foreign policies of the Roosevelt administration toward the war raging in Europe and Asia.[27]

When the Reciprocal Trade Agreements Act came up for renewal and extension in 1937, it again won the votes of some leading isolationists, including Senators Clark of Missouri, La Follette of Wisconsin, Norris of Nebraska, and Wheeler of Montana. But the issues were more clearly drawn than in 1934. There was little mention of manufacturers who may have been hurt by the trade agreements; the focus was almost exclusively on the harmful effects on agriculture. General Motors, United States Steel, and the House of Morgan liked the program, and so did the cotton-producing South. But legislators with substantial farming constituencies in the North generally did not. They charged that agreements opened America's doors to agricultural imports in exchange for tariff concessions abroad favorable for American industrial exports. With both heavy industry and agriculture important in his state, Michigan's Republican Senator Vandenberg pointed to that split with particular clarity. In 1937 he told his fellow senators that "the automobile industry has been most generously and sympathetically treated by the State Department in all the agreements thus far negotiated. . . . The press of my State, in its metropolitan sectors, very generally favors the Hull policy. . . . but I believe Michigan agriculture very generally disapproves of the Hull policies." He charged that agriculture was "the chief victim of the plan." Arthur Capper, whose political base in Kansas was predominantly agricultural, had voted for reciprocity in 1934, but in 1937 he spoke and voted against it. He conceded the importance of foreign markets for both agriculture and industry, but he had reached the conclusion "that agriculture has suffered some distinct losses and has been placed at serious disadvantage by the terms of the agreements" that had been made. Representatives of farm organizations generally opposed the legislation. Senators Key Pittman and Pat McCarran from the western mining state of Nevada and Joseph C. O'Mahoney of Wyoming had voted for reciprocity in 1934, but shifted to the opposition in 1937.[28]

Legislative opponents objected to the unconditional-most-favored-nation clause and to the delegation of treaty-making authority to the president. They wanted agreements subject to approval by two-thirds vote of the Senate. Amendments were easily defeated, however, and the joint resolution extending the reciprocity program won approval by even wider margins in 1937 than in 1934 (285 to 101 in the House, and 58 to 24 in the Senate).[29]

Early in 1940 when Congress debated and voted another three-year extension of the program, conditions had further changed both at home and abroad. The undeclared Sino-Japanese war was raging in Asia; Germany had begun World War II in Europe with its conquest of Poland. Within the United States economic conditions were better than they had been earlier, but many found it hard to convince themselves that the depression had really ended. Growing political opposition had brought Roosevelt's New Deal program very nearly to a standstill. And most of Roosevelt's personal and political bonds with western progressive isolationists were parting.

Secretary Hull and other administration leaders continued their efforts to persuade farmers, miners, and small manufacturers that they benefited from reciprocal trade agreements. And they had the support of the president. In January, 1939, he authorized Lowell Mellett, director of the White House's National Emergency Council, to initiate an informational campaign to win support for the trade agreements program: "Please do all you can." Roosevelt told Jim Farley to "go down the line with our Senators and Congressmen in support of our trade agreement policy."[30]

Most farmers, miners, raw material producers, and their organizations outside the South remained unconvinced. The negotiation of a reciprocity agreement with Great Britain provoked irritation all around. The British complained that American special interests pressed unreasonably for access to the British market, while American agricultural and mining interests complained that the Ottawa agreements gave preferential treatment in Britain to agricultural and mineral products from Canada, Australia, and other Commonwealth countries. General Robert E. Wood, head of Sears, Roebuck and Company in Chicago and later national chairman of the America First Committee, argued for a bilateral barter agreement that would have sent American lard and cotton to Germany in exchange for barbed wire, nails, and other similar manufactured products. Senate minority leader Charles L. McNary from Oregon repeatedly complained that reciprocity agreements "brought the farmers of America into direct competition with the agricultural producers of other countries" and that heavy industry benefited "at the expense of the producers of farm crops." He and other agrarian spokesmen were as tenacious in their opposition to reciprocity as Hull was in support of it.[31]

Insofar as the reciprocal trade program may have coincided with American internationalism, the debates and votes of 1940 in Congress could not have provided President Roosevelt, Secretary Hull, and the internationalists with much ground for confidence or satisfaction. Both houses voted to extend the reciprocal trade program three more years, but the margin of victory was much closer than before. The vote in the House of Representatives on February 23, 1940 (218 for and 168 against) revealed an opposition increased by more than 66 percent over 1937.[32]

Key Pittman of Nevada, Democratic chairman of the Foreign Relations Committee, led the opposition in the Senate in 1940. He had always been an economic nationalist and had objected to the unconditional-most-favored-nation provision. But under pressure from Roosevelt he had reluctantly voted for reciprocity in 1934. In 1937 he had voted against extension, but had not played a major role in Senate debates. By 1940, however, constituent interests, personal conviction, and political advantage moved him to leadership for the opposition. Mining interests in Nevada (like agricultural interests in other states) objected that the trade agreements brought minerals, metals, and raw materials to compete on the American domestic market in exchange for foreign markets for American industrial output. But objections on those grounds had had little effect on individual trade agreements and had completely failed to block the basic legislation. So Pittman and other opponents of reciprocity determined to focus on the constitutional issue. He explained the tactics in a letter to a constituent early in 1940: "We must realize all the time that there are a very few people engaged in producing metal by comparison with those engaged in all other industries in the United States."[33]

Senate opposition to extending the reciprocal trade program in 1940 continued to emphasize the harmful effects of the program on agriculture and mining. But the main focus was on the contention that the legislation unconstitutionally delegated treaty-making authority to the executive. Pittman and others urged that the legislation be amended to require that the trade agreements be subject to approval by two-thirds vote of the Senate as required for treaties. All proposed amendments were defeated, however, and on April 5, 1940, the Senate voted forty-two to thirty-seven to extend the reciprocity program three more years.[34]

Secretary Hull's associates in the State Department warmly congratulated the old gentleman for his victory in winning extension of the program. The affirmative votes in the Senate included such isolationists as Clark of Missouri, Norris of Nebraska, Reynolds of North Carolina, and Walsh of Massachusetts. But it had been a close, hard fight; the opposition was stronger in 1940 than it had been in 1934 or 1937. The thirty-seven negative votes represented an increase of more than 54 percent over the opposition three years earlier. A shift of three votes in the Senate from the affirmative to the negative column would have defeated the legislation. Senators Wheeler of Montana and La Follette of Wisconsin had voted for reciprocity in 1934 and 1937, but both were paired against in 1940. Democratic Senator Homer

Bone of Washington had voted for the legislation in 1934 and 1937, but he cast his vote against it in 1940. Senator Shipstead of Minnesota had voted for reciprocity in 1934, but he voted against in 1940—and so did the new junior senator from Minnesota, Ernest Lundeen. Robert A. Taft of Ohio and D. Worth Clark of Idaho had not been in the Senate in 1934 or 1937, but they voted against it in 1940.[35]

Roosevelt's artful political skill in winning support from western agrarian progressives in the early years of his administration, and the presence of George N. Peek in that administration, divided and weakened opposition to Hull's internationalist reciprocal trade program initially. And the administration never failed to win the votes needed to continue the program. But the lines were more sharply drawn by 1940 than before. If the reciprocity program was an indication of the strength of internationalism, then Roosevelt, Hull, and the internationalists had little cause for optimism on April 5, 1940. But Hitler helped boost internationalist (or interventionist) strength four days later when he sent his German blitzkrieg into Denmark and Norway.

Chapter 9

The League and World Court Reconsidered

Franklin D. Roosevelt could see no wisdom and feel no satisfaction in fighting for lost causes. Quixotic crusades or the martyr's shroud were not for him. The image of nobly falling on his sword while heroically leading a bloody charge against an impregnable fortress did not inspire him. He fought to win what he could with tactics that seemed most likely to accomplish practical results. If the costs of a frontal assault seemed excessive or the odds against victory too great, he did not hesitate to turn, instead, to indirection, stealth, dissembling, and compromise if they seemed more likely to accomplish advances. Indeed, he seemed often to prefer or delight in indirection. And he really did not like confrontations. As he maneuvered, Roosevelt allowed himself few utopian expectations even if victory were complete. He would feel no great surprise if he found that the roof leaked and that the castle teemed with rodents once he captured the keep.

So it was with the president's contest with isolationists over the League of Nations and the Permanent Court of International Justice. Like Woodrow Wilson earlier, Roosevelt favored American participation in the league and World Court. But his expectations from such participation were never so optimistic as Wilson's had been. During his years in the White House, Roosevelt displayed less candor, demonstrated greater patience, and (after his death) won greater accomplishment than Wilson had. That ultimate triumph may have resulted as much from changed conditions at home and abroad as from his leadership. And the contributions of world organizations to peace and security may have fallen short of even his modest hopes. But the general positions he served ultimately prevailed over isolationist opposition.

As the Democratic party's vice-presidential nominee in 1920, young Roosevelt had urged American approval of the Versailles treaty and membership in the League of Nations. He retained that attitude in the decade that followed. In 1930, he wrote England's Viscount Robert Cecil urging him to accept the League of Nations Association's invitation to speak in the United States on behalf of the league. In his letter Governor Roosevelt emphasized "that the general spirit which underlies the League and the World Court should be kept alive." Some who were isolationists in the 1930s (including Senator Gerald P. Nye and historian Charles A. Beard) had endorsed American membership in the League of Nations in 1919. Prominent statesmen in both political parties, distinguished American scholars, and many others supported the League of Nations Association in the 1920s and later. Some internationalists hoped the Kellogg-Briand Pact of Paris of 1928 might draw the United States into joint peace-keeping efforts with cosigners of that multilateral pact "outlawing war."[1]

By the 1930s, however, there was no practical possibility of any formal United States commitment to the League of Nations or to any other meaningful collective security arrangement with England and France. William E. Borah, Hiram W. Johnson, and George W. Norris had led Senate opponents of the league in 1919–20, and they never abandoned their opposition. In the 1930s, neither the Democratic nor the Republican party platforms endorsed American membership in the League of Nations.[2]

Despite his earlier support for the league, on February 2, 1932, in an address before the farmer's Grange in Albany, New York, Governor Roosevelt publicly stated that he no longer favored American membership in the league. He said the league too often had been "a mere meeting place for the political discussion of strictly European political national difficulties. In these the United States should have no part." He contended that "American participation in the League would not serve the highest purpose of the prevention of war and a settlement of international difficulties in accordance with fundamental American ideals." That speech was a direct result of pressure from isolationist publisher William Randolph Hearst and was a conscious effort to win political support from Hearst and other isolationists for his nomination and election to the presidency.[3] At no time while he was president did Roosevelt publicly advocate American membership in the League of Nations.

The Roosevelt administration did try to cooperate with the League of Nations informally, unofficially, and inconspicuously. It tried to avoid undercutting league peace-keeping efforts. But it did so with a sharp eye on American public opinion. Even during the Republican years under Presidents Harding, Coolidge, and Hoover, the United States ministers to Switzerland served as informal, unofficial liaisons with the League of Nations. That procedure continued under the Roosevelt-Hull administration from 1933 onward. Arthur Sweetser, an American employed by the league in Geneva, performed a similar informal and unofficial liaison service between American officials and the league in the 1920s and 1930s.[4]

Norman H. Davis's major policy statement at the World Disarmament Conference in Geneva on May 13, 1933, did not explicitly focus on the League of Nations. But with the approval of Roosevelt and Hull, Ambassador Davis announced that if the conference reached agreement on general disarmament, the United States would be "willing to consult the other states in case of a threat to peace with a view to averting conflict." He also declared that "in the event that the states, in conference, determine that a state has been guilty of a breach of the peace in violation of its international obligations and take measures against the violator, then, if we concur in the judgment rendered as to the responsible and guilty party, we will refrain from any action tending to defeat the collective effort which such state may make to restore peace."[5] The president was convinced that antileague sentiment in the United States and in Congress would not permit him to go any further at that time.

The necessity for caution was underscored by an episode in September, 1933. On August 17, Arthur Sweetser had had lunch with the president. Roosevelt had lauded the league and said he had been thinking of ways he might encourage it without making any political commitments. He had considered asking Congress to authorize a payment to the league for expenses for causes from which the United States benefited. He had also considered appointing Minister Hugh R. Wilson to serve officially as the president's personal representative at all league meetings in which the United States had an interest, but without any authority to commit the United States. The State Department also had been quietly exploring the possibilities of similar lines of cooperation with the league.

In mid-September, however, after Sweetser had returned to his post at the league in Geneva, someone there gave out a statement describing American plans for cooperation with the league, but making them seem firmer, more sweeping, and more public than either Roosevelt or Hull had intended. State Department officials were convinced that Sweetser was responsible for the leak, though he denied it. Whatever its origins, the statement provoked an uproar in the United

States, and Secretary Hull felt obliged to deny the whole thing. He gloomily concluded that the "outlook for any sort of international cooperation" was "near its lowest ebb." Jay Pierrepont Moffat, chief of the Division of Western European Affairs in the State Department, feared that Sweetser's "indiscretion" would "put back the matter he desires for years."[6]

In November, 1933, after a discussion among members of the internationalist-oriented Century Club in New York, Spencer Van B. Nichols discreetly inquired how they might serve the president in building sentiment in line with league principles. Roosevelt's secretary, Marvin H. McIntyre, responded that he was "sure that all the President could ask is intelligent cooperation and support, and if this carries with it criticism that is constructive, it would still be helpful and not unwelcome." In other words, the president would welcome friendly criticism prodding him and the American people in internationalist and league directions.[7]

On December 28, 1933, in an address before a Woodrow Wilson Foundation dinner in Washington, President Roosevelt praised Wilson's efforts on behalf of peace and called the League of Nations "a prop in the world peace structure" that "must remain." Roosevelt mentioned that the United States was not a member and did not "contemplate membership" in the league. But he said the United States was "giving cooperation to the League in every matter which is not primarily political and in every matter which obviously represents the views and the good of the peoples of the world as distinguished from the views and the good of political leaders, of privileged classes and of imperialistic aims."[8]

But members of the Woodrow Wilson Foundation, the League of Nations Association, and the Century Club—and Franklin D. Roosevelt himself—held views on the league that most Americans did not share—and Roosevelt knew it. Though more blunt than many, Senator Borah of Idaho was more nearly in tune with majority sentiment when he wrote in December, 1933, that "the League of Nations cannot be changed, reformed, or made over so as to receive my support." In April, 1934, Senator Couzens of Michigan wrote a constituent that he was "unwilling to have our country tied up with any League of Nations which is controlled by foreign countries many thousands of miles away." A year later when Undersecretary of State Phillips asked the White House about including an American on a committee of trade experts to be appointed by the Economic Committee of the League of Nations, Roosevelt worried whether it might be "going too far towards official membership in a direct official Committee of the League itself."[9]

When the undeclared Italian-Ethiopian war erupted in the fall of 1935, the United States under President Roosevelt and Secretary Hull pursued an independent policy that technically conformed to the letter of America's Neutrality Act of 1935. The administration deliberately invoked the Neutrality Act, including its mandatory arms embargo, *before* the league voted economic sanctions against Italy. Isolationists and pacifists applauded the administration action in the name of peace and noninvolvement. Roosevelt and Hull, however, saw the course as an unspoken way of cooperating informally with league sanctions against Italy. By acting in advance of the league, the administration disarmed isolationists who might have accused it of following the league's lead. Since Ethiopia did not have shipping access to American war goods anyway (and Italy did), the arms embargo had the effect of working against Mussolini's Italy much as league sanctions did. Roosevelt and Hull regretted that the embargo did not extend to oil and other nonmunitions war materials that Italy needed. They tried to fill that gap by means of a "moral embargo," though it was not very effective. Hull's fear of isolationist opposition helped prevent the Roosevelt administration from explaining publicly that the United States policies involved de facto cooperation with the league in that crisis.[10]

Hull's fears were not without justification. Senator Gerald P. Nye, for example, voiced "emphatic opposition" to any American cooperation with league sanctions against Italy. Senator Henrik Shipstead of Minnesota pointed to the Italian-Ethiopian war as evidence that the league and World Court provided paths to war and not to peace. He urged the United States to stay out of the league and to refrain from aiding its sanctions. Senator Arthur H. Vandenberg of Michigan warned: "We cannot pursue neutrality worthy of the name except as it be an independent, American program unrelated to the League of Nations or any program dictated by dominant League powers." Early in 1936, after Hitler's Germany remilitarized the Rhineland in violation of existing agreements, Senator Hiram Johnson of California reaffirmed his opposition to the Versailles treaty and reasserted his conviction that the league was designed as a "hypocritical institution to maintain the status quo."[11]

In mid-September, 1936, in the midst of the presidential election campaigns, Roosevelt considered issuing a statement at his press conference encouraging efforts for peace at the forthcoming meeting of the League of Nations Assembly. In the statement Roosevelt intended to emphasize that though the United States was "not participating in these discussions," it was following them with "an eager hope that the statesmen engaged in them may find ways of contributing to world peace." And Roosevelt planned to announce that his government stood "ever ready to participate in any effort which promises to contribute towards either a reduction of the armaments which now threaten world peace or the removal of the economic barriers which stifle world trade." Before deciding to issue the press statement, however, he asked his assistant secretary, Stephen T. Early, to speak to him about it. In fact, the president did not issue the statement to the press; it went unused into the White House files.[12]

More than a year later, Senator Borah wrote to a New York attorney that he thought "an international police force" was not practicable and that he "certainly would not be willing to trust the affairs of the United States to an international body over which the people of the United States would have no control." He believed that if other countries attacked America, it could take care of itself "under all circumstances." In company with other western progressives, Borah firmly believed that the United States could "pursue the Jeffersonian policy,—peace, friendship and commerce with all nations, and entangling alliances with none." Even as George W. Norris was beginning to turn away from his earlier isolationism by 1938, the old Nebraska senator wrote that he was "not in favor of the League of Nations. I opposed it when it was proposed. I still believe we were right in not joining it."[13]

In April, 1940, after World War II had erupted in Europe, various American devotees of the league, including Mary Woolley and Clark Eichelberger, set in motion plans to organize a committee to raise money to help humanitarian activities of the league. They won the sympathetic ear of the president and, through him, the active assistance of Assistant Secretary of State Adolf A. Berle. At their request Roosevelt agreed to provide a letter supporting their fund-raising efforts. But he made it clear that America's long efforts "to cooperate in the world-wide technical and humanitarian activities of the League" had been undertaken "without in any way becoming involved in the political affairs of Europe."[14]

Though the United States under President Roosevelt encouraged humanitarian activities of the league, and though the United States under his leadership cautiously pursued independent foreign policies that paralleled league actions on particular issues, there was not the slightest possibility that isolationist sentiment would permit American membership in the League of Nations during the 1930s. After that the league was dead—and no isolationist shed any tears at its passing.

Isolationist opposition to the League of Nations also extended in diluted form to American adherence to the protocols of the Permanent Court of International Justice. Frustrated in their efforts to bring the United States into the league, many internationalists saw adherence to the World Court as a limited but potentially helpful first step toward a more active and responsible role by the United States in world affairs. Pacifists who objected to alliances or collective security arrangements found the legal approach of the World Court appealing. Isolationists worried less about the direct effects of membership in the World Court than about the possibility that it might be a vehicle for involving the United States in the league system and in European turmoil. The World Court only had authority to treat legal disputes covered by treaties or international law that parties to the disputes might voluntarily bring before it; it had no collective security or political powers. The court's limited authority made it appear less hopeful as an instrument of world peace in the eyes of nonpacifist internationalists and less of a danger to American sovereignty and freedom of action in the eyes of isolationists. Writing early in 1935, the British ambassador to the United States, Sir Ronald Lindsay, doubted whether American membership would "make any immediate difference," but thought that in "the longer view" American adherence to the World Court "must have some educative value to the American public, and should be a considerable help to the Administration in its perpetual struggle against the extremer forms of isolationism." He warned the British Foreign Office against imagining that American adherence would indicate "any tendency at this moment on the part of Congress towards closer co-operation in world affairs. No such tendency is to be observed, and no particular enthusiasm for the Permanent Court."[15]

Both Democratic and Republican party platforms endorsed American adherence to the protocols. The Republican presidential administrations of Harding, Coolidge, and Hoover all recommended Senate approval, and so did the Democratic administration of Roosevelt. On January 27, 1926, the Senate voted seventy-six to seventeen to approve membership in the World court. Even Senators Norris, Wheeler, and Capper voted for adherence. But Senators Borah, Johnson, La Follette, Nye, Shipstead, and others voted against approval. And they helped attach reservations that were unacceptable to major European states.[16] President Hoover's administration recommended approval of the court, but the Senate took no action on it during the months that remained to the beleaguered administration.[17]

Franklin D. Roosevelt had long favored American adherence to the Permanent Court of International Justice, and he continued to do so after he became president in 1933. But his hopes for that organization were never so optimistic as his wife's were; her tone was that of the internationalist peace groups with which she identified. Late in March, 1933, during the Hundred Days, Democratic Senator Joseph T. Robinson of Arkansas urged the Foreign Relations Committee to report out a World Court resolution. That elicited vigorous objections from Senators Johnson, Borah, Shipstead, and other isolationists on the committee. President Roosevelt did not want to endanger his New Deal program by alienating his western progressive supporters. At a White House dinner party the jovial president leaned across the table and laughingly told Hiram Johnson, "Now Senator I want you to enjoy your dinner. I know you will enjoy it when I tell you that the World Court will remain for the present at least in the Foreign Relations Committee." He was as good as his word. The president asked Senator Robinson not to press action in committee on the World Court that session because it would interfere with more urgent domestic legislation.[18]

With encouragement from State Department officials (especially Secretary Hull and Assistant Secretary Sayre), from Mrs. Roosevelt, pacifists, and various internationalists, the president from time to time considered trying to get Senate action on the World Court. Generally, he concluded that the political situation was not right or that priority should go to more pressing New Deal concerns. Senator Key Pittman of Nevada, Democratic chairman of the Foreign Relations Committee, reinforced Roosevelt's caution.

In September, 1934, Secretary Hull, Assistant Secretary Sayre, and Assistant Secretary R. Walton Moore won the president's permission to press the issue at the next session of Congress. They drafted an appropriate resolution. In conversations with Senator Johnson, however, Roosevelt minimized the importance he attached to the matter and emphasized that his action was undertaken to fulfill his party's platform pledge.[19]

In the first week of January, 1935, Roosevelt, Hull, and Sayre ran into difficulties with their plans even before the Foreign Relations Committee and the Senate began formal deliberations. Senator Pittman refused to assume leadership on the matter because he did not believe the administration's proposal contained adequate safeguards against advisory opinions by the World Court in cases involving the United States. Pittman agreed to be "a friendly neutral," but he suggested that Roosevelt ask Senator Robinson to lead the fight in the Senate. On January 5, at a White House conference, the president agreed to that arrangement. Senate Majority Leader Robinson and Senate Minority Leader Charles McNary, after preliminary tallies, had concluded that the opposition could count on only about fifteen to twenty votes—not enough to block approval. The moment seemed right.[20]

On January 9, the Foreign Relations Committee (without conducting further hearings) voted fourteen to seven to report out the World Court resolution to the full Senate. The opposition in committee included Johnson, Borah, Cutting, Shipstead, and La Follette. As proposed by the administration and as reported by committee, the resolution called for the United States to adhere to the protocols of the Permanent Court of International Justice "with the clear understanding" that the court "shall not, over an objection by the United States, entertain any request for an advisory opinion touching any dispute or question in which the United States has or claims an interest." Even Pittman approved it in that form.[21]

On January 10, Senator Robinson reported the resolution to the Senate with the committee's recommendation that it be approved. He opened Senate consideration of the issue on January 14 and 15, and on January 16 the president sent a message to the Senate urging approval. In his letter Roosevelt emphasized that "the sovereignty of the United States will be in no way diminished or jeopardized by such action." Robinson orchestrated tactics on behalf of the resolution. The debate proceeded in an almost leisurely fashion, and all who wished had the opportunity to be heard. Though the longer and more powerful presentations came from opponents, speeches rather evenly divided between opponents and proponents. And most on both sides assumed that the resolution for adherence would win the necessary two-thirds vote.[22]

Senator Johnson, who led the opposition, saw himself as fighting a lonely battle for a just but hopeless cause. He boasted that when he opened the debate for the opposition on January 16, he "started alone." The Californian's feelings may have been reinforced when, contrary to his prior understanding, the president sent his letter to the Senate on behalf of the World Court on the very day that Johnson rose to deliver his major address. Johnson's speech against adherence was in the grand traditions of Senate oratory. He began by noting the coincidence that the day was also his grandson's twenty-first birthday and that he could not "do better" by his descendant and others like him than to dedicate his energies and talents "to the endeavor to preserve the traditional policy of the American Republic and to keep this country free and independent in its every action in regard to other nations." Johnson boasted that he did not speak as "a citizen of the world," but rather "as a citizen of the United States." He called it "the League of Nations Court" and an "adjunct of the League of Nations." Adherence, he insisted, would draw the United States toward involvement in the league, and through the league into the turmoil and wars of Europe.[23]

Though Johnson excelled in his moving drama, none was so impressive and formidable in oratory as William E. Borah. The Idaho Republican focused particularly on the advisory opinion issue and on legal subtleties that persuaded him that neither the protocols nor the Senate resolution sufficiently guarded American interests and independence. Borah charged that the World Court was more of a political organ of the league and its member states than a court of law. He was convinced that its political character would harm the United States and draw it into the caldron that was Europe. Arthur Vandenberg, Henrik Shipstead, Robert R. Reynolds, and others added the power of their oratory to the opposition in the senate.[24]

Opponents proposed various amendments and reservations generally designed to guard American sovereignty and freedom of action if the resolution were approved. The Senate rejected most of those proposed amendments, including one by Senator Nye that would have required that "the code of law to be administered by the World Court shall not contain inequalities based on sex." Senator Norris had voted for the court in 1926, had supported President Roosevelt on most issues, and had been expected to vote for adherence again in 1935. He introduced an amendment that would have required all recourse to the court in cases involving the United States to be accomplished through treaties subject to two-thirds vote of the Senate. When the Senate rejected his admendment, Norris indicated he would oppose adherence —an unsettling development for devotees of the court. Only an interpretative amendment introduced by Vandenberg won approval. It was essentially a restatement of America's traditional policy of isolation and noninvolvement.[25]

As the debate began to run down, some wanted a final vote on Friday, January 25. Johnson objected, however, and pressed Robinson to put off the vote until after the weekend. Robinson acquiesced, but with the provision for limitation of debate beginning on Monday. The World Court, as amended, did not come to a vote until Tuesday, January 29, 1935.[26]

The battle was by no means limited to the Senate floor. In the final hectic days and hours the tempo of activity accelerated on both sides. Pacifist organizations urged their members to write or telegraph their senators supporting the court, and spokesmen for peace groups earnestly buttonholed individual senators to persuade them to vote for the court (or to make certain that their resolves to vote right did not falter). Mrs. Roosevelt met with groups of women and with peace organizations. She delivered a nationwide radio address on behalf of adherence. The president met in the White House with individual senators. Hull, Sayre, Robinson, and others on the administration side shared in the effort.[27]

Opponents were even more active (and effective). A Movietone newsreel in which Johnson and Robinson voiced their differing views helped the opposition (at least Johnson thought it did). The humor of cowboy Will Rogers may have been more effective in opposition than some more angry blasts. William Randolph Hearst threw the weight of his newspapers into the fray. He sent Edward Coblentz from New York to organize an efficient staff in the Mayflower Hotel in Washington against the World Court. Father Charles E. Coughlin of Royal Oak, Michigan, appealed to his huge radio audience to make opposition known. His broadcast on Sunday, January 27, brought thousands of letters and telegrams to senate offices opposing the court.[28]

Senator Robinson had estimated that only about eight Democratic senators would vote against the administration, and McNary believed the opposition would not get much more than eight Republican votes. Johnson thought he could count twenty-eight votes against the court, but was fearful lest the administration get to individual legislators to reverse their positions. According to Johnson, an unnamed Republican leader offered an additional bloc of five votes if the California senator could assure him it would be enough to defeat the administration on the issue. After conferring name by name on their tallies, they concluded that it could be done. Their forces held on Monday. On Tuesday, January 29, 1935, Johnson nervously checked and rechecked and found his lines holding firm.[29]

The final vote came at 6:15 P.M. Fifty-two senators voted for the World Court resolution as amended, and thirty-six voted against. The affirmative vote was seven fewer than the required two-thirds, so the opponents triumphed over the administration. Robinson, Pittman, and McNary voted for the resolution, but so did isolationists Vandenberg, Capper, and Couzens, who were satisfied with its amended form. The opposition included, among others, Senators Johnson, Borah, Norris, Nye, Wheeler, La Follette, Shipstead, Long, and Walsh. The negative votes included twenty Democrats, fourteen Republicans, one Progressive, and one Farmer-Laborite.[30]

There were the usual postmortems. While conceding roles by others, Johnson was inclined to see the outcome as little more than his own one-man triumph. He boasted in a letter to his son that he had "won the toughest and the biggest and most far-reaching contest legislatively in which ever I have been engaged." Many blamed Robinson for blundering in leading the floor fight; by allowing delay of the vote until after the weekend, he gave the opposition more time to organize and make its voices heard. Most credited Hearst and Father Coughlin for turning the tide. The day after the vote, Senator Borah sent warm messages to Coughlin and Hearst thanking them for their help. Two years later, however, Borah contended privately that "the vote would have been the same" whether Coughlin and Hearst had taken part in the effort or not. He thought the effect of propaganda in the contest was "fearfully overestimated." In a letter to old Elihu Root a few days after the vote, President Roosevelt wrote that "the deluge of letters, telegrams, Resolutions of Legislatures, and the radio talks of people like Coughlin turned the trick against us." McNary explained the final vote partly as a slap at the president and partly due to poor organization of the debate on the part of the administration. Assistant Secretary of State Moore thought the World Court would not have been defeated in the Senate "if some people very close to the President had exerted themselves a little more instead of giving the impression that the President was indifferent." Britain's Ambassador Lindsay thought the president had not "exerted quite as much pressure on it as might have been expected." The ambassador believed that though Roosevelt "earnestly desired that the United States should join the court, he also had his eye on his future influence over Senators for support on domestic questions, and the manner in which that influence might be impaired if he pressed them vigorously on a foreign question."[31]

Administration supporters, internationalists, and pacifists saw the vote as a serious and damaging setback. Hull saw the defeat as "another heavy blow to our efforts at international cooperation."

William E. Dodd, United States ambassador to Germany, considered resigning in protest against the insistence "of a minority of the Senate on their right to govern the country." Former Secretary of State Henry L. Stimson described it as a "tragedy" and feared the "repercussions around the world will be bad." He saw some benefit, however, in "the fact that the opponents of such an honest effort for peace as the World Court are now lined up in full view."[32]

President Roosevelt's defeat on the World Court at the hands of Senate isolationists came the day before his fifty-third birthday. Norman Davis found the president "furious" at the opposition senators; Undersecretary Phillips described him as "very indignant with the Senate for throwing out the World Court and seemed to want to fight back." At the cabinet meeting later that week, Secretary of Interior Ickes "thought the President distinctly showed that the defeat of the World Court Protocol had cut pretty deeply. At times there seemed to be a bitter tinge to his laughter and good humor and perhaps a little showing of willingness to hurt those who brought about his defeat." In a letter to Senator Robinson the day after the vote, Roosevelt wrote that if the senators who voted against the World Court "ever get to Heaven they will be doing a great deal of apologizing for a very long time—that is if God is against war—and I think He is." In another letter Roosevelt wrote "that at the present time we face a large misinformed public opinion and we can only hope that this will change." To Stimson he concluded that "common sense dictates no new method for the time being—but I have an unfortunately long memory and I am not forgetting either our enemies or our objectives." In a letter to Elihu Root, Roosevelt wrote that "in time we shall win the long fight for judicial decision of international problems—but today, quite frankly, the wind everywhere blows against us."[33]

As he had written to Stimson, Roosevelt did have a "long memory." The rejection of the World Court sparked a lively and wide-ranging discussion at a small dinner gathering in the home of brains truster Rexford G. Tugwell on the evening of February 1. One of the guests was the historian and United States ambassador to Germany, William E. Dodd. A doctrinaire Wilsonian internationalist, Dodd predicted that America's rejection of the World Court would lead to war. Convinced by the vote that the United States would not take a stand in Europe, Hitler would, Dodd contended, feel free to move against Austria, Czechoslovakia, and Poland. If Britain then concentrated its strength against Hitler in Europe, Japan could move against China in

Asia. Others at the dinner gathering thought Dodd was too emotional and exaggerated the significance of the vote. But they thought Roosevelt probably shared Dodd's general point of view.[34]

In striking contrast to Dodd, another of the dinner guests, Senator Burton K. Wheeler, who had voted against the World Court, thought Europe would have to recognize Germany's great power and permit its expansion in Central Europe. He thought the United States should stay out of it. John Franklin Carter, another of the guests, thought the exchange demonstrated "that there was complete irreconcilability between the Wheeler nationalistic view and the Dodd internationalist view. Each believed that his way was the way to prevent war and that the other way would involve us in war."[35]

The next day at the White House Ambassador Dodd reported the conversation to Roosevelt. Six years later at a press conference on January 31, 1941, in response to persistent queries by newsmen, the president alluded to Wheeler's comments. As he recalled Dodd's rendition six years before, Roosevelt thought Wheeler's comments tantamount to favoring Nazi domination of Europe. That was not the way Tugwell remembered it.[36] But by 1941 that image helped inflame the developing feud between the president and the senator.

In that same 1935 conversation at Tugwell's home, Wheeler had criticized Roosevelt's failure to lead boldly in progressive directions on the domestic front. Wheeler charged Roosevelt with being close to big business and unfriendly to progressives. Consequently, the senator thought a third party could form on the left in 1936 under Huey Long, Father Coughlin, Upton Sinclair, and the La Follettes. As Carter reported it, another of the guests, Jerome Frank, concluded that they had to make up their minds whether to "go Inca or go Morgan, internally and externally"—and not to continue their "vain efforts to do two contradictory things at the same time."[37]

After the Senate defeat of the World Court in 1935, some State Department officials explored the possibility of accomplishing their goal through a joint resolution that would require only a simple majority in both houses of Congress, rather than a two-thirds vote in the Senate. Hull approved the idea, but the president rejected it. In his memoirs Hull wrote that they "kept tab on the prospects in the Senate for ratification. . . . But the forces of isolation grew stronger rather than weaker. The opportunity that seemed so bright in January, 1935, was not to recur."[38] The Roosevelt administration never again pressed for a vote on the World Court. At the close of World War II after the defeat of the Axis powers and the death of Roosevelt, the American people and the United States Senate overwhelmingly approved American membership in the United Nations organization and in a new International Court of Justice. But during the Roosevelt era, when the Axis states were challenging world peace and security, isolationists successfully prevented United States membership in both the League of Nations and the Permanent Court of International Justice.

Chapter 10

The New Deal

Disarmament, international stabilization, war debts, reciprocity, and the World Court all won headlines and the earnest attention of statesmen, diplomats, and newsmen. They were important. But most people had more pressing concerns closer at hand—finding a job, buying food and fuel, paying the rent or mortgage, patching worn clothing, making do with what one had, growing accustomed to the fact that "we can't afford it." Farmers on the Great Plains had their own special concerns of paying high interest and big mortgages with farm products that brought prices lower than production costs—and drought, grasshoppers, and dust storms often left them with no products to sell at any price. Norman Davis flitted from capital to capital, from conference to conference; countless others who owned little more than the clothes on their backs flitted from town to town, from door to door, seeking work or handouts—and they were not necessarily lazy or incompetent. Comfortable elites could afford the luxury and fascination of preoccupation with realpolitik; they could ridicule the parochial concerns of lesser folk. But food, clothing, and shelter were practical necessities for all. State Department officials, Foreign Service officers, professional scholars, career military officers, and financiers might take such necessities for granted; the man (and woman and child) in the street could not. And neither could politicians whose election or reelection depended on the votes of those common folk. Most of those concerns were close at hand. Insofar as they reached national levels, they concentrated on the New Deal—and on President Franklin D. Roosevelt who gave leadership and hope through his domestic New Deal program.

Neither isolationists nor internationalists united in their attitudes and actions toward the New Deal during Roosevelt's first term. There were conservative isolationists who criticized much of the New Deal—

Senator Arthur H. Vandenberg of Michigan, for example. But prominent internationalists also opposed the New Deal—Henry L. Stimson of New York, among others. Independent progressive Republicans could not be depended upon to rubber-stamp any broad political or economic program. Nonetheless, leading isolationists generally supported Roosevelt's New Deal. When western progressive isolationists broke with the president on particular domestic issues, they generally did so on the grounds that the individual proposal was not consistent with their conceptions of progressivism.

Their progressive perspectives were more commonly agrarian and Jeffersonian than urban and Hamiltonian. Generally, they favored programs beneficial to farmers, small businessmen, debtors, workers, and the little guy. They were hostile to monopoly and critical of big business and big finance. In the crises of the Great Depression, western progressive isolationists urged federal government action. But they tended to fear bigness of almost any sort—including big business, big government, big military, and eventually (for many of them) big unions. Their compassion for the weak and downtrodden led them to vote for federal relief programs, social security legislation, and the Wagner Labor Relations Act. Their sympathy for farmers moved them to support a wide variety of farm legislation. They favored regulating banking and security exchanges. Within limits they favored inflation, including silver legislation and devaluation of the dollar. But collectivization, centralized government planning, permanent government subsidies, prolonged relief programs, government-enforced production controls, and massive federal deficits did not appeal to them. In their attachment to the individual, in their emphasis on constitutional restraints on federal authority, in their skepticism about deficit financing, in their attachment to "little *d* democracy," and in their misgivings about socialism or strong federal controls, many of those progressive isolationists had domestic values that would make them outsiders as the United States (under both Democrats and Republicans, from both business and labor perspectives, in both peace and war) moved toward ever bigger government, more government regulation, more government spending, and ever larger federal debts.

Those differences with the directions the government was to take were dampened and obscured during the frenetic gyrations of the New Deal during Roosevelt's first term. Most leading isolationists supported the president's New Deal proposals most of the time during his first term in office. President Roosevelt frequently consulted with various western progressive isolationists and took them into account in shaping the political tactics for implementing his New Deal program.

The Agricultural Adjustment Administration benefited many farmers. But the plow-up and kill program to get it into operation quickly in 1933 drew widespread criticism. Farm spokesmen charged that industrial prices increased more rapidly than farm prices and left farmers worse off than before. In 1934 and 1936, severe droughts in the Middle West and Great Plains did more to reduce farm production than did AAA acreage controls. Few really liked the acreage controls —at a time when millions at home and abroad were hungry or starving. In January, 1936, the United States Supreme Court killed the AAA by declaring its processing tax unconstitutional. There had been little enthusiasm among leading isolationists for the Agricultural Adjustment Act when President Roosevelt had signed it into law in May, 1933; they shed few tears when it died at the hands of the court in January, 1936.

The provisions of the so-called inflation amendment to the farm bill were largely discretionary, and its effects proved less helpful in increasing commodity prices than its sponsors had hoped. Similarly, the silver agreement concluded by Senator Pittman at the World Economic Conference in 1933 had little effect on commodity prices or world trade. Legislators serving inflationary and silver interests (overlapping but really different interests) met repeatedly to plan tactics. The Reverend Father Charles E. Coughlin made emotional appeals for inflation in his popular radio broadcasts, in his correspondence, and in personal contacts. His nationwide following was not to be treated lightly, whatever one thought of the wisdom of his nostrums.[1]

In January, 1934, Senator Wheeler of Montana introduced another silver purchase amendment, this one attached to a monetary bill. Again the president, through Senate Majority Leader Joseph T. Robinson of Arkansas, opposed the amendment and urged that they "wait a little while to see how the Pittman agreement works out." Again Roosevelt prevailed over Wheeler. On January 27, the Senate voted forty-five to forty-three to reject his amendment. Though Father Coughlin of Michigan supported Wheeler's amendment, Michigan's Senators Vandenberg and Couzens (both Republicans and both isolationists) voted against it. Vandenberg boasted that he and Couzens from Coughlin's state "saved the President's program." But most progressive isolationists voted with the minority in favor of silver and in opposition to the president.[2]

In response to President Roosevelt's silver message of May 22, 1934, Congress quickly passed a Silver Purchase Act, which he signed into law on June 19, 1934. The vote in the House was 263 to 77, and in the Senate 55 to 25. The Senate votes for the Silver Purchase Act included those of Bone, Borah, Capper, Clark, Costigan, Frazier, La Follette, Long, Norbeck, Norris, Nye, Pittman, Reynolds, Shipstead, and Wheeler, among others.[3] Pittman, Wheeler, Thomas, and others continued their silver and inflationary efforts throughout the 1930s.

In practice, the silver legislation as implemented by the Roosevelt administration subsidized western silver producers and contributed to financial havoc for China's silver monetary system. In the United States it did little to promote inflation, limit imports, promote foreign purchases of American products, or restore prosperity. It was one of the issues on which Roosevelt reluctantly made halfhearted political gestures to appease western legislators (many of whom were isolationists) without really satisfying them of his good faith and trustworthiness on the issue.[4]

Western progressive isolationists supported New Deal relief and public works programs, with Senator Robert M. La Follette, Jr., of Wisconsin providing leadership for larger and more effective programs. Progressives complained that the relief programs were inadequate and that Harold L. Ickes moved too slowly and conservatively in undertaking public works projects. By the end of 1934, Roosevelt wanted "the abolition of relief altogether" and to "substitute work for relief." The major action by Congress to attempt that change was the adoption of legislation creating the Works Progress Administration, which the president signed into law on April 8, 1935. Roosevelt appointed Harry Hopkins to administer WPA. Among leading isolationists only Republicans Arthur Vandenberg of Michigan in the Senate and Hamilton Fish of New York in the House opposed the legislation in clearly conservative terms. Vandenberg charged that it was "an unconscionable surrender of the legislature's functions, and a corresponding concentration of equally unconscionable power in a relatively irresponsible bureaucracy." He thought it would not produce adequate relief and would retard recovery. He worried about the steady legislative surrender of power to the president. He thought those patterns contained "the seeds of fascism." Besides, in his view, "the prescription did not work"; there were more unemployed than there had been when Roosevelt began his New Deal two years earlier.[5]

Other isolationists proposed amendments to the WPA bill that reflected their special perspectives, but they supported the basic proposal. Senator La Follette thought the appropriation was not large enough. He introduced an amendment suggested by his brother, Governor Philip La Follette of Wisconsin, that would have more than doubled the appropriation from $4 billion to $9 billion. His amendment won only eight votes, including those of progressive isolationists Costigan, Frazier, La Follette, and Nye. Senator Homer T. Bone of Washington, an active member of Nye's munitions investigating committee, proposed an amendment calling for federal loans to states and municipalities for public power facilities, but it was rejected without record vote. Senator Borah introduced an amendment calling for repeal of the provision in the National Industrial Recovery Act that exempted NRA codes from the antitrust laws. The Senate rejected his amendment, but most progressive isolationists either voted for it or did not vote against it. Senators Thomas of Oklahoma and Wheeler of Montana proposed silver and inflationary amendments, but failed to get what they wanted. All of those progressives, however, supported the basic administration proposal.[6]

On March 23, 1935, the Senate approved WPA by sixty-eight to sixteen, and on April 5 voted the conference report sixty-six to thirteen. All of the progressive isolationists voted for it. The House approved the resolution and the conference report by wide margins, with Hamilton Fish voting with the minority in opposition. Hiram Johnson confided to his son that he voted for the legislation because of his views "about relieving distress," but he worried about "giving to one man the largest sum that has been accorded an individual in the history of the world." Others complained of political partisanship, inefficiency, and inequities in the operation of WPA. Nonetheless, progressive isolationists shared in the enactment and continued support for the relief and public works programs of Roosevelt's New Deal.[7]

Progressive Senators La Follette, Nye, Borah, and others favored enactment of the Wagner labor relations bill before Roosevelt did. When the Supreme Court killed NIRA in May, 1935, Roosevelt endorsed the Wagner bill, and Congress quickly passed it with little debate and little opposition. In the only roll call vote on the Wagner bill, the Senate on May 16, 1935, approved it sixty-three to twelve. All progressive isolationist senators voted for the bill; among leading isolationists only Vandenberg voted against it.[8]

Similarly, progressive isolationists voted for Social Security when it was adopted in the summer of 1935. Even Vandenberg voted for Social Security. Both the Senate and House approved Social Security by wide margins.[9]

Of special interest to many leading isolationists (and to President Roosevelt) was the Saint Lawrence Seaway project. In 1932, the

Hoover administration negotiated and signed a treaty with Canada calling for the construction of that inland waterway system. The Senate had not yet acted on it when Roosevelt became president. The project had two main features: it would provide for a deep-channel linkage via the Saint Lawrence River and the Great Lakes for ocean-going ships between the upper Middle West in America's heartland and foreign markets abroad, and it would provide public hydroelectric power at low cost for private and business consumers in New York. The commercial-shipping features won enthusiastic support from the Middle West—from Ohio, Michigan, Indiana, Wisconsin, Minnesota, and other states. Progressives (and conservatives) from that region favored construction of that transportation system to compete with railroads that, in their judgment, charged excessive rates harmful to western prosperity. Those same progressives applauded public power facilities that would undercut private utility companies controlled by J. P. Morgan and other eastern financiers. The Saint Lawrence Seaway might do for the Northeast in public power what the Tennessee Valley Authority was doing for the Tennessee Valley, Boulder Dam was doing for the Southwest, and Grand Coulee Dam was to do for the Northwest.

Not surprisingly, the Saint Lawrence Seaway project sparked spirited opposition from competing interests. Private utility companies in the Northeast—including those controlled by J. P. Morgan and Company—opposed the public power features. In East Coast port cities from Maine to Texas, business, labor, shipping, and political interests (including both Republicans and Democrats, both chambers of commerce and labor unions) feared competition from the proposed inland system. Railroad corporations and the railroad brotherhoods fought against creation of that competition. Cities tied to use of the Mississippi River (including Chicago, St. Louis, and New Orleans) feared loss of traffic and water diverted from that great river system. Other parts of the country less likely to be affected directly were reluctant to approve appropriations or taxes necessary for construction of that huge project. Neither party lines nor class lines nor liberal-conservative lines nor isolationist-internationalist lines held firm in the controversies surrounding the Saint Lawrence Seaway; self-interests of specific individuals, groups, and sections carried the day. Nonetheless, internationalists (many from coastal regions of the East and South) commonly opposed the seaway, and leading isolationists (many from the upper Middle West and Great Plains) generally supported the Saint Lawrence Seaway. It was a bit ironic that leading isolationists spoke out for the promotion of foreign commerce and for the economic and industrial developments to be gained by that trade, while at the same time internationalists (including Democratic Senator Robert F. Wagner of New York) found ways to argue against the development. President Roosevelt aligned with proponents of the treaty, though it was never at the top of his priorities.

Roosevelt, as governor of New York, had played an important role in the public power features of the project; he continued his interest and efforts after he became president. In the Senate, Robert M. La Follette, Jr., of Wisconsin, Arthur H. Vandenberg of Michigan, Henrik Shipstead of Minnesota, George W. Norris of Nebraska, Arthur Capper of Kansas, Gerald P. Nye of North Dakota, and Burton K. Wheeler of Montana (isolationists all) were among the legislators who urged the administration to action, shared in legislative maneuvers for the treaty, battled for the project—and failed in their efforts during the Roosevelt years. Senators J. Hamilton Lewis of Illinois, Bennett Champ Clark of Missouri, Huey Long of Louisiana, and Robert R. Reynolds of North Carolina (Democrats all) were among the isolationists whose constituents' interests put them in opposition to the seaway.

There was no question about Roosevelt's approval of the Saint Lawrence Seaway, but the acute economic crises in the spring and summer of 1933 demanded priority. In April, 1933, at the president's request, the House of Representatives approved a resolution arranging New York State's contribution to the costs of the project in the event the treaty should win approval. As time passed and the president failed to press the Senate to action, Senators Vandenberg, La Follette, Wheeler, Shipstead, Duffy, Norris, Costigan, and Cutting formally urged the president to add the treaty to the administration's priority items for the special session. But Roosevelt hesitated. When queried by newsmen on May 24, he told his press conference: "There is no question about my being for the St. Lawrence Treaty. . . . I would like to see it go through now. On the other hand, if it means two weeks of debate with the question of whether it goes through in the end in doubt, I think it better not to take it up." In response to a letter from La Follette, Roosevelt on June 8 wrote the Wisconsin senator endorsing both the treaty and the House resolution. And he gave La Follette permission to use his letter. The very next day La Follette attached the House resolution as an amendment to the NIRA bill then under consideration in the Senate and arranged to have the president's letter printed in the *Congressional Record*. The Senate promptly rejected La Follette's amendment, but nearly all western isolationists voted for it.

The Senate adjourned without approving either the House resolution or the treaty.[10]

Proponents of the seaway continued their efforts. Vandenberg and others urged Roosevelt to use public works funds to begin construction in advance of Senate action, but he thought that would violate congressional intent.[11] Concerned senators and administration leaders conferred endlessly on timing and tactics. They arranged for various studies and reports to provide data to support Senate action. At the same time, public power interests, railroads, labor, port cities, and Mississippi River interests mounted formidable propaganda and lobbying campaigns against the project.

Though all persons involved realized that the margin would be close and the possibilities for failure very real, in 1934 the president and his associates made their move. On January 10, Roosevelt sent a message to the Senate urging approval of the treaty on "broad national" grounds. He urged Senator Key Pittman to "make a rip-snorting, 20 carat, 100%, speech on the St. Lawrence Treaty—*We* ought not to let the Progressives bear the brunt of the attack!" Pittman opened the Senate debate with a speech on January 12. It was a weak presentation, however, rather than the "rip-snorting" performance Roosevelt had called for. Senator J. Hamilton Lewis responded on behalf of Chicago's special interests with an eloquent oration opposing the treaty on the grounds that it would provide the waterway through which the British navy could sail in assaulting the United States directly in its heartland. That ludicrous idea won ridicule from the treaty's advocates and embarrassed its opponents. But anti-British and anti-foreign arguments were conspicuous weapons in the arsenal of treaty opponents.[12]

Though Pittman's opening remarks got the debate off to a shaky start, others spoke with much greater effectiveness. In a report to the Foreign Office on the progress of the debate, the British ambassador to the United States noted that the president "enjoys the strong support of the insurgent Republicans in the matter, and is anxious to retain them under his wing in view of the elections in November." And most of those insurgent Republicans were isolationists. Using the language of the agrarian radical he was, Senator Shipstead of Minnesota blamed the opposition on "the banking interests in the large financial centers of the country" who controlled the railroads, steel, oil, and other groups lobbying against the treaty. Senators La Follette, Vandenberg, Capper, Wheeler, Nye, and Norris (among others) added their voices and legislative talents to the effort. Pittman complained to the White House that they had "not had sufficient support upon the floor of the Senate to indicate seriously that it was an Administration measure, in spite of the President's very strong message." As the debate progressed, it became increasingly apparent that the proponents did not have, and might not be able to get, the necessary two-thirds vote. Opponents pressed for an early vote, while proponents wanted to delay, hoping to win more support. Senator Clark proposed reservations as part of his opposition, but withdrew them when it became apparent that the treaty would fail.[13]

The final Senate vote on the Saint Lawrence Seaway treaty came on March 14, 1934. The forty-six affirmative votes fell short of the required two-thirds, and the treaty failed. But those yea votes included most of the leading isolationists, including Senators Bone, Borah, Capper, Costigan, Couzens, Frazier, Johnson, La Follette, Norris, Nye, Vandenberg, and Wheeler. Senators Barbour, Clark, Long, McCarran, McNary, Reynolds, Walsh, and White were among the forty-two who voted against the treaty.[14] Neither the president nor Senators La Follette, Vandenberg, Shipstead, Pittman, and their colleagues abandoned their efforts on behalf of the project in the years that followed. But none of those efforts prevailed while Roosevelt lived. With his usual caution, Key Pittman, chairman of the Foreign Relations Committee until his death in 1940, could be depended upon to warn the president of his weak position in the Senate on the issue. In July, 1935, Roosevelt wrote a Wisconsin constituent that he thought it would not "be at all advisable to inject this into the present session," but believed "we should keep it a live issue." He kept it alive—but just barely.[15]

Progressive hostility to big business and big finance manifested itself even more vividly in the battle for the public utility company legislation. Influences leading to the legislation were many and varied—including revelations about the Insull utility empire and findings of a probe by the Federal Trade Commission. It was an important part of the president's legislative program for 1935. Tom Corcoran and Benjamin Cohen were the principle authors of the complex 150-page bill. Sam Rayburn of Texas, Democratic chairman of the House Interstate Commerce Committee, led the fight for the legislation in the lower house; Montana Democrat Burton K. Wheeler, chairman of the Senate Interstate Commerce Committee, led the fight in the upper house.

Senator Wheeler was one of those leading progressives with whom the president had conferred frequently at the White House in planning legislative tactics for the early New Deal. By 1935, however, relations between Roosevelt and Wheeler had cooled considerably. Silver was a point of difference. Wheeler complained of difficulty in getting access to the president. Roosevelt and some close to the White House were uneasy about the possible course of western progressives in the up-coming presidential election of 1936. At the suggestion of Felix Frankfurter and David K. Niles, Roosevelt arranged a special White House meeting on the evening of May 14 with the senators who had been members of the National Progressive League for Franklin D. Roosevelt in the 1932 compaign. The gathering included Senators Costigan, Johnson, La Follette, Norris, and Wheeler—all western progressives and all isolationists. Secretary of Agriculture Wallace and Secretary of Interior Ickes also attended, along with Niles and Frankfurter. All thought the evening's discussions improved rapport between Roosevelt and the progressives. They helped.[16] Wheeler led the fight for the administration's holding company bill boldly, loyally, and skillfully. It was a major triumph for the administration, for Wheeler, and for progressives—many of whom were isolationists.

Wheeler had his own bill, but deferred to White House urgings to substitute the Corcoran-Cohen draft, which was tougher and better prepared. It contained a so-called death sentence provision (section 11) banning holding companies that were not parts of geographic or economically integrated systems. Utility companies and their financial and political allies spent millions in massive lobbying efforts against the legislation. But Wheeler and Roosevelt stood their ground and carried the battle.

Wheeler's Interstate Commerce Committee held hearings and reported the bill favorably to the Senate late in May. In his address on May 29, urging Senate approval of the bill, the Montana Democrat called holding company practices "legalized thievery against the people of the United States." He urged that America "stop the present trend toward monopoly and get back to an economic democracy." Wheeler said his bill did not seek "further concentration of power in the hands of the Government of the United States," but rather would "make these power-holding companies decentralize, so that they can be controlled by local communities, or can be controlled in a small number of States where they carry on their operating facilities." Five days later Senator Norris of Nebraska told the Senate that he had "been unable to find a single instance where a holding company in the second degree is of any benefit to society. On the contrary, it is always a great danger, and affords a strong temptation for dishonest men, or men moved only by the desire to create great wealth for themselves, and to perpetrate a great injustice upon the people of the country." On June 5, Democrat Homer Bone told the Senate that for years the "Power Trust" had "made a mockery and travesty of government" in his state of Washington. He thought attempts at regulation were "futile." Bone charged that "holding company control has destroyed local autonomy, local initiative, and local responsibility, and has set up a system of absentee management remote from local control and responsive to local need." He insisted that if the "trend toward concentrated business patronage" were "not reversed" there was "danger of an economic feudalism in this country far worse than any goblin of state socialism these men profess to fear."[17]

As the legislative contest progressed, the opposition took heart from rumors that Roosevelt was not firmly committed to the death sentence provision. Brains truster Raymond Moley later wrote that neither the president nor Corcoran and Cohen had really expected that provision to win approval in Congress; they had included it as a tactical bargaining device. But Wheeler took his assignment (including the death sentence provision) seriously. As rumors accumulated about the president's position, the Montana senator confronted him on the issue. As Wheeler described the scene later, "FDR was sitting in bed, propped up by pillows, his cigarette and holder jutting up out of his mouth and cigarette ashes dropping on the bed-spread." Wheeler told the president that he would change the bill any way he wanted it, but that if Roosevelt wanted the death sentence clause, he must make his position clear publicly. Roosevelt was not willing to make a public broadcast on the subject. But he took pencil and paper in hand and scribbled a note for Wheeler's use: "To verify my talk with you this morning, I am very clear in my own mind that while clarifying or minor amendments to section 11 cannot be objected to nevertheless any amendment which goes to the heart or major objective of section 11 would strike at the bill itself and is wholly contrary to the recommendations of my message." Armed with the president's note, Wheeler stood firm. On June 11, when the Senate voted on amendments to eliminate the death sentence provision, the Montana senator produced the president's note to beat back the opposition by the one-vote margin of forty-four to forty-five. All progressive isolationists voted to retain the death sentence; among leading isolationists only Clark, Reynolds, Vandenberg, Walsh, and White voted with the minority against it. The Senate also approved an amendment proposed by Senators Borah, Norris, and Wheeler further tightening that section. With the death sentence provision included, the Senate then adopted the holding company bill fifty-six to thirty-two, with all progressive isolationists voting for it, and Clark, Reynolds, Vandenberg, Walsh, and White against.[18]

The House of Representatives then substituted discretionary provisions for the Senate's mandatory death sentence provision. The conference committee named to reconcile the Senate and House versions very nearly deadlocked. Felix Frankfurter urged the president to compromise on the issue, while Wheeler urged him to stand firm. At one point the president advised Wheeler to take the bill back to the Senate for another vote—which would have killed the death sentence provision. The final conference report was a compromise. It prohibited holding companies beyond the second degree, but gave the Securities and Exchange Commission power to prohibit them beyond the first degree if they were not necessary. The compromise disappointed all progressives—including Wheeler, Norris, and Borah. But it was the best they could get. Both houses approved the conference report on August 24, 1935, and the president promptly signed it into law.[19]

Similar patterns evolved that summer in Roosevelt's relations with progressive isolationists on tax policies. On June 19, the president sent a message to Congress urging various tax reforms—corporation surplus taxes, heavy inheritance and gift taxes, increased surtaxes on large incomes, and graduated corporation income taxes. Critics saw the proposals as political, punitive, vindictive, and economically unwise; proponents saw them as shifting the tax burden to those who could most afford it. Leading Senate progressives eagerly pressed for action on the president's soak-the-rich proposals. A luncheon meeting attended by Senators Norris, Johnson, Borah, and La Follette produced the idea for a round robin on behalf of the tax program. Senator Nye of North Dakota helped line up support from twenty-two senators from four parties urging Congress to stay in session until the proposals were enacted. Those who endorsed the round robin included all leading progressives (most of whom were isolationists on foreign affairs)—Wheeler, Costigan, Bone, Borah, Nye, Capper, Frazier, Norris, La Follette, Shipstead, and others. Senator Nye predicted that the president's course on that issue would "decide whether he can hope to have the Progressive Republicans with him" in the 1936 presidential election.[20]

Conservatives and even moderate liberals objected. Senator Vandenberg criticized the proposals. General Robert E. Wood of Sears, Roebuck and Company and later national chairman of the America

First Committee had voted for Roosevelt in 1932 and had supported much of his early New Deal. But on July 18, he wrote the president opposing the graduated corporation tax as "silly, unfair, and unjust," with "very little revenue producing possibility," and "useless as a matter of social reform." He wrote the president's secretary Marvin McIntyre, "Those of us business men who are liberals are very much in the position of the man without a country. We do not want to go back to the old order of things. On the other hand, there are so many factors in the President's course during the past three or four months, that it is hard to go along with him." Publisher William Randolph Hearst instructed the editors of his newspapers and news services "that the phrase 'SOAK THE SUCCESSFUL' be used in all references to the Administration's Tax Program instead of the phrase 'SOAK THE THRIF-TY' hitherto used." He also wanted "the words 'RAW DEAL' used instead of 'NEW DEAL.'" The White House promptly expressed its displeasure by releasing the Hearst statement to the public.[21]

In practice both isolationists and internationalists divided on the tax issue. In the final analysis the president got far less than he and the progressives wanted, but his proposals strengthened his bonds with progressives as the elections of 1936 drew nearer.

Throughout Roosevelt's first term western progressives supported much of the early New Deal program, and the president in turn initiated and pressed for progressive legislation partly to strengthen their support for his administration. When progressives broke with the president on domestic issues, they did so on grounds that his proposals were not sufficiently in tune with their conceptions of progressivism and were not bold enough in combating the old order. Liberal internationalists (particularly from the urban Northeast) were also prominent in supporting the New Deal, and there were conservative isolationists who opposed it (Vandenberg, Walsh, and White among them). On balance, however, leading isolationists tended to be more radical than the president on domestic issues in the 1930s. Their sympathies were with farmers, small businessmen, and workers. Generally, they preferred antitrust policies, inflation, and tax reforms rather than the government regulation and controls that were more attractive to urban liberals. Those patterns were to project themselves into foreign affairs; the big government, big military, federal regulation, large government expenditures, and huge deficits that came with American participation in World War II were as much a defeat for the western progressive domestic programs as they were a defeat for their programs in foreign affairs.

Chapter 11

Munitions Makers, International Bankers, and Presidents

The Senate Investigation of the Munitions Industry headed by Republican Gerald P. Nye of North Dakota from 1934 to 1936 marked the high point for isolationist strength in the United States during the presidential administration of Franklin D. Roosevelt. Like America's earlier isolationism, the munitions investigation emerged from such widely shared grass-roots attitudes and emotions that it encountered little open opposition during its early phases. Business conservatives, militarists, internationalists, and administration leaders who might have dissented found it expedient to muffle their objections and feign approval. Department of State misgivings generally were masked; it would have been politically unwise to have taken a different tack.

Initially the language of the probe was much like that which young Roosevelt had often used in addressing farmers and villagers early in his New York political career. It meshed perfectly with antibusiness views so commonplace in the Great Depression. It was wholly in tune with attitudes of western agrarian progressives, whose political support Roosevelt had solicited so assiduously. And it was consistent with many of the assumptions and actions of Roosevelt's early New Deal. Initially President Roosevelt gave little attention to the munitions investigation. He promised the cooperation of his administration and never publicly opposed it.

Nonetheless, the investigation stepped on many toes. As it probed ever more deeply, it antagonized industrialists, financiers, military leaders, foreign statesmen, State Department officials, administration leaders, internationalists, and Democratic politicians. By 1936, when it focused on big government, the executive branch, the presidency, and more specifically on the record of President Woodrow Wilson, criticisms of the investigation became intense. Reactions to the committee attacks on what later generations would call the military-industrial complex and the imperial presidency brought about its undoing.

The attitudes and assumptions of the Nye munitions investigation extended far back in European and American history, with organized agitation dating from World War I and before. The investigation grew out of disillusionment with the results of World War I. It was part of a general distrust of Europe. It resulted from a passionate determination to prevent the United States from becoming embroiled in any future European wars.

In addition, the investigation grew out of domestic considerations within the United States. It was based on economic and psychological interpretations of the causes for wars. It assumed that munitions manufacturers and financiers encouraged armament races, imperialism, international friction, and wars in their quest for profits. In 1934, the investigation was as antibusiness as it was antiwar. Western agrarian radicals had been denouncing big business and Wall Street for many years; the munitions investigation provided the perfect vehicle for projecting their views into foreign affairs. The stock market crash of 1929 and the Great Depression that followed in the 1930s descredited big business in the eyes of millions of Americans all over the country. The antibusiness character of the inquiry grew out of both rural and urban values and included both liberal and radical patterns. The munitions investigation emerged in part from the same general conditions and attitudes that produced the New Deal. The Nye committee acknowledged the importance of noneconomic causes for wars, but it contended that the drive for profits played a large role in involving the United States in foreign wars. It focused its attacks on shipbuilders, munitions manufacturers, and international bankers, but it insisted that war prosperity affected foreign policy attitudes of many in all sectors of the population.

In 1935–36, the investigation also began to attack the war-making proclivities of the executive branch of the government. It criticized the War Department, the Navy Department, the Department of Commerce, the Department of State, and even the president. At first it considered the president an unfortunate victim of pressures from urban economic interests. By the latter part of the 1930s, however, Nye and many other isolationists began to view the president as a force for war quite as dangerous as munitions makers and international bankers.[1]

Many individuals contributed to the effort that culminated in the Senate munitions investigation, but among the more important were

Dorothy Detzer, Senator Norris, Senator Nye, and Senator Vandenberg. Dorothy Detzer was executive secretary of the Women's International League for Peace and Freedom. As early as World War I, that pacifist organization had urged investigation and regulation of the international munitions traffic. In 1932 and 1933, it adopted resolutions calling for a Senate investigation. Other pacifist organizations, including the National Council for the Prevention of War, the Fellowship of Reconciliation, and World Peaceways, added their strength to the effort. Bright, able, and energetic, Miss Detzer tried to persuade one or another of the senators to introduce the necessary legislation and push it through. Those initial efforts failed, partly because senators feared the consequences might harm them politically.

In December, 1933, Miss Detzer conferred again with aging Senator Norris, telling him of her failures and discouragement. He favored an investigation, and although too old to undertake it himself, went over a list of the ninety-six senators with her, systematically crossing off the names of his colleagues as he eliminated them from consideration for one reason or another. When Norris finished, only one name remained—that of Senator Nye of North Dakota. Nye had criticized the role of munitions makers in international relations as early as 1920, and he had repeated his criticisms many times in the ensuing years. Senator Norris told Miss Detzer: "Nye's young, he has inexhaustible energy, and he has courage. . . . He may be rash in his judgments at times, but it's the rashness of enthusiasm." Norris pointed out that Nye did not come up for election for four years. By that time, Norris believed, the investigation would help him because "there isn't a major industry in North Dakota closely allied to the munitions business."

Nye had already turned her down twice, but armed with Norris's backing, at a third meeting in early January, 1934, she finally persuaded him. When he began the munitions investigation, Nye was forty-two years old with eight years of Senate experience. He had already directed two inquiries and was firmly convinced of the importance of legislative investigations.[2]

Born in Hortonville, Wisconsin, in 1892, young Nye had absorbed the values of Fighting Bob La Follette's progressivism in that state. After graduation from Wittenberg High School in 1911, Nye followed his father's footsteps into the newspaper business, editing small town papers in the farming states of Wisconsin, Iowa, and North Dakota for nearly fifteen years. He supported President Woodrow Wilson's domestic reforms and foreign policies and became increasingly active in the Nonpartisan League in North Dakota. That agrarian radical organization's hositility to eastern big business interests influenced both his domestic and foreign policy views. Not quite thirty-three years old in 1925 when first appointed, Nye served in the United States Senate for nearly twenty years, until 1945.

Though a Republican, Nye battled against the conservative, pro-business policies of the Coolidge and Hoover administrations. He supported much of Roosevelt's New Deal. When he criticized it (as he did the National Recovery Administration), he did so from the point of view of an agrarian radical who thought the New Deal reforms did not go far enough to help workers, farmers, and small businessmen. On the relatively few occasions when Senator Nye spoke on foreign affairs during his first eight years in office, his views directly reflected his agrarian frame of reference. Repeatedly he opposed foreign policies that seemed to benefit urban financial and business groups at the expense of farmers. The munitions investigation of 1934–36 was a logical foreign policy projection of Nye's long crusade against big business, international bankers, and Wall Street.

Lean, youthful, and energetic, Nye stood five feet, ten and one-half inches tall and kept his brown hair smoothly combed. He became one of the better-dressed senators, tending toward dark double-breasted suits and colorful ties. Never very active in Washington social life, he found relaxation in fishing, developed into a good golfer, played bridge, and was a heavy smoker. Serious, earnest, and direct, he was also considerate, generous, and had a sense of humor. He spoke in a soft, low-pitched voice and was a good listener. Sensitive about not attending college and awed by his distinguished colleagues, Nye was never very effective in accomplishing legislative goals. But he had abundant energy, physical endurance, and courage. With his more cautious colleagues often urging him on from the safety of the sidelines, Nye spoke out candidly on explosive issues. His frankness made good copy for newsmen. He recognized the value of publicity and won more than his share of headlines. He enjoyed public speaking and became a powerful and moving orator. And from the time he participated in final phases of the Teapot Dome inquiry in the 1920s, Nye became increasingly skilled and dogged in directing Senate investigations.[3]

Drawing on drafts already prepared by the Foreign Policy Association, the Women's International League for Peace and Freedom, and other peace groups, Senator Nye tried his hand at drafting the necessary legislation for the munitions investigation. On January 17,

1934, he conferred with Joseph C. Green of the Department of State. A devotee and protégé of Herbert Hoover, Green had taught at Princeton and was the State Department's authority on international arms traffic. He agreed to help draft the legislation, but emphasized that his cooperation was "entirely personal" and should not be seen as involving the Department of State. Nye too thought it best to keep Green's role confidential. Though not speaking for Secretary Hull, Green told the senator that "such an investigation might bring out facts which might be useful to the Department" and that "the Department would stand ready to supply the investigating committee with such pertinent material as it had at its disposal."[4]

On February 8, 1934, Nye submitted his Senate Resolution 179 calling for an investigation of the munitions industry by the Foreign Relations Committee. The handful present in the Senate at the time paid little attention. Without objection the resolution was referred to the Foreign Relations Committee under Senator Pittman of Nevada.[5]

Hull let it be known that he was sympathetic to the idea for such a probe. Pittman did not want responsibility for the investigation, however, and arranged to have the resolution referred to the Military Affairs Committee (on which Nye served). Its supporters then urged that a special committee, rather than a standing committee, conduct the investigation. They also suggested that Nye's resolution be combined with one introduced earlier by Senator Vandenberg of Michigan. Vandenberg's resolution, endorsed by the American Legion, advocated taking the profits out of war, a proposal that Nye wholly approved. If the resolutions were combined, and so appealed for support from such disparate groups as the American Legion and the pacifists, the chances for adoption would improve. Nye and Vandenberg agreed to those moves, and on March 12, Nye introduced a new combined Senate Resolution 206. The Military Affairs Committee promptly reported it out favorably.[6]

At the same time, popular enthusiasm and organized pressure for an investigation were reaching massive proportions. An article on European munitions makers, "Arms and the Men," published in the March, 1934, issue of *Fortune* magazine, was reprinted, distributed, and quoted. Senator Borah delivered a powerful oration in the Senate on the subject. *Merchants of Death*, a sensational book by H. C. Englebrecht and F. C. Hanighen, was widely read and discussed. Petitions, meetings, letters, telegrams, editorials, and personal appeals urged an investigation. The State Department endorsed the idea.[7]

A showdown in the Senate occurred on April 12, 1934. Senator Pat

Harrison of Mississippi, chairman of the Finance Committee, was impatiently pushing for a vote on the pending revenue bill, but was frustrated by lengthy debate on amendments to his bill. Nye spoke for over an hour supporting his amendment calling for a 98 percent tax on all incomes over ten thousand dollars a year during wartime. Vandenberg then took the floor and spoke at length on Nye's amendment. As Vandenberg spoke on, Harrison's impatience grew. Finally he consulted Nye on the Senate floor and learned, to his horror, that eleven senators planned to speak for Nye's amendment and that that would probably consume five days. To head off the filibuster, Harrison proposed that the Nye-Vandenberg munitions investigation resolution be adopted immediately and that Nye's tax amendment be referred to the committee appointed to conduct the investigation. That was exactly what Nye and Vandenberg wanted. With Harrison's cooperation, the Senate promptly adopted Senate Resolution 206 on April 12, without a record vote and without dissent.[8]

The resolution alleged that "the commercial motive" was "an inevitable factor in considerations involving the maintenance of the national defense" and was "one of the inevitable factors often believed to stimulate and sustain wars." It empowered the vice-president to appoint seven senators to a special committee to investigate all aspects of the manufacture, sale, and distribution of armaments and munitions. The resolution also directed the committee to study and report on the adequacy of existing legislation and treaties on the subject, instructed it to review the findings and recommendations of an earlier commission concerned with taking the profits out of war, and authorized it to consider the desirability of a government monopoly in the manufacture of munitions.[9]

Vice-President John Nance Garner of Texas, Nye, and Vandenberg determined the compositon of the committee. The four Democrats chosen were James P. Pope of Idaho, Homer T. Bone of Washington, Bennett Champ Clark of Missouri, and Walter F. George of Georgia, and the three Republicans were Nye, Vandenberg, and W. Warren Barbour of New Jersey. That committee overrepresented agricultural sections of the country and underrepresented urban industry, finance, and labor. Five of the seven were from south of the Ohio River or west of the Mississippi (four from west of the Mississippi). The Northeast and the South were internationalist strongholds, but only two of the seven came from those sections. Both of the members with the most substantial industrial constituencies, Barbour and Vandenberg, were fervent protectionists. Their two states, New Jersey and Michigan, both had huge industries that profited from munitions production and foreign markets. But Barbour was a manufacturer of light consumer goods. Vandenberg's home was in Grand Rapids, famed for its protected furniture manufacturing industry. Henry Ford of Dearborn was an isolationist. Michigan was also a leader in the processing of agricultural dairy and cereal products. All seven members participated in committee affairs, but the most active and influential were two Republicans (Nye and Vandenberg) and two Democrats (Clark and Bone). Of those four, Nye and Bone were progressives; Vandenberg was conservative but not a reactionary.

Vice-President Garner left the choice of a chairman up to the committee. The Democrats controlled the White House, both houses of Congress, and a majority on the committee; one might have expected that a Democrat would head the probe. Instead, at a brief meeting on April 23, the committee unanimously chose Nye as chairman. Secretary Hull was deeply disappointed that a Republican isolationist was made chairman. He later wrote that the appointment of Nye was "a fatal mistake" and that he would have opposed the investigation had he known that would happen.[10]

Nevertheless, as Hull wrote in his memoirs, the administration "went beyond the usual limits" to cooperate with the Nye committee. According to Hull, he and Roosevelt felt that their "only feasible step was a sort of marking time. There was no hope of success and nothing to be gained in combating the isolationist wave at that moment. To have done so would only have brought a calamitous defeat and precipitated a still more disastrous conflict on the whole basic question of isolation itself." Hull directed Joseph Green to serve as liaison with the committee. Hull assured Nye that he could "rely upon the fullest and most cordial cooperation of the Department in supplying you with any information in our possession, which may aid you in connection with the investigation."[11]

On May 18, in a message drafted by Green in the State Department, President Roosevelt informed the Senate that he was "gratified" that "a committee has been appointed to investigate the problems incident to the private manufacture of arms and munitions of war and the international traffic therein." He "earnestly" recommended that it "receive the generous support of the Senate," and he promised that "the executive departments of the Government will be charged to cooperate with the committee to the fullest extent." In his message to the Senate, the president charged that "the private and uncontrolled manufacture of arms and munitions and the traffic therein" constituted "a serious source of international discord and strife." Roosevelt warned, however, that it was "not possible . . . effectively to control such an evil by the isolated action of any one country." It was "a field in which international action" was necessary. He urged Senate approval of the Convention for the Supervision of the International Trade in Arms and Ammunition and in Implements of War that had been signed at Geneva in 1925. And he expressed hope that a "much more far-reaching" convention on the subject might be concluded at the World Disarmament Conference in Geneva. The president's message to the Senate contended: "The peoples of many countries are being taxed to the point of poverty and starvation in order to enable governments to engage in a mad race in armaments which, if permitted to continue, may well result in war. This grave menace to the peace of the world is due in no small measure to the uncontrolled activities of the manufacturers and merchants of engines of destruction, and it must be met by the concerted action of the peoples of all nations." In a circular telegram, the secretary of state informed the American ambassadors to Great Britain, France, Germany, and Italy and the American delegate to the Geneva Disarmament Conference of the substance of the president's message. In a letter to Senator Nye on that same date, May 18, Hull reemphasized his "genuine interest in the investigation" and restated his assurances of "the whole-hearted cooperation of the Department" in supplying the committee "with all pertinent information available to us."[12]

The committee named Stephen Raushenbush of New York to be its secretary and chief investigator. A tall, keen-minded, and experienced investigator in his late thirties, Raushenbush undertook much of the work of directing research, planning hearings, and preparing reports for the committee. He had graduated from Amherst, served in the ambulance corps in France during World War I, and had investigated and written on the power trust in America. He gathered an able and dedicated staff of experienced workers for the committee. The legal assistant on his staff for a few months was a brilliant young Harvard Law graduate named Alger Hiss, who was borrowed temporarily from Jerome Frank's staff in the Agricultural Adjustment Administration. The committee also appointed an advisory council of three experts to consult with the committee. Of the three, only John T. Flynn of the *New Republic* played a major role in the committee's work.[13]

At its meeting on June 1, the Nye committee adopted a resolution asking for an executive order from the president giving full access to income tax returns of all firms and individuals believed involved in matters within the purview of the investigation. On June 6, the full committee met with President Roosevelt to seek "full help from the various departments." According to the diary of the State Department's J. Pierrepont Moffat, at that White House meeting Roosevelt "told them at length about his sympathy with their idea of clipping the wings of the arms manufacturers." According to Moffat the president even told committee members "that he was in favor of the complete abolition of all aviation." With Roosevelt's support and cooperation, the Nye committee gained access to virtually all government documents it sought in its investigation, including income tax returns.[14]

The committee staff began examining State Department records on June 1. It agreed not to publish material from department files without first checking with the department. During the summer of 1934, Raushenbush and his staff scoured files of various corporations and agencies in their search for documents and evidence. Public hearings before the Nye committee began on September 4, 1934, and continued through September 21. It then adjourned for two months but resumed its hearings on December 4 and continued them regularly for nearly five months. Late in April, 1935, the committee adjourned and held no hearings for eight and one-half months until January 7, 1936. It heard its final witness on February 20, 1936, a year and one-half after the hearings first began. During those eighteen months the Nye committee questioned nearly two hundred witnesses and spent more than $130,000; the testimony and exhibits, when published, filled thirty-nine volumes, totaling 13,750 pages of fine print. The du Ponts (the brothers Irénée, Pierre, and Lammot, and their cousin Felix), who testified in 1934–35, were the biggest of the industrial giants examined. The appearance of J. P. Morgan and his senior partners in January and February, 1936, was the high point of the committee's exploration into financial aspects of the munitions traffic. Officers of many other firms also testified. Newspapers from all over the United States and from other countries gave the hearings detailed coverage, providing readers throughout the world with a daily round of headlines and sensations.[15]

The examination of du Pont Company records worried the War Department. On August 8, 1934, even before the hearings began, Army Chief of Staff General Douglas MacArthur expressed concern to Nye lest the inquiry reveal secret War Department procurement plans. MacArthur also informed the head of the du Pont Company "that the secret data in his files must be safeguarded."[16]

From their beginnings in September, 1934, the Nye committee

hearings provoked a storm of diplomatic protests from abroad. Evidence and testimony introduced in the hearings alleged corruption, bribes, and rake-offs by officials of various governments in dealings with agents of American munitions firms. Some of that evidence was accurate; some was unsubstantiated rumor and hearsay. True or not, however, allegations embarrassed and angered officials in countries with which the United States had friendly relations. A communication from a source in Warsaw introduced as evidence before the committee alleged that King George V of England had personally intervened with the Polish ambassador in London to help win a munitions contract for a British rather than a competing American firm. British officialdom protested against the publicity given to the rumor concerning the king's role.[17] The committee's probings and revelations also elicited protests from some Latin American governments, endangering the Good Neighbor policy.[18]

Secretary Hull was away from Washington when the committee hearings began, and after his return exploded with wrath upon learning of the various protests from foreign governments. "It was refreshing," Moffat later recorded, "to watch oath after oath pour out of his rather saintlike countenance and then to have him smile and say, 'It's not more than once every six months that I use language like that!'" Top State Department officials conferred as they helped ready Hull's response to the Nye comittee. As Moffat explained it, Hull needed to avoid "two pitfalls. On the one hand, he must not seem to be blocking the inquiry which in general is along the lines the Department desired. On the other hand, he must protect our good name and friendship." During noon recess in the hearings on Septermber 11, Secretary Hull spent nearly two hours discussing the problem with the committee. He then issued a statement to the press stating that neither the committee nor the United States government wanted to offend foreign governments or their officials. At the same time, Hull made public a letter from Nye in which the senator emphasized that the insertion in the record of statements by foreign agents of American companies did not necessarily imply that those statements were true.[19]

Secretary Hull, Secretary of Commerce Daniel C. Roper, and Green again met with the committee for more than an hour on September 14, on a different matter. The committee had wanted permission to put into the record a confidential report by Douglas Miller, the American commercial attaché in Berlin, on German purchases of airplanes. At their meeting Hull and Roper flatly refused to authorize publication of the report. They emphasized that if the report were published, it would end Miller's usefulness and dry up valuable sources for confidential information both in Germany and in other parts of the world. They also discussed other difficulties relating to the committee's activities. The Nye committee had discovered that the Argentine president's son received a 10 percent commission on certain sales in that country. Hull and Roper contended that publishing such information would not advance the committee's purposes, but could damage United States efforts to improve relations with that important South American government. The many diplomatic protests and Secretary Hull's closed sessions with the Nye committee provoked speculation that the committee was being asked to soft-pedal its findings. Nye denied that. Though the committee and the State Department tried to cooperate with each other, problems continued to strain the relationship throughout the entire investigation.[20]

Between the adjournment of the committee's first series of hearings on Friday, September 21, 1934, and the beginnings of the next set of hearings on December 4, Senator Nye addressed public meetings and radio audiences all over the United States. In the fall of 1934 he went on the first of his many nationwide speaking tours arranged through private lecture agencies. Nye enjoyed those speaking engagements, they added to his income, and they provided opportunities for him to take his foreign policy views to the people. From 1934 through 1941 many tens of thousands of Americans heard his addresses, and millions more heard him on local and national radio broadcasts. In speech after speech, citing evidence from the findings of the munitions investigation, Senator Nye drove home his theme: "There may be doubt as to the degree but there is certainty that the profits of preparation for war and the profits of war itself constitute the most serious challenge to the peace of the world." To preserve peace the senator urged the United States to "be as severe with income and property as we are with lives in time of war."[21] At the same time that the Senate committee was continuing its probe, the Department of State, with Roosevelt's encouragement, was pressing for international action to control the munitions traffic.[22]

Throughout the investigation, Senators Nye and Vandenberg and their colleagues probed the methods and profits of private businesses engaged in the manufacture, trade, and finance of munitions. The committee also turned up data that reflected critically on administrative departments. From December, 1934, onward, Senator Nye and his committee became increasingly concerned about the role of the federal government in the munitions traffic.[23] When Nye and his committee first expressed concern about the role of the government, they singled out the War Department, the Navy Department, and the Department of Commerce. They did not immediately criticize the presidency. Even as the committee's fears about the direction and strength of presidential influence on foreign affairs steadily increased, its members initially sympathized with the chief executive's difficulties in withstanding pressures from powerful urban economic interests.

Though he had not focused much attention on the investigation, President Roosevelt had publicly endorsed the inquiry, had met with the committee, and had admonished departments of his administration to cooperate fully. Eight days after the hearings resumed in December, however, an unexpected White House action sharply heightened the committee's growing concerns about the government's role. In a surprise move at his press conference on December 12, 1934, President Roosevelt announced the appointment of a separate committee of prominent administrative officials under Wall Street's Bernard Baruch to consider the possibility of legislation to take the profit out of war. It included no senators or congressmen. Many feared it was an administration effort to undercut the Senate inquiry.[24]

Nye's reaction was prompt and vigorous: "The departments of our government are really codefendants with the munitions industry and the profiteers. . . . When I view, in part, the personnel of the conference, I cannot but think how unfortunate it is that [John] Dillinger is dead. He was the logical person to write the anti-crime laws." Letters flooded the White House protesting any effort to block the Senate munitions investigation. At Roosevelt's invitation, Nye conferred with him at the White House on December 26, 1934. Roosevelt assured the North Dakota senator that the Baruch committee would not undermine the Senate inquiry. The Baruch group did not actually function, but the episode increased the Nye committee's uneasiness about the administration.[25]

Early in January, 1935, Nye told a reporter: "I suppose nothing [in the munitions investigation] has astonished me so much as to discover the large amounts of evidence which indicate that, instead of munition-makers promoting the military activities of governments, governments—especially our own war and navy departments—have been actively promoting the munitions-makers, for years." He contended that the munitions business "would not be what it is without the support of government officials" and "that certain departments of our government are co-defendants with the munitions industry and its profiteers in this great 'trial.'" On January 15, 1935, he told the

Senate that "the most vicious feature of all the disclosures as a result of this investigation has been the revelation of a partnership that exists in the munitions business. . . . the partnership which our Government—your Government and mine—has in the business of selling American munitions of war." From 1935 onward Nye and his committee wanted to restrain *both* business and government in the name of peace.[26]

On February 23, 1935, President Roosevelt directed a brief memorandum to Secretary Hull asking him to speak with him "about the advisability of a message on war profits and kindred subjects." He attached a memorandum drafted by Bernard Baruch.[27] Three weeks later, on March 15, Hull handed the president a detailed response. In his memorandum Hull advised Roosevelt not to send a message to Congress concerning the international arms traffic. He feared it "would not serve any useful purpose and might result in a head-on collision with the Nye Committee." Pointing out that the Nye committee planned to submit a preliminary report on April 1, Hull suggested that a presidential message at that time "could easily be misconstrued as an attempt to take the wind out of the sails of that Committee." He thought the Senate probably would not act in any event until the munitions committee had reported.

The secretary of state advised President Roosevelt to meet with the Nye committee within the next week or two. He thought such a White House meeting could strengthen the American delegation negotiating in Geneva on arms traffic. It might "help check any tendency on the part of the Committee to adopt a program of Government monopoly." Such a meeting would make clear that the Roosevelt administration was not leaving the arms traffic matter entirely in the hands of the Senate committee. Hull believed a White House meeting "would demonstrate to the public that the Administration is to some degree cooperating with the Committee."[28]

Roosevelt invited the Nye committee to meet with him on March 19, 1935. All seven committee members attended. In his conversation with the committee, however, Roosevelt did not follow the guidance Hull had outlined for him. The particular problem that most troubled the State Department, the committee, and the British government at the moment involved examination of documents in files of American banks relating to loans to Allied governments in World War I. But the president did not discuss that subject at all with the committee. The meeting touched only briefly on control of the international arms traffic. Instead, the discussions focused largely on methods for taking the profits out of war (which Hull had advised Roosevelt to hold in abeyance) and on neutrality legislation (which was not really in the Nye committee's jurisdiction).

During the White House meeting, Senator Nye outlined for the president a twelve-point program prepared for the committee by John T. Flynn for taxing the profits out of war. It was far more drastic than the price-fixing approach recommended by Bernard Baruch. Much to Senator Nye's surprise, Roosevelt "expressed emphatically his approval of the several portions of that scheme." He further suggested that legislation taking profits out of war should cover both when the United States was at war and when it was a neutral in wars between other states.

The president then discussed American neutrality policy at length and told the committee "that he had come around entirely to the ideas of Mr. Bryan, in regard to that matter." Roosevelt encouraged the Nye committee to consider neutrality policy, "with a view to the introduction of appropriate legislation." As Green learned the day after the meeting, Senator Nye was "enthusiastic in regard to the attitude of the President." The committee members "had left the President with the definite impression that he was disposed to cooperate with the Committee."[29]

One can speculate on reasons for the president's performance. He may have been voicing his personal convictions at that time on the issues involved. Perhaps he had not done his homework properly, despite the help Hull had provided. After his tactical mistake in appointing the competing Baruch committee in December, and after his defeat on the World Court issue in January, he may have feared provoking isolationist opposition further. He may have had the political needs of his New Deal program in mind in appeasing isolationist inclinations of the committee. He may partly have been swept along by his own personality as he charmed committee members. When newsmen the following day asked the president about his meeting with the Nye committee, Roosevelt was vague, general, and ambiguous.[30] Reading the transcript of the press conference, one wonders whether Roosevelt were deliberately obfuscating, whether he had not made up his mind on some of the issues, or whether he really was a bit fuzzy-minded about the whole matter. One does not get the impression that the issues involved in that White House meeting with the Nye committee were foremost in his attention at that time. In any event, his performance fitted the patterns of his dealings with western progressive isolationists during his first term. And his performance surely disappointed and displeased Hull, Green, and other State Department officials.

In March, 1935, and continuing through the year, the Nye committee examined records of American banks involved in loans to Allied governments while the United States was a neutral in World War I. Specifically, the probe involved files of the Guaranty Trust Company of New York on loans to Britain, records in the custody of Central Hanover Bank and Trust Company of New York on loans to France, records of Lee Higginson and Company relating to an Italian loan, files of J. P. Morgan and Company, Federal Reserve Bank records, and others. The British, French, and Italian governments variously objected to the committee's examination. The State Department would have preferred that the Nye committee be willing to forego examination of those files completely, but the committee would not do that. Nye considered it "perhaps the most important part of the investigation" and insisted that "it was absolutely essential that the Committee proceed." The Department of State was caught in the middle between the committee, private banks, and European governments.[31]

Roosevelt and Hull met with Senators Nye, Clark, and Pope of the committee again on April 13. In advance of that White House meeting Hull and Green provided the president with a detailed nine-page "Memorandum Cooperation with the Nye Committee." It focused on four phases of Nye committee activity—neutrality, taking profits out of war, control of the arms traffic, and investigation of private American loans to the Allies during World War I. The general tenor of the memorandum was cautious and foot-dragging. It advised the president not to support any specific neutrality legislation at that time, it recommended "complete neutrality" on legislation to take the profits out of war, it advised the president to endorse the legislation Green had drafted for registering firms involved in the arms traffic, and it recommended that the president press the committee not to proceed with its examination of the files of J. P. Morgan and other banks. At their White House meeting on April 13, Roosevelt and Hull urged the senators not to go further with the committee's examination of the bank records. But Nye and his colleagues would neither yield nor delay.[32]

Nonetheless, in March and April, Hull and Green worked out reasonably acceptable arrangements for handling the problem. The Nye committee and its staff proceeded with its examination of the records. It agreed not to make public any documents originating with foreign governments, however, until it had first informed the State Department and had given Hull the opportunity to determine whether there were objections from the foreign government involved. The arrangement was not entirely satisfactory either to the committee or to the European governments, but it functioned.[33] In mid-August 1935, they developed a different procedure for handling examination of British and French commercial accounts in the files of J. P. Morgan and Company.[34]

Despite continued official courtesy and efforts at cooperation, differing views and interests extending over the long months of the inquiry led to increased tension and irritation on all sides. Roosevelt's direct relations with the committee and its members were cordial and cooperative. But he may have come closer to expressing his personal feelings in a letter he wrote to Colonel Edward M. House in September, 1935. House had been President Wilson's closest adviser and a chief delegate to the Versailles conference after World War I. Roosevelt wrote House that "some of the Congressmen and Senators who are suggesting wild-eyed measures to keep us out of war are now declaring that you and Lansing and Page forced Wilson into the war! I had a talk with them, explained that I was in Washington myself the whole of that period, that none of them were there and that their historical analysis was wholly inaccurate and that history yet to be written would prove my point." He complained "that they belong to the very large and perhaps increasing school of thought which holds that we can and should withdraw wholly within ourselves and cut off all but the most perfunctory relationships with other nations. They imagine that if the civilization of Europe is about to destroy itself through internal strife, it might just as well go ahead and do it and that the United States can stand idly by."[35] By January, 1936, when J. P. Morgan and his senior partners testified at committee hearings based on the Morgan files, Joseph Green wrote his friend Moffat that Nye was "having his Roman holiday and the circus proceeds. The Secretary and Judge Moore are both so furious against the Senator and his Committee that they are now unwilling to admit that I accomplished anything whatever in the interests of the Department by cooperating with the Committee."[36]

In mid-January, 1936, a sensational episode marked the final phases of the munitions investigation. It gave opponents their best opportunity to attack Nye and his comittee, helped them make it a more partisan issue, and brought the probe to an early end. The crisis did not involve munitions makers, shipbuilders, international bankers, or any other economic group directly. Rather, it concerned the political leader of the United States during World War I, President Woodrow Wilson. At the committee hearings on January 15, Senator Clark read documents and evidence into the record showing, among other things, that President Wilson, Secretary of State Robert Lansing, and Colonel Edward M. House knew of the Allied "secret agreements" very early. He based his statement on "information from official sources which has not yet been released for publication, which I am therefore unable to put into the record." The document Clark alluded to was a memorandum of May 18, 1917, from British Foreign Secretary Arthur J. Balfour to Lansing in the State Department files. The Nye committee wanted to make it public, but the British government had refused to grant the necessary permission. At the hearings Nye then said that "the Committee is informed by the highest possible sources that Secretary Lansing and President Wilson were fully apprised by Balfour of the secret treaties, to which Great Britain had been committed, and the record that has been made and is yet to be made will all clearly reveal that both the President and Secretary Lansing falsified concerning this matter, and declared upon occasion that they had no knowledge prior to their visit to the Peace Conference in Paris."[37]

Senator Nye's statement that "the President and Secretary Lansing falsified" about their knowledge of the secret treaties set off explosive repercussions. Newspapers charged that Nye had said that President Wilson "lied." The next day Tom Connally of Texas rose from his seat in the Senate and gave Nye a scathing tongue-lashing for "efforts of this kind to besmirch the memory of the man Woodrow Wilson." The altercation continued the following day when Nye took the floor to defend himself. Nye refused to apologize or retract his statement about Wilson. He said the committee had to study the Wilson administration to determine the effects of the arms traffic on the government's foreign policies. He reminded his listeners that as a newspaperman he had supported Wilson and his foreign policies. He said, "when we go in search of pertinent truths we ought not dodge them when we encounter them—we ought not let partisan prejudices blind us to those truths, however embarrassing they may be to a mere political party." He promised to pursue the truth whatever "the degree of threat or intimidation." Connally repeatedly interrupted and criticized Nye's speech.[38]

The heaviest blast on that second day came from Senator Carter Glass of Virginia. The background of Glass's performance was signif-

icant. He was a conservative southern Democrat who opposed isolationism. He had served as secretary of treasury in President Wilson's
cabinet. In May, 1935, Russell C. Leffingwell of J. P. Morgan and
Company wrote to Glass about the munitions investigation. Leffingwell had been assistant secretary of the treasury from 1917 to 1920
in the Wilson administration before he became a Morgan partner in
1923. In his letter to Glass he expressed concern about possible attacks
by the Nye committee on the loan policies of the Treasury Department
during the Wilson administration. But Glass wrote back assuring
Leffingwell that he need not "worry about Nye's investigation" and
promising that if Nye made "any attack on the Wilson Administration
you may be sure that McAdoo and I will be prepared to meet the
issue." He was as good as his word. On January 17, the old senator
trembled with emotion as he told the packed galleries that Nye's
allegation about Wilson was the most "shocking exhibition" that had
occurred in his thirty-five years in Congress. Connally and Glass
vigorously opposed giving the Nye committee any more funds. During
his impassioned oration Glass pounded his desk so violently that his
hand bled. Other senators joined in the fray, and it continued a third
day on the Senate floor with some echoes still later.[39]

The State Department objected to the reference by Nye and Clark
to the Balfour memorandum that the British government had explicitly refused to release for publication. Hull indicated that State Department cooperation with committees was conditional upon the cooperation that those committees gave the depatment. He told newsmen he
had always maintained "the highest regard" for President Wilson's
"patriotism and scrupulous honesty." At Green's request, Raushenbush returned all copies of the Balfour memorandum and other
documents from State Department files that had not been approved
for public use. Two Democrats on the Nye committee (Pope and
George) criticized Nye and disassociated themselves from "head hunting or using an instrumentality of the United States Senate to promote
the bias, prejudice, or animus of any member of the committee."
Even old Senator Hiram Johnson in a letter to his son criticized "the
unfortunate mode of expression of Nye in regard to certain evidence
being produced." He wrote that Nye's reference to Wilson "gave the
opportunity to the Democrats to tear him to tatters." The sympathetic
Senator George Norris feared that Nye's "unfortunate" and "unnecessary" remark might reduce the good results he hoped would
come from the committee's probe. Joseph Green believed that Nye
had "lost any influence which he may ever have had with his col-

leagues,'' but that his "popular support" was "not only undiminished, but continues to grow."[40]

Senator Nye's statement about Wilson was factually correct, and none of his critics cited any evidence to disprove it. When the episode occurred, the inquiry was nearly completed, and the committee was able to finish its hearings and issue its final reports. But the senator's statement was a political blunder. It strengthened and unified the previously scattered opposition to the munitions investigation. Nye's criticism of a Democratic president helped drive Democrats into opposition. The committee heard its last witness on February 20, 1936.

The Munitions Investigating Committee had submitted a brief preliminary report on April 1, 1935.[41] It submitted seven major reports—two in the spring and summer of 1935 and five more before the end of June, 1936. Those reports (averaging more than two hundred pages each) treated the committee's findings and recommendations on naval shipbuilding, methods for taking the profits out of war, activities and sales of munitions companies, War Department wartime industrial mobilization plans, neutrality legislation, and the roles of big financiers. The seventh and final report submitted on June 19, 1936, dealt with the question of government manufacture of munitions.[42]

In its reports the Nye committee insisted that private shipbuilders should either "be policed" or "be cut off entirely from the building of ships for the Navy." It suspected some shipbuilders "of willingness to wave the flag or to circulate war scares in the plain and simple interest of their own pocketbooks, regardless of results." The committee insisted that there was "no effective profit-limitation law" and that the profits of shipbuilding firms were too high—21.8 percent to 36.9 percent on the ships it studied.[43]

The central issue on taking the profits out of war concerned the relative merits of price controls and taxation. Administration departments generally favored primary reliance on price controls; the Nye committee believed controls would not be adequate and recommended extremely high wartime taxes in addition to price controls.[44]

The committee reported "that almost without exception, the American munitions companies investigated have at times resorted to . . . a form of bribery of foreign governmental officials or of their close friends in order to secure business." It conceded that the evidence did "not show that wars have been started solely because of the activities of munitions makers and their agents," but insisted that it was "against the peace of the world for selfishly interested organizations to be left free to goad and frighten nations into military activity.'' The committee charged that munitions companies had ''secured the active support of the War, Navy, Commerce, and even State Departments in their sales abroad.'' In the interests of American neutrality, the committee recommended detailed restrictions on economic groups and on the administration in relations with belligerents in any war. It emphasized ''the importance of determining a neutrality policy before war has begun and the desirability of mandatory rather than discretionary legislation.''[45]

After probing the activities of J. P. Morgan and Company before the United States entered World War I, the committee concluded that ''loans to belligerents militate against neutrality.'' The committee recommended the continuation and extension of neutrality laws restricting loans and exports to belligerents to help preserve American neutrality in future wars.[46]

The majority on the committee (Nye, Clark, Bone, and Pope) favored government ownership of munitions industries, while the minority (George, Vandenberg, and Barbour) favored reliance on strict government control of private munitions companies. Those who favored government ownership were all (in varied degree) liberals or progressives from states west of the Mississippi River. Those who opposed government ownership were conservatives from east of the Mississippi. The senators with the largest farming constituencies outside of the South favored government ownership, while the senators with the most substantial industrial constituencies opposed it.[47]

The State Department's Joseph Green correctly predicted in April, 1936, ''Nothing will come of it.'' The Nye committee proposed specific legislation designed to implement its recommendations, but Congress did not enact any of the committee's bills. On June 19, 1935, Senator Vandenberg introduced two bills for the committee designed ''to prevent collusion in the making of contracts'' and ''to prevent profiteering in the construction of naval vessels in private shipyards.'' Both bills died in the Senate Naval Affairs Committee.[48]

On April 9, 1935, the House adopted the McSwain bill representing the administration approach on price controls to discourage wartime profiteering. Senator Nye arranged to have the McSwain bill referred to the munitions committee, which then completely rewrote it. As amended, the lengthy document called for sharply increased wartime taxes, including virtually 100 percent tax rates on all corporate profits over 6 percent and on all personal income of more than ten thousand dollars a year during a war. Nye submitted the amended resolution to the Senate on May 3, 1935. It was referred to the Military

Affairs Committee and then to the Finance Committee. But it failed to win adoption. During the next five years Nye and his colleagues reintroduced bills to tax the profits out of war, but Congress never enacted them.[49]

In 1937, Senator Nye introduced a bill that would have provided for government ownership of shipbuilding and munitions manufacturing facilities. Public opinion polls in 1936 had concluded that the overwhelming majority of the American people in all sections of the country favored government ownership of munitions industries. The administration opposed government ownership, however, and Congress never acted on Nye's bill.[50] The Senate Foreign Relations Committee claimed authority in the area of neutrality, so the Nye committee did not formally propose legislation. It did, however, make general recommendations, two of its members (Nye and Clark) individually introduced neutrality resolutions, and the Nye committee and its staff did much of the behind-the-scenes work in fighting for the neutrality laws of 1935 and 1936.[51]

In his memoirs published after the end of World War II, Cordell Hull wrote that the Nye committee hearings produced some benefits "in revealing hitherto undisclosed methods employed in the traffic in arms." But he strongly emphasized the "disastrous effects" of the hearings. Hull wrote: "The Nye Committee aroused an isolationist sentiment that was to tie the hands of the Administration just at the very time when our hands should have been free to place the weight of our influence in the scales where it would count. It tangled our relations with the very nations whom we should have been morally supporting. It stirred the resentment of other nations with whom we had no quarrels. It confused the minds of our own people as to the real reasons that led us into the First World War. It showed the prospective aggressors in Europe and Asia that our public opinion was pulling a cloak over its head and becoming nationally unconcerned with their designs and that therefore they could proceed with fuller confidence." He also wrote that "the Nye Committee hearings furnished the isolationist springboard for the first Neutrality Act of our present epoch." Senator Connally in his memoirs described the Nye committee as "probably the most effective medium for channeling American public opinion into isolationism during this period." Connally wrote that the munitions investigation "had accomplished what Nye wanted. Momentarily he had been in the limelight and he had promoted the cause of isolationism."[52]

After it was all over, Senator Arthur Vandenberg wrote in his diary that he was "proud to be a member of the Munitions Committee." In his farewell address to the Senate a decade after the investigation began, Senator Gerald P. Nye said he was "more proud of having been connected with the work of the Munitions Investigating Committee than of any other service in my 20-year career as a United States Senator."[53] Nye, Vandenberg, and their colleagues on the committee failed to secure enactment of any of the committee's bills for regulating the shipbuilding industry, for taxing the profits out of war, and for government ownership of munitions industries. But the committee, its hearings and reports, the speeches and legislative activities of its members, and the press coverage dramatically publicized its isolationist and noninterventionist analyses. The investigation appealed to and helped arouse pacifist and isolationist sentiment in the United States. Individual members of the Nye committee played prominent roles in adoption of the neutrality legislation in the 1930s. The attitudes, interests, and strength that the Senate Munitions Investigating Committee represented were more formidable than President Roosevelt was prepared to challenge head-on during his first term in the White House.

Chapter 12

Neutrality Legislation

The Neutrality Acts of 1935, 1936, and 1937 tried to combat economic, political, and psychological influences that many believed had drawn the United States into World War I two decades earlier. The same general atmosphere that gave rise to the munitions investigation also led to adoption of the neutrality laws. Senators Gerald P. Nye of North Dakota, Bennett Champ Clark of Missouri, Arthur H. Vandenberg of Michigan, and Homer T. Bone of Washington from the Munitions Investigating Committee, along with Stephen Raushenbush and others from the committee staff, provided essential initiatives to accomplish the legislation. And the laws reflected widespread antiwar, antibusiness, anti-Europe, and antiinterventionist sentiments in the United States.

Most political leaders in the 1930s said they favored neutrality legislation, but they differed widely on the kinds of legislation they wanted. Internationalists led by President Roosevelt and Secretary Hull wanted to guard peace and security through discretionary authority to discriminate against aggressor states in support of victims of aggression. Traditionalists led by Hiram W. Johnson, William E. Borah, Edwin M. Borchard, and John Bassett Moore wanted to preserve conventional neutral rights, including the right to trade with belligerents in noncontraband goods. More extreme isolationists led by Senators Nye and Clark wanted mandatory legislation to restrict both the president and urban economic groups in the interests of peace. They thought the discretionary authority sought by internationalists could put the United States on one side in a war and bring the country into that war. They did not think neutral rights were worth defending if that defense put the United States in a war. In the interests of noninvolvement they wanted to abandon neutral rights on the high seas and bind the president to treat all belligerents alike.

The Neutrality Acts were not so binding on the president nor so sweeping in their economic restrictions as the more extreme isolationists wanted. By 1937, however, the legislation included an arms embargo, a loan ban, a ban on travel by Americans on belligerent ships, a National Munitions Control Board, and cash-and-carry. It limited the president's discretionary powers far more than internationalists would have preferred. The laws restricted American freedom of action on the high seas more than nationalists such as Borah and Johnson wanted. The neutrality laws were compromises between various conflicting approaches.

Ironically, early initiatives for revamping America's traditional concepts of neutral rights came from internationalists and from the Hoover-Stimson and Roosevelt-Hull administrations. Within limits set by his temperament and by the times at home and abroad, Roosevelt identified with and provided leadership for moderate internationalist perspectives on the issue. But his performance was more low key, more cautious, and less bold than internationalists would have preferred.[1]

The actual legislation did not coincide so clearly with the perspectives of either the isolationists or the administration as it did with those of Key Pittman, the tall, lean, alcoholic Democratic senator from America's least populous state of Nevada. Neither an isolationist nor an internationalist, Pittman's nationalism, his political shrewdness, and his position as chairman of the Foreign Relations Committee from 1933 to 1940, enabled him to play a more central role in shaping the legislation than either the president of the United States or the chairman of the Munitions Investigating Committee. To a remarkable degree Pittman personified the struggle between isolationism and internationalism, and the controversy over congressional versus presidential control of neutrality policies. Though critical of isolationists, Pittman's position and advice reinforced caution and restraint in the president's dealings with foreign policy opponents in Congress.[2]

Internationalist critics point to the fact of American involvement in World War II to demonstrate the ineffectiveness and futility of the neutrality laws. But under Roosevelt's leadership (with the support of the majority of the American people) Congress had repealed virtually all the restrictions in the neutrality legislation *before* the Japanese attack on Pearl Harbor officially brought the United States into the war. Axis aggression abroad and interventionist influences at home defeated the almost desperate efforts by isolationists to prevent erosion of the neutrality laws. One may debate whether or not neutrality laws could or could not have kept the United States out of World War II without damaging vital interests and national security. But in reality the neutrality laws themselves were unable to survive the impact of developments abroad and at home before the United States declared war on the Axis states. From 1934 to 1937, President Roosevelt played significant roles in the enactment of those laws; from 1939 through 1941, he played even larger leadership in the repeal of that legislation.

As part of its disarmament initiative in May, 1933, the Roosevelt administration was prepared under certain circumstances to forgo exercise of traditional neutral rights, and to that end it urged adoption of discretionary arms embargo legislation. The Foreign Relations Committee under Senator Pittman blocked that move, however, when it approved the Johnson amendment that would have required that the embargo apply to all belligerents alike.

The Council on Foreign Relations arranged a high-level meeting in New York on January 10, 1934, to discuss American neutrality policies. Former Secretary of State Henry L. Stimson presided; Charles Warren, who was assistant attorney general during World War I, led off with a formal presentation; and Allen W. Dulles served as secretary for the meeting. The small, prestigious group included businessmen, financiers, government officials (past, present, and future), legislators, and journalists—most of them from the Northeast. There were sufficient diversity and privacy to encourage thoughtful and fruitful discussion. Stimson and Norman Davis wanted emphasis on America's role in preserving peace, while Warren and Borchard (from different perspectives) emphasized preserving neutrality. Copies of the report of that meeting circulated to all participants, as well as to Secretary Hull. Warren's remarks were published in the April issue of the council's journal *Foreign Affairs* and received distribution and study at the highest levels. Davis, Warren, Borchard, and others forwarded memoranda to Roosevelt, Hull, and State Department officials. The Council on Foreign Relations conducted a second discussion dinner meeting on April 16, but it added little new.[3]

In April, 1934, the secretary of state asked Undersecretary William Phillips, Assistant Secretary R. Walton Moore, Legal Adviser Green H. Hackworth, and J. Pierrepont Moffat of the Western European Division to study and make recommendations on neutrality policies. That group of four in the State Department felt no great urgency and believed Congress would not act on the matter that session. Phillips persuaded Warren to prepare a detailed study of neutrality, which he presented in the form of a 198-page memorandum early in August. That document (and a briefer resumé of it) went to the president and Hull, and it served as a starting point for the departmental group's deliberations.[4]

In a memorandum to Hull on September 25, 1934, President Roosevelt wrote: "This matter of neutral rights is of such importance that I wish you and Phillips and Judge Moore would discuss the whole subject and let me know if you think I should recommend legislation to the coming session of Congress." The departmental group set to work in earnest. By mid-November it had prepared draft legislation and was seeking reactions and suggestions from Davis, Warren, Walter Lippmann, Bernard Baruch, and others, as well as from the Justice, War, and Navy Departments.[5]

Throughout those deliberations the issues revolved around the relative weight that neutrality legislation should give to preserving peace on the one hand and to keeping the United States out of foreign wars on the other. Intimately related was the question of whether the legislation should give the president discretionary authority to discriminate between aggressors and victims of aggression, or whether it should be mandatory in binding the president to treat all belligerents alike in the effort to avoid involvement. The navy disliked the draft legislation and saw no point in neutrality legislation at all. The army also criticized the State Department draft. Walter Lippmann thought the draft legislation was too permissive to win public approval and that rejection by Congress could have damaging consequences. Norman Davis believed the United States was "more apt to keep out of war by collaborating to a reasonable extent in collective efforts to preserve peace and curb the activities of nations that want to run amuck and disregard international treaties." He thought "it a mistake to base a problem of neutrality to such a large extent upon arms and munitions." He feared that denial of discretionary authority to the president would "be construed as a repudiation of the spirit, if not the letter" of the statement he had made in Geneva in May, 1933, "with the approval of, and on behalf of, the President."[6]

Divided and changing sentiments within the State Department and the administration (to say nothing of Congress and the public) led Assistant Secretary Moore to advise Hull in February, 1935, that it would be best for the president to defer recommending any neutrality legislation.[7] Until February, 1935, formal deliberations on the issue had been conducted quietly within the State Department, the administration, and elite circles in the Northeast. Neither President Roosevelt nor the Nye munitions committee was prominently involved to that point. That changed.

The Nye munitions investigation within the United States and the looming Italian-Ethiopian war abroad finally forced action on neutrality legislation. In 1935, Adolf Hitler repudiated the Versailles treaty, and Nazi Germany rearmed in violation of that treaty. Benito Mussolini revealed Italy's aggressive goals in Africa that made an Italian-Ethiopian war likely and a general European war disturbingly possible. Confronted with those international crises, the League of Nations floundered ineffectively. The United States had never joined the league; Japan and Germany withdrew from it; most distrusted the collective security proposals of the Soviet Union after it gained membership; and divisiveness and indecision characterized the performances of Great Britain, France, and smaller countries in the league.

The Senate Investigation of the Munitions Industry under Senator Nye was not explicitly authorized to deal with neutrality legislation. But it was directed to "investigate and report upon the adequacy or inadequacy of existing legislation, and of the treaties to which the United States is a party, for the regulation and control of the manufacture of and traffic in arms, munitions, or other implements of war within the United States, and of the traffic therein between the United States and other countries."[8]

In April 1934, Secretary Hull had urged Senator Pittman to press for favorable action by the Foreign Relations Committee and by the Senate on the Convention for the Supervision of the International Trade in Arms and Ammunition signed in Geneva in 1925. Later in 1934, the State Department proposed to the Geneva Disarmament Conference a more stringent convention for supervising and controlling the arms traffic. Senator Nye had mixed feelings on the relative merits of international agreements versus national legislation for control of the arms traffic. On January 15, 1935, he told the Senate: "We should hope for, we should anticipate, ultimate international agreement. It will simplify matters very, very much indeed. Surely, however, we can proceed in a domestic way in very large measure to straighten out and bring into the line of fair play and decency our own munitions makers." On February 20, Nye asked Joseph C. Green of the Department of State to prepare a memorandum for the munitions committee on legislation that might precede or supplement a treaty to control munitions manufacture and traffic. Secretary Hull gave Green permission to draft the memorandum and legislation that Nye had requested.[9]

Ironically, a suggestion by President Roosevelt triggered the Nye committee's decision to plunge headlong into the whole matter of neutrality legislation. In a memorandum on February 23, the president asked Hull to speak with him "about the advisability of a message on war profits and kindred subjects." Hull responded with a detailed memorandum. He advised the president not to send a message to Congress on the international arms traffic, contending that such a message "would not serve any useful purpose and might result in a head-on collision with the Nye Committee." With the Nye committee planning to submit a preliminary report on April 1, Hull feared that a presidential message "could easily be misconstrued as an attempt to take the wind out of the sails of that Committee." Hull did advise the president, however, to encourage approval of the legislation on registration and licensing of munitions makers and traders that Green had drafted at the committee's request and with Hull's approval. Hull also encouraged Roosevelt to meet with the Nye committee at the White House. He thought such a meeting could serve several useful purposes, including demonstrating "that the Administration is to some degree cooperating with the Committee."[10]

The president did invite the Nye committee for a White House meeting with him on March 19, 1935. The president was in great form, and everything went swimmingly—*except* that Roosevelt strayed far from the paths that Hull had recommended. The discussion centered on methods for taking profits out of war and on American neutrality legislation. Senators Nye and Pope reported that Roosevelt had said "he had come around entirely to the ideas of Mr. Bryan" on neutrality policy and "was preparing to propose legislation which would prohibit American ships or citizens from visiting belligerent countries in time of war." While encouraging the committee to study neutrality policies and formulate appropriate legislation, the president asked that it consult him before introducing bills on the subject. A few days later Stephen Raushenbush told Green "that the President had pushed the Committee into the study of this subject of neutrality which, up to the time of their conference with him, they had not considered in connection with their program of proposed legislation." As a result the Nye committee was "hot on the trail" of the neutrality matter. Green advised delay until it had been "threshed out more thoroughly" with the president, but Raushenbush doubted whether the committee . would be willing to wait.[11]

In a major address in Lexington, Kentucky, on March 30, 1935, Senator Nye warned that German rearmament made it necessary for the United States "at once to consider and write law such as would largely guarantee our neutrality in the event of European hostilities." He told his audience that President Roosevelt had "voiced a determination to keep America out of another war at all costs" and had urged his committee to study the neutrality question. Nye recommended a loan ban, withholding passports of Americans planning to travel in war zones, and an arms embargo applying to all belligerents. In a letter to Professor Borchard on April 1, Senator Borah took a more clearly isolationist position than he had in 1932 and 1933. He feared that neutrality legislation would permit "too much delegation of power and too much discussion as to use." He asked Borchard if it would be possible to draft a law "not depending for its effect upon somebody's discretion." He wanted a "permanent law" that "could deal with the actions of belligerents in our territory and around our borders, the actions of foreigners, also the questions of loan and to some extent possibly of trade." Senator Johnson sought the views of John Bassett Moore on neutrality legislation. He worried that "those internationalists who love every country but their own" would try to formulate "neutrality policies and treaties for the introduction of lopsided embargoes and nebulous definitions of 'aggressor.' "[12]

Encouraged by its conference with Roosevelt, the Nye committee planned that its preliminary report on April 1, 1935, would contain a general statement indicating that it was approaching agreement on possible neutrality legislation. Senators Pittman and Borah complained, however, that neutrality legislation belonged in the hands of the Foreign Relations Committee rather than with Nye's committee. Consequently the munitions committee toned down its reference to neutrality legislation. The preliminary report indicated that the committee was "in substantial agreement on a principle to govern the export of munitions and contraband in case of a major war" and expected to recommend Senate action on that matter. But it emphasized that that was "the only phase of the neutrality problem which the committee considers to be within its jurisdiction."[13]

Because Pittman's committee firmly claimed jurisdiction, the munitions committee decided not to sponsor neutrality legislation of its own. The joint resolutions on neutrality policies cosponsored by

Nye and Clark technically were introduced by the individual senators —not on behalf of the munitions committee—and were referred to the Foreign Relations Committee for consideration. But the vital role of Nye's committee in the enactment of neutrality laws should not be obscured by the parliamentary tactics. The munitions hearings helped stimulate public interest in the general subject. The committee's staff did much of the work and planning behind the scenes. Nye and his colleagues on the munitions committee helped force legislative action on neutrality policies. Given the prevailing public attitudes and political patterns, President Roosevelt and Secretary Hull would have preferred no neutrality legislation except for the registration and licensing of munitions makers and shippers. Without the Nye committee, Congress probably would not have adopted neutrality legislation. And if it had acted, the neutrality laws probably would have been significantly different from what they were.

Senators Nye and Clark cosponsored four resolutions on American neutrality policies in 1935. Nye introduced two of them on April 9. The first (S.J.Res. 99) would have required the president to withhold passports from American citizens traveling in war zones or on belligerent ships. Nye and Clark hoped it would avoid the loss of American lives that had resulted from incidents such as the sinking of the British *Lusitania* in World War I. The second (S.J. Res. 100) would have prohibited private American loans and credits to all belligerents at the outbreak of war. It reflected the theory that the United States had entered World War I partly because of its financial involvement on the side of the Allies. On May 7, Senator Clark introduced Senate Joint Resolution 120, which would have prohibited American export of arms and ammunition to all belligerents at the outbreak of war. That proposed arms embargo was consistent with the theory that profits and prosperity from the sale of munitions to belligerents had helped involve the United States in World War I. That resolution also would have required exporters of nonembargoed contraband to ship their goods at their own risk or at the risk of the belligerent to which they were sent. The resolutions were mandatory, and their application was not to be left to the president's discretion. They would have applied to all belligerents—not just to aggressors. The fourth resolution (S. 2998) had been drafted by Green and was introduced on June 5, by Senator Pope for himself, Nye, Clark, Bone, and George. It provided for the establishment of a National Munitions Control Board under the secretary of state to register and license munitions makers and shippers.[14]

The day after Nye and Clark introduced their passport and loan ban resolutions, Pittman forwarded them to Hull for his recommendations. The following day, April 11, Hull provided Roosevelt with a nine-page memorandum on cooperation with the Nye committee. The first of the four sections in that detailed document focused on neutrality. It advised the president not to support "any specific legislation in respect to neutrality at this time." Both the president's advisers and the general public were divided on the subject. Senate leaders opposed "the raising of any question of foreign policy which would result in delaying action on necessary domestic legislation." The memorandum contended "that in view of the present situation in Europe, discussion of this question at this time would tend to arouse unjustifiable fears of imminent war." Hull was "not prepared to advocate" any specific neutrality legislation at that time. The president agreed to indicate that he did not wish to propose neutrality legislation that session. McReynolds promised that his House Foreign Affairs Committee would not report neutrality resolutions if the Senate committee followed the same course. Senator Pittman agreed to take no action on the matter. All seemed secure.[15]

At the same time, the Department of State repeatedly prodded the president, the Nye committee, and the Foreign Relations Committee for action on registration and licensing of munitions makers and shippers—the bill that Green had drafted for the Nye committee. The third part of the State Department memorandum of April 11 urged Roosevelt to support that legislation. It won approval from President Roosevelt and from the Departments of War, Navy, Commerce, Treasury, and State. The Foreign Relations Committee reported it out favorably on June 20. It appeared as though all might fall into place as the administration wished.[16]

But it seems that Nye and Clark never got the word, and the message apparently did not filter through to Pittman's committee clearly enough. On June 26, Senator Nye spoke on behalf of Senate Joint Resolutions 99 (passports) and 100 (loans and credits) at a meeting of the Foreign Relations Committee. Contrary to the wishes of Roosevelt, Hull, and top State Department officials, the committee reported both resolutions out favorably. Pressed for time, it delayed consideration of Senate Joint Resolution 120 (arms embargo) until July 10.[17]

Pleased and encouraged by that initial success, Nye directed his committee staff under Raushenbush to prepare a memorandum on the resolutions. That thirteen-page mimeographed document over the names of Nye and Clark went to Pittman and the other members of the Foreign Relations Committee a week before Senate Joint Resolution 120 was scheduled for consideration. The memorandum said that the three resolutions formed "a unified program designed to avoid the entangling economic alliances created by the growth of a vast trade in munitions, by the granting of huge loans and credits which link our financial and economic interests with one group of warring nations and by the activities of private citizens who involve the nation in their pursuit of war profits." It emphasized the importance of mandatory provisions to help the president resist the "tremendous pressure" that would accompany the drive for "profitable trade in war materials after war has broken out." While the bans on munitions and loans to belligerents were mandatory and absolute, warring countries could purchase "cotton or wheat or machinery" and "make their own arrangements about securing their safe shipment."[18]

At the same time, the Roosevelt administration brought heavy (and decisive) pressure upon Pittman and his committee to block the Nye-Clark neutrality resolutions. Norman H. Davis, acting for the State Department, spent several hours with Pittman on June 27, to persuade him to "stifle" the resolutions. Roosevelt met with Pittman on June 29, and Hull also talked to the senator to seek his cooperation. The secretary of state and Assistant Secretary Moore both testified at the Foreign Relations Committee meeting on July 10, opposing the neutrality resolutions under consideration. The Nye-Clark forces suffered a "complete rout." The committee not only refused to vote out Senate Joint Resolution 120, but it also recalled Senate Joint Resolutions 99 and 100 for further consideration. On July 17, it appointed a subcommittee composed of Pittman, Borah, Johnson, Robinson, and Connally to consider neutrality proposals. Borah and Johnson opposed internationalist approaches, but they did not share the determination of Nye and Clark to restrict drastically American shipping and commerce in the interests of peace.[19]

Nye and his colleagues were shaken and discouraged by their reverse. Raushenbush wrote that "now it looks like a real scrap and that is something we have not had yet. At least the people of the country will be made conscious that an endeavor is being made to keep them out of war, which they don't seem to realize at the moment." Nye and Clark prepared to fight. They gained active support from Senators Bone, La Follette, Norris, and others. Senator Nye arranged to delay Senate action on the munitions control resolution (S. 2998) so that neutrality amendments might be attached to it if the Foreign

Relations Committee failed to report out a bill before Congress adjourned.[20]

As an alternative to the Nye-Clark resolutions, the State Department produced the discretionary neutrality resolution it had drafted and submitted it on July 31. The subcommittee rejected the State Department resolution on August 7, and there was a mad scramble to prepare a compromise measure that might win committee approval. The subcommittee was much too divided to be able to agree on any draft legislation when it reported back to the full Foreign Relations Committee on August 14. The next day Assistant Secretary Moore took a State Department draft for a discretionary arms embargo to the White House. Roosevelt approved it, but in response to Moore's query the president told him to accept a mandatory embargo if Pittman insisted. Moore then took the discretionary draft to Pittman, who refused it, saying that his committee overwhelmingly favored mandatory provisions. The senator rephrased the resolution to make it mandatory. Moore rechecked with the White House and received word that Roosevelt had changed his mind; he had decided to drop the matter rather than settle for a mandatory arms embargo. On August 17, however, Congressman McReynolds reported to Moore that Pittman did not object to introduction of the State Department bill.[21]

The alarming Italian-Ethiopian crisis abroad, divided sentiments in the Foreign Relations Committee and in the State Department, differences among isolationists between the Nye-Clark and the Borchard-Johnson positions, the determination of the Nye-Clark group to win action on mandatory neutrality legislation, the eagerness of Hull and Green to win approval for the munitions control bill, the earnest efforts by Davis and other internationalists to obtain discretionary powers for the president, the preoccupation of Congress and the public with the depression and domestic matters, Pittman's foot-dragging (and drinking), the indecisiveness and caution of Roosevelt's leadership on the issue, and the weariness of Congress and its eagerness to adjourn—all combined into a confusing political mess that seemed unlikely to produce anything—at least anything that anyone could be entirely happy about. In that situation Roosevelt, Hull, and Pittman would have preferred to have neutrality resolutions introduced for the record to appease public sentiment and to have Congress then adjourn without taking action. But Nye, Clark, and their isolationist colleagues were determined not to permit that.

The whole controversy in 1935 climaxed in the week beginning on Monday, August 19. In a letter to Pittman released to the press on that day, Senators Nye and Clark insisted that if "Congress imposes no restrictions on munitions sales and shipments before a war breaks out in Europe, it will be impossible for Congress to form a policy later without incurring representations that such a new policy involves the taking of sides against one particular belligerent."[22]

On that same day Hull handed Roosevelt a letter urging him to "make a vigorous effort" to secure legislation that would give the president discretionary authority to embargo shipment of arms and munitions to Italy and Ethiopia. The White House immediately consulted Pittman by telephone about Hull's proposal and found the senator vehemently opposed. He agreed to introduce the resolution as an administration measure if Roosevelt were determined to proceed. He contended, however, that both the Foreign Relations Committee and the full Senate would reject it and that that "would do great harm to our foreign policy." In a personal note to the president's secretary, Stephen Early, Pittman said he had been "trying to harmonize things and get away from that fool Munitions Committee," but he warned that "the President is riding for a fall" if he determined "on designating the aggressor in accordance with the wishes of the League of Nations." Pittman insisted that the president would "be licked as sure as hell." Confronted with that ominous evaluation from the chairman of the Senate Foreign Relations Committee, the president yielded.[23]

Instead, after prolonged and heated discussion at its meeting on August 19, the Foreign Relations Committee agreed to report out a compromise neutrality resolution (S. J. Res. 173) including a mandatory arms embargo. Senator Pittman was to draft the resolution in accord with specifications approved by his committee and report it to the Senate the next day. In the rush to complete action on domestic legislation and adjourn later that week, the months of detailed deliberation in the Department of State and the work by the Nye committee were largely set aside. The final bill was to be drafted in a few hours by the Nevada Democrat. The tensions and strain of it all turned Pittman to the bottle even more than was his custom; the resolution was certain to fall short of the desires of all concerned—with the possible exception of Pittman. The enormity of it all was tempered by the fact that neither Pittman, his committee, the State Department, nor the president really expected or wanted Congress to pass Senate Joint Resolution 173 before it adjourned. It was designed largely to appease public opinion.[24]

Senators Nye, Bone, Clark, Vandenberg, and other isolationists, however, had absolutely no intention of permitting Congress to adjourn without voting on neutrality—and they had the voices to back their determination. At three o'clock on Tuesday afternoon, August 20, Bone and Nye, with other senators in reserve, began a filibuster to force consideration of the neutrality resolution. "We hold the whiphand," Nye boasted, "and we intend using it to the limit." Nye promised that until it voted on neutrality, "nothing will happen in the Senate." And he was not bluffing. Consequently they won unanimous consent to have the chairman of the Foreign Relations Committee present the neutrality resolution for Senate action the next day before proceeding with pending legislative matters. The filibuster accomplished its purpose.[25]

On Wednesday morning, August 21, Senator Pittman rose to present his bill as a substitute for the several neutrality resolutions that had been referred to his committee. The Senate gave unanimous consent to his motion to lay aside consideration of the Guffey coal bill long enough for quick action on neutrality. The Senate then promptly passed Senate Joint Resolution 173 without debate, without objection, and without record vote. There was no discussion of the specific provisions of Pittman's resolution; most of the senators had not read it and had no real knowledge of its detailed provisions and language.[26]

The Senate neutrality resolution then went to a House of Representatives that was equally eager to adjourn. Republicans Hamilton Fish of New York and George Tinkham of Massachusetts represented the isolationist views on the House Foreign Affairs Committee. And on Wednesday morning, August 21, the very day the Senate approved Senate Joint Resolution 173, the president received a delegation of nine representatives headed by Democrats Fred J. Sisson of New York, Frank Kloeb of Ohio, and Maury Maverick of Texas, who urged approval of the mandatory Senate resolution. During their White House discussion Roosevelt defended discretionary authority.[27]

The chairman of the House Foreign Affairs Committee, Democrat Sam D. McReynolds of Tennessee, was not an isolationist. He was miffed at times by the priority the White House gave to working through Pittman and his Senate committee. And the House committee had its own political divisions and difficulties. But McReynolds was fully prepared to cooperate with the Roosevelt administration. With strong presidential support McReynolds probably could and would have guided his Foreign Affairs Committee and the House of Representatives either to block the mandatory Senate resolution or to pass discretionary legislation. Given McReynolds's cooperative tone, the president's leadership became controlling for action in the House. But Roosevelt's capacity to lead was affected by Pittman's evaluation of political realities in the Foreign Relations Committee and in the Senate. Over it all was the priority that Roosevelt (and most others) gave to the depression and New Deal. And finally there was the eagerness of Congress to adjourn.

On Wednesday evening, August 21, the president met at the White House with Secretary Hull, Assistant Secretary Moore, and Congressman McReynolds to decide their course and tactics. Rather than block the mandatory Senate resolution or press for discretionary legislation in those closing days of the session, Roosevelt decided to have the House amend the resolution so the embargo would expire in six months, on March 1, 1936. The four of them also agreed to certain changes in language to strengthen the remnants of Green's munitions control resolution included in Pittman's resolution.[28]

That day's developments dismayed Secretary Hull and his colleagues in the State Department. Green wrote to Davis the next day that he had "never seen the Secretary so dejected as he is today." Green wrote: "Considerations of domestic politics must apparently take precedence over more important considerations." In a personal note to former Secretary of State Stimson, Cordell Hull berated "the blind and extreme nationalistic sentiment which renders it exceedingly difficult for our government to function in a constructive, sane and practical way at all to the extent desirable."[29]

On Thursday, August 22, the House Foreign Affairs Committee under McReynolds took up consideration of the Senate resolution. The committee split three ways: Tinkham led an isolationist group urging adoption of the Senate resolution unchanged; McReynolds and his followers pressed for the compromise that Roosevelt had approved the night before; and Democrat Luther Johnson of Texas led a group that wanted to fight for the discretionary provisions that the State Department (and Roosevelt) really wanted. The House committee named a subcommittee under Johnson to amend the Senate resolution in accord with the compromise Roosevelt had endorsed, including the mandatory arms embargo, munitions control provisions, and the six-month limit. The subcommittee quickly accomplished its task.[30]

At that juncture Roosevelt telephoned McReynolds to report that he and Pittman had discussed the matter at length over lunch at the White House and that he was sending Pittman to McReynolds with definite instructions on what the president wanted. When Pittman met with the subcommittee later that afternoon, he insisted that no changes be made in the Senate resolution except for ending the embargo on February 29. In a long session Pittman's persistence wore down the subcommittee members. They acquiesced, winning only minor changes in the munitions control provisions. In that form the Foreign Affairs Committee reported the resolution to the full House which adopted it quickly, unanimously, and without record vote on Friday, August 23.[31]

The changes in the House then required Senate approval. Gerald P. Nye told the Senate that if Congress were not so eager to adjourn and "if world conditions were other than they are," he would object to the House amendment. Under the circumstances, however, he urged approval, believing it "the most important bit of legislation with which this session of Congress has dealt." He promised that when Congress convened in January, there would be "a large army in both the Senate and the House of Representatives striving with all their might" to make the legislation permanent and to add provisions covering contraband, loans, and credits. Hiram Johnson told the Senate that the neutrality resolution would not do much harm or good. He believed the United States was not going to get into any war between Italy and Ethiopia, or into any other foreign war in the immediate future—with or without the resolution. Johnson thought the resolution was useful largely as a statement of "the policy of the United States of America to keep out of European controversies, European wars, and European difficulties." As a policy statement he saw adoption of the resolution as "the triumph of so-called 'isolationists.'" But he warned against "the delusion that war is going to be prevented or that the millennium has come because of it." He considered it "a makeshift, at best." In diverse and even conflicting ways most others in the Senate (and in the State Department and the White House) were also dissatisfied with the 1935 neutrality resolution and determined to make changes the next year. In that spirit, on Saturday, August 24, the Senate quickly approved Pittman's motion to concur in the House amendments to Senate Joint Resolution 173. The vote was seventy-nine yeas, two nays (Democrats John Bankhead of Alabama and Peter Gerry of Rhode Island), and fifteen not voting. The yeas included most of the isolationists, but most internationalists as well.[32]

Democratic Senator Tom Connally of Texas and others hoped the president would veto the bill. But on Wednesday, August 28, Roosevelt told newsmen that the neutrality resolution was "entirely satisfactory, except that it does not include any power over loans for financing.'' He said that the embargo ''against two belligerents meets the needs of the existing situation [that is, between Italy and Ethiopia]. What more can one ask? And, by the time the situation changes, Congress will be back with us, so we are all right.'' In a personal letter that same day Roosevelt wrote: ''The Senate Resolution has been much modified and an actual reading of it shows that it takes away little Executive authority except the embargo on certain types of arms and munitions (the type to be determined by me) between now and next February. Discretion must, of course, remain in the Executive in the long run.''[33]

On August 24, the White House had written Secretary Hull to determine whether he objected to Senate Joint Resolution 173 in its final form. With the help of Moore and Green, Hull composed a reply describing, explaining, and evaluating the neutrality resolution. Since Roosevelt had publicly called it ''entirely satisfactory'' except for the lack of a loan ban, they did not feel free to make their objections so strong as they might have preferred. In his response to the president on August 29, however, Hull wrote that he considered the mandatory arms embargo ''an invasion of the constitutional and traditional power of the Executive to conduct the foreign relations of the United States'' and that its inflexible provisions ''would tend to deprive this Government of a great measure of its influence in promoting and preserving peace.'' He regretted the ''random'' excerpting from S. 2998. But Hull concluded, *''In spite of my very strong and, I believe, well founded objections to this Joint Resolution, I do not feel that I can properly in all the circumstances recommend that you withhold your approval.''* He expressed hope that ''satisfactory legislation to replace these two sections can be enacted at the next session of Congress.''[34]

When the president signed the neutrality resolution into law on August 31, 1935, he issued a statement drafted for him by the State Department. But he added stronger language of his own, warning that ''the inflexible provisions might drag us into war instead of keeping us out. The policy of the government is definitely committed to the maintenance of peace and the avoidance of any entanglements which would lead us into conflict. At the same time it is the policy of the Government by every peaceful means and without entanglement to cooperate with other similarly minded governments to promote peace.''[35]

The Neutrality Act of 1935 was a scissors-and-paste combination of the Nye-Clark resolutions, the State Department's proposals,

Green's munitions control resolution, and innovations by Pittman. It was more mandatory than the administration wanted, but it was less sweeping and more discretionary than Senate isolationists wanted. It included the mandatory arms embargo specified in the Nye-Clark resolution, parts of Green's munitions control resolution, and restrictions on American travel on belligerent ships comparable to those sought by Nye and Clark. Unlike Senate Joint Resolution 120, it did not deal with the export of nonmunitions contraband. It did not include the ban on loans and credits that would have been provided by Senate Joint Resolution 100. The omission of those financial restrictions was partly covered, however, by the Johnson Act of 1934. Although the Neutrality Act of 1935 did not permit the president to discriminate against aggressors in the application of the arms embargo, it did give him authority to determine when key provisions of the act should become operative. For example, he was to invoke the arms embargo when a foreign war began "or during the progress of war." He could also determine what specific munitions would be embargoed, whether and when the embargo should be extended to states that later became involved, and whether and when the restrictions on travel on belligerent ships would be invoked.[36]

Neither isolationists nor internationalists, neither the administration nor legislators were satisfied with the new law. But most could identify reasons to be resigned to it until Congress could enact more satisfactory legislation the next year. D. G. Osborne of the British Embassy in Washington analyzed the patterns in his report to the Foreign Office in London: "The debate is chiefly important for Senator Robinson's solemn warning to Europe that the United States will not contribute to the adjustment of European controversies other than by peaceful means and will not be used or drawn to the support of causes, or to the settlement of controversies, which do not involve American interests, rights or welfare. . . . Senator Robinson did not exclude American contribution to the adjustment of European controversies 'by peaceful suggestion or action.' I am not sure that Senator Borah and the isolationist majority throughout the country would approve even this degree of interest or intervention in European affairs. . . . But the latitude allowed by Senator Robinson for peaceful contribution to the maintenance of peace certainly corresponds to the wishes of the President and the State Department, who endeavoured, although in vain, to secure congressional agreement to the award to the President of discretionary powers for the imposition of the embargo. . . . However, as always here, presidential and Administration policy is inevitably conditioned by the exigencies of domestic politics. Next year Mr. Roosevelt must present himself for re-election, and he must be more than ever cautious in the conduct of his foreign policy not to offend the electorate to play into the hands of his adversaries."[37]

The growing tensions between Benito Mussolini's Fascist Italy and Emperor Haile Selassie's Ethiopia in East Africa loomed as an increasingly ominous war cloud over American deliberations on neutrality legislation during 1935. The eruption of the undeclared Italian-Ethiopian war early in October provided the occasion for testing the Neutrality Act of 1935 in a real-life situation. The particular circumstances made it possible for both the Roosevelt administration and the isolationists to be reasonably pleased with the application of the law in that unequal contest. Italy had both the financial resources and shipping facilities for obtaining munitions from abroad; Ethiopia did not. Consequently, the practical effect of invoking the embargo was to close Italy's access to munitions produced in the United States, while depriving Ethiopia of nothing it might have obtained without the embargo. Technically, it applied to both belligerents alike, but in reality the law worked to the disadvantage of Italy. While acting in accord with the letter of the law just as the isolationists wished, the Roosevelt administration consciously pursued a course consistent with collective security. The administration professed devotion to noninvolvement and at the same time independently reinforced League of Nation actions against Italy. Under the Neutrality Act of 1935 the administration was able to function in accord with the policies outlined by Norman Davis in Geneva two and one-half years earlier.[38]

After Congress had adjourned, Roosevelt had left on a vacation cruise in the Pacific aboard the U.S.S. *Houston*. Before he sailed, the president signed undated proclamations to invoke the provisions of the Neutrality Act in the likely event that war erupted between Italy and Abyssinia while he was away. The outbreak of fighting in Africa, on October 3, provided the occasion for intense deliberations at top levels in the State Department, punctuated by frequent communications with the president aboard his ship, and with American diplomats in Europe. All agreed on issuing the proclamations; differences concerned their timing relative to League of Nations action in the crisis. After exhaustive deliberations, the president ordered release of his proclamation on October 4, in advance of an independent of league actions. That timing was calculated to head off any possible charges from isolationists that the United States was acting in cooperation with or following the lead of the league. The president's proclamations banned sale of munitions to both Italy and Ethiopia and warned Americans that any transactions with either belligerent would be at their own risk. Under the law the embargo applied only to "arms, ammunition and implements of war" and did not apply to such war goods as oil, cotton, and steel. That was a matter of regret (for different reasons) to both internationalists and isolationists. Some urged Roosevelt and Hull to define the law broadly enough to include oil, but neither the president nor his advisers believed such a broad definition could be justified under the law. They did, however, strongly discourage Americans from selling or shipping oil and other war products to the belligerents.[39]

The administration's course won approval from both isolationists and internationalists. Senator Norris of Nebraska wrote that the president's proclamation "ought to receive the approval of all peace-loving citizens." Senator Nye wired Hull his congratulations for "the spirit in which the neutrality policy laid down by congress just before adjournment is being invoked." At the same time he warned against "joining in League sanctions." While isolationists applauded, so did internationalists. Norman Davis believed "that under the circumstances we have acted as wisely as was possible." In a letter drafted for him by the State Department, Roosevelt summed up the administration's position: "The policy which we have adopted has been based upon the Neutrality Act of August 31 and the measures which we have taken have been taken independently and on our own initiative. At the same time we view [in Hull's words] 'with sympathetic interest the individual or concerted efforts of other nations to preserve peace or to localize or shorten the duration of war.'"[40]

When the Italian ambassador called on Secretary of State Hull on November 22, complaining of the unneutrality of America's application of the Neutrality Act, Hull responded in terms that could have pleased almost any isolationist. As he recorded it afterward, Hull told the Italian ambassador that "the people of this country are in no state of mind to engage in any activities or steps except those primarily looking towards keeping out of the war and in a secondary or subordinate sense manifesting proper interest in peace and the shortening of the duration of the war in the light of our obligations under the Kellogg Pact." He reminded the ambassador that the United States had "pursued its own separate, independent course and initiative with respect to all phases of the controversy between Ethiopia and Italy" and that it "had no agreement whatsoever, directly or indirectly, with Geneva or London or Paris." Hull pointed out that even "the bitterest critics of the Executive branch of the Government and the most extreme isolationists who are demanding that all Americans stay entirely away from the war zone do not in the slightest question the integrity of the neutrality policies of this Government as they are being carried out in accordance with the letter or the spirit, or both, of the Neutrality Act." Roosevelt congratulated Hull for his "splendid job in making our position clear" to the ambassador. Hull was correct in his analysis—but so was the ambassador.[41]

Both Roosevelt and the isolationists could find reason to be pleased with the patterns. Nye, Clark, and their colleagues had forced legislative action on the neutrality resolution. The president invoked it independently for the United States in the Italian-Ethiopian war, and the United States had not become involved in the hostilities. Roosevelt, in turn, successfully appeased the isolationists in the enactment of the neutrality legislation and in invoking it in the war in Africa. He shared isolationist satisfaction that the conflict had not spread to a general war and had not involved the United States. He had invoked the Neutrality Act so skillfully that his performance had pleased isolationists while at the same time following a course that was consistent with and did not undercut the League of Nations efforts in the crisis. His parallel but independent course did not prevent Italian conquest of Abyssinia—but neither did the efforts of the League of Nations. Roosevelt and Hull regretted that the Neutrality Act did not apply to nonmunitions war goods such as oil; leading isolationists shared that regret and would have made the legislation more sweeping in other respects as well. The experiences during the Italian-Ethiopian war of 1935–36 provided superficial appearances of an antiinterventionist consensus in the United States sufficient to allay isolationist misgivings about Roosevelt on foreign affairs through the important presidential election year of 1936. Behind that facade, however, the lines were beginning to be drawn between Roosevelt and his isolationist adversaries.

In the early winter of 1935, while the temporary neutrality law was being tested by Italian aggression in Africa, both administration and congressional leaders laid plans for renewed struggles on the issue when Congress reconvened early in 1936. In preparing revised draft legislation, State Department officials tried to find what Joseph Green called "the impossible compromise between what the Administration wants and what we can presumably get through the Senate." At a White House meeting on December 31, 1935, President Roosevelt,

Secretary Hull, Assistant Secretary Moore, Senator Pittman, Congressman McReynolds, and Congressman John O'Connor of New York decided on the main provisions of the administration neutrality proposal. In his annual message that the president delivered before a joint session of Congress on January 3, 1936, Roosevelt warned of serious threats to peace and security posed by "nations which are dominated by the twin spirits of autocracy and aggression." He told Congress that the United States was "following a two fold neutrality towards any and all nations which engage in wars that are not of immediate concern to the Americas. First, we decline to encourage the prosecution of war by permitting belligerents to obtain arms, ammunition or implements of war from the United States. Second, we seek to discourage the use by belligerent nations of any and all American products calculated to facilitate the prosecution of a war in quantities over and above our normal exports of them in time of peace." He expressed hope that those objectives would "be carried forward by cooperation between this Congress and the President." On that same day, January 3, Key Pittman introduced the administration's neutrality resolution in the Senate and Sam McReynolds introduced it in the House.[42]

At the same time, isolationist leaders also prepared for renewed efforts on neutrality legislation. Senators Nye and Clark authorized Stephen Raushenbush to draw up a revised neutrality resolution. The Munitions Committee changed the schedule for its hearings so that J. P. Morgan would testify before Congress acted on neutrality proposals. On January 6, Nye and Clark introduced their revised neutrality resolution, and Representative Maury Maverick of Texas presented an identical measure in the House. Both the Senate Foreign Relations Committee and the House Foreign Affairs Committee conducted extended closed hearings at which Secretary Hull and his top aides testified at length. Nye and Clark also appeared before the Foreign Relations Committee.[43]

By 1936 the administration believed it was politically impossible to win discretionary authority to apply the arms embargo only against aggressors, so the Pittman-McReynolds bill omitted that provision. Like the Nye-Clark resolution, the administration measure called for an embargo on the shipment of arms to all belligerents and a ban on loans and credits. The most obvious administration innovation in 1936 was a provision giving the president discretionary power to limit to normal peacetime levels the export to belligerents of nonembargoed war materials (not including food, medical supplies, and clothing). It could have limited the export of such nonmunitions commodities as oil, cotton, iron, steel, and copper that were as essential to war as munitions. Roosevelt and Hull had attempted to restrict the flow of these goods to Italy through a "moral embargo," but they believed statutory authority was needed to make it fully effective. The Nye-Clark resolution contained a comparable provision, though it would have extended to all nonmunition materials (including food, medical supplies, and clothing) and would have been mandatory (not discretionary). Despite administration concessions, the issue of mandatory versus discretionary provisions remained central in the controversy of 1936. In nearly every part of the proposed legislation, the Pittman-McReynolds bill would have given the president greater discretion than the Nye-Clark-Maverick resolution.[44]

Both the Pittman and Nye resolutions encountered heavy going in committee. Congressmen and administration leaders were cautious in that election year. Italian-Americans vigorously opposed severe restrictions on trade with their mother country. While the arms embargo and loan ban would directly restrict only urban segments of the economy, the provisions limiting export of nonmunitions war materials could affect diverse economic groups in all sections of the United States—industrialists, miners, oil producers, cotton planters, traders, and laborers.

Senator Hiram Johnson from the oil-rich, cotton-producing, state of California led the opposition in the Foreign Relations Committee. He consulted Borchard and Moore frequently for legal guidance during the controversy. The three of them objected both to the administration and to the Nye approach on neutrality legislation. Johnson boasted that he was "absolutely alone" in his opposition in the committee at first and that he was "the only one" on the Foreign Relations Committee "who had any knowledge" on the subject. Pleased with the bill as finally reported, Johnson wrote that it "came from doggedly fighting without considering the odds, and pertinaciously, day after day, hammering our views, which our opponents could not logically refute." Though "knocked out by a wretched and acute attack of rheumatism" he "hobbled over to the Senate" to do his duty. When the battle was over, Johnson modestly claimed that he was "the main instrument" in "the two set-backs the President has received in his efforts with Congress." He neglected to mention that Senator Borah shared his general views and contributed to the opposition. Borah insisted that "neutrality does not mean that the neutral must give up the sea to the exclusive use of the belligerents" and that "a neutral has a right to trade and to use the sea for trade in non-contraband goods." Borah (and Johnson) believed, "Neutrality is not synonymous with cowardice."[45]

Early in February, 1936, Senator Pittman summarized the situation concisely when he wrote that "the necessity for foreign commerce is so great and political pressure at this particular time is so strong that possibly it is advisable to avoid weeks of acrimonious debate with probably no accomplishment, and simply extend the existing law for one year." That was very nearly the course followed. The House Committee reported out the Pittman-McReynolds resolution on January 28. The Foreign Relations Committee, however, did not report either the Pittman bill or the Nye-Clark resolution. Instead, on February 12, it unanimously reported a measure that extended the main provisions of the 1935 act, with certain modifications and amendments, until May 1, 1937.[46]

The next day Senator Nye summoned a dozen senators to plan a last-ditch battle from more sweeping neutrality legislation. His group included eight Democrats, two Republicans in addition to Nye, one Progressive, and one Farmer-Laborite. Prominent in his group were Senators Clark, Bone, La Follette, Frazier, Capper, and Pope. Senators Norris and Vandenberg were absent but supported Nye's group. All but four of the fifteen represented states located west of the Mississippi River. Only one (Rush Holt, a young West Virginia Democrat) was not from the West or Middle West. They decided to seek a sixty- to ninety-day extension of the 1935 act to give Congress time to adopt a permanent neutrality measure before it adjourned. If that effort failed, they proposed amendments to make the committee bill more acceptable to the peace bloc. They decided against a filibuster because that might cause the existing law to expire without anything to take its place.[47]

On February 14, the House Foreign Affairs Committee unanimously approved a stopgap bill similar to the one reported in the Senate. Its sponsors arranged to push it through the House under a suspension of the rules that severely limited debate and barred amendments. Representative Maverick protested to the president that it was "the cruelest type of gag rule." He said the steamrolling tactic "may help in a few districts like New York City, Boston, and San Francisco but it will definitely hurt politically in all agricultural districts." But Roosevelt replied that it would be "improper" for him to "take part in legislative procedure." The House adopted the measure by a vote of 353 to 27 on Monday, February 17, 1936.[48]

To speed action in the Senate, Pittman substituted the House resolution for the slightly different one reported by his committee and pushed for an immediate vote. The Senate easily defeated all amendments proposed by Nye and his colleagues; Senator Clark marshaled only sixteen votes for his amendment to extend the 1935 act until June 1, 1936. After only four hours of consideration, the Senate on Tuesday afternoon, February 18, 1936, adopted the House bill without a record vote.[49]

On February 29, President Roosevelt signed the Neutrality Act of 1936. Like its predecessor, it was a temporary measure. In extending the main provisions of the 1935 law until May 1, 1937, the act of 1936 included certain changes and substantive amendments. The new law gave the president some discretion in putting its key provisions into effect by stating that they would become operative "whenever the President shall find that there exists a state of war." It added a mandatory loan ban to the earlier arms embargo. It exempted American republics from the application of the law when they were involved in war with a non-American state. It made it mandatory for the president to extend the arms embargo to states that became involved in a foreign war after it started.[50]

The Neutrality Act of 1936 did not restrict abnormal export of nonmunition war materials to belligerents. The Roosevelt administration had different objectives from Senators Nye and Clark in urging such a restriction. Roosevelt and Hull expected it to hurt aggressor Italy more than Ethiopia; Nye and Clark saw it as another step to prevent economic entanglement in a foreign war. Nye also opposed the discretionary features of that provision of the Pittman bill, while the administration objected to the mandatory character of the provision in the Nye-Clark resolution. The political powers of particular economic and ethnic groups that feared the effects of the restrictions helped Senator Johnson and others block both the administration's internationalists and Nye's more extreme isolationists on that issue.

Enactment of permanent neutrality legislation was put off until May 1, 1937. By that time Mussolini's Fascist Italy had completed its military conquest of Ethiopia, and the failure of the League of Nations peace-keeping efforts was apparent to all. Also by that time the 1936 presidential campaigns and election were over; the political inhibitions encouraged by isolationist opinion weighed less heavily on Roosevelt as he faced war in Asia and Europe during his second term in the White House.

Chapter 13

Progressive Politics

The T.W.A. DC-2 airliner took off into a dark night at 9:15 P.M. on May 5, 1935, after refueling at Albuquerque, New Mexico. The plane never reached its scheduled destination at Kansas City. Flying blind on instruments through the clouds, its two-way radio was inoperative. With weather deteriorating and fuel running low, the pilots tried to reach safety by flying below the clouds. But mist and fog forced them to tree-top levels in the darkness over rolling terrain in Missouri. The left wing dragged the ground; the plane was thrown out of control and crashed into an embankment at 3:30 in the early morning on May 6. Five persons died in the crash, including both pilots and Senator Bronson M. Cutting of New Mexico.[1] The tragedy gave dramatic publicity to continuing and growing personal and political difficulties between Franklin D. Roosevelt and western progressives—most of whom were Republicans and most of whom were isolationists.

A wealthy and urbane Republican, Cutting was a respected member of the progressive bloc. He worked effectively with Senators Norris, Borah, Johnson, and Wheeler, and was an especially close friend of Philip and Robert La Follette. Six years younger than the president, he had known Roosevelt since boyhood. The senator campaigned for Roosevelt's election in 1932, and the president-elect had offered him appointment as secretary of interior. Cutting declined, but like other western progressives, he generally voted for New Deal legislation. He had, however, taken sharp issue with Roosevelt's effort to slash veterans' benefits in the economy bill of 1933. Cutting led the fight to restore the veterans funds, and most western progressives voted with him in overriding the president's veto in 1934. Roosevelt interpreted reports of Cutting's comments during the controversy as reflecting critically on his compassion for wounded and disabled veterans. Others had parted company with the president on specific issues without significantly provoking his ire, but Roosevelt and Farley pressed a relentless political drive in an unsuccessful effort to defeat Cutting's bid for reelection in 1934. He won by a narrow margin over Dennis Chavez, but the administration shared with Cutting's New Mexico and Senate opponents in contesting the results. The senator had traveled to New Mexico to get affidavits for his defense against the challenge and was on his way back to Washington when the airplane crashed, killing him.[2]

Even Roosevelt's warmest admirers among progressives had protested his treatment of Cutting. Norris, Ickes, Johnson, and La Follette were among those who tried to persuade Roosevelt to desist. They failed. And they could never fully understand Roosevelt's almost vengeful performance.[3] It was significant that the episode was a domestic political matter that had nothing to do with foreign affairs directly. The progressives who were most shaken by Roosevelt's treatment of Cutting, however, were nearly all isolationists who opposed Roosevelt's foreign policies before and during World War II.

The political alliance between Roosevelt and western progressive isolationists was always an uneasy one. It required constant tending. In dealings with progressives, Roosevelt had the continuing task of trying to convince them that he was truly as devoted to progressivism as they were, of allaying their worries about his trustworthiness on progressive issues. Given their long and often courageous devotion to progressivism and given Roosevelt's readiness to compromise on almost any issue, they felt uneasy about the directions he might take. In turn, the doctrinaire, inflexible, self-righteous, independent patterns of progressives made it difficult for them to work with each other, to say nothing of working with the wealthy, eastern, aristocrat in the White House.

Those patterns were complicated by the committee system in Congress and by the party system nationally. To win enactment of his legislative program the president had to work with Democratic leaders who chaired Senate and House committees. Most leading progressives were not Democrats, and most of the Democrats who chaired standing committees were not progressives—or New Dealers. Particularly during his first year in office, Roosevelt consulted frequently with progressive leaders of all parties and included them in top-level deliberations on legislative tactics. In 1934 and 1935, however, he consulted less regularly. They often felt left out and complained of having difficulty getting to see the president. Neither Democratic National

Chairman James A. Farley of New York, Senate Majority Leader Joseph T. Robinson of Arkansas, Finance Committee Chairman Senator Pat Harrison of Mississippi, nor White House Secretary Marvin H. McIntyre really empathized with progressives. Secretary of Agriculture Henry A. Wallace lunched with Senators Wheeler, Bone, and Shipstead on January 26, 1935. He noted in his diary that all three (two Democrats and one Farmer-Laborite) "indicated considerable dissatisfaction with the administration," but had nothing to suggest "on a unifying program on which they could stand affirmatively." Wallace concluded that progressives were "splendid critics but very poor builders." Two weeks later Republican newsman William Allen White from Kansas wrote to Secretary Ickes that "Roosevelt can't win next year without the progressive Republican votes of the Middle West from Ohio to the Coast, but particularly the Mississippi basin north of Tennessee." Ickes responded that he hoped the president would see "the necessity of holding the Progressive West to his cause." At the suggestion of Felix Frankfurter, Ickes conferred with his friend Hiram Johnson about "the political situation in the West."[4]

At Frankfurter's urging, the president invited the senators who had been members of the National Progressive League for Franklin D. Roosevelt in the 1932 campaign to dinner at the White House on Tuesday evening, May 14, to clear the air. Attending were Senators Costigan, Johnson, La Follette, Norris, and Wheeler. (Frankfurter's initial suggestion approved by Roosevelt would have included Cutting, but he died in the crash just eight days before the dinner.) Also present were Secretary of Agriculture Wallace from Iowa, Secretary of Interior Ickes of Illinois, David K. Niles of Massachusetts, and Frankfurter. Dinner and conversation lasted until nearly midnight. Senators La Follette and Wheeler did much of the talking. They made it clear that they thought "the time had come" for the president to assert more positive leadership. When Wheeler complained that he could not get past McIntyre to see the president, Roosevelt promised to be more readily available and advised the Montana Democrat to make arrangements through his personal secretary, Marguerite "Missy" Le Hand. Ickes left the gathering "with a distinct impression that it is the President's intention to take a firm stand on his progressive policies and force the fighting along that line." Frankfurter considered the dinner a "high success" and reported that La Follette called it "the best, the frankest, the most encouraging talk we have ever had with the President."[5]

Just six days later, however, Senators Norris, Johnson, La Follette, Nye, and Shipstead conspicuously walked out of the chamber
in protest when Dennis Chavez took the oath of office to replace Cutting in the Senate. Senator Borah made a point of not being present on
the occasion. Senator Norris, one of Roosevelt's most devoted
followers, explained that it was the only way he could show his "condemnation of the disgraceful and unwarranted fight that was made to
drive Senator Cutting out of public office." He called it "the greatest
case of ingratitude in history" and "a blot upon the record of the
Roosevelt administration."[6]

Over lunch a month later in June, 1935, Senators Norris, Johnson,
Borah, and La Follette conceived an idea to organize progressives to
force legislative action on the president's soak-the-rich tax program.
On their initiative twenty-two legislators (fourteen Democrats, six
Republicans, one Progressive, and one Farmer-Laborite) signed a
round robin urging Congress to stay in session until it adopted the tax
program. Senator Nye said that what the president did on the tax
question would "decide whether he can hope to have the Progressive
Republicans with him next year."[7]

Roosevelt faced a different problem when progressives were up for
reelection in 1934 and 1936. There was no real difficulty when the progressive was a Democrat such as Burton K. Wheeler of Montana in
1934. But most were Republicans, La Follette a Progressive, and Shipstead was Farmer-Labor. Often their Democratic opponents were
more conservative and less sympathetic to Roosevelt's New Deal than
they were. It was awkward for a Democrtic president to support candidates (however progressive and pro–New Deal) against Democrats.
Roosevelt thought it best not to take part in Jefferson Day celebra-
tions in 1934 because "the recovery and reconstruction program is being accomplished by men and women of all parties" and he had
"repeatedly appealed to Republicans as much as to Democrats to do
their part." He wrote Colonel Edward M. House that "much as we
love Thomas Jefferson we should not celebrate him in a partisan
way." In practice Roosevelt skillfully arranged things so he did not
have to come out against leading progressives, whatever their political
labels. Circumstances varied from state to state, but he was able either
to support or not to oppose the nomination and election of Senators
Wheeler, Johnson, La Follette, and Shipstead in 1934 (Cutting was a
conspicuous exception to that pattern). In 1936 Roosevelt strongly
urged the reelection of Norris in Nebraska.[8]

The presidential election of 1936 presented a special problem in relations between Roosevelt and progressives. Western progressives were not noted for their party loyalty; they took dim views of both major parties. They had several political alternatives—none of them satisfactory. Conceivably, Republican progressives might shift parties and become Democrats. None did. Most progressives believed that without Roosevelt the Democratic party would be as conservative as it had been in the 1920s. Some were from states where the Republican party dominated so completely that they had to win election on a Republican ticket if they were to hold public office at all. At the same time the Republican party, in the progressive view, was dominated by big business, financiers, reactionaries, and special interests that had enriched the few at the expense of the many and had led America to the disaster that was the Great Depression.

Conceivably, progressives might turn to a third-party movement; most gave thought to that possibility at one time or another. Hiram Johnson had been Theodore Roosevelt's vice-presidential running mate in the Bull Moose movement in 1912, and Burton K. Wheeler had run with old Fighting Bob La Follette on a Progressive ticket in 1924. Gerald P. Nye and others had been active in the Nonpartisan League, though it had worked through the Republican party rather than as a third party. The La Follette brothers in Wisconsin and Henrik Shipstead in Minnesota successfully worked through third parties. Several of those progressives toyed with the third-party alternative in 1935–36, and some were suggested as presidential candidates for third-party tickets.

At the same time, particularly in the first half of 1935, Roosevelt and his political advisers worried about the possibility of a third party forming under the leadership of Democratic Senator Huey "Kingfish" Long of Louisiana, Father Charles E. Coughlin of Michigan, and Dr. Francis E. Townsend. All three had supported the election of Roosevelt in 1932; all had approved of much of his early New Deal. But all had grown impatient with what they saw as Roosevelt's excessive caution; each in separate ways urged more drastic innovations than Roosevelt was prepared to endorse. Long's share-the-wealth program, Father Coughlin's inflationary proposals and social justice movement, and Dr. Townsend's scheme for subsidizing recovery through old age pensions captured the fancy of many—but not Roosevelt. During FDR's first term, Long often aligned with noninterventionists on foreign policy issues, and Coughlin increasingly identified with extreme forms of isolationism. All in separate ways were demagogues who appealed to workers, farmers, wage earners, and small businessmen. The appeal of Townsend's old-age program forced many politicians to come out in favor of some kind of care for the elderly. Father Coughlin reached the homes and emotions of millions with his radio broadcasts. And Huey Long may have been the most formidable of all. Solidly in command of his home state, he had national political ambitions and was sufficiently able (and ruthless) so his challenge had to be taken seriously.[9]

Huey Long aligned with Senate progressives, but he was particularly close to Burton K. Wheeler. The Montana Democrat was fascinated by the man and liked him. The two had first met in 1929 when Long was governor. Wheeler helped win Long to the Roosevelt cause early in 1932 and claimed that the Louisiana senator helped hold the Mississippi and Arkansas delegations for Roosevelt in the course of the balloting at the Chicago convention. In his memoirs Wheeler described Long as a boastful, "flashy personality" who "loved to swagger." He wrote that Long's "mind was so brilliant he could discourse endlessly on everything from the silver issue to the dunking of cornpone in potlikker." As a debater "no one wanted to take him on. He would talk forever and sometimes would resort to a form of backwoods vilification that would make any victim blanch." He "always put on a good show." "There was a lot of bluff in the 'Kingfish,'" but Wheeler insisted that Long had "never lied" to him. According to Wheeler, "Long had far less racial prejudice in him than any other Southerner in the Senate" and "was one of the most liberal Southerners." Wheeler believed Long "was sincere in espousing welfare programs—some of them admittedly pretty radical—to do something for the kind of poor people he sprang from. Perhaps he fancied himself a kind of Robin Hood of the bayous."

Senator Long was never enthusiastic about Roosevelt and broke with him early. According to Wheeler, "FDR feared Huey Long as a dangerous type of liberal. . . . Huey, for his part, openly distrusted Roosevelt and never had any use for him from the start. They were, of course, polar opposites in background, manners, taste, etc."[10] As early as 1932, Roosevelt had told a confidant that he considered Long one of the two most dangerous men in America (the other being Douglas MacArthur). Administration leaders were particularly concerned early in 1935 about Long's challenge. The Democratic National Committee conducted a secret poll that indicated Long could win three to four million votes at the head of a third party and that the strength extended to industrial and farm areas in the North as well as in the South.[11]

In February, 1935, William Allen White wrote Ickes of a reliable report that Huey Long's strategy was "to run for President in '36 with no expectation of being elected but hoping to draw enough radical votes from Roosevelt to permit the election of the Republican nominee. Long's price will be the dispensation of southern patronage by which he expects to build an invincible machine for 1940." White feared "that a reactionary victory in '36 would be followed by a Fascist victory under some demagogue like Long in '40 and then the devil would be to pay." Ickes agreed that Long could not "be laughed off" and that "just now he and Father Coughlin make a formidable team."[12]

Analyzing the political opposition at that time, Roosevelt wrote Colonel House that "progressive Republicans like La Follette, Cutting, Nye, etc." were "flirting with the idea of a third ticket anyway with the knowledge that such a third ticket would be beaten but that it would defeat us, elect a conservative Republican and cause a complete swing far to the left before 1940." Roosevelt thought all the Republican elements were "flirting with Huey Long and probably financing him. A third Progressive Republican ticket and a fourth 'Share the Wealth' ticket they believe would crush us and that then a free for all would result in which case anything might happen." He thought it "a dangerous situation" but that when it came to a showdown "these fellows cannot all lie in the same bed and will fight among themselves with almost absolute certainty."[13] In April, Johnson wrote his son that "the administration is fretting and worrying about Long, but I think by next year, unless they make a martyr of him, he will be out of the picture." At the White House dinner gathering on May 14, La Follette said (according to Ickes) "that the best answer to Huey Long and Father Coughlin would be the enactment into law of the Administration bills now pending."[14]

Johnson and La Follette proved to be correct—but not the way they had expected. Roosevelt's legislative program in 1935 (including Social Security and the Wagner Act) was sufficiently liberal to appease many who earlier believed his New Deal had not gone far enough. That expanded New Deal program, combined with positive efforts by Roosevelt to smooth ruffled feathers, improved his relations with individual progressives. On September 8, 1935, an assassin gunned down Huey Long in the Louisiana State Capitol in Baton Rouge.

Progressives did give thought to the idea of a national third party

—but not for 1936. Though they worked with him on legislative matters, progressives were not inspired by the presidential ambitions of Huey Long. They believed a progressive third party in 1936 could not win, would draw votes away from Roosevelt, and could lead to a Republican victory that (as Senator Nye phrased it) "would throw the government back into the hands of the reactionaries." North Dakota progressive Representative William Lemke was the presidential candidate on a Union party ticket in 1936, but he won little support and no electoral votes.[15]

Another possible alternative for progressives might have been to capture control of the Republican party and take it out of the hands of conservatives. That did not prove politically possible on the national level in 1935 and 1936. After its reverses in the elections of 1930, 1932, and 1934, the Republican party was a feeble vehicle by 1936. But weak or strong, progressives had not been able to dominate it (or even influence it very much). Progressive Republicans repeatedly urged reorganizing and liberalizing the party, and Republican reverses in the elections of 1934 added weight to those urgings. Arthur Capper of Kansas, for example, wrote that the belief "that the Republican party is controlled by the reactionary forces and the great financial interests of the country" helped account "for the defeat of many of the Republican Senators who lost out in 1932 and many others who went out in 1934." Among progressives, Senators Borah and Nye were particularly outspoken in urging liberalizing the GOP. They saw no hope for the party under the leadership of Herbert Hoover and his policies. Nye was among those mentioned as a possible progressive Republican presidential candidate.[16] But it was old Senator William E. Borah of Idaho who made the strongest progressive bid for the GOP presidential nomination in 1936. His effort failed.

A politician seeking the Republican presidential nomination for the contest with Roosevelt in 1936 was in much the same situation as a heavyweight boxer at that time seeking a fight with Joe Louis; it would be an exciting once-in-a-lifetime adventure and would bring national attention—with almost no chance to win. The likelihood of defeat made Republican contenders less eager to get the nomination and more philosophical about delaying their presidential moves for some more propitious time. Whatever the odds, however, there were always those who would make themselves available. In 1935–36 the politicians most mentioned for the GOP nomination were Governor Alf M. Landon of Kansas, Chicago newspaper publisher Frank Knox, former President Herbert Hoover, Senator William E. Borah of Idaho, and Senator Arthur H. Vandenberg of Michigan. Robert A. Taft was a favorite-son candidate in Ohio's presidential primary, but at that time he had his eyes on the senate or gubernatorial races of 1938 rather than on the presidency. Hoover may have hoped for a vindicating groundswell of support for him, but that was never a serious possibility. Vandenberg's chances rested on the possibility of a deadlock among front-runners. The East provided no real contender; many thought the party's slim chances for victory lay in getting a nominee who might challenge Roosevelt's hold on the West.

Four of those six individuals (Hoover, Borah, Vandenberg, and Taft) in varied ways were isolationists or noninterventionists who battled against Roosevelt's increasingly internationalist foreign policies before World War II. Knox was a nationalist who would become one of the most interventionist members of Roosevelt's cabinet in 1940. Despite the endorsement he won from William Randolph Hearst, Landon was a moderate internationalist. But foreign policy considerations scarcely entered into their contest for the nomination. The depression, New Deal, and Roosevelt provided focal points for their attention. Senator Borah saw himself as the only real spokesman for progressivism and the common people running in opposition to various politicians representing (and financed by) special interests and the GOP Old Guard.

Borah was one of the most impressive, scholarly, and powerful of the western progressives. Born on a farm in Illinois in 1865, he never abandoned the devout Presbyterian religious faith or the habits of hard work that he learned as a child. Serious, self-righteous, and a loner, in 1885 he went west to study at the University of Kansas. Despite his straight-A record, overwork and tuberculosis cut short his studies after a year, and he never graduated. Instead, he read law and was admitted to the bar in 1887. More important were values he absorbed in that restive period in Kansas history. The combination of drought, heavy farm indebtedness, high interest rates, declining farm prices, and declining real incomes were laying the groundwork for agrarian protest movements and for William Jennings Bryan's Populist party. The farm boy from Illinois had no difficulty seeing justice in the farmers' objections to eastern urban business dominance and exploitation. That background helped shape his approach to both domestic and foreign affairs throughout his later public career. In 1887 he moved further west to Idaho, where he practiced law and became increasingly active in Republican party politics. First elected in 1906, Borah served as United States senator from Idaho for thirty-three years until his death in January, 1940.[17]

Borah was five-feet, ten-inches tall and weighed about 165 pounds, but his massive head, craggy features, and natural dignity made him seem more formidable physically than he was. He was one of the greatest orators ever to serve in the Senate.

Proudly independent, he was never a good party man; he denounced conservative, probusiness leadership of his own Republican party more vehemently than he did the opposition Democratic party. He took the progressive side on public issues, but it was little-*d* democratic progressivism, not paternalistic welfare progressivism. He was such a poor organization man that even his fellow progressives despaired of being able to depend on him in a showdown. One person described him "as a 'three round man,' he never goes ten. He starts many things but never finishes any." Hiram Johnson once referred to him as their "spearless leader." Old Bob La Follette described Borah as a man "who shook his lionlike mane, drew his sword, called for a charge on the enemy's breastworks, and stopped in his tracks before he got there."[18]

Borah became a member of the Senate Foreign Relations Committee in 1911 and remained a powerful member of that committee until his death. As a nationalist he approved the defense of American neutral rights from 1914 to 1917, but he vigorously opposed the Versailles treaty, the League of Nations, and the Permanent Court of International Justice. With the death of Henry Cabot Lodge, Sr., in 1924, Borah became chairman of the Foreign Relations Committee until the Republicans lost their Senate majority in 1933. During those years no Republican president or secretary of state made any major move in foreign affairs without consulting Borah and seriously considering his reactions. He provided the initiative that eventually led to the Washington Naval Conference of 1921–22 and to Senate approval of the three major treaties emerging from that conference. In the 1920s he was the leading Senate advocate for extending diplomatic recognition to the Soviet Union. He was the key senator in the background and approval of the Kellogg-Briand Pact of Paris of 1928. From 1933 until his death he was the ranking minority member of the Foreign Relations Committee.[19]

Roosevelt never courted Borah with the same energy and warmth he had used in winning Norris, Johnson, and La Follette. And Borah, in turn, never developed enthusiasm for Roosevelt. The Idaho Republican often voted for the president's New Deal proposals, but Roosevelt's personal persuasiveness and artfulness played little part in winning Borah's votes. Urged on by one of the senator's friends, Roosevelt had Borah to lunch at the White House on March 22, 1935, but the visit had no visible beneficial effects on the political course of either of them or on their relations with each other.[20]

In an article in the spring of 1936, Walter Lippmann came close to capturing the approaches of the two: "The two men are alike in their general feeling that large corporate wealth has exercised too much power. But they are radically different in their general feeling as to how to deal with the problem.

"Senator Borah is, in the main . . . a lineal descendant from the earliest American liberals, an individualist who opposes all concentration of power, political or economic, who is against private privilege and private monopoly, against political bureaucracy and centralized government. It is the tradition of Jefferson and Lincoln, of Bryan and Wilson. It is grass-roots progressivism. Mr. Borah believes in the Bill of Rights. He believes in the principle of the Sherman Act. He believes in widely distributed private property. He believes in competition. He believes in a government of limited powers, above all in the distinctly American theory that the Government itself is under the law and must be held to the law. . . .

"Mr. Roosevelt on the other hand, has no such instinctive appreciation of American liberalism in this, its oldest and most authentic, sense. He is disposed to think that these old liberal principles no longer fit the modern world, that they belong to a horse-and-buggy age, and that the future is to bring a very highly organized society controlled by a very powerful government. Thus he is not much concerned about the old safeguards of liberty. What he is really concerned about is sufficient power to provide security and the good things of life for everybody."[21] What Lippmann did not note in that particular piece was that the foreign policy projections of those two perspectives were as different as their domestic aspects. In a personal letter in May, 1936, Borah drew his thoughts together concisely when he wrote: "I am perfectly satisfied we are facing one of two propositions in this country in case we do not deal with the question of monopoly, and that is, regimentation by private interests or regimentation by the government."[22]

Despite Borah's distinction as a leading progressive, it was difficult to take his candidacy at face value. His forte had been that of the loyal opposition. He was the master dissenter; his experience as a leader and administrator was negligible. And he was past seventy years of age. There was reason to believe that Borah never really expected to win the Republican presidential nomination in 1936. More likely, he hoped to build enough strength so he could play a large role in choosing the party's nominee and in shaping its program.

Whatever the intent or hopes, local Borah-for-President clubs began to emerge, and in January 1936, a National Borah-for-President Committee was organized in Washington. Congressman Hamilton Fish played an active role both in New York and nationally. Senator Nye endorsed Borah and urged the Nye-for-President clubs to switch to the Idaho Senator.[23]

In Republican presidential primaries, Borah did well in Wisconsin and Oregon. But he concentrated his major efforts in Illinois and Ohio. In Illinois conservative Republicans lined up behind Knox in opposing him, and in Ohio Taft represented the opposition to Borah and his progressivism. The Idaho Republican lost to the home-state contenders in both states. But the patterns reinforced his conviction that the GOP could not beat Roosevelt with Old Guard candidates and programs. In Illinois Borah was stronger than Knox among rural and small-town voters outside of Chicago. Roosevelt's voting strength in the Democratic primary was more than three times that of Knox (or Borah), and Borah and Roosevelt combined won five times Knox's total. Borah's defeat in Ohio essentially knocked him out of contention. But he won approximately 40 percent of the Republican votes, and the combined total for Borah and Roosevelt was three times that cast for Taft and the conservatives. The progressive challenge in presidential primaries to Old Guard control of the GOP was turned back. In 1936 the Republicans probably could not have beaten Roosevelt, whomever they nominated. But the combined strength of progressive Borah and New Deal Roosevelt made it clear that the Republicans had no chance with a conservative candidate and program. Borah made his point, even as he lost his battle. And foreign affairs had nothing to do with the outcome.[24]

At the Republican National Convention in Cleveland, Governor Alf M. Landon of Kansas won the presidential nomination on the first ballot; the vice-presidential nomination went to Frank Knox of the *Chicago Daily News*. Both had made their peace with the eastern wing of the party, but both were from the Middle West, where leaders thought any chances for the party's victory lay. Neither was an isolationist—though that did not determine their selection. They and other leaders tried to increase the party's appeal in the West by deferring to Borah's wishes as much as possible in the platform. He wrote the plank calling private monopoly "indefensible and intolerable" and warning that monopolies would "utterly destroy constitutional government and the liberty of the citizen."[25]

Borah also wrote the foreign policy plank. It pledged "to promote and maintain peace by all honorable means not leading to foreign alliances or political commitments" and emphasized that "America shall not become a member of the League of Nations nor of the World Court nor shall America take on any entangling alliances in foreign affairs." The failure to mention neutrality or taking the profits out of war disappointed Senator Nye—and illustrated the differing emphases of Borah and Nye within isolationist ranks. Nye and others were displeased that the platform did not endorse construction of the Saint Lawrence Seaway and blamed that omission on power interests. The platform called for "repeal of the present Reciprocal Trade Agreement Law." As Senator Norris's long-time secretary had correctly predicted, Borah's efforts had not been able "to reform the Republican party." And few thought the GOP had any chance for election victory unless Roosevelt beat himself.[26]

At the Democratic National Convention in Philadelphia, Franklin D. Roosevelt and John Nance Garner were renominated by acclamation. Senator Robert F. Wagner's Committee on Resolutions made little change in the platform originally drafted in the White House. Senator Norris made suggestions to Wagner, but they did not focus on foreign affairs. Secretary Hull, Ambassador Josephus Daniels, and others provided drafts for the foreign policy plank. But the final document did not incorporate Hull's language. Hull had cause for disappointment with the product. The Democrats promised to "observe a true neutrality in the disputes of others." The platform pledged "to work for peace and to take the profits out of war; to guard against being drawn, by political commitments, international banking or private trading, into any war which may develop anywhere." Even its endorsement of the administration's trade program was guarded. Nye should have felt more comfortable with the foreign policy plank than Hull did.[27]

Landon and the Republicans were no match for Roosevelt, the New Deal, and the Democrats during the 1936 campaign—and foreign affairs had little to do with it. Jobs and recovery held center stage, not diplomacy and foreign wars. Charisma was more essential to the outcome than statecraft. Roosevelt and Landon each made one major foreign policy address during the campaign—Roosevelt at Chautauqua, New York, in August; Landon in Indianapolis, Indiana, in October. Neither speech was an entirely frank statement of the candidate's policy convictions, and neither changed the outcome of the election.

Roosevelt's Chautauqua address on August 14 was part of his continuing efforts to win and retain the political support of western progressives. At Roosevelt's suggestion the nonpartisan progressive organization that had worked for his election in 1932 was revived and reformed as the Progressive National Committee under Senators Norris of Nebraska and La Follette of Wisconsin. Secretary of Interior Ickes, however, believed Gerald P. Nye would be a better chairman for the group. Ickes saw Nye as a "party Republican," which La Follette and Norris were not. And Nye was "one of the outstanding leaders of peace sentiment in the country." If Roosevelt made a strong peace statement expressing firm determination not to intervene in another European war and if Nye endorsed the president for his peace stand, Ickes believed it "would go a long way toward assuring his re-election." Ickes contended that Nye could "help as well as, or better than, any other man in the country." He discussed his scheme with Senator Nye on Thursday morning, August 6. On Monday morning Ickes had a long conference with the president in which he pressed his suggestion. The president was "very impressed with this idea." They discussed it at length, and Roosevelt said he would use his scheduled appearance at Chautauqua the next Friday as the occasion for that peace statement. At that same White House session Ickes also got the president to agree to two irrigation projects that Norris wanted and urged Roosevelt to telephone the ailing Hiram Johnson.[28]

But Ickes, Nye, and concern for progressive support provided only part of the background of the Chautauqua speech. Others were conferring with the president on foreign affairs from quite different perspectives. For example, on Friday, August 7, the president met with Clark M. Eichelberger of the League of Nations Association. In a letter to the president five days later, Eichelberger summarized the views he had advanced at the White House. He too urged a speech on foreign affairs. He too was concerned with peace—but with a difference. He wanted emphasis on world cooperation as the way to preserve world peace and democracy. Eichelberger believed the United States could not "be morally neutral to the great effort that is being made to preserve peace and save democracy.''[29] Though both were devoted to peace, the methods proposed by Eichelberger and by Nye were radically different. FDR, however, had both in mind in delivering his Chautauqua speech. He also had in mind winning the election in November.

Roosevelt's Chautauqua address on Friday evening, August 14, 1936, was based on a draft (much shortened and revised) prepared by William C. Bullitt. The president told his audience (as he had told others in personal correspondence and conversations) that he was ''more concerned and less cheerful about international world conditions than about our immediate domestic prospects.'' He spoke pridefully of the peaceful accomplishments of the Good Neighbor policy. He said very nearly all that Ickes and Nye could have wanted to hear. ''We shun political commitments which might entangle us in foreign wars; we avoid connection with the political activities of the League of Nations.'' He said ''we are not isolationists except insofar as we seek to isolate ourselves from war.'' In vivid language he described the horrors of war that he personally had seen. ''I hate war.'' He told his audience that he has ''passed unnumbered hours'' and would ''pass unnumbered hours thinking and planning how war may be kept from the United States of America.'' Congress had given him ''certain authority to provide safe-guards of American neutrality in case of war.'' Roosevelt berated war profits ''that caused the extension of monopoly'' and promised that ''if we face the choice of profits or peace, this Nation will answer—this Nation must answer—'we choose peace.' ''

But in that same address, delivered in an isolationist America in the midst of a presidential election campaign, Roosevelt also said certain things in tune with internationalism. He spoke of assisting international movements to prevent war and of cooperating ''to the bitter end'' in the disarmament conferences. He spoke with pride of wholehearted cooperation ''in the social and humanitarian work at Geneva.'' He warned that ''so long as war exists on earth there will be some danger even to the nation that most ardently desires peace, danger that it also may be drawn into war.'' Reminiscent of the Norman Davis pledge at Geneva in 1933, Roosevelt told his audience that he could ''at least make certain that no act of the United States helps to produce or to promote war'' and that ''any nation that provokes war forfeits the sympathy of the people of the United States.'' He praised the trade agreements program and contended that ''without a more liberal international trade, war is a natural sequence.'' Though

Congress adopted the neutrality legislation, Roosevelt emphasized that "the effective maintenance of American neutrality depends today, as in the past, on the wisdom and the determination of whoever at the moment occupy the offices of President and Secretary of State." He warned that "no matter how well we are supported by neutrality laws, we must remember that no laws can be provided to cover every contingency, for it is impossible to imagine how every future event may shape itself."[30] Isolationists applauded Roosevelt's Chautauqua speech, but so did internationalists. And with good cause.

Three days after the address, at Ickes's urging, the president invited Senator Nye to visit him at Hyde Park. Ickes hoped the meeting would cause the senator to "give out a statement endorsing the President for re-election on the basis of his peace record and his peace talk" and showing "very clearly that those elements in this country who would profit from a war, namely, the international bankers and the munitions makers, are all on the side of Landon." In response to the president's invitation, Nye traveled from Yellowstone Park, where he was vacationing, and met with Roosevelt in his Hyde Park home on Friday, August 21.[31]

The following week the president departed on an extended personal inspection tour of the drought areas in the Middle West and Great Plains. He met with governors and senators. On August 27, he conferred with Senators Nye, Wheeler, Frazier, and others at Bismarck, North Dakota, about the drought situation. He expressed concern and promised aid.[32] Roosevelt probably won more votes as he commiserated with hard-pressed farmers and townspeople in that parched region than he gained there from his Chautauqua speech. But he did not win the backing of Senator Nye.

Early in September the North Dakota progressive Republican announced that he would continue to keep hands off the presidential race and would not endorse either Roosevelt or Landon. Conceivably Nye was not satisfied with Roosevelt's position on neutrality legislation and taking the profits out of war. The senator may have feared that endorsing the Democratic presidential candidate might jeopardize his chances for winning the Republican presidential nomination in 1940. Part of the explanation involved the complicated political situation in North Dakota, where Nye faced reelection in 1938. Whatever his reasons, Nye limited his campaigning in 1936 to the state level— largely in North Dakota.[33]

There were other western progressive isolationists whose endorsements Roosevelt did not win, notably Capper, Borah, and

Johnson. Arthur Capper was seeking reelection in 1936 to another term in the Senate. Running on the same Republican ticket with Alf Landon, his friend and fellow Kansan, one could not have expected Capper to endorse Roosevelt.[34] Borah too was running for reelection on the Republican ticket in Idaho. He had become increasingly bitter against Landon in the course of the contest for the presidential nomination. Despite repeated efforts to persuade him to endorse Landon, he never did so. Some close to Borah thought a gesture from Roosevelt and withdrawal of the Democratic candidate from the Senate race in Idaho could win Borah's support for Roosevelt. Wheeler, among others, discussed the possibility with the president. But the Democratic candidate for Senate would not withdraw. Neither Landon nor FDR won endorsement or support from Borah in 1936.[35] There was never any possibility that the more conservative Michigan Republican Arthur H. Vandenberg would endorse Roosevelt.[36]

The Capper, Borah, and Vandenberg performances were predictable, but Roosevelt had reason to expect something better from Hiram Johnson. None of the western progressive isolationists had been more warmly courted by Roosevelt than Johnson. The California Republican always had mixed feelings and reservations about Roosevelt, but on balance he was favorably impressed. Johnson and Roosevelt enjoyed each other's company and maintained good humor in their relationship. As professional politicians they could disagree without getting personal or petty. The Democrats did not run a candidate against Johnson in the 1934 senate race in California. The senator was delighted with the foreign policy speech that Roosevelt delivered in San Diego on October 2, 1935. In that address the president said that "despite what happens in continents overseas, the United States of America shall and must remain, as long ago the Father of our Country prayed that it might remain—unentangled and free." Johnson found it "refreshing . . . to hear a President of the United States finally quote the immortal words of our first President." The old California Republican was included in Roosevelt's various efforts to smooth relations with progressives in 1935 and 1936.[37]

Somewhere along the line, however, the two men got out of phase. Perhaps it was inevitable, but neither intended it that way. Early in May, 1936, in a letter to his son outlining the preconvention political situation, Johnson wrote: "What a child of destiny Roosevelt is! He blunders along here with half-baked and oftentimes half-finished policies, and I give him due credit for his adventurous spirit, and desire to accomplish things, and, more than that, for being funda-

mentally right.'' In June, 1936, Mrs. Johnson broke her arm, and the
senator fell seriously ill with intestinal toxemia. He was under continuing medical care at the Naval Medical Center and aged markedly during the course of the year. Before departing on his tour of the drought
areas late in August, Roosevelt telephoned the ailing senator, but the
old man had retired for the night. Mrs. Johnson, ''the Boss,'' had
never really liked or trusted Roosevelt. By the summer of 1936, the
senator wrote that his wife had ''conceived a tremendous prejudice
against Roosevelt, which, in many instances, I do not share.'' ''The
Boss'' did not control the senator's views, but he respected her judgment. When Farley wrote the senator, he responded by explaining that
his doctors had told him he could not be active during the campaign.
He was seeing no one save his own household and medical personnel.[38]

As he followed the news, Johnson confidently predicted that
Roosevelt would be reelected. He thought the Republicans were
''bungling the campaign.'' Early in October Johnson wrote his son:
''What this Administration will try to do is to take us into the League
of Nations, or some equivalent of it. It is an international administration. . . . I am afraid of what he will do to this Country in the next
four years.''[39]

On October 7, in conversation with Ickes about Johnson, the
president commented, ''Surely, he cannot be too sick to make a statement.'' On October 26, Roosevelt wrote a nice note to the senator and
''the Boss'' sympathizing with their difficulties and inviting ''any
statement'' Johnson might make to ''put the finishing touches to the
picture in California, Oregon, and Washington.'' But Mrs. Johnson
telephoned the president's personal secretary explaining that the
senator was ''in such a highly nervous state that the doctors had for-
bidden him to even read letters.'' Neither Roosevelt nor Ickes really
believed he was that sick. The president speculated that perhaps
Johnson ''knew that he was finishing his last term and he wanted to be
absolutely independent during the next four years.'' Ickes was not
convinced, and neither could really understand the senator's silence.
On October 24, Senator Johnson voted for Roosevelt against Landon
by absentee ballot, but he cast his vote ''with many misgivings.''[40]
After the election-year experiences, relations between Roosevelt and
Johnson were never the same again.

If Roosevelt had certain difficulties with progressives in the 1936
campaign, Landon had greater difficulties with them. Despite his

Middle West base, within his party he was stronger in the Northeast than in the West. Moderately progressive, he had admired Borah, Norris, and others. He did everything he could to win the endorsement of Borah. But Landon and his party were much less appealing to most progressives than Roosevelt and his New Deal were. His monetary and tariff views did not mesh with the Republican platform and alienated Borah and other progressives.[41] Landon and his supporters focused their campaign almost exclusively on domestic affairs.

If Landon had spoken out more on foreign affairs, he might have had additional difficulties. His own moderate internationalist views, if advanced fully and frankly, would not have been acceptable to western progressives. And if he had embraced the peace and neutrality views that progressives held, he could have alienated the eastern internationalist wing of his party—and probably would not have won the progressives anyway. Former Secretary of State Henry L. Stimson of New York voted against Roosevelt in 1936, but he did not campaign for the GOP. He wrote: "The Republicans, in coming out against the World Court and cooperation with the League as well as in their attack on the reciprocal treaties, pretty effectively stopped my mouth from speech making. If the foreign issues had been the only ones in the campaign, I should have voted the other way."[42] The conservative American Liberty League threw its support to Landon. Like him, it focused almost exclusively on domestic issues. But its membership and funds came overwhelmingly from the urban Northeast, and its leaders generally were internationalists.[43] With much to lose and little to gain, Landon avoided the foreign policy issue.

After much prodding, and with help from such varied and even contradictory sources as former Undersecretary of State William R. Castle, former Secretary of State Frank B. Kellogg, former Undersecretary of State J. Reuben Clark, William Allen White, Arthur H. Vandenberg, James P. Warburg, and Hamilton Fish Armstrong of the Council on Foreign Relations, Landon's foreign policy speech took shape. White wrote him that there were "more unattached votes hovering between Roosevelt with his big navy expenditures and Norman Thomas with his pacific ideas who would go to you if you make this straightaway declaration . . . than any other one block now drifting around waiting for someone to grab it off." In Indianapolis late in October, the Kansas governor compromised his convictions, made the appropriate gestures on neutrality and peace, and delivered his foreign policy speech. In an already losing effort, however, his speech got little attention and was no match for FDR's moving Chautauqua address. It won no new converts in progressive or isolationist circles.[44]

As the campaign entered its final phases, Roosevelt's standing with progressives was better than it had been for some time. Though Republicans Nye, Borah, and Johnson did not endorse Roosevelt for reelection, neither did they endorse Landon. And Johnson, at least, voted for Roosevelt. The president helped persuade old George Norris to run for another term. Early in 1936, Norris wrote (as he had many times before and as he would many times later): "I am deeply interested in the reelection of President Roosevelt. I supported him in 1932 and while I do not agree with everything his Administration has done or tried to do, I still believe it would be a serious mistake for the country if he were to be defeated for reelection. I want to do everything within my power to assist in his reelection." And he did. Norris served as honorary chairman of the Progressive National Committee supporting the reelection of Roosevelt. He lauded the president and made a national broadcast criticizing Landon. Roosevelt, in turn, made a moving appeal to Nebraska voters, urging them to keep Norris, running as an Independent, in the Senate. He had a tough fight; it was a close contest. After the election the president wrote to his old friend that "of all the results on November third, your re-election gave me the greatest happiness. Naturally I was worried and the last thing I did before going to bed at 3 A.M. was to put in a special call to Nebraska and to get assurances that you were safely ahead."[45]

In September, Wisconsin Progressives Robert M. La Follette and Philip La Follette helped organize a major Progressive conference in Chicago that urged reelection of Roosevelt. Senator La Follette served as chairman of the national committee of the Progressive National Committee, and he and Philip (who was running for another term as governor) campaigned vigorously for Roosevelt. Democratic Senator Burton K. Wheeler of Montana campaigned for and with FDR in 1936. Farmer-Labor Senator Henrik Shipstead of Minnesota, Democratic Senator Homer T. Bone of Washington, and Republican Senator James Couzens of Michigan all urged reelection of Roosevelt. Couzens's support for Roosevelt and much of his New Deal contributed to his own defeat in the Republican primary in his bid for another term.[46]

On November 3, 1936, the American voters gave Franklin D. Roosevelt, his New Deal, and the Democratic party an overwhelming victory at the polls. As Democratic National Chairman James A.

Farley correctly predicted, Roosevelt and Garner won the electoral votes of every state except Maine and Vermont in New England. The urban strength in Roosevelt's national sweep was of fundamental significance. The president carried both rural and urban America, but in the North he won his most overwhelming support among lower-income voters in the cities. Both major parties were becoming more urbanized, but that urban orientation was particularly striking in the Democratic party in the North. The party also increased its majorities in both houses of Congress.[47]

Though Couzens was eliminated in Michigan and W. Warren Barbour defeated in New Jersey, leading isolationists of all parties did well in the elections of 1934 and 1936. Senators Wheeler, Johnson, La Follette, Shipstead, Frazier, Vandenberg, and Bone, among others, had won reelection in 1934. Senators Norris, Borah, and Capper were reelected in 1936, and Ernest Lundeen of Minnesota moved up from the House to the Senate. FDR's bête noire in his home district, Hamilton Fish, won another term in the House (and in its Foreign Affairs Committee) despite Democratic efforts to beat him.

With the president's overwhelming victory in 1936 and with his impressive urban strength, he felt less obliged to cater to the wishes of western progressives than he had during his first term. That was particularly true as he refocused his attention away from domestic matters to the increasingly alarming developments on the world scene. The rural, small-town, and small-business America for which most western progressive isolationists spoke was declining in population and power. That augured ill for both the progressivism they represented and the foreign policies they endorsed. During the closing months of 1936, Roosevelt and the progressives enjoyed as close and mutually beneficial personal and political relations as they could reasonably have expected. After that the patterns changed.

Old Hiram Johnson anticipated those forthcoming difficulties in a letter he wrote to his son a few days after the election: "And now will come the test of the President. He loves the dramatic. His mentality is so restless it has to have something new daily. He has delusions of grandeur which make him dissatisfied with dealing with domestic problems alone, and which will constantly urge a wider field. Like Wilson he'll see himself the arbiter of the world. With his power and the vote he has received, the views of men like myself will receive scant attention. . . . I'm going to be very lonely and very poorly equipped for the job. I don't look forward with very great interest to the part I shall play.''[48] Johnson's analysis focused on Roosevelt's temperament and power; he did not mention socioeconomic changes at home and international developments abroad in his explanation of the president's course or of the difficulties Johnson and his fellow isolationists were to face. If one discounts the subjective and pejorative tone, however, the senator's analysis had a certain prescience. Relations between Roosevelt and the isolationists were to travel a much rougher road during the president's second term than during his first. And the first major issue to set the pattern for that more difficult relationship was, characteristically, a domestic matter—the so-called court-packing controversy of 1937.

Part II: A Parting of the Ways

Chapter 14
Court Packing

Crises leading to war in Asia and Europe, and World War II itself, were fundamental to Franklin D. Roosevelt's refocus away from the New Deal toward foreign affairs and to his break with isolationists. But domestic developments were part of that transition as well. If any single domestic political episode marked a turning point in Roosevelt's relations with isolationists, that episode was the so-called court-packing battle of 1937. Most who fought against the president's proposal to reorganize the judicial branch were conservatives who were not identified either with progressivism or with isolationism. Some prominent isolationists (notably Senator Robert M. La Follette, Jr., of Wisconsin) supported Roosevelt throughout the controversy. But most isolationist leaders (both progressive and conservative, both Republican and Democratic) opposed the President on court packing. And progressive Democratic Senator Burton K. Wheeler of Montana led the opposition. It became a heated, emotional, bitterly fought contest—on both sides. Neither Roosevelt nor his opponents forgot or entirely forgave after it was over. Motives were mixed for all involved. Nonetheless, for isolationists who already feared concentrated power in almost any form and who increasingly feared presidential power in foreign affairs, the court-packing fight emphasized a theme that was to become more and more prominent in arguments against Roosevelt's conduct of American foreign affairs.

After working so hard and successfully to bring the New Deal into being, both the president and his supporters were shaken and even angered in 1935 and 1936 when the United States Supreme Court wiped out important parts of the administration's program by finding them unconstitutional. Most notably, in May, 1935, it struck down the National Industrial Recovery Act, and in January, 1936, it ruled against the Agricultural Adjustment Act. The decision against NIRA was unanimous, but AAA fell before a six-to-three vote in the court. The president feared that the court jeopardized his whole social and economic program.

Long before Roosevelt became president, liberals and progressives had called for methods to bypass or override the court's obstruction of reform efforts. Progressive parties in 1912 (with Hiram Johnson as its vice-presidential candidate) and in 1924 (with old Fighting Bob La Follette and Senator Wheeler heading its ticket) had endorsed constitutional amendments to that effect. Late in January, 1935, Roosevelt spoke favorably to Senator Norris about such an amendment. In May, 1936, Senator Norris wrote that he would be glad if the "judicial question" were to be "one of the prominent issues" of the presidential election campaign that fall. Roosevelt, Norris, and many others explored various alternatives. But Roosevelt and the Democrats did not make judicial reform an issue in the 1936 campaign. Ultimately, Roosevelt decided against seeking a constitutional amendment, believing the procedure would be too slow and the dangers of defeat too great.[1]

Conservatives rallied in defense of the court and the Constitution in the controversy, whatever their views on foreign affairs. For example, former Secretary of State Henry L. Stimson of New York was a Republican, a conservative, and a Hamiltonian in his "belief in a strong central American government within those matters where centrality and strength are necessary." He was never an isolationist. Under both Theodore Roosevelt earlier and Franklin D. Roosevelt later, Stimson favored strong presidential authority in foreign affairs. But in June, 1935, Stimson wrote to FDR opposing any moves "to change the constitution in a vital and fundamental respect" and warning against "the danger of further centralization resulting in building up of an irresponsible bureaucracy."[2] Though the two differed sharply on foreign affairs, isolationist Republican Senator Arthur H. Vandenberg of Michigan was very nearly as conservative as Stimson on domestic issues. In a network broadcast in March, 1936, Vandenberg predicted that if the Supreme Court were ever denied the authority to declare legislation unconstitutional, it would "be a sad day for popular government, and for the perpetuation of American liberties."[3]

On February 5, 1937, without formally conferring with congressional leaders in advance, President Roosevelt presented his judicial reorganization plan to Congress. He later wrote that he considered that message to Congress "one of the most important and significant events of my administration on the domestic scene" and "a turning point in our modern history." The plan was shaped by the president, Attorney General Homer B. Cummings, and Solicitor General Stanley F. Reed. In his message Roosevelt said his proposals were needed to improve efficiency and to speed efforts to keep up with the case load; he did not portray it as a way to get a more liberal court that would sustain the New Deal. Among his proposals, the president recommended that Congress authorize him to appoint an additional justice to the Supreme Court for each one that failed to resign or retire within six months after his seventieth birthday. The proposal would have allowed the president to name up to six additional justices, thus enabling him to increase the size of the court from nine to a maximum of fifteen.[4]

In addition, Roosevelt explained his proposals to newsmen at press conferences. He spoke on behalf of his plan at a Democratic victory dinner in Washington on March 4. He went to the people in a fireside chat broadcast nationwide on March 9. And he used persuasion, pressure, and patronage to win legislators to his side and to discourage them from breaking ranks. It was a maximum political effort.[5]

Given the huge Democratic majorities in both houses of Congress after the elections of 1936, the administration's chances for winning adoption of its judicial proposal seemed excellent. The massive vote that Roosevelt had rolled up in winning reelection to a second term might have made moderates politically fearful of opposing his plan. And if western progressive isolationists (who generally supported the New Deal and criticized the court's performance) fell into line, Roosevelt's chances for victory seemed overwhelming. But things did not work out that way.

The morning after Roosevelt submitted his plan to Congress, former President Herbert Hoover telephoned Senator Vandenberg eager to war against court packing. Other Republicans, including Alf M. Landon, wanted to help. The American Liberty League was ready to throw its resources into the fray. Senator Borah, a member of the Judiciary Committee, was expected to lead the fight. But Borah, Vandenberg, and Senate Minority Leader Charles L. McNary of Oregon conferred and decided on different tactics. They agreed that they had "no hope if it is trade-marked in advance as a 'Hoover fight' or a 'Republican fight.'" They persuaded Hoover to stay in the background and Landon to pull his punches. Democratic Senator Carl A. Hatch of New Mexico, a member of the Judiciary Committee, was inclined to oppose the president's proposal, but he warned Vandenberg that "you Republicans and particularly Mr. Hoover must not make it too hard for me." Republican leaders agreed to "stay in the background for a week or ten days and let the revolting Democrats make their own record."[6]

As the Republicans hoped, Democrats led the opposition. Conservative Democrats caucused and decided they could be more effective if a liberal Democrat led their battle. At dinner in the home of Senator Millard E. Tydings of Maryland, Democratic Senators Harry F. Byrd of Virginia, Walter F. George of Georgia, Kenneth D. McKellar of Tennessee, Royal S. Copeland of New York, Edward R. Burke of Nebraska, and Tydings chose progressive Democratic Senator Wheeler to lead the fight.[7]

The White House tried to persuade Wheeler not to go against the president on the issue and to let a Republican lead the opposition. The Montana Democrat believed that he endangered his political future by opposing the popular president's plan. He took on the task nonetheless. Feisty Mrs. Wheeler, who distrusted Roosevelt much as Mrs. Johnson did, strengthened her husband in his resolve. Roosevelt was reported to have called Mrs. Wheeler the "Lady Macbeth of the Court Fight." But Wheeler made his own decision. Hiram Johnson returned from convalescing in Florida to condemn court packing, charging the president with trying to make the court subservient to him.[8] With Wheeler, Borah, Johnson, and other progressives in opposition, Roosevelt's formidable political position on the issue weakened. Conservative Republicans, conservative and moderate Democrats, and western progressives lined up against court packing, confronting the president with his toughest political battle since he took office four years earlier.

As chairman of the Senate Interstate Commerce Committee, Wheeler helped arrange network broadcast time for opponents of the president's plan. Progressive Senator La Follette gave a radio address supporting the president. Wheeler asked progressive Republican Senator Nye to deliver a broadcast against court packing. Vandenberg had thought that after leaving the initiative to Democrats for a week or two, it would be appropriate for Republicans to loose their fire. He prepared a speech and arranged broadcast time over NBC for Sunday evening, February 21. Wheeler and Borah advised against it, however, and persuaded him to transfer his network time to Nye. They wanted to get Nye on record against the president's proposal. And though he was a Republican, Nye's status as a progressive fit the tactics of keeping conservative Republicans out of the forefront. Not a lawyer, Nye got Republican attorney Seth W. Richardson, formerly of North Dakota, to help prepare his speech. The White House called Nye to meet with the president on Saturday, February 20. Roosevelt urged the North Dakota Senator not to give the address and suggested he claim a sprained ankle as an excuse for canceling the speech. The next morning, as the senator was completing preparations for his broadcast, William Thatcher of the Farmers' Union called on him. He too urged Nye not to speak against the president's proposal, fearing it could hurt North Dakota farmers. In making his case, the farm organization leader used some of the same language Roosevelt had used the day before, even to the point of suggesting a sprained ankle as an excuse for canceling. But Nye persisted.[9]

In his radio address on Sunday evening, Senator Nye contended that "the individual is the key to the proper understanding of our Government." He thought it "essential to limit strictly the power of the Executive" as "opposed to a Fascist government where supreme power exists in the executive." Nye said he was "completely out of sympathy with those processes by which the Supreme Court majorities have thwarted the will of the people when they have sought to build for better opportunity for themselves and to win a larger share of reward for their labors." He endorsed the constitutional amendment proposed by Senator Wheeler that would have enabled Congress, after an intervening election, to pass laws by two-thirds votes in both houses over the court's opposition. Nye concluded, "However foreign to the President the thought of dictatorship may be, in connection with this present request, it is good warning to look out, not for him necessarily, but for those who would in other days have opportunity to use the power which he would have us now extend."[10]

Mail reaction to Nye's address was largely favorable. But in addition to pressure from Thatcher of the Farmers' Union, A. F. Whitney of the Brotherhood of Railroad Trainmen, Daniel J. Tobin of the Teamsters Union, and other farm and labor spokesmen urged the North Dakota Senator to reverse his stand. Nye wavered, and by May, 1937, Roosevelt's legman Thomas Corcoran assured Secretary Ickes that Nye would vote for court packing.[11]

On March 2, with Wheeler's approval, Senator Vandenberg delivered his radio address opposing the president's plan. He was the first regular Republican senator to broadcast for the opposition. Like Nye earlier, Vandenberg included a sympathetic reference to the constitutional amendment Wheeler was proposing in place of the president's plan. Vandenberg had serious misgivings about the amendment, but he considered Wheeler *"absolutely essential* to us in this fight. He has taken a courageous stand against the President and is entitled to *any* co-operation we can give him." The Michigan senator recorded that his mail was running about fifty to one in opposition to court packing. In a letter Vandenberg wrote that it was "the 'zero hour' for the American system." He contended: "With 'law and order' in jeopardy in Michigan and with 'Nine old men' marked for slaughter in Washington, this certainly is a moment when the old maxim is right: 'Now is the time for all good men to come to the support of their country'."[12]

Senator Wheeler took to the airwaves to answer the president's broadcast on behalf of the judiciary proposal. He expressed fear that it would be a weapon that could "extinguish your right of liberty of speech, or thought, or action, or of religion; a weapon whose use is only dictated by the conscience of the wielder."[13]

The Judiciary Committee under Senator Henry F. Ashurst of Arizona began hearings on the president's proposal on March 10, with Attorney General Cummings and Assistant Attorney General Robert H. Jackson as the first witnesses on behalf of the plan. Senator Borah, ranking minority member of the committee, handled arrangments for opposition testimony. Senator Wheeler was scheduled to be the first opposition witness. On Saturday, March 20, two days before Wheeler testified, Mrs. Louis Brandeis, wife of the oldest, most progressive, and most respected of the associate justices on the Supreme Court, told the senator's daughter that she thought Wheeler was "right about the Court bill." The senator's daughter telephoned the word to her father, who promptly called on Judge Brandeis. Wheeler asked if he and Chief Justice Charles Evans Hughes would testify against the president's proposal. The old gentleman declined. But he urged the senator to call Hughes and assured him that the chief justice would provide him with a letter he could use. Wheeler had opposed the appointment of Hughes in 1930 and was reluctant to call him. So Brandeis took matters in hand. He personally telephoned and arranged for Hughes to receive Wheeler at his home that very afternoon. The distinguished chief justice greeted the progressive Democratic senator warmly and quickly agreed to prepare a letter. Sunday afternoon Hughes called Wheeler to his home and provided him with a letter, endorsed by Justices Brandeis and Van Devanter, opposing the president's plan.[14]

The impressive caucus room of the Senate Office Building was packed on Monday morning, March 22, when Wheeler took his seat to testify against the president's judicial reform proposal. He emphasized his friendly relations with Roosevelt, his support for most of his program, his campaign activities for Roosevelt, and his continued "high regard for the President." He was reluctantly parting company with Roosevelt on that issue as a matter of principle, opposing what he considered an "illiberal" proposal. "If a President could make both branches of government subservient," Wheeler wrote later, "totalitarianism could happen here as well as anywhere else." He caused a sensation when he produced and read Chief Justice Hughes's letter. The senator thought the letter "put the bill's backers on the defensive." He reported that Assistant Attorney General Jackson told him later that the Hughes letter "did more than any one thing to turn the tide in the Court struggle." In his memoirs James A. Farley described the Hughes letter as "a bombshell" and "a staggering blow."[15]

The following day Raymond Moley testified against the president's proposal, urging the constitutional amendment route instead. Moley, then editor of *Today*, had earlier broadcast along similar lines over the NBC network, charging that the proposal "strikes at the heart of democratic government." He supplemented his speeches and testimony with critical editorials.[16]

Hiram Johnson was not on the Judiciary Committee, and he was still too weakened from his illness to play the formidable role he could have in his younger years. But the California Republican left no doubt where he stood on the issue. In letters he wrote that America was "on the road to dictatorship. I will fight it until I die." To his son the old progressive wrote that the big thing was "the absorption of one of the coordinate branches of the government by the Executive. We can not deny he already has the legislative branch, and he whips it about as a schoolmaster would whip a recalcitrant boy. Give him now the judicial branch and all the power of government would be his. This way dictatorship." He was skeptical of polls showing a majority in California favoring the president's proposal; his own constituent mail ran heavily against the president.[17]

Senator Arthur Capper of Kansas firmly opposed court packing, as did young Democratic Senator Rush D. Holt of West Virginia. Illness kept Farmer-Labor Senator Henrik Shipstead away from Washington through much of the session, but he recorded his opposition to the president's plan. Robert A. Taft of Ohio was not yet in the Senate, but his father had served both as president and as chief justice of the Supreme Court. The future senator strongly objected to Roosevelt's proposal. He saw it as "a mere subterfuge to conceal" the "real purpose." He considered the move as designed "to change the opinions of the Supreme Court on New Deal legislation." Taft concluded that "if the present attempt succeeds, it will practically mean an end of the Constitution and of judicial independence."[18]

Probably no one close to the president was more torn and troubled by the controversy than Senator George W. Norris of Nebraska. He and Roosevelt discussed the problem many times and explored various alternatives in depth. Norris did not like what the court was doing to the New Deal, he sympathized with the president's social and economic goals, and he agreed with Roosevelt that the amendment process was too slow and uncertain. At the same time Norris did not like the court-packing scheme or consider it the best or only legislative way to handle the problem. Unlike most western progressives, Norris did not join the opposition. In letter after letter, the old Nebraska progressive wrote that he "would not favor the President's plan except as a last resort," but that he "would favor the President's plan rather than do nothing whatever about it." Norris denied that Roosevelt was "trying to become a dictator." His efforts to accomplish a compromise on the issue were not successful. With the passing years Norris had found the hot, humid Washington summers increasingly unbearable. As the court-packing controversy dragged on into the summer, he became ill. In July he fled to Wisconsin for his health and did not return until after the Senate had disposed of court packing.[19]

Things had started badly for Roosevelt's proposal—and they got worse. Progress on other legislative matters very nearly came to a standstill as both congress and the administration concentrated on court packing. Conferences, caucuses, rumors, counting and recounting expected vote patterns, arm twisting, button-holing, persuasion, and pressure went on constantly on both sides, in and out of the Capitol and the White House. For the first time in his life, Wheeler's income tax return was audited. In March and April, the Supreme Court reversed itself (or Hughes and Roberts did) and began sustaining New Deal measures in five-to-four decisions, including rulings upholding the Wagner Labor Relations Act and the Social Security Act. On May 18, 1937, the day the Judiciary Committee scheduled its vote on the plan, Associate Justice Willis Van Devanter submitted his resignation. With the court reversing itself and with the resignation giving the president his first opportunity to appoint a liberal to replace one of the conservatives on the court, court packing seemed less essential than before. The Judiciary Committee rejected all major amendments, and on May 18, it voted ten to eight to report the bill unfavorably. Borah was one of the ten who voted against the president's plan in committee. But still Roosevelt persisted.[20]

In the Senate, administration forces led by Majority Leader Joseph T. Robinson of Arkansas, pressed for approval of a compromise measure. Opponents would have none of it. Robinson was less than enthusiastic about court packing, but he was a good soldier and did his best to carry out Roosevelt's wishes. He had long hoped to win appointment to the Supreme Court, and Farley informed him confidentially that Roosevelt would appoint him to the seat vacated by Van Devanter when the judicial reform fight was over. On July 14, however, the hard-pressed Arkansas senator died. And the administration's fading chances for victory in the contest died with him.[21]

On July 15, the day after Robinson's death, Roosevelt stirred further irritation with his "Dear Alben" letter to Senator Barkley of Kentucky, acting majority leader. His letter was a slap at congressional opponents, a renewed appeal for action on judicial reform, and a show of preference for Barkley over Pat Harrison of Mississippi as successor to Robinson as Senate majority leader. Roosevelt got his way on the latter matter on July 21, when Senate Democrats voted thirty-eight to thirty-seven to elect Barkley majority leader. But the close vote underscored the sharp division in the majority party over the judicial reform issue and over the president's leadership.[22]

The final blow fell on July 22, 1937. Rejecting all compromise proposals, the Senate voted seventy to twenty to send the judicial reform bill back to the Judiciary Committee—essentially killing court packing. Among the twenty senators voting on behalf of the administration's position against recommitting were isolationist Senators Bone of Washington, La Follette of Wisconsin, and Lundeen of Minnesota. Among the five senators not voting was Norris, who was resting in Wisconsin, but he had indicated that if he had been present, he would have voted against sending the bill back to committee. All other leading isolationists voted against the president in favor of recommitting the bill—including Senators Borah, Capper, Clark, Frazier, Holt, Johnson, McNary, Nye, Reynolds, Shipstead, Vandenberg, Walsh, Wheeler, and White. Old Hiram Johnson arose from his seat to make certain that a vote to recommit referred to the Supreme Court as well as to lower courts. He was assured that it did. When it was clear that "the Supreme Court is out of the way," Johnson brought a round of applause when he exclaimed, "Glory be to God!"[23]

That was not Roosevelt's response to the vote. Though FDR got the more liberal Supreme Court he wanted, there was no denying that he had suffered a major defeat. And it showed on the man. Two days before the Senate vote Ickes found the president looking more tired and nervous than he had ever seen him before. Ickes thought it "quite evident that he is feeling the strain under which he has been working." And Roosevelt's personal secretary Missy Le Hand told Ickes that "she didn't see how anyone could stand" twelve years of the presidency.[24]

Most were surprised when the president nominated liberal Democratic Senator Hugo L. Black of Alabama to fill the seat on the Supreme Court left vacant by Van Devanter's resignation. Objections by Senators Johnson and Burke forced consideration by the Judiciary Committee and made it possible for opponents to record their opposition. The Judiciary Committee reported quickly and favorably on the nomination, however, and on August 17, the Senate approved the appointment by a vote of sixty-three to sixteen. All leading isolationists present voted for approval except Borah, Johnson, and White. Among those not voting were Norris (paired for), Tydings (paired against), Vandenberg, Walsh, and Wheeler.[25]

Though Roosevelt continued to be good-humored and affable in relations with legislators who had opposed his judicial proposal, he did not forget or forgive. He directed his ire more against Democrats who had parted company with him than he did against Republicans. During the latter part of September and early October, 1937, Roosevelt made a tour through the Middle West and Far West. In the course of the trip he made a point of not including legislators who had opposed him on court packing. For example, in Montana he invited Democratic Senator James E. Murray, and Democratic Congressmen James F. O'Connor and Jerry J. O'Connell aboard his train, but he conspicuously omitted Senator Wheeler. Wheeler also felt the President's displeasure on patronage matters. Democrats who had opposed court packing and who came up for reelection in 1938, including Senators Tydings of Maryland and George of Georgia, were among those that Roosevelt tried unsuccessfully to purge.[26]

The court-packing controversy did not mark a final or total breach between Roosevelt and individual isolationist leaders. Even Wheeler continued to cooperate with Roosevelt later on specific legislative matters. And those who displeased (and were displeased by) the president in the court fight were by no means limited to isolationists. Democratic Senator Tom Connally of Texas was not an isolationist, and he battled aggressively for President Roosevelt's foreign policies before and after the United States entered World War II. But he had opposed the president on court packing and was one of those the president snubbed after it was over. Not until 1939 was the Texan again drawn into frequent personal dealings with Roosevelt—largely on foreign policy matters.[27] Nonetheless, the whole court-packing controversy was an important part of the growing estrangement of Roosevelt and isolationists. It increased isolationist fears about the dangers of excessive power in the hands of the president.

That growing fear of presidential power evidenced itself in deliberations on other domestic legislation as well. The president's proposal for reorganization of the executive branch was a clear example. Roosevelt had forwarded his recommendations to Congress early in 1937, but they were buried under the protracted court-packing controversy and made little progress during the special session late in the year. The Senate finally passed a revised version of the reorganization bill on March 28, 1938, by a margin of 49 to 42. On April 8, however, the House of Representatives killed it by voting 204 to 196 to recommit—to send it back to committee.[28]

Conservatives and those opposed to New Deal innovations could have been expected to fret about the proposal. One should not have expected otherwise from Vandenberg, for example. But the increasing anxieties of western progressives about concentrated presidential power and their growing fears of Roosevelt's power-grabbing proclivities added those isolationists to the opposition. Legislators proposed amendments that would have restricted presidential authority in the reorganization process. Most amendments were defeated, but the patterns found leading isolationists voting with the minorities in favor of the amendments. For example, Senator Wheeler introduced an amendment that would have required that presidential reorganization orders would not become effective until approved by majorities in both houses of Congress. The amendment was defeated 43 to 39. Senators La Follette and Norris voted against the amendment, and then voted for the administration bill later. Senator Lundeen of Minnesota voted against the Wheeler amendment, but then turned around and voted against the final bill as well. Most of the rest of the isolationists (both conservative and progressive, both Democratic and Republican) voted for the Wheeler amendment on March 18 and ten days later voted against the administration bill. They included Senators Bone, Borah, Capper, Clark, Frazier, Holt, Johnson, McNary, Nye, Vandenberg, Walsh, and Wheeler, among others. Democratic Senator Walsh of Massachusetts called the administration's proposal "the antithesis of Democracy and a dangerous excursion along the road to the totalitarian state.'' California's Hiram Johnson wrote his son that ''the Reorganization Bill is the small crack in the dike that will let through the torrent. It was presented contemporaneously with the Court Packing Bill. The two, if adopted would literally have made of the President a Dictator.'' Isolationist Congressmen Hamilton Fish of New York and George Tinkham of Massachusetts were among the 204 in the House who voted to send the bill back to committee.[29]

Those fears of excessive presidential power became increasingly emotional and increasingly directed against President Franklin D. Roosevelt personally. They extended to both domestic and foreign policy concerns. Those fears were evident as Congress and the administration shaped permanent neutrality legislation in 1937. And as Japan, Germany, and Italy mounted their challenges to the international status quo, Roosevelt initiated policies and used methods in foreign affairs that isolationists saw as evidence of the dangers of what, in different hands and in different contexts much later, would be called the ''imperial presidency.''

Chapter 15

Permanent Neutrality

The court-packing controversy very nearly brought legislative action on other matters to a standstill during the early months of 1937. Among the comparatively few substantive legislative accomplishments of that session of Congress was the enactment of two neutrality laws. The first was emergency legislation to embargo shipment of arms to both sides in the civil war raging in Spain. The second was the so-called permanent Neutrality Act of 1937. The Neutrality Act of 1937 carried further the general patterns already set in motion by the laws of 1935 and 1936. The Spanish embargo, however, moved both the Roosevelt administration and leading isolationists into postures that seemed very nearly the reverse of those they had taken earlier and were to take later.

Erupting in July, 1936, the Spanish civil war dragged on until the final triumph by the Nationalists under Franciso Franco in 1939. It was a horribly bloody and bitterly fought contest. It had disturbing international ramifications that made it a precursor, a squall line, for World War II later. Though the Spanish provided the impetus and leadership (and endured most of the suffering), other peoples and states also played roles and felt its effects. The Loyalist republican government of Spain won military and material aid from Stalin's Soviet Russia. And Franco's forces got military help from Mussolini's Fascist Italy and from Hitler's Nazi Germany. The anticlerical violence and policies of the Spanish government alienated Roman Catholics the world over. Socialists and liberals attracted by Communist-supported popular front movements backed the Loyalist regime against Franco's fascists. Even Norman Thomas at the head of the Socialist party in the United States (which abjured popular front enticements and was skeptical of working with Communists) shared that general perspective. One might have expected internationalists (including the Roosevelt administration) to have sympathized with collective security efforts to sustain the Spanish government against the fascist challenge. That was the course urged by the United States ambassador to Spain, Claude G. Bowers. And one might have expected isolationists to have favored extending American neutrality restrictions to the Spanish civil war in the interests of noninvolvement by the United States. The actual patterns were the reverse of those expectations. The Roosevelt administration spoke the language of neutrality and noninvolvement, while isolationists led by Senator Gerald P. Nye urged policies that would have had the effect of helping the Loyalist government against Franco's Nationalists. Only with the final triumph of Franco's forces in 1939 did the Roosevelt administration end what Sumner Welles later called "our blind isolationist policies" toward the Spanish civil war.[1]

Initially the Roosevelt administration's policies toward the Spanish civil war were (like its policies toward the Italian-Ethiopian war earlier) designed to move the United States independently into channels paralleling and supplementing multilateral policies initiated by Britain and France. Still shaken by the fear that the Italian-Ethiopian war might have spread to a general European war and by the failure of the League of Nations sanctions against Italy, the British and French governments determined to confine the Spanish upheaval by organizing a general European noninterventionist policy. The Department of State kept abreast of those developments without formally becoming a part of them. The Neutrality Act of 1936 did not apply to civil wars, so the administration could not invoke its embargo provisions in the Spanish conflict. Knowing the general policies the British and French proposed to pursue, on August 7, 1936, the Department of State telegraphed American consular and diplomatic officials in Spain that "in conformity with its well-established policy of non-interference with internal affairs in other countries, either in time of peace or in the event of civil strife, this Government will, of course, scrupulously refrain from any interference whatsoever in the unfortunate Spanish situation." The State Department advised potential exporters that sale of munitions in Spain "would not follow the Government's policy." The United States independently initiated that noninterventionist policy early in August before the British and French finalized their organization of the twenty-seven-state Nonintervention Committee. The British and French kept the United States informed of their policies and actions. But they carefully refrained from inviting the United States to become a party to their multilateral arrangement in their efforts to avoid provoking isolationist reactions that might complicate matters for the Roosevelt administration in pursuing its "parallel but independent" noninterventionist policies in Spain.[2]

When Socialist Norman Thomas complained late in 1936 about the policy of discouraging sale of arms to the Spanish government, President Roosevelt responded that the State Department's policy had his "entire approval." In a letter drafted for him by Acting Secretary of State R. Walton Moore, Roosevelt was able to write Thomas that the policy was initiated "some weeks before the non-intervention pact among the several European nations came into effect and while the policy of those nations toward the Spanish conflict was still uncertain and undetermined. No suggestion was made to us by any European country in regard to the attitude which we should adopt at that time nor have there been any subsequent suggestions of such nature. Our stand was taken as a completely independent measure which arose naturally and inevitably from our policy of non-intervention and from the spirit of the recent neutrality laws." Using language that isolationists used in different situations earlier and later, Roosevelt wrote that "a policy of attempting to discriminate between parties would be dangerous in the extreme" and would "be involving ourselves directly in that European strife from which our people desire so deeply to remain aloof."[3]

Until December,1936, interested businesses and exporters honored the "moral embargo," and it successfully prevented the flow of arms directly from the United States to either side in Spain. In December, however, Robert Cuse of the Vimalert Company applied for licenses to export airplanes and engines valued at nearly $3 million to the Loyalist government of Spain (not to Franco). Since the shipment did not violate existing law, the State Department had to grant the licenses. A second applicant sought licenses for even larger shipments of planes and arms.[4]

On December 29, the day after the department gave public notice of issuing the first export licenses, the president commented on the matter at his press conference. It was, he said, "a rather good example of the need of some power in the Executive." He charged that the businessman involved was doing "what amounts to a perfectly legal but thoroughly unpatriotic act."[5]

The Spanish ambassador to the United States was unhappy about the administration's objections to the shipments. The British, the French, and the Roosevelt administration were unhappy that the

United States lacked legal authority to deny the export licenses. Senator William E. Borah of Idaho said the department "did the right thing. It obeyed the law." But he thought that "the mandatory principle worked the wrong way" in that instance, and that there was "a limit to 'mandatory' legislation."[6]

On December 30, the president met with Acting Secretary of State Moore, Senator Key Pittman, and Congressman Sam McReynolds. They agreed on the necessity for legislation to ban arms shipments to Spain. Further deliberations on January 5 determined that Pittman would introduce emergency legislation calling for an embargo on shipment of arms and munitions to Spain, and McReynolds would handle the matter in the House.[7]

On Wednesday, January 6, 1937, Pittman hoped to win quick unanimous consent to his resolution. Much to the displeasure of Pittman and Tom Connally of Texas, Senator Gerald P. Nye of North Dakota took the floor to register his thoughts and reservations. In August, 1936, Nye had joined nine other senators and congressmen in a telegram to Roosevelt urging "every possible effort on the part of the government to prevent shipment of war supplies to Spain." From all sections of the country outside the South, the ten legislators included eight Democrats, one Republican, and one Farmer-Laborite. On December 30, Nye had written Acting Secretary of State Moore asking for "the times and names of persons or corporations indicating to the State Department during the past six months an interest in or desire for license to export arms or implements of war to Spain." Moore responded on January 5, outlining the department's general policies on the matter, but omitting the names that Nye had sought.[8]

In his brief comments to the Senate on January 6, Nye spoke out against cooperative undertakings with the British and French, preferred more sweeping neutrality legislation rather than emergency action applying only to Spain, and denied that the Spanish embargo would be neutral. He insisted that he was not moved by sympathy for one side or the other in Spain. He feared that cooperation with Britain and France conceivably could lead to the sale of arms to the Loyalists on the grounds that others were helping Franco. Nye wished the United States would handle the matter "by writing an embargo policy that would apply automatically to every country when trouble like that in Spain may come anywhere upon the earth." He agreed to support the Spanish embargo if it were conceived as "an effort to keep the hands of the United States clean and removed from the danger of being drawn quickly into that war or strife in Europe." He insisted that it was not neutrality, however, and implied that it would, in effect, aid Franco's rebels against the Loyalist government.[9]

Senators Pittman and Connally were angered by Nye's remarks and by the fact that he took the floor at all on the matter. Pittman heatedly denied that his resolution involved any cooperative course with Britain and France. He denied that the resolution "was drafted with the intent of siding with the so-called insurgent elements in Spain." With the flurry surrounding Nye's comments concluded, the Senate approved the Spanish embargo by a vote of 81 to 0, with 12 not voting. Nye cast his vote for the resolution. The House approved the embargo 404 to 1. The lone negative vote was cast by Minnesota's Farmer-Labor Congressman John T. Bernard.[10]

The resolution prohibited the sale and export of all arms, munitions, and implements of war to either side in Spain. It also banned sale of munitions to neutrals for transshipment to Spain. Under the legislation the licenses already issued by the Department of State were invalidated. It would be binding until the president declared the emergency in Spain ended.[11]

A legal technicality briefly delayed transmission of the resolution to the White House. On January 8, 1937, President Roosevelt signed it into law. He voiced none of the reservations or misgivings he had indicated when signing the Neutrality Acts of 1935 and 1936. The one-day delay gave Cuse time to ship part of his cargo on its way from New York aboard the Spanish steamship *Mar Cantábrico*. Ironically, those planes eventually were captured by Franco's forces and never reached the Loyalist government that had contracted for them.[12]

If America's embargo and Europe's Nonintervention Committee were designed to prevent the Spanish conflict from spreading to involve Britain, France, and the United States in the flames of a general war, they may be seen as successful—in the short run. Most doubted that noninterventionist policies represented neutrality between the combatants in Spain. Their practical effect was to deny the Loyalist government access to military equipment from Britain, France, the United States, and other Western countries at the same time that Franco's Nationalist forces won increasing military help from Fascist Italy and Nazi Germany. Italian and German aid were known before enactment of the Spanish embargo, but Axis military involvement became more massive and effective as the weeks and months passed. Many, including American Ambassador Claude Bowers, were convinced that the rebel forces would have been crushed quickly had it not been for Germany and Italy (who were parties to the Nonintervention Committee). Bowers believed most Spanish favored the Loyalist government over the Nationalists, that Italian and German power turned the military tide against the republican government.[13]

Among the more vocal critics of American policies in 1937 and 1938 were isolationists and pacifists, notably progressive Republican Senator Gerald P. Nye and pacifist Socialist Norman Thomas. Late in March, 1937, with Germany and Italy in mind, Nye introduced Senate Resolution 100, asking the secretary of state "whether the existing neutrality laws of the United States are sufficient to provide an embargo against nations whose armed forces are engaged in active warfare in a nation where a state of civil war exists, which state of civil war has caused our Government to declare embargoes against exportation of arms, ammunition, and implements of war to that nation." Though Pittman forwarded the resolution to Secretary Hull, Nye and the Senate never received a clear and explicit response to the inquiry.[14]

On March 30, 1937, Senator Nye introduced Joint Resolution 120, to prohibit the export of "arms, ammunition, or implements of war from any place in the United States, except to nations on the American continents engaged in war against a non-American state or states." It would have encompassed German, Italian, and Soviet military involvement in Spain, but its sweeping language was much broader than that. It was a further extension of Nye's consistent drive for national legislation to stop the international munitions traffic.[15]

Pittman forwarded Senate Joint Resolution 120 to the secretary of state. In his response nearly six weeks later on May 4, Hull firmly opposed Nye's joint resolution. He pointed out that a broad definition of arms, ammunition, or implements of war "would destroy our export trade in such articles intended for commercial use." It would "add to the number of restrictions upon normal peace-time international trade—restrictions which it has been our policy to reduce to a minimum." It would conflict with Hull's trade policies. He also believed it "would not promote the cause of world peace, and might indeed have the contrary effect." Two weeks later, on motion by Senator Tom Connally, the Foreign Relations Committee postponed action indefinitely on Nye's joint resolution. The committee restored it to its calendar two weeks later, but the committee never reported it, and the Senate never voted on it.[16]

With Nye's Senate Joint Resolution 120 stalled in Pittman's committee, Norman Thomas independently pressed along similar lines by going directly to President Roosevelt. Ohio-born Thomas had been a Presbyterian minister and had become the leader of democratic socialism in the United States. He was the Socialist party candidate for president every four years from 1928 through 1948. A comparison of Nye and Thomas throws light on differences, similarities, and co-operation between isolationists and pacifists in opposition to Roosevelt's foreign policies. Thomas and Nye differed in many ways. Thomas was a socialist; Nye a progressive. Thomas was a pacifist; Nye an isolationist. Thomas graduated from Princeton University and Union Theological Seminary; Nye never attended college after graduating from Wittenberg High School in Wisconsin. Thomas made his headquarters in New York City; Nye had his base in the Great Plains agricultural state of North Dakota. In addition, however, there were many similarities between the two men. In the 1930s both Thomas and Nye were to the left of Roosevelt and the New Deal. Both had faith in little-*d* democracy, were skeptical of elitism, and opposed authoritarian methods. Both emphasized domestic economic bases for military expenditures and involvement in foreign ventures. Both became noninterventionist opponents of Roosevelt's foreign policies before Pearl Harbor. Both supported the United States government after it declared war in December, 1941. On some issues Nye's views were closer to those of Thomas and other pacifists than they were to fellow isolationists Borah and Johnson. Despite their different images and reputations, it is difficult to identify foreign policies between 1932 and 1945 on which Norman Thomas and Gerald P. Nye disagreed.[17]

On June 9, after returning from a trip to the Soviet Union and Europe, Thomas wrote to President Roosevelt about American policies toward Spain. Thomas was convinced that "a state of real, if undeclared, war exists between the legitimate Loyalist government of Spain and Germany and Italy, or to be more accurate, Hitler and Mussolini." He urged that "unless the German and Italian governments markedly change their policy we should apply the principles of neutrality as against them. If we are not prepared to do that we should scarcely apply neutrality against Loyalist Spain." He thought America's embargo policies were "a kind of left-handed aid to Franco, the Fascists, and the dictators who are supporting him."[18]

After receiving the letter, Roosevelt asked his secretary to arrange a White House appointment for Thomas. On June 29, in a memorandum to Cordell Hull marked personal and confidential, FDR wrote: "For many reasons I think that if Mussolini or the Italian Government or Hitler or the German Government have made or make any official admissions or statements that their Government armed forces are actually taking part in the fighting in Spain on the side of Franco, or are engaging in the Spanish war, then in such case we shall have to act under the Neutrality Act." He did "not think we can compound a ridiculous situation if after the fight is established, Great Britain and France continue to assert solemnly that they 'have no proof' of Italian or German participation in the Spanish War.'' He asked Hull if they ought to cable America's ambassadors in Italy and Germany "to ask for categorical answers.'' The view that Roosevelt suggested in his memo to Hull was precisely the point that Nye had been trying to make through his resolutions and Thomas had been trying to make in his letters and meeting with the president. In response to the president's memo, the State Department did cable the American ambassadors in European capitals. On into the spring of 1938, Nye continued to prod Pittman for action on his joint resolution, and the State Department persisted in its opposition.[19] Throughout the Spanish civil war the Roosevelt administration continued the policies it had initiated in August, 1936, and had firmed up with the enactment of the Spanish embargo in January, 1937.

During the early months of 1937, while controversy swirled about the wisdom and effects of the Spanish embargo and while the court-packing fight continued to overshadow and stymie legislative action on other matters, Congress and the administration labored over so-called permanent neutrality legislation. The Neutrality Act of 1936 would expire on May 1, 1937. Isolationists had momentum on the issue. Assistant Secretary of State Francis B. Sayre could "strongly doubt whether neutrality laws can save us from being swept into the war.'' But leading internationalists from President Roosevelt and Secretary Hull on down were driven reluctantly to the conclusion that it was not politically possible to win enactment of legislation authorizing the president to use the power of the United States to try to preserve world peace and thereby make American involvement in foreign wars less likely.[20] By 1937, the administration thought it futile and tactically unwise even to propose draft legislation of its own.

The Senate Munitions Investigating Committee made specific recommendations for neutrality legislation before Congress convened in January, 1937. The Nye committee's fifth report, submitted in June, 1936, included detailed proposals for extending, clarifying, and tightening existing neutrality laws. It particularly emphasized "the importance of determining a neutrality policy before war has begun and the desirability of mandatory rather than discretionary legislation.'' The committee's sixth report made comparable recommendations for financial, export, and shipping controls—including "limiting exportations of commodities other than medicines and hospital supplies to belligerents to the normal amount exported to such nations during a typical peacetime period.''[21]

By 1937 there was no practical possibility that Congress would pass neutrality legislation in tune with the internationalist views of Roosevelt, Hull, and Davis. The administration and Department of State deliberately stayed in the background, refrained from recommending specific legislation, and generally left the initiative to congressional leaders. As Hull explained in his memoirs later: "I felt that Congress was determined on neutrality legislation of an inflexible nature, and our arguments in favor of flexible neutrality legislation that would leave the widest possible discretion to the Executive would have little effect. Where we could, we obtained slight modifications more in conformity with our ideas."[22]

Senator Key Pittman introduced his proposals (S.J. Res. 51) on January 22, 1937. It was not an administration bill and had not been prepared in the State Department. Pittman had drafted his resolution after only brief and rather vague consultation with Acting Secretary of State R. Walton Moore. Pittman presented it as "a basis for the consideration of the whole subject." He hoped his resolution would prevent favorable committee action on the "much more radical" resolution likely to be introduced by leading isolationists. About all Roosevelt suggested was that he strongly favored "permissive legislation."[23]

Ten days later, on February 1, Democratic Senator Bennett Champ Clark of Missouri introduced Senate Joint Resolution 60 for himself, Nye, Vandenberg, and Bone. All four (two Democrats and two Republicans) had served on the Munitions Investigating Committee. Clark had teamed with Nye in sponsoring earlier neutrality legislation. The son of Champ Clark, long-time speaker of the House, Clark was over six feet tall and weighed more than two hundred pounds. He had been an Army colonel in World War I and was a charter member and former national commander of the American Legion. After developing a successful law practice in St. Louis, he went to the Senate in 1933. Round-faced and amiable, Clark lacked Nye's intensity and capacity for hard work, but he had a keen mind and plenty of political courage.[24]

Both the Pittman resolution and the one introduced by Clark and his colleagues were in the form of amendments to the existing Neutrality Act. Senators Elbert D. Thomas of Utah and J. Hamilton Lewis of Illinois introduced separate bills to replace the existing law. Comparable measures were introduced in the House of Representatives. Pittman's joint resolution did not allow nearly so much discretionary authority for the president as the administration and internationalists would have preferred. The Clark resolution was not so rigidly mandatory nor so sweeping in its controls as Nye would have preferred.

Each was limited by what its sponsors thought Congress might be willing to adopt.

The Senate Foreign Relations Committee met in executive session on February 13, 1937, to consider the four proposals. R. Walton Moore and Green H. Hackworth represented the State Department at the meeting. Moore urged permissive legislation, but acknowledged that "in all human probability the Congress is going to retain the mandatory provisions." He warned against "legislation which will induce all the other nations of the world to channel their trade to other markets than the American markets." Under the circumstances he considered the Pittman resolution reasonably satisfactory. Late in February the Foreign Relations Committee favorably reported the Pittman bill, modified as a result of detailed committee consideration. Senator Johnson voted against the joint resolution in committee; Borah opposed it, but was not present for the vote.[25]

Senators Clark, Nye, Vandenberg, Bone, Johnson, and Borah all considered the Pittman bill too discretionary. In addition, Borah and Johnson both opposed the cash-and-carry provision that Nye, Clark, and Vandenberg enthusiastically favored. All shared in trying to amend the resolution on the Senate floor. Still weakened by his prolonged illness, Senator Johnson spoke as vigorously as he could against the resolution. The Senate rejected amendments proposed by Vandenberg and by Borah. On March 3, 1937, the Senate adopted Pittman's Senate Joint Resolution 51 by a vote of sixty-three to six. Clark, Nye, Bone, Vandenberg, and most others voted for the bill despite their misgivings, but the negative votes included those cast by Senators Borah, Johnson, Warren Austin of Vermont, Peter Gerry of Rhode Island, Henry Cabot Lodge, Jr., of Massachusetts, and Styles Bridges of New Hampshire. Assistant Secretary of State Moore wrote Roosevelt that the resolution was "a fairly liberal measure and the best that anyone knowing the situation could expect the Senate to pass."[26]

A similar measure introduced by Sam McReynolds, passed in the House of Representatives 376 to 12. It allowed slightly greater presidential discretion than the Pittman resolution, particularly in the application of cash-and-carry. A House-Senate conference committee wrestled for weeks with the task of reconciling the two measures. Senator Borah of Idaho and Congressman Fish of New York served the isolationist views on the conference committee. President Roosevelt urged Senator Joseph T. Robinson of Arkansas to try to persuade Pittman to yield as far as possible to the House bill and authorized Robinson to use the president's name if he thought it advisable in talking with the Nevada senator. In line with Roosevelt's wishes, the conference report on April 28 generally compromised in favor of the more discretionary House resolution.[27]

A "mandatory" bloc led by Senator Nye and including five of the seven members of the old Munitions Investigating Committee (Clark, Bone, Pope, and Vandenberg, in addition to Nye) vigorously opposed the conference report. Nye told the Senate that it was not "possible to draft and enact a neutrality policy which will be a genuine cure-all and assure our nonparticipation in more foreign wars." He insisted, however, that if they really determined to stay out of foreign wars, Americans must give up "any taste of the profit from other people's wars before we get into them" and must reduce presidential discretion "so far as we can." He believed Americans must "do more than we have done in our pending neutrality program" if the United States hoped to stay out of foreign wars.[28]

In spite of the opposition, however, the House and Senate both adopted the conference report on April 29, 1937. Forty-one senators (including Borah and Pope) voted for the report. Fifteen senators (including Bridges, Capper, Clark, Frazier, Holt, Johnson, Lodge, Nye, White, and others) voted against it. McNary, La Follette, Lundeen, Norris, Shipstead, Vandenberg, Walsh, and Wheeler were among the thirty-nine not voting. Despite certain "features which cannot be considered entirely satisfactory," Secretary Hull recommended that Roosevelt approve it. The president signed it into law on May 1, 1937.[29]

That "permanent" Neutrality Act of 1937 retained many of the provisions of the earlier laws—a mandatory arms embargo, a ban on loans and credits to belligerents, continuation of the National Munitions Control Board, and a ban on travel by Americans on belligerent ships. It also prohibited the arming of American merchant ships trading with belligerents and the use of American ships for transporting munitions to belligerents. In addition it gave the president discretionary authority to put the sale of nonembargoed goods to belligerents on a cash-and-carry basis—that is, title to the goods had to be transferred to non-American hands, and the goods had to be carried to the belligerent in non-American ships. That law also gave the president discretionary authority to prohibit use of American ports by armed belligerent ships. Like the 1936 law, it did not apply to a war between an American republic and a non-American state. But unlike the 1936 law, it did apply to civil wars in addition to international conflicts. Most of its provisions were "permanent," but cash-and-carry would expire in two years on May 1, 1939. On May 10, Clark, Nye,

Bone, and Vandenberg sponsored an amendment that would have made cash-and-carry mandatory, but the State Department opposed and Congress never adopted it.[30]

Two years later, in a letter to columnist Walter Lippmann, Senator Nye protested against associating his name with the Neutrality Act of 1937. He pointed out that he had voted against the conference report. Most other leading Senate isolationists had either voted against the conference report or had not voted for it. "Could I have my way about it," Nye wrote, "the neutrality law would forbid all trade with nations at war as well as financing through loans or credits. In the absence of chance for this complete accomplishment, I should have to be content with a strict forbiddance of loans, credits and munitions sales to belligerents with a provision that All other commodities be placed on a strict cash and carry basis, with no right or power left with the President to determine what commodities should be included in the cash and carry category, and all of the provisions to be invoked when once a state of war existed, not at the discretion in whole or in part of the President." Nonetheless, Nye thought the Neutrality Act of 1937 was "far better than having no law in its field whatever."[31]

From May 1, 1937, until April 1, 1939, both the Spanish embargo of January, 1937, and the Neutrality Act of May, 1937, barred sale and shipment of arms and munitions from the United States to both sides in Spain. The Roosevelt administration had initiated that policy as part of its independent efforts to parallel and supplement the Anglo-French nonintervention policies. Both the Nonintervention Committee in Europe and the Roosevelt administration persisted in those policies long after it was apparent that they were, in effect, denying the Loyalist government needed equipment at the same time that Fascist Italy and Nazi Germany were aiding and warring for Franco's fascist rebels. The administration found it easier to get into that awkward situation than to get out of it. Furthermore, as the fighting continued, Franco's forces gained control of Spain's coastal areas and port cities, thus blocking access to the Loyalists even if the United States had lifted its embargo.

In addition, domestic patterns in the United States made it politically risky to lift the embargo. Polls showed that a large percentage of the American people had little interest in the Spanish developments. Those who did note them were rather evenly divided in their sentiments. A minority, however, felt passionately on the subject. Many on the left from liberals through Socialists to Communists fervently favored aid for the Loyalists against Franco's fascists and urged repeal of the embargo. At the same time, most Roman Catholics were equally passionate in their hostility against the Loyalist government of Spain and determined that the embargo be continued. They were moved by anti-Communist considerations. Moreover, most Italian-Americans and many German-Americans were Roman Catholics. The predominantly Catholic Irish-American population abhorred the idea of supplementing British policies anywhere. And the anti-church actions of the Loyalist government had alienated most Roman Catholics. The White House, congressmen, and senators received thousands of cards, letters, and telegrams opposing any relaxation of the embargo. Some of that mail was inspired by organized groups, but much of it expressed powerful individual feelings. When some seventy congressmen and senators signed a greeting to the Spanish parliament early in 1938, the storm of protests from Catholics and Catholic organizations forced a lot of backing and hauling by individual legislators. Though the administration's policies initially grew out of informal cooperation with Britain and France, those policies were continued long after their futility was apparent, partly because of the passionate feelings expressed by many thousands of Roman Catholics. The administration had more than enough political difficulties in 1937 and 1938, without alienating the large Roman Catholic population. By 1938, Secretary of Interior Harold Ickes had become thoroughly disenchanted with the embargo and had discussed the matter repeatedly with Roosevelt and others. He became convinced that the fear of losing the Catholic vote was decisive in continuing the embargo.[32]

Senator Nye's North Dakota included a large German and German-Russian Catholic population. He could not be insensitive to their views, particularly since he faced a strong adversary in his bid for re-election to another term in the fall of 1938. Nonetheless, he pressed ahead on the Spanish issue along the general lines he had been pursuing very nearly from the beginning. Unable to overcome administration opposition to Senate Joint Resolution 120, in 1938 Nye initiated a different and more direct approach. On May 2, 1938, the North Dakota progressive introduced Senate Joint Resolution 288, which would have repealed the Spanish embargo. It would have called on the president to "raise the embargo against the Government of Spain" (while continuing it against Franco's Nationalists), with the proviso that all sales and shipments to Spain be on a cash-and-carry basis. In presenting his resolution, Nye told the Senate that he was "not promoted by the interest of either side involved in Spain," but "only by a desire to right an injustice growing out of the embargo program." The embargo resulted "in aid for one side as against another, and neither neutrality nor non-intervention is accomplished."[33]

For Senator Nye to urge repeal of an arms embargo seemed out of line with his long crusade earlier and later against the international arms traffic (just as Roosevelt's support for the embargo seemed out of character). Nonetheless, just as the administration's course becomes comprehensible on closer examination, so with Nye's. By 1938 it had become easier for Nye to fall into an anti-Roosevelt posture than it had been earlier. Like other isolationists, Nye objected to cooperative ventures with Britain and France—even when the Anglo-French policy was noninterventionist. In his peace efforts Nye consulted and cooperated frequently with pacifists, many of whom were also Socialists who were critical of the Spanish embargo (though Nye insisted later that they had not influenced him). Recalling the episode many years later, Nye found the immediate explanation for his repeal resolution in a Masonic dinner meeting he had attended along with Democratic Senator Tom Connally of Texas. As he recalled it in 1959, Nye said that he and Connally had attended a Masonic dinner together. At that meeting there was much criticism of the Spanish embargo and much discussion of how unneutral it was. A few days after the dinner meeting, as Nye recalled, Connally approached him and urged him to introduce a resolution repealing the embargo. Nye invited the Texas senator to join with him, but Connally declined. As a result of the discussions at the Masonic dinner, however, and as prodded by Connally, Nye introduced his Senate Joint Resolution 288.[34]

The Nye resolution provoked heated controversy both in and out of government. The White House and Capitol were inundated with mail on the issue. There were flurries of conferences in the State Department. Hull and his advisors spent much time carefully revising several drafts for the department's response to Pittman's inquiry about its reaction to the Nye resolution. As J. Pierrepont Moffat phrased it in his diary: "Few if any documents are politically as dangerous[,] for the bitterness inspired by this Spanish strife among the Left Wingers on the one hand and the Catholic conservative elements on the other surpasses anything I have seen for years." Hull cleared his letter with both Roosevelt and Pittman before he sent it.[35]

In his letter to Pittman dated May 12, Secretary Hull opposed Nye's resolution and opposed repeal of the Spanish embargo. Hull pointed out that Nye's resolution, if enacted, would continue the embargo against Franco but lift it to permit sale of arms to the Loyalist government. Hull wrote: "In view of the continued danger of international conflict arising from the circumstances of the struggle, any proposal which at this juncture contemplates a reversal of our policy of strict non-interference which we have thus far so scrupulously followed, and under the operation of which we have kept out of involvements, would offer a real possibility of complications." Hull also suggested that rather than repeal the Spanish embargo, it might be better to reconsider the whole neutrality legislation matter—something Nye did not want to do at that time.[36]

Pittman carefully guarded the contents of Hull's letter until his Foreign Relations Committee met on Friday morning, May 13, 1938. He then solemnly provided each senator with a mimeographed copy of the letter. Each read it carefully, and all concluded its perspective was sound. Someone suggested that Nye might wish to testify before the committee acted on his resolution, but he was in North Dakota at the time, so the committee decided not to wait. It voted seventeen to one to postpone consideration of the resolution indefinitely (Idaho's Senator Pope cast the lone negative vote). The committee agreed that Nye could ask for reconsideration when he returned if he wished, but the committee was not likely to reverse its decision.[37]

Nye continued his efforts. In a broadcast over NBC on May 20, he said he wanted to end "the policy of coming to heel like a well trained dog every time England whistles." By that time Borah considered the original Spanish embargo a mistake. He believed, however, that with Franco in control of Spanish ports and shipping, repeal would help the Nationalists (not the Loyalists).[38]

As Franco and his Nationalist forces gradually triumphed over the Loyalist government and as pressure mounted in the United States, Roosevelt gave further thought to the possibility of repeal. On November 28, he wrote Attorney General Cummings asking him to study the legal aspects of the Spanish embargo situation and talk to him about it. Roosevelt thought, "No written opinion seems advisable."[39]

By January, 1939, Senator Borah wrote that nothing had troubled him "so much as to know what to do with reference to the Spanish Embargo." He claimed he was guided by just one consideration: "How will this or that course affect the interests of the United States?" But he found that "most difficult to determine" in the Spanish situation. "It is earnestly contended by one side that to lift the embargo is to favor communism and tacitly approve the mass murders and persecutions of religionists in Spain. On the other hand, it is contended that if we do not lift the embargo, we are favoring Franco, who is supported by the fascists. I want nothing to do with either outfit and

I do not want, if it is possible, to favor either of these forces. The fascists and communists are all the same to me when I come to consider the interests of my own country." He did not know what his course would be at that time. On January 25, Senator Nye repeated his appeal for lifting the embargo. He pointed out that under the Neutrality Act of 1937 the president had the power "if he chose to do so" to lift the embargo. He emphasized that while he favored repeal of the Spanish embargo, he opposed repeal of the Neutrality Act of 1937 and the Johnson Act of 1934. In February, 1939, Senator George Norris of Nebraska wrote that he was "in favor of lifting the Spanish embargo" and thought "it ought to have been lifted long ago."[40]

At his cabinet meeting on Friday, January 27, 1939, the president discussed the Spanish embargo at length. According to Ickes's account of the meeting, Roosevelt "very frankly stated, and this for the first time, that the embargo had been a grave mistake." According to Ickes, Roosevelt told his cabinet "that the policy we should have adopted was to forbid the transportation of munitions of war in American bottoms. This could have been done and Loyalist Spain would still have been able to come to us for what she needed to fight for her life against Franco." Though Ickes did not say so, that was very nearly the policy that Nye had urged in his Senate Joint Resolution 288."[41]

Not until April 1, 1939, after Franco completed his triumph over the republican government, did the Roosevelt administration finally lift the Spanish embargo. Throughout the entire Spanish controversy the administration took a noninterventionist position and used arguments much like those used by isolationists in other situations. At the same time, the effects of Nye's proposals would have been consistent with opposition to the spread of fascist power in Europe. For the administration, the initiatives lay in the Department of State; with court packing and other matters absorbing his attention, President Roosevelt did not give either the original Spanish embargo or the Neutrality Act of 1937 priority in his thinking. The Italian-Ethiopian war and the Spanish civil war provided early occasions for testing the application of neutrality laws. As the Spanish civil war ran its bloody and unsettling course, violence erupted in a more distant part of the world with the beginning of the undeclared Sino-Japanese war in East Asia. It confronted Roosevelt and the isolationists with a new and different situation to test their foreign policy perspectives, to apply their conceptions of neutrality, and to strain their relations with each other.

Chapter 16
The Sino-Japanese War

Isolationism took shape as Americans looked across the Atlantic toward Europe; those patterns blurred a bit when they looked westward across the Pacific toward Hawaii, the Philippines, Japan, and China. Similarly, relations between Roosevelt and the isolationists were most sharply defined as they contested over policies toward Europe. Those patterns spilled over into the Pacific, but they were modified in the process.

Outside the Western Hemisphere, Franklin D. Roosevelt (like most Americans) gave priority in foreign affairs to developments in Europe rather than in Asia. Threats to peace and security from Hitler's Nazi Germany and, to a less extent, from Mussolini's Fascist Italy concerned him more than challenges from militarist Japan. In Roosevelt's thinking the security and survival of Britain and France were more vital to the United States than China's security in East Asia. As international conditions worsened, the president wanted no military involvement in Asia that would reduce the power available to check the Axis in Europe. Those same priorities prevailed in the thinking of most American internationalists. At the same time, however, the earlier shipping and trading businesses of Roosevelt's ancestors in the Pacific gave him a sentimental attachment to China. And in 1941, developments in the Pacific (rather than in the Atlantic) brought war to the United States—and violently dramatized the ultimate triumph by Roosevelt over the isolationists.

Isolationists were not entirely united in their policy views toward Europe; they were less so toward Asia. Isolationists and pacifists opposed involvement in the Sino-Japanese war that erupted in 1937. Senator Gerald P. Nye and other isolationists who were close to the pacifists particularly opposed strong policies toward Japan. But in their noninvolvement proposals even Nye and Senator Arthur H. Vandenberg unintentionally played into the hands of those whose hard-line approaches eventually provoked Japan into striking at the United States. Some nationalistic isolationists, particularly from the Far West, took hard-line views in opposition to the Japanese. That was the case with Senator Hiram Johnson of California.

Key people through whom Roosevelt worked had varied inclinations in dealing with Asia. America's ambassador to Japan, Joseph C. Grew, did not want involvement in the Sino-Japanese war. An experienced and judicious career diplomat, Grew generally encouraged continued efforts to avert war through patient diplomatic negotiations. Nelson T. Johnson, United States ambassador to China, took a strongly anti-Japanese stance. But those diplomats were not controlling voices in shaping Roosevelt's policies. Secretary of State Cordell Hull personally conducted negotiations with Japanese representatives, and he did not want war in the Pacific. But his moralistic perspectives made his guidance and performance more doctrinaire and less flexible than successful negotiations might have required. Hull's top State Department adviser on Far Eastern affairs, Stanley K. Hornbeck, favored hard-line policies toward Japan. Senator Key Pittman of Nevada, chairman of the Foreign Relations Committee, had different perspectives toward Asia than toward Europe. He cautioned Roosevelt and Hull against initiatives in Europe that might provoke isolationist opposition. At the same time, Pittman was impatient with the president for his failure to take stronger stands against Japanese expansion sooner and more boldly than he did. As the months and years passed, others around Roosevelt encouraged tough policies against Japan. Those included Secretary of War Henry L. Stimson, Secretary of Navy Frank Knox, Secretary of Interior Harold L. Ickes, and Secretary of Treasury Henry Morgenthau, Jr. All of that was made more explosive by the triumph of hard-liners in Japanese leadership and by expansionist opportunities that war in Europe and civil war in China provided for Japan.[1]

On July 7, 1937, a minor shooting skirmish between Japanese and Chinese troops at the Marco Polo Bridge ten miles west of Peiping triggered the undeclared Sino-Japanese war. Nearly ten million people died as a result of that terrible conflict before it ended with the final defeat of Japan more than eight years later. Roosevelt and the isolationists explored various alternatives as the United States (and its territories in the Pacific—Hawaii, Midway, Guam, the Philippines, and Samoa) faced Japan's expanding power. Most believed the United States could and should stay out of the war. Americans overwhelmingly opposed Japan and sympathized with China, but not to the extent of going to war to help China. Until 1941, the United States pursued independent policies toward the Sino-Japanese war rather than entering into commitments with other states. Few thought Japan was any direct threat to continental United States, but many doubted the ability of the United States to defend the Philippines in the western Pacific in the event of war. With rare exceptions, most did not anticipate any Japanese strike at Hawaii.

President Roosevelt did not invoke the Neutrality Act in the Sino-Japanese war, in contrast to his course in the Italian-Ethiopian war. The Sino-Japanese conflict was not a formally declared war—but neither was the Italian-Ethiopian war. The president was required to invoke the law when he found "that there exists a state of war." Presumably he found such a condition in East Africa earlier, but not in East Asia. The reason for the administration's course, however, did not lie in the state of war. The reason lay in the conviction (as Roosevelt wrote privately later, but did not state publicly at the time) that "while the cash and carry plan works all right in the Atlantic, it works all wrong in the Pacific." The Neutrality Act would have worked against China to the advantage of Japan. Invoking the arms embargo would have had little effect on Japan, which had industrial facilities to manufacture its own munitions; it would have handicapped China, which was deficient in that industrial capacity. The loan ban could have handicapped China's war effort; Japan had sufficient financial resources independent of the United States. Under cash-and-carry Japan would have had both the money to buy and the ships to transport nonmunitions goods from the United States; China lacked both the cash and the ships.[2] The differing effects of neutrality provisions on the wars in Africa and in Asia illustrated why internationalists (and the Roosevelt administration) wanted the president to have discretionary authority in the application of the laws. The administration's unneutral motives and differing courses in the two situations were precisely the reasons that isolationists, pacifists, and noninterventionists wanted mandatory neutrality laws and opposed giving the president discretionary authority in the application of the legislation.

On July 16, 1937, Secretary Hull issued a statement outlining the administration's policies. He asserted that there could "be no serious hostilities anywhere in the world which will not one way or another affect interests or rights or obligations of this country." In his statement Hull summarized the fundamental principles of international conduct that he had advanced earlier and would repeat many times later: "national and international self-restraint"; "abstinence by all nations from use of force in pursuit of policy and from interference in the internal affairs of other nations"; adjusting international problems by "peaceful negotiation and agreement"; "faithful observance of international agreements"; upholding "the sanctity of treaties"; "revitalizing and strengthening of international law"; promotion of "economic security and stability the world over"; "lowering or removing of excessive barriers in international trade"; and "limitation and reduction of armament." He asserted that the United States avoided "alliances or entangling commitment" but believed "in cooperative effort by peaceful and practicable means in support of the principles" he outlined. In his memoirs later, Hull wrote that one of his purposes "in constantly reiterating these principles" was "to edge our own people gradually away from the slough of isolation into which so many had sunk." He considered those principles "as vital in international relations as the Ten Commandments in personal relations" and thought there was "untold value" in "preaching" them. Hull firmly believed "that international morality was as essential as individual morality."[3]

Senator Pittman also issued a statement and delivered a radio address explaining and defending the administration's policies. Senator Borah of Idaho, Pittman's predecessor as chairman of the Foreign Relations Committee, wanted the United States to do "everything within reason" to stay out of the war in Asia. As long as he believed the president was "acting in the interest of peace," however, Borah did "not intend to quarrel with him about the technical observance of the neutrality law."[4]

Most isolationists and pacifists urged the president to invoke the Neutrality Act and berated him for failing to do so. For example, on August 18, Senators Gerald P. Nye, Bennett Champ Clark, and Homer T. Bone issued a statement arguing the case for applying the neutrality law to the Sino-Japanese war. They reasoned that the existing legislation would have "an adverse effect on both parties to the war." If the Neutrality Act's lack of an embargo or limit on export of nonmunitions war products (such as scrap iron and oil) benefited Japan to the disadvantage of China, the senators urged enactment of more sweeping legislation (which they had wanted all along anyway) rather than withholding application of the law. They criticized "munitions interests" and "those who wish us to act as policemen for the world.'' Nye also wanted American evacuation of Shanghai and withdrawal of troops and ships.[5]

On October 5, 1937, President Roosevelt made his first major statement relative to the Sino-Japanese war in his famous quarantine address in Chicago, Illinois. From the beginning of his administration in 1933, Roosevelt had had a continuing concern about world affairs and about America's role in international developments. Throughout his first term and on into the early months of his second term, however, he generally gave front stage to domestic matters and the New Deal. When the requirements of domestic and foreign affairs competed, he often compromised on foreign affairs in the interests of political support for his domestic program. Western progressive isolationists were both instruments for and beneficiaries of those priorities. But Roosevelt was always an internationalist. So far as his public performance was concerned, his quarantine speech marked a turning point. That transition did not represent a change in FDR's domestic or foreign policy views; it did represent a change in the relative weight and priority that he gave to the one over the other.

The transition symbolized by the quarantine address was a product of both domestic and international developments. On the domestic scene his defeat on court packing and the growing opposition to his New Deal made it politically dangerous and impracticable to press ahead on that front. Despite the recession late in 1937, the economy no longer seemed to require emergency actions. Many of the innovations urged by the president and his domestic advisors had been enacted into law. At the same time, the Italian-Ethiopian war, German rearmament, remilitarization of the Rhineland, the Spanish civil war, and the Sino-Japanese war all portended increasingly alarming dangers abroad. At the very moment when further progress on the domestic scene was becoming more difficult and damaging politically, developments on the world scene demanded the attention of the president and the American people.

In those changing circumstances, Roosevelt was alert to the economic and political advantages to be derived from a refocus from domestic to foreign priorities. His shift did not represent any fundamental change in his general values on either domestic or foreign affairs. It was not crass political opportunism or cynicism. But circumstances were changing at home and abroad. And ever the realist, Roosevelt adjusted to what he saw as the requirements of those changing circumstances. Among the consequences of that adjustment was a realigning of his political base. A product of that realignment was his personal and political break with leading isolationists. The domestic New Deal program, more often than not, had provided a basis for accord between Roosevelt and isolationists; priority to foreign affairs destroyed that accord.

As with so many of FDR's actions, various individuals (perhaps correctly) claimed credit for advising him to make the Chicago address. He was receptive to their suggestions. In his memoirs later, Cordell Hull wrote that in 1937 he "was becoming increasingly worried over the growth of isolationist sentiment in the United States" and about the effects that isolationism "would have on nations abroad." In September, he and Norman Davis urged Roosevelt to "make a speech on international cooperation" in his trip west that fall and recommended that it be delivered "in a large city where isolation was entrenched." Roosevelt liked the idea and asked Hull and Davis to prepare data for such a speech—which they did.[6]

Others also urged that course on the president. Clark Eichelberger of the League of Nations Association had conferred with him shortly after the beginning of the Sino-Japanese fighting. He urged Roosevelt to make "a dramatic statement" that would "lead the world on the upward path." Eichelberger thought the Asian conflict might "be sufficient to scare statesmen into a greater readiness to return to cooperation for the solution of the world's problems." In a letter written in mid-September, Bishop Frank W. Sterrett of Bethlehem, Pennsylvania, so effectively urged the president along similar lines that FDR quoted an excerpt from the bishop's letter in his address.[7]

Secretary of Interior Harold L. Ickes had been scheduled to deliver a speech on October 9 for the dedication of the new Outer Link Bridge constructed in Chicago with PWA funds. Ickes suggested that the president deliver the address instead and arranged to change the date to October 5, when FDR would be returning from his trip through the West. In discussing the international situation with Roosevelt before the trip, Ickes suggested the quarantine analogy. According to Ickes's diary, the president was so taken by the idea that he immediately made a note of it.[8]

President Roosevelt's address in Chicago on October 5, 1937, was his most important foreign policy speech since taking office. Much of it had been drafted for him in the State Department, but FDR made major changes in the Hull-Davis draft. Hull did not know of the quarantine reference until he heard the broadcast.[9] In his powerful oration, Roosevelt warned of the worsening international situation, without specifically naming Japan, Germany, or Italy. "The land-marks and traditions which have marked the progress of civilization toward a condition of law, order, and justice are being wiped away. Without a declaration of war and without warning or justification of any kind, civilians, including women and children, are being ruthlessly murdered with bombs from the air."

Roosevelt warned, "If those things come to pass in other parts of the world let no one imagine that America will escape, that it may expect mercy, that this Western Hemisphere will not be attacked, and that it will continue tranquilly and peacefully to carry on the ethics and the arts of civilization." There could be "no escape through mere isolation or neutrality." He insisted that peace-loving states "must work together for the triumph of law and moral principles in order that peace, justice, and confidence may prevail in the world." In Hull's terms, FDR said "national morality is as vital as private morality."Roosevelt told his listeners of "a solidarity and inter-dependence about the modern world, both technically and morally, which makes it impossible for any nation completely to isolate itself from economic and political upheavals in the rest of the world, especially when such upheavals appear to be spreading and not declining."

He charged, "The peace, the freedom, and the security of 90 percent of the population of the world is being jeopardized by the remaining 10 percent, who are threatening a breakdown of all international law and order." The 90 percent "can and must find some way to make their will prevail." The situation was "definitely of universal concern."

In the most quoted part of the speech, the president said: "It seems to be unfortunately true that the epidemic of world lawlessness is spreading. When an epidemic of physical disease starts to spread, the community approves and joins in a quarantine of the patients in order to protect the health of the community against the spread of the disease." He called war "a contagion, whether it be declared or undeclared." "We are determined to keep out of war," he said, "yet we cannot insure ourselves against the disastrous effects of war and the dangers of involvement." In powerfully moving tone and measured words the president concluded his address: "America hates war. America hopes for peace. Therefore, America actively engages in the search for peace."[10]

At his press conference the next day, newsmen tried to get FDR to be more specific. He would not comment except "completely off the record.'' Though prodded by questioners, he insisted that in calling for a quarantine of aggressors he was not necessarily advocating economic sanctions, a conference, or repudiation of neutrality. About as far as he would go in being specific with newsmen was to reemphasize the final sentence of his speech: "Therefore America actively engages in the search for peace.'' In response to questions, he described it as "an attitude, and it does not outline a program; but it says we are looking for a program.'' He said there were "a lot of methods in the world that have never been tried yet'' and that they could be in "a very practical sphere.'' He explained his perspective two weeks later in a letter to Colonel Edward M. House: "I thought, frankly, that there would be more criticism [of the speech] and I verily believe that as time goes on we can slowly but surely make people realize that war will be a greater danger to us if we close all the doors and windows than if we go out in the street and use our influence to curb the riot.''[11]

Many then and later thought the president in his press conference was evasive and backing off from the bolder tone he had used in his address. That may have been partly correct, but there was more to the patterns. Roosevelt did not lock into rigid formulas or styles of thinking. He explored a wide range of possibilities without necessarily endorsing or rejecting them. For years he had been groping for methods consistent with both the political situation at home and international requirements abroad that might enable the United States to play a larger and more positive role in trying actively to preserve peace and security. Both the intractable problems abroad and isolationist strength at home made that groping difficult in the extreme. But Roosevelt was trying.[12]

The president's quarantine speech elicited both vehement denunciations and lavish praise. Isolationists railed against it. Professor Edwin M. Borchard of Yale University wrote that the speech indicated that Roosevelt "really never had any use for neutrality" and had "no compunctions about flouting Congress.'' He charged that in foreign affairs the United States was "under as complete a dictatorship as Germany or Italy.'' Senator Borah wrote that if quarantine included "the idea of boycotting Japanese goods,'' the United States was "fooling with dynamite'' and "would be adding fuel to the flame.'' He advised moving "cautiously and with patience.'' Senator Nye told newsmen that "there can be no objection to any hand our Government may take which strives to bring peace to the world so long as that hand does not tie 130,000,000 people into another world death march.'' But he feared "that we are once again being caused to feel that the call is upon America to police a world that chooses to follow insane leaders." Nye said, "We reach now a condition on all fours with that prevailing just before our plunge into the European war in 1917." Even Alf Landon, while rejecting isolationism, feared that "collective action through a quarantine means economic sanctions—which means a blockade if it is to be successful—which means war." He thought critical reactions to the speech would cause the president to back off, and it would "be a mere gesture."[13]

In response to an inquiry from Raymond Moley, Senator Hiram Johnson telegraphed: "The levying of sanctions means their enforcement and their enforcement means the Navy's activity. At once then you have war. My sympathy for China is so great that I would do anything short of war and our people will not have war." He thought the quarantine idea was "the product of restless mentality" and had "not been thought through." He feared that "the President with his delusions of grandeur sees himself the savior of mankind." Ever the nationalist, however, Johnson felt uncomfortable that "a lot of pacifists" were taking the same position he had assumed, and he did not want "to be mixed up with them." Consequently he emphasized that he "was for a big Navy" but "wanted no alliances at this time." Johnson suspected that the quarantine speech and subsequent actions were designed by Roosevelt to divert public attention from domestic problems. Former Undersecretary of State William R. Castle wrote that if the president were "able to carry out his ideas," it would "inevitably lead this country into war."[14]

Secretary Hull initially liked the speech, but he was troubled that by moving too boldly the president may have strengthened the isolationist opposition. Writing in his memoirs a decade later, Hull concluded that the quarantine speech "had the effect of setting back for at least six months our constant educational campaign intended to create and strengthen public opinion toward international cooperation."[15]

As Roosevelt correctly noted at the time, however, favorable responses to his quarantine speech were more widespread and powerful than one might have expected in that isolationist era. Even pacifists with internationalist bent applauded the speech. Pacifist Oswald Garrison Villard telegraphed the White House that it was "the greatest speech" the president had made and that "if followed up," it might "easily become a great turning point in the worlds history." Columbia's international law professor Philip C. Jessup, who opposed Roosevelt's policies before Pearl Harbor, applauded the speech as "admirable, " while recognizing that "the framing of a precise program" would be "enormously difficult."[16]

The conservative nationalist Republican publisher Frank Knox of Chicago wrote that though he had "differed widely with the President on many of his domestic economic policies," he found himself "in thoroughgoing accord with him" on the quarantine matter. Senator Pittman responded to the speech by urging an economic quarantine of Japan and predicting that "the quarantine would be successful in itself in stopping the Japanese invasion of China in thirty days" without "a single shot fired." Clark Eichelberger of the League of Nations Association applauded the speech and thought the American people supported the president. British Foreign Secretary Anthony Eden expressed his government's "warm appreciation of President Roosevelt's speech."[17]

President Roosevelt was uncertain exactly where his groping would take him in shaping American foreign policies. And abundant evidences of isolationist strength encouraged caution, secrecy, and even deviousness as he shaped his course. But he pressed on. After his return to Washington on Friday morning, October 8, Roosevelt conferred for two hours with Secretary Hull, Undersecretary Sumner Welles, and Norman Davis. As Moffat recorded in his diary, the president had "certain definite ideas which he wants suggested to the British without delay."[18] Roosevelt envisioned actions both in Europe and in the Pacific. He advanced both in utmost secrecy.

Roosevelt and Welles proposed to invite all diplomats accredited to Washington to meet with the president at the White House on Armistice Day, November 11, 1937, At that meeting he intended to urge agreement on fundamental principles to be observed in international relations, on methods for limiting and reducing armaments, and on methods for assuring equal access to raw materials and other economic necessities. In deference to isolationist sentiment, Roosevelt would promise that the United States would continue to remain free from political involvement abroad, while pledging American cooperation. Hull objected to the conference, particularly without prior consultation with Britain or France, so the president set aside his initiative temporarily. In January, Roosevelt revived the proposal in slightly modified form.[19]

In the Pacific, the president conceived an idea for a long-distance Anglo-American naval blockade of Japan. The American navy would be responsible for the line from the Aleutian islands through Hawaii to Wake and Guam. The British navy would cover the line westward to Singapore. Roosevelt had begun to form his idea as early as July, 1937, but delayed suggesting it until he could build necessary public sentiment. He secretly communicated his naval blockade idea to the British government near the end of 1937 and very early 1938.[20]

With Foreign Minister Eden out of the country on vacation, Prime Minister Neville Chamberlain rejected both of Roosevelt's proposals. Chamberlain had little confidence in the United States, partly because of the inhibiting strength of American isolationists. He feared the initiatives could work at cross-purposes with his continuing efforts to appease the Axis states. In striking contrast, Eden attached great importance to involvement of the United States in European and world affairs. On February 20, 1938, Eden resigned his position as foreign secretary in Chamberlain's cabinet, partly because he disagreed with the prime minister's policy of giving priority to appeasement over building Anglo-American cooperation in world affairs. With what Welles called Chamberlain's "douche of cold water" on the president's initiatives, with the Anschluss on March 11, 1938, incorporating Austria into greater Germany, and with continued isolationist strength in the United States, both of Roosevelt's secret proposals died a quiet death.[21] But neither developments abroad or at home diverted President Roosevelt from pursuing (however cautiously) his increasingly internationalist course in the face of the growing Axis challenges abroad.

Isolationism at home and timidness abroad (those patterns reinforced each other) moved Roosevelt to secrecy and brought failure for his conference and blockade schemes. But another product of his quarantine speech was the Brussels Conference of November, 1937. That conference failed in its immediate goal to accomplish a peaceful settlement of the Sino-Japanese conflict. That failure probably did not surprise Roosevelt. In a different sense, however, the conference may have accomplished part of what he hoped to gain from it. It helped identify Japan as the villain of the piece, arouse moral sentiment against aggressor states, and educate public opinion in the United States and abroad. In that sense Roosevelt saw the conference and America's participation as part of his efforts against appeasement abroad and isolationism at home.

The League of Nations had been grappling with the problem of the Sino-Japanese conflict since it had erupted in July. With its leading members preoccupied with European concerns, with Britain's Chamberlain and others still hopeful about appeasement, with the

United States not a member of the league, and with that organization enfeebled by its earlier failure in the Italian-Ethiopian war, the League of Nations seemed unlikely to be effective in dealing with the Asian conflict. Roosevelt's quarantine speech on October 5, however, encouraged hope that the United States under his leadership might be willing to play a larger role in trying to end the conflict than many had thought. Consequently the league moved to turn the problem over to a meeting of states that were party to the Nine Power Treaties Relating to China of 1922. Those ageements had the advantages of being specifically concerned with China and East Asia and (unlike the league) included the United States. The arrangements for calling the Nine Power Conference at Brussels were handled in England and Europe, but the United States was consulted closely at every stage. It was a full (but independent) party to the initiatives and planning that made the Brussels conference a reality.[22]

Germany rejected the invitation to attend; Italy was hostile to the aims of the conference; France was preoccupied with developments in Europe; smaller states feared it might involve them in distant controversies; and Japan virtually destroyed the conference before it began by refusing to attend or participate. Japan insisted that the conflict be resolved bilaterally with China. In the Japanese view, the slim chances that the Brussels Conference might be impartial in its quest for peace were reduced by what they saw as the anti-Japanese stance of the United States manifested in Roosevelt's quarantine speech and Hull's policy statements.

Despite probable failure, Britain dramatized the importance it attached to the meeting by sending Foreign Secretary Anthony Eden to head its delegation, while the Soviet Union was represented by its commissar for foreign affairs, Maxim Litvinov. Secretary Hull did not attend, but President Roosevelt named Norman Davis to represent the United States (his last major diplomatic mission).

In addition to written instructions and briefings in the State Department, Davis spent two hours conferring with Roosevelt at Hyde Park before he departed on his mission. The president emphasized that neither the conference nor the United States should consider sanctions or collective actions against Japan. Roosevelt and Davis were determined that Britain and other states should not maneuver the United States into accepting responsibility either for actions against Japan or for failure on the conference. The United States was to share with the other states at the conference in trying to accomplish a peaceful resolution of the conflict between China and Japan. If those

efforts should fail (and they did), Roosevelt instructed Davis to pro-
long the conference as long as possible so that it might strengthen the
moral climate against war-making states and educate public opinion.
The fine line between rejection of sanctions and collective action on
the one hand and efforts to mobilize moral sentiment against war-
making states on the other made Davis's diplomatic assignment
delicate and difficult. Britain's Eden valued the conference particularly for the role it might play in drawing the United States under
Roosevelt into collective security roles with Britain and other states.

The conference failed. Japan would not participate, would not accept mediation, and insisted that the controversy be settled bilaterally
between China and Japan. And Davis was not able to protract the
conference deliberations so long as Roosevelt had hoped.[23] Just how
effective it was in educating public opinion on the menace of the lawlessness posed by Japan and the other Axis states cannot be measured
precisely. But the conference did help dramatize the cleavage between
Axis states and their adversaries. It did make the United States a
prominent party to multilateral efforts to restore peace. It was a long
way from full United States participation in actions against Axis
states, a long way from abandonment of appeasement, and a long way
to the defeat of American isolationism. But the Brussels conference
was an early step toward the accomplishment of all those tasks.

On December 12, 1937, three weeks after the Brussels conference
ended, Japanese military airplanes bombed, strafed, and sank a
United States Navy gunboat, the U.S.S. *Panay,* and three Standard
Oil Company tankers. Three Americans died, and dozens more were
injured. The incident occurred on the Yangtze River as Americans fled
the Japanese military advance on Nanking. Japanese leaders insisted
that it was a tragic mistake, but the ships were clearly marked, their
location and identity known to the Japanese. President Roosevelt expressed shock and concern. He called for Japanese apologies, com-
pensation, and guarantees against such attacks in the future. The sink-
ings intensified already strong anti-Japanese sentiments in the United
States. The incident underscored Roosevelt's warnings about the
growth of international lawlessness and its consequences. It dramatized the dangers posed by military conflicts in distant lands. But most
Americans did not see it as cause for war or military action by the
United States against Japan.[24]

Isolationists shared the shock and anti-Japanese sentiments. For
them, however, the incident added weight to arguments against involvement in foreign wars. It strengthened their convictions on the

need for stronger and more sweeping neutrality legislation binding the president to avoid such incidents in the future. Senator Nye placed the responsibility on President Roosevelt. "We had the machinery all set to handle a situation like that in the Neutrality Act," the North Dakota Republican said, "which the President failed to invoke." He reemphasized his theme that the legislation should be mandatory rather than discretionary. Senator Borah wrote an Idaho constituent that he was "not prepared to vote to send our boys into the Orient because a boat was sunk which was traveling in a dangerous zone. That which happened might be expected to happen under such circumstances." But he thought the administration had "done all that a government could do" in the situation.[25] The *Panay* incident also ignited a final isolationist-pacifist flame on behalf of efforts to legislate noninvolvement, before the spread of war abroad and socioeconomic-ideological developments within the United States, under President Roosevelt's leadership, gradually smothered that flame. That effort came in the form of the Ludlow amendment in the House of Representatives.

Chapter 17

The Ludlow Amendment

On Monday, January 10, 1938, congressmen voted 209 to 188 against a resolution that would have allowed members of the full House of Representatives to consider, debate, and vote on the Ludlow amendment. That proposed amendment to the Constitution, sponsored by Democratic Representative Louis L. Ludlow of Indiana, would have required that a declaration of war passed by Congress would have to be approved by a majority vote of the people before it could go into effect, except in case of attack or threatened attack. Public opinion polls at the time indicated that some 73 percent of the American people favored such a course. In his memoirs Cordell Hull called the episode "a striking indication of the strength of isolationist sentiment in the United States." Ambassador Sir Ronald Lindsay in reporting to the British Foreign Office on the significance of the House vote concluded that the "size of minority shows that isolationist elements in Congress are impressively strong."[1] And so they were.

But the vote could also be viewed from a different perspective. Less than nine months after adoption of the Neutrality Act of 1937, President Franklin D. Roosevelt and internationalists successfully defeated a bid to allow the full House of Representatives even to consider the amendment on the floor. The Ludlow amendment was never formally debated or voted on in the House of Representatives. If the House vote revealed isolationist strength, it also revealed President Roosevelt's growing power relative to the isolationists. In 1938, the president was more successful in blocking the Ludlow amendment than he was in winning enactment of additional New Deal legislation. Never again would isolationists be able to push through new independent schemes to legislate neutrality or noninvolvement in foreign wars. The war between Roosevelt and the isolationists was a long way from over; the toughest battles lay ahead. But Roosevelt had gained high ground and momentum. Isolationists won skirmishes now and then, but developments abroad, socioeconomic-political trends at home, and Roosevelt's able leadership combined to assure his ultimate triumph in the war against the isolationists.

The idea of deciding war or peace by direct vote of the people was not new in 1938. Populist-Democrat William Jennings Bryan had urged it long before. In 1917, progressive Republican Congressman Charles A. Lindbergh, Sr., of Minnesota (the famed aviator's father) had introduced a resolution calling for an advisory referendum before the United States declared war on Germany. Senator Robert M. La Follette, Sr., of Wisconsin, along with his running mate Senator Burton K. Wheeler of Montana, had included the proposal in their unsuccessful bid to win the presidency on a third party Progressive ticket in 1924. Pacifist organizations adopted resolutions urging the war referendum scheme, but they inspired few outside their own ranks.[2] In 1935 however, Louis L. Ludlow took up the cause.

Ludlow was getting up in years by the time his crusade began to win headlines. Born in rural Fayette County, Indiana, in 1873, he had a long career as a newspaperman before winning election to the House of Representatives in 1928. For nearly thirty years he was Washington correspondent for the *Indianapolis Sentinel* and other newspapers. In 1929, he moved from the press gallery to the House of Representatives. Both as a newsman and as a congressman, Ludlow was well liked. He was a devout Methodist and a dedicated Jeffersonian. Through his long careers as newsman and legislator, he had won no great prominence. His persistence in pressing the war referendum amendment provided his claim to a place in history.[3]

Congressmen James A. Frear of Wisconsin, Hamilton Fish of New York, and others had urged adoption of war referendum resolutions earlier.[4] When Frear retired in 1935, Ludlow took up the cause and pressed it with unexpected energy. He introduced war referendum resolutions in 1935 and again in 1937. Each was referred to the House Judiciary Committee, under Chairman Hatton W. Sumners of Texas. It held brief hearings, but never acted. Each year the Indiana Democrat tried to get the 218 required signatures on petitions to force it out of committee. To colleagues he wrote that his war referendum resolution would do more "to keep American boys out of slaughter pens in foreign countries than any other measure that could be passed. It is based on the philosophy that those who have to suffer and, if need be, to die and to bear the awful burdens and griefs of war shall have something to say as to whether war shall be declared."[5] But he never came close to winning enough signatures for his discharge petitions in 1935 and 1936. In 1934, Senator Nye had introduced a comparable resolution, and Senators Capper, La Follette, Clark, and others did so later. They were no more successful than Ludlow in getting action.[6]

The movement for the war referendum amendment highlighted the marriage of convenience between isolationists and pacifists in opposing involvement in foreign wars. And it sharpened the growing cleavage within the peace movement between those who compromised their internationalism in the interests of noninvolvement in foreign wars and those who compromised their pacifism in the interests of meeting the Axis challenges. Unlike isolationists, most pacifists were internationalists. They generally approved the League of Nations initially and favored the international law approach represented by the Permanent Court of International Justice. When the World Court was the issue, it was logical to find Clark Eichelberger of the League of Nations Association working comfortably on the same side as Frederick J. Libby of the National Council for the Prevention of War. Mrs. Eleanor Roosevelt's personal sympathy for the peace movement put her in company with them in support of the World Court. They opposed isolationists who battled against membership in the World Court. Cleavages within the peace movement manifested themselves over neutrality legislation in the mid-1930s. Those differences became sharper when the Ludlow amendment was under consideration. Clark Eichelberger and Eleanor Roosevelt opposed the amendment, while Frederick Libby, Dorothy Detzer, and other pacifists threw their weight behind it. Much organized agitation in favor of the amendment came from pacifist and religious groups (the two often overlapped). Ludlow was not a pacifist, and neither were most of the others in the House and Senate who favored the war referendum amendment. By 1938, pacifists who temporarily turned away from their traditional internationalism worked closely with isolationists. Both pacifists and isolationists recognized their differences and often felt uncomfortable working together. They cooperated, however, in the interests of noninvolvement in foreign wars. Some isolationists (Gerald P. Nye, for example) held foreign policy views that differed little from those of leading pacifists (Frederick J. Libby, for example).[7] And some whose personal values and perspectives were quite different (Socialist Norman Thomas and Colonel Charles A. Lindbergh, for example) developed respect and affection for each other in the course of their separate but shared efforts to oppose American intervention in foreign wars.

With the outbreak of the Sino-Japanese war in July, 1937, Congressman Ludlow and peace groups stepped up their efforts to win signatures to discharge petitions. On September 11, Ludlow wrote President Roosevelt commending him for warning Americans in China "to leave the danger zones or otherwise remain at their own risk." He urged Roosevelt to issue "a proclamation of neutrality directed to the two belligerent nations in the Orient." He believed that "as a Christian nation we should arise above the sordid profits of war trade and we should not be a party, even indirectly to the slaughter of human beings which we are when we furnish munitions and loans to warring nations." Roosevelt responded in friendly but noncommital terms.[8]

When the second session of Congress ended in August, they still had only 185 signatures on the discharge petition. By Monday morning, December 12, there were 205 signatures—13 fewer than the 218 required. Headlined news of the sinking of the *Panay* that day gave the Indiana congressman his chance. Within two days the additional signatures were forthcoming, the 218th provided by Republican Congressman Dudley A. White of Ohio.[9]

With House consideration of Ludlow's discharge resolution scheduled for Monday, January 10, 1938, both proponents and opponents stepped up efforts to hold their congressmen in line and to win over those who might waver on the opposing side. The battle focused on the House of Representatives, but sympathetic senators on both sides tried to help. On November 30, under sponsorship of the National Council for the Prevention of War, Senator Capper broadcast from Washington, urging approval of the war referrendum amendment. The Kansas Republican told his listeners: "It is the people who fight the wars who offer their lives as a sacrifice in case of war. It is the people who pay the other terrible costs of war. So I say it is the people who are entitled to say when the United States should go to war."[10]

In December, Ludlow announced the formation of a National Committee for the War Referendum, under the chairmanship of Major General William C. Rivers (retired). In the statement issued with the announcement, General Rivers called the war referendum "a wise and practical step for our people." He insisted that "it would in no way interfere with or affect action for the defense of this country against attack," but "it would prevent hasty action by the government in a moment of emotional stress." He believed "the effect of the people having the right to vote on war would make any administration more hesitant to follow a line of policy likely to result in a war situation."[11]

On January 9, 1938, fourteen church leaders released a statement supporting the war referendum amendment. The clergymen included Dr. John Haynes Holmes of Community Church of New York, Dr. Ernest F. Tittle of First Methodist in Evanston, the Reverend John N. Sayre of the Fellowship of Reconciliation, Charles F. Boss of the Methodist Episcopal Church Commission on World Peace, the Reverend A. J. Muste of Labor Temple, Dr. Albert W. Palmer of Chicago Theological Seminary, and others. In their statement the clergymen contended that "as free men capable of choosing between right and wrong, they [the American voters] have the competence and should be given the opportunity to exercise freedom of choice on this matter which affects their own welfare more vitally than any other choice they could make."[12]

Still others battled to defeat the amendment. And just as support cut across sectional, party, ethnic, and religious lines, so did opposition. Both Alf M. Landon of Kansas and Frank Knox of Illinois, the GOP presidential and vice-presidential candidates in 1936, opposed the Ludlow amendment.[13] Frank Knox's enthusiasm for the president's foreign policies (and disdain for isolationism) was already beginning to overshadow his abhorrence of Roosevelt's New Deal. In his *Chicago Daily News,* Knox vigorously denounced the fifty-four Republicans who had signed the discharge petition (including the five from Illinois). He thought the "folly of the project itself is beyond definition and action of that sort right now in the face of our crisis with Japan is little short of treason."[14] That portrayal of the isolationists as treasonous was a theme that was to be used with increasing frequency and effectiveness as the United States drew closer to involvement in World War II.

Former Secretary of State Henry L. Stimson of New York recorded his opposition to the Ludlow amendment in a letter published in the *New York Times.* In his memoirs a decade later, Stimson saw the movement for the war referendum amendment as "the high point in the prewar self-deception of the American people." The national commander of the American Legion charged that the Ludlow amendment was "impracticable, would tend to destroy our whole plan of national defense and without question would invite war." The Veterans of Foreign Wars opposed the amendment on the grounds that it would "invite aggressor nations flagrantly to violate the rights of the United States" and would "lead to wars otherwise avoidable rather than being any assurance of peace." Not all isolationists favored the amendment. Republican Senator Arthur H. Vandenberg of Michigan wrote that "it would be as sensible to require a town meeting before permitting the fire department to face a blaze."[15]

The controversy over the Ludlow amendment highlighted foreign policy inclinations of metropolitan newspapers. Roosevelt had often complained that the press opposed him and his New Deal. But most leading metropolitan newspapers supported the president in opposition to the Ludlow amendment and continued to support him on most of the positions he took on foreign policy issues thereafter. Among the many newspapers that came out against the Ludlow amendment were the *New York Times, New York Herald Tribune, Christian Science Monitor, Washington Post, Atlanta Journal, New Orleans Times-Picayune, Los Angeles Times, San Francisco Chronicle, St. Louis Post-Dispatch, Minneapolis Tribune, Milwaukee Journal, Detroit Free Press, Cincinnati Inquirer,* and the *Cleveland Plain Dealer.* Roosevelt had a better press for his foreign policies during his second and third terms than he had had for his New Deal earlier.[16]

The Roosevelt administration threw its weight against consideration of the Ludlow amendment. As Cordell Hull explained in his memoirs a decade later, he and the president saw the amendment as "a disastrous move toward the most rigid form of isolationism" that would "hamstring the nation's foreign policy." If it were adopted in the House, they feared "it would indicate to the world that the nation no longer trusted the Administration to conduct its foreign affairs" and that it "would serve notice on the aggressor nations that they could take any action anywhere in the world in direct violation of our rights and treaties, with little if any likelihood of any concrete reaction from Washington."[17]

At the presidential press conference on December 17, a reporter asked Roosevelt whether he thought the Ludlow amendment was consistent with representative government. He responded with an emphatic "No!" and declined to elaborate. On January 6, in a letter drafted in the State Department, the president wrote to Speaker of the House William B. Bankhead of Alabama opposing the war referendum amendment. Two days later Secretary Hull wrote to Democratic Congressman Sam D. McReynolds of Tennessee, chairman of the House Committee on Foreign Affairs. Hull quoted a statement he had made to the press that "from the standpoint of promoting peace and keeping this country out of war, I am unable to see either the wisdom or practicability of this proposal."[18]

On Sunday, January 9, the day before the House vote on the discharge resolution, the president telephoned James A. Farley, postmaster general and chairman of the Democratic National Committee. FDR knew the House vote the next day could be "very close." He asked Farley to do all he could "to help defeat it. Call Hague and Kelly and get their delegations lined up. We must beat this resolution as it will tie our hands in dealing with international affairs." Farley promised to do all he could—and he did.[19]

As FDR had requested, Farley called Mayor Frank Hague of Jersey City and Mayor Edward J. Kelly of Chicago to solicit their help. Farley telephoned Democratic congressmen urging them to support the administration. His efforts continued even as the vote got under way early Monday afternoon. Altogether he talked to seventy-eight legislators, most of whom had signed the discharge petition. He tried unsuccessfully to reach thirty-two additional Democratic congressmen. Farley correctly guessed that most of those he could not reach were avoiding him; nearly all of them voted against the administration on the issue in the House that afternoon.[20]

Shortly after the House met at noon on Monday, January 10, the speaker of the house recognized congressman Ludlow to begin the twenty-minute deliberations alloted to his resolution to discharge his war referendum amendment resolution (H.J. Res. 199) from committee so it could be considered by the full House. Ludlow began with a brief statement in which he expressed hope that the debate would "be conducted without criminations and recriminations." Ludlow contended that the war referendum amendment could be "a valuable contribution to the cause of peace" and "a practical and dependable means of keeping out of war."[21]

Opponents of the war referendum amendment produced greater drama when Speaker of the House William Bankhead stepped down from his place at the podium to take the floor. He called it "the gravest question that has been submitted to the Congress of the United States" during the more than twenty years he had served in the House. It was, he said, a "radical" and "revolutionary" "attack upon the fundamental basic principle of a representative democracy for a free people." He then dramatically read the letter he had received from "the Chief Executive of this Nation, our Commander in Chief, a man who loves peace as passionately and devotedly as any man that breathes the air of God in America this day or anywhere else in the world." In the letter Bankhead read to the House, Roosevelt described the proposed amendment as "impracticable in its application and incompatible with our representative form of government." He expressed his conviction that the proposed amendment "would cripple any President in his conduct of our foreign relations, and it would encourage other nations to believe that they could violate American rights with impunity." Roosevelt conceded that sponsors of the amendment sincerely believed it would help keep the United States out of war. But the president was "convinced it would have the opposite effect."[22]

Speaker Bankhead's reading of the president's letter overshadowed all that followed. After only twenty minutes divided between opponents and proponents, the House voted. The totals were 188 in favor of the discharge resolution, 209 opposed; 4 voted "present," and 30 did not vote. The discharge resolution failed.[23]

Those who saw the vote as evidence of formidable isolationist strength pointed out that a shift of only eleven votes would have reversed the outcome. The Ludlow forces won more that 47 percent of the yea / nay votes cast. In reality, however, there was never the slightest possibility that the war referendum amendment could have become a part of the Constitution. The letters from President Roosevelt and Secretary Hull might have been enough by themselves to defeat the discharge resolution. Thirty-four of the congressmen that Farley telephoned (most of whom had signed the discharge petition) voted against the resolution. Some had no strong opinions on the matter and willingly acceded to the administration's wishes. Others personally favored the Ludlow amendment, had strong constituent pressures for the amendment, or had put themselves on record for the amendment so unequivocally that it was awkward for them to vote as the administration wished. But some of them did nonetheless. In addition, two of the individuals Farley called cooperated by not voting (not casting the affirmative votes they had intended). Farley's efforts were as effective as they were largely because he was speaking on behalf of the president. But Vice-President John Nance Garner probably was correct when he told the cabinet meeting that Farley turned the tide against the discharge resolution.[24]

Even if the House had approved the resolution, there was no possibility that the war referendum amendment would have won two-thirds majorities in both houses of Congress over the opposition of the Roosevelt administration. And if it had, there still would have remained the task of winning approval in three-fourths of the states. The Ludlow amendment never had a chance. Isolationist and pacifist strength along with Ludlow's persistence gave the idea its brief moment at center stage. But the finality with which it was struck down was more significant. The tide was beginning to turn in the contest between Roosevelt and the isolationists.

Ludlow in the House and La Follette, Capper, Nye, Bone, Frazier, Shipstead, Wheeler, and others in the Senate continued their efforts on behalf of war referendum resolutions from 1938 through 1941. But they had no chance for success. In October, 1939, Senator La Follette proposed an advisory war referendum as an amendment to pending neutrality legislation, but the Senate rejected it by a vote of seventy-three to seventeen. In 1941, the noninterventionist America First Committee urged approval of resolutions calling for an advisory referendum on war or peace. But none of those resolutions ever got out of committee, reached the floor of either house, or was voted on in either house of Congress.[25]

The vote on the discharge resolution not only revealed the president's growing power versus isolationists', it also threw light on sectional and political patterns that were essential to Roosevelt's ultimate triumph over the isolationists. The patterns were quite different from those that had accomplished his New Deal earlier. Proportionately, the discharge resolution won its greatest strength in the Great Plains and upper Mississippi Valley. All the representatives from Kansas, South Dakota, North Dakota, and Wisconsin voted for the discharge resolution. In Minnesota and Nebraska only one representative each voted against the resolution. All the Farmer-Labor party representatives from Minnesota and all the Progressive party representatives from Wisconsin voted for the discharge resolution. In striking contrast, only 17 percent of the representatives from the South voted for the resolution, and only about 35 percent from Middle Atlantic states voted for it. New England and the Far West divided their votes almost equally for and against the resolution. Three-fourths of the Republican congressmen voted for the discharge resolution, while nearly two-thirds of the Democrats voted against it.[26] Those general patterns prevailed on most foreign policy issues from 1938 through 1941.

Congressman Ludlow and his colleagues hoped the war referendum amendment would give the people sufficient power to check the war-making proclivities of munitions makers, financiers, militarists, and the president. Implicit in their perspective was the conviction that if the United States did not meddle in distant parts of the world, it could successfully defend itself militarily in the Western Hemisphere. But Ludlow and other isolationists had conceptions of America's military and naval requirements that were quite different from those of Roosevelt and his advisors. Writing to his son James just ten days after the House vote, the president explained: "National defense represents too serious a danger, especially in these modern times where distance has been annihilated, to permit delay and our danger lies in things like the Ludlow Amendment which appeal to people who, frankly, have no conception of what modern war, with or without a declaration of war, involves." In that same letter, Roosevelt also contended that popular passions, when aroused, could be a force for war just as surely as they might be for peace. In reference to the Spanish-American War, he saw William McKinley as "a weak President" and the conflict "an unnecessary war." As Roosevelt saw it, "Under a Ludlow proposition, we would have gone to war anyway. If we had happened to have a strong President, he could have averted war. So you see it works both ways."[27]

Chapter 18

Naval Preparation

On Sunday, November 28, 1937, Franklin D. Roosevelt had traveled by rail south from Washington to Florida to spend a few days on a fishing cruise in waters off Miami. The president was tired. He had been troubled by a badly infected tooth. On shipboard he had read, worked on his stamps, rested, and reflected. He had enjoyed his companions, did some fishing, and was exceptionally lucky in poker. His spirits and vitality had revived as the days passed pleasantly. He seemed refreshed by the time he got back to his desk in December.

But more than a bad tooth and weariness had troubled the president. Secretary of Interior Harold Ickes was included in the president's party and was "a good deal worried about the President" on the trip. On the train from Washington to Miami, FDR "looked bad and he seemed listless." Ickes thought he had "the appearance of a man who had more or less given up." At the last cabinet meeting of the year, after Roosevelt's return from his cruise and after the special session of Congress had adjourned, Vice-President John Nance Garner bluntly said, "Before you went to Florida, Mr. President, you were both scared and tired. You were willing to give up on taxation, on holding companies." The economy was suffering a serious recession. Things were not going well in Congress. Roosevelt got none of the New Deal legislation he had sought from the special session. Secretary Ickes and Assistant Attorney General Robert H. Jackson worried that Roosevelt might back off from the administration's anti-monopoly efforts and New Deal reforms; Postmaster General James Farley, Vice-President Garner, and others were worried that he was further alienating businessmen and thereby slowing recovery and damaging the administration politically. The presidency was a terrible responsibility. It was particularly frustrating and discouraging for

Roosevelt on the domestic front in November and December, 1937.[1] And then there was the world scene.

On November 10, 1937, Roosevelt had written Commander George C. Sweet in New York State: "If it were only what they call the 'domestic situation,' I would be a lot happier because I know it is not as desperate as a good many people make out and because I know that given time the center of the hurricane is going to pass around us and disappear to windward. But on top of all this I am really worried about world affairs. The dictator nations find their bluffs are not being called and that encourages other nations to play the same game. Perhaps you will be back in uniform yet—and thank the Lord the Navy and, incidentally, the Army, have made a lot of real progress in the past four years."[2] Roosevelt did not want war abroad, armaments at home, or involvement by the United States in conflagrations anywhere. But facing up to the dangers abroad was more challenging and envigorating for Roosevelt (and for millions of American people) than suffering the squabbling, frustrations, and reverses on the domestic scene. It was also better politics.

The Sino-Japanese war and mounting tensions in Europe moved the Roosevelt administration to step up its naval building program. The adoption of that program further alienated isolationists and demonstrated the president's growing power compared to them. Roosevelt never failed to get from Congress what he asked for in the way of naval authorizations and appropriations. Some isolationists supported his moves to build naval power, but others fought him all the way. They lost.

Roosevelt had loved the seas and ships since childhood and was convinced of the importance of sea power long before he served as assistant secretary of navy during World War I. As president he demonstrated continuing interest, knowledge, and activity on behalf of American naval power. Though he pressed for armament limitations, FDR was displeased that the United States had failed to maintain its fleet at levels permitted by the naval limitations treaties of 1922 and 1930. He had not yet completed his first year in the White House when he allocated $238 million in Public Works Administration funds for naval construction. He won enactment of the Vinson-Trammel naval construction bill of 1934, and more in the years that followed. He emphasized that construction was necessary to reach treaty levels and to replace obsolete equipment. When Japan gave notice that it would end the Washington and London naval treaties in 1936, when it began building beyond treaty levels, and when it warred against China in 1937, President Roosevelt made his move.[3]

At the cabinet meeting on December 10 (the first after Roosevelt's return from Florida), the discussion focused largely on foreign affairs. Secretary of State Hull and the president both spoke out at the meeting in favor of building American naval power. On December 28, the president alerted the chairman of the House Appropriations Committee that he might have to increase and speed America's naval construction program. Roosevelt began his annual message to Congress on January 3, 1938, by emphasizing that "in a world of high tension and disorder, in a world where stable civilization is actually threatened," the United States must keep "adequately strong in self-defense." In his budget message that same day he warned that world conditions might make it necessary for him "to request additional appropriations for national defense."[4]

On January 28, 1938, President Roosevelt presented his special national defense message to Congress. In it he referred to his continuing diplomatic efforts to limit armaments—and the failure of those efforts. He reported that armaments were increasing "at an unprecedented and alarming rate" and that "at least one-fourth of the world's population is involved in merciless devastating conflict." In that alarming situation he found it his duty to report that America's national defense was "inadequate for purposes of national security and requires increase for that reason." He asked that "the existing authorized building program for increases and replacements in the Navy be increased by 20 percent." He also asked Congress to "authorize and appropriate for the laying down of two additional battleships and two additional cruisers during the calendar year 1938" and for funds for newer types of small ships. In addition, the president asked Congress "to enact legislation aimed at the prevention of profiteering in time of war and the equalization of the burdens of possible war."

Explaining his program, the president told Congress, "Adequate defense means that for the protection not only of our coasts but also of our communities far removed from the coast, we must keep any potential enemy many hundred miles away from our continental limits." He warned that the United States could not "assume that our defense would be limited to one ocean and one coast and that the other ocean and the other coast would with certainty be safe. We cannot be certain that the connecting link, the Panama Canal, would be safe." He promised that protection of the United States would "be based not on aggression but on defense."[5] The president's messages in January, 1938, called for the largest peacetime naval and military appropriations in American history to that time. Congress approved the military authorizations and appropriations he requested. But the president was no more successful in winning legislation to prevent "profiteering in time of war" and "equalization of the burdens of possible war" than the Senate Munitions Investigating Committee and its members had been earlier. And he focused much less energy on those matters than they had.

Isolationists endorsed military and naval forces adequate to defend the United States against foreign attacks in the Western Hemisphere. Those from coastal states (Atlantic and Pacific) and from industrial states were more likely to favor naval preparedness than those from inland and agricultural states. Democratic Senator David I. Walsh of Massachusetts, chairman of the Naval Affairs Committee, shared Roosevelt's big navy views. In a spirited peroration on behalf of the Vinson-Trammel naval bill of 1934, Hiram Johnson of California told the Senate that any man from his part of the country who did not favor building up to treaty limits did not understand "what may occur in the great Pacific and in the Orient within a brief period in the future." Johnson gloried in the great American navy and said the Roosevelt administration deserved "the very highest praise" for urging Congress to adopt the naval construction bill. And he voted the way he spoke. So did Senators Frederick Steiwer of Oregon, Homer Bone of Washington, Robert Reynolds of North Carolina, Millard Tydings of Maryland, John Townsend of Delaware, Warren Barbour of New Jersey, David Walsh of Massachusetts, Wallace White of Maine, and Arthur Vandenberg of Michigan. Seventy-eight percent of the senators present and voting cast their votes for the administration's Vinson-Trammel bill of 1934.[6] During the Roosevelt years the minority in opposition generally could not win much more than the eighteen negative votes it managed to corral that time. And even in their opposition isolationists emphatically denied that they were pacifists or that they opposed building adequate defenses for the United States.

Nonetheless, most leading isolationists challenged the necessity, motives, and consequences of very large military preparations, particularly naval construction. They feared that the Roosevelt administration wanted a large navy, not for defense, but for meddling in foreign wars thousands of miles from American shores. None of them believed America's first line of defense lay in Europe or Asia. They believed that Nazi Germany, Fascist Italy, and militarist Japan could not successfully attack a prepared America in the Western Hemisphere. They insisted that excessive military and naval preparations provoked armament races, international tensions, and war. They particularly emphasized that American naval construction worsened relations with Japan, strengthened the military in Japan, and provoked that Asian country into further construction and expansion.

Isolationist leaders suspected that many who wanted larger military and naval forces for the United States were serving selfish interests other than national defense and security. Even before the munitions investigation, they charged that military appropriations were designed to line the pockets of shipbuilders and munitions makers. They feared the influence of professional military and naval officers who wanted expensive new trinkets to play with. And by the latter part of the 1930s they accused President Roosevelt of using naval and military expenditures to combat the domestic depression that his New Deal had failed to end.

Those misgivings about naval appropriations were by no means limited to Congress. In February, 1934, the White House referred to the State Department more than two hundred letters and telegrams a day that it received on the Vinson-Trammel bill. Jay Pierrepont Moffat reported to Secretary Hull that nearly all of those communications opposed the naval bill on the grounds that the money should be spent more constructively, the expenditures were not consistent with America's disarmament goals, and naval armaments would not preserve peace. According to Moffat the letters and telegrams came from all parts of the country, from all social classes, and were "usually hand written and in individual styles." Hull forwarded Moffat's report to the president without comment.[7]

Opposition, in Congress and out, to the administration's military and naval proposals persisted each year during Roosevelt's first term in office and on into his second term. But he always got what he asked for on the issue from Congress, despite opposition maneuvers and orations. For example, only eleven senators voted against the administration's naval appropriations bill in 1937. Hugo Black of Alabama was the only southern senator and the only senator from a coastal state to vote in opposition. The other ten were Senators William Bulow of South Dakota, Arthur Capper of Kansas, Bennett Champ Clark of Missouri, Lynn Frazier of North Dakota, Rush Holt of West Virginia, Edwin C. Johnson of Colorado, Robert La Follette of Wisconsin, Ernest Lundeen of Minnesota, Gerald P. Nye of North Dakota, and Elbert D. Thomas of Utah. Six of the eleven were Democrats, three Republicans, one a Progressive, and one a Farmer-Laborite.[8]

In 1938, isolationists quickly established their positions on the president's naval proposals. Among the more prominent and important in those initial moves were Senators George W. Norris of Nebraska, Gerald P. Nye of North Dakota, and Hiram W. Johnson of California, along with Congressman Louis Ludlow of Indiana.

Senator Norris unexpectedly came out in favor of enlarged naval construction even before President Roosevelt presented his message to Congress. No one in either house of Congress had more bona fide and respected isolationist credentials than Norris. His opposition to American involvement in foreign wars and alliances preceded his vote against entry into World War I and his opposition to the Versailles treaty. He did not abandon those positions in the two decades that followed World War I. Nonetheless, in 1937–38, Norris began to edge a bit away from his earlier perspectives. He revealed that gradual and limited shift in a statement carried in newspapers on New Year's Day, January 1, 1938, commenting on Roosevelt's indications that he might seek additional naval construction. Norris said that with Japan "running amuck," the United States should maintain a strong navy and "must not decrease" its naval expenditures. The seventy-six-year-old progressive said the United States should firmly maintain the rights of American citizens in China.[9]

Norris's comments pleased Roosevelt and internationalists, but provoked disappointed and even angry responses from pacifists and isolationists who had admired and supported him over the years. In countless long letters the senator explained and defended his changing perspectives. He emphasized that circumstances were different in 1938 from what they had been in World War I, and those changed circumstances called for different responses. He still wanted "the limitation of armaments, and a decrease instead of an increase of the amount of money expended for armaments." But he could not close his eyes "to what has been going on in the world." As he explained in a letter to a Nebraska constituent: "The size of our navy must necessarily depend somewhat upon the size of the navies of other countries. Recent events have shown that some countries, particularly Japan, have no respect for anything except force." In his view, "A war with Japan would be a war upon the sea. Neither her army nor ours would be used, in all probability." Norris feared that there was "a secret agreement between Japan, Italy, and Germany, and that they will help one another in the conquest which they contemplate, and that they will stand together as a unit." He thought it "imperative for us to make some preparation, at least for our own protection, against any such unreasonable and unwarranted attack as may come from Japan, or from a combination of nations similar to Japan." In a letter to Yale's Professor Edwin M. Borchard, the old progressive underscored his moral abhorence of Japan's actions. "The slaughter by Japan of hundreds of thousands of innocent people, many of them women and children, is so repugnant to me that I cannot refrain from expressing my condemnation of the course she had pursued and is pursuing."[10]

Senator Norris was virtually alone among leading isolationists in thus modifying his views on the issue. It is impossible to enter the hidden recesses of his mind to determine why he moved in different patterns from fellow isolationists. From a cynical perspective one might argue that Roosevelt had bought Norris with the Tennessee Valley Authority and with continuing political support for the senator and his progressive program. But Norris had too much integrity; he could not be bought—not even by FDR with TVA. From an internationalist perspective one might reason that Norris simply commanded the intelligence, realism, wisdom, and compassion to see what was happening in world affairs as they were and to adjust his perspectives to those changing circumstances.

Roosevelt surely was part of the explanation for the senator's course. No progressive isolationist won Roosevelt's warm affection more than Norris did in the 1930s. The dynamic New York patrician and the old Nebraska progressive had countless relaxed conversations on many subjects over the years. Norris helped educate FDR on progressivism, and Roosevelt helped educate Norris on international politics. The senator had found ample reason to trust and respect the president's wisdom and good faith. Roosevelt never won over Borah, Johnson, Wheeler, Capper or Nye on foreign affairs; to a degree he did win Norris. Conceivably, Norris's statement to the press may have been a part of the administration's groundwork for its navy proposals; Senator Key Pittman made a similar statement two days before Norris commented. Ironically, however, after the Senate concluded its deliberations and after overwhelming approval was assured, Norris voted against the administration's navy bill on May 3, 1938.[11]

In the Senate no one spoke longer or battled more earnestly against the administration's naval program than Gerald P. Nye. In a radio address nearly two weeks before President Roosevelt submitted his special message to Congress, Senator Nye described the navy as "an outstanding illustration of bureaucracy that grows and grows, regardless of whether the additional ships asked for are actually necessary to our defense or not." He insisted that enlargement of the navy was not necessary for defense and that an enemy could not successfully attack the United States. He charged that the administration's big naval construction program was "part of a campaign of getting the United States ready for a slaughter of its men on foreign fields."[12]

Nye never slackened his efforts, either in organizing the opposition or in speaking out against the administration's proposals. Late in April, as the Senate vote drew near, he and others delayed action by their prolonged orations. Much of what he and others said he summarized briefly for the Senate on April 20: "I want my country adequately prepared at any hour successfully to defend itself against any attack, singly or jointly, by a foreign foe or foes. . . . I think we have such a degree of preparedness today. . . . What is proposed in addition to what we have is most emphatically a preparation, not to defend ourselves, but to carry on aggressive warfare thousands of miles away from the shores and the homes for which national defense should be provided." A week later he told the Senate: "Our naval program must of necessity be linked directly with our foreign policy. If our foreign policy . . . is one which dictates the need for an increase of one and a quarter billion dollars in our Naval Establishment, I say that that foreign policy is one which directly jeopardizes the future of America. In that event the policy is one which contemplates fully and completely America's participation in other people's wars."[13]

By 1938, old Hiram Johnson of California no longer had the health, strength, and energy to match young Nye's pace. But none got to the core of the issue from an isolationist perspective more effectively than Johnson did. The day after the president submitted his special message to Congress, Johnson wrote his son that Roosevelt "slowly but surely is taking us into a league of nations. . . . While I favor a big Navy, I am somewhat alarmed by his activity in that direction now. We may need it to whip the Japs, but we don't need it as an auxiliary of Great Britain." Two days later on January 31, the old California Republican rose briefly in the Senate to ask in connection with the president's naval message "what the foreign policy of the

United States is." He thought "the Senate ought to assert itself and learn the foreign policy of the United States before it embarks on a journey which parallels one we took in 1917."[14]

The following day Senator Key Pittman took the floor in his capacity as chairman of the Foreign Relations Committee. He told Johnson that when Roosevelt first took office in 1933, "he announced what I consider the fundamental foreign policy of our Government— noninterference and nonintervention in the affairs of other governments." Pittman said he knew "of no instance so far of that policy being violated." Johnson found Pittman's assurances at odds with the president's quarantine speech, however, and Pittman conceded that he was speaking for himself and was not authorized to speak for the administration. Senator Borah underscored Johnson's misgivings by citing the British secretary of foreign affairs who had told the House of Commons, according to Borah, that the United States and Britain had "an understanding or relationship" and were daily "in consultation with reference to our foreign policy." Borah said "we want no alliance, open or secret, written or oral, and furthermore we do not want the world to think we have any such alliance."[15]

A week later Johnson formally introduced Senate Resolution 229 asking the Secretary of State "(a) whether or not any alliance, agreement, or understanding exists or is contemplated with Great Britain relating to war or the possibility of war; (b) whether or not there is any understanding or agreement, express or implied, for use of the Navy of the United States in conjunction with any other nation; (c) whether or not there is any understanding or agreement, express or implied, with any nation, that the United States Navy, or any portion of it, should police or patrol or be transferred to any particular waters or any particular ocean." Without waiting for the Senate to act on Johnson's resolution, on February 8, Hull answered an unequivocal no to each of Johnson's questions. Hull sent his letter less than a month after President Roosevelt's secret idea for a joint Anglo-American long-distance naval blockade of Japan had been torpedoed by Prime Minister Chamberlain in England and by continued isolationist strength in the United States. Johnson accepted Hull's response without question. And the chairman of the Naval Affairs Committee, David I. Walsh of Massachusetts, hoped the Johnson-Hull exchange would "be effective in quieting the claim of a naval alliance and making the issue solely what it ought to be—whether the time has come for a reasonable expansion of our Navy in the interest of our own insurance, and not an adventure into a naval program which may be involved with or part of an agreement or understanding with other powers."[16]

Two days later, however, Johnson again took the floor. He feared that he and the secretary of state had been "taken for a ride," and that "perhaps something was in the wind" that neither of them knew about. "Events occurring since the resolution was presented" led Johnson to that view. He reemphasized that he "was for a good Navy, a large Navy," but he was "not for this Navy of ours being used in connection with any other country on earth." He was "not for any alliance with any other country on earth." Writing to his son after the exchange, Johnson indicated that, following Hull's response, he had learned "that there really was a 'gentlemen's agreement' between us and Great Britain, in relation to the disposition of our fleet in case hostilities broke out," but that "it is very likely that it consists of an oral agreement which was noted by the parties and not in any formal writing." In all of that, the nationalist Johnson felt uncomfortable "that a lot of pacifists are taking the position" that he had taken; he did not "want to be mixed up with them" and reemphasized that he "was for a big Navy," but "wanted no alliances at this time."[17]

From the House of Representatives Democratic Congressman Louis Ludlow of Indiana raised a similar question. In a letter to Hull he asked whether the naval increases were needed for defense of the American homeland and territories, or whether any naval forces were to be used in cooperation with any other country in any part of the world. Hull replied that the ships were needed for the national defense of the United States and its possessions, that they would help keep the United States out of war, and that "in our foreign policy there is not any disposition or intent to engage in warfare." But he also insisted that the United States should continue to try to contribute to peace, order, and security in the world. Hull wrote: "This Government carefully avoids, on the one hand, extreme internationalism with its political entanglements, and, on the other, extreme isolation, with its tendency to cause other nations to believe that this nation is more or less afraid; that while avoiding any alliances or entangling commitments, it is appropriate and advisable, when this and other countries have common interests and common objectives, for this Government to exchange information with Governments of other countries, to confer with those Governments, and, where practicable, to proceed on parallel lines, but reserving always the fullest freedom of judgment and right of independence of action."[18]

In his memoirs a decade later, Hull described the Johnson resolution and the Ludlow letter as "samples of the suspicion that dogged our every step toward international cooperation." He wrote that in its foreign policies the administration "sought to keep reasonably ahead of public opinion, even while seeking to educate public opinion to the importance of our position in the world and to the fatal fallacy of isolating ourselves. But we could not get too far ahead. To do so brought an inevitable reaction and made the situation worse than before because it caused the aggressor governments to believe that our people would not follow us in any strong action in the foreign field."[19]

In addition to Norris, Nye, Johnson, Borah, Walsh, and Ludlow, many other isolationists actively participated in consideration of Roosevelt's naval program in 1938. Senators Arthur H. Vandenberg of Michigan, Robert M. La Follette of Wisconsin, and Lynn J. Frazier of North Dakota, among others, spoke out. But the outcome was never in doubt in either house of Congress. On March 21, the House of Representatives approved the bill by a vote of 294 to 100—nearly 75 percent voting for the proposal. On May 3, the Senate approved it 56 to 28—exactly two-thirds of those voting approving the resolution. Senators Hiram Johnson and Burton Wheeler were absent, but Johnson had indicated that if present, he would have voted for the resolution while Wheeler would have voted against it. The 28 negative votes included seventeen Democrats, seven Republicans, two Farmer-Laborites, one Progressive, and one Independent Republican. None of the senators from the five Great Plains states voted for the resolution (Democrat Edward Burke of Nebraska was absent). None of the four senators from Minnesota and Wisconsin voted for the resolution (and none of the four was a Republican). Only 8 of the 28 votes were from east of the Mississippi River. Only 3 of the votes came from coastal states—1 each from Oregon, Delaware, and North Carolina. Only 3 votes came from the South; none from New England. Among those voting against the administration's naval resolution were Senators Borah, Capper, Clark, Frazier, Holt, Johnson of Colorado, La Follette, Lundeen, McNary, Norris, Nye, Pope, Shipstead, Townsend, and Vandenberg.[20] They were beaten. And they were beaten on every other major military and naval appropriation and authorization sought by the Roosevelt administration before and during World War II.

Chapter 19

Kennedy, Lindbergh, Roosevelt, and Munich

Japanese assaults on China shocked Americans. Mussolini's Italian conquest of Ethiopia and his military aid to Franco in Spain alarmed them. But it was Nazi Germany under the dictatorship of Adolf Hitler that most frightened and shocked the moral sensibilities of Europeans and Americans alike. Many in Europe and the United States shared Hitler's anti-Communist views and sympathized to a degree with part of his resentment of the Versailles settlement. But Hitler's vicious anti-Semitism, his brutal totalitarianism, his militarism, his chauvinism, and his terrifying expansionism challenged all who treasured democracy, religious tolerance, individual freedom, peace, and security. That the three aggressor states might join forces was an alarming possibility that few could lightly dismiss. And it was by no means certain that the fanatic Hitler and his Nazis could be dealt with in normal, civilized, rational ways.

Officially, Hitler had come to power through legal and constitutional means in January, 1933. But he quickly converted the Weimar Republic into a Nazi dictatorship and quashed all opposition. He suppressed Jews, promised to eliminate indignities that the Versailles treaty had imposed on Germany, and determined to reestablish Germany's place in Europe and the world. Germany withdrew from the League of Nations and the World Disarmament Conference. By 1935, Germany under Hitler's leadership was rapidly rearming in violation of the Versailles treaty. In 1936, his still-weak forces remilitarized the Rhineland in violation of existing treaties. He shared with Mussolini in aiding Franco's Nationalists in the Spanish civil war (and in the process tested German men, military equipment, and tactics). Those alarming developments, however, were only preludes for even more terrifying crises in 1938 and after.

In March, 1938, Hitler bullied Chancellor Kurt von Schuschnigg into acquiescing in the military moves incorporating Austria into greater Germany. Italy's Mussolini felt uneasy as the Anschluss extended Germany to Italy's borders at the Brenner Pass, but he stood firm with Hitler, and the bond between the dictators grew stronger. At the Munich conference at the end of September, after a succession of crises and war scares, Hitler badgered Britain's Neville Chamberlain and France's Edouard Daladier into yielding Czechoslovakia's German-populated Sudetenland to Germany. Each of his military and territorial moves through 1938 conceivably could be seen as steps to right the wrongs of Versailles. In March, 1939, however, when Hitler violated his Munich promises and dismembered the rest of Czechoslovakia, he had gone beyond any possible Versailles rationale. Appeasement had run its course—and had failed. Even Britain's Chamberlain could find no further hope for appeasement in coping with Hitler's seemingly insatiable demands.[1]

Both the Anschluss and Munich in 1938 were products of European statecraft and diplomacy; the United States and its leaders played only marginal roles. Nonetheless, certain Americans (both private citizens and government officials) participated in the developments. From President Roosevelt on down, their actions generally had the effects of encouraging appeasement in efforts to avoid war. Two Americans (one an ambassador and the other a private citizen) were to emerge from the crucible as prominent spokesmen for American isolationism and noninterventionism before Pearl Harbor. Those two were Joseph P. Kennedy, United States ambassador to Great Britain from 1938 through 1940, and Colonel Charles A. Lindbergh, America's most famous aviation hero.

Born in Boston in 1888 of Irish Catholic descent, Joseph P. Kennedy demonstrated a striking genius for making money. He attended Boston Latin School and graduated from Harvard in 1912. Both his father and father-in-law had been active in Democratic politics, and Kennedy shared their interest. A bright, talented, aggressive, and sometimes ruthless financier and entrepreneur, Kennedy was a bank president by the age of 25. His involvement in shipbuilding during World War I brought his first contacts with then Assistant Secretary of Navy Franklin D. Roosevelt. With foresight (and luck) he managed to survive the stock market crash more successfully than most. His talent for financial manipulation that made him a multimillionaire was matched by devotion to his large family of four sons and five daughters.

Kennedy was drawn into the Roosevelt political camp even before the nominating conventions of 1932. He contributed generously of his money and energies campaigning with and for Roosevelt both in 1932 and 1936. The president rewarded him by naming him to head the new Securities and Exchange Commission in 1934 and as chairman of the United States Maritime Commission in 1937.[2]

With the resignation and death of Robert W. Bingham late in 1937, President Roosevelt appointed Kennedy to serve as United States ambassador to Great Britain, a position he filled during the crucial years from 1938 through 1940. Kennedy's lack of diplomatic experience did not make the appointment unusual; the position had never gone to career foreign service officers and usually had been a patronage appointment rewarding a wealthy member of the majority party. It was unusual, however, to name an Irish-American Catholic to the position, especially at a time when Anglo-American accord was so important to both countries.

The appointment won quick approval when submitted to the Senate in January, 1938. Kennedy did his homework in conferences with Roosevelt, Hull, and State Department officials. The president encouraged him to communicate directly with him, not just through State Department channels—and Kennedy did not hesitate to follow that procedure. Jay Pierrepont Moffat, chief of the Division of European Affairs in the State Department, encouraged him to broaden the embassy's contacts and to include analysis, interpretation, and forecasting in his reports to Washington. The new ambassador presented his credentials on March 8, 1938, just as Europe faced Nazi Germany's imminent take-over of Austria.[3]

Kennedy got off to a good start in London despite his inexperience in foreign affairs. British leaders found his warmth, energy, and enthusiasm engaging and refreshing. His attractive family, and the hole-in-one he shot in golf shortly after his arrival, did not detract from his appeal.[4] He entertained lavishly and was soon much at home (and graciously accepted) in leadership circles in and out of government. He quickly established good relations with Prime Minister Neville Chamberlain and with Britain's new Foreign Secretary Lord Halifax. He found himself in tune with their appeasement policies, and they welcomed his encouragement and support.

Three days after presenting his credentials, the new ambassador wrote to Roosevelt giving his reactions to European and British developments. He thought Austria's Chancellor Schuschnigg would "eventually give in unless there is some indication that France and England are prepared to back him up"—which they were not. Hitler and Mussolini had "done so very well for themselves by bluffing" that, in Kennedy's opinion, they were "not going to stop bluffing until somebody very sharply calls their bluff." Commenting on the resignation of Eden from Chamberlain's cabinet, Kennedy wrote that "Eden maintained a policy always looking at the outside of Britain and Chamberlain makes his policy looking at the political situation here." The ambassador was "thoroughly convinced" that the United States "would be very foolish to try to mix in."[5] With neither Britain, France, the United States, President Roosevelt, Secretary Hull, nor the American people prepared to take a strong and effective stand in defense of Austria's continued independence, Kennedy's thoughts in his letter to Roosevelt could hardly have seemed inappropriate.

For all of that, however, neither President Roosevelt nor Secretary Hull approved what was happening to Austria. Ambassador Sir Ronald Lindsay reported to the British Foreign Office that "the President's mind is strongly anti-German and is revolted at what the German Government are doing but that at the same time he fully appreciated limitations which public opinion places on his policies and actions."[6]

Secretary Hull was troubled by what he considered isolationist statements that Ambassador Kennedy proposed to include in his first major speech in England. Kennedy had worked hard preparing his speech for a dinner meeting of the Pilgrim Club and submitted its text to the State Department for approval in advance. The secretary of state thought it too isolationist and at odds with a speech he himself proposed to deliver about the same time. At Hull's request the president reviewed and approved revisions suggested by the State Department. Hull cabled Kennedy that "with the President's approval" he was making a speech that would "set forth as our Government policy our effort to avoid the extremes of isolationism and internationalism . . . and, while having no idea of policing the world, indicating that we should cooperate in every practical way with peace seeking nations in the establishment of these principles." Roosevelt suggested that Hull inform Kennedy: "I have shown this to the President and he heartily approves."[7]

The new American ambassador had the audacity, however, to telephone across the Atlantic to ask Hull to postpone his address. Some suspected that Kennedy wanted Hull's speech canceled "in order that his own which was more isolationist in trend would receive a better play." Hull consulted Roosevelt and won the president's agreement "that domestic considerations outweighed the foreign ones." That is,

Roosevelt and Hull believed it was essential to try to move the American people away from isolationism. Hull delivered his address in the United States on Thursday, March 17; Kennedy delivered his speech in London the next day. Erupting during Kennedy's first month at his post, the incident pointed to differences and difficulties that were to grow more acute in the future.[8]

If Kennedy's speech was not what Hull and Roosevelt would have preferred, it did please Senator William E. Borah. After the Anschluss the Idaho progressive wrote a constituent, "It was natural . . . for Hitler to take Austria. Austria was really a German state and the Versailles peacemakers had ruined, crippled and dismembered it, and [it] could not stand alone." He did not think Hitler's seizure of Austria was "nearly as serious as is generally supposed." Borah wrote that "what we ought to do is to attend closely to our own business, rehabilitate our own people, give some degree of contentment and prosperity to our own citizens, and, if we can succeed along those lines, we need not have much fear of communism or fascism." Borah considered Kennedy's speech "the only sensible American speech which has been made abroad recently." In April, Ambassador Kennedy wrote the Idaho Republican that "the more I see of things here, the more convinced I am that we must exert all of our intelligence and effort toward keeping clear of any kind of involvement." He claimed that Chamberlain, Halifax, and other high British officials understood American public opinion and were "going ahead with their plans without counting on the United States to be either for or against them."[9] That may have been true of Chamberlain; it was not true of Churchill and Eden.

In tracing Kennedy's early diplomatic performance, however, it would be misleading to emphasize his letter to Borah or Hull's displeasure with his speech. Kennedy provided the State Department with detailed factual reports of his conversations and observations. His reports during 1938 were no more isolationist or noninterventionist than those from other American diplomats abroad such as Ambassador William C. Bullitt in Paris and Ambassador Hugh R. Wilson in Berlin. J. Pierrepont Moffat, chief of the Division of European Affairs in the State Department, thought highly of Kennedy. Adolf A. Berle, newly appointed assistant secretary of state, shared noninterventionist perspectives for the United States in 1938.[10] Neither President Roosevelt nor Secretary Hull favored committing the United States in European affairs to give the British and French the courage and strength to stand firm in opposition to Hitler's demands on Austria and Czechoslovakia. Furthermore, Kennedy's foreign policy views generally were consistent with those of Britain's Prime Minister Chamberlain. He was in tune with, not alienated from, the government to which he was accredited and its foreign policies. Not until later, after Munich, did he come under substantial suspicion and criticism in Britain on the grounds that he was an "isolationist."

The other American who played a role in developments that led to Munich and who later became the leading isolationist was Colonel Charles A. Lindbergh. The tall, slender young aviator had won fame with his unprecedented solo flight across the Atlantic from New York to Paris on May 20–21, 1927. He had studied engineering briefly at the University of Wisconsin, but left to begin a career in aviation. After barnstorming through the South and Middle West in an old Jenny biplane, he trained as a pursuit pilot in the Army Air Service, graduating at the top of his class in 1925. While serving as an airmail pilot on the route between St. Louis and Chicago, he conceived the idea of competing for the Orteig prize for the first nonstop flight from New York to Paris. That solo flight in his single-engine *Spirit of St. Louis* brought Lindbergh worldwide acclaim. Promoted from captain to colonel in the Air Corps Reserve, decorated by President Coolidge, awarded the Medal of Honor, and cheered by millions in Washington, New York, and St. Louis, Lindbergh became one of the great heroes in American history. In 1929 he married Anne Morrow, the daughter of Dwight W. Morrow, United States ambassador to Mexico and former senior partner of J. P. Morgan and Company.[11]

The acclaim and hero-worship accorded to Lindbergh helped his efforts to promote aviation, but they destroyed the privacy of a very private person. Newsmen, photographers, and curiosity-seekers dogged his every step. In 1932, tragedy struck when their infant son was kidnapped and murdered. The sensational trial of Bruno Hauptmann brought more headlines, newsmen, photographers, and crackpots. There were threats on their second son, Jon. A normal life seemed impossible for the young family in America. In December, 1935, Charles, Anne, and Jon slipped quietly out of the United States and sought temporary refuge in England.[12]

England provided them with privacy, tranquillity, and personal security they had lost in the United States. But an invitation from the United States military attaché in Germany, Major Truman Smith, drew Colonel Lindbergh into the developing European maelstrom. The attaché had never met Lindbergh, and the airman had never been in Germany. But Smith was not satisfied with the information he was getting about military aviation in Germany. He hoped the Germans might reveal more to the famous aviator. In May, 1936, after clearing the idea with both German and American officials, Major Smith invited Lindbergh to visit Germany to inspect civil and military aviation developments there. Lindbergh accepted the invitation and made three major inspection visits to Germany in July and August, 1936, October, 1937, and October, 1938, not long after Munich.

As Smith had hoped, the Germans from Hermann Goering on down proudly showed Colonel Lindbergh (always accompanied by the American military attaché or his air attaché) their finest planes and aviation research and manufacturing facilities. They allowed Lindbergh to pilot some of their airplanes, including the Me-109 which was to be a first-line fighter throughout World War II. He may have been the first American to learn about and examine the Ju-88, the finest and most versatile of the Luftwaffe's light bombers.[13]

In addition to his observations in Germany, Lindbergh knew much about military aviation in England, France, and the United States. And in August, 1938, in the midst of the Sudeten crises, he and Anne flew to the Soviet Union to study aviation developments there. On that trip they had brief visits in Poland and Czechoslovakia. Lindbergh and his wife always traveled as private citizens, but in cooperation with American diplomatic and military officials. He reported his findings to leaders in and out of government in the United States, Britain, and France. Initially he studied the developments as part of his continuing interest in aviation. His findings in the midst of the alarming international crises, however, aroused his deep concerns about possible consequences of war in Europe. He became convinced that German air power surpassed that of all other European states. He feared that a war between Germany on one side and Britain and France on the other could destroy Western civilization and open floodgates for the spread of Soviet power and communism in Europe.[14]

Lindbergh's fame and his wife's family brought them into upper social and political circles in England, France, and other countries they visited. On May 5, 1938, Charles and Anne attended a dinner in London given by Lord and Lady Waldorf Astor. Among the other guests were Ambassador Kennedy, Ambassador Bullitt, Mr. and Mrs. George Bernard Shaw, and the editor of the *Times*. The Lindberghs liked Kennedy. The Kennedys invited the Lindberghs to a dinner at the American Embassy on May 17 honoring Foreign Secretary Lord Halifax. On May 23, they met King George VI and Queen Elizabeth at a dinner and ball given by Lord and Lady Astor at their home at St.

James's Square. And on June 1, they attended a ball at Buckingham Palace. On those and other occasions they got better acquainted with the Kennedys. Colonel Lindbergh spoke out about his fears of German air power and of the possible consequences of war in Europe. In addition he corresponded on the subject with many both in Europe and in the United States.[15]

In June, 1938, the Lindberghs moved from England to the small island of Illiec off the coast of France. And in August they made their trip to the Soviet Union, returning to Paris on September 8, when all Europe was tense with the fear of war over Hitler's demands for the Sudetenland.[16]

They had planned to fly on the next day, but the American ambassador, William C. Bullitt, persuaded them to stay an extra day to visit with the French air minister, Guy La Chambre. At dinner and late into the night the French minister and the American aviator discussed aviation developments in France, Germany, and the Soviet Union. Lindbergh concluded that the French situation was "desperate." He thought it impossible for the French to catch up with German military aviation "for years, if at all," and was convinced that German air power was "stronger than that of all other European countries combined." In his opinion, "The opportunity of stopping the extension of German control to the east passed several years ago."[17]

La Chambre reported Lindbergh's analysis to others in the French cabinet, and the American aviator was quoted in the Chamber of Deputies. Lindbergh was neither the first nor the last to report such findings or to advance such views. Nonetheless, he helped confirm the fears of many, including Foreign Minister Georges Bonnet, and shake the confidence of others. Premier Edouard Daladier thought Lindbergh's analysis "seemed unduly pessimistic," but he did not treat it lightly. The British military attaché in Paris wrote that "the Fuhrer found a most convenient ambassador in Colonel Lindbergh, who appears to have given the French an impression of its [the German air force's] might and preparedness which they did not have before, and who at the same time confirmed the view that the Russian Air Force was worth almost exactly nothing." When the Lindberghs got back to Illiec, the colonel wrote of his findings at length to the American air attaché in London and to various friends and officials in England and in the United States.[18]

On Monday, September 19 (after Chamberlain's first trip to confer with Hitler on the Sudetenland at Berchtesgaden), Ambassador

Kennedy sent an urgent telegram asking Colonel Lindbergh to come to London. The Lindberghs arrived late Tuesday night and had lunch with Ambassador and Mrs. Kennedy on Wednesday (the day before Chamberlain made his second trip to see Hitler at Godesberg). They discussed the diplomatic and military situation at length. Kennedy believed Hitler would wage war if he did not get what he wanted in Czechoslovakia, that Chamberlain wanted to avoid war, but that public pressure was against further concessions. Lindbergh emphasized that Britain and France were not prepared to cope with German air power in war successfully at that time. They shuddered at the consequences that war would have for all concerned. Lindbergh thought it would be "the beginning of the end of England as a great power." Mrs. Lindbergh feared that with the first air raid on either side the United States would "be shocked into the war, too." Later as they walked down crowded Piccadilly, she felt as though she were "seeing the doomed" and trembled at the thought that "it might all be interrupted with bomb holes and shattered buildings in another week." At Kennedy's request, Lindbergh drafted a letter summarizing his analysis. The ambassador promptly cabled it to the secretary of state on Thursday, September 22, and referred to Lindbergh's views again in a trans-Atlantic telephone conversation with Hull two days later.[19]

In the portions that Kennedy cabled to Hull, the aviator wrote that "without doubt the German air fleet is now stronger than that of any other country in the world," and "greater than that of all other European countries combined." Lindbergh believed that the United States was "the only country in the world capable of competing with Germany in aviation." He feared, however, that Germany was "rapidly cutting down the lead we have held in the past." In Lindbergh's opinion France was "in a pitiful condition in the air." England was "better off" but not equal to Germany. He did "not place great confidence in the Russian air fleet," though the Soviet Union probably had "a sufficient number of planes to make her weight felt in any war she enters." Kennedy's cable of Lindbergh's letter concluded: "Germany has such a preponderance of war planes that she can bomb any city in Europe with comparatively little resistance. England and France are far too weak in the air to protect themselves." Kennedy suggested to Hull that Lindbergh's opinions might "be of interest to the President and to the War and Navy Departments."[20]

During the days immediately preceding the Munich conference, Ambassador Kennedy also arranged for Colonel Lindbergh to confer with other top British military and political leaders. On September 22, the American flier spent two hours with John Slessor of the Air Ministry (later marshal of the Royal Air Force) and with the private secretary of Britain's chief of the air staff. The next day he lunched with Air Marshal Sir Wilfred Freeman, conferred with others in the Air Ministry and Air Intelligence, and visited with American air attaché Colonel Raymond Lee. Each day Lindbergh conferred with Kennedy, and the ambassador was in touch with Chamberlain and Halifax. As the Munich conference drew near, Lindbergh concluded that Ambassador Kennedy had "taken a large part in bringing about the conference," that the English liked Kennedy, and that they were pleased that the United States had "at last sent a real man to represent us."[21]

Back in the United States, President Roosevelt, Secretary Hull, and the Department of State followed the European developments closely. It was the sort of war crisis that Roosevelt had feared, and the sort that he had hoped he might help prevent or resolve. Most internationalists and the greater part of the metropolitan press were critical of Chamberlain and appeasement. At the same time, however, there were few who were prepared to commit the United States to war on the side of Britain and France to block Hitler's take-over of Czechoslovakia's Sudetenland in Central Europe.

As tensions mounted, both the president and the secretary of state spoke out in general terms. In a radio broadcast on August 16, Hull had pointed to the dangerous developments that threatened "the very foundations of our civilization." Hull reminded Americans "that an isolationist position would not protect them from the effects of a major war elsewhere." And he warned Axis powers that "they could not count us out in pursuing their plans for conquest."[22]

Two days later in an address at Queen's University in Kingston, Ontario, Canada, President Roosevelt reinforced that general view. The president said, "Civilization, after all, is not national—it is international." He reminded his listeners that "the vast amount of our resources, the vigor of our commerce and the strength of our men have made us vital factors in world peace whether we choose it or not." America and Canada, Roosevelt said, resolve "to leave no pathway unexplored . . . which may, if our hopes are realized, contribute to the peace of the world."[23]

On September 2, Ambassador Kennedy had proposed to say in an address in Scotland, "I can't for the life of me understand why anybody would want to go to war to save the Czechs." Neither Roosevelt nor the State Department liked the statement; they struck it from the speech before delivery. They feared America's Irish-American ambassador had drawn much too closely to Chamberlain and his appeasement policies. Roosevelt and Hull also verbally spanked Kennedy for giving an exclusive story to the Hearst International News Service.[24]

Neither President Roosevelt nor Secretary Hull really believed that appeasement would produce enduring peace and security for Europe and the world. At the time of Chamberlain's visit with Hitler at Berchtesgaden, Roosevelt wrote Ambassador William Phillips in Italy that it "may bring things to a head or may result in a temporary postponement of what looks to me like an inevitable conflict within the next five years."[25]

Throughout his presidency Roosevelt had sought opportunities to contribute to enduring peace and security in the world. Those hopes were frustrated by circumstances in Europe that gave him little substantial to work with and by circumstances within the United States, including the priority of domestic New Deal programs and the strength of American isolationism. The Sudeten crises provided a new chance for American involvement on behalf of peace and security. Ambassador Bullitt suggested that President Roosevelt propose a meeting at The Hague, with a United States presence (presumably Bullitt) to explore peaceful resolution of the Sudeten difficulties. But circumstances at home and abroad blocked implementation: isolationists would have fought such an American involvement in Europe. In a later communication, Bullitt pointed to a moral problem that could not lightly be disregarded. Concluding a long communication to Secretary Hull on September 19, Bullitt wrote: "It is entirely honorable to urge another nation to go to war if one is prepared to go to war at once on the side of that nation but I know of nothing more dishonorable than to urge another nation to go to war if one is determined not to go to war on the side of that nation, and I believe that the people of the United States are determined not to go to war against Germany."[26] And Roosevelt, Hull, Chamberlain, Daladier, and Hitler knew that Bullitt was correct at that time on that issue.

Both Ambassador Kennedy in Britain and Ambassador Bullitt in France, along with the other American diplomats in Europe, reported regularly in detail to Secretary Hull and to President Roosevelt. Kennedy and Bullitt also communicated frequently with Roosevelt, Hull, and Welles by trans-Atlantic telephone. Kennedy, Bullitt, and Ambassador Anthony Biddle, Jr., in Poland, among others, reported their conversations with Lindbergh to Hull and probably to Roosevelt. At least two of Lindbergh's letters reached Roosevelt's eyes before Munich. Early in 1938, before he took up his duties as ambassador, Kennedy forwarded to President Roosevelt a four-page excerpt from a letter written by Lindbergh after his second trip to Germany and before his trip to the Soviet Union. Lindbergh wrote that Germany was "probably the strongest air power in Europe"; he thought Germany could produce "many more [planes] than in any other country, not excluding the United States." He doubted "that any country in Europe will be able to catch up with them during the next few years." The president forwarded copies of Lindbergh's letter to Chief of Naval Operations Admiral William D. Leahy and to Army Chief of Staff Malin Craig. Both found the data in Lindbergh's letter was accurate.[27]

On September 27, the president saw an eight-page letter from Colonel Lindbergh to Admiral Emory S. Land, Kennedy's successor as chairman of the United States Maritime Commission and Lindbergh's second cousin and friend. In that letter Lindbergh wrote "that it would be difficult to paint a more depressing picture." He did "not believe there will be a general European war in 1938, but war in 1939 seems probable." Though rejecting pacifism, Lindbergh thought it "absolutely essential to avoid a war next year if there is any possibility of doing so." He feared that "a general war in Europe would leave the participating countries prostrate." Colonel Lindbergh thought "the German air fleet is more supreme in air than the British fleet at sea," and could "level a city such as Paris, London, or Prague." If France attacked on the German front, Lindbergh thought that "a Communistic Europe is far from a remote possibility." Lindbergh believed that Germany intended "to extend her influence still further to the east within the next year." In his opinion "there would be nothing gained by a military attempt on the part of France and England to stop the German movement toward the east. The opportunity to do this was lost several years ago when German policies went unopposed." The American aviator concluded, "This is no longer a question to be decided by our traditional ideas of what is legally right or wrong. It is now a question of the survival of European nations and races." Roosevelt saw Lindbergh's letter the day after the president's first letter to Hitler and the very day of his second letter to Hitler and his communication to Mussolini.[28] Whether Lindbergh's views, as they reached Roosevelt directly and indirectly, affected the president's course or not cannot be determined with certainty. But Lindbergh's analyses were consistent with reports the president got from other sources.

Within the constraints at home and abroad, President Roosevelt earnestly tried to promote peace. He did so without either endorsing or rejecting any specific diplomatic solution of the Sudeten controversy, without explicitly endorsing either appeasement or collective security. On September 26, President Roosevelt sent identical messages to Chancellor Hitler in Germany, to President Beneš of Czechoslovakia, and through Hull to Prime Minister Chamberlain in Britain and Premier Daladier in France. While emphasizing that the United States had "no political entanglements," Roosevelt wrote that there was "no problem so difficult or so pressing for solution that it cannot be justly solved by the resort to reason rather than by the resort to force." He urged "not to break off negotiations looking to a peaceful, fair, and constructive settlement of the questions at issue."[29]

The responses from Britain, France, and Czechoslovakia were wholly favorable. Hitler in his reply, however, placed the blame entirely on Czechoslovakia for its treatment of Sudeten Germans and on the Allies for the treaties they had imposed in 1919. The Nazi dictator insisted that responsibility for war or peace lay entirely with Czechoslovakia, not with Germany.[30]

Nonetheless, President Roosevelt determined to press on with his efforts to avert war. Tuesday afternoon, September 27, he sent a personal message to Mussolini in Italy. In deference to American isolationist strength, Roosevelt noted that the United States "followed a determined policy of refraining from political entanglements," but he urged Mussolini to "help in the continuation of the efforts to arrive at an agreement of the questions at issue by negotiations or by other pacific means rather than by resort to force." At the same time, with the president's approval, Secretary Hull sent a circular telegram with a similar message to all American diplomatic missions abroad. And Tuesday night President Roosevelt sent a second message to Hitler. He noted that the United States had "no political involvements in Europe" and would "assume no obligations in the conduct of the present negotiations," but that it recognized its "responsibilities as a part of a world of neighbors." Again Roosevelt urged Hitler to continue negotiations to resolve the Sudeten differences peacefully without resort to war.[31]

On Wednesday morning, September 28 (in response to urgings

from Britain's Chamberlain, some hours before America's Ambassador Phillips was able to present Roosevelt's message to the Italian leader), Mussolini had interceded by telephone with Hitler. He persuaded Hitler to delay his threatened military move into Czechoslovakia and to agree to a four-power meeting in Munich the next day, on September 29. After midnight at that Munich conference, Hitler, Chamberlain, Daladier, and Mussolini reached accord on the transfer of the Sudetenland from Czechoslovakia to Nazi Germany. Hitler got what he wanted. Chamberlain returned to England with "peace for our time." War in Europe was postponed for eleven months.[32]

The actual course of events in that alarming crisis was shaped and controlled by European statesmen, not by President Roosevelt, Ambassador Kennedy, Colonel Lindbergh, or the United States. Given the continued strength of isolationism in the United States, President Roosevelt could not and did not commit America's power to bolster British, French, Czech, and Russian resistance to Hitler's demands in Central Europe. Mussolini's intercession with Hitler on Wednesday morning that led to the Munich conference was in response to British initiatives and preceded the presentation of Roosevelt's personal message to Mussolini.[33] Both British and French intelligence reported the superiority of German air power before Lindbergh briefed them on his observations and conclusions.[34] And Chamberlain had set on his appeasement course before Ambassador Kennedy added his encouragement.

Nonetheless, insofar as key Americans from President Roosevelt on down entered into the flow of events, their efforts had the effects of encouraging appeasement in the Sudeten crisis. Ambassador Kennedy wholly approved Prime Minister Chamberlain's policies and encouraged him in his efforts. In somewhat different patterns, the same was true of Ambassador Bullitt in France. Colonel Lindbergh's alarming analyses of the relative air power of the several European states increased acute fears about the consequences of war in Europe. Neither President Roosevelt nor Secretary Hull believed that appeasement would lead to enduring peace and security in Europe. As they had during the preceding six years, both of them wanted the United States to play a larger and more active role in preserving international peace and security. President Roosevelt's initiatives on September 26 and 27 were consistent with those desires. Neither Roosevelt nor Hull explicitly endorsed any specific diplomatic arrangement involving the Sudetenland; neither explicitly endorsed appeasement. In pressing so earnestly for continued negotiations in those troubled times, however, the Roosevelt administration's influence had the effect of encouraging appeasement.

Most Americans from President Roosevelt on down (like most Europeans and their leaders) were relieved that the Sudeten crisis had passed without war. But many (including Roosevelt and Hull) were skeptical about the permanence of the peace that Chamberlain and Daladier had purchased from Hitler at the cost of Czechoslovakia's Sudetenland. In a letter to Prime Minister Mackenzie King of Canada, President Roosevelt wrote that "we in the United States rejoice with you, and the world at large, that the outbreak of war was averted." But he was still concerned about "prospects for the future." To King George VI the president wrote of his happiness "that Great Britain and the United States have been able to cooperate so effectively in the prevention of war—even though we cannot say that we are 'out of the woods' yet."[35]

Colonel Lindbergh was "not surprised, but very much relieved" by news of the Munich conference. He hoped "England would wake up after the experience she has gone through. If she does not wake up now, there is no hope." On September 29, the day of the Munich conference, Ambassador Bullitt telephoned Lindbergh and asked him to come to Paris. The ambassador wanted to draw Colonel Lindbergh into discussions with Air Minister La Chambre and Jean Monnet about a plan for building aircraft factories in Canada near Detroit and Buffalo to manufacture military planes for France. Bullitt had already communicated the idea to President Roosevelt, including the possibility of including Lindbergh in the project. The scheme would bypass the arms embargo in America's Neutrality Act in the event of war. It could increase production so that France need not feel so inadequate in air power in the event of future crises in relations with Germany. After careful deliberation, Lindbergh decided not to participate in the project—partly because the publicity that surrounded his every action would make it difficult to keep it out of the news. In reality the project never materialized anyway.[36]

In the middle of October, 1938, Colonel and Mrs. Lindbergh made their third major visit to inspect aviation developments in Germany. During their two weeks there Lindbergh piloted the Me-109, inspected the Ju-88, and was awarded a medal by Field Marshal Hermann Goering for his services to aviation (an award that was to be the subject of much criticism in the months and years that followed).[37]

Lindbergh had considered moving with his wife and sons to Berlin for the winter in his efforts to learn more about the Germans. He canceled those plans, however, after the Nazis violently stepped up their persecution of Jews early in November. The Lindberghs instead spent the winter of 1938–39 in Paris. The colonel did, however, make two brief trips to Berlin that winter for secret negotiations to purchase German aircraft engines for France. The French and Lindbergh hoped the purchase might improve relations between France and Germany. Ambassador Bullitt had misgivings about the idea. When President Roosevelt declined to estimate the impact of the purchase on American public opinion, and when in March Hitler dismembered the rest of Czechoslovakia, the project fell through.[38]

In April, 1939, as war in Europe drew closer, the Lindberghs returned to the United States. At the request of General Henry H. Arnold, Colonel Lindbergh served five months with the Army Air Corps helping increase and improve American military aircraft research, design, and production. On April 20, near the beginning of that service, Lindbergh had his only personal meeting with Roosevelt in a fifteen-minute visit at the White House. Many years later the aviator recalled Roosevelt as friendly and affable. But he found it difficult to size up the man; it was, he said, like talking to a person who was wearing a mask. In September, 1939, Lindbergh began his public efforts to oppose American intervention in World War II—efforts that continued until the Japanese attack on Pearl Harbor twenty-seven months later.[39]

After Munich the secretary of state congratulated Ambassador Kennedy, Ambassador Bullitt, and others under his authority for their able work during those difficult times. But it was already clear that Kennedy's perspectives on American policies toward Europe did not coincide with those of Roosevelt and Hull. On October 19, 1938, in his first major speech after Munich, Ambassador Kennedy told his listeners at a Trafalgar Day dinner of the British Navy League that it was "unproductive for both the democratic and dictator countries to widen the division now existing between them by emphasizing their differences." He thought they should "bend their energies toward solving their common problems by an attempt to re-establish good relations on a world basis." In the atmosphere that prevailed in 1938, Kennedy's statement (like Lindbergh's comparable thoughts and efforts at the same time) provoked heated protests. Hull, Welles, and Moffat had all cleared Kennedy's speech in advance, but they had "slipped up" in their performance. Objections to Kennedy's statements were loud and clear. Individuals wrote to Roosevelt and Hull urging that Kennedy be fired and recalled. Republican Frank Knox of the *Chicago Daily News* wrote Hull calling Munich "a world tragedy from which we as well as the rest of the world will suffer for years to come." He published an editorial "suggesting a muzzle for both Kennedy and Bullitt."[40]

Matters got worse when it was learned that Kennedy had played a role in having antiappeasement statements cut from a Paramount newsreel in the midst of the Sudeten controversy. Charges of censorship fell on the ambassador. One writer summed up his feelings in a letter to Kennedy (with a copy to the president): "Between Lindbergh's ill-timed comment upon the superior German air forces, your suppression of newsreels and Chamberlain's lack of true wisdom, it is no wonder that Hitler gets what he wants."[41]

With the beginning of the European war in September, 1939, while Chamberlain continued as prime minister, Kennedy came under increasing criticism in British leadership circles for being an "isolationist." Stigmatized as an "appeaser," an "isolationist," and a "defeatist," his status and influence steadily waned. In October, 1939, Roosevelt told Secretary of Treasury Henry Morgenthau, Jr., that Kennedy "always has been an appeaser and always will be an appeaser. . . . he's just a pain in the neck to me."[42]

Kennedy continued to report faithfully to the State Department and to advance his views in personal letters to Roosevelt. But neither the president nor the secretary gave much credence to his guidance. Increasingly they bypassed him by working through the British Embassy in Washington. More important, from 1939 onward Roosevelt's direct personal communications with Winston Churchill reduced the roles of the ambassadors in both countries. Kennedy continued to serve as ambassador partly because Roosevelt did not like to fire people, and partly because of Kennedy's standing with the large Irish-American and Roman Catholic voting population in the United States. Roosevelt may have continued him as ambassador partly to keep him leashed during the presidential campaign. In October, 1940, Kennedy returned to campaign for the reelection of Roosevelt.[43] But the president and the ambassador had long since taken sharply diverging paths in foreign affairs. Joseph P. Kennedy's public service under Franklin D. Roosevelt was rapidly drawing to an end.

Chapter 20

Political Signals

In 1938, President Roosevelt's efforts to purge Democrats who had fought him on court packing failed. And the Democratic party did poorly in congressional elections. It maintained majorities after the elections, but its margins were cut sharply in both houses. Between defeats on court packing and other administration proposals, the recession of 1937–38, the failure of the purge, and setbacks in the congressional elections, things were not going at all well for Roosevelt on the domestic front. That boded ill for the president's legislative program and caused serious concerns for the Democratic party (and Roosevelt) about the upcoming 1940 presidential contest.

Foreign affairs had little to do with the results of the primaries and elections of 1938. But the challenges abroad provided Roosevelt with politically promising alternatives. If he pressed ahead relentlessly with his domestic New Deal program, his party faced the serious possibility of defeat in 1940. FDR continued to cherish liberal economic and social goals and to speak out for them. Most voters and congressmen did not want to throw out the New Deal or go back to the policies of Coolidge and Hoover. The continued strength of isolationism made certain that FDR would face strong opposition if he shifted priorities to foreign affairs. One could reasonably contend that by the end of 1938 foreign threats were so ominous that they required his foremost attention, regardless of developments at home. And one could reasonably argue that he had successfully accomplished enough of his domestic program to make continued efforts along those lines less essential. Circumstances abroad in 1938–39, however, did provide the president and his party with politically advantageous alternatives at a time when his domestic New Deal program was becoming a serious political liability.

Roosevelt's attempted purge of conservative Democrats was designed to provide a more liberal Congress that would adopt legislation to accomplish the administration's social and economic goals for America. It was also an angry slap at Democrats who had fought the president on court packing. The most prominent of those Democratic opponents, Burton K. Wheeler, did not come up for reelection until 1940. Others faced the voters in 1938, notably Walter George of Georgia, Millard Tydings of Maryland, Guy Gillette of Iowa, and Bennett Champ Clark of Missouri. Though Clark, and sometimes Tydings and Gillette, had differed with the president on foreign affairs, foreign policy considerations did not give rise to the purge. Court packing did. Despite Roosevelt's persistent efforts, the purge failed. George, Tydings, Gillette, and Clark, among others marked for defeat, won renomination in the Democratic primary elections.[1]

The emaciated Republican party had its own difficulties. Former President Herbert Hoover and former GOP nominee Alf M. Landon jockeyed for position in their separate efforts to lead the party toward stronger programs. But each was skeptical of the other, neither could win the presidential nomination again, and both were identified with defeat at the hands of Roosevelt. William E. Borah and Gerald P. Nye wanted to throw out conservative Old Guard leadership and replace it with progressive Republican leadership, while at the same time opposing Hamiltonian big government and dictatorial patterns they identified with Roosevelt. They were no more successful in 1938 than they had been in their earlier efforts along those lines. Conservative Arthur H. Vandenberg spoke out for a new coalition cutting across old party lines in opposition to the president's program. As an admirer of Hamilton, Vandenberg did not speak the language of Jefferson. But neither did he embrace the big government patterns represented by Roosevelt and the New Deal. He called for a coalition that might merge the better parts of Hamiltonian and Jeffersonian values.[2]

In Wisconsin, the energetic and ambitious Progressive Governor Philip La Follette was impatient with what he considered Roosevelt's timid leadership. In December, 1936, after a White House meeting of state governors with the president, La Follette persuaded himself that the progressive cause would not be served in the long run by Roosevelt and the Democratic party. After that meeting he concluded that "Roosevelt had no more real interest in the common man than a Wall Street broker. He was playing the same kind of game as Big Business, only he sought, got, and intended to keep *power*, rather than money." He resolved that he "would never again support him politically." In

1938, Governor La Follette (with his brother Bob's reluctant and skeptical assent) organized a new National Progressive party. On April 28, it initiated its call with much fanfare at a mass meeting in Madison, Wisconsin. Senator Robert La Follette did not attend, but sent a message endorsing the movement.[3]

Philip invited Mayor Fiorello La Guardia of New York, but the mayor asked Adolf A. Berle, Jr., to represent him. Then serving as assistant secretary of state in Washington, Berle consulted Roosevelt before committing himself. The president advised him to attend. According to Berle, Roosevelt thought its methods "were hardly adapted to the eastern situation," but that it "was all right if the movement did not get too far away from shore so that the forces could not be joined." FDR thought it well for Berle to attend quietly and unofficially "to have someone there who would generally keep the lines parallel."[4]

The meeting attracted a large and receptive audience of progressives from across the country, and the governor delivered what he considered one of his best addresses. Some were uneasy, however, about the flag-flying emotional fervor of the proceedings, and thought the new party's cross-in-a-circle symbol looked disturbingly like a Nazi swastika. Though sympathetic with the La Follettes and their progressivism, Berle thought a "third party would become logical" only "if and when the Democratic Party repudiated the Roosevelt leadership." And he was troubled that Governor La Follette's program was surprisingly "close to that of the Italian fascist." By prior arrangement Berle reported his observations and reactions to the president by telephone after he left Madison. Roosevelt followed the developments closely, but does not seem to have viewed the National Progressive party as a particularly worrisome challenge. And it wasn't. Philip La Follette was defeated in his bid for a fourth term as governor by the Republican candidate. Others running for offices in Wisconsin and elsewhere under the Progressive aegis fared poorly in the November elections. It never really developed as a national political force and petered out before the 1940 presidential contest got underway.[5]

Leading isolationists who faced the voters generally did well in 1938 (as most had who had come up in 1934 and 1936). Six of the seven members of the old Senate Munitions Investigating Committee (all except Vandenberg) ran in 1938; five of the six were victorious (Nye, Clark, Bone, Barbour, and George). Only Pope of Idaho was ousted, and he lost in the Democratic primaries to D. Worth Clark, who proved to be a more outspoken and unequivocal isolationist than Pope had been. Republican Robert A. Taft of Ohio won election to his first term in the United States Senate. And the ranking minority member of the Foreign Affairs Committee, Republican Hamilton Fish from Roosevelt's home district in New York, won another term in the House seat he had filled since 1920. Foreign affairs, however, were not decisive in any of those contests. Nye's national prominence as chairman of the munitions investigation was a political asset in North Dakota, but his most formidable opponent in the election, William Langer, was fully as isolationist as Nye was. And the election turned on the highly emotional issue of whether one was for or against the controversial Langer.[6]

From a Democratic perspective the election results on November 8 were worse than either Roosevelt or Farley had expected. The Democrats retained some 75 percent of the seats in the Senate and nearly 60 percent in the House. But the Republicans gained eight Senate seats from the Democrats, and eighty-one seats in the House. Democratic reverses were most striking among rural and small-town voters. The Democrats were unable to win any of the seats held by Republicans in the Senate. With conservative Democrats holding their own in the primaries and with Republicans gaining ground in the general elections, the president was certain to face increased difficulties with Congress on domestic issues in 1939.[7]

Democratic National Chairman Jim Farley set out to find out what had gone wrong. He wrote personal letters to hundreds of state and local Democratic leaders throughout the country seeking their explanations for the reverses. They responded thoughtfully and helpfully, but not very cheerfully. Local, state, and personal considerations were involved in the election results; often they were decisive. Most of Farley's correspondents did not consider the vote as a slap at Roosevelt personally. The letters rarely mentioned foreign policy issues one way or the other. There were strong criticisms of specific New Deal programs and policies, particularly the way they were being administered. Farmers were dissatisfied with agricultural policies and prices. They complained of the impact of relief rolls on farm labor costs and of the administration's lenient policies toward urban labor and unions. Small businessmen shared those views. Works Progress Administration relief programs came under particularly sharp criticism, both from those on relief who thought they got too little and from others who thought WPA workers got too much for doing too little on projects of questionable merit.[8]

Though the Democratic reverses were greater than Roosevelt had expected, he kept his optimistic spirit and did not appear discouraged by the results. At his first cabinet meeting after the elections, discussion focused particularly on foreign affairs. The president did not take up the political situation until near the end of the meeting. He explained the election results in terms of "local conditions." Late in November and early in December, FDR relaxed in Warm Springs, Georgia, and conferred with friends and advisers about the political situation. He read many of the early postelection letters that Farley was receiving from across the country. He wrote Farley advising him to "resume the tactics of 1930, 1931 and 1932, getting the utmost publicity out of attacks on these new men and basing the attacks on their definitely reactionary policies." In that memorandum responding to analyses in those letters he had read, Roosevelt did not mention either WPA or foreign affairs one way or the other.[9]

Looking at the domestic scene from the perspective of Emporia, Kansas, the wise old Republican editor, William Allen White, analyzed the president's political situation in a letter written after the 1938 elections. White concluded that Roosevelt was mistaken in believing that he was "making the Democratic party a national weapon of liberalism." In White's opinion it could not be done because Roosevelt had "to use the Old South which is certainly not liberal and the Tammanies which certainly have no great convictions" to get "a national victory." White may have been correct in terms of domestic policies at that particular time. In an unintended way, however, the old Kansas newsman alluded to the new bases that were to give Roosevelt, his administration, and his party renewed political strength and vitality as the president shifted priorities from domestic reform to a more active role by the United States in world affairs.[10]

Though FDR continued to speak the language of liberalism the rest of his life, he also stepped up efforts to build ties with the urban business and financial community and with conservative southern Democrats. And it was that alliance between the urban Northeast (including labor, business, finance, academia, and the press) and the South that provided the rockbed political base for the president's increasingly internationalist foreign policies. Western progressives and their isolationism were left behind without sufficient strength to prevail either in their progressivism, their rural and small town values, or in foreign affairs.

In his annual message to Congress on January 4, 1939, President Roosevelt artfully hinted at his refocus away from domestic affairs toward foreign affairs, a transition that developments abroad (including Munich) and at home (including the elections of 1938) had already mandated. In moving terms he spoke on both foreign and domestic affairs, but he meshed them together with emphasis on the alarming challenges abroad. War and aggression threatened religion, democracy, and international good faith. He called for "a united democracy" and described his "program of social and economic reform" as "a part of defense, as basic as armaments themselves." He tended to refer to reforms in terms of past accomplishments. When Roosevelt said, "We are off on a race to make democracy work, so that we may be efficient in peace and therefore secure in national defense," he was giving a different emphasis than he had in 1933. The call "to bring capital and man-power together" was more palatable to businessmen than the earlier New Deal vocabulary. Businessmen and financiers could find encouragement in his contention that "investment for prosperity can be made in a democracy." In contrast to earlier priorities, the president explained, "Events abroad have made it increasingly clear to the American people that dangers within are less to be feared than dangers from without."[11] Millions of Americans agreed with him, especially in the South and the urban Northeast. Isolationists did not. His change in priorities strengthened their conviction that not only were socioeconomic problems at home still America's most important concerns but that the president himself was increasingly part of the "dangers within" that they feared.

Chapter 21

Frontier on the Rhine

The airplane was a prototype for a twin-engine light bomber designed and built to Army Air Corps specifications by the Douglas Aircraft Company. Later production models were used by the Army Air Forces throughout World War II as the A-20. In the British Royal Air Force it saw service as the Havoc. Nearly three thousand of the planes went to the Soviet Union under lend-lease for use against the Germans in Eastern Europe. But the earliest production models went to France as the DB-7. Not yet ordered by the air corps, on January 23, 1939, a company plane flown by a civilian pilot spun out of a turn when performing a low level engine-out test. It crashed in a parking lot at North American Aviation's plant at Mines Field, later part of Los Angeles International Airport. The pilot was killed when he attempted to parachute at low altitude. Pulled from the wreckage before it burst into flames was a badly injured Frenchman, Paul Chemidlin. He was a member of a French purchasing mission headed by Jean Monnet in the United States secretly to buy American-made military planes for the French air force. Headlines of the crash, and news of the Frenchman's presence in the plane, brought the first public awareness of the secret French mission. Three weeks earlier the president had referred to "methods short of war, but stronger and more effective than mere words" in his annual message to Congress. But the crash in California was the most dramatic early public revelation of Roosevelt's aid-short-of-war policy.[1]

President Roosevelt and Secretary Hull had attempted a wide range of methods that might enable the United States to play positive and active roles in efforts to preserve peace and guard security in international affairs over opposition from isolationists. Disarmament, trade reciprocity, conference diplomacy, presidential messages, and independent but parallel actions all were approaches the administration explored in its efforts to make America's voice and weight effective in trying to preserve peace and check the Axis. Of all those varied tactics, the most central and effective in President Roosevelt's foreign policies from 1939 to December, 1941 was American aid-short-of-war to the victims of Axis aggression.

In Roosevelt's artful hands the aid-short-of-war method proved to be the near-perfect formula for providing the maximum assistance against the Axis that public opinion and Congress would permit. It meshed with the nearly unanimous American hostility to Hitler's Nazi Germany, Mussolini's Fascist Italy, and militarist Japan. And it was consistent with the overwhelming desire by the American people to stay out of foreign wars. On the surface, at least, it had the potential for allowing the United States "to have its cake and eat it too." Its flexibility fitted changing circumstances at home and abroad as well as Roosevelt's undoctrinaire style. When isolationist and peace sentiment was particularly strong in the 1930s, the early aid-short-of-war formula could take such guarded forms as Norman Davis's Geneva statement in 1933, the administration's decision to invoke the Neutrality Act of 1935 in the undeclared Italian-Ethiopian war, and its decision not to invoke the Neutrality Act of 1937 in the undeclared Sino-Japanese war. As Axis aggression led to war that threatened to engulf the whole world and as American hostility and fear of the Axis menace grew more acute, the president enjoyed greater freedom to undertake bolder actions to help the British, Chinese, and Russians in their battles for survival. By 1941 it included lend-lease aid and an American undeclared naval war against Germany in the Atlantic.

One could contend that the method was fundamentally flawed in that it mistakenly led the American people to believe (or hope) that aid-short-of-war could be sufficient to accomplish the defeat of the Axis without full United States involvement in World War II. By encouraging that hope, opposition to a declaration of war remained overwhelming both in Congress and in public opinion right down to the moment the Japanese attacked Pearl Harbor. It could also be seen as misleading insofar as it encouraged Americans to believe (or hope) that aid-short-of-war would not (or need not) bring the United States into war abroad. But if aid-short-of-war was not sufficient to accomplish the defeat of the Axis powers (and it wasn't), the method had the capacity of being pushed to the point where it could (and did) provoke Axis retaliation that would move the American people, the Congress, and the president to war on the Axis. And it was the near-perfect method for enabling Roosevelt to contest with isolationist opposition without a potentially disastrous direct frontal assault on the isolationist stronghold on the issue of whether the United States should or should not declare war. Isolationists could (and did) charge that Roosevelt's methods short-of-war were actually steps to war and oppose his various actions on noninterventionist grounds. But the president and his followers could (and did) insist that aid-short-of-war provided America's best hope for staying out of World War II. And increasingly the majority of the American people and the majority in Congress followed the president's lead on the method. Roosevelt was not entirely frank and candid with either Congress or the American people. But he played the aid-short-of-war instrument with the finesse that Fritz Kreisler used in playing his Stradivarius. The aid-short-of-war formula failed insofar as it may have been designed to accomplish the defeat of the Axis without a United States declaration of war or without the use of United States armed forces in combat. It failed insofar as it may have been designed to keep the United States out of war. But insofar as the aid-short-of-war formula was designed to overcome isolationist opposition, it was successful.

The gestation for Roosevelt's aid-short-of-war ideas was long, slow, and obscure. Throughout his administration he wrestled with the question of how he might effectively lead the United States to a constructive role in striving for world peace and security. Nationalism, depression, xenophobia, weak leadership, and appeasement abroad gave him something less solid to work with in foreign states than he required. And the depression, New Deal, and isolationism hampered him at home. But he never ceased groping. In hundreds of conversations and conferences in the White House, at Hyde Park, on his travels, and on cruises he tried out ideas and listened to the thoughts of others. No one then or now can know just how his thinking formed as he reflected in the solitude of his mind on ocean cruises, while fishing, or while working on his stamp collections. He seems to have communicated his thoughts on the subject more frankly to foreign visitors than to Americans, certainly more so than he did to the American public.

Roosevelt's quarantine speech was a phase in the development of the idea. His scheme late in 1937 for a joint Anglo-American long-distance naval blockade of Japan was an early specific application of the idea that failed to materialize because of British reticence abroad and isolationist strength at home. In mid-September, 1938, during the Munich crisis, the British ambassador to the United States, Sir Ronald Lindsay, reported to Foreign Minister Viscount Halifax that the president had told a French visitor; "You may count on us for everything except troops and loans." Lindsay believed that was "a true reflection" of Roosevelt's feelings, but that "he ought to have added a reservation: 'Subject to dictates of our public opinion and our own domestic politics.'" The president, according to Lindsay, found that Americans had "already been aroused by Germany's brutal diplomacy, and hostilities of the same character would only accelerate the process thereto."[2]

On the evening of September 19, 1938, the president explored possible United States actions in a White House conversation with Ambassador Lindsay. The conversation was so secret that Roosevelt asked Lindsay to tell nobody and warned him that if it became "known to anyone that he has even breathed a suggestion" he "would almost be impeached and the suggestion would be hopelessly prejudiced." If the Western powers were forced into a war, he thought "they should carry it on purely by blockade and in a defensive manner." Roosevelt believed conducting the war by blockade would "meet with approval of the United States if its humanitarian purpose were strongly emphasized." Though he could not initiate the plan, FDR told the British ambassador that he could on his own authority as president recognize the blockade as effective and thereby help the blockading powers.[3]

It would be easier for him to help the British and French, the president said, if they could avoid declaring war, perhaps by calling their actions "defensive measures or anything plausible but avoid actual declaration of war." Even if Germany declared war and the British and French refrained from doing so, "he might yet be able to find that we [the British] were not at war" and thus not invoke the Neutrality Act. Roosevelt pointed out that he "had already been able to give himself wide latitude in the interpretation of the Neutrality Law in the Far East and in Ethiopia and if the law was not changed he would be disposed to do so again." According to Lindsay, "Several times in the conversation he showed himself quite alive to the possibility that somehow or other in indefinable circumstances the United States might again find themselves involved in an European war." If Germany invaded Britain in force, "such a wave of emotion might arise, that an American army might be sent overseas."[4]

Ambassador Lindsay reported his conversation with the president to the Foreign Office, marking it "most secret." At his suggestion the foreign minister authorized the ambassador to "convey to the President my great appreciation of his having taken you so far into his confidence." He wrote that "should His Majesty's Government be drawn into any conflict, their major role would probably be enforcement of blockade, as President foresees." He found it "of great encouragement to know that the President has been giving thought to these questions."[5]

At his cabinet meeting a few days later, the president discussed his idea for an Anglo-French defensive war in Europe and emphasized his concern (according to Ickes's diary) about "the overwhelming preponderance of Germany and Italy in the air." Like Lindbergh at the same time, Roosevelt believed "Germany alone has an air fleet much greater than the combined fleets of England, France and Russia and can turn out airplanes two or three times faster than those of three countries."[6]

In October, 1938, at Roosevelt's invitation, Colonel and Mrs. Arthur Murray were guests at Hyde Park. Active in the British Liberal party, Murray had served in the Foreign Office under Sir Edward Grey in World War I and had been an assistant military attaché in Washington during and after the war. Alarmed by the Nazi menace and critical of Chamberlain's appeasement policies, Colonel Murray had maintained friendly contact with Roosevelt over many years. On October 21, Roosevelt discussed German air power with Murray, including ways the United States as a neutral might be able to help Britain in the event of war. The president asked Murray to tell Prime Minister Chamberlain that he would have "the industrial resources of the American nation behind him in the event of war with the dictatorships," insofar as it was within Roosevelt's power to achieve it. Roosevelt wanted Chamberlain "to know that privately," though the prime minister (and the president) "couldn't say it publicly." Roosevelt also asked Colonel Murray to tell the prime minister of the growing awareness of the American people to the Axis threat to the Western Hemisphere in the event those aggressors triumphed elsewhere. Roosevelt told Murray that "one of his difficulties . . . was that the last democracies to be really hit would be the United States."[7] On December 14, Murray met with Chamberlain and left him a memorandum of the conversation with Roosevelt.[8] Chamberlain and his office were not much impressed, but the episode does provide a peek at Roosevelt's evolving thoughts—a glimpse that was more candid than the American people or Congress had had to that time.

In the same month of October that he visited with Murray, in the days and weeks immediately following Munich, French needs and perspectives were brought vividly to the president's attention. The United States ambassador to France, William C. Bullitt, was more intimately informed on French thought and policies than any other American in public life. It was his invitation that had brought together French Air Minister Guy La Chambre, Jean Monnet, and Colonel Charles A. Lindbergh, as well as Premier Daladier and others, to discuss ways of meeting France's needs for increased air power. Though Lindbergh decided against participating in the scheme for building French aircraft factories in Canada and though nothing came of the plan directly, the deliberations in Paris did lead in October to Monnet's mission to the United States and to his personal conferences with Roosevelt and other top American officials.[9]

Ambassador Bullitt returned to the United States and on October 13 reported to the White House and conferred late into the night with the president. Three days later Bullitt went to Hyde Park with Roosevelt and others. At his sessions with FDR, Bullitt presented his impressions of German air power superiority, French aviation weakness, the importance of air power in deliberations leading to Munich, and the urgent necessity for building French (and British and American) air power in confronting future Axis challenges. Bullitt drew on various sources for his information, but among those was Colonel Lindbergh. At the very time Bullitt was conferring with the president, Lindbergh and his wife were in Germany for their third and last major inspection tour of aircraft and aviation research and production facilities there. On October 26, Colonel Lindbergh sent an eighteen-page hand-written letter addressed to Ambassador Bullitt in Paris describing his latest observations and findings on German air power. In November, Lindbergh also wrote to General H. H. Arnold, recently appointed chief of the Army Air Corps.[10]

Those reports from Bullitt and others and indirectly from Lindbergh affected Roosevelt's thinking. That was evidenced in his comments at cabinet meetings and in his conversations with Britain's Anthony Eden who visited the United States in December. The British embassy reported that in talking with Eden the president had "harped upon the great inferiority in air power of Great Britain and France as compared with Germany" and urged Britain to "do everything possible" to strengthen its air power.[11]

Earlier in 1938 the French had contracted for the purchase of one hundred Curtiss Hawk 75 pursuit planes (export versions of the P-36, of which the Army Air Corps had only three at the time). In early November after he had returned to Paris from the United States, Monnet reported that he believed France could get a thousand airplanes from American manufacturers by the end of July, 1939. Premier Daladier authorized him to purchase the planes, and, with encouragement from President Roosevelt, Monnet returned to the United States in December at the head of a small mission of aviation experts—including Paul Chemidlin. Through Acting Secretary of State Sumner Welles, Roosevelt authorized the Treasury Department under Secretary Henry Morgenthau, Jr., to assist Monnet and his mission. Morgenthau arranged for Monnet to confer with the Treasury Department's acting director of procurement. They began to explore the possibilities of French purchase of military bombers, fighters, and trainers from American manufacturers. In their efforts to step up expansion of American air power, the Army Air Corps under General Arnold and the War Department under Secretary of War Harry Woodring objected to having the still puny output of American aircraft factories siphoned off to fill European orders. With encouragement from Morgenthau, however, the president on December 21 authorized the French to inspect and buy American planes, providing their orders did not interfere with upcoming American orders. And on January 16, 1939, the President pressed his insistence "that every effort be made to expedite the procurement of any types of plane desired by the French government." With firm authority from the president channeled through Secretary Morgenthau, Secretary Woodring and General Arnold reluctantly authorized the French inspection of the Douglas bomber and other aircraft.The prototype did not include the secret Norden bombsight. Since the plane had not yet been purchased by the air corps, legal restrictions on foreign sales of American military aircraft presumably did not apply. All of that was accomplished secretly. Not until the plane crashed in California on January 23 was it brought vividly to the attention of Congress and the public.[12]

Even before the crash, however, Congress had been alerted to the general problem. On January 10, 1939, Ambassadors Bullitt and Kennedy had given secret testimony at an executive session of a joint meeting of the Senate and House Military Affairs Committees.The two American ambassadors (both fully and personally informed by Lindbergh of his findings) provided the legislators with a gloomy portrait of the inferiority of British and French air power relative to Germany and implied the urgent necessity for vastly increasing American air power. Leaks from that meeting alluded to Lindbergh's reports on German air power.[13]

Two days later, on January 12, the president submitted his message calling for additional defense appropriations in excess of a half billion dollars. The largest part of that was to be allocated for the purchase of airplanes for the Army Air Corps.[14] Isolationists generally approved building American air power, in contrast to their skepticism about big navy construction. But except for his annual message calling for "methods short of war, but stronger and more effective than mere words" for "bringing home to aggressor governments the aggregate sentiments of our own people," the president had not yet given major emphasis to his aid-short-of-war idea. Though isolationists might support and even applaud appropriations for continental defense, aid to Britain and France and channeling American airplane production to them were quite different matters. News of the secret French purchase mission threatened to lead to a full-scale Senate investigation.

Though the senior and most prestigious Senate isolationists served on the Foreign Relations Committee, the isolationist perspective was vigorously represented by younger isolationists on the Senate Military Affairs Committee under the chairmanship of Morris Sheppard of Texas. Among members of that committee were Senators Gerald Nye of North Dakota, Bennett Clark of Missouri, Ernest Lundeen of Minnesota, Edwin Johnson of Colorado, Robert Reynolds of North Carolina, and Henry Cabot Lodge, Jr., of Massachusetts.[15]

After the crash, in response to questioning from Senator Clark, General Arnold told the Military Affairs Committee that the Frenchman "was out there under the direction of the Treasury Department, with a view of looking into possible purchase of airplanes by the French Mission." That caused an uproar in the committee, in the Treasury Department, and in the White House. The air corps chief feared he might be fired. At a White House meeting with Secretaries Morgenthau and Woodring with military brass present, the president emphasized the necessity for cooperation on sale of aircraft abroad.[16]

On Friday, January 27, the president explained the matter at his press conference. On that same day, with committee chairman Sheppard presiding, the Military Affairs Committee proposed to get at the heart of the matter. Present at the committee meeting were Secretary Morgenthau, Secretary Woodring, Army Chief of Staff Malin Craig, and others. General Arnold was not present. Senators Clark, Reynolds, and Nye pressed the questioning. Secretary Morgenthau explained that the Procurement Division of the Treasury Department was helping the French "meet manufacturers and carry out its mission" as a helpful action to "a friendly nation." He traced authority for his department's role to Acting Secretary of State Sumner Welles and to President Roosevelt.[17]

With the controversy still raging, President Roosevelt met at the White House with members of the Military Affairs Committee on Tuesday, January 31, 1939. He took the unusual precaution (for him) of having a verbatim transcript made of the statements at that meeting. FDR spoke to the senators with unusual candor and forthrightness. He asked them to keep his comments "confidential"; he did not want "to frighten the American people." He did, however, want Americans "to gradually realize what is a potential danger." It was his most frank and advanced statement on foreign policy to any legislative committee during his first two terms in office.[18]

President Roosevelt told the senators that he was "very much exercised over the future of the world" and did "not belong to a school of thought that says we can draw a line of defense around this country and live completely and solely to ourselves." He said that about three years earlier they had "got the pretty definite information that there was in the making a policy of world domination between Germany, Italy and Japan." There were, he said, two possible ways of viewing the challenge. One was "the hope that somebody will assassinate Hitler or that Germany will blow up from within." The other way, FDR said, was to "try to prevent the domination of the world—prevent it by peaceful means."[19]

Elaborating on that second approach, Roosevelt posed the question, "What is the first line of defense in the United States?" For the Pacific he described that first line of defense as "a series of islands, with the hope that through the Navy and the Army and the airplanes we can keep the Japanese—let us be quite frank—from dominating the entire Pacific Ocean and prevent us from having access to the west coast of South America." Turning to the Atlantic and Europe, Roosevelt described America's first line of defense as "the continued independent existence of a very large group of nations." He named them: Finland, Latvia, Estonia, Lithuania, Sweden, Norway, Denmark, Holland, Belgium, Hungary, Czechoslovakia, Poland, Romania, Bulgaria, Greece, Yugoslavia, Turkey, Persia, France, and England.[20]

Roosevelt then discussed the air power weakness of France and England relative to Germany at the time of Munich, using figures proportionately much like those that Lindbergh had used. He contended that if British and French air power had been twice what it had been, "there would not have been any Munich." If Britain, France, and other still independent states decided to fight to block Hitler's next moves, the outcome could go either way. If Hitler and Mussolini triumphed, "it would be primarily because of the air force." If the Axis conquered Europe, Africa would automatically fall. Next would be Central and South America. Roosevelt traced steps by which Hitler conceivably might bring the individual Latin American states under his control. He described that hypothetical process as "the gradual encirclement of the United States by the removal of first lines of defense."[21]

So far as America's rearmament program was concerned, Roosevelt told the senators that the United States needed the production capacity to mass-produce military airplanes. He thought Germany had "enough mass production factories to turn out forty thousand planes a year on a three-shift basis." He thought if American factories were put on a mass-production basis at that time, they might "turn out nine or ten thousand planes a year. None of them has ever been in mass production, so we do not know."[22]

The president explained that nearly two years earlier the British and French had sent people to the United States to place small orders with American aircraft manufacturers. The United States approved because factories were idle and could complete the foreign orders before starting work on American orders. Also the United States wanted "France to continue as an independent nation. . . . Therefore, it is to our interest, quite frankly, to do what we can, absolutely as a matter of peace, peace of the world, to help the French and British maintain their independence. Literally, their independence is threatened today." The president promised to do everything possible "to prevent any munitions from going to Germany or Italy or Japan." And he would do everything he could "to maintain the independence of these other nations by sending them all they can pay for on the barrelhead, to these about forty or fifty now independent nations of the world. Now, that is the foreign policy of the United States." He hoped France got the best planes America could produce and got them quickly. "It may mean the saving of our civilization." Roosevelt said, "We will help them to rearm against the threat of dictators in this world. It is our policy." He assured the senators "that about the last thing that this country should do is ever to send an army to Europe again."[23]

The president had been boldly frank in his comments to the Senate Military Affairs Committee. He had described in alarming terms the seriousness of the Axis challenge. He had explained the policies he intended to follow in the face of that foreign menace. He told the senators what America's foreign policy was and why. It was a concerned group of senators that left the president that Tuesday afternoon.

Senators Clark, Nye, and Reynolds were together as they walked out of the White House. An hour later Senator Nye wrote an eleven-page memorandum summarizing his thoughts from the meeting. In his memorandum Nye expressed concern both about the policies the president had outlined and the secrecy surrounding those policies. The progressive Republican Senator from North Dakota thought Roosevelt had called the session primarily to block efforts to get the correspondence on the episode. Nye was convinced that Roosevelt was "determined to utterly ignore the neutrality law" and "to aid the so-called democracies" in a pending European war. He found it "shocking" that "even before that war comes the President considers our first line of defense to be in France." The "short of war" assurances by Roosevelt would be insufficient restraint, in Nye's view, if they were prefaced by the word "anything." Noting Roosevelt's usual charm, Nye wrote: "His talk today was as one who knows just what is coming and just what to do. His program was carefully charted." In his memorandum the senator wrote that after the meeting he had limited himself to one sentence for newsmen: "To be confined to secrecy at a time when there is so much that ought to be said is distressing." He believed that "secrecy on such scores as were discussed today is not in the best interests of the country." Nye concluded his personal memorandum by writing; "Get the uniforms ready for the boys."[24]

The next day Nye took the floor in the Senate to protest against secrecy on "a matter which quite properly might have been left wide open to the press and to the public." He announced that he would withdraw "from all executive committee meetings of the Military Affairs Committee in its present consideration of national defense measures, and to maintain that withdrawal until such time as a reasonable part of the record, devoid of any military secrets of those meetings, shall be available to the people." He determined to protect himself "from a position that is intolerable and completely out of step with what ought to be practice under a democratic representative form of government."[25]

Though Nye limited his immediate public reaction to objecting to the secrecy, at least one other senator was less inhibited. Newsmen swarmed as the senators left the meeting with the president. And headlines the next day quoted an unidentified senator as saying that Roosevelt had told them that America's frontier was on the Rhine or in France. The president had discussed America's first line of defense and had listed countries much further east than France or the Rhine whose continued independent existence was important to the United States. According to the White House transcript, however, Roosevelt had not said that America's frontier was on the Rhine. There was much speculation about who had made the statement to newsmen. Some suspected Nye. He (both then and later) denied that he had made the remark. He thought Senator Lundeen of Minnesota had done so. Whoever was responsible, it caused a tremendous uproar—in the press, in Congress, in the public, and in the White House.[26]

At his press conference on February 3, Roosevelt called the allegation a "deliberate lie." Contrary to his usual procedure, he authorized newsmen to quote him on that. He charged that "Some boob got that off" and denied that the phrase summed up what he had actually told the senators. He provided the newsmen with what he called "a comparatively simple statement" of American foreign policy. It included no "entangling alliances," "maintenance of world trade for everybody," "complete sympathy with any and every effort made to reduce or limit armaments," and sympathy "with the peaceful maintenance of political, economic and social independence of all nations in the world."[27] That was a different statement of American foreign policy than he had provided for the Military Affairs Committee three days before.

The White House also made arrangements for Democratic Congressman Thomas C. Hennings, Jr., of Missouri to deliver an address over the Columbia Broadcasting System that evening defending the president and attacking his critics. Stephen Early, the president's secretary, provided Hennings with the text for his broadcast, arranged network time for him in New York, and advised the congressman on getting the speech to wire services and newspapers.[28]

Senator Hiram Johnson of California found that constituents in Los Angeles were eager to have the sale of planes to France consummated. But he did not share that view. Like Nye, Johnson particularly objected to the secrecy with which the administration had handled the matter. He was concerned that if the planes went to France, they would not be available for America's own air corps. He wrote his son that the lines were divided "with all the Jews on one side, wildly enthusiastic for the President, and willing to fight to the last American, both Germany and Italy; and those of us—a very considerable number—who are thinking in terms of our own country, and that alone." For his son, Johnson elaborated on the Jews: "Naturally, like any normally constituted human being, I hate the persecutions to which the Jews have been put, and I will go any fair lengths, save the ruin of my own country, to aid them; but I will not go to the length of fighting citizens of other nations, who have been badly and shamefully treated, nor that these citizens of other nations may vindicate their rights or punish their wrongdoers. This is the basis of the struggle here, and I don't know but what somebody ought to say it openly, but everybody is afraid—I confess I shrink from it—of offending the Jews." He was convinced that Roosevelt "cares no more for what may happen to us in a war, than the man in the moon. He has developed the dictator complex, and he has found, at last, the class which cheers him vociferously for aiding their people, who neither live here, nor have anything in common with our country. He will do anything for applause, and it is this very group at present which applaud him to the echo."[29]

At his press conference on February 17, President Roosevelt elaborated more fully on what he had told the Military Affairs Committee. He insisted, however, that his comments be "off the record" because "in the hands of an unscrupulous person like Nye or Bennett Clark, on this particular subject . . . it can be so completely twisted around as to be an awfully dangerous thing." He then restated his view that the "continued independence" of "thirty or forty" countries was "of tremendous importance to the safety of the United States." He again denied "that the frontiers of the United States are on the Rhine or in France," charging that the phrase was coined to "make political capital."[30]

Senator Nye got a different impression of the president's comments to newsmen. As he understood it, Roosevelt had told his press conference that he did not know who leaked the statement but that the person was a "boob" and a "liar" and "spelled his name N-y-e." Nye insisted that he had not leaked the statement and was angered by what he understood to be Roosevelt's reference to him. When Marvin McIntyre, the president's secretary, later called Nye and said Roosevelt would like him to come to the White House to talk over matters, the senator refused the invitation. He believed that if Roosevelt considered him a "boob" and a "liar," nothing would be accomplished by further discussion. After that refusal, Nye was never again invited to the White House for consultation. The episode marked the final break in personal relations between Roosevelt and Nye.[31]

President Roosevelt had been moving slowly, cautiously, and skillfully in shaping and implementing the early patterns for his aid-short-of-war policy. The plane crash in California blew the cover of secrecy that had hidden his thoughts and actions from the American public and isolationists. In an effort to quiet the uproar, he explained his policies and actions with unusual frankness to members of the Military Affairs Committee. That backfired with the leak of the "frontier on the Rhine" phrase. His efforts to smooth things over at his press conferences won the cooperation of most newsmen, but did not assuage isolationists. As in the aftermath of his quarantine speech, so in the wake of the "frontier on the Rhine" episode President Roosevelt was not deterred from pursuing increasingly internationalist policies in the face of Axis challenges abroad. His boldness and innovativeness continued in his actions abroad. And he and other administration leaders continued their effforts to educate the American public away from isolationism. But the furor at home made him more cautious (and even devious) in his tactics for dealing with isolationists, with Congress, and with the American public. Those patterns were apparent in his efforts to accomplish revision of the neutrality legislation in 1939.

Chapter 22

Eroding Neutrality

The Neutrality Act of 1939 was an important part of President Roosevelt's aid-short-of-war policy. Signed into law on November 4, it repealed the arms embargo and thereby enabled warring Britain and France to buy armaments and munitions in the United States. It reenacted the cash-and-carry provisions that had expired six months earlier. It was the first in an uninterrupted succession of Roosevelt administration triumphs over isolationists in legislative contests on neutrality and aid-short-of-war. Though they could still delay action on the president's proposals and though they might deter him from pressing particular legislation, from 1939 onward isolationists were never able to defeat any presidential aid-short-of-war proposal actually put to a vote in Congress. The initiative and advantage had shifted to the president. Isolationists fought tenaciously in a losing struggle as Roosevelt's forces relentlessly drove them back in engagement after engagement.

The initial administration moves to revise neutrality legislation in 1939 were so cautious, and isolationist strength was so great before the European war began, that the opposition temporarily prevailed. The president and Secretary Hull would have preferred complete repeal of the Neutrality Act or discretionary authority to apply the arms embargo only against aggressor states. Senator Key Pittman and others, however, warned that such legislation could not be passed at that time. Pittman believed the most that could be hoped for was repeal of the arms embargo and the application of cash-and-carry to all exports, including munitions, from the United States to belligerents. Administration leaders were persuaded that Pittman's political analysis was correct, and they cooperated with his cautious strategy. Even those limited changes faced formidable opposition. Not until after war erupted in Europe in September, 1939, were administration forces able to overpower isolationists on the issue. Congress and the nation hotly debated the issue before the President and his supporters carried the day. To accomplish his goal, the president was less than frank with the American people. Both interventionists and noninterventionists correctly identified the administration's moves as designed to extend American aid to the victims of Axis aggression. The president phrased it in those terms in private conversations and correspondence with those he trusted. His public stance, however, was that the changes in neutrality legislation would be more likely to keep the United States out of war and were more in tune with traditional international law. The neutrality debates in 1939 set general patterns that were to be repeated over and over again until the Japanese attack more than two years later officially brought the United States into World War II.[1]

The permanent Neutrality Act of 1937 had no sooner become law than many on all sides wanted to revise or repeal it. In the fall of 1938 the Department of State named a subcommittee to study options and make recommendations. That subcommittee concluded that repeal of the neutrality law or legislation giving the president discretionary authority to apply the provisions of the law against only one side in a foreign war could not win approval in Congress. Repeal of the embargo and strengthening cash-and-carry seemed the most that might be obtained. Senator Pittman, chairman of the Foreign Relations Committee, advised R. Walton Moore, counselor of the Department of State, that he thought the Senate would not give the president "any larger discretion under our so-called 'Neutrality Legislation.'"[2]

In his annual message to Congress on January 4, 1939, President Roosevelt said, "We have learned that when we deliberately try to legislate neutrality, our neutrality laws may operate unevenly and unfairly—may actually give aid to an aggressor and deny it to the victim. The instinct of self-preservation should warn us that we ought not to let that happen any more." When Secretary of State Cordell Hull conferred with Senator Pittman a few days later, however, the Nevada Democrat thought the chances for success might be greater if the administration left the initiative to him and his committee. Hull and Roosevelt deferred to Pittman's wishes.[3] Later in January, just after the bomber crash in California, V. A. L. Mallet of the British Embassy in Washington explained in a dispatch to the Foreign Office in London that the president and secretary of state were "anxious to do what they can to help but are obsessed by the risk of going too far ahead of public opinion and thus losing control of Congress." As the British diplomat saw it, "President Roosevelt evidently feels he must exercise greatest care not to give a handle to the isolationists and he presumably feels he has in his speech of January 4th said as much as he safely can for the present."[4]

On March 20, after consulting Moore in the State Department, Pittman introduced his neutrality resolution (S.J. Res. 67). It had the administration's tacit approval. It would continue most of the provisions of the earlier neutrality legislation, but provided for repeal of the arms embargo and extension of cash-and-carry. Pittman presented his resolution as "The Peace Act of 1939," rather than as aid-short-of-war.[5]

A few days later in a memorandum to Hull and Welles, FDR wrote; "The more I think the problem through, the more I am convinced that the existing Neutrality Act should be repealed in toto without any substitute." He authorized them to pass his views on to Pittman and other congressional leaders. Though Senators King of Utah and Lewis of Illinois had introduced separate bills calling for repeal of the existing Neutrality Act, Pittman and others thought that was not politically practicable in 1939. Senator Elbert D. Thomas of Utah had introduced a resolution designed to authorize the president to apply the arms embargo only against states waging war in violation of treaties to which the United States was a party. Neither Pittman nor the State Department officials thought it could win approval in Congress.[6]

In January, Senator Nye had reintroduced his earlier resolution calling for a complete ban on export of all munitions from the United States at any time in peace or war to any country outside the Western Hemisphere. On March 28, Senator Nye, Bone, and Clark sponsored a less drastic resolution. It would have retained most of the provisions in the Neutrality Act—including the arms embargo and cash-and-carry. But it would have increased the powers of Congress and restricted presidential authority in implementing neutrality policies. Nye charged that the Pittman resolution was designed to provide "American help for England and France especially."[7]

In their separate analyses, Roosevelt and Nye understood in general terms what the other was doing, neither could see the wisdom of the others's course, each took a jaundiced view of the other and his perspective, and each determined to battle the other's approach with all the ability he could command. Each felt righteous in his efforts; each thought the other unwise or worse.[8] There was at least the possibility that by 1939 each was beginning to realize that the president and his approach would prevail, that Nye and the isolationists would go down to defeat as war raged abroad and the United States was drawn (or led) into that maelstrom.

With the administration and State Department cautiously staying in the background, Pittman's Senate Foreign Relations Committee prepared to conduct public hearings. On April 5, the first to testify was former Secretary of State Henry L. Stimson of New York. A conservative, Republican, urban-oriented, internationalist, Stimson shared Roosevelt's opposition to isolationism but was more frank and straightforward in expressing his views. Stimson preferred the Thomas amendment that would have given the president authority to discriminate against aggressor states. His second choice was repeal of the Neutrality Act.[9] Stimson's testimony intensified isolationist fears about internationalist-interventionist intentions in revising neutrality legislation and about possible consequences for the United States if those intentions were carried out.

Crusty old Hiram Johnson thought the committee hearings made little difference and that neutrality legislation itself had little import. But he tried to use the hearings "as a sounding board for the refrain— we won't go into the war." He was convinced that Roosevelt was determined to take the United States into war "unless some of us here can make him realize that it is not a popular thing." In a letter to his grandson he wrote, "The first casualty of war is always truth, and then would come the loss of our own democracy. We would have whipped one dictator abroad, and set up another here." To his son he wrote that "we would be just as well off if we repealed the laws and depended upon international law."[10] That view coincided generally with those of the international law authorities John Bassett Moore and Edwin M. Borchard, with whom Johnson and Borah often corresponded and consulted.

Young Robert M. La Follette, Jr., of Wisconsin, on the Foreign Relations Committee, also made clear his disagreement with the administration. In a form letter La Follette wrote that he was "unalterably opposed to the United States becoming involved in another war except in actual defense of the United States, its possessions and this hemisphere." He favored "mandatory neutrality legislation" and opposed "in any way broadening the discretion of the President in the enforcement of neutrality laws." He urged adoption of "drastic legislation which will tax war profits to the limit in case this country becomes involved in war."[11]

As the hearings ran their course, Pittman, while keeping the initiative in his committee, cautiously opened the door for testimony by

Secretary Hull. Hull insisted that his testimony be given in closed executive session. He and his advisers spent days painstakingly preparing a statement he might make before the committee. But things got out of hand. As Moffat described it in his diary on May 3: "The neutrality situation seems to be going from bad to worse. . . . The President obviously is afraid to enter the picture for fear of the reaction against his personal wishes. The Secretary has had a series of talks with a group of Senators but has gotten nowhere. Pittman's leadership has broken down."[12]

On May 7, State Department officials completed the draft of the statement Hull might make at committee hearings. He invited Pittman to confer with him on Monday morning, May 8. The Nevada Democrat spent two and one-half hours at the State Department, and everything fell apart. Pittman did not like the statement Hull proposed to make. The committee wanted Hull's testimony in open, not closed, session. Believing that such a confrontation on the administration's policies and aims would be dangerous and unwise, Pittman advised Hull not to testify. Given the political situation as they saw it, Roosevelt and Hull concurred with Pittman's advice. The committee took no action. The efforts to work through Pittman and his Foreign Relations Committee stalled.[13]

The administration then turned to the House Foreign Affairs Committee. Democrat Sam McReynolds had been a loyal and effective instrument for the administration's foreign policies as chairman of that committee during Roosevelt's first six years in office. His health had failed, however, and in 1939 Democratic Congressman Sol Bloom of New York served as acting chairman. Bloom rejected isolationism and was eager to cooperate with the administration, but he lacked McReynold's political expertise. Roosevelt and Hull conferred with Bloom and other Democratic House leaders urging repeal of the embargo to help prevent war in Europe or, if war erupted, to make an Axis victory less likely.[14]

On May 27, Secretary Hull sent a letter to Senator Pittman and Congressman Bloom on neutrality revision. It had been the object of long and careful work by Hull and his advisers. They cleared the letter with FDR, who considered it "excellent." Hull wrote that the United States could not "disassociate" itself from world events, that America's neutrality policies would inevitably affect other countries. He warned against rigid and inflexible legislation. Hull thought the legislation "should conform, so far as possible, to traditional concepts of international law adhered to by this Government." He wrote that "a complete embargo upon all exports would obviously be ruinous to our economic life.'' He urged repeal of the arms embargo and called for reenacting most of the other provisions of the existing law, including cash-and-carry. He believed his recommendations would "help to keep this country out of war and facilitate our adherence to a position of neutrality.'' Hull made his letter public in a press release.[15]

With help and guidance from the State Department and the White House, Bloom moved his committee to action. On June 13, in a straight party vote of twelve to eight, the Foreign Affairs Committee reported Bloom's neutrality bill favorably. It included the provisions Roosevelt and Hull had hoped for, given the prevailing political situation.

But matters got out of hand when it reached the floor of the House of Representatives. The neutrality issue got mixed up with the silver issue.[16] Even the visit to the United States early in June by the popular king and queen of England failed to help matters in Congress. The House adopted the Bloom neutrality resolution on June 30, but only after it had attached an amendment introduced by Republican Congressman John M. Vorys of Ohio partly restoring the arms embargo. Passed by the narrow margin of 159 to 157 in a late night session after many of the Democratic congressmen had already gone home, the Vorys amendment removed the embargo on "implements of war," but maintained it on arms and ammunition.[17]

After midnight on June 30, according to the presidential diaries of Henry Morgenthau, Jr., Roosevelt told his treasury secretary on the telephone: "On these Monetary and Neutrality bills, I will bet you an old hat, and tell your people to spread the word around, that Hitler when he wakes up and finds out what has happened, there will be great rejoicing in the Italian and German camps. I think we ought to introduce a bill for statues of Austin, Vandenberg, Lodge and Taft—the four of them—to be erected in Berlin and put the swastika on them." That guilt-by-association pattern of identifying leading isolationists with Hitler and the Nazis was to become an increasingly effective and devastating tactic used by interventionists and the Roosevelt administration to demolish their isolationist opponents. In a letter to Congresswoman Caroline O'Day on July 1, Roosevelt wrote, "The anti-war nations believe that a definite stimulus has been given to Hitler by the vote of the House, and that if war breaks out in Europe, because of further seeking of territory by Hitler and Mussolini, an important part of the responsibility will rest on last night's action." He wrote that the House vote "was a stimulus to war and that if the result had been different it would have been a definite encouragement to peace.'' On July 1, the president wrote Attorney General Frank Murphy asking, ''If we fail to get any Neutrality Bill, how far do you think I can go in ignoring the existing act—even though I did sign it?''[18] Blocked in the House, the administration turned once again to the Senate. Both Roosevelt and Hull actively tried to win favorable action from Pittman and individual members of his committee.[19]

At the same time, Senators Johnson, Nye, Clark, and La Follette called a meeting of senators in Johnson's office on Friday morning, July 7, to plan opposition to neutrality revision. Fourteen attended the meeting, but they claimed the support of twenty other senators. Johnson felt uncomfortable working with some in the group and ''would much rather be a lone wolf.'' But he knew the necessity for the strength of numbers. Those attending the meeting were Senators Johnson, Nye, La Follette, Bennett Clark of Missouri, D. Worth Clark of Idaho, Borah, Bone, Shipstead, Capper, Lodge, White, Holt, Clyde Reed of Kansas, and John Danaher of Connecticut. They issued a statement opposing repeal of the arms embargo and objecting to ''any discretion being lodged in the hands of any Chief Executive to determine an aggressor or aggressors during any war abroad.''[20]

Senator Pittman scheduled a meeting of his Foreign Relations Committee for July 11 to consider neutrality proposals. When his committee met that morning, senators expected him to propose consideration of either his own resolution or Bloom's. Instead, he asked whether any neutrality measure should be considered or recommended in view of the fact that the Neutrality Act of 1937 was still binding except for cash-and-carry. Surprised by Pittman's tack, the senators hesitated as they gathered their thoughts. Democrat Tom Connally of Texas moved that the committee consider the Bloom resolution, but he got no second. Before he could press his proposal, Senator Clark of Missouri, recently named to the committee, moved that consideration of neutrality legislation be postponed until the next session of Congress met six months later in January, 1940. His motion was quickly seconded, discussed, and passed by a vote of twelve to eleven.

Clark's motion won the votes of all five Republicans on the committee—Borah, Johnson, Capper, Vandenberg, and White—as well as those of Progressive La Follette and Farmer-Laborite Shipstead. Five Democrats also voted for the motion—Clark, Robert Reynolds of North Carolina, Frederick Van Nuys of Indiana, Walter George of Georgia, and Guy Gillette of Iowa. Roosevelt had opposed the renomination of four of the five Democrats in his attempted purge in 1938 of conservative Democrats who had opposed his court-packing plan. Given their generally even-handed approaches on foreign affairs, George and Gillette conceivably might have gone either way in the committee vote. But both voted with the isolationists for the Clark motion. Two years after the defeat of court packing, FDR was still paying a political price, this time in foreign affairs, for his bungled attempt to reorganize the federal judiciary and for his unsuccessful efforts to purge Democrats who broke with him on court packing. With the exception of one New England vote (White) and two from the South (Reynolds and George), all the votes for the Clark motion were from the Middle West, Great Plains, or Far West. The twelve senators were not all isolationists and were not in agreement on what ought to be done about neutrality legislation when it came up for consideration. But isolationists were delighted by the committee's action. Senator Nye told newsmen that the committee vote and House approval of the Vorys amendment served "notice to France and Great Britain that we are not going to fight any more of their wars."[21] Roosevelt, Hull, and American diplomats in Europe believed that those actions were similarly noted by Germany and Italy, thereby increasing the danger that they might provoke war in Europe.[22]

Though blocked in both the Senate and the House, Roosevelt and Hull were not prepared to give up their efforts. The president called in Democratic leaders of both houses to express his disappointment in their actions. On July 14, he forwarded to Congress with his endorsement a long statement by Secretary Hull vigorously urging neutrality revision and repeal of the embargo. And on Tuesday evening, July 18, at a lengthy meeting in the White House, Roosevelt and Hull made a final earnest effort to move Senate leaders to action before Congress adjourned. At the meeting were President Roosevelt, Vice-President John Nance Garner of Texas, Secretary of State Cordell Hull, Senate Majority Leader Alben Barkley of Kentucky, Senate Minority Leader Charles McNary of Oregon, Assistant Minority Leader Warren Austin of Vermont, Chairman of the Foreign Relations Committee Key Pittman of Nevada, and ranking minority member of the Foreign Relations Committee William E. Borah of Idaho.[23]

According to Hull's account in his memoirs, the president began the discussion by mentioning Senator Nye's extreme isolationist views that were blocking repeal of the embargo. Borah interrupted, "There are others, Mr. President." In an exchange between the two of them Borah voiced his opposition to repeal of the embargo and contended that there would be no European war in the near future. Roosevelt turned to Hull for his comments on that. The secretary of state emphasized that the cables from abroad crossing his desk revealed an extremely dangerous and explosive international situation. The Idaho Republican responded, however, that he had private information that made clear to him that there would be no European war in the near future. Hull interpreted Borah's statement and tone as a reflection on the State Department and on the quality of its diplomatic reporting. Proud of his Department and concerned about the war clouds abroad, Hull had a bad temper when sufficiently provoked. He scarcely knew whether to explode or cry. He did neither, but it was apparent to all that he restrained himself only with great difficulty.[24]

Apparently one of Borah's sources of information was a mimeographed publication in London called the *Week*. It was edited by Claud Cockburn and generally followed the Communist party line. It was a source for the image of the appeasement proclivities of the Cliveden Set at the estate of Lord and Lady Astor. And it had triggered a heated controversy when it reported a garbled version of Charles A. Lindbergh's evaluation of the Soviet Union and its air power after his visit to Russia in 1938.[25]

The discussion in the president's study that Tuesday night in July, 1939, continued amicably enough, but it became clear to all present that Roosevelt simply could not garner sufficient votes to accomplish repeal of the arms embargo during that session of Congress. The president stressed that failure to repeal the embargo would prevent the United States under his leadership from contributing effectively to the prevention of war in Europe. He wanted it clear that responsibility for that failure rested with Congress.[26] When the White House meeting ended shortly before midnight, the initial phase of the administration's efforts to revise the Neutrality Act had failed.

The White House released a statement by Senator Barkley that "the consensus of opinion on the part of those members of the Senate present was that no action on neutrality legislation can be obtained in the Senate at the present session and that a majority of the Senate would concur in this view." Senator McNary endorsed that opinion. They agreed that the Senate would consider neutrality legislation at the next session. In a personal letter the day after the meeting, Senator Borah wrote: "We are in real danger. And, in my candid opinion, the danger is by reason of conditions happening in the United States." Presumably the danger he feared centered in the White House, not in the Senate. In contrast, the president and secretary of state, in the statement released by the White House, reemphasized "that failure by the Senate to take action now would weaken the leadership of the United States in exercising its potent influence in the cause of preserving peace among other nations in the event of a new crisis in Europe between now and next January.'' After World War II had ended, Hull wrote in his memoirs: "Here was the last effective stand of the powerful isolation movement in the United States. The movement continued its fight by every means at hand and it remained a danger, but after war came in Europe it was never again able to thwart an Administration proposal.''[27]

That fruitless months-long controversy between the Roosevelt administration and the isolationists over revision of the Neutrality Act seethed against a backdrop of increasingly ominous war clouds abroad. On March 15, 1939, Hitler's Nazi Germany dismembered the rest of Czechoslovakia in violation of his promises at Munich. Hitler stepped up his pressure on Poland for Danzig and the Polish Corridor that separated the two parts of Germany. On April 14, President Roosevelt called on Hitler and Mussolini to promise not to attack or invade any of thirty-one states he listed in Europe and the Middle East. One of those was Poland. FDR's appeal did not deter Hitler. The president's messages late in August were similarly unsuccessful. As Britain and France stiffened in the face of German pressures, Stalin's Soviet Union opened the floodgates for Hitler's next move east by concluding a nonaggression pact with Nazi Germany on August 23. With the Soviet Union temporarily out of the picture, with Poland incapable of defending itself successfully against German might, and with Britain and France not in positions to help Poland effectively in East Europe, Hitler made his move. He loosed the German blitzkrieg against Poland early on Friday morning, September 1, 1939. When Hitler rejected Anglo-French demands that he withdraw his forces from Poland, they declared war, and the long-feared World War II was a reality. As expected, the German Luftwaffe quickly destroyed the antiquated Polish air force and battered its cities from the air. Hitler's mechanized divisions with devasting tactical air support overwhelmed Polish forces. Britain and France were in no position to help effectively. In less than a month Poland fell. It remained to be seen where and when Hitler would strike next.

Roosevelt first learned of the German invasion of Poland when he was awakened at 2:50 in the early morning by a call from Ambassador Bullitt in France. He quickly aroused Secretary Hull and other top administration leaders. By 4:30 A.M. the president had authorized messages to the governments of Britain, France, Germany, Poland, and

Italy urging them to refrain from aerial bombardment of civilian populations and unfortified cities. His press conference later that morning included a swipe at Senator Borah. In response to the question of whether the United States could stay out of war, Roosevelt said that "I not only sincerely hope so, but I believe we can; and that every effort will be made by the Administration to do so." He authorized the newsmen to quote him on that. He was in a somber mood when he met with his cabinet early in the afternoon; there was none of the jocular banter that so often opened those meetings.[28]

During the first eight months of 1939, the California plane crash, the "frontier-on-the-Rhine" episode, and the muddled efforts to revise the Neutrality Act had represented something less than a high point in Roosevelt's contest with isolationists. During those months FDR was, in effect, on a political shakedown cruise as he worked out bugs and perfected techniques for maneuvering his aid-short-of-war approach. With the eruption of the European war in September, 1939, however, Roosevelt was the supreme political master as he guided Congress and the American people along paths the United States was to pursue in foreign affairs during the twenty-seven months before Pearl Harbor. He was less than frank with Congress and the public, but he slowly educated them on the dangers of the Axis menace and on the wisdom of extending aid short-of-war to the victims of Axis aggression. Behind that public performance, Roosevelt was bold and innovative in building what Robert E. Sherwood called a "common-law alliance" with Britain in its war against the Axis. Isolationists then and revisionist critics later saw his tactics as dishonest obfuscations that undermined democracy at home while leading America to war. Interventionists then and internationalist defenders later considered him less devious than his critics charged and, in any event, believed that, given the frightful Axis challenge abroad and blind isolationist opposition at home, the end justified the means. However one evaluates his methods, President Roosevelt performed with impressive political skill and artfulness in accomplishing the repeal of the arms embargo in the fall of 1939.

In his fireside chat to the nation on September 3, Roosevelt did not advocate aid to Britain, France, and Poland, but he warned, "When peace has been broken anywhere, the peace of all countries everywhere is in danger." He urged "that partisanship and selfishness be adjourned; and that national unity be the thought that underlies all others." He promised that the United States would remain neutral, but unlike President Wilson a quarter of a century earlier, he did not call for neutrality in thought. "Even a neutral cannot be asked to close his mind or his conscience." He concluded his broadcast in the moving terms of peace: "I have said not once, but many times, that I have seen war and that I hate war. I say that again and again. I hope the United States will keep out of this war. I believe that it will. And I give you assurance and reassurance that every effort of your Government will be directed toward that end. As long as it remains within my power to prevent, there will be no black-out of peace in the United States."[29]

The president was in no hurry to invoke the Neutrality Act. He gave Britain and France as much time as possible to get munitions in the United States before the law's restrictions went into effect. Not until September 5, two days after war was declared, did he invoke the legislation. In doing so, however, he was careful to adhere to the full letter of the law so that he would not make his administration vulnerable to isolationist attacks.[30]

Though the president called a special session of Congress to revise the neutrality law, he moved carefully, taking time to prepare the political groundwork first. He conferred individually with Senate and House leaders to get their judgment of likely political alignments on the issue. He and Hull briefed legislators to win them to the cause. Not until September 13 did he sign the proclamation calling a special session of Congress to meet on Thursday, September 21. At the same time he sent telegrams inviting leaders in both parties to meet informally with him at the White House a day earlier.[31]

On September 14, Senator Borah broadcast his conviction that neutrality was possible, that American involvement was not inevitable, that repeal of the embargo was designed to aid one side in the war against the other, and that that would lead to American involvement in the war. The White House promptly arranged to have the Republican presidential and vice-presidential candidates of 1936, Alf M. Landon and Frank Knox, answer Borah with statements to the press after the broadcast. The White House saw to it that former Republican Secretary of State Stimson and others were lined up to reply to the Idaho isolationist.[32] Nothing was left undone in planning the administration's moves.

On Wednesday afternoon, September 20, fifteen Democratic and Republican leaders met at the White House with President Roosevelt and his secretary, Stephen Early, to confer about the special session scheduled to convene the next day. Most in attendance were from the Northeast and South. Only four were from the Middle West and Great

Plains, and they included Republicans Alf Landon and Frank Knox, who were not isolationists. In contrast to his meetings with the Military Affairs Committee in January and with Senate leaders in July, none of the more outspoken Senate isolationists was included that September afternoon. Roosevelt was marvelously effective in leading the discussions, but he was not nearly so candid as he had been when he had met with the Military Affairs Committee eight months earlier. He did not mention aid-short-of-war or the continued independent existence of particular countries.[33]

In his opening remarks the president underscored his "plea to forget partisanship, for a while anyway." He spoke of the seriousness of developments abroad. He said he wanted to sustain the economy at a high level. FDR called for the kind of neutrality that was "based on the fundamental principles of international law." As he explained it, the United States had followed that kind of neutrality throughout its history except for departures in the Jeffersonian era early in the nineteenth century and after adoption of the Neutrality Act of 1935. So far as the Neutrality Act was concerned, Roosevelt said; "I regret that the Congress passed that Act. I regret equally that I signed that Act." Roosevelt, Hull, and Pittman blamed Nye, Clark, and their Munitions Investigating Committee for the legislation; they emphasized that they had gone along with the enactment of the neutrality laws only to prevent the more extreme Nye-Clark proposals from winning approval.[34]

As he had done earlier and as he was to do many times later, Roosevelt used the guilt-by-association device to discredit his isolationist opponents, associating them with both Germany and the Communist party. He said the German press was "displaying on the front page . . . every remark that Bennett Clark makes, that Borah makes, that Hiram Johnson makes, that Hamilton Fish makes . . . as pro-German." He complained that under the neutrality laws the United States was "handing a navy to Germany." He also said the Communists were doing "everything in their power to prevent the repeal of the embargo."[35]

So far as specific legislation was concerned, the president thought he had the executive authority to pursue the kind of neutrality he favored with or without authorization from Congress. When one of those present said he wanted to "get rid of the whole thing," Roosevelt reminded him that there were not enough votes to do that. Another conferee thought they could get the necessary votes in both houses for repeal of the Neutrality Act, but that the legislators would spend months talking about it. The president wanted to avoid that. Roosevelt preferred flexible legislation without rigid provisions that might draw the United States into war. He said very little about the arms embargo, but one of the conferees put it concisely and accurately when he said that "the only big issue now, that we have got on the calendar, is the repeal of the embargo."[36]

Burned by reporting of the meeting with the Military Affairs Committee in January and anticipating the questions of newsmen after they left the White House, the group approved a statement for the press. As Roosevelt said, "They will write their own story if you don't write it for them." The statement released by the White House at the close of the meeting declared, "The conference had the unanimous thought that the primary objective is keeping the United States neutral and at peace." It called for "a wholly nonpartisan spirit." And it proclaimed "that the most important subject is the repeal of the embargo and a return to processes of international law." The statement made no mention of extending aid to the victims of Nazi aggression.[37]

Just after noon the next day, Thursday, September 21, when President Roosevelt addressed the joint session opening the special session of Congress, he said many of the same things he had told the smaller group at the White House the day before. It was a moving performance. He conceded honorable motives to those who disagreed with him, and hoped they would be similarly generous. "Let no group assume the exclusive label of 'peace bloc.' We all belong to it." He briefly reviewed the international crises and the administration's policies toward those crises. "The Executive Branch of the Government did its utmost, within our traditional policy of non-involvement, to aid in averting the present appalling war. Having thus striven and failed, this Government must lose no time or effort to keep our nation from being drawn into the war. In my candid judgment we shall succeed in those efforts." He told of his efforts to win revision of the neutrality law before war began. He described and lamented departures from traditional neutrality policies in the earlier Jeffersonian era and in the more recent Neutrality Acts. Again he said: "I regret that Congress passed that Act. I regret equally that I signed that Act." He asked Congress to change "that part of the Act which is wholly inconsistent with ancient precepts of the law of nations—the embargo provisions." He noted the material advantages that would accrue from repeal of the embargo. In answer to allegations that repeal of the embargo would bring the United States closer to war, President Roosevelt said: "I give you my deep and unalterable conviction, based on years of experience as a worker in the field of international peace, that by the repeal of the embargo the United States will more probably remain at peace than if the law remains as it stands today. I say this because with the repeal of the embargo, this Government clearly and definitely will insist that American citizens and American ships keep away from the immediate perils of the actual zones of conflict.'' In that key statement Roosevelt was citing the noninterventionist advantages of cash-and-carry in arguing for repeal of the embargo, even though the two were not directly related except politically. With repeal of the embargo he also called for reenacting the other provisions of the Neutrality Act of 1937, including cash-and-carry.[38]

As he had earlier, Senator Key Pittman at the head of the Foreign Relations Committee firmly admonished the administration to leave the initiative to him and his committee. He drafted the legislation with help from the other Democrats on his committee, though he excluded Missouri's isolationist Senator Bennett Champ Clark. Most of the provisions were the same as those in the Neutrality Act of 1937. The key changes were elimination of the arms embargo and reinsertion of cash-and-carry. In an effort to reduce opposition, Pittman included more stringent shipping restrictions than the administration preferred. The Nevada Democrat presented his neutrality resolution to the Foreign Relations Committee on Monday morning, September 25. It held no hearings and on Friday, September 29, voted sixteen to seven to report it favorably.[39]

On Monday, October 2, Pittman presented it to the full Senate. He said the embargo was not necessary to keep the United States out of war and that it was a departure from international law. He expressed confidence in the president's intention "to do everything in his power to keep us out of war." He did not portray repeal of the embargo in terms of aid to Britain and France. The president, Secretary Hull, and others in the administration and State Department worked tirelessly behind the scenes.[40]

A few prominent isolationists went along with Roosevelt on repeal of the embargo. Republican Robert A. Taft of Ohio, in the first year of his first term in the Senate, emphasized his noninterventionist perspective. He doubted that American entry into the war would preserve democracy, and he believed there was "real danger to American democracy from our participation in a war." Even if Germany triumphed over Britain and France, Taft thought the United States need not fear successful military invasion or economic domination by Hitler. At the same time, however, he contended that repeal of the embargo and reenactment of cash-and-carry would not be unneutral. He thought the embargo was "unfair as between other nations." In his opinion, "Removal of the arms embargo is not in any way calculated to increase the chances of our getting into war." He criticized specific details in the proposed legislation, but on balance favored repeal of the embargo and reenactment of cash-and-carry. Assistant Minority Leader Senator Warren R. Austin of Vermont had attended the White House meetings with Roosevelt both in July and in September; he went along with the president on the issue.[41]

New Jersey's W. Warren Barbour had served on Nye's Munitions Investigating Committee and was torn on the issue. Late in September he was receiving four thousand letters a day. Half of them he discounted as inspired by pressure groups, but those that seemed to express strong individual convictions ran about twenty to one against repeal. At the same time, heavy industry in New Jersey stood to benefit from armament production and sales; those interests made their views clearly known to him. In a radio address on October 24, he followed the example of President Roosevelt in citing the virtues of cash-and-carry as arguments for repeal of the embargo. Ultimately he followed the president on the issue.[42]

George W. Norris continued his gradual shift from his earlier isolationism to a cautiously hopeful endorsement of Roosevelt's general perspectives on the war abroad. In a radio address on October 3, the Nebraska progressive expressed confidence in the patriotism and good faith of people on both sides in the debate. There could be no doubt about his earnest desire to keep the United States out of the war. He endorsed revision of the Neutrality Act partly to keep out of war and partly to put the United States "on the side of humanity and civilization." In his view the proposed new legislation contained "safeguards against all of the causes that carried us into the last war." In a letter to a constituent, Senator Norris wrote: "If we repeal it, we are helping England and France. If we fail to repeal it, we will be helping Hitler and his allies. Absolute neutrality is an impossibility. If we have a right to do either one, which I think we have without any question, what heathens we would be if instead of taking the course that would be helpful to the friends of humanity we would take the course that would help the murderers of men, women, and children, and the destroyers of civilization!"[43]

Most leading isolationists, however, fought Roosevelt on revision of the neutrality legislation with all the intensity, determination, and organization they could command. It was to be Senator William E.

Borah's last battle. He had been seriously ill for some months in the middle of 1938. As he passed the age of seventy-four, his strength and vigor were diminished. But he retained his reputation for magnificent oratory, his showmanship, his nationalism, and his unwavering opposition to alliances and intervention in foreign wars. On September 1, the day Germany attacked Poland, Borah issued a statement emphasizing the desire of the American people to stay out of the war and insisting that it was the duty of public officials to serve that wish. He warned that if Congress repealed the arms embargo, "our boys would follow our guns into the trenches."[44] From that day onward no day passed without speeches, press interviews, articles, radio addresses, or (after the special session began) orations in Congress by noninterventionists opposing repeal of the embargo.

Even before Roosevelt formally called the special session of Congress, leading Senate isolationists began meeting together to plan and organize their opposition. Senators Nye, Johnson, La Follette, and Vandenberg were particularly active in initiating calls and providing leadership for those caucuses. The group generally met in Johnson's office. The senators met twice on the first day of the special session and generally met every two or three days thereafter. Twenty-four were present at their morning meeting on September 21, and usually ten to fifteen gathered for the meetings that followed. Among those attending were Johnson, Borah, Nye, La Follette, Vandenberg, Clark, Lundeen, McCarran, Danaher, Shipstead, Sheridan Downey of California, and John Overton of Louisiana.[45]

With a full quota of individualists, the group had difficulties keeping all working together. Johnson wrote that he had "been every hour engaged in trying to draw together again our scattered forces. I have not been very successful except with the 'die-hards.'" La Follette wrote his wife that it was "hard to get any group action out of the Senators opposed to repeal of the Arms Embargo. In the first place they are only agreed on that issue, in the second place as you well know it is like driving two wild horses to try and keep Borah and Johnson pulling together." La Follette thought they should not only fight repeal in the Senate but should also organize public opinion to bring pressure against the administration proposal. He called in his brother Philip La Follette to plan a national committee. Chester Bowles of the advertising firm of Benton and Bowles came in to share in the organizing effort. Some of the senators feared, however, that they might be accused of manufacturing the opposition response. Consequently, both Senators Borah and Nye advised against public organizational efforts by their group. La Follette thought that decision was a mistake and that "the fight was lost right there."[46]

Despite differences within the group, their lines held remarkably well. Individual noninterventionists delivered radio addresses opposing repeal. They franked many thousands of copies of their speeches to people all over the country. A private source provided three thousand dollars for a research bureau to aid them with data against repeal. Senator Nye canceled scheduled speaking engagements in the Middle West so he could be close at hand in Washington during the battle. Administration leaders feared a possible filibuster. The group decided, however, that that would not be the best tactic unless driven to it by administration effort to limit debate. Instead, through Minority Leader Charles McNary they won assurances from Senator Pittman and Majority Leader Alben Barkley that there would be unhampered opportunity for full debate. The group of noninterventionist senators carefully planned their speaking schedules on the floor with each sharing the oratorical responsibilities. They introduced various amendments to the Bloom-Pittman joint resolution.[47]

The Roosevelt administration, the isolationists (with the notable exceptions of Borah and Johnson),[48] and most of the American people favored reenactment of cash-and-carry, so the only real issue was repeal of the embargo. Internationalists and interventionists contended that the embargo helped the Axis against the democratic Allies, that repeal would not involve the United States in war, and that it would enable the United States to expand its munitions manufacturing facilities essential for national defense. Following the president's lead, most who urged repeal of the embargo did not explicitly justify it in terms of aiding the Allies against the Axis. In striking contrast, isolationists or noninterventionists insisted that repeal would be an unneutral attempt to aid the Allies, that it would be a step toward war for the United States, and that the Allies were not fighting for democracy but for the defense of their empires and power dominance.

International law authorities Edwin Borchard, Philip C. Jessup, and Charles C. Hyde wrote that changing the neutrality law after war began with the intent or effect of aiding one belligerent against the other would be a violation of international law.[49] On September 3, Senator Clark told an audience in Missouri, "If we again set out upon the path of being merchants of death we are setting our feet upon the path which sooner or later will lead us into war with all of its horrid consequences." He feared that "we might win a war and lose our liberties." In mid-September, Senator Nye said: "If we repeal the act, we will not be able to avoid subsequent steps which will lead us into war. If we make it a cash and carry proposition, it will be only a matter of weeks until they ask us to repeal the 'cash' part. The next step will be to throw the 'carry' part out the window and then the repeal of the Johnson act. The last step will be a declaration of war." In a network broadcast on October 24, Senator Johnson said: "The repeal of the embargo can serve but one purpose, and in Washington that is frankly and freely avowed, to have us take sides in a war to which we are not parties by 'methods short of war' at first, but inevitably by methods that will make us wholly partisans."[50]

On September 15, 1939, in the privacy of his diary, Senator Vandenberg wrote: "My quarrel is with this notion that America can be half in and half out of this war. . . . I hate Hitlerism and Naziism and Communism as completely as any person living. But I decline to embrace the opportunist idea—so convenient and so popular at the moment—that *we* can stop these things in *Europe* without entering the conflict with everything at our command, including men and money. There is no middle ground. We are either *all the way in* or *all the way out.*" Other isolationists advanced variations of those views over and over again in the course of the debate on revision of the neutrality legislation.[51]

In the midst of that heated controversy Colonel Charles A. Lindbergh made his first noninterventionist addresses. Since his return to the United States in April, Lindbergh had been serving the Army Air Corps in its efforts to build American air power. Important as those efforts were, after the European war began he believed it was even more important to keep the United States out of the war. He discontinued his work with the air corps, and on Friday evening, September 15, he delivered his first nationwide radio broadcast opposing American involvement in the European war. A few hours before his speech the Roosevelt administration (through the channels of Secretary of War Woodring, General Arnold, and Colonel Truman Smith) had attempted unsuccessfully to buy Lindbergh's silence with the proffer of appointment as the first secretary of air in the president's cabinet (a position that did not yet exist). The aviator rejected the offer and went ahead with his scheduled broadcast, "America and European Wars." A month later on Friday evening, October 13, Colonel Lindbergh broadcast an address, "Neutrality and War." In that speech Lindbergh (like former president Hoover at the same time) distinguished between offensive and defensive armaments. He urged continuing the embargo on offensive armaments (such as bombers) and endorsed repeal of the embargo on defensive armaments (such as antiaircraft guns). He favored reenactment of cash-and-carry. The famed aviator became President Roosevelt's most formidable and controversial adversary in the foreign policy debates during the twenty-seven months before the Japanese attack on Pearl Harbor.[52]

Newspapers throughout the country and abroad provided front-page coverage of the neutrality controversy, and Senate galleries filled with interested spectators during the first few days of the debates. As they dragged on through much of October, however, the arguments on both sides became repetitive, and interest lagged. Everything had been said, and most had made up their minds on the issue. Mail at the White House and most Senate offices ran heavily against repeal. But polls indicated that a majority of the American people favored repeal of the embargo, and nine out of ten favored cash-and-carry. A month after the president addressed the special session of Congress, a Gallup poll found that 62 percent of the people believed the United States should do everything it could to help Britain and France win the war, except go to war itself.[53]

Chances for a noninterventionist victory might have been greater if cash-and-carry (which nearly all favored) had been voted separately from embargo repeal (on which sentiment sharply divided). Republican Senator Charles W. Tobey of New Hampshire introduced an amendment to treat the two separately, but it was defeated in mid-October by sixty-five to twenty-six. Various other amendments proposed by isolationists were also voted down. On October 27, in the final vote, H.R. 306 passed the Senate sixty-three to thirty. Among noninterventionists who voted for repeal were Senators Norris, Taft, Austin, and Barbour. Included among the thirty voting in opposition were Senators Borah, Capper, Clark of Idaho, Clark of Missouri, Frazier, Holt, Johnson, La Follette, Lodge, Lundeen, McCarran, McNary, Nye, Reynolds, Shipstead, Tobey, Vandenberg, Walsh, Wheeler, White, and Wiley. Nearly half of the negative votes came from seven states, both of whose senators voted in opposition: Wisconsin, Minnesota, North Dakota, Idaho, Oregon, California, and Massachusetts. Fifty-four of the sixty-nine Democratic senators voted for repeal, as did eight of the twenty-three Republicans, and one independent (Norris). The negative votes were provided by twelve Democrats, fifteen Republicans, two Farmer-Laborites, and one Progressive.[54]

On November 2, the House of Representatives acted favorably by a vote of 243 to 181. The House-Senate conference committee submitted its report the next day, though two of its senators (Borah and Johnson) and two of its representatives (Fish and Eaton) did not sign it. The Senate approved the report 55 to 24, and the House approved 243 to 172. President Roosevelt signed it into law on November 4, 1939.[55]

Britain's Prime Minister Chamberlain wrote Roosevelt on November 8 that repeal of the embargo was "not only an assurance that we and our French Allies may draw on the great reservoir of American resources; it is also a profound moral encouragement to us in the struggle upon which we are engaged." In a letter to Buckingham Palace, FDR wrote that the opposition to revision of the neutrality legislation "was in many cases mere political partisanship but in many other cases was an honest belief that we could build a high wall around ourselves and forget the existence of the rest of the world."[56]

In the postmortem, isolationists were discouraged, but they thought their efforts had been worthwhile. Democratic Senator Walsh of Massachusetts said the long debate had "aroused the country to an active opposition to participation with our military forces in the European war." In his diary Senator Vandenberg wrote that he and his fellow noninterventionists had "won a great moral victory." He believed that "because of our battle it is going to be much more difficult for F.D.R. to lead the country into war. We have forced him and his Senate group to become vehement in their peace devotions— and we have aroused the country to a peace vigilance which is powerful." And Senator Borah, writing less than three months before his death in January, 1940, expressed the view that despite their defeat on the embargo repeal, "it was well to have the fight made." He wrote: "If the war should run along for any great length of time, I do not see how it is possible for us to stay out of it. The tremendous influences which will be exerted by the nations abroad to draw us into the war and the influences at home to the same effect, will require every American citizen who wants to stay out to be vigilant every moment against any acts or deeds which are calculated to take us into the war."[57]

Chapter 23

Negotiated Peace

Secretary of Agriculture Henry A. Wallace was waiting in the White House to see the president. Seated near him was William Rhodes Davis. The two struck up a conversation, and the middle-aged Davis explained that he was an international oil entrepreneur involved in the marketing of Mexican oil abroad. His appointment with Roosevelt was before Wallace's, so the secretary of agriculture continued to wait while Davis conferred with the president and with Assistant Secretary of State Adolf A. Berle. When Wallace finally was ushered into the president's office, Roosevelt was excited. "The man who has just been in here," he told Wallace, "brought me the most amazing story about the possibility for peace that you ever heard. Probably nothing will ever come of it but I am going to follow it up just the same."[1]

As FDR predicted, nothing positive came of it. Wallace did not learn any of the details until he read columnists' versions in the newspapers five months later. But that episode was a part of a succession of futile efforts to prevent or end the war in Europe through mediation or negotiation. The Munich conference a year before, Congressman Hamilton Fish's abortive peace explorations a month before, the much-publicized diplomatic mission by Undersecretary of State Sumner Welles five months later in 1940, and the incredible flight and parachute jump into Scotland by Hitler's Nazi associate Rudolf Hess on May 10, 1941, were all parts of the long trail of fruitless quests for the phantom of a negotiated peace. Those efforts all failed. They affected evolving patterns in relations between Roosevelt and the isolationists, however, and were parts of the sequence of events that helped the president triumph over isolationists.

The possibility of a presidential role in the prevention of war abroad had been in Roosevelt's mind from the beginning of his service in the White House, and when wars erupted, he searched for ways he might help restore peace. His early explorations on methods, however, stumbled because of the timidity of British and French leadership, the intractable German and Italian leaders, and the inhibiting strength of isolationists at home. He feared rebuff abroad and insisted that the results of any peace initiative must show promise of enduring—not transient—beneficial results. In March, 1936, he wrote America's Ambassador William E. Dodd in Berlin: "If in the days to come the absolutely unpredictable events should by chance get to the point where a gesture, an offer or a formal statement by me would, in your judgment, make for peace, be sure to send me immediate word. But the peace must be not only peace with justice but the kind of peace which will endure without threat for more than a week or two." In December to James M. Cox he wrote that "until there is something I can hang my hat on, I must keep away from anything that might result in a rebuff of an offer of help."[2]

Roosevelt's peace initiative early in 1938 foundered on precisely the sort of rebuff he had feared. Even as he readied that abortive initiative, he reminded a correspondent that he did "not want the kind of peace which means definite danger to us at home in the days to come," and he argued against "peace at any price."[3]

In actively encouraging continued negotiations, Roosevelt was part of the compound that produced the Munich settlement in the fall of 1938. He was pleased to have a role and glad that hostilities had not erupted, but he had serious doubts about the durability of the peace that Chamberlain had claimed for that time. His skepticism about the possibilities for negotiating an enduring peace increased when Hitler dismembered the rest of Czechoslovakia in March, 1939, and when appeals later in that same year failed to check the Nazi dictator's ambitions in Poland.

Just exactly when Roosevelt gave up on the practical possibility of preserving or regaining enduring peace by means of diplomatic negotiations with Hitler and Mussolini cannot be determined with certainty. Surely that possibility faded to almost nothing in Roosevelt's mind when war erupted in September, 1939. His momentary curiosity about the peace mission of William Rhodes Davis and his decision to send Sumner Welles to explore the possibilities for negotiating peace early in 1940 were grasping at straws to assure himself, the American people, and the world that he had exhausted every honorable diplomatic effort for peace. They may also have been designed to help educate the American people on the futility of trying to deal with Hitler. When the Welles mission failed to produce grounds for enduring peace (as Roosevelt and Welles probably anticipated), the president put "negotiated peace" on the same shelf with "appeasement" and "isolationism" as discredited shibboleths unworthy of further consideration. Axis aggression combined with the inspiring leadership of Winston S. Churchill in England and Franklin D. Roosevelt in the United States to make "negotiated peace" more and more unthinkable. Its increasingly unsavory connotations further disarmed and discredited appeasers in England and isolationists in the United States. At the same time, the president's jaundiced view of the possibilities for a negotiated settlement further confirmed pacifists and isolationists in their fears about his warlike and interventionist intentions.

A month before the Davis peace mission and two weeks before war erupted in Europe, isolationist Republican Congressman Hamilton Fish of New York became involved in an unsuccessful peace effort of his own. Some seven years younger than the president, Fish represented Roosevelt's home district in the House of Representatives and had an even more distinguished background. The grandson of President Ulysses S. Grant's able secretary of state, the tall, broad-shouldered Fish had been an All-American football player at Harvard and graduated cum laude in 1910 before studying law there. Elected to the New York State Assembly, he helped organize and lead a black infantry unit in combat in World War I, winning the Croix de Guerre and Silver Star in the process. He served in the House of Representatives for a quarter of a century after the war. He spoke out for minority rights and was an early advocate for creation of a homeland for Jews in Palestine. Fish was passionately anti-communist and highly critical of Roosevelt's increasingly internationalist policies. As ranking minority member, he played a role in the House Foreign Affairs Committee during the Roosevelt years roughly comparable to the roles of Borah and Johnson in the Senate Foreign Relations Committee.[4]

In 1939, as the newly elected president of the American delegation to the Interparliamentary Union, Fish anticipated a peace negotiation effort. Established in 1889 to promote democratic institutions and peace, the organization held annual conferences; delegations from the United States drawn from both houses of Congress and from both parties participated prominently. En route to its 1939 conference in Oslo, Norway, Fish conferred with British Foreign Minister Lord Halifax in London, French Foreign Minister Georges Bonnet in Paris, and others. While in France he was invited to meet also with German Foreign Minister Joachim von Ribbentrop. On Monday afternoon,

August 14, Fish spent an hour and one-half talking with Ribbentrop at the Nazi official's mountain villa near Salzburg. Fish's conversations in the various European states underscored for him the alarming state of international affairs, the likelihood of war in the immediate future, the probable destructiveness and tragedy of that war, and the pressing need for effective moves to preserve peace. Fish also explored possibilities for establishing a homeland for Jewish refugees in Africa.[5]

At the Oslo conference, Fish introduced a resolution calling for a thirty-day moratorium on war to give more time for peaceful settlement of the dispute over Danzig and the Polish Corridor. When the British and Norwegian delegations opposed the resolution, however, he felt it useless to press it. Then and later he suspected Roosevelt of playing a part in Britain's opposition to the proposed moratorium.[6]

Roosevelt later wrote to Bernard Baruch that he wished "this great Pooh-bah would go back to Harvard and play tackle on the football team. He is qualified for that job."[7] Instead, Congressman Fish had departed Europe just as war erupted, and he continued with increased vigor to battle against what he saw as Roosevelt's warlike interventionist policies. Fish grew ever more convinced that the president had been responsible for the Anglo-French hard-line policies that moved Poland to destruction by rejecting Hitler's demands for Danzig and the Polish Corridor.[8]

Though Fish's initiative was unconventional and outside normal channels, the peace efforts of William Rhodes Davis were even more unorthodox. Davis had been doing business in Germany for some seven years and knew Goering and other top Germans. In the course of negotiating a credit arrangment with the Mexican government in the summer of 1939, the oil entrepreneur was concerned about the possible effects of war. Consultation with Germans in Mexico and communications with both private and official contacts in Germany encouraged Davis to explore the possibility of an initiative to determine grounds for preserving or restoring peace in Europe. With encouragement from Berlin, Davis sought an appointment with President Roosevelt in Washington late in August before the European war began. Unable to get an appointment, Davis's business took him on to New York, back to Mexico, and (after war began) once again to New York and Washington. This time he turned for help to John L. Lewis, the burly, beetle-browed labor leader who headed the Congress of Industrial Organizations. Both Davis and Lewis had contributed to FDR's campaign for reelection in 1936, but Lewis commanded far more political clout than Davis. When Lewis telephoned the White

House on the afternoon of September 14, his call was put through directly to Roosevelt, and he arranged an appointment for Davis for the next day. As a precaution Roosevelt asked Assistant Secretary Berle to be present.[9]

On September 15, Davis explained to Roosevelt and Berle the background and purpose of his visit. He believed Field Marshal Hermann Goering was increasing his power in the German government, displacing Goebbels and Ribbentrop in influence, and conceivably even taking over from Hitler. Goering, through Joachim Hertslet, had encouraged Davis to determine whether President Roosevelt might mediate an end to the European war.

President Roosevelt reminded Davis of the efforts he had made for peace in April and August of 1939 and said he could not deal with the matter unless it came through a government. According to Berle's account, Roosevelt told Davis: "The British and the French were not fighting for Poland, primarily; they were fighting in order to have some assurances for the future against continual interruptions of peace. Proposals on the basis of the *status quo* at present, or the like, did not contain any such assurance, nor could they." Davis asked whether he might explore the situation and inform the president of his findings. Roosevelt said he was interested in any information, but that he could not act until a proposal reached him through some government.[10]

President Roosevelt did not authorize Davis to speak for him, did not send him as a peace emissary, and really did not expect anything helpful to come from the effort. But neither did he entirely close the door on Davis at that time.[11] Davis went on his way, however, as thrilled by his adventure in high diplomacy as Raymond Moley had been in 1933 and even more than Welles was to be a few months later.

The oil entrepreneur arrived in Rome on Tuesday afternoon, September 26. There German officials arranged for him to meet with Goering in Berlin. He traveled by rail to Munich and then by air to Berlin.[12]

In Berlin, Davis had three meetings with Goering on successive days, the first beginning at noon on Sunday, October 1 (after Germany had completed its conquest of Poland). According to the account in his letter to Roosevelt, Davis explained to Goering that he was "not in position officially or unofficially to guarantee any results whatsoever in this matter," that is, on Roosevelt's possible role of mediation. But Davis assumed greater authority than he actually had. His tone in the conversation was sympathetic with Germany and critical of the British and French. He overstated Roosevelt's determination to negotiate peace and made the president appear more amenable to Hitler's terms than he actually was. Davis's presentation was a mixture of Roosevelt and Davis, with much more of the latter than the former. The only point at which Davis suggested possible departures from Germany's every wish was when he indicated that Poland and a Czech state should be reconstituted.[13]

Goering expressed surprise at Davis's rendition, inasmuch as "the impression in Germany is that Mr. Roosevelt's feelings are now against Germany and that he is sympathetic to England and France." Again at their second meeting Goering said that until then Germany had "believed that Mr. Roosevelt is pro-English and pro-French and is an enemy of ours." Davis's words had, in Goering's view, produced "a completely new situation." It would have been new to Roosevelt, too, had he been listening in on Davis's performance.[14]

If Davis were reporting FDR correctly, Goering thought the president's views corresponded "substantially to the views of Mr. Hitler and his Government. A world conference appears under the circumstances to be the only practical medium through which these mutual hopes for peace can be achieved. Germany will welcome the aid of Mr. Roosevelt in bringing about such a conference." According to Goering, "The fundamental and motivating purpose of such a conference must be to establish a new order in the world designed to assure an enduring peace. A pre-requisite to that aim is the complete liquidation of the 'Versailles System.' Naturally such parts of this Treaty as already have been liquidated by Germany cannot appear on the agenda for reconsideration." The "colonial question must also be on the agenda of the world conference" though they had "no fixed or arbitrary views." As he explained it, "We want not a single village from France and we have no desire to weaken the British Empire." At their third and final meeting on Tuesday, October 3, Goering said that when Hitler addressed the Reichstag on Friday of that week, he would make general suggestions for a peace and would "embody some of the points" that Goering and Davis had discussed. If Roosevelt believed "the suggestions of Mr. Hitler afforded a reasonable basis for a peace conference, he will then have the opportunity which we have provided to take the initiative in bringing about a settlement." Goering and Davis agreed that if a conference were held, it should meet in Washington with President Roosevelt presiding. Goering would represent Germany.[15]

Wednesday morning, October 4, Davis departed Berlin for Rome aboard a plane provided by Goering. He then took the Clipper to New York and went on to Washington. Unsuccessful in his efforts to get an appointment with Roosevelt, he was received at the State Department on Thursday, October 12, by Assistant Secretary Berle and J. Pierrepont Moffat. Davis produced a long letter addressed to the president tracing his adventures from Mexico through Washington to Rome and Berlin and back again, including a detailed account of the meetings with Goering. During the session Davis's secretary brought in a second letter summarizing other views he wanted to report. Berle and Moffat quickly read the letter, noting certain inaccuracies and emphasizing that the trip and meeting abroad were "not at the President's suggestion or the suggestion of anyone in the Government." Berle also corrected Davis's summation of the president's views. Berle repeated that the president could consider mediation only if officially asked by governments involved. Davis thought the consequences of war in Europe could be disastrous and urged that the president mediate peace. Now that Roosevelt knew what Germany would and would not accept, he could, Davis insisted, "write the ticket." An hour and one-half after he arrived, Davis departed Berle's office. The mediation conference that he thought he had engineered never materialized.[16]

Even before Davis got back to the United States, the F.B.I. provided Roosevelt with a cable from Davis to the effect that the President was the only person who could save civilization by making peace at that time. Roosevelt exploded. According to Berle, "He said these Germans were probably plain fools. They were trying to soft-soap him with a little third-rate flattery to make him the agent in some kind of intrigue." In his report of his meeting with Davis, Berle wrote: "The Germans have made an extremely clumsy use of this man in endeavoring to try to get the President committed to something which would serve their own desire. At the present this is a desire to end the West Front war, on their own terms. There is practically nothing in it." When Berle later read to Roosevelt that part of Davis's letter that summarized FDR's views, "the President squarely hit the roof." He advised "stringing it along for a week or so." As Berle summarized it: "Davis obviously had made himself a real part of a real intrigue; the question is whether we should accept our end of it. We are not, of course."[17]

During the six-month interval, or so-called phoney war, in the West after the defeat of Poland and before the German conquest of Denmark, Norway, the Low Countries, and France in the spring and early summer of 1940, there were other unofficial appeals urging Roosevelt to mediate an end to the war. There were rumors about possibilities for peace.[18]

Pacifists and isolationists pressed the president to take steps to help restore peace. For example, on October 7, Senator Nye told newsmen he "would very much like to see the President take that job" of mediator. He thought "now is the logical time to move." The next day Socialist pacifist Norman Thomas wrote a powerfully moving letter urging Roosevelt "to explore every road of mediation for peace." Circumstances at the time, according to Thomas, would give unique weight to FDR's "efforts in mediating first a truce, and then a better peace than Hitler suggested, and infinitely better than the virtual distruction of Europe by a continuance of war." After spending time in England and the Netherlands early in the fall, pacifist noninterventionist Oswald Garrison Villard radioed the president pleading with him to try to bring the combatants together to avert the complete disaster that continued war would represent. John L. Lewis, through Berle, urged Roosevelt to act on the Davis mediation proposal. There were others with similar appeals.[19]

In reality nothing constructive came of Davis's efforts—or of any other peace initiatives, rumors, or suggestions. Roosevelt's failure to act further convinced noninterventionists of his warlike and interventionist inclinations. In the 1940 presidential election year, Davis saw to it that copies of his letters to the president reached key figures in the Republican party, including former President Hoover, GOP politico Samuel Pryor, Iowa newsman Verne Marshall (who later led the ill-fated No Foreign War Committee), and probably labor leader John L. Lewis. They urged using FDR's failure to act on Davis's peace plan as a political weapon against Roosevelt in Wendell Willkie's presidential campaign. Willkie decided not to use it, however, fearing it could backfire. Davis continued his antics until August 1, 1941, when he died suddenly and unexpectedly in his Houston, Texas, hotel. There were those who suspected foul play. Over the years that followed, Verne Marshall made repeated efforts to arouse public interest in the president's alleged role in killing the chances for peace that Davis claimed to have brought back from Berlin in October, 1939. But Marshall accomplished nothing.[20]

Though President Roosevelt never acted on Davis's peace scheme, nor on any other peace initiative at that time, he made his own distinctive move when he sent Undersecretary of State Sumner Welles on a special diplomatic mission to Rome, Berlin, Paris, and London late in

February and early March, 1940. On February 2, 1940, the president called British Ambassador Lord Lothian to meet with him at the White House. He told the ambassador that "to satisfy himself and public opinion here that every possibility of ending war had been made," he had decided to send Undersecretary Welles to visit leaders in the major European capitals to determine "whether there was any possibility of ending the war in the near future." Welles would be "authorized to make no proposal or commitment in the name of United States and would report on his return solely to President and Secretary of State." He assured the ambassador "that his ideas about peace were practically the same" as the British "that any peace must include restoration of freedom to Czechoslovakia and Poles in some real form and guarantees that there would be no renewal of aggression during any of our life-times. It would have to include restoration in Europe of what he called the four freedoms." Roosevelt explained that he was "not hopeful of Under-Secretary of State being able to find any basis of agreement which he or the Allies could accept but if that proved to be so he would be able to issue a statement on Under-Secretary of State's return, making it clear that Germany was the obstacle to peace and that the Germans were being made to fight not for security and integrity of their own country but for aggression."[21]

Prime Minister Chamberlain was pleased that Roosevelt believed any peace settlement must include "'guarantees that there would be no renewal of aggression during any of our lifetimes.' That is really the kernal of the difficulty." Chamberlain wrote that he could not "imagine how such assurance could be attained so long as Germany remains organised on the present lines and is under the direction of her present rulers." That is, he believed an end to Hitler's Nazi dictatorship in Germany probably was a prerequisite to any acceptable peace settlement.[22] Others in England, France, and the United States had serious doubts about the wisdom of the president's course. Secretary Hull and Ambassador Bullitt in Paris were among those with misgivings. Some speculated that the president was moved by considerations of domestic politics.[23] If they had in mind the presidential election of 1940, the question might be debated; if they meant that Roosevelt was acting partly to combat the political challenge of isolationists to his foreign policies, there could be little doubt.

They need not have worried. Neither Roosevelt nor Welles had any intention of making matters more difficult or less secure for Britain, France, or the United States. The career diplomat and former ambassador to Nazi Germany, Hugh R. Wilson, summed up the situation well in his diary: "In the first place, Sumner. . . . has a wise head and a cool one on his shoulders. In the second place, he can keep his mouth shut, and in the third place—and to me this is the most important one—he won't commit the United States one inch. I don't think there is one chance in twenty that he will find sufficient ground for agreement or desire therefor on the part of the fighting states to do anything positive. The other nineteen chances are that he will satisfy himself and the President that there is nothing that can be done usefully at the present moment."[24] A British Foreign Office minute put it more bluntly when it reported private information from a "very reliable American journalist" with "excellent sources of information" that Welles's mission was "based mainly on domestic considerations. President Roosevelt knows an early peace to be impossible, but he has to demonstrate this to American opinion; he would never consent to any proposals which would allow Germany to preserve the status quo. It is part of the President's campaign to wake up American opinion to the difficulties of ultimately keeping out of the war."[25]

Wealthy, brilliant, urbane, aloof, and superior in manner, Sumner Welles was some ten years younger than Roosevelt and had known him since childhood. They had attended the same schools and moved in similar social circles. Welles was an able career foreign service officer. He was not awed by Roosevelt and moved in and out of the president's office more freely than Hull did. Welles's easy access to the president and the contrast between his aristocratic background and that of the Tennessee hill country politico who headed the State Department made friction between him and Secretary Hull almost inevitable. It culminated in 1943 with Welles's resignation. But Roosevelt's confidence in Welles's professional competence was fully justified.[26]

The president announced the mission in a statement to the press on February 9, explaining that Welles's visit to Italy, Germany, France, and Great Britain was "solely for the purpose of advising the President and the Secretary of State as to present conditions in Europe." He emphasized that Welles had no authority to make "proposals or commitments in the name of the Government of the United States" and that his findings would "be communicated by him solely to the President and the Secretary of State."[27]

Arriving in Rome on February 25, Welles's journey took him on to Berlin, Paris, London, and back through Paris to Rome again with his final session on March 19, before returning to Washington on March 29. In his travels he met with the king and queen of England, the king of Italy, and Pope Pius XII; with Mussolini, Hitler, Daladier, and Chamberlain; with the foreign ministers in each of the states; and with many lower-ranking officials (including Winston Churchill and Anthony Eden, who were soon to become Britain's wartime prime minister and foreign minister, respectively). Out of it all Welles (and Roosevelt) found no real grounds for negotiating an enduring peace. The stumbling blocks, in Welles's view, were security and disarmament. Specific political and territorial differences conceivably might have been resolved through hard negotiations. Hitler insisted he had no desire to destroy Britain or the British Empire. The British and French insisted they did not want to destroy the German state and people. The Italians did not want war and sought peace. But German leaders were so persuaded of the hostility of the British and French that they insisted German security and interests could only be served by victory over the Allies. The British and French, having suffered Hitler's broken promises and insatiable demands too often, could envisage no security or enduring peace until Hitler and his Nazi regime were crushed and ousted. That added up to a general insecurity that each state thought could be resolved only through military triumph over the adversary. That meant more war (very soon) and no negotiated peace. That is probably what Roosevelt, Hull, and Welles had expected before the mission.[28]

Harry L. Hopkins served as the president's secretary of commerce, personal adviser, and speech writer. In the middle of 1940, Hopkins drew the talented playwright Robert E. Sherwood into the tiny group that shared in helping prepare the president's speeches. In that capacity Sherwood came to know Roosevelt intimately. In his later award-winning book, *Roosevelt and Hopkins*, Sherwood wrote that after the European war began, Roosevelt's "greatest fear then and subsequently was a negotiated peace, another Munich."[29] After the Welles mission, however, the president's position on that issue was much stronger. He could act and speak on the subject with greater authority; he was in a stronger position when confronted by demands that he mediate peace.

Even before Welles completed his mission, the president broadcast to a Christian Foreign Service Convocation, on March 16, an address designed to reassure those who feared disruptive consequences from the Welles mission. In his speech Roosevelt said: "Today we seek a moral basis for peace. It cannot be real peace if it fails to recognize brotherhood. It cannot be a lasting peace if the fruit of it is oppression, or starvation, or cruelty, or human life dominated by armed camps. It cannot be a sound peace if small nations must live in fear of powerful neighbors. It cannot be a moral peace if freedom from invasion is sold for tribute. It cannot be an intelligent peace if it denies free passage to that knowledge of those ideals which permit men to find common ground. It cannot be a righteous peace if worship of God is denied."[30] That moral tone helped seize the high ground from pacifists and noninterventionists. After Welles reported to him on March 29, the president issued a brief and appreciative statement. It contained no encouragement that there was any more than "scant immediate prospect for the establishment of any just, stable, and lasting peace in Europe."[31]

Less than two weeks later Adolf Hitler once again loosed his blitzkrieg and Luftwaffe, that time against Denmark, Norway, the Netherlands, Luxembourg, Belgium, and France. With the British evacuation of Dunkirk, the Italian declaration of war on June 10, the French surrender on June 22, and the beginning of the Battle of Britain in the skies and seas, the slight possibilities for negotiated peace essentially disappeared. On December 29, 1940, after his election to a third term, President Roosevelt delivered one of his more moving fireside chats. It was part of his groundwork for winning approval of lend-lease early in 1941. It was also a powerful attack on appeasement, isolationism, and any thought of negotiated peace. In that nationwide broadcast Roosevelt asserted; "The Nazi masters of Germany have made it clear that they intend not only to dominate all life and thought in their own country, but also to enslave the whole of Europe, and then to use the resources of Europe to dominate the rest of the world." Consequently, according to Roosevelt, "the United States had no right or reason to encourage talk of peace, until the day shall come when there is a clear intention on the part of the aggressor nations to abandon all thought of dominating or conquering the world." He called talk of a negotiated peace "Nonsense!" He asked, "Is it a negotiated peace if a gang of outlaws surrounds your community and on a threat of extermination makes you pay tribute to save your own skins?" In his view: "Such a dictated peace would be no peace at all. It would be only another armistice, leading to the most gigantic armament race and the most devasting trade wars in all history. And in these contests the Americans would offer the only real resistance to the Axis powers."[32] By the time Rudolf Hess parachuted into Scotland a few months later, that desperate effort on behalf of a negotiated peace was seen as almost ludicrous or pathetic madness that few were prepared to take seriously.

Many pacifists and isolationists, however, continued to urge a negotiated peace and blamed Roosevelt and his policies for prolonging the war in Europe. Among the more prominent of the noninterventionists who urged a negotiated peace were democratic Senator Burton K. Wheeler of Montana, General Robert E. Wood of Chicago at the head of the America First Committee, and Colonel Charles A. Lindbergh.

On December 30, 1940, Senator Wheeler broadcast a reply to Roosevelt's fireside chat. He underscored his dislike for "Hitler and all that he symbolizes" and emphasized that his "sympathy for the British is both deep and genuine." He insisted, however, that Germany could not successfully invade the United States and that involvement in the wars abroad would destroy democracy in America. In Wheeler's opinion, "The offer of a just, reasonable and generous peace will more quickly and effectively crumble Hitlerism and break the morale of the German people than all the bombers that could be dispatched over Berlin." He proposed an American initiative to bring peace and outlined an eight-point plan for such a peace. It included restoring Germany to its 1914 boundaries, with Alsace-Lorraine going to France. It called for arms limitations with no indemnities or reparations. Early in January, 1941, Wheeler again called for a negotiated peace. He insisted that "before we lend or lease arms and before we lend or lease American boys to England, we should know whether it is possible to have a negotiated peace. We should know the terms of peace demanded by both sides. We should act as peacemakers, not war-mongers." On May 23, 1941, Wheeler told an audience at an American First Committee rally in Madison Square Garden in New York that Roosevelt "could bring about the peace of the world" if he would.[33]

As late as September, 1943, after the United States had become a full belligerent in the war, Senator Wheeler continued to press his point. Citing statements from both Pope Piux XII and the Soviet Union, the Montana Democrat telegraphed President Roosevelt that "the time has now come for you to define unconditional surrender and appeal to the people to abandon the false path of militarism, intolerance and brutality." He contended that Roosevelt "as a champion of democracy, and opponent of totalitarism and tyrany can now bring about peace in Europe and establish democracy through out that war torn continent." The White House made no reply to Wheeler's telegram.[34]

In an address before the New York Board of Trade on December

11, 1940, General Wood expressed his opinion that if the United States entered the European conflagration, the war might last two to five years; if the United States decided not to enter the war, there could be a negotiated peace "in the spring." He suggested that the persons to work for a negotiated peace were the pope or the president of the United States. Addressing a meeting of the National Association of Manufacturers, General Wood again predicted that if the United States made it clear to Britain that it would not enter the war, peace would be negotiated. In a letter to Roy Howard of the Scripps-Howard newspapers at the same time, Wood encouraged press discussion of "a hypothetical compromise peace." He speculated that "if peace could be arranged today on the basis of Norway, Denmark, Holland and Belgium being restored, England keeping all her colonies with the exception of perhaps two of the old German colonies (which would be submitted to neutral mediation for a decision), wouldn't it be better to arrange peace on such terms than for England to continue the battle? And if she refused such terms, why should we go to her assistance?" He thought complete victory by either Britain or Germany would not result in a just or durable peace. In his opinion, "A stalemate, with neither side completely victorious and with a negotiated peace, would probably offer the best chance of a just peace." In a major address on July 7, 1941, General Wood said: "Either we should decide to go into the war as an active ally of England or we should decide to stay out. If we decide to stay out, we should advise England to make a negotiated peace. . . . If England can retain her independence, her fleet and most of her colonies she should make peace. Whether such a peace is practicable I do not know, but it ought to be ascertained whether it is possible within the next few months."[35]

Colonel Charles A. Lindbergh repeatedly urged a negotiated peace. In testifying against lend-lease before the Foreign Relations Committee on February 6, 1941, he told the senators that he thought a complete victory by either side in the war would leave Europe prostrate and Western civilization shattered. "That is why I say that I prefer a negotiated peace to a complete victory by either side." In an address before an America First rally in New York on April 23, Lindbergh said: "I have said before, and I will say again, that I believe it will be a tragedy to the entire world if the British Empire collapses. That is one of the main reasons why I opposed this war before it was declared, and why I have constantly advocated a negotiated peace. I did not feel that England and France had a reasonable chance of winning. . . . I have been forced to the conclusion that we cannot win this war for England, regardless of how much assistance we extend.'' Late in 1941, as Soviet armies retreated in the face of advances by German forces in eastern Europe, Lindbergh wrote General Wood: "The collapse of the Russian armies may easily bring the demand in England for negotiation. If so, I think we should be ready to support that demand over here." Though he ceased his noninterventionist activities and supported the war effort after Pearl Harbor, Lindbergh did not abandon his personal convictions on the disastrous consequences of prolonging the war.[36] Senator Nye, Senator D. Worth Clark, John T. Flynn, Chester Bowles, most pacifists, and others also advocated a negotiated peace before Pearl Harbor.[37]

Nonetheless, the noninterventionist America First Committee never conducted a major drive on the issue. Negotiated peace in Europe was a matter for the belligerents; the committee's concern was to serve American interests by opposing intervention in the war. One of the explanations for reticence on the issue was the fear by R. Douglas Stuart, Jr., the committee's founder and national director, that it would bring the damaging charge of appeasement down upon the antiinterventionist organization.[38] Military analysts and so-called realists after the war were critical of Roosevelt's unconditional surrender policy. But Hitler's duplicity and anti-Semitism, Nazi German aggression and atrocities, Churchill's inspiring leadership, Britain's courageous performance in the Battle of Britain, and President Roosevelt's skillful leadership—all combined to discredit talk of a negotiated peace and to make isolationists who countenanced such a course seem suspect. A Gallup poll in January, 1941, showed that nearly four of every five Americans thought England should keep on fighting in the hope of defeating Germany. Only 15 percent thought England should try to make the best possible peace with Germany at that time.[39] Roosevelt's skillful handling of the issue was a significant part of the processes by which he gradually triumphed over his noninterventionist opponents.

Chapter 24

Scrap Iron and Japan

On August 10, 1937, a month after the beginning of the Sino-Japanese war, Gerald P. Nye took the Senate floor to complain about the increase in shipment of scrap iron and steel from the United States. "There is no secret about where this scrap iron is going. A great part of this raw material is going into the making of war. It is being shipped very largely to Japan." The North Dakota Republican told the assembled senators that he thought "the only return we may expect from a continuation of this exportation, aside from the munificent return in dollars to the several exporting companies, is the probability that one day we may receive this scrap back home here in the form of shrapnel in the flesh and in the bodies of our sons." Senator Nye repeated that statement in noninterventionist speeches and broadcasts throughout the country. Years later, long after the Japanese attack on Pearl Harbor and after Nye had been turned out of office by the voters, many Americans favorably recalled the North Dakota Senator's warning.[1]

Senator George W. Norris of Nebraska urged Americans to express their objections to Japanese aggression and atrocities by boycotting Japanese products, by refusing to buy products made in Japan. Since a boycott would be a voluntary action by individual Americans rather than official government policy, it would not, in Norris's opinion, give Japan grounds for complaint. He thought such a boycott "would result in Japan's being compelled to cease her warlike acts." If one accepted the old progressive's reasoning, American women held Japan's future in their hands—or on their legs. "The principal product of export from Japan is silk. Without the money which she gets from this, she could not carry on this or any other war. The principal customers for this silk are the women of America. I understand that 85 per cent of the silk exported from Japan is sent to the United

States. Every cent of money going to Japan will probably be used in the killing and slaughtering of innocent people, including women and children and other non-combatants."[2]

On July 18, 1939, some two years after Nye first voiced concern about the consequences of sale of scrap iron to Japan, Republican Arthur H. Vandenberg of Michigan introduced Senate Resolution 166 urging the Roosevelt administration to give formal six-month notice of its intention to abrogate the trade treaty of 1911 between the United States and Japan.[3]

Though Norris was gradually changing his views as he followed Roosevelt's leadership in the face of Axis aggression, Nye, Norris, and Vandenberg were all noninterventionists. They wanted the United States to stay out of the Sino-Japanese war after it began in 1937 and out of the European war that erupted two years later. They opposed economic sanctions, and they objected to any participation in collective actions against aggressor states, fearing such policies might involve the United States in war abroad. Nonetheless, both Senator Nye's dramatic warning against sale of scrap iron abroad and Senator Vandenberg's resolution calling for abrogation of the trade treaty played into the hands of internationalists who wanted the United States to throw its weight short-of-war against aggressor states. They unintentionally reinforced their interventionist adversaries and contributed to defeat of their own noninterventionist cause.

Most Americans shared Nye's opposition to selling scrap iron to Japan. Sentiment overwhelmingly opposed Japan's aggression in China. Specific reasoning underlying objections to sale of scrap iron varied widely, however. Americans objected on moral and humanitarian grounds to Japan's aggression, bombings, and atrocities. Nye's view was consistent with his criticisms of traffic in war goods, profiteering from those sales, and the danger that such sales might involve the United States in war abroad. Internationalists saw a ban on the sale of scrap iron as a way of bringing America's weight to bear against Japanese aggression. Economic self-interest of independent iron and steel producers led them to favor stopping that drain on American resources (and on their profits). On the other side, cotton producers and exporters worried about the damaging effects of restrictions on their profitable export trade with Japan. Many feared that any trade ban might increase the dangers of war between the United States and Japan. And an embargo could violate the trade treaty of 1911.[4]

Nye was by no means the first to object to sale of scrap iron and steel. Even before the Sino-Japanese war began, Democratic Congressman Herman P. Kopplemann of Connecticut and Democratic Senator Lewis B. Schwellenbach of Washington had introduced separate resolutions that would have restricted sale of scrap iron abroad. Both the War and Navy Departments endorsed the legislation, though they favored amendments to give the president greater flexibility and discretion. In 1937, however, the report of an interdepartmental committee advised against an embargo.[5] Opinion divided within the Roosevelt administration, the Department of State, and the Foreign Service. All objected to Japanese actions, but disagreed on the wisdom and possible consequences of an embargo. Secretary Hull was cautious on the issue. With his Europe-first emphasis, President Roosevelt generally concurred in Hull's approach.

Some of the most vigorous and effective efforts on behalf of hardline policies toward Japan came from outside the administration, from a foreign policy pressure group and from the chairman of the Senate Foreign Relations Committee. Organized in 1938, the American Committee for Non-Participation in Japanese Aggression drew heavily for its leadership and support from former missionaries, educators, businessmen, and diplomats to China. Under the able leadership of Harry B. Price, the son of a missionary and himself a financial adviser and educator in China, the organization had its national headquarters in New York City. Henry L. Stimson served as its honorary chairman, and among others prominent in its leadership were Roger S. Green, Walter H. Judd, Willian Allen White, and Admiral Harry Yarnell. A comparative handful of persons controlled its course and made it effective. Its most helpful contact in the Department of State was Stanley K. Hornbeck, adviser on political relations. Among its many legislative contacts, most important were Democratic Senators Key Pittman of Nevada and Lewis B. Schwellenbach of Washington. Both cooperated with the pressure group in its efforts to block the flow of war materials to Japan.[6]

Pittman's priority in public life was to serve American silver interests. Though not an isolationist, he was not a doctrinaire internationalist either. He repeatedly advised caution for the Roosevelt administration in its dealings with isolationists in shaping policies toward Europe. He was vehemently anti-Japanese, however, and was impatient with Roosevelt and Hull for their failure to take stronger stands against Japanese aggression sooner and more boldly than they did.[7]

As chairman of the Foreign Relations Committee, Senator Pittman led the administration's efforts to revise neutrality legislation in 1939. Both President Roosevelt and the American Committee for Non-Participation in Japanese Aggression pointed out to him that repeal of the embargo and reenactment of cash-and-carry could help Britain and France against Germany in Europe but would benefit Japan against China in East Asia. Pittman believed that difficulty could best be handled through adoption of separate legislation applying to the war in Asia.[8] In January, 1939, Congressman Hamilton Fish introduced a resolution "to prohibit the exportation of pig iron, scrap iron, and scrap steel to China and Japan." Secretary Hull advised the chairman of the House Foreign Affairs Committee to postpone consideration of Fish's resolution until Congress got around to considering "our neutrality policy in all its aspects."[9]

With detailed help from Harry Price of the American Committee for Non-Participation in Japanese Aggression, Pittman drafted and, on April 27, 1939, introduced Senate Joint Resolution 123 to authorize the president to restrict trade with any state, party to the Nine Power pact of 1922, that violated that treaty. The Nine Power pact had given the authority of a multilateral treaty to the earlier Open Door policy in China; both the United States and Japan were parties to the pact. On June 1, Senator Schwellenbach introduced a similar Senate Joint Resolution 143. On July 11, Pittman amended his resolution to specify the materials the president might embargo—including arms, ammunition, implements of war, iron, steel, oil, gasoline, scrap iron, scrap steel, and scrap metal. In an effort to assuage concerns of southern producers and exporters, it did not mention cotton or cotton products.[10]

At that juncture Senator Hiram Johnson moved that the Foreign Relations Committee ask the secretary of state whether enactment of the Pittman or Schwellenbach resolutions would violate any treaty. When the query reached Hull, the Foreign Relations Committee had already approved the Clark motion postponing further consideration of neutrality legislation until the next session of Congress met in January, 1940. The White House meeting of Senate leaders on the evening of July 18 had concluded that the administration could not get enough votes at that time to revise the neutrality legislation. Understandably discouraged, Secretary Hull wrote Pittman suggesting that State Department comment on the Pittman and Schwellenbach resolutions might "be offered to a better advantage when Congress at its next session is ready to give full consideration to these and related proposals."[11] That was the context in which Senator Vandenberg, on July 18, introduced his resolution calling on the administration to give six-month notice of its intention to terminate the trade treaty of 1911 with Japan.

Arthur H. Vandenberg was one of the leading isolationists during most of the years that Roosevelt was president of the United States. Born of Dutch lineage in Grand Rapids, Michigan, Vandenberg was two years younger than Roosevelt. He attended the University of Michigan for a time, but never graduated. Instead (like Nye) he turned to the newspaper business and edited the *Grand Rapids Herald* more that twenty years from 1906 until he went to the United States Senate. He became fascinated with the career of Alexander Hamilton and in the 1920s wrote books on his hero. Active in Republican party politics, he was appointed to the United States Senate in 1928.[12]

A big, hard-working, impressive man, Vandenberg was more handsome than most. Those who liked him said he looked like a president; others found him a bit pompous and posturing. He was not given to small talk. With limitless energy and self-confidence, he had hopes for winning the presidency. Unlike western progressive isolationists, he was a conservative on domestic issues and voted against most of Roosevelt's New Deal measures.

Vandenberg was a member of the Foreign Relations Committee for nearly a quarter of a century. During his first fifteen years in the Senate he was a consistent and outspoken isolationist (though he preferred the term "insulationist").[13] With Nye he was cosponsor of the resolution calling for the Senate investigation of the munitions industry in 1934 and was one of the more active members of that investigating committee. He urged adoption of the neutrality laws. He opposed repeal of the arms embargo in 1939 and enactment of the lend-lease in 1941. Like most isolationists, he warned against excessive presidential power and discretion in foreign affairs. With others, he feared that steps to aid Britain short-of-war would become steps to war. Vandenberg never explicitly repudiated or apologized for his prewar foreign policy views or actions.

Senate Resolution 166 that Vandenberg introduced on July 18, if adopted, would have had the Senate recommend giving Japan the six-month notice required for ending the trade treaty of 1911 "so that the Government of the United States may be free to deal with Japan in the formulation of a new treaty and in the protection of American interests as new necessities may require.'' The resolution also would have had the Senate suggest that the Brussels conference of 1937 be reassembled.[14]

In response to Pittman's inquiry, Secretary Hull promised to give careful consideration to the Senate's advice if Vandenberg's resolution were passed. Though the resolution was never voted out of committee and was never voted in the full Senate, Secretary Hull (with the president's authority) acted without it. On July 26, eight days after Vandenberg had introduced his resolution, Hull gave formal notice to Japan that the United States would end the trade treaty in six months on January 26, 1940.[15] By itself that action did not end or restrict trade between the two countries. It did, however, leave the United States free to apply trade restrictions when the treaty ended. It was, in effect, tacit warning that if Japan endangered American interests, the United States could retaliate with damaging economic restrictions.

Republican William R. Castle, former undersecretary of state during the Hoover administration, wrote Vandenberg criticizing the resolution. Castle feared that if the United States "put an embargo on trade with Japan it would almost certainly have the effect of bringing about a defensive and offensive alliance with Germany and Italy—and this brings war closer." He was sure "that these pin pricks are just what will bring war in the end."[16] Other isolationists were similarly critical of Vandenberg's resolution and feared its interventionist consequences.

The Michigan Republican defended his action in a reply to Castle. He agreed that it was "none of our business to prod and prick the dictators every twenty minutes." Vandenberg wrote that the United States should "keep out of other peoples' troubles and other peoples' wars." But he thought there were "inevitable American interests in the Far East (as distinguished from Europe) which can cause us trouble and that we had better write a *new* treaty with Japan based on the realities of 1939." Vandenberg wrote that he had "always opposed any one-sided embargo against Japan" and did not think "there are very many things we can safely do 'short of war' in dealing with a country like Japan." He contended that the United States either had "to get out of the Far East entirely one of these days or we have got to have a reasonable recognition of our rightful interests and I think we should abrogate the Treaty of 1911 so as to untie our hands to the end that we may be free to at least *consider* the appropriate subsequent course to pursue." He confessed, however, that he would "be much more comfortable about such a prospectus if it were in the hands of some other President" than Roosevelt.[17]

As Vandenberg's uneasiness about the administration's course increased, on August 7 he wrote to Secretary Hull emphasizing that his "own theory of abrogation is definitely predicated upon earnest efforts to agree upon a new engagement." He explained that he "would not be interested in a mere arbitrary prelude to a subsequent one-sided embargo." When he received no reply, Vandenberg sent Hull a second letter ten days later.[18]

On August 22, Acting Secretary of State Sumner Welles replied in a letter tracing the background and course of events. He complained of Japan's disregard for American rights and interests and concluded, "The question of moving toward conclusion of a new treaty must be considered and will be considered in the light of all known facts and circumstances and of future developments." Vandenberg considered the State Department's response too vague and imprecise (which is what the department intended it to be). The Michigan Senator believed the administration could not justify ending the trade treaty if there were not "a vigorous good faith effort on our part toward 'the formulation of a new treaty.'" In September, Vandenberg again nudged Hull to initiate efforts to negotiate a new treaty. But that was not to be.[19]

Early in 1940 the issue between what Vandenberg claimed to have intended in his resolution and the use made of the initiative by the Roosevelt-Hull administration was further highlighted in an exchange between Walter Lippmann, the syndicated newspaper columnist, and Vandenberg. Lippmann wrote that the United States was in an "extremely dangerous position" as a result of ending the treaty with Japan, and he traced the difficulty to Vandenberg's resolution. According to Lippmann everyone (except perhaps Vandenberg) saw the resolution as designed to clear the way for imposing an embargo against Japan. Lippmann thought it unwise for the United States to take such an active role in the Far East at a time when war smoldered in Europe; he feared the administration's course could lead to a two-ocean war for the United States or other harmful consequences. Vandenberg denied responsibility for the State Department's use of his resolution. He wrote that he had hoped his resolution would avoid an embargo through the negotiation of a new treaty.[20]

In March, 1940, Vandenberg got into a donnybrook on the issue with still another newspaper columnist, Drew Pearson. Pearson charged that Vandenberg had "clamored for aggressive action against Japan." The senator flatly denied the charge. He pointed out that he had never favored one-sided embargoes against Japan and had repeatedly urged the State Department to initiate efforts to negotiate a new and more satisfactory treaty.[21]

During the special session in the autumn of 1939 after the European war began, Roosevelt wanted Congress to concentrate exclusively on revision of neutrality legislation and not be diverted to other matters. In accord with the president's wishes, Senator Pittman advised Harry Price of the American Committee for Non-Participation in Japanese Aggression not to press Far East concerns at that time. But Price and his organization moved into action even before the president affixed his signature to the Neutrality Act on November 4, 1939. In letters dated November 1, Price reminded Pittman and other legislators that the European war "greatly increased Japan's dependence upon the United States for essential war supplies" and that revision of the neutrality law did not affect America's "role as Japan's economic ally for the war against China." After the ending of the trade treaty with Japan in January, according to Price, "the decks will be cleared for measures to end this unholy partnership." He cited a Gallup poll indicating that 82 percent of the American people favored government action to stop the flow of war materials from the United States to Japan.[22]

Under auspices of Price's organization, Stimson hosted a dinner in New York on November 9 to discuss and plan tactics. Illness prevented Pittman from attending, but by telephone and a telegram he endorsed and guided their efforts. In contrast to his earlier recommendations on neutrality laws, Pittman favored increasing the president's discretion and power in dealing with Japan. He advised postponing legislative action until the trade treaty expired on January 26. He opposed any thought of "appeasing" Japan. Price's organization sponsored another conference in January when the trade treaty ended. Again Pittman telegraphed guidance for the meeting. He thought enactment of his resolution would "indicate opposition on the part of Congress to the conduct of Japan and it psychologically would encourage the Chinese and possibly the peace element in Japan." He contended that "even if Japan should declare war on the United States sound strategy would not require that we send a single soldier outside of the United States."[23]

Roosevelt and Hull shared Pittman's objections to Japan's actions, but were more cautious in dealing with them. In June, 1938, the State Department had initiated a moral embargo, asking American companies voluntarily not to sell or export airplanes and aeronautical equipment to countries engaged in bombing civilian populations. That moral embargo was expanded to include additional products late in 1939. The ending of the trade treaty and the failure to negotiate a new treaty left Japan uncertain about the future of its commercial relations with the United States.[24] Contrary to the wishes of Pittman, Stimson, Price, and Hornbeck, however, Roosevelt and Hull did not recommend enactment of the Pittman or Schwellenbach resolutions. The Nevada senator believed Congress would pass his resolution if it won administration support, but not without that support.[25]

In the alarming weeks of May and June, 1940, when Hitler's military forces were overrunning Western Europe, Congress and the Roosevelt administration settled on a formula that provided legal authority for the president to do what Pittman and Price wanted but without the frankly coercive rationale that the Pittman and Schwellenbach resolutions had included. Rather than prohibit sale of munitions and war materials to countries that violated the Nine Power pact, the draft prepared in the planning branch of the War Department would authorize the president to "prohibit or curtail" the export of any products or materials when he determined that it was "necessary in the interest of national defense." The provision was included as a section in House Resolution 9850, "To Expedite the Strengthening of the National Defense." On May 24, it passed in the House of Representatives 392 to 1. The lone negative vote was cast by Vito Marcantonio of the American Labor party in New York.[26]

In the Senate, at the suggestion of Schwellenbach, it was modified slightly to make certain that it authorized the president to prohibit the export of gasoline and oil. In response to a question from Senator Vandenberg, it was clear that the president was not required to treat all countries the same in the application of the law, that the president could "apply a one-sided embargo rather than a general embargo" when he considered it necessary in the interest of national defense. Even with Schwellenbach's modification and the clarification elicited by Vandenberg's question, the roll call tally in the Senate recorded no opposition in the final vote on June 11. On that day, just after Mussolini's Italy entered the European war against the rapidly crumbling French military resistance and after British forces had been driven off the continent at Dunkirk, none of the isolationist senators voted against it.[27]

The resolution then went to a Senate-House conference committee to reconcile differences in language. The conference report was approved in the House on June 21, and in the Senate the following day—just as France was surrendering to Hitler in Europe. There was no record vote on the conference report in either house; no isolationist was recorded as voting against it.[28] At that time, when Hitler and Mussolini were triumphant in Western Europe, when the British under Churchill were bracing for the expected Nazi assault on their home islands, and when Americans under President Roosevelt were increasingly alarmed at the threat posed by the Axis powers, isolationists were losing their majority position in American public opinion. Roosevelt and his aid-short-of-war approach had the upper hand.

President Roosevelt signed the National Defense Act on July 2, 1940. That same day under the new law he signed the first proclamation prohibiting the export of some forty categories of war materials and products, except by license. He added to that list as the months passed. Scrap iron and oil were not on that first list.[29] A heated contest raged in 1940 and 1941 between hard-liners headed by Morgenthau, Ickes, and Stimson, who wanted to clamp down severely on exports, and the more cautious, represented by Hull and Welles, who feared that drastic export restrictions would drive Japan to further expansion and to military retaliation and war against the United States.[30]

In the autumn of 1940, after Japanese troops had moved into northern French Indochina and after Japan had concluded its Tripartite Pact with Germany and Italy, President Roosevelt added all scrap iron and scrap steel to the prohibited list. Hard-liners were pleased, but not content. On November 12, two days after the ailing Key Pittman died, Eleanor Roosevelt sent her husband a pointed note: "Now we've stopped scrap iron, what about oil?" The president replied that if the United States stopped all oil shipments, Japan would increase its purchases of Mexican oil and "may be driven by actual necessity to a descent on the Dutch East Indies. At this writing, we all regard such action on our part as an encouragement to the spread of war in the Far East."[31] But the ban on oil would come eight months later, and the Japanese attack on American forces at Pearl Harbor came less than five months after that.

The interventionist flood might have burst through inevitably sooner or later. But the roles of Senators Nye and Vandenberg in helping inadvertently to open a tiny crack in the noninterventionist dike and the failure (or inability) of isolationists to stop up that crack as it widened with the National Defense Act of 1940 were crucial mistakes or failures in their continuing battle against American intervention in World War II. The deluge that swept through that fissure was to drown the still struggling isolationists in a torrent that carried the United States into war in the Pacific and Asia, as well as in the Atlantic and Europe.

Chapter 25

Latin America—Side Door
to Internationalism

The foreign policy contest between Roosevelt and the isolationists centered on Europe. To a lesser degree the Pacific and Far East were of concern in the contest, and ultimately developments there violently projected the United States into war in both Asia and Europe. Latin America in the Western Hemisphere was not central to the foreign policy debates between Roosevelt and the isolationists. In subtle but increasingly significant ways, however, Roosevelt's policies toward Latin America helped educate the American people on the wisdom and practical benefits of a more active leadership and multilateral peace-keeping role by the United States. It accomplished that from a direction the isolationists were not well prepared to defend.

Many policies of the Roosevelt administration toward Latin America were so consistent with attitudes of isolationists that they either did not recognize or were in a weak position to meet his challenges. While isolationists were concentrating their main strength on the European front and while forces were building that would overwhelm them on their less well defended Asian front, those same isolationists were being outflanked by Roosevelt's artfully camouflaged maneuvers by way of Latin America. Isolationists may have blundered or stumbled in coping with Roosevelt at the back door of Asia, but they scarcely realized that they were also being overrun through the side door of Latin America.[1]

For more than a century before Franklin D. Roosevelt became president, United States policies toward Latin America generally had been consistent with the Monroe Doctrine, as interpreted and applied in changing circumstances over the decades. President James Monroe's original statement in 1823 warned against extending European political systems to the Western Hemisphere. It promised that the United States would not intervene in European affairs. Though it warned against further European colonial expansion in America, it did not rule out the possibility of expansion by the United States. It was a unilateral United States policy and did not call for multilateral policies and actions. Early in the twentieth century under the Roosevelt Corollary the Monroe Doctrine was used to justify intervention by the United States in Latin American countries. Those traditional policies—nonintervention in Europe, unilateralism, assumption of the moral and political superiority of the New World, emphasis on differences between European and American values and interests, and warning against further European expansion in America—were consistent with American isolationism. President Roosevelt did not repudiate the Monroe Doctrine; he used it as a foundation upon which he helped build an internationalist superstructure.[2]

Isolationists varied widely in their views on specific applications of the Monroe Doctrine in Latin America. Western progressive isolationists, however, tended to be antiimperialists. Most of them opposed United States military intervention in Latin America, particularly intervention to defend the interests of businessmen and financiers. For example, in 1928 Gerald P. Nye introduced a Senate resolution urging that "it shall never be the policy of the United States to guarantee nor protect by force the investments and properties of its citizens in foreign countries." At the same time, Senator George W. Norris wrote that "our President [Coolidge] is carrying on an unauthorized and indefensible war against Nicaragua. We are establishing a precedent down there that will some day plunge thousands of our young boys into war and bring about untold bloodshed, for certainly, if the President of the United States can carry on war in Nicaragua, without the consent of Congress, he can do the same thing with many other countries." Early in FDR's first term, Senator William E. Borah wrote to President Ramón Grau San Martín of Cuba that he believed "Cuba can best solve her own problems and is entitled to live her own life in her own way. We shall always be deeply interested in the Cuban people, and certainly would always want to be a good and helpful neighbor, but the policy of exploitation upon the part of certain private interests and the period of interference with your governmental affairs ought to have an end."[3]

Isolationists were not united in their policy views, however, and even western progressives sometimes went in confusing directions. Early in 1935 Borah introduced a resolution calling for a Senate probe of antireligious activities under the government of Mexico. On behalf of his resolution he wrote that Mexico "should not be permitted under the guise of religious reform to confiscate the property of American citizens, imperiling their lives and persecuting them.'' He based his resolution upon "the effect of this religious persecution upon American citizens.'' Secretary Hull advised against approval of the Borah resolution. It was never voted out of committee and never passed the Senate.[4]

Senators Hiram Johnson, Bronson Cutting, Burton Wheeler, Gerald Nye, and other progressive isolationists also became active on behalf of bondholder committees working to protect Americans who had invested in Latin American securities. Cuba, Mexico, Brazil, and other Latin American countries won attention from committees serving the interests of American bondholders. Those progressives saw themselves as trying to protect small lenders who were being ruined by Latin American irresponsibility, by big financiers who reaped gains marketing unsound bonds while transferring the losses to smaller lenders, and by the United States government that sanctioned transactions so damaging to the little guy.[5]

The Roosevelt-Hull Good Neighbor policy toward Latin America evolved through two overlapping phases, one partly building upon the other. The first phase and much of the second were consistent with attitudes of most western progressive isolationists. Beginning with Roosevelt's first inaugural address and continuing through 1938 (really throughout Roosevelt's presidency), the first phase turned away from America's earlier "big stick" interventionist policies toward Latin America. During Roosevelt's first six years in office, priority went to emphasizing the sovereignty and right of self-determination for all states in the Western Hemisphere and to abandoning rights by the United States to intervene in the internal affairs of Latin American countries. At the Seventh International Conference of American States at Montevideo, Uruguay in December, 1933, Secretary Hull voted for a convention that asserted: "No state has the right to intervene in the internal or external affairs of another.'' He reserved only such rights as the United States had "in the law of nations as generally recognized and accepted.'' Three years later at the Inter-American Conference at Buenos Aires, the United States under the leadership of Roosevelt and Hull formally endorsed an even stronger noninterventionist protocol without attaching any reservations. In 1934 the United States withdrew the last of its military forces from Haiti. It concluded agreements giving up its earlier treaty rights to intervene in Cuba (1934), Panama (1936), and Mexico (1937). It turned away from coercive de jure diplomatic recognition policies in Central

America back to its earlier de facto recognition policies that passed no judgment on the morality or legality of the methods by which governments came to power. Its commitment to nonintervention was severely tested by Mexico's expropriation of foreign oil holdings in 1938. The Roosevelt administration passed that test by resisting pressures from oil companies and nationalists to intervene on behalf of property owners, insisting only that Americans be paid for their lost properties. Most western progressive isolationists approved the administration's noninterventionist policies toward Latin America.[6]

The second phase of the Roosevelt-Hull Good Neighbor policy began with the extraordinary Inter-American Conference for the Maintenance of Peace, at Buenos Aires, Argentina in December, 1936. That second phase converted the Monroe Doctrine from a unilateral United States policy into a multilateral policy in which all states shared in shaping and implementing actions to guard peace and security in the Western Hemisphere. Under Roosevelt's leadership that multilateral approach in the Western Hemisphere was placed in a world setting.

In proposing the Buenos Aires conference, the president wrote that it "would advance the cause of world peace, inasmuch as the agreements which might be reached would supplement and reinforce the efforts of the League of Nations and of all other existing or future peace agencies in seeking to prevent war." On December 1, 1936, he personally addressed the delegates at the conference. He told them, "The madness of a great war in other parts of the world would affect us and threaten our good in a hundred ways." He urged that "the Americas make it . . . clear that we stand shoulder to shoulder in our final determination that others who, driven by war madness or land hunger might seek to commit acts of aggression against us, will find a hemisphere wholly prepared to consult together for our mutual safety and our mutual good." In the deliberations that followed, the delegates to the Buenos Aires conference unanimously approved a convention agreeing to consult "to preserve the peace of the American Continent" in the event it were threatened by war either inside or outside the Western Hemisphere.[7]

The Eighth International Conference of American States meeting in Peru in December, 1938, adopted the Declaration of Lima, which provided machinery for that consultation. Secretary of State Cordell Hull headed the United States delegation. It also included, among others, Alf M. Landon, the Republican presidential nominee two years earlier. The appointment of Landon was part of the administration's efforts to draw Republican leaders into foreign policy roles to build bipartisan unity and to discredit dissenters. Landon accepted the appointment as "a patriotic duty to present a united front." Assistant Secretary of State Berle later wrote that Landon had "successfully conveyed the impression that political differences at home do not mean a divided house when we deal with foreign affairs. This was just what he was there for; he did it admirably." That use of cooperative leaders of the opposition party to build bipartisan unity and undercut opposition was a tactic that President Woodrow Wilson had neglected a generation earlier; Roosevelt (and later Truman) used that method with impressive effectiveness against isolationist opposition. All agreements concluded at the Lima conference were in the form of resolutions, declarations, or recommendations; they were not treaties or conventions that would have required Senate approval in the United States. That procedure reduced opportunities for opponents to question, challenge, or defeat the administration's policies. Under the Declaration of Lima, any American government could call a meeting of ministers of foreign affairs when it believed "the peace, security or territorial integrity of any American Republic is threatened by acts of any nature that may impair them." That consultative machinery was soon put into operation.[8]

The very day that Britain and France declared war in Europe, the Roosevelt administration initiated actions that culminated in the First Meeting of Ministers of Foreign Affairs held in Panama from September 23 to October 3, 1939. Summer Welles headed the United States delegation. In an impressively cooperative spirit, the meeting approved a General Declaration of Neutrality. It also adopted the Declaration of Panama, proposed by the United States, that established a neutral zone extending some three hundred nautical miles into the oceans surrounding the Western Hemisphere. The declaration directed that the zone should be "free from the commission of any hostile act by any non-American belligerent nation, whether such hostile act be attempted or made from land, sea, or air." It provided for consultation among American states and for sharing responsibilities for patrolling the zone. In the emphasis on neutrality and on efforts to keep hostilities away from America, those declarations were consistent with isolationism. But in their multilateral character, in initiating Atlantic patrols, and in supplementary agreements, they were consistent with internationalism and opposition to Axis activities. The General Declaration of Neutrality rejected "any selfish purpose of isolation."[9]

The Second Meeting of Ministers of Foreign Affairs gathered in Havana, Cuba in July, 1940, just after the Axis powers in Europe had conquered Denmark, Norway, the Low Countries, and France. The Battle of Britain was getting under way. The immediate concern was that Germany and Italy might seize colonies of the Netherlands and France in the Western Hemisphere. With Secretary Hull heading the United States delegation, the meeting adopted the Act of Havana, authorizing any American country to take over and administer any European colony in the Western Hemisphere if it were threatened by a change of sovereignty. Except for the multilateral procedure, isolationists could easily approve that effort to guard American security. It never became necessary to invoke the Act of Havana, but it underscored the hardening United States and Latin America line against the Axis. Furthermore, the meeting approved a less-noted but more fundamental resolution that "any attempt on the part of a non-American state against the integrity or inviolability of the territory, the sovereignty, or the political independence of an American state shall be considered as an act of aggression against the states which sign this declaration." Isolationists would have fought vigorously against such a commitment for the United States in Europe or Asia; they probably would have objected to it even in the Western Hemisphere if it had been brought to a vote in the Senate. That general formula, approved so quietly at Havana in 1940, was to be used repeatedly in collective security accords during the years and decades that followed. It was the antithesis of isolationism. Through executive agreement the United States was party to the formula in the Western Hemisphere long before isolationist strength had waned sufficiently to permit its use for American policies in other parts of the world.[10]

President Roosevelt rarely gave a foreign policy speech without alluding to the successes of the Good Neighbor policy in building friendship and in maintaining peace and security in the Western Hemisphere. His policies toward Latin America provided an appealing bridge over which he led the American people from their traditional isolationism toward a more positive and active multilateral role for the United States in world affairs.

Chapter 26

The Turning Point—
at Home and Abroad

The middle half of 1940 was one of the most dramatic, terrifying, tragic, heroic, and crucially important times in the modern history of Western civilization. It was also the time when isolationism lost its majority position in American public opinion.

On April 9, 1940, Adolf Hitler loosed his blitzkrieg against Denmark and Norway; Denmark offered no military resistance, and Norway fell after a few weeks of fighting. On May 10, Hitler sent German panzer divisions and the Luftwaffe into the Low Countries; the next day they roared into France. That same day, May 10, Winston Churchill replaced Neville Chamberlain as Britain's wartime prime minister, offering the British nothing but "blood, toil, tears and sweat." He called for victory, for "without victory there is no survival." By the end of May, British forces were being evacuated from the continent at Dunkirk, leaving their equipment behind. Mussolini's Italy declared war on June 10. On June 16, Marshal Henri Pétain replaced Paul Reynaud as French premier. Less than a week later he took France out of the war when he accepted the armistice imposed by Hitler.

By the middle of August, the Battle of Britain was raging in the skies over England, and German U-boats were taking a heavy toll of British shipping. The British people and their military forces braced for the Nazi invasion that Hitler was preparing. In powerfully moving words Churchill promised that Britain would fight on "until, in God's good time, the New World, with all its power and might, steps forth to the rescue and the liberation of the Old."[1]

Temporarily secure behind its Russo-German nonaggression pact, Stalin's Soviet Union built its strength in Eastern Europe. Japan continued its expansion in Asia. And the giant United States, officially neutral, pondered its course in the war-torn world. If the Axis triumphed and Britain fell, the United States and Latin America could look across the oceans at a world controlled by menancing totalitarian states emboldened aggressively by their victories. The American people and their leaders faced a critical situation that could determine the future and survival of their country, their values, their lives, and those of their children.

When German bombers hit London late in August, Churchill ordered the Royal Air Force to retaliate with raids on Berlin. Reich Marshal Goering then blundered when he redirected the Luftwaffe away from its assaults on air installations and factories to major bombing raids on London and other cities. That gave the RAF's dwindling band of fighter pilots a slight respite. By the end of September it was clear that the German Luftwaffe could not successfully win control of the skies over England. Hitler postponed and then called off his invasion plans. The danger of imminent defeat for Britain had passed. There was no assurance, however, that Britain could hold out indefinitely. And the possibility of a military triumph over Axis forces on the European continent seemed remote—even unlikely—at that moment. From a British—and a worldwide—perspective, the future could be determined by the course of the United States under the leadership of President Franklin D. Roosevelt. And America's course could be determined by the outcome of the contest between Roosevelt and the isolationists.

At no time before the Japanese attack on Pearl Harbor on December 7, 1941, did a majority of the American people favor a declaration of war by the United States on the Axis states. Before Germany invaded the Scandinavian and Low Countries in the spring of 1940, more than 90 percent of Americans opposed a declaration of war by the United States. During most of 1940 and 1941 about 80 percent of the American people opposed a declaraton of war.[2] At the same time, however, the majority favored extending aid-short-of-war to victims of Axis aggression. Specific percentages in the polls varied, but generally about two-thirds favored aid-short-of-war.

A fundamental shift occurred in 1940 on the relative weight Americans gave to staying out of war on the one hand, and to helping the Allies on the other. As late as May and June, 1940, the high tide of German military triumphs in Western Europe, nearly two-thirds of Americans thought it more important for the United States to stay out of war than to aid Britain at the risk of war. But the proportions changed. In August, September, and October, Americans divided almost evenly on the question. From then on, however, the majority held that it was more important for the United States to aid Britain at the risk of war than it was to stay out of war. And in 1941 polls indicated that a majority would favor American entry into World War II if it were necessary to prevent the defeat of Britain and to accomplish the defeat of the Axis. Though isolationists were strongest in the Middle West and Great Plains and weakest in the South, those were only differences in degree; the general patterns prevailed in all sections of the country. Except on the specific question of whether the United States should declare war, the isolationists and noninterventionists had fallen to a minority position in American public opinion.[3]

The immediate cause of the decline of isolationism lay in the alarming military developments abroad, particularly in Europe and England. Churchill's inspiring leadership and the magnificent performance of the English people had their impact. Long range socioeconomic developments in the United States, including urbanization and industrialization, laid fundamental groundwork for those changes. Educational, informational, and propagandistic facilities moved the thoughts and emotions of Americans. But central to the developments, bringing it all together and guiding the patterns, was the leadership of Roosevelt and his administration.

None save Churchill was more effective than Roosevelt in using the spoken word to inspire and move those opposed to Axis aggression. The president's fireside chats, broadcasts, and messages to Congress were sources of information, inspiration, guidance, and leadership for Congress and the American people—and irritants and targets for his noninterventionist opponents. In an almost endless stream of personal conversations and conferences he left his imprint. He pressed his perspective in countless personal and official letters. And in the election year of 1940 Roosevelt drew prominent Republicans into the task of guiding the American people away from isolationism toward support for a larger and more active role for the United States in world affairs.

Some would have had the president create powerful government propaganda organs to shape American thought; Roosevelt preferred to encourage and assist the efforts of private individuals and groups that shared his perspectives on foreign affairs. If those individuals were Republicans, and if they were from the Middle West or Great Plains, so much the better in terms of their potential effectiveness in isolationist circles.

One such person was the Kansas newspaper editor, William Allen White. Born less than three years after the Civil War, White had edited the *Emporia Gazette* since 1895 and had followed his region and Theodore Roosevelt in the paths of progressivism. He earned and enjoyed the friendship and confidence of many in all sections and strata of society. Most of America's presidents since Cleveland had listened to his counsel. An active Republican, he was neither so progressive as leading agrarian radicals on the Great Plains nor so conservative as leaders of his party. The veteran newsman had supported Roosevelt's Republican opponent in each of his elections.[4]

White never lost his ties with the people of Kansas or America's heartland, but his experiences and concerns also extended to Europe and beyond. He was a long-time member of the League of Nations Association. That organization brought him into contacts with Clark M. Eichelberger, James T. Shotwell, Hamilton Fish Armstrong, Frederic Coudert, and other internationalists. In the fall of 1939 they persuaded him to head a Non-Partisan Committee for Peace through the Revision of the Neutrality Law. He worked effectively to marshal public and legislative support for repeal of the arms embargo. The committee disbanded after the Neutrality Act of 1939 became law, and Roosevelt wrote the old Kansan thanking him for the "grand job" he had done.[5]

A month later in mid-December, FDR wrote a long and thoughtful personal letter inviting White to spend a night at the White House on his next trip east: "Let me sit you on the sofa after supper and talk over small matters like world problems." The president recognized that the world situation was "getting rather progressively worse." He worried "that public opinion over here is patting itself on the back every morning and thanking God for the Atlantic Ocean (and the Pacific Ocean)." He wrote that he and Hull "fully expect to keep us out of war—but, on the other hand, we are not going around thanking God for allowing us physical safety within our continental limits." Roosevelt explained to White that his problem was "to get the American people to think of conceivable consequences without scaring the people into thinking that they are going to be dragged into this war."[6]

White was pleased by the president's letter. He had no immediate plans to go to Washington and did not make a special trip in response to the president's invitation. But he did write back in a similar tone. "I fear our involvement before the peace, and yet I fear to remain uninvolved letting the danger of a peace of tyranny approach too near." Those divided feelings were shared in one form or another by most Americans—and probably by Roosevelt as well. White supposed that "if we can help the Allies surreptitiously, illicitly and down the alley by night, we ought to do it." Late in January, 1940, Roosevelt again wrote commending White for an editorial on the reciprocal trade agreements program. FDR expressed satisfaction that there were "strong voices like yours which are willing and ready, irrespective of any partisan consideration, to speak out courageously in defense of constructive and far-sighted policies."[7] The president explored the public opinion problem with others as well. Early in February he asked Rexford Tugwell how "the country could be brought to the realization that the Allies may well lose this war." Tugwell thought FDR was "puzzling a good deal over ways to wake the country up to its world position."[8] Many were independently puzzling over that problem, but the president's attitude undoubtedly encouraged them in their concerns.

By mid-May, 1940, Clark Eichelberger and others from the earlier temporary committee had successfully persuaded William Allen White to serve as national chairman of a new and more powerful Committee to Defend America by Aiding the Allies. Eichelberger was executive director. It won a distinguished list of prominent Americans to its banner. Local chapters were organized throughout the country, and it won hundreds of thousands of members. The organization's name was so cumbersome and White's role so prominent that it was commonly called the White Committee. It was the leading so-called interventionist mass pressure group before Pearl Harbor. It adhered closely to Roosevelt's official position on foreign affairs, generally staying a step ahead of the president's public proposals. White, Eichelberger, and others in the committee often conferred with administration leaders. It served, in effect, as an unofficial public relations organ for the Roosevelt administration's foreign policies.[9]

On June 20, 1940, as French military resistance crumbled in Europe and as political parties prepared for their national conventions in the United States, the White House announced the appointment of two leading Republicans to the president's cabinet. Roosevelt named seventy-two-year-old Henry L. Stimson of New York to replace isolationist Harry H. Woodring as secretary of war, and sixty-six-year-old Frank Knox of Chicago to succeed Charles Edison as secretary of navy. Both were prominent in the Republican party and had been devotees of Theodore Roosevelt. An aristocratic member of the law firm that Elihu Root had headed before his death, Stimson moved easily from his distinguished law practice in New York to top appointive government positions in Washington and back again. He had served as secretary of war under President William Howard Taft from 1911 to 1913, and as President Herbert Hoover's secretary of state from 1929 to 1933. Knox, the publisher and editor of the *Chicago Daily News*, had been the GOP vice-presidential nominee on the same ticket with Alf M. Landon in 1936. Both Stimson and Knox had voted against FDR in 1932 and again in 1936. Though both were conservatives on domestic issues and opposed much of the New Deal, both applauded Roosevelt's foreign policies from 1937 onward. Neither was an isolationist, both believed peace and security required the defeat of the Axis powers, both favored American aid-short-of-war, and both were more boldly interventionist than Secretary of State Hull, William Allen White, or President Roosevelt (at least more than the president's public stance).[10]

The appointments of Stimson and Knox were designed to strengthen the administration's military preparedness programs. Like FDR's actions to help draw the Republican White into efforts to arouse support for the administration's policies, the naming of Republicans Stimson and Knox was designed to give bipartisan image to the administration's policies. The appointments could underscore the administration's appeal for national unity in those critical times and discredit noninterventionists who attacked Roosevelt's policies.

Stimson had conferred with FDR in 1933 and 1934, both before and after Roosevelt was inaugurated. The two shared common foreign policy attitudes. They did not confer at any length again until 1940, but they corresponded, and Stimson was consulted by Hull and others in the State Department. His name had not been among those that Roosevelt had mentioned in discussing cabinet posts. On May 3, 1940, however, Justice Felix Frankfurter arranged for Stimson to join him for lunch with Roosevelt at the White House. Conversation focused on foreign affairs. On June 1, Stimson wrote the president commending to his attention an editorial from Knox's *Chicago Daily News* that urged strong presidential leadership in the current international crisis. Roosevelt was still considering various persons, but Frankfurter strongly recommended Stimson for the position. On June 18, Stimson delivered a radio address advancing his foreign policy views. He was, as he wrote later, "well out in front of the President and most other leaders in the debate—at least ahead of their published opinions." On June 19, Frankfurter telegraphed FDR urging him to read Stimson's address—which he did. That afternoon Stimson received a telephone call from the president offering him the position of secretary of war. That evening he accepted.[11]

While Stimson moved into the War Department with the noblesse oblige tone of an old statesman being called back to duty in time of national crisis, Knox's move into the Navy Department savored a bit more of climbing ambition, albeit ambition combined with a high sense of public service. At Roosevelt's invitation, Knox had conferred at the White House after his trip to Europe in 1934. From time to time from 1937 onward Knox had written to Hull commending his conduct of foreign affairs and had met with Hull, Ickes, and others in the administration. He applauded the administration's foreign policies in editorials he published in his newspaper, and he saw to it that appropriate editorials were brought to the attention of Roosevelt and Hull. The president had included both Landon and Knox at the meetings of leaders who gathered at the White House on September 20, 1939, and had considered adding both of them to his cabinet. But neither Roosevelt nor Landon was pleased by the performance of the other at that White House gathering or after; the president made no appointments.[12]

Three months later, on December 10, Roosevelt asked Knox to accept appointment as secretary of the navy. Knox advised delay, however, until international crises might make it seem more critically essential for the national interest. FDR let the matter stand for a while.[13] Knox kept in touch with Roosevelt, Hull, and others in the administration. And on June 20, Roosevelt nominated him as secretary of the navy.[14]

Isolationists saw the appointments as further efforts by FDR to turn the United States away from its traditional noninterventionist policies toward involvement in war abroad. With isolationists still vocal and with Roosevelt still talking in terms of aid-short-of-war, Stimson and Knox had to demonstrate restraint in testifying before the Senate committees on their appointments. They rejected isolationism, embraced military preparedness, favored aid-short-of-war, and denied any desire to have the United States enter war abroad. Isolationist senators were highly skeptical, but they were unable to draw either Knox or Stimson into statements that might have blocked approval of their appointments. On July 9, the Senate confirmed the Stimson appointment fifty-six to twenty-eight; the next day it acted favorably on Knox by a vote of sixty-six to sixteen.[15]

From 1940 onward, Stimson and Knox provided skilled administrative leadership for their departments in building America's military strength. They also added to interventionist muscle within the administration. The two of them joined Secretary of Treasury Morgenthau and Secretary of Interior Ickes as the boldest interventionists in the president's cabinet. Three of those four were Republicans; three of the four were born and reared east of the Hudson River. Unlike Secretary of State Hull in the cabinet and William Allen White at the head of the Committee to Defend America by Aiding the Allies, they pressed the president to move aggressively and unequivocally against the Axis. That was precisely what leading isolationists and pacifists feared—and what Roosevelt had reason to expect. The appointments did not silence isolationists, but they added strong interventionist voices within President Roosevelt's administration.

The destroyers-for-bases deal between the United States and Great Britain announced on September 3, 1940, brought together many of the influences and patterns in the contest between Roosevelt and the isolationists. The destroyer deal was a reaction to the alarming aggression by Hitler's Nazi Germany. It was a response to persuasive initiatives of Winston Churchill. It had importance both in helping meet immediate needs in combating submarine attacks that endangered Britain's lifelines and Britain's larger need to draw the United States more fully into the struggle against the Axis. It was an expression of sympathy for the British and of awareness of Britain's significance for American interests and security. It provided a classic demonstration of Roosevelt's views and tactics at home and abroad. It was a major action to aid Britain short-of-war. It used the bipartisan tactics through active roles by Republicans William Allen White and Frank Knox and through the tacit cooperation of the Republican presidential candidate, Wendell Willkie. Sophisticated legal interpretations maximized presidential authority and avoided the necessity for seeking legislation from Congress where isolationists would have had their say. Arranging the deal by executive agreement avoided the necessity for winning the Senate approval that a formal treaty would have required. In the House or the Senate isolationist voices would have delayed and might have blocked action. Legislative debates also might have divided the American people more sharply. Like other aid-short-of-war initiatives, the destroyer deal was not nearly enough to accomplish the defeat of the Axis. But it was the most that Roosevelt thought he could do in that election year without risking defeat and without further dividing the American people. The destroyer-for-bases deal won widespread approval. The potential value of the bases for defense of the Western Hemisphere even muted isolationist objections a bit, leaving them to complain of the methods Roosevelt used, the loss of destroyers to America's own use, and the danger that it moved the United States one step closer to war.[16]

On May 14, 1940, French Premier Paul Reynaud had urged the sale or loan of American destroyers. The next day, in his very first communication to Roosevelt after becoming prime minister, Churchill wrote of Britain's immediate need for "the loan of forty or fifty of your older destroyers." He repeatedly emphasized Britain's acute need for the destroyers from that time on until the deal was consummated nearly four months later. FDR's initial response was negative; he thought it would require "the specific authorization of the Congress" and he was "not certain that it would be wise for that suggestion to be made to the Congress at this moment." Furthermore, he doubted whether American defense requirements in the Western Hemisphere would permit even temporary disposal of the destroyers.[17]

Churchill understood FDR's difficulties with public opinion; within limits set by Britain's requirements, he tried to be helpful. In a circular telegram on June 7, he informed British Commonwealth governments that he was considering "launching a judicious campaign designed to show that it is neither to our interests nor our wish that U.S.A. should become involved in totalitarian warfare. By depriving Isolationists of their main argument, it is hoped that Congress would thus be able to move faster over measures designed to help us." In a communication to FDR on June 15, Churchill wrote: "When I speak of the United States entering the war I am, of course, not thinking in terms of an expeditionary force, which I know is out of the question." Even Britain's King George VI added his voice to the urgent appeals for "some of your older destroyers." In the negotiations Roosevelt and Churchill largely bypassed America's isolationist Ambassador Joseph P. Kennedy in London. William Allen White's Committee to Defend America by Aiding the Allies became active on the issue, as did the more militant Century Group in New York under Francis Miller and others.[18]

At a cabinet meeting on Friday afternoon, August 2, the president earnestly sought a way to get action. The cabinet members agreed "that the survival of the British Isles under German attack might very possibly depend on their getting these destroyers." They believed legislation was necessary to authorize transferring the destroyers to Britain and that such legislation faced defeat or delay unless handled well. They also agreed that Roosevelt should seek the help of William Allen White to win approval for the plan from Republicans Wendell Willkie, Charles McNary, and Joe Martin. Roosevelt thought the legislation "would fail if it had substantially unanimous Republican opposition."[19]

Soon thereafter the idea of authorizing the United States to lease bases in British possessions in the Western Hemisphere was introduced into the deliberations. That innovation made the transaction more palatable to Americans (including isolationists) by strengthening American defense in the Western Hemisphere. Initially it was not seen as eliminating the need for legislative actions. Isolationists earlier had initiated an "island-for-war debts" campaign, calling on European governments to pay their war debts by transferring their island colonies in the Western Hemisphere to the United States. The scheme proposed in the destroyer deal was different, but it fell within that general spectrum.[20]

Though both British and American leaders determined to get the destroyers to Britain, there were difficulties rooted largely in domestic public opinion considerations in both countries. To reassure Americans, Roosevelt wanted public assurances from Churchill that in the event of a British defeat the Royal Navy would not be destroyed or permitted to fall into the hands of the Axis. Churchill would go as far as he had in his "we shall fight on the beaches" speech—but no further. He could not guarantee what a later British government might do if Britain were defeated. The kind of public statement FDR wanted could undermine British morale and raise doubts about Churchill's confidence in their ability to throw back the Nazis. Churchill also preferred to make the bases a gift to the United States as an expression of friendship, rather than as an exchange for the destroyers. If it were not done as an exchange, however, it seemed unlikely that Roosevelt or the navy could legally justify disposing of the destroyers. Within the United States, at Roosevelt's request, William Allen White conferred with the Republican presidential candidate, Wendell Willkie. White found no significant differences between Roosevelt and Willkie on the issue, but he was not able to get from Willkie the firm commitment on the matter that Roosevelt wanted.[21]

Late in August, however, most of the difficulties were resolved or bypassed. In a letter to Secretary of Navy Knox on August 17, Attorney General Robert H. Jackson gave his opinion that the chief of naval operations could certify that the destroyers were "not essential to the defense of the United States if in his judgment the exchange of such destroyers for strategic naval and air bases will strengthen rather than impair the total defense of the United States." That is, though the chief of naval operations could not declare the destroyers of no defensive value by themselves, he could declare that America's strength would be increased if the destroyers were traded to England for bases. Consequently on August 21 and in different form on September 3, Chief of Naval Operations Admiral Harold R. Stark sent the necessary opinion to the president that "an exchange of fifty overage destroyers for suitable naval and air bases on ninety-nine year leases in Newfoundland, Bermuda, the Bahamas, Jamaica, St. Lucia, Trinidad, Antigua, and in British Guiana, will strengthen rather than impair the total defense of the United States," and on those grounds he certified that the destroyers were "not essential to the defense of the United States."[22] The difficulty over whether the bases should be gifts from Britain or exchanges for the destroyers was resolved by dividing them into two packages. Land for bases in Newfoundland and Bermuda would be British gifts to the United States; the others would be leased in exchange for the destroyers. Secretary of War Stimson and Ben V. Cohen brought to Roosevelt's attention the opinion of four lawyers (including Dean Acheson and George Rublee) that he did not require authority from Congress. On August 27, at the president's request, Attorney General Jackson provided his legal opinion that Roosevelt had the necessary constitutional and statutory authority to conclude the arrangement by executive agreement "without awaiting the inevitable delays which would accompany the conclusion of a formal treaty." Secretary of State Hull, Secretary of Navy Knox, and Ambassador Lothian worked out the final details of the exchange of notes that constituted the executive agreement between the governments headed by Roosevelt and Churchill. It required no legislation or appropriation by Congress, and no Senate approval. The agreement was concluded and made public on September 3, 1940.[23]

Just exactly how valuable the old destroyers were for Britain's sea war against German submarines may be debated. But in his memoirs, published after the war, Winston Churchill wrote that more important than the destroyers and bases was the fact that the deal "brought the United States definitely nearer to us and to the war." In his words, "It marked the passage of the United States from being neutral to being non-belligerent."[24] That was precisely why American isolationists objected. They also objected to the methods the administration used that gave neither Congress nor the American people direct voices in the matter.

Two weeks before the agreement was announced, Senator Vandenberg criticized "the hypocrisy which tries to cover up all of these things as being purely 'peaceful' and always 'short of war.'" He favored aid that was truly short-of-war, but he opposed "any of the things which would logically take us into the present conflict." And he opposed "entering the war unless and until the war comes to the Western Hemisphere."[25]

Opposition from Senator David I. Walsh was of greater concern; he was chairman of the Senate Naval Affairs Committee. Roosevelt had included the Massachusetts Democrat on a refreshing three-day Potomac cruise, but that did not soften the senator's objections. He wrote FDR that the transfer of the destroyers would "be politically harmful." He thought the Democratic party would "lose many votes because of the belief that we are either excessively war-minded, or, at least, pursuing policies that will tend to involve us in the present European war." Roosevelt wrote back explaining that "as President and as Commander-in-Chief I have no right to think of politics in the sense of being a candidate or desiring votes." He insisted that the islands were "of the utmost importance to our national defense as naval and air operating bases." He discounted the danger of German retaliation. Roosevelt hoped Walsh would not oppose the destroyer deal, contending that it was "the finest thing for the nation that has been done in your lifetime or mine." The president wrote that he was "absolutely certain that this particular deal will not get us into war and, incidentally, that we are not going into war anyway unless Germany wishes to attack us." FDR's letter did not change Walsh's views.[26]

Senator Nye charged that transferring the destroyers would "plant" the United States "in the middle of war as an actual belligerent" and would "seriously weaken our own defenses." As he said many times before and later, Nye contended that the steps short-of-war were "marching us straight into a war of European power politics."[27]

On September 25, the noninterventionist America First Committee sponsored a network broadcast by Republican Senator Henry Cabot

Lodge, Jr., of Massachusetts that later was printed and distributed as a pamphlet by the committee. In his address Lodge boasted that he and Senator McNary had been the first to introduce legislation calling for the acquisition of naval bases in the Western Hemisphere. But he strongly criticized the administration's destroyers-for-bases deal. He objected to depleting the American navy to get the bases and denied that the ships were obsolete for training purposes. Furthermore, Lodge insisted "that if weapons are to be sent abroad, it should be done in the open, after debate, with public participation by consent of Congress." He worried that "if the Executive can do these things without action by Congress, can he not also declare war without Congress?" He insisted that the United States should concentrate on building its own military preparedness and providing "a leadership which thinks first of America always." He feared involvement in the war could destroy "everything we prize."[28]

Other noninterventionists spoke out in similar terms. But the alarming Axis aggression, Britain's precarious situation, Churchill's magnificent leadership, and the courageous performance of RAF fighter pilots and the British people all combined to persuade most Americans that the destroyer-for-bases deal was the right thing to do at that time. By drawing key Republicans into the process, by keeping the matter out of the hands of Congress and the Senate, and by tying the transfer of destroyers to the lease of bases designed to strengthen America's defenses in the Western Hemisphere, President Roosevelt muffled the opposition. According to opinion polls the overwhelming majority in the United States approved the deal. In his memoirs Roosevelt's new Secretary of War Stimson wrote that it "was the President at his best."[29]

On September 16, 1940, two weeks after the destroyer deal, the president signed the first peacetime selective service, or conscription, bill into law. Coming in the midst of Roosevelt's campaign for election to an unprecedented third term, the action could have seemed politically bold or even foolhardy. In the context of world events, however, and with bipartisan support both inside and outside the adminstration, it may have won as many votes as it lost. As with many of FDR's accomplishments, the initiative for selective sevice did not originate with him or the White House. He responded helpfully to those who did initiate the move, however, and when the time and circumstances were right, he went public on the issue. His presidential influence made the difference.

The prime mover behind compulsory military service legislation was Grenville Clark of the New York law firm of Root, Clark, Buckner and Ballantine. A Republican and "an old-fashioned liberal," he was not attuned to the New Deal. But he and FDR had been friends for many years; Clark had graduated from Harvard just a year ahead of Roosevelt. They shared common preparedness views. Clark had been an army officer in World War I and was active in the Military Training Camps Association that pushed the so-called Plattsburg idea based on the voluntary military training camps before the United States had entered the First World War. Though a private civilian association, the Plattsburg camp group worked closely with the War Department. It had a national membership, but its leadership centered in New York.[30]

Clark arranged a dinner meeting at the Harvard Club for some one hundred members of the old Plattsburg group on May 22, 1940, at the time the German blitzkrieg was smashing resistance in Western Europe. Clark wrote to the president before the meeting explaining that its purpose was to consider "recommending and supporting compulsory military training" and to "discuss the public support of a concrete set of measures 'short of war' to aid the Allies." He invited FDR's comments. Roosevelt responded promptly in a letter marked "private and confidential" to "Dear Grennie." He had no objections, but thought that if it was to be called "compulsory" there was "a very strong public opinion for universal service of some kind so that every able bodied man and woman would fit into his or her place." Roosevelt wrote, "The difficulty of proposing a concrete set of measures 'short of war' is largely a political one—what one can get from the Congress."[31]

Clark and his group required no further encouragement. The meeting was a huge success. Among those attending was Henry L. Stimson. It created an emergency committee under Clark to raise funds (they hoped for $275,000) for a national campaign for enactment of conscription. In June, Clark and his associates drafted legislation that was introduced in the Senate by Democrat Edward R. Burke of Nebraska and in the House of Representatives by conservative Republican James W. Wadsworth, Jr., of New York.[32]

Roosevelt moved more slowly in giving his support than Stimson and Clark wished. But he gave his go-ahead early in July, and the Senate and House Military Affairs committees began hearings on the Burke-Wadsworth bill. On July 19, in his address accepting the Democratic presidential nomination, Roosevelt said that "most right thinking persons are agreed that some form of selection by draft is as necessary and fair today as it was in 1917 and 1918." At his press conference on August 2 (the same day that he and his cabinet considered the destroyer deal so carefully), the president endorsed "a selective training bill" and hoped Congress would "do something about it, because it is very important for our national defense." On August 23, Roosevelt told newsmen that he "absolutely opposed" postponing conscription to give the volunteer system more time to work; volunteers would not provide enough men as soon as they were needed. The administration was uneasy about Wendell Willkie's possible tack on the matter, but on August 17 Willkie endorsed selective service in his address accepting the Republican presidential nomination. With support from both Republican and Democratic leaders, with public opinion polls indicating that nearly two-thirds of Americans favored some sort of selective service program, and with war raging in Europe and Asia, approval of the Burke-Wadsworth bill seemed probable.[33]

It faced vigorous opposition, however. Opposition came from pacifists such as Norman Thomas, Oswald Garrison Villard, Frederick J. Libby, and the peace organizations they led. Equally outspoken were isolationists who were not pacifists. Among leading isolationists who battled against selective service were Senators Norris, Wheeler, Vandenberg, La Follette, Taft, and Nye, and Congressman Fish. Noninterventionist legislators conferred in planning their tactics; peace groups worked to arouse public opposition to conscription. They tried earnestly but unsuccessfully to persuade Willkie to oppose selective service. They argued that the necessary manpower for America's armed forces could be obtained through volunteers; at least they believed more efforts to recruit volunteers should be attempted before resorting to the draft. Noninterventionists feared conscription as a militaristic threat to American freedom and democracy at home and as a step toward involvement in war abroad.[34]

Despite his continued friendship with Roosevelt and his growing concern about the Axis menace, George Norris battled against conscription. On August 12, he delivered a major address in the Senate opposing the Burke-Wadsworth bill, and his office franked thousands of copies of the speech to people in Nebraska and elsewhere. He wrote to a constituent that the United States was not confronted by "such imminent danger as to justify" peacetime draft. He feared the growth of militarism in the United States. In time selective service "would change the very nature of most of our citizens. We would become warlike, and when we had become warlike, there would be no doubt that we would soon be fighting with somebody."[35]

Norman Thomas expressed his concerns in an exchange of letters with President Roosevelt that failed to change the opinions of either of them. On August 5, Thomas wrote FDR that he did "not think the case is adequately made that conscription is necessary for defense and I do think that its actual, and still more, its potential dangers to democracy are enormous."[36]

Democratic Senator Vic Donahey wrote the president that the Burke-Wadsworth bill was "fraught with political disaster in Ohio" and that letters were pouring in from Ohio at a rate of one hundred to one against conscription. Roosevelt wrote back that he would be derelict in his duty if he "did not tell the American people of the real danger which confronts them at the present time." He urged Donahey "to banish political considerations" from his mind. Roosevelt sent copies of that exchange of letters to Senate Majority Leader Alben Barkley and to Senator James F. Byrnes of South Carolina.[37]

Senators La Follette, Taft, Walsh, and others all believed that attractive inducements could win enough volunteers without conscription. La Follette complained in a letter to his family, "They will draft the boys but let profits off with a slap on the wrist."[38]

In a similar vein Senator Nye told a public meeting that there would "be a much better taste in the American mouth if, at the same time the man draft is undertaken, a far-reaching draft of profits is forwarded at the same time." He told the Senate that peacetime conscription could fasten "a yoke of militarism upon us that will not be easily, if ever, cast off."[39]

On August 15, in a network broadcast sponsored by the Keep America Out of War Congress, Senator Wheeler charged that peacetime conscription was not only another step in the direction of war, it was also "the greatest step toward regimentation and militarism ever undertaken by the Congress of the United States." He feared it would "slit the throat of the last Democracy still living." California's Hiram Johnson wrote his son that it was "the most insidious act that has been passed in my long service here."[40]

Noninterventionists in both houses of Congress proposed various amendments; most were defeated easily.[41] On August 28, the Senate approved the Burke-Wadsworth bill by a vote of 58 to 31. The negative votes included nearly all of the familiar isolationist names, including western progressives. Their followers gradually were falling away, however, and their images were changing. The same persons who had been seen as noble spokesmen for peace in the middle of the 1930's were, by 1940, seen as partisan, unsavory, and possibly as Nazi sympathizers. The changing images, along with shrinking numbers, were part of the erosion of isolationist strength. The House approved the bill as amended on September 7 by a vote of 263 to 149, with Congressman Fish voting with the majority. On September 14 the Senate approved the conference report 47 to 25, and the House approved it 233 to 124. The president signed it into law on September 16, 1940.[42]

In its final form the Selective Service Act required the registration of all male citizens and aliens residing in the United States who were between the ages of 21 and 36. Those inducted would serve in the armed forces for twelve months. The law provided that draftees would not serve outside the Western Hemisphere except in territories and possessions of the United States.[43] It was a far cry from a new American Expeditionary Force to Europe, but noninterventionists feared that it pointed in that direction.

On September 4, 1940, the day after announcement of the destroyer deal, twelve days before the president signed the Selective Service Act, and nearly four months after creation of the White Committee, isolationists announced the formation of the American First Committee. During the fifteen months preceding the Japanese attack on Pearl Harbor the American First Committee was the leading isolationist, or noninterventionist, mass pressure group battling against the foreign policies of the Roosevelt administration. Though there were many local, regional, and other national groups on all sides of the foreign policy debate, the America First Committee was to the isolationist or noninterventionist cause what William Allen White's Committee to Defend America by Aiding the Allies and later the Fight for Freedom Committee were to the internationalist, or interventionist, cause.[44]

With its national headquarters in Chicago, the America First Committee grew out of an earlier student organization at Yale University led by R. Douglas Stuart, Jr., a twenty-four-year-old law student and son of the first vice-president of Quaker Oats Company. During the summer of 1940, young Stuart won the support of prominent Middle West business and political leaders for a national organization. General Robert E. Wood, chairman of the board of Sears, Roebuck and Company, served as national chairman of America First, and Stuart was national director.[45]

Born in Kansas in 1879, Wood graduated from West Point in 1900. He served in the Philippines during the insurrection and in Panama while the canal was being built. During World War I he was acting quartermaster general. After the war he retired from the army and became vice-president of Montgomery Ward and Company before moving to Sears, Roebuck as vice-president in 1924. He became president of Sears in 1928 and chairman of the board in 1939. Though a Republican and a businessman, Wood considered himself a liberal. He voted for Roosevelt in 1932, supported much of the early New Deal, and with growing misgivings voted for Roosevelt again in 1936. He had no love for the House of Morgan and other Wall Street financiers, and he had much sympathy for farmers in the Middle West and Great Plains. Though dedicated to American capitalism, he did not believe that "the charge of socialism, communism, or regimentation should be hurled at every new proposal or reform." He was a skilled administrator, and despite his duties at Sears, Roebuck he kept in close personal touch with the operation of the America First Committee. He commanded the respect of other leaders of the committee and tempered differences among them that might have reduced its effectiveness.[46]

R. Douglas Stuart, Jr., had studied government and international relations at Princeton University, where he graduated in 1937. He spent several months traveling in Europe before entering the Yale University Law School in 1938. He held an Army Reserve Officers Training Corps commission. Handsome, personable, and idealistic, Stuart gave the limit of his capacities in the committee's battle against intervention in World War II. Some criticized his youth and his lack of administrative experience, but his judgment on matters of policy generally was sound. And he had a capacity to learn.[47]

General Wood, Stuart, and five others from the Middle West (mostly businessmen) formed the executive committee that shaped and supervised America First policies. A total of more than fifty prominent individuals served at one time or another on a larger national committee. Among the more prominent members of the national committee were George N. Peek, General Hugh S. Johnson, Alice Roosevelt Longworth, Mrs. Burton K. Wheeler, Mrs. Bennett Champ Clark, Chester Bowles, Edward Rickenbacker, John T. Flynn, Hanford MacNider, Kathleen Norris, and Lillian Gish. Henry Ford was a member for a time in the fall of 1940, but the committee dropped him in an effort to reduce its vulnerability to the charge of anti-Semitism. Colonel Charles A. Lindbergh initially was not a member, but he joined the national committee in April, 1941. Others also advised committee leaders on policies. Stuart relied heavily on the advice of Chester Bowles, then an advertising executive, and William Benton, vice-president of the University of Chicago. Philip La Follette, former Governor of Wisconsin, and Samuel B. Pettengill, former Democratic congressman from Indiana, were particularly influential. Among the more prominent and active speakers at major America First rallies were Democratic Senator Burton K. Wheeler of Montana, Republican Senator Gerald P. Nye of North Dakota, and Colonel Charles A. Lindbergh.[48]

The committee financed its battle against intervention through voluntary contributions both to national headquarters and to local chapters. William H. Regnery, president of the Western Shade Cloth Company and a member of the America First executive committee, was the largest financial backer. H. Smith Richardson of the Vick Chemical Company in New York contributed large sums, and General Wood contributed more than $10,000. J. M. Patterson, president of the *New York News*, and Colonel Robert R. McCormick, publisher of the *Chicago Tribune*, each contributed $4,000. Altogether the America First national headquarters received around $370,000 from approximately twenty-five thousand contributors. Local chapters were largely self-supporting through voluntary contributions and were more dependent on small contributions than was the national headquarters.[49]

In the fall of 1940 the committee placed full-page advertisements in major newspapers and sponsored radio broadcasts. By November it began to organize local chapters in cities and towns all over the United States. The committee's greatest growth occurred between December, 1940, and May, 1941. By December 7, 1941, the America First Committee had approximately 450 chapters and subchapters. Its total national membership was around 800,000 to 850,000. The committee had members in every state and organized chapters in most of them, but it won its greatest strength in the Middle West. It was least successful in the interventionist South.[50]

Its original public announcement in September, 1940, included the following statement of the America First Committee's principles:

1. The United States must build an impregnable defense for America.
2. No foreign power, nor group powers, can successfully attack a *prepared* America.
3. American democracy can be preserved only by keeping out of the European war.
4. "Aid short of war" weakens national defense at home and threatens to involve America in war abroad.[51]

The newly formed committee did not take a stand on either the destroyer deal or selective service. It appealed for support from both Republicans and Democrats and tried to be nonpartisan in the presidential campaign of 1940. General Wood and Stuart, however, hoped that the committee's full-page newspaper advertisements in October would help inject the foreign policy issue into the campaign.[52] Given the alarming wars raging abroad and the heated foreign policy debates within the United States, foreign affairs were certain to have prominence and importance both for and against Roosevelt's campaign for election to an unprecedented third term as president of the United States.

Chapter 27

Third Term

In 1940 the military triumphs by Nazi Germany under the dictatorship of Adolf Hitler inadvertently led to Franklin D. Roosevelt's election to an unprecedented third term as president of the United States. Without Hitler there would have been no third term. Without Hitler, Roosevelt and the internationalists would not have triumphed over isolationists in the United States so quickly or completely as they did. Furthermore, without Hitler and World War II the urban bases for that larger and more active role for the United States in world affairs might not have grown so rapidly, and rural and small town bases for isolationism might not have eroded as fast as they did.[1]

The defeat of Roosevelt's court-packing proposal in 1937, the economic recession and unemployment in 1937–38, the growing criticism of the New Deal, the failure of FDR's attempted purge of conservative Democrats, and Democratic reverses in the elections of 1938 combined to leave both Roosevelt and the Democratic party weakened politically as they faced the elections of 1940. Viewed from the perspective of domestic issues, a Republican victory in 1940 was not outside the realm of possibility. More conservative patterns seemed likely, whichever party won the election. In those circumstances Roosevelt's personal preference for retirement from the presidency when his second term ended probably would have been honored.

Speculation about possible successors to Roosevelt, and about the possibility of a third term, began almost as soon as the results of his overwhelming election to a second term were apparent. As usual, the concerns involved both domestic and foreign policies. Conservative isolationists such as Senator Vandenberg of Michigan wanted a coalition of Republicans and conservative Democrats to block any more of the hated New Deal. Progressives such as Senators Norris of Nebraska, Borah of Idaho, Nye of North Dakota, and La Follette of

Wisconsin deliberated on how to continue America on progressive paths. So long as domestic issues were in the forefront, conservatives tended to be hopeful, while progressives and liberals were more pessimistic about the political future. For example, early in 1940 Norris asked Roosevelt what liberals would do if he did not run again. FDR responded, "Did you ever stop to think that if I should run and be elected I would have much more trouble with Congress in my third term and much more bitterness to contend with as a result of my running for a third term than I have ever had before?"[2] Most of those seriously considered for the Democratic presidential nomination if Roosevelt did not run (including Cordell Hull, James A. Farley, and John Nance Gardner) were not really New Dealers and would not be likely to continue domestic reform with the ardor and boldness that urban liberals and western progressives wanted.

By 1940 war in Asia and Europe overshadowed those domestic concerns. Internationalists (both conservative and liberal) worried about isolationist strength and increasingly looked to Roosevelt for continuing leadership in foreign affairs. Conservative internationalists who opposed both the New Deal and isolationism could have problems, however, if FDR ran again. One Democatic New York attorney phrased the difficulty clearly in a letter to a leading interventionist: "What shall we do if we have to choose between a third term for the New Deal and a Republican Party espousing the Isolationism of Borah et al?"[3]

Western progressives faced a comparable dilemma. A third term could help the progressive cause, but they feared it could also mean danger of American involvement in war abroad. If Roosevelt did not run again, the Democratic party could join the Republican party in conservative patterns with progressives blocked whichever way they turned. That concern helped produce Philip La Follette's National Progressive party, but it foundered in the elections of 1938 and faded to national insignificance by 1940. New Republican leadership might have eased progressive concerns, but that seemed unlikely. And as war abroad threatened to engulf the United States, foreign affairs grew increasingly important—both to isolationists and to internationalists.

In that context both conservative and progressive isolationists worried more and more about increased presidential power in general and President Roosevelt's power in particular. In his domestic policies and in his conduct of foreign affairs, Roosevelt personified a larger role for the the president and weaker role for Congress than either progressive isolationists or conservative isolationists wanted. They feared the danger of Roosevelt for democracy within the United States on both domestic and foreign policy issues. None of the leading isolationists approved dictatorship by Hitler in Germany or by Mussolini in Italy, but by 1940 many of them believed that Roosevelt was more of a danger to democracy within the United States than either Hitler or Mussolini was. For leading isolationists the dangers posed by the growing power of the presidency in the hands of Roosevelt—dangers to democracy at home and dangers of involvement in war abroad—overshadowed other considerations as they faced the third term issue in the election year of 1940.

Roosevelt discussed his possible successors during conversations with close friends and confidants. But he never completely revealed his personal thoughts, did not lock his plans into rigid forms, and he kept his options open throughout. Newsmen tried to draw him out on the subject at his press conferences, but they were no match for Roosevelt in that cat-and-mouse game. As he told Morgenthau early in 1940: "It is a game with me. They ask me a lot of questions, and I really enjoy trying to avoid them."[4]

As a possible successor Roosevelt may have favored Secretary of Commerce Harry L. Hopkins for the Democratic nomination, but his poor health and political unpopularity made that impracticable. Among others considered for the nomination, Roosevelt probably preferred Cordell Hull despite the Tennesseean's conservatism on domestic issues. He did not consider Farley qualified for presidential responsibilities, and he opposed both Garner and Wheeler. In considering imperfect alternatives FDR preferred a relatively conservative internationalist (Hull) over a progressive isolationist (Wheeler), though considerations other than foreign affairs and the New Deal helped determine that preference.[5]

Senator Burton K. Wheeler of Montana won considerable attention as a possible Democratic presidential candidate if Roosevelt did not run again, and as a possible vice-presidential running mate if Roosevelt ran for a third term. As early as November, 1937, not long after the court-packing fight, Wheeler and Frank Knox conferred about cooperation between Republicans and anti-Roosevelt Democrats in 1940. In January, 1938, isolationist Amos R. E. Pinchot wrote Wheeler that he was "the logical candidate for the presidency, and the only man that can deal with Roosevelt on equal terms over the radio." In May, 1938, Alf Landon had a confidential talk with Wheeler on cooperation between Republicans and Democrats for senatorial candidates "who stood up to the President." In June, 1939, George Norris unofficially asked Wheeler whether he would consent to run as vice-president if FDR ran for a third term. Others raised that question in conversations with the Montana progressive.[6]

In November, 1939, Wheeler approved formation of a Wheeler-for-President organization, but said he would support Roosevelt if he ran again. Among others, John L. Lewis of the CIO and Senator Hiram Johnson (both isolationists and both increasingly critical of FDR) commended consideration of Wheeler for the presidency. Though running for another Senate term in 1940, Wheeler savored the speculation about his possible candidacy and in speeches and inter-views helped keep the idea alive.[7]

In June, 1940, before the national conventions, Senator and Mrs. Wheeler attended a dinner in the home of columnist Robert E. Kint-ner. Among the guests were Leon Henderson of the Securities and Ex-change Commission, Edward Foley of the Department of Treasury, and Benjamin V. Cohen, New Dealers all. As Wheeler recalled the evening many years later, the four agreed that Wheeler would be nominated for vice-president and that he would have to accept the nomination. He got the impression that they were speaking for the White House. They posed the possibility that after the international emergency had ended Roosevelt would resign and Wheeler would become President. He responded by asking whether they thought FDR would let Wheeler decide when the emergency was over. Ben Cohen's account of the dinner conversation was slightly different, and made clear that they had not been speaking for the White House.[8]

Wheeler had good credentials as a Democrat, a progressive, and an isolationist. At the same time, his battle against court packing had won approval from conservatives. Both then and later Wheeler in-sisted that his battle against court packing had not irreparably dam-aged his relations with the president. The two continued to confer on legislative matters. Roosevelt turned to Wheeler to lead the fight for railroad legislation that culminated in the Transportation Act of 1940.[9]

But the president and the western senator had been getting out of phase with each other even before the court-packing fight; in private conversations with others each gave evidence of increasing irritation with the other. Despite surface affability, Roosevelt never entirely forgave or forgot after the court-packing fight, and Wheeler's distrust of the president grew sharper. From time to time in private conversa-tions friends would try out Wheeler's name with Roosevelt as a possi-ble presidental nominee if FDR did not run, or as a possible vice-presidential nominee if he ran for a third term. Roosevelt did not favor the Montana Democrat either as a presidential nominee or as a vice-presidential running mate. Until after the Democratic party had approved a platform acceptable to him in 1940, Wheeler was equally adamant in rejecting the possibility of running for the vice-presidency with Roosevelt.[10]

During the 1930s Wheeler had not been so prominent in Senate leadership on foreign policy matters as other isolationists such as Borah, Johnson, Nye, or Vandenberg. He was not a member of the Foreign Relations Committee. When he voted on foreign policy matters, however, he usually joined with other western progressives on the isolationist side. As talk about him for the Democratic presidential nomination increased in 1939 and early 1940, isolationists turned to him in opposition to the president's foreign policies. And in 1940 Wheeler was fully persuaded, if he had not been before, that Roosevelt would lead the United States to war.

As Wheeler recalled many years later, two particular episodes in 1940 helped arouse his alarm about the president's policies. Late in May, Rear Admiral Stanford C. Hooper, a senior communications officer in the navy, called on Wheeler. He told the senator that Roosevelt was "going to get us into the war." When Wheeler asked about the Axis threat to American security, the admiral told him that the Germans did not have a bomber that could fly more than a thousand miles—far short of the range needed to attack the United States. If German forces moved by way of Dakar in Africa to Brazil in South America, they would still be further from New York than they had been in Berlin. He contended that Roosevelt was using the fear of a Nazi invasion of the United States as a tactic to get the United States to join the Allies in the European war. Hooper said Wheeler could block the president's road to war by speaking out on the issue. "You licked him on the Court issue and you can lick him again." At Wheeler's request the admiral provided the senator with a handwritten memorandum of data supporting his allegations on Nazi air power.[11]

A few days later, on June 7, while Nazi forces were smashing toward Paris, Senator Wheeler broadcast a major address attacking the president's policies toward the European war. He berated the "mad hysteria" that was being "produced in New York and Washington." He urged his audience not to be panicked by "bogey stories" about swarms of Nazi planes bombing American cities. His address brought a flood of letters and telegrams—and a visit from another military officer.[12]

On June 8, an Army Air Corps captain called on Wheeler. He urged the senator to continue his battle against intervention in the European war and provided data that reinforced the admiral's earlier analysis. The captain told Wheeler, "We haven't got a single, solitary plane that's fit for overseas service. You've got to have three things—armor plate, self-sealing fuel tanks, and fire power. We haven't got a single, solitary plane that has all three." He provided the senator with specific data on American military aircraft—and provided more information later. The admiral and the captain convinced Wheeler that not only was Germany not capable of invading the United States, but that the United States was not prepared at that time to war successfully against the Axis in Europe. That was essentially the same theme that Colonel Charles A. Lindbergh had pressed in a nationwide radio broadcast on May 19. The Senator continued his speechmaking against intervention in the European war, addressing a Keep America out of War Congress rally in Chicago on July 1.[13]

The Montana progressive may not have needed much persuading, but years later Wheeler recalled his separate conversations with the admiral and the captain as he recounted his decision to lead noninterventionist opposition to President Roosevelt's policies. By June, 1940, there was little chance that Wheeler could win the Democratic presidential nomination, and neither he nor Roosevelt favored his candidacy for the vice-presidency. He could not block the renomination if Roosevelt chose to run for a third term, but Wheeler determined to make certain that the Democratic platform clearly opposed American involvement in war abroad.

Even Roosevelt's closest friends were not certain just when he decided to run for a third term. It seems likely that he reached that decision in June, 1940, after Hitler's forces struck west in Europe, after Churchill took the reins in England, after the British had evacuated their forces from Dunkirk, after Mussolini's Italy entered the war, after France surrendered late in June, and just as the Battle of Britain was about to begin.

On June 19 Farley wrote: "It looks as if the President will accept the nomination. Everything points in that direction, although insofar as I know, he hasn't said a thing of a definite nature to anyone." As late as June 20 Roosevelt told Hull that he wanted him as his successor and gave no indication that he intended to run again. On June 28 Secretary of Treasury Morgenthau, one of FDR's closest friends and confidants, concluded that sometime during the preceding thirty days Roosevelt "had made up his mind to run." Even at that late date neither Morgenthau nor Roosevelt's personal secretary, Missy Le Hand, really knew for certain whether he would run or not. At lunch with the president on July 3, however, Hull for the first time noted a change in Roosevelt's tone and concluded that he had decided to run. According to Hull's memorandum written after the conversation, Roosevelt thought that "he could win unless the war should stop, but in that event Willkie might defeat him."[14]

Senator Norris of Nebraska was alone among leading isolationists in favoring a third term for Roosevelt even before the national conventions, and one of very few among them who supported him after the conventions. In July, 1939, before the European war began, the seventy-eight-year-old progressive told newsmen that though there were others he would prefer, he hoped Roosevelt would be reelected in 1940. At that time he thought FDR did not want to run. In a letter to Democratic Senator Claude Pepper of Florida on August 28, Norris wrote: "I am a firm believer in the principles of government for which President Roosevelt has stood and for which he has fought, and, admitting that he has made mistakes, something which is common to all humanity, I have nevertheless never doubted his sincerity, his wisdom, or his courage. The cry that is being made by his enemies that he is trying to set himself up as a 'dictator' to my mind is entirely without foundation and under all the circumstances seems to me to be utterly foolish." After the European war began in September, he wrote Ickes that anyone who charged that Roosevelt wanted to get the United States into the war "was either malicious or crazy, or too ignorant to have his opinions respected." He thought that "those who want a liberal are driven, logically, forcibly, into a realization of the fact that to get a liberal who will win, we must come to Roosevelt."[15]

Most leading isolationists sharply disagreed with Norris on Roosevelt and a third term. In April, 1940, Hiram Johnson was convinced that "the nomination of Roosevelt was settled by the activities of Hitler in the Scandinavian countries." He predicted that the United States would "be in the war either just before or just after the election." He wrote his son that Roosevelt was "bending every effort now, and by every trick and device known, to get us into it."[16]

Speaking at a dinner meeting of the Federation of Young Republican Clubs of Greater New York in February 1940, Senator Nye quoted George Washington in warning against both a third term and American involvement in European disputes. On June 21, as news of the French armistice reached the world and as the Republican National Convention was about to begin, the North Dakota progressive

Republican delivered a major address in the Senate urging Roosevelt to resign and turn over the presidential responsibilities to Vice-President Garner. In his speech Nye denied any sympathy for Hitler or Mussolini and insisted that he was only interested in the United States. He charged that Roosevelt's foreign policies had "brought disaster upon France" by promising military support from America that the president could not deliver. He feared Roosevelt was then encouraging Britain to fight on in anticipation of American aid. With the defeat of France, Nye said, Roosevelt could demonstrate his patriotism by turning over his duties to Garner to "restore the national unity and national confidence in governmental leadership." Nye concluded his address by saying that he had "but one wish, one cause to serve, that is, the cause of keeping my country out of this war, on this lone theory that when the war shall have ended there will be nothing of democracy, there will be nothing of stability, left for any country which permits itself to participate in the war." He predicted that communism would be the only ideology to triumph from the ashes of war.[17] Roosevelt had no intention of being guided by Nye's advice on that or any other matter at that time. But the president continued to play his sphinx-like role on the third term issue a bit longer.

Criminal prosecutor Thomas E. Dewey of New York was the front runner for the Republican presidential nomination before the convention. He had strength in the West, but his largest following was in the Northeast. He was not an isolationist, but his positions on foreign policy issues were not drawn sharply enough to inspire either much hostility or enthusiasm from isolationists (or internationalists). Nonetheless, the Republican party had plenty of prominent isolationists available for the nomination. Until his death early in 1940 Borah had his supporters. In 1939 there were those who worked to win the nomination for Gerald P. Nye, but he never got enough of a following to be a real factor. Hanford MacNider of Mason City, Iowa, was a manufacturer, a much-decorated hero in World War I, a former national commander of the American Legion, and had served as United States minister to Canada under President Hoover. Later he helped lead the America First Committee and served as its vice-chairman in 1941. Friends and admirers organized a favorite son movement for him, but it won little attention outside the Middle West. Former President Herbert Hoover may have had slim hope for renomination, but few shared those hopes. More likely possibilities among isolationists were Senator Arthur H. Vandenberg of Michigan and Ohio's first-term Senator Robert A. Taft. Though Taft supported repeal of the arms embargo in 1939, both Taft and Vandenberg were convinced noninterventionists. Both were conservatives, but if western progressives had to decide between a conservative isolationist and a liberal internationalist in 1940, most would choose the former. Before his death Borah privately assured Vandenberg of his support for the nomination. Nye, Capper, and others worked for his nomination.[18]

As leading isolationists turned to Vandenberg or Taft, however, internationalists were equally determined to block them. Neither of the party's 1936 nominees, Landon or Knox, wanted an isolationist. Internationalists (including Landon) preferred Dewey to Hoover, Taft, Vandenberg, Nye, or MacNider, but there were those who hoped to do better. The result was the well-financed and skillfully organized drive to nominate the former Democrat Wendell Willkie of Indiana and New York City. As head of Commonwealth and Southern Corporation, he had battled against Roosevelt's TVA. He had more charisma than any of the other contenders for the nomination. A member of New York's Century Club, Willkie was an internationalist and shared Roosevelt's general policy views toward the European war. With enthusiastic support from Oren Root, Jr., of New York, Russell Davenport of *Fortune* magazine, Henry Luce and his *Time-Life* publications in New York, the Gardner Cowles family and its publications in Iowa and Minnesota, and from other internationalists, the movement to nominate Willkie came on fast and overtook the front-runners at the wire in the hectic and exciting Philadelphia convention.[19]

Isolationists hoped to portray Roosevelt's Democratic party as the war party and to identify the GOP with America's traditional policies of nonentanglement and nonintervention in European wars. Republican internationalists, however, battled against wedding the party to isolationism. By way of compromise the emphasis went to attacking the Roosevelt administration for failing to build adequate military defenses for America. The party platform approved in Philadelphia berated Roosevelt for leaving "the Nation unprepared to resist foreign attack." It contended, "To establish a first line of defense we must place in official positions men of faith who put America first." It urged that America's "national defense must be so strong that no unfriendly power shall ever set foot on American soil." It emphasized that the Republican party was "firmly opposed to involving this Nation in foreign war." The Republicans endorsed extending aid "to all peoples fighting for liberty, or whose liberty is threatened," providing that aid did not violate international law or conflict with the requirements of America's own defense.[20]

At the beginning of the GOP convention, according to Vandenberg's account, Dewey tried to make a deal with the isolationist Michigan senator. He sent Senator Styles Bridges of New Hampshire to tell Vandenberg that if he would run for vice-president on the same ticket with Dewey, he could have anything he wanted. Dewey thought (or hoped) that ticket could "sew up the whole thing on the first ballot." Vandenberg preferred to stay in the Senate rather than become vice-president. But he told Bridges that if Dewey would take the vice-presidential place on the ticket with Vandenberg, he could "write his own ticket and have anything he wants." Vandenberg would pledge to be a one-term president so Dewey could move on to the presidency in the election of 1944. Vandenberg also told Bridges that if Dewey could not agree to that arrangement, Vandenberg was willing to meet the New Yorker and "flip a coin to see which end of the ticket we each take." That ended that! Vandenberg heard no more from Dewey until the last night of the balloting, when Dewey made frantic calls urging him to do something to help stop Willkie. It was too late.[21]

Dewey led on the first ballot, Taft was second, and Willkie third. The line-up was the same on the second ballot, but Dewey lost ground, and Willkie gained. On the third ballot Willkie moved ahead of Taft into second place. The galleries packed with Willkie supporters were filling the convention hall with resounding cries of "We want Willkie!" On the fourth ballot Willkie pulled ahead of Dewey. Last-minute efforts to check the avalanche failed. Willkie won the Republican presidential nomination on the sixth ballot. It was a victory for internationalists and the urban Northeast; it was a defeat for isolationists and western progressives. The choice of Charles L. McNary of Oregon for vice-president appeased the West and agriculture, but did not significantly soften the significance of the Willkie nomination for isolationists.[22]

The Democratic convention in mid-July was a confusing, poorly handled affair. Roosevelt was so coy and so determined to avoid any impression of seeking a third term that he provided little leadership for the convention in Chicago. Though there was no definite word, there was little serious doubt that Roosevelt would accept a third nomination for the presidency. From their suite in the Blackstone Hotel, Harry L. Hopkins with help from Senator James F. Byrnes of

South Carolina provided unofficial leadership for Roosevelt's cause at Chicago. It was Senator Alben W. Barkley of Kentucky, in his address as permanent chairman of the convention, who read FDR's statement that he did not wish to be a candidate again and that the delegates were "free to vote for any candidate." That was a backhanded way of saying that Roosevelt was available, an "invitation to the draft." Senator Lister Hill of Alabama formally nominated Roosevelt. Senator D. Worth Clark of Idaho had prepared to nominate Wheeler, but at the last minute, when the outcome was apparent to all, Wheeler firmly asked Clark not to place his name in nomination. When the voting was over on the night of July 17, Roosevelt had won the Democratic nomination on the first ballot with an overwhelming 946 votes; Farley, Garner, Tydings, and Hull scattered the remaining 148 votes among them.[23]

Opposition to Roosevelt manifested itself less in the party's presidential nomination than in shaping its platform and in reactions to FDR's choice for vice-president. Senator Robert F. Wagner of New York was chairman of the Resolutions Committee that had responsibility for drafting the Democratic platform. He also chaired the subcommittee charged with drafting the foreign policy plank. Among other members of that subcommittee were the administration's internationalist Secretary of Agriculture Wallace of Iowa and isolationist Senators Wheeler of Montana and Walsh of Massachusetts. With Wheeler and Walsh leading the attack, the subcommittee rejected the foreign policy plank proposed by the White House. In a rugged battle Wheeler and Walsh carried the day for isolationists; Wheeler even threatened to walk out of the convention if the interventionists had their way on the foreign policy plank. As finally approved, the Democratic platform proclaimed: "The American people are determined that war, raging in Europe, Asia and Africa, shall not come to America. We will not participate in foreign wars, and we will not send our army, naval or air forces to fight in foreign lands outside of the Americas, except in case of attack." The phrase "except in case of attack" was added at the insistence of administration spokesmen. The platform contended, "The direction and aim of our foreign policy has been, and will continue to be, the security and defense of our own land and the maintenance of its peace." It did not mention selective service one way or the other.[24]

But the foreign policy plank was not without merit from an internationalist perspective. It rejected "appeasement" and pledged to extend "all the material aid at our command, consistent with law and not inconsistent with the interests of our own national self-defense" to "the peace-loving and liberty-loving peoples wantonly attacked by ruthless aggressors." Neither Roosevelt nor Hull liked the foreign policy plank; Hull was particularly unhappy about it. But it had enough variety and ambiguity to give even a literal-minded president (which Roosevelt was not) room to maneuver on foreign affairs. Wheeler was so pleased with the plank that he may have given further thought to the possibility of accepting second place on the Democratic ticket with Roosevelt. FDR had not favored Wheeler for vice-president earlier; he did not turn to Wheeler after the fight on the foreign policy plank.[25]

Instead, Roosevelt chose Secretary of Agriculture Henry A. Wallace of Iowa as his running mate. Wallace was a New Deal liberal on domestic issues, an idealistic internationalist on foreign affairs, and was as identified with agriculture and the West as McNary was on the Republican ticket. Wallace did not appeal to city bosses or experienced party workers. He aroused so much opposition that Roosevelt threatened to refuse the presidential nomination if the convention rejected Wallace. It did his bidding, but without enthusiasm. From the perspective of Roosevelt's continued efforts for the New Deal and internationalism, Wallace was a logical choice.[26]

The party faithful had mixed feelings as they departed convention headquarters in Chicago. The nomination of Roosevelt gave them an internationalist, a liberal, and a proven winner; the vice-presidential nominee provided a liberal, an internationalist, and sectional balance. But the third term and Wallace's public image would be liabilities. The platform was more isolationist than internationalists preferred. In 1940, however, that noninterventionist but ambiguous platform may have been more of a political help than a hindrance.

No campaign in which Franklin D. Roosevelt was a candidate could be entirely dull or boring, and the campaign of 1940 was not that. For the first time Roosevelt faced a Republican presidential nominee who could almost match him in vitality and charisma. Wendell Willkie's political inexperience led to mistakes, but he conducted a lively, spirited campaign. His general agreement with FDR on most issues, domestic and foreign, reduced his appeal for many who opposed Roosevelt, but he attracted support from some liberals and many internationalists who had reservations about a third term. Conservatives and isolationists really had no one else to turn to if they hoped to defeat Roosevelt.

In different circumstances the third-term issue might have dominated the campaign (but in different circumstances FDR might not have sought a third term). The issue was prominent in 1940 and determined the votes of many. But with the Battle of Britain raging in Europe, with Japan driving south into Indochina, and with the Tripartite Pact drawing the Axis states closer together in opposition to the United States, foreign affairs loomed larger than in any presidential election since 1920. Before the campaign ended, foreign affairs overshadowed the third term issue.

Initially Willkie tried not to play politics with foreign affairs (or he played politics by trying to win internationalists to the Republican banner). He resisted efforts by isolationists to move him in directions that Taft or Vandenberg would have taken. His acceptance speech, delivered on August 17 at Elwood, Indiana, generally pleased Republican internationalists. Roosevelt's Republican Secretary of War Henry L. Stimson confided to his diary that the speech was "fine, brave and sensible" and had "gone far to hamstring the efforts of the little group of isolationists to play politics."[27]

Not surprisingly, Senator Hiram Johnson took a different view. Though he expected to be for Willkie ultimately, Johnson confided to his son that Willkie had "raised hell with us here by adopting the Roosevelt foreign policy, and being for conscription, etc. He really broke the back of the opposition to the conscription law." Johnson would have been even more angered had he known of a confidential message that Willkie had sent to the British ambassador to the United States, Lord Lothian. As Lothian reported the message to Foreign Secretary Halifax and Prime Minister Churchill, Willkie "was personally in favour of doing everything possible to see that Great Britain did not get beaten in the war because he realised that the continued existence of Great Britain and its Navy was essential to the safety and security of the United States." Because "of the overwhelming desire of the United States not to get involved in the war," however, Willkie thought it "necessary to convince the American people about every particular step, which inevitably took time." Willkie promised the ambassador that he would not oppose the destroyer deal, but he was "most insistent that this statement of his views should not in any circumstances be allowed to leak out because it would certainly be used against him in the campaign."[28] During the early weeks of his campaign Willkie's speeches gave neither the British nor American internationalists cause for displeasure. Isolationists had less ground for satisfaction.

As the campaign progressed, however, it became increasingly clear that Willkie would go down to defeat unless he could accomplish some sort of breakthrough. Prodded by isolationists, during the last month of the campaign Willkie stepped up his attacks on FDR's foreign policies. He berated the president for failing to build adequate defense forces for the United States. And he warned repeatedly that if Roosevelt were reelected, the United States would soon be at war. For example, in Chicago he charged that if Roosevelt's promise "to keep our boys out of foreign wars is no better than his promise to balance the budget, they're almost on the transports!" He repeated such charges many times in the closing weeks and days of his campaign, and others who urged his election shouted that theme in even more strident terms.[29]

Isolationists could make those charges with honest conviction. For Willkie, who shared the president's views, however, such language grew out of isolationist pressures, out of his desperate determination to win election, and out of emotions aroused in the heat of the campaign. Three months after the election, he told the Foreign Relations Committee, in response to a question from Senator Nye, that his prediction that America would be at war by April, 1941, if FDR were elected had been "a bit of campaign oratory."[30] Willkie's standing on the polls did improve as the campaign neared its close. Though isolationists had lost their majority position, most Americans still hoped the United States could somehow stay out of the war. In a contest between two internationalists running on noninterventionist platforms, isolationist appeals conceivably could bring out the vote and determine the victor in a close election. So Willkie may have reasoned, and so Roosevelt began to fear.

The president did not propose to campaign in the usual sense, and he never traveled further than a twelve-hour train trip from Washington before the election. Nonetheless, he was by no means inactive or passive. From July 19, when he broadcast his midnight address accepting the Democratic nomination, until election day on November 5, Roosevelt conducted his own kind of campaign with an effectiveness that Willkie and the Republicans could not match. He made numerous trips to inspect military installations and defense plants, giving warm and moving speeches along the way. He delivered radio broadcasts. He conducted both regular and special press conferences. In the final weeks of the campaign he delivered five major campaign speeches. Even his decision to stay close to Washington underscored the sense of crisis and emergency that made his continued service as president seem more essential. And his almost continuous round of inspection trips dramatized his efforts to build American defense. In his acceptance speech he spoke of the call of public duty and patriotism that moved him to serve despite his personal preference for retirement to private life. At the same time he portrayed opponents as "blind" and "partisan" and denounced "appeaser fifth columnists" who had charged him with "war-mongering." That acceptance speech, and Roosevelt's later speeches during the campaign, continued the tactic of identifying his foreign policy opponents with all that was evil, sinister, and even subversive.[31]

Roosevelt had little difficulty with the language in the Democratic platform. As he had been doing before, he could and did emphasize his earnest desire and efforts for peace, his abhorrence of the tyranny of the dictators, his actions to aid democratic peoples resisting aggression, and his determination to build military strength to guard American freedom. The campaign in the midst of the war abroad required only slight shifts in emphases. He had never said that he favored American intervention in the war; he did not say so during the campaign. He had often voiced his hope and determination that the United States would stay out of the war; he repeated such statements in the campaign.

In his acceptance speech Roosevelt said that during his administration the government "had the courage openly to oppose by every peaceful means the spread of the dictator form of Government." He hoped "untried hands, inexperienced hands" would "not substitute appeasement and compromise with those who seek to destroy all democracies everywhere, including here." He spoke pridefully of his efforts to prevent war, to limit its spread, to condemn aggression, to sympathize with free peoples resisting aggression, to aid victims of aggression, and "to awaken this country to the menace for us and for all we hold dear." The president said that America faced choices of "people versus dictatorship," "freedom versus slavery," and of "religion against godlessness; the ideal of justice against the practice of force; moral decency versus the firing squad; courage to speak out, and to act, versus the false lullaby of appeasement."[32] His were bold and inspiring words—and from an isolationist perspective increased fears that FDR would lead the United States to war.

Roosevelt's main speech writers during the campaign were Samuel I. Rosenman, Harry L. Hopkins, and the poet and playwright Robert

E. Sherwood. All were talented, all were completely devoted to the president, and all fully shared his antipathy for isolationists and isolationism. Roosevelt devoted much time and energy to the preparation of those speeches and worked closely with his writers as they revised draft after draft. The products were Roosevelt's in content, tone, and spirit. Assistant Secretary of State Adolf Berle occasionally shared in the preparation of foreign policy speeches and often helped write antiisolationist speeches initiated by the White House but delivered by others. In his diary on October 29 Berle described the president's speech writers in stark terms; he saw Hopkins, Rosenman, and Sherwood, along with Felix Frankfurter and William O. Douglas as "a highly intelligent crew—and, except for Sam Rosenman, as unscrupulous a crew as ever put together. Rosenman is square. Harry Hopkins is nice and likeable, but would commit murder for the President. The rest of the bunch would commit murder on general principles, either for the President or for themselves. How you can put any of the saving grace of solidity of character into this bunch is a question that I have been totally unable to solve. I am afraid we shall get one of these clever, progressive administrations in which the end always justifies the means." That was more cutting than they deserved. But there was no doubt of their complete loyalty to Roosevelt, or of their ruthlessness when contending with his opponents—including isolationist opponents.[33]

Repeatedly in speech after speech during the fall of 1940, Roosevelt stressed his commitment to building America's defenses, his abhorrence of the aggressor states, his sympathy for the victims of aggression, his determination to keep America out of war, and his disdain for "appeasers"—the term he used when referring to his isolationist opponents during his campaign. When he addressed a meeting of the Teamsters Union on September 11, the president told his listeners: "I hate war, now more than ever. I have one supreme determination—to do all that I can to keep war away from these shores for all time." He quoted and endorsed the noninterventionist plank of the Democratic platform. He called for "an end to the sort of appeasement that seeks to keep us helpless by playing on fear and by indirect sabotage of all the progress we are making. 'Appeasement' is a polite word for misdirected partisanship."[34]

Devoted followers urged FDR to soothe Italian-Americans who had been angered by his stab-in-the-back speech at Charlottesville, Virginia, after Mussolini's Italy had joined the war against France.

Consequently, on Columbus Day, October 12, the president issued a statement praising the contributions of Italian and Spanish people to American development. He also lauded them in a campaign speech that day in Dayton, Ohio. In that speech he appealed for national unity and attacked those "who suggest that the course the Americas are following is slowly drawing one and all of us into war with some nation, or nations beyond the seas." He emphasized that "this country wants no war with any nation" and that "keeping this nation and the other Republics at peace with the rest of the world" was "uppermost" in his mind. He rejected "the doctrine of appeasement" and called it "a major weapon of the aggressor nations."[35]

Many who favored FDR's election urged him to speak out more on the peace issue, particularly as Willkie stepped up attacks. For example, the interventionist newspaper columnist Robert S. Allen wrote the president on October 19. He had just returned from a political survey and believed that Roosevelt's chances of carrying the Middle West in the election were "very doubtful." Allen believed Roosevelt still might win Ohio, Michigan, Illinois and Indiana, however, if he made a trip to Illinois and Indiana, and if "from now on until election day you pound away with all your eloquence that *you are for peace.*" Allen thought the third-term issue was not counting much, that the people were "concerned only about one thing—war." That issue concerned a "very large percentage of undecided votes in each state." FDR rejected urgings to travel to the Middle West or further, but he wrote Allen that his suggestion that he stress peace was "excellent" and promised to do so "with even greater emphasis." And he did.[36]

When he swung fully into the campaign with his address in Philadelphia on October 23, he said he did so to point out some of the "more fantastic misstatements" by his political opponents; he thought them "deliberate falsifications." In line with his procedure of identifying his opponents with evil foreign influences, in Philadelphia Roosevelt said, "Certain techniques of propaganda, created and developed in dictators countries, have been imported into this campaign." He debunked allegations that the government had entered into secret agreements with foreign states and lit into "the charge that this Administration wishes to lead this country into war." Roosevelt assured Americans that he was "following the road to peace." He once again quoted the noninterventionist plank in the Democratic platform, and concluded: "It is for peace that I have labored; and it is for peace that I shall labor all the days of my life."[37]

In a radio address to the *New York Herald Tribune* Forum on October 24, the president quoted Abraham Lincoln in warning against "appeasers." He appealed for unity and "free inquiries and free debate," but at the same time attacked "foreign propagandists who seek to divide us with their strategy of terror." As he did many times before and later, Roosevelt blurred the distinction between foreign subversives and Americans who dissented from his foreign policies.[38]

At Madison Square Garden in New York City on October 28, Roosevelt set out "to nail up the falsifications that have to do with our relations with the rest of the world and with the building up of our Army, our Navy and our air defense." He denied that American rearmament was lagging or would be unable to meet threats from abroad. "Those are the whisperings of appeasers." He charged that if the Republicans had controlled Congress, the military forces would still be almost as weak as they had been in 1933. He quoted Fish, Hoover, Vandenberg, and Taft to sustain his allegation. He pointed out that Senators McNary, Vandenberg, and Nye, along with Congressman Fish, had voted against his naval expansion program of 1938. FDR insisted that "the Republican leaders played politics with defense in 1938 and 1939. I say that they are playing politics with our national security today." In contrast to his public position in the fall of 1939, he described repeal of the arms embargo in the context of aiding the allies. He identified Senators McNary, Nye, Vandenberg, Johnson, and "Congressmen Martin, Barton and Fish" as opposing that action. As he phrased it, "Great Britain and a lot of other nations would never have received one ounce of help from us—if the decision had been left to Martin, Barton and Fish." He said that "through all the years since 1935, there has been no entanglement and there will be no entanglement." He traced the alarming course of Axis aggression and war since 1937. He warned Americans not to risk America's future "in the inexperienced hands of those who in these perilous days are willing recklessly to imply that our boys are already on their way to the transports."[39]

In Boston on October 30 Roosevelt delivered his most controversial and most quoted campaign speech. He described his accomplishments for military preparedness. He named cities scattered across the land that were building planes, engines, and military equipment. Roosevelt said: "And while I am talking to you mothers and fathers, I give you one more assurance. I have said this before, but I shall say it again and again and again: Your boys are not going to be sent into any foreign wars."[40]

In his campaign speech in Cleveland on November 2, Roosevelt denounced "certain forces within our own national community, composed of men who call themselves American but who would destroy America." He said there was "nothing secret" about America's foreign policy and outlined it for his listeners: "The first purpose of our foreign policy is to keep our country out of war. At the same time, we seek to keep foreign conceptions of Government out of the United States. . . . The second purpose of this policy is to keep war as far away as possible from the shores of the entire Western Hemisphere. . . . Finally, our policy is to give all possible material aid to the nations which still resist aggression, across the Atlantic and Pacific Oceans." He promised "to commit none of the fatal errors of appeasement," and he reaffirmed his faith in democracy.[41]

Senator Norris of Nebraska and, to a less extent, Senators La Follette of Wisconsin and Clark of Missouri supported FDR. In September, after consulting Mayor Fiorello La Guardia of New York and others, Norris initiated a call to recreate the organization of independent progressives that had urged the election of Roosevelt in 1932 and 1936. Norris served as honorary chairman of the National Committee of Independent Voters for Roosevelt and Wallace. La Guardia was chairman, and David K. Niles was executive assistant. Unlike the organizations they had led in 1932 and 1936, however, it included none of the leading western progressive isolationists except Norris, and its roster included prominent interventionists. Critics asked why he had taken the lead against a third term in 1928 when Coolidge was president and now urged a third term for Roosevelt; Norris's response was clear and to the point: "At that time there was no emergency. . . . At the present time we are confronted with an emergency fraught with as much peril and danger as has ever confronted our country since its birth." Given FDR's support for the Tennessee Valley Authority and Willkie's prominence in battling against TVA, it was little wonder that the aged Nebraskan opposed the Republican presidential nominee. Norris spent the weeks preceding the election actively campaigning for FDR in the West. Roosevelt muffled possible criticisms from his isolationist Ambassadors Joseph P. Kennedy and John Cudahy by delaying their resignations while not naming them to new positions. Late in the campaign Kennedy made a major broadcast urging the election of Roosevelt.[42]

Most other leading isolationists strongly opposed the election of Roosevelt to a third term. They were handicapped in their campaign efforts, however, by the fact that they were no more confident of Willkie on foreign affairs than they were of FDR. Consequently, though they attacked Roosevelt's foreign policies, they focused particularly on the third-term issue—often without positively endorsing Willkie. The positions of several on the national election were affected by the fact that they were running for reelection on the state level. Among others, Senators Vandenberg, Shipstead, La Follette, Johnson, Walsh, and Wheeler (and of course Congressman Fish) were all running for reelection.

Wheeler had a particularly difficult situation. He abhorred Roosevelt, but as a Democrat, he was running on the same ticket with him. After winning the fight on the foreign policy plank at the Democratic national convention, he had promised to support the party's national ticket. And he found Willkie unsatisfactory. He feared "that the same crowd of interventionists that are pushing Roosevelt into the war are also for Willkie one hundred percent." As he said, it was "a pretty hard choice." On election day Senator Wheeler voted for Socialist Norman Thomas, a noninterventionist with whom the Montana Democrat could agree on many domestic issues as well.[43]

Farmer-Labor Senator Henrik Shipstead of Minnesota had supported the election of Roosevelt in 1932 and 1936. In 1940, however, he abruptly bolted the Farmer-Labor party and ran for reelection as a Republican. Willkie did not appeal to him, but he opposed the election of Roosevelt to a third term.[44]

Though Senator Hiram Johnson of California had had Roosevelt's political blessings in 1934, the president made a point of speaking out against him in 1940. In response to a question at his press conference on August 2, Roosevelt said he did "not think anybody in his wildest dreams could consider him [Johnson] as being in any way a liberal or progressive Democrat in the year 1940." Roosevelt said that Johnson had been "a grand old liberal and progressive for a great many years" and he professed to be "still very fond of him." But FDR thought Johnson had "changed an awful lot in the last four or five years," and guessed that that was "pretty generally recognized." Johnson was shaken by the president's comments and was convinced the newsman's question had been planted by the White House. Senator Wheeler promptly came to Johnson's defense—but Wheeler's progressivism was similarly suspect in the president's eyes. Johnson could not stomach Willkie or his foreign policy views, but he delivered one major radio address during the campaign opposing the election of Roosevelt to a third term.[45]

Senator Nye faced a complicated political situation in North Dakota. He did not come up for reelection until 1944, but his bitter political opponent William Langer had beaten out Lynn Frazier's bid for another Republican nomination in the Senate race. In his efforts to block Langer, Nye campaigned for William Lemke as an independent for the United States Senate. Nye also campaigned for Willkie against Roosevelt. He said there was "a million times larger chance that America can stay out of war with Wendell Willkie and Charles McNary at the helm and Mr. Roosevelt a private citizen." He said the "real emergency" confronting the United States was "not in the danger of attack upon us by any foreign power or group of powers. The threat to our democracy lies within our own borders. It is largely economic." Nye charged that the president "has assumed powers that were never intended to be that of the Executive, has assumed them without even consulting a Congress, has seemed to want to make himself the policeman of all the world." In his view, "The third-term candidate talks sweetly of peace, but his acts for the past two years have been acts taking us ever closer to war."[46]

Iowa-born labor leader John L. Lewis of the United Mine Workers and the CIO had vigorously supported FDR in 1936, but the two had broken by 1940. Lewis gave his support to the reelection campaigns of isolationist Democratic Senators Walsh in Massachusetts and Wheeler in Montana. And in his efforts to get workers to vote against Roosevelt, on October 25 he pledged to resign as president of the CIO if Roosevelt won reelection.[47]

Colonel Charles A. Lindbergh did not participate in party campaigns in 1940, and he did not mention either Roosevelt or Willkie by name in any of his speeches that year. He felt momentary encouragement when both parties adopted noninterventionist foreign policy planks for their platforms. Though he did not like Willkie's acceptance speech and did not think Willkie understood Europe's problems very well, Lindbergh preferred the Republican nominee to Roosevelt. During 1940 the famed airman delivered five major addresses opposing American involvement in the European war (three nationwide radio broadcasts, a speech at a mass meeting in Chicago, and a talk to a large audience at Yale University). Two of those were during the month preceding the election, and Lindbergh voted for Willkie on November 5.[48]

The America First Committee organized in the midst of the campaign was nonpartisan and appealed for support from noninterventionists in both parties. With the nominations of Willkie and

Roosevelt, however, frustrated isolationists turned to the committee as a vehicle for opposing both Roosevelt and his foreign policies. The committee urged voters "to support those candidates on November 5, regardless of party, who stand for defense at home, and, by their acts as well as by their words oppose war in Europe or Asia." It placed full-page advertisements in major newspapers across the country in its efforts to inject the foreign policy issue more prominently into the presidential campaign. It rejected a request to sponsor a network broadcast in which John T. Flynn of its national committee would oppose the election of Roosevelt without endorsing Willkie. But most of the leaders and members of America First opposed the reelection of FDR. Both General Wood, its national chairman, and R. Douglas Stuart, Jr., its national director, favored Willkie over Roosevelt.[49]

On Tuesday, November 5, American voters elected Roosevelt to a third term as president of the United States. His margin of victory was closer than it had been in 1932 or 1936, but he carried all but ten states. Except for Maine and Vermont, Roosevelt carried all of the Northeast, all the electoral votes of the South, and all states west of the Rocky Mountains. Willkie won the electoral votes of his home state of Indiana and of Vandenberg's Michigan. Wallace's home state of Iowa gave its electoral votes to Willkie. Roosevelt lost all four of the northern Great Plains states of North Dakota, South Dakota, Nebraska, and Kansas despite the efforts of Nebraska's Norris on behalf of FDR. The Mountain and Plains state of Colorado completed Willkie's list. Roosevelt was stronger in cities than he had been in his previous elections and weaker in rural areas and small towns outside the South.[50]

In the Senate some leading isolationists fell in 1940. Farmer-Labor Senator Ernest Lundeen died in a plane crash in August. Democrat Rush D. Holt of West Virginia was voted out of office. No senator had voted more consistently on the isolationist side of public issues during FDR's first two terms than progressive Republican Lynn J. Frazier of North Dakota. He was turned back within the GOP by William Langer, but in conviction and action Langer was fully as isolationist as Frazier had been. Most other leading isolationist senators won reelection in 1940, including Johnson of California, La Follette of Wisconsin, Shipstead of Minnesota, Vandenberg of Michigan, Walsh of Massachusetts, and Wheeler of Montana. Wheeler carried every county and city in his state and received nearly three times the vote of his opponent. He ran stronger in Montana than he had six years earlier and much stronger than FDR in the state. C. Wayland "Curly" Brooks, a Republican isolationist, won election to the Senate from Illinois. Republican Hamilton Fish of FDR's home district in New York won reelection to another term in the House of Representatives despite concerted efforts by Democrats and internationalists to try to defeat him.[51]

Isolationists felt frustrations during the conventions, the campaigns, and the election. The parties did not provide voters with clear alternatives on foreign affairs (they rarely had in American history). Though both Willkie and FDR made noninterventionist pledges in the final weeks of the campaign, both were internationalists. Despite equivocation on foreign policy issues in the campaign (or because of that equivocation), the election of 1940 assured Roosevelt four more years as president to meet both the challenges of war abroad and of the isolationists at home. By the end of 1940 war between the United States and the Axis states was drawing perilously closer; ideological and political war between Roosevelt and the isolationists was already raging.

Part III: Victor and Vanquished

Chapter 28

Lend-Lease

The battle between Roosevelt and the isolationists stepped up its furious pace during 1941. As he completed his eighth year in the White House and prepared to begin his third term, FDR faced strident opposition from isolationists. He had the upper hand and, given developments abroad and socioeconomic and political changes at home, his triumph may have been very nearly inevitable. By the time the president died in April, 1945, he had crushed and discredited opponents of his foreign policies. But the isolationists went down fighting. They did not concede defeat before Pearl Harbor. And throughout their lives most leading isolationists continued to believe that they had been right on foreign affairs and had been justified in their indictments of Roosevelt, his policies, and his methods.

Isolationist leadership changed some during the Roosevelt years, but there was much continuity. Senator William E. Borah had died early in 1940, and Senator Ernest Lundeen was killed in a plane crash later that same year. In 1936, Republican Senator James Couzens had lost his primary bid for another term and died before the general election. Lynn J. Frazier lost his Senate seat in 1940. Senators Hiram Johnson and Arthur Capper continued to speak and vote against Roosevelt's policies, but they were some seventy-five years old and no longer commanded the strength and energy required to battle so effectively as before. Senator George W. Norris did not entirely depart his earlier foreign policy perspectives, but advancing years, devotion to Roosevelt, and his changing views substantially removed him from noninterventionist ranks.

Nonetheless, most prominent isolationist leaders continued their battle against Roosevelt and his foreign policies with increased aggressiveness. And new spokesmen emerged to fill gaps left by those who had wearied or fallen in the battle. Gerald P. Nye, Robert M. La

Follette, Jr., Bennett Champ Clark, and Arthur H. Vandenberg had been among the younger Senate isolationists; they had gained increased experience and legislative know-how by the time Roosevelt began his third term. Nye replaced Borah on the Foreign Relations Committee, joining Johnson, Capper, La Follette, Vandenberg, White, Shipstead, Clark, Reynolds, and Gillette on the noninterventionist side in that powerful Senate committee. David I. Walsh continued as chairman of the Senate Naval Affairs Committee. In the 1930s Senator Burton K. Wheeler had focused his energies largely on domestic affairs, but from 1940 onward he was one of the more able and outspoken noninterventionist leaders. Robert A. Taft, D. Worth Clark, William Langer, and C. Wayland Brooks came on the Senate scene later than the others, but they were no less active in opposing the president's foreign policies. In 1940 voters in West Virginia ousted young Rush Holt from the Senate, but he was as outspoken against intervention out of office as he had been in. Congressmen Hamilton Fish, Karl E. Mundt, Dewey Short, and others continued their battles against intervention, and Fish was the ranking minority member of the House Foreign Affairs Committee. The newly organized America First Committee under the leadership of General Robert E. Wood provided a public forum through which many thousands of people outside of Congress opposed Roosevelt's policies. Older pacifist organizations shared in those efforts. Colonel Robert R. McCormick's *Chicago Tribune* and the newspapers of William Randolph Hearst battled against the president and his policies. And Colonel Charles A. Lindbergh was the most prominent, controversial, and formidable opponent of Roosevelt's foreign policies.

By 1941 the isolationists were fighting a losing battle. The president relentlessly drove them back in engagement after engagement. The Japanese attack on Pearl Harbor shattered them. By the time Roosevelt died near the end of World War II, the isolationists were a battered remnant shorn of the power and prestige they had once commanded. They never gave up, but Roosevelt won his war against them as decisively as he led the United States toward victory in war against the Axis.

In the course of that torrid contest Roosevelt was even more successful in destroying the public image of leading isolationists than in reducing their numbers. The terrifying Axis challenges from abroad and Roosevelt's inspiring leadership at home did not cause most leading isolationists to change their opinions or abandon their struggles; millions of Americans continued to believe that the isolationists were right. But those Axis challenges and Roosevelt's leadership did combine to shatter the more attractive public image that isolationist leaders had enjoyed earlier. By the time Roosevelt began his third term, isolationists were widely viewed as narrow, self-serving, partisan, conservative, antidemocratic, anti-Semitic, pro-Nazi, fifth columnist, and even treasonous. That image distorted the truth, but it formed nonetheless. Roosevelt and his followers helped create that jaundiced view, and it contributed to the declining status and power of isolationism and isolationists then and later.

In 1939 isolationists had predicted that repeal of the arms embargo would be followed by proposals to repeal the "cash" requirement on sales to belligerents, and then by repeal of the "carry" provision. They were correct. After the election of 1940 the administration gave growing thought to the policies it should follow when Great Britain no longer had enough cash to pay for goods it needed. Late in November British Ambassador Lord Lothian warned of the seriousness of his country's financial situation. On December 7, 1940, in a long letter to President Roosevelt, Prime Minister Winston Churchill described Britain's needs in detail and warned that the time was coming when England would "no longer be able to pay cash." Reminding the president "that the defeat of the Nazi and Fascist tyranny is a matter of high consequence to the people of the United States and to the Western Hemisphere," Churchill expressed confidence that Roosevelt would find the "ways and means" to cope with the crisis.[1]

His letter reached the president while he was relaxing aboard the U.S.S. *Tuscaloosa*. FDR was aware of Britain's financial problems, but Churchill's letter and the opportunities for reflective thought while cruising in the Caribbean helped Roosevelt draw his thoughts together on the matter. At his press conference on December 17, after his return to Washington, the president emphasized the necessity for doing everything possible to help Britain. Though the details had not yet been worked out, Roosevelt described his plan "to eliminate the dollar sign" in aiding Great Britain. Using an analogy that Harold Ickes had suggested to him earlier, Roosevelt compared his lend-lease plan to lending one's garden hose to help a neighbor put out a fire in his home. The president said the plan would not take the United States into the war any more than it already was.[2]

On December 29, the president broadcast a fireside chat to the nation. In powerfully moving terms he warned of the dangers posed by Axis aggression. "If Great Britain goes down," the president said, "the Axis powers will control the continents of Europe, Asia, Africa,

Australasia, and the high seas—and they will be in a position to bring enormous military and naval resources against this hemisphere." In that event, Roosevelt said, all the Americas "would be living at the point of a gun. He pointed out that the distance from Dakar in Africa to Brazil in South America was "less than from Washington to Denver, Colorado—five hours for the latest type of bomber," and that "at the North end of the Pacific Ocean America and Asia almost touch each other." According to the president even then the United States had "planes that could fly from the British Isles to New England and back again without refueling." He warned that America could not escape the danger "by crawling into bed and pulling the covers over our heads."[3]

With the isolationists in mind, Roosevelt warned against "American citizens, many of them in high places, who, unwittingly in most cases, are aiding and abetting the work of these [foreign] agents. I do not charge these American citizens with being foreign agents. But I do charge them with doing exactly the kind of work that the dictators want done in the United States." In his opinion "a nation can have peace with the Nazis only at the price of total surrender." He called talk of a negotiated peace "Nonsense!"[4]

President Roosevelt promised that there was "far less chance of the United States getting into war, if we do all we can now to support the nations defending themselves against attack by the Axis than if we acquiesce in their defeat, submit tamely to an Axis victory, and wait our turn to be the object of attack in another war later on." According to the president, there was "no demand for sending an American Expeditionary Force outside our own borders. There is no intention by any member of your Government to send such a force. You can, therefore, nail any talk about sending armies to Europe as deliberate untruth. Our national policy is not directed toward war. Its sole purpose is to keep war away from our country and our people." In moving terms the president told the American people, "We must be the great arsenal of democracy."[5]

In presenting his lend-lease idea in his annual message to Congress on January 6, 1941, the president was even more direct in his attacks on isolationism and more sweeping in his utopian internationalism. He told the Congress, "Today, thinking of our children and of their children, we oppose enforced isolation for ourselves or for any other part of the Americas." He charged that it was "immature—and incidentally, untrue—for anybody to brag that an unprepared America, single-handed, and with one hand tied behind its back, can hold off the whole world." He warned, "We must always be wary of those who with sounding brass and a tinkling cymbal preach the 'ism' of appeasement." Roosevelt denounced "slackers or trouble makers in our own midst" and proposed in dealing with them "first, to shame them by patriotic example, and, if that fails, to use the sovereignty of Government to save Government."[6]

The president asked Congress "for authority and for funds sufficient to manufacture additional munitions and war supplies of many kinds, to be turned over to those nations which are now in actual war with aggressor nations. . . . The time is near when they will not be able to pay for them all in ready cash. We cannot, and we will not, tell them that they must surrender, merely because of present inability to pay for the weapons which we know they must have."[7]

The most moving and quoted part of the president's annual message was his call for "a world founded upon four essential human freedoms"—freedom of speech and expression, freedom of worship, freedom from want, and freedom from fear. He called for the accomplishment of each of the four freedoms "everywhere in the world." He said it was "no vision of a distant millennium. It is a definite basis for a kind of world attainable in our own time and generation."[8]

The initiatives that led to lend-lease came from England's Winston Churchill and Lord Lothian; the idea was Roosevelt's; the actual drafting of the legislation was accomplished in Morgenthau's Treasury Department, particularly by Edward H. Foley and Oscar S. Cox; and as with most of the bolder efforts to aid Britain, Hull's State Department was out of the center of things. Cordell Hull's doctrinaire internationalism was decidedly antiisolationist, but he was cautious in dealing both with isolationists in America and with the Axis states abroad. Always bolder against the Axis abroad and the isolationists at home were Secretary of the Treasury Henry Morgenthau, Jr., Secretary of the Interior Harold L. Ickes, Secretary of War Henry L. Stimson, Secretary of Navy Frank Knox, and Harry L. Hopkins. Although Hull continued as secretary of state and although Roosevelt moved less boldly than militant interventionists preferred, it was to Morgenthau, Ickes, Stimson, Knox, and Hopkins, among others, that he turned increasingly as he shaped American policies during his third term as president. According to Morgenthau, Roosevelt explained that he wanted the legislation "in the blank check form." That was the way Foley and Cox drafted it.[9]

On January 10, 1941, identical lend-lease bills were introduced in the House of Representatives as H.R. 1776 and in the Senate as S. 275. During the next two months the United States witnessed one of the most spirited and important debates in the history of American foreign affairs. In and out of Congress, Americans argued the need, the merits, and the dangers of the president's proposal. The House Foreign Affairs Committee under the chairmanship of Sol Bloom of New York conducted hearings from January 15 through January 29. The Senate Foreign Relations Committee hearings were delayed a bit by the illness of its chairman, Walter F. George of Georgia; he had won the post after the death of Key Pittman the preceding November. Though neither Bloom nor George was an isolationist, neither ran his committee with the strong hand that interventionists would have preferred. Each provided full opportunities for both proponents and opponents of lend-lease to make themselves heard. Most assumed the bill would pass both houses of Congress by wide margins, probably with clarifying but not crippling amendments attached. Public opinion polls indicated a comfortable but not overwhelming majority of the American people supported lend-lease and that support grew in the course of the debate. The administration was in a strong position and Roosevelt was properly confident of the outcome. The principal concerns were how long it might take and how devisive the deliberations might be.[10]

The isolationists inside and outside of Congress mounted a massive drive against lend-lease. Not since repeal of the arms embargo in the fall of 1939 had noninterventionists worked so hard to try to defeat an administration proposal. Most of them sympathized with Britain and favored aid-short-of-war. But they feared that lend-lease would lead the United States toward involvement in war abroad and toward dictatorship at home. On December 28, General Wood for the America First Committee sent a telegram to President Roosevelt expressing hope that in his fireside chat FDR would reassert his "pre-election statements that under no conditions will you involve our nation in war abroad." The president's broadcast on December 30, however, was not what Wood and America First wanted. The general called Roosevelt's speech "virtually a personal declaration of undeclared war on Germany." On January 11, 1941, General Wood announced that the America First Committee would oppose lend-lease "with all the vigor it can exert." He charged that the president was "not asking for a blank check, he wants a blank check book with the power to write away your man power, our laws and our liberties."

The committee sponsored countless public meetings and broadcasts, distributed thousands of pieces of anti-lend-lease literature, circulated petitions, encouraged members to write letters, helped organize the opposition in Congress, and was represented in both the House and Senate hearings. Guided and encouraged by America First, many thousands of Americans wrote letters to the president and to their congressmen and senators. The White House received much more mail opposing lend-lease than favoring it.[11]

On Friday evening, January 10, Senator Wheeler invited Senator Johnson and eight other noninterventionists for dinner to organize opposition to lend-lease. When Johnson declined to lead the fight, Wheeler agreed to do so. Two days later in a radio debate on "The American Forum of the Air," Senator Wheeler made the most quoted isolationist attack on lend-lease. He called it "the New Deal's triple 'A' foreign policy—it will plough under every fourth American boy." That infuriated Roosevelt. At his next press conference, on January 14, FDR said he regarded Wheeler's statement "as the most untruthful, as the most dastardly, unpatriotic thing that has ever been said. Quote me on that. That really is the rottenest thing that has been said in public life in my generation." The feud between the president and the senator raged from then on.[12]

As ranking minority member of the House Foreign Affairs Committee, Hamilton Fish helped arrange for witnesses to testify against lend-lease. Hanford MacNider and William R. Castle represented America First before the House committee. They both expressed sympathy for Britain, and both favored aid-short-of-war. Both favored building American military defenses. But both feared lend-lease would put the United States into war abroad and would undermine American freedoms. MacNider, a much-decorated hero in World War I and a former commander of the American Legion, said, "No foreign powers nor group of powers will ever attack a prepared America." He feared that enactment of lend-lease "would mean the beginning of the end of the Republic with consequent disaster not only to the American people but to free men everywhere." Castle, who had served as undersecretary of state for President Hoover, called lend-lease a war measure that "signs away our freedom, creates a dictatorship, does not enable us to help Britain more than we are doing now except insofar as it permits the President to ignore such laws as he pleases and thus to make war." He thought the Soviet Union was the only country that would gain from a prolonged war.[13]

The most prominent American to testify against lend-lease was Colonel Charles A. Lindbergh. Not yet a member of America First, he had been conducting his own independent battle against intervention since September, 1939, just after the European war began. He based his noninterventionist arguments partly on his observations during the nearly three and one-half years he and his family lived in England and France from December, 1935, until April, 1939. During those years he had unique opportunities (in cooperation with United States military and diplomatic officials) to inspect military aviation developments on three major visits to Nazi Germany. He also inspected aviation developments in France, the Soviet Union, Czechoslovakia, and England. And for nearly five months in the middle of 1939, at the request of General H. H. Arnold, he served with the United States Army Air Corps helping plan and develop modern military aviation equipment.

In Lindbergh's prepared statement before the House Foreign Affairs Committee on January 23, he discussed "the effect of aviation upon America's position in time of war." He distinguished between air invasion of America on the one hand and "trans-oceanic bombing" on the other. Because of aviation, Lindbergh said, America's position was "greatly strengthened for defense and greatly weakened for attack." He reasoned that an invading army and its supplies would have to be transported by sea and that air power made it "more difficult than ever before for a navy to approach a hostile shore." He said flatly, "I do not believe there is any danger of an invasion of this continent, either by sea or by air, as long as we maintain an army, navy, and air force of reasonable size and in modern condition, and provided we establish the bases essential for defense." He urged construction of an air force of about ten thousand modern fighting planes plus reserves. He pointed out that there had "never been an invasion of enemy territory by air alone." Lindbergh reasoned, "If air invasion alone could be successful, it would have been used by the Germans against England many months ago." He insisted that "an air invasion across the ocean" was "absolutely impossible" at that time or "in any predictable future."[14]

Colonel Lindbergh conceded that it was "perfectly possible, today, to build bombing planes that could cross the ocean, drop several tons of bombs, and return to their starting point" and that such raids "could do considerable damage on peacetime standards." But he thought such raids "would have very little effectiveness on wartime standards." As he explained it, "The cost of trans-oceanic bombing would be extremely high, enemy losses would be large, and the effect on our military position negligible. Such bombing could not begin to prepare the way for an invasion of this continent. He reasoned, "If England is able to live at all with bases of the German air force less than an hour's flight away, the United States is not in great danger across the Atlantic Ocean." He pointed out that "not a single squadron of trans-oceanic bombing planes exists anywhere in the world today."[15]

Turning to the task of invading Hitler's Europe, Colonel Lindbergh believed that "almost every advantage we have in defense would be a disadvantage to us in attack." He did not think it was "possible for either America or Europe to invade the other successfully by air, or even by a combination of air, land, and sea, unless an internal collapse precedes invasion." In that sense, he contended, aviation had "added to America's security against Europe, and to Europe's security against America." In the course of his testimony Lindbergh said that the United States "should go to war with all of our resources" if there were "any attempt to establish a foreign base in North or South America." He favored building a two-ocean navy.[16]

In response to questions, Lindbergh shook many of his listeners when he said that he preferred "to see neither side win" in the war abroad and "would like to see a negotiated peace." He feared that "a complete victory on either side would result in prostration in Europe such as we have never seen." He opposed lend-lease, believing it would be a step away from democracy and a step closer to war. The aviator was on the witness stand for four and one-half hours. When Lindbergh stepped down, Congressman Bloom told him that he had "made one of the best witnesses that this committee could possibly ever hear."[17]

As ranking minority member of the Senate Foreign Relations Committee, Hiram Johnson helped plan and direct opposition to lend-lease in its hearings that began on January 27. He asked individual isolationists on the committee to assume responsibility for questioning one or another of the administration spokesmen. Johnson thought all of the examinations were "poorly conducted," and he tried to "round out" each one at the conclusion.[18]

Senator Johnson also helped arrange for witnesses to testify against lend-lease beginning on February 3. He had some difficulty getting enough qualified and distinguished witnesses for the opposition.[19] As the foreign policy debate grew in intensity, as isolationists came under increasingly damaging attacks, and as their public image grew more tarnished, the fainthearted were reluctant to speak out on the noninterventionist side. Theoretically, freedom of speech prevailed on foreign policy issues, but in practice by 1941 any individual who spoke out on the noninterventionist side was suspect and had to be prepared to have his reputation besmirched and his wisdom and even his loyalty questioned. Individuals who had spent lifetimes building distinguished reputations were reluctant to endanger their public images by speaking out on the wrong side of the debate. By 1941 it took real courage (or brashness) to be identified prominently with the noninterventionist position.

Among those who did testify against lend-lease before the Foreign Relations Committee were Philip La Follette of Wisconsin, Socialist Norman Thomas, historian Charles A. Beard, Hanford MacNider, and Alf M. Landon. General Robert E. Wood testified as national chairman of the America First Committee. And at the invitation of Senator George, Colonel Lindbergh testified before the Senate committee as he had earlier before the House committee. The opponents "ran out of witnesses" by the time the Senate hearings ended on February 9. According to Johnson, "We could have had all sorts of cranks and crackpots, and a couple of these were put upon the stand . . . against my advice, but fortunately they did us no particular harm."[20]

Those who testified against lend-lease in the Senate hearings repeated many of the arguments advanced before the House committee. They particularly objected to the lack of specific limits on the authority it would give the president. Charles A. Beard said the lend-lease bill should be entitled: "All provisions of law and the Constitution to the contrary notwithstanding, an Act to place all the wealth and all the men and women of the U.S. at the free disposal of the President, to permit him to transfer or carry goods to any foreign government he may be pleased to so designate, anywhere in the world, to authorize him to wage undeclared wars for anybody, anywhere in the world, until the affairs of the world are ordered to suit his policies, and for any other purposes he may have in mind now or at any time in the future, which may be remotely related to the contingencies contemplated in the title of this Act." General Wood charged that the bill would give "the President a blank check on the American taxpayers' money for the defense of Britain with no safeguards or checks." He worried about the language in the bill that said, "notwithstanding the provisions of any other law." He urged that American aid be limited in terms of time, countries to be aided, and the amount of money to be spent.[21]

Lindbergh again was the star witness for the opposition as he had been earlier in the House hearings. He opposed lend-lease because he thought it was "a step away from the system of government in which most of us in this country believe" and he believed it would "weaken rather than strengthen our nation." Unlike most isolationists, Lindbergh opposed extending aid to Britain. He thought such aid weakened the United States at home and added to bloodshed abroad without changing the course of the war. In Lindbergh's opinion "An English victory, if it were possible at all, would necessitate years of war and invasion of the continent of Europe." He thought that "would create prostration, famine, and disease in Europe—and probably in America—such as the world has never experienced before." That was why he preferred "a negotiated peace to a complete victory by either side." He thought that Britain was in no position to win the European war. In aiding Britain, Lindbergh said, the United States was "giving up an ideal defensive position in America for a very precarious offensive position in Europe." In closing his prepared statement, Colonel Lindbergh told the Senate committee: "I advocate building strength in America because we can be successful in this hemisphere. I oppose placing our security in an English victory because I believe that such a victory is extremely doubtful. I am opposed to this Bill because I believe it endorses a policy that will lead to failure in war, and to conditions in our own country as bad or worse than those we now desire to overthrow in Nazi Germany. I do not believe that the danger to America lies in an invasion from abroad. I believe it lies here at home in our own midst." In response to questions, Lindbergh said that the United States should not and could not "police the world." He thought many people were "using the phrase 'short of war' to make us take steps that will inevitably lead us to war." He urged a negotiated peace in Europe. He was "against appeasement," but was even "more strongly against an unsuccessful war."[22]

The Foreign Affairs Committee had reported H.R. 1776 favorably to the House of Representatives at the end of January, and the House passed it with clarifying amendments on February 8, 1941 by a vote of 260 to 165. One hundred and thirty-five Republicans, twenty-five Democrats, three Progressives, one Farmer-Laborite, and one from the American Labor Party voted against the bill.[23]

Opponents of lend-lease met in Hiram Johnson's office three days before the Senate debate began. Eight Republicans (Brooks, Capper, Johnson, Nye, Shipstead, Taft, Tobey, and Willis), six Democrats (Bulow, Clark of Idaho, Clark of Missouri, Gillette, Walsh, and Wheeler), and one Progressive (La Follette) met to plan the noninterventionist floor fight. The full Senate began its deliberations on February 17, and the debate lasted some three weeks. Near the end of the second week, fifteen noninterventionist senators met in Gerald Nye's office to plan the final phases of their efforts. Nye was willing to filibuster, but most opposed using that tactic. As the debate dragged on, some proponents of lend-lease considered trying to limit debate through cloture. Senator Vandenberg warned southern Democratic interventionist senators, however, that he would revive the anti-lynching bill if they did.[24]

Senator Nye listed some seventeen drastic powers he contended the president would have under the lend-lease law, including the power "to give away the United States Navy," "to give to foreign governments all our military plans," "to send naval convoys into war zones," "to saddle upon the United States the costs of a foreign government's war," "to ignore or repeal any existing law which the President considers interferes with his conduct of national defense," and "to govern through administrative proclamation." Those were, Nye charged, the powers "of a dictator," and they concealed "the power to take this country into war." When Roosevelt ridiculed the idea that he would ever use all the powers that conceivably could be exercised under the law, Nye then asked why such broad powers should be granted if there was no intention to use them. Nye emphasized his belief that emotions of fear and hate, fostered by propaganda and leadership, were moving the United States toward war. As the debate neared its close, he told the Senate: "What I object to most strenuously in the pending bill is the surrender of constitutional powers by the Congress to the President. . . . I am now more alarmed by the encroachments upon our constitutional status, and the impairment of the regular processes of our Government by the forces within the Government itself, than about possible aggressions against us by potential, but not necessarily probable, foreign foes. . . . What we need in America today are more Nathan Hales and fewer Caesars." He complained that "hatred dominates this hour" and quoted at length from bitter attacks made upon him in the press.[25]

Senator Henrik Shipstead told the Senate that if it approved lend-lease, "we will pay the bill with our money, our resources and the precious blood of American boys." Senator Johnson wrote his son that lend-lease was "a wicked bill" and was "founded upon hypocrisy and put over by misrepresentation." Senator Robert A. Taft and others proposed amendments designed to limit the president's authority, preserve powers for the legislature, and reduce the danger that it might lead to war. The administration accepted certain amendments to increase support on the issue, but it successfully blocked or watered down all that might have emasculated the measure. Writing in his diary on the day of the final vote, Senator Vandenberg described it as "the most tragic hour in 150 years of our history." The day after the Senate vote, Johnson wrote his son: "We assassinated liberty under the pretext of aiding a belligerent in the war."[26]

All during the House and Senate deliberations on lend-lease, countless persons outside of Congress all over the country from every point of view earnestly and even desperately made their views known to members of Congress and to the White House. The Committee to Defend America by Aiding the Allies was inspiring support for lend-lease while the America First Committee and peace groups were marshaling opposition. Meetings, discussions, debates, broadcasts, pamphlets, leaflets, newsreels, articles, and editorials exhorted the American people, and they in turn wrote and telegraphed their legislators and the White House to make their wishes known. Roosevelt and key cabinet members closeted with senators to win or retain their support. It was democracy in action, and no nonviolent method was neglected by either side in the battle for the minds and votes of senators.[27]

On Saturday, March 8, the Senate approved H.R. 1776 by a vote of sixty to thirty-one. The negative votes were cast by seventeen Republicans, thirteen Democrats, and one Progressive. More significant, most of those voting against lend-lease were from agricultural and mining states. Twenty-four of the thirty-one votes were cast by senators from the Middle West, Great Plains, and Far West. One of the important exceptions was George W. Norris of Nebraska, who voted for lend-lease. Five negative votes were from New England, one from Pennsylvania, and one from the South (Reynolds of North Carolina).[28]

The Lend-Lease Act that President Roosevelt signed on March 11, 1941, authorized him, "notwithstanding the provisions of any other law" to "sell, transfer title to, exchange, lease, lend, or otherwise dispose of" any "defense article" to "the government of any country whose defense the President deems vital to the defense of the United

States." Only nine senators voted against the first lend-lease appropriation of seven billion dollars on March 24.[29]

Lend-lease was very nearly an act of war by the United States against the Axis; so the isolationists charged, and so the Axis states could have contended if it had been in their interests to do so. Secretary of State Cordell Hull considered it "one of the most revolutionary legislative actions in American history." As President Roosevelt told the annual dinner of the White House Correspondents' Association, the "great debate" on lend-lease "was not limited to the halls of Congress. It was argued in every newspaper, on every wave length, over every cracker barrel in all the land; and it was finally settled and decided by the American people themselves."[30] And so it was. On the president's part, however, the debate was accompanied by attacks on "appeasers" and "defeatists." His appeals for "unity" would have left little room for dissent on the issue. Isolationists in turn railed at his warmongering and his grasp for dictatorial powers. Pending a formal declaration of war (opposed by 80 percent of the American people), isolationists continued their battle against Roosevelt and his foreign policies with undiminished vigor.

Chapter 29

Battle of the Atlantic

Lend-Lease resolved the problems of financing and allocating aid to Britain and to other victims of Axis agression. There remained, however, the task of assuring that American aid actually reached its intended destinations and was not sent to the bottom of the oceans by German bombs or torpedoes. German submarines, surface raiders, and bombers took heavy tolls in the waters around the British Isles and in the North Atlantic. On December 13, 1940, as Roosevelt was shaping his thoughts on lend-lease, Prime Minister Winston S. Churchill wrote the president: "North Atlantic transport remains the prime anxiety. Undoubtedly Hitler will augment his U-boat and air attack on shipping and operate even further into the ocean." Later, in his memoirs, Churchill wrote that "the only thing that ever really frightened me during the war was the U-boat peril. . . . The losses inflicted on our merchant shipping became most grave during the twelve months from July '40 to July '41, when we could claim that the British Battle of the Atlantic was won."[1] During the spring of 1941 the issue of the use of United States naval vessels to escort convoys of merchant ships all or part of the way to England held center stage. President Roosevelt emphasized that delivery of goods to England must be assured. Isolationists insisted that use of United States naval vessels to escort convoys would inevitably lead to shooting incidents, to the loss of American lives, and to war.

Though public opinion overwhelmingly favored aid to Britain, opposition to convoys (stimulated by the America First Committee and isolationist leaders) was sufficiently formidable so that the president equivocated and masked his moves in his efforts to muffle objections. Nonetheless, through Atlantic patrols, occupation of Greenland and Iceland, the shoot-on-sight policy, and repeal of vital provisions of the Neutrality Act, the president and the British got much of what they wanted. By the autumn of 1941 the United States under President Roosevelt was waging an undeclared naval war against German submarines in the Atlantic to assure delivery of aid to Britain. That was accomplished over unrelenting opposition from noninterventionists.[2]

Roosevelt initiated most of his actions under his constitutional authority as commander in chief of American armed forces. The president did not turn to Congress for authority until the autumn of 1941, when he asked for repeal of key portions of the Neutrality Act. By then the undeclared naval war in the Atlantic between the United States Navy and German submarines had grown to the point where it seemed only a matter of time before it became a full-fledged declared war. That was what isolationists feared and opposed.

Steps to bypass shipping restrictions in the Neutrality Act had been initiated as early as 1939. Over objections from isolationists the government allowed merchant ships to change from United States registry to Panamanian registry to avoid "carry" restrictions in cash-and-carry; flying the flag of Panama, those ships could transport products all the way from the United States through the war zones to Great Britain.[3] The destroyer deal announced in September, 1940, provided the British navy with more warships to guard its supply lines. With enactment of lend-lease in March, 1941, the issue came fully to the fore.

Despite their defeat on lend-lease, isolationists determined to continue their battle against Roosevelt's policies that they believed were leading to involvement in war abroad. Senators Wheeler, La Follette, D. Worth Clark, Shipstead, Clyde M. Reed of Kansas, and William J. Bulow of South Dakota invited all who had voted against H.R. 1776 to meet in the Senate Office Building on Tuesday evening, April 1, 1941, to plan future noninterventionist efforts. Seventy-one legislators attended the meeting (fourteen senators and fifty-seven representatives). They determined to concentrate their energies against convoys. They named an executive committee to lead the noninterventionist group in a "concerted drive to inform the people of this country of their nearness to war, and to enlist their support to halt the few remaining steps that will lead to actual participation in the fighting."[4]

As a consequence of that meeting several legislators in both houses of Congress introduced anticonvoy resolutions. Republican Senator Charles W. Tobey of New Hampshire carried the main burden in the Senate opposition to convoys. If Tobey's anticonvoy resolution were defeated, Senator Nye proposed a resolution that would have prohibited navy escort of convoys without consent of Congress.[5]

The America First Committee vigorously opposed convoys and formally endorsed Tobey's anticonvoy resolution. An America First pamphlet flatly asserted: "Convoys mean war—a shooting, bloody war." During the spring of 1941 Senators Wheeler, Nye, Clark, and others went on nationwide speaking tours addressing public meetings and rallies sponsored by America First. They rallied against use of the American navy to escort convoys. They quoted President Roosevelt's statement that convoys would mean shooting and that shooting "comes awfully close to war." America First urged members of local chapters to write to the Senate Foreign Relations Committee supporting Tobey's resolution. The White House received much more mail opposing convoys than it got from people supporting them. On April 29 a Senate-House Joint Steering Committee against War composed of Wheeler, La Follette, Taft, Bulow, Hamilton Fish, Karl Mundt, Knute Hill, James F. O'Connor, and James E. Van Zandt called a second major meeting of all senators and representatives opposed to lend-lease and convoys.[6]

President Roosevelt was acutely alert to the need and difficulty of protecting supply lines to Britain. He was receptive to Churchill's appeals. His experience as assistant secretary of the navy during World War I had given him technical knowledge and experience in dealing with problems and possibilities for combating the German submarine threat to convoys. Secretary of War Stimson, Secretary of Navy Knox, and others inside and outside the cabinet pressed him to initiate naval escort for convoys. But in early April he concluded that public opinion was not yet ready to approve convoys and that Congress would reject any resolution authorizing him to use the United States Navy for that purpose. Instead, he initiated a plan to extend America's security zone and patrols to the mid-Atlantic. United States ships and planes began to patrol waters of the North and South Atlantic as far as 25° west longitude and reported the location and movements of German vessels in those waters. At the same time, the United States took over defense of Greenland, a possession of Denmark, in the North Atlantic. The United States removed the Red Sea from the list of combat zones and so enabled American merchant ships to carry products to British forces in Egypt and the Middle East. On April 11 the president informed Churchill of those decisions. So far as possible, Britain moved its convoys west of that line so American patrols could provide maximum assistance.[7]

At his press conference on April 25, President Roosevelt explained his moves as no more than an extension of the patrols that had been operating for "the defense of the American hemisphere" since September, 1939. He did not explain the patrols in terms of defending supply lines to Britain. FDR insisted that patrols were not the same as convoys any more than cows were the same as horses. In the course of that press conference FDR ridiculed "appeasers" and defeatists; he called them "dumb."[8]

With Roosevelt's consent, Secretary of State Hull advised the Foreign Relations Committee under Senator Walter F. George not to approve the Tobey anticonvoy resolution. He wrote that "its passage would be misunderstood abroad." Consequently on Wednesday, April 30, the committee voted thirteen to ten against reporting the resolution to the full Senate. The minority favoring the resolution consisted of Senators Capper, Clark, Gillette, Johnson, La Follette, Nye, Reynolds, Shipstead, Vandenberg, and Frederick Van Nuys of Indiana.[9]

Senator Tobey wanted to force a vote on his resolution by proposing it as an amendment to pending legislation. According to Ruth Sarles, the America First Committee's liaison with Senate leaders, Tobey was "not looked upon as a first-rate strategist, and unfortunately breaks out in a rash of moral indignation at the drop of a hat." Though sharing Tobey's opposition to convoys, Senators Taft, Wheeler, La Follette, Nye, Clark, and others advised against pressing for a vote. They feared that the administration might interpret a vote against the anticonvoy resolution as positive approval for convoys. Secretary of War Stimson had urged that tactic on the president, and Roosevelt had assured him that he could successfully block approval of any anticonvoy resolution. General Wood of America First praised Tobey, but urged him not to press for a vote fearing that if the vote lost, "it might be taken as permission from Senate to President to convoy." Consequently Senator Tobey reluctantly decided not to offer his resolution as an amendment to pending legislation.[10]

Throughout the years preceding American entry into World War II, President Roosevelt was inundated with advice from far and near on what he should do in foreign affairs and how he should do it. He encouraged direct communications from many in and out of government at home and abroad. His White House staff helped draw significant items to his attention. Advice came from pacifists and isolationists. By 1941, however, he was so completely committed to the defeat of the Axis that he blanked out suggestions from isolationists except as they revealed arguments he had to overcome. But even among those who rejected isolationism, there were wide differences of opinion on tactics and timing. Some, including Secretary of State Hull, were decidedly internationalist and anti-Axis, but were cautious and fearful about moving too fast for public opinion or moving too boldly against the Axis. Others, including Secretary of War Stimson, Secretary of Navy Knox, Secretary of Treasury Morgenthau, and Secretary of Interior Ickes, wanted Roosevelt to be more frank and direct in explaining to the American people the dangers abroad and the urgent need for a larger and bolder role by the United States to help defeat the Axis. They grew impatient with FDR's steps-short-of-war approach and believed that defeat of the Axis required full United States military participation in the war. If the president used his marvelous leadership abilities and persuasive powers to explain things as they were, the American people would, they contended, unite behind him to meet the challenge and crush the Axis.[11]

Those patterns of thought and advice were evident on the public scene as well as within the administration. In April, 1941, those patterns led to the organization of Fight for Freedom Incorporated, a new interventionist foreign policy pressure group. The Fight for Freedom Committee grew out of earlier interventionist activities of prominent individuals in the Century Club group in New York City. Francis P. Miller and others from that Century Club group were active in the Council on Foreign Relations in New York. Frederic R. Coudert of that group and Fight for Freedom was legal adviser to the British consul general in New York. Ulric Bell of the *Louisville Courier-Journal* served as chairman of the executive committee of the Fight for Freedom Committee. Episcopal Bishop Henry W. Hobson of southern Ohio was national chairman, and Democratic Senator Carter Glass of Virginia was honorary chairman. The Fight for Freedom Committee won its greatest support in states along the Atlantic seaboard. Much of its leadership identified with the eastern urban establishment and tended to represent relatively elitist perspectives. In 1941 individual leaders of Fight for Freedom had easy access to the Roosevelt administration and had particularly cooperative relations with Secretary Ickes. At the same time, financial resources and access to the administration for the Committee to Defend America eroded somewhat. Both the Committee to Defend America by Aiding the Allies and the Fight for Freedom Committee attacked isolationism and isolationists. Both considered defeat of the Axis essential for the United States. But the Committee to Defend America continued to adhere to Roosevelt's aid-short-of-war formula, while Fight for Freedom insisted that aid-short-of-war would not be enough to defeat the Axis and urged full United States involvement in the wars abroad. The Fight for Freedom Committee and its leaders also were much more aggressive and vicious in their attacks on the America First Committee and on isolationist leaders such as Lindbergh, Wheeler, and Nye. By comparison the Committee to Defend America seemed almost bland.[12]

President Roosevelt's official stance was much like that of the Committee to Defend America; he never publicly advocated a declaration of war until after the Japanese attack on Pearl Harbor on December 7, 1941. As Roosevelt told Morgenthau on May 17, "I am waiting to be pushed into this situation." After the cabinet meeting on May 23, Secretary Stimson wrote in his diary that he was worried "because the President shows evidence of waiting for the accidental shot of some irresponsible captain on either side to be the occasion of his going to war."[13] Though Roosevelt continued to adhere to his tried and tested aid-short-of-war formula, by 1941 his closest advisers and confidants shared the general approach of the Fight for Freedom Committee.

In May, 1941, Roosevelt was buffeted by extreme interventionists who were impatient with what they saw as his excessive caution, indecision, and reluctance to lead. He was troubled both by the restiveness of extreme interventionists (bolstered by creation of Fight for Freedom, Inc.) and by attacks from isolationists (bolstered late in April when Colonel Charles A. Lindbergh began speaking at huge America First rallies across the country). Roosevelt was tired and ill with a persistent cold. While confined to bed, he read many letters (often from prominent people) urging him to lead more boldly. Among those pressing him to lead were Henry L. Stimson, Harold L. Ickes, Adlai E. Stevenson, Lewis W. Douglas, James B. Conant, Felix Frankfurter, Thomas W. Lamont, Samuel Eliot Morison, Hamilton Fish Armstrong, William C. Bullitt, Reinhold Niebuhr, and many others. For example, on April 28 Ickes wrote Roosevelt: "The Lindberghs and the Wheelers and the Nyes are carrying on what appears to be a well financed and carefully planned campaign. They are preaching defeatism. . . . Only you can give leadership and direction to the moral forces of the country, which in my opinion, are more important than the armed forces." On May 1, Professor Morison of Harvard University wrote FDR that he wished "we might move a little faster toward a full partnership in the war, which seems to be necessary if the Axis is not to win." He thought "that a strong message to Congress, based on the Japanese 'peace terms' and on the abundant evidence in possession of the State Department on Axis designs toward us, would be the way to obtain authorization for an all-out naval and air patrol of the Atlantic, or a declaration of war." On May 19, Thomas W. Lamont of J. P. Morgan and Company wrote to the president reporting a conversation with Morgan in which the New York financier had said "the people were awaiting a fresh call to action" and had quoted Paul's words from the New Testament: "For if the trumpet give an uncertain sound who shall prepare himself for the battle?" On hearing of Morgan's comments, according to Lamont, Eve Curie had exclaimed, "Ah yes, is it not amusing? The Morgans getting at Roosevelt through God!" On May 21, William C. Bullitt wrote to FDR: "There is a desire to know the facts—*from you*—, and an intense desire to know what you think ought to be done, and a readiness to follow you wherever you may lead." On May 24, Stimson wrote the president: "The people of the United States are looking to you then to lead and guide them in a situation in which they are now confused but anxious to follow you. Under these circumstances I think it would be disastrous for you to disappoint them. They are not looking for a statement of expedients or halfway measures." Many others added their pens and voices to the effort to move Roosevelt to bolder leadership against the Axis—and against the isolationists.[14]

Writing for a British audience, American news commentator Raymond Gram Swing analyzed FDR's situation thoughtfully at the time: "If he should assume the leadership now, and appear to be 'taking' the country into war, the public would turn on him later, and reproach him for having brought the country to its dark hours. At such times, the only possibility of maintaining unity and morale is that the President shall not have whipped up sentiment for the war, that he should appear to have yielded to public insistence, and that the war should be an enterprise of partnership, rather than something entered at his behest. . . . America must come in, if it comes, after full discussion, with a feeling of having known the facts, and having been allowed to make up its mind. That is the democratic way. It is the way which Roosevelt understands and values, not only as an ideal, but as the hardest kind of political realism. . . . Impatience with Roosevelt in American political life, now paradoxically becomes part of the Roosevelt strategy. He needs all the impatience which can be mustered. The more his friends are in anguish about his inscrutable delay, the better they serve him. . . . He feels that the public is not yet aware enough of the dangers and the gravity of the hour for him to move now." Roosevelt's friend and confidant Harry Hopkins noted Swing's analysis and had it placed with other materials they would use in preparing the president's next speech.[15]

After conferring with the president in his bedroom in mid-May, FDR's speechwriter Robert E. Sherwood thought he did not seem ill. He asked Roosevelt's personal secretary Missy Le Hand what was wrong with him. She responded, "What he's suffering from most of all is a case of sheer exasperation." His illness and exasperation (and perhaps his own personal uncertainties) led FDR to postpone until May 27 the Pan American Day speech he had been scheduled to deliver on May 14. The postponement drew increased attention to the speech. With help from Hopkins, Rosenman, Sherwood, Hull, Welles, Berle, Stimson, and Frankfurter, the speech went through several drafts before FDR delivered it on Tuesday evening, May 27.[16]

In his address President Roosevelt did not go so far as the more extreme interventionists wanted, but it was a powerful oration that left no doubt about his conception of the Nazi menace. He explained that the Nazis were waging "a world war for world domination," that "unless the advance of Hitlerism" were "forcibly checked" the Western Hemisphere would "be within range of the Nazi weapons of destruction." He warned of the oppressive terms a victorious Hitler would impose.[17]

The president told his listeners that the Axis states could "never achieve their objective of world domination unless they first obtain control of the seas. . . . and to achieve it, they must capture Great Britain." The Axis would be defeated, however, if it failed to gain control of the seas. He proposed to meet the Nazi challenge on the seas by speeding and increasing America's shipbuilding program and "by helping to cut down the losses on the high seas."[18]

Roosevelt said American forces were only for defense "to repel attack." But he defined "attack" in terms of "the lightning speed of modern warfare." "Our Bunker Hill of tomorrow may be several thousand miles from Boston." He announced, therefore, that the United States had extended patrols in the Atlantic and was steadily adding more ships and planes to that patrol. He emphasized that "the delivery of needed supplies to Britain" was "imperative" and that it "can be done; it must be done; and it will be done."[19]

Roosevelt warned against "a small group of sincere, patriotic men and women whose real passion for peace has shut their eyes to the ugly realities of international banditry and to the need to resist it at all costs." In nearly the same breath he linked those "sincere, patriotic" noninterventionists with "the enemies of democracy in our midst—the

Bundists, the Fascists, and the Communists, and every group devoted to bigotry and racial and religious intolerance.''[20]

President Roosevelt reasserted "the ancient American doctrine of freedom of the seas" and closed his address by proclaiming "an unlimited national emergency." He said America would "expect all individuals and all groups to play their full parts."[21]

Roosevelt was pleased with the responses to his speech. When Sherwood visited him in his bedroom later that night, FDR was surrounded by hundreds of telegrams he had received. "They're ninety-five percent favorable! And I figured I'd be lucky to get an even break on this speech." The responses were, indeed, favorable; there was a slight rise in the percentage of Americans willing to aid Britain even at the risk of war. But polls also indicated a growing intensity of feeling on both the interventionist and noninterventionist sides of the foreign policy debate.[22]

Isolationists were by no means comforted by the speech. General Wood said it was "the least war-like of any of his utterances since election," but most isolationists were less sanguine. The America First Committee insisted that the declaration of unlimited national emergency did not give the president authority to go to war, restrict freedom to dissent, or to institute convoys. The day after Roosevelt's speech the noninterventionist group headed by Senator Wheeler called a third major meeting of senators and representatives opposing American entry into the war. Some fifty legislators attended the meeting in the old House office building caucus room. They were encouraged by the conviction that the strength of noninterventionist opposition had helped postpone the speech and may have discouraged Roosevelt from announcing the use of the navy to escort convoys. They determined to continue to speak out to give strength to popular antiwar sentiment. Roosevelt watered down the impact of his address by equivocating at his press conference the next day. Roosevelt and the interventionists were gaining ground in their contest for the minds and emotions of the American people. But the isolationists and pacifists did not give up the battle; they fought the president every inch of the way.[23]

In the spring of 1941, as part of the defense of supply lines to Britain, the Roosevelt administration considered taking over defense of Iceland, the Azores, and the Cape Verde Islands. The possibility that American troops might have to fight to get into Portugal's Azores or Cape Verde Islands, combined with the fact that Hitler did not invade either Spain or Portugal, deterred the president from moving there. Iceland, however, lay along the North Atlantic supply lines between the United States and Britain. Occupation of Iceland could strengthen the effectiveness of American naval protection of supply lines that far across the North Atlantic. After meeting conditions set by the government of Iceland and after the initial contingent of American marines reached Iceland, the president on July 7 informed Congress that United States forces were supplementing and would eventually replace the British there. He told Congress that as commander in chief he had ordered the navy to take "all necessary steps . . . to insure the safety of communications in the approaches between Iceland and the United States, as well as on the seas between the United States and all other strategic outposts."[24]

On July 3, four days before the president's announcement and before American forces reached Iceland, Senator Wheeler had called in newsmen to inform them that he had learned that American troops were to embark later in July to take over Iceland. The White House made clear its displeasure at Wheeler's action, and Fight for Freedom called it treasonable.[25]

Though Iceland could as reasonably be seen as an extension of Europe as of America, the administration's action provoked less uproar than it might have expected. But isolationists were quick to respond. John T. Flynn, chairman of the America First chapter in New York and a leading member of the America First national committee, called the president's "audacious act" possibly "the beginning of the end of Constitutional Government in the United States." According to Flynn: "If the President, without the consent of Congress, can occupy Iceland, he can occupy Syria or Ethiopia. He could not do this if the Congress of the United States had not been reduced to the state of a servile shadow of the august institution which it was intended to be under our Republican form of Government." He charged that the move into Iceland was designed "to stick America's neck far out into the European continent" and was "but one more cunning device to try to inch us into the European war." The America First Research Bureau feared that next Roosevelt would insist that the United States occupy Ireland, Norway, or Scotland to protect Iceland. It charged that the occupation of Iceland was "another evasion of the convoy issue" and insisted that is was not essential to American defense. Former President Hoover and Senator Taft explored the possibility of attaching riders to military appropriations confining their use to the Western Hemisphere—presumably not including Iceland, the Azores, or the Cape Verde Islands. A resolution adopted by a national meeting of America First chapter leaders called for removal of American troops from Iceland.[26] As usual, however, FDR prevailed over his opponents.

During the summer of 1941, while the Battle of the Atlantic was raging, the war took on a whole new dimension when Nazi Germany struck east against the Soviet Union. Hitler's decision to loose his blitzkrieg against Soviet forces early on Sunday morning, June 22, 1941, ranked with the attack on Poland in 1939, the Battle of Britain in 1940, the Japanese attack on Pearl Harbor on December 7, 1941, and the dropping of the atomic bombs on Hiroshima and Nagasaki as pivotal events in Word War II. Conceivably a German victory over the Soviet Union might have made the Axis virtually invincible; most experts expected Russia to fall before the German assault. In the summer and autumn of 1941, German forces drove deep into Soviet territory and caused terrible physical destruction and loss of life. By the time it ended four years later, more people had died in the Russo-German war in Eastern Europe (soldiers and civilians on both sides) than in all other parts of World War II combined. Few were prepared to rule out the possibility that a ravenous Nazi Germany, having feasted on Russia and replenished itself from the vast resources in the Soviet Union, might turn once again on the British Isles and eventually on the Western Hemisphere.

In those awful times Prime Minister Churchill for the United Kingdom and President Roosevelt for the United States determined that Hitler's Nazi Germany was still the most dangerous menace to their survival. They saw in the Russo-German war increased hope for the defeat of the Axis, and they promised aid to Joseph Stalin's Soviet Union as it fought for survival against the German assaults. As Churchill phrased it when the Russo-German war began: "I have only one purpose, the destruction of Hitler, and my life is much simplified thereby. If Hitler invaded Hell I would make at least a favourable reference to the Devil in the House of Commons." In a personal letter to editor Fulton Oursler on June 25, Roosevelt concisely revealed his views: "If I were at your desk I would write an editorial condemning the Russian form of dictatorship equally with the German form of dictatorship—but, at the same time, I would make it clear that the immediate menace at this time to the security of the United States lies in the threat of Hitler's armies, and that we should not forget that fact in retaining the immediate objective of the United States, which is to prevent world domination by Hitler." Neither Churchill nor Roosevelt was so pessimistic as their military advisers about Russia's chances for survival in the war. Both determined to aid Communist Russia's

military resistance to Nazi Germany. President Roosevelt's decision
not to invoke the Neutrality Act in the Russo-German war made it
possible for American merchant ships to carry war goods through
submarine-infested waters all the way to Soviet ports in both Europe
and Asia. He sent Harry Hopkins to Russia to confer with Stalin, and
lend-lease aid was soon on its way. Neither the English nor Americans
had much love for Communist Russia, but they generally supported
their government's priorities in aiding Soviet military resistance to
Nazi Germany.[27]

American noninterventionists, however, took a different view of
the Russo-German war and its significance for the United States. They
saw it as one more reason the United States should not enter the European war. Lindbergh and other isolationists were skeptical of viewing
the conflict abroad as a war for democracy; with Communist Russia
fighting on the same side as Great Britain, they found it even more
difficult to see it as a war for democracy. Though they shared the
widespread skepticism about the Soviet Union's ability to check Nazi
Germany in war, they opposed extending aid to that totalitarian Communist regime. They preferred to sit back and let the two hated
dictatorships destroy each other. The idea of defending freedom and
democracy by aiding Stalin's totalitarian Communist regime seemed
ludicrous and almost profane to them.

The day after Germany attacked the Soviet Union, the America
First executive committee approved a statement issued by General
Robert E. Wood: "The entry of Communist Russia into the war certainly should settle once and for all the intervention issue here at
home. The war party can hardly ask the people of America to take up
arms behind the red flag of Stalin. With the ruthless forces of dictatorship and aggression now clearly aligned on both sides the proper
course for the United States becomes even clearer. We must continue
to build our own defenses and take no part in this incongruous European conflict. . . . In the name of the four freedoms are we now to
undertake a program of all-out aid to Russia" Senator Arthur Capper
of Kansas wrote: "I am against Hitler and hope he will finally be
crushed. I have no sympathy for Stalin. The latest developments confirm me in the conviction I long have held that these European wars
are not our wars. We should stay out of them." Senator Hiram Johnson wrote his son: "Russia has been the admitted awful example of a
ruthless tyranny against which we have ever inveighed. I hasten to add
that I consider Hitler no better, and so far as I am concerned, I would
leave these two scoundrels Hitler and Stalin to fight it out." In a radio

broadcast former President Herbert Hoover said that the collaboration between Britain and Russia in war "makes the whole argument of our joining the war to bring the four freedoms to mankind a gargantuan jest." Some forty Senate and House isolationists generally agreed with those reactions when they held another major meeting on July 1.[28]

In a network broadcast Congressman Hamilton Fish of New York said: "I am opposed to Nazi-ism, and can think of nothing too bad to say against its aggressions and ideology, but there is one thing worse, and that is the bloody hand of Communism. American mothers will not willingly sacrifice their sons to make the world safe for Communism, or to fight and die for the red flag, Joe Stalin and world revolution under the guise of democracy." He said it was "preposterous to think of America being aligned with Soviet Russia and Joseph Stalin as our pal and comrade, with his hands dripping with blood of murdered priests and nuns and the same dagger in his hand which he plunged into the backs of Poland, Latvia, Estonia, Lithuania and our friend the little honest Republic of Finland." On July 1, at an America First rally in San Francisco, Charles A. Lindbergh thought it incongruous that "the idealists who have been shouting against the horrors of Nazi Germany, are now ready to welcome Soviet Russia as an ally." He charged that Communist Russia's "record of cruelty, bloodshed, and barbarism" was "without parallel in modern history." Lindbergh opposed alliances with any foreign countries, but said he "would a hundred times rather see my country ally herself with England, or even with Germany with all her faults, than with the cruelty, the godlessness, and the barbarism that exist in Soviet Russia." Before an America First audience in Brooklyn, Senator Bennett Champ Clark asked if anyone could "conceive of American boys being sent to their deaths singing 'Onward Christian Soldiers' under the bloody emblem of the Hammer and Sickle."[29]

Communists dutifully followed the party line. Before the Russo-German war when the Soviet Union was neutral, American Communists were noninterventionists; when Germany attacked the Soviet Union, they immediately became fervent interventionists. On June 21, they saw Roosevelt as a warmonger; by June 23 William Z. Foster at the head of the Communist party called on the American people to give "full support and cooperation with the Soviet Union in its struggle against Hitlerism." But few Americans were swayed by Communist appeals.[30]

The majority, however, followed President Roosevelt's leadership

in supporting aid-short-of-war to the Soviet Union's military resistance to German aggression. The Russo-German war complicated ideological alignments, but it did not significantly enhance isolationist
strength. The United States extended aid to the Soviet Union, Americans applauded Russian courage in fighting German aggression, and
they worried that Nazi Germany might triumph over the Soviet Union
as it had done over other continental states.[31] The foreign policy debate in the United States (and the contest between Roosevelt and the
isolationists) moved on to new concerns and new controversies.

In July and August, Roosevelt contested with isolationists on the
issue of draft extension. The original Selective Service Act of 1940
provided that draftees would serve one year and would not be required
to serve outside the Western Hemisphere. Secretary of War Stimson
and Army Chief of Staff General George C. Marshall pressed for removal of those restrictions. Both Roosevelt and the isolationists had
tactical difficulties on the issue. Roosevelt agreed with Stimson and
Marshall but was troubled by the political problems. In January,
1941, he recommended postponing reconsideration of the selective
service legislation for six months.[32] Deliberations early in July among
administration, legislative, and military leaders made clear both the
army's desires and the political difficulties. It appeared that Congress
would not remove the ban on using selectees outside the Western
Hemisphere. That elicited from Roosevelt sharp criticism of the
America First Committee and its activities, but he decided not to press
for that change in the law. The isolationists won that skirmish without
having to fight it out on the floor of Congress. With prodding from
Stimson and Marshall, however, the president did seek authority from
Congress to extend the period of service for each draftee for as much
as eighteen months beyond the year called for by the original legislation. Even that time extension faced strong opposition, particularly in
the House of Representatives.[33]

Most isolationists and all pacifists opposed any extension of selective service—either length or place of service. General Wood, national
chairman of America First, however, had misgivings about all-out opposition to changes sought by the army and the Roosevelt administration. A graduate of West Point and a retired professional military officer who had served overseas in the Philippines, Panama, and later in
Europe during World War I, General Wood was no pacifist. He favored military preparedness to defend United States security in the
Western Hemisphere. He opposed any new American Expeditionary
Force overseas, but he did not want to oppose changes that army

leaders believed were essential for American defense in the Western Hemisphere. He feared that opposition to revision of the selective service law would make America First vulnerable to charges that it was obstructing American defense efforts.[34]

Early in July, General Wood issued a statement for America First opposing repeal of the ban on overseas service for draftees. "Here at last is the Administration's bald request for a new A.E.F. . . . The net effect of the proposal is to empower the President to send American troops to wage undeclared war in whatever part of the world he may choose." It would, he contended, be "a fraud upon America's one million draftees" who had been inducted under legislation "which excluded service overseas."[35]

On the question of extending the period of service, however, General Wood took a different position from many local chapters and grass-roots members. Largely because of General Wood, the America First national committee did not take an official position on extending the period of service. In bulletins to local chapters the America First national headquarters in Chicago explained: "This is a military problem involving the defense of the United States. The America First Committee has always stood for as strong a national defense as possible, while opposing any legislation which might mean sending our boys to foreign battlefields." When John T. Flynn of the New York chapter objected to that policy, R. Douglas Stuart, Jr., wrote back explaining: "The policy [was] laid down by General Wood. The General's decision that the America First Committee should not take a position opposing the Chief of Staff of the United States Army was based on the feeling that this is an issue which would impress the public as being one of defense rather than foreign policy."[36]

In practice, however, the America First Committee was not really neutral on the issue. Even members of the staff at America First national headquarters provided ambiguous counsel. In writing to chapter leaders one staff member explained: "The National Committee has taken no stand on the extension of service for draftees. However, I suggest personally that you push every single effort to stop the passage of this extension of service proposal. I think we can win this fight and if we do, it will be a terrific blow against the administration forces." Most America First members and chapters leaders shared his general views, as did pacifist organizations. Many local chapters, including the New York chapter under Flynn, flatly opposed any changes in the selective service law—including any change that would lengthen the period of service for draftees.[37]

The America First Research Bureau in Washington, D.C., under Ruth Sarles prepared *Did You Know* releases arguing against all the changes sought by the Army and the administration. It charged that removal of the ban against service outside the Western Hemisphere would "authorize a new A.E.F. should the Administration desire it. . . . It is designed to give the President power to put the country into war." The research bureau argued against extending the period of service because it would not be fair to those who went into the army expecting to serve only one year. The research bureau insisted that the army would not be crippled if draftees were discharged at the end of one year. According to its calculations, "Only 19,327 men need be mustered out before January, 1942, and those only in November and December 1941. By then, those men can be replaced by new selectees who by then will have had more training than the selectees who were inducted between April and June, 1941, now have." It concluded that there seemed "no justification for the proposed Resolutions, unless military ventures into foreign lands are planned."[38]

The America First Research Bureau also argued that in the summer of 1941 the danger of any Axis military invasion of the United States or the Western Hemisphere seemed "far less that it was a year ago—if there was any danger then." In a *Did You Know* release it contended: "Hitler can make no attempt to invade this Hemisphere as long as Britain holds out. Any attempt by Hitler to invade Britain seems indefinitely postponed. To attack America, Hitler must first defeat not only Britain but the Soviet Union with its 182,000,000 people and its huge Red Army. And a defeated Soviet Union would have to be policed by hundreds of thousands of Nazi troops. A year ago, France had already fallen and British cities were being blasted by the Luftwaffe. This summer the RAF has bombed Germany far more severely than the Luftwaffe has bombed Britain. This summer British shipping losses have been dropping. A year ago we did not possess the new Atlantic bases. A year ago our own armament program was not even a book of blueprints, but now it is beginning to take effective shape—effective for defense at least." It insisted that America need fear no invasion by way of Siberia and Alaska, Iceland and Greenland, the Caribbean, or by way of Dakar and Brazil.[39]

The New York chapter's *America First Bulletin* also challenged the administration's allegation that the United States was in greater danger than it had been when the original selective service legislation was adopted in 1940. "A year ago not a soldier on the continent—save the Greeks—was opposing Germany. Today Russia's millions have joined England. Yet the President says the situation is worse. If Russia cannot beat Germany with five or six million soldiers right on her own ground, with her own defenses built through the years and within a short distance of her bases and supplies, how many will we have to send to Europe to beat Germany 3,000 to 4,000 miles from our bases and fighting on her own ground?''[40]

In the debate over draft extension Roosevelt and the isolationists conceived of "defense" in radically different terms. The America First Committee and other isolationists referred to the military forces necessary to repel any attacks on or attempted invasions of the United States or the Western Hemisphere. In contrast, President Roosevelt conceived of "defense" in terms of the military forces needed to defeat Hitler and Nazi Germany in Europe, a task that he considered essential to American defense and world peace.

Secretary Stimson, General Marshall, and others pressed Roosevelt to send a message to Congress to get legislative action on draft extension. He did so on July 21. In urging extension of the period of service for selectees, the president insisted that the international situation was "far more grave than it was a year ago." He reminded Congress of the "German conquests or attacks—which have continued uninterruptedly throughout several years—all the way from the coup against Austria to the present campaign against Russia" and contended that "each elimination of a victim has brought the issue of Nazi domination closer to this hemisphere." He argued that the danger to American national security was "infinitely greater" at that time than it had been a year before.[41]

Leading noninterventionists in the Senate and House of Representatives who cooperated with America First battled vigorously against draft extension. They had little chance to win in the Senate, but the contest in the House of Representatives promised to be very close. At a meeting on July 30, Senator Nye and other isolationist legislators determined to make a fight of it in the Senate to encourage noninterventionists in the House, where they had a real chance to defeat the administration on the issue.[42]

General Marshall was the most important administration spokesman for draft extension at the hearings before the Senate Military Affairs Committee under the chairmanship of isolationist Senator Robert R. Reynolds of North Carolina. General Wood did not testify, but Major General Thomas S. Hammond of the America First executive committee did. He testified as an individual rather than as a spokesman for America First. He had retired from military duty with the Illinois National Guard in 1940. He had had twenty-five years of military service, including combat experience in France during World War I. In his Senate testimony on July 24 General Hammond emphasized the need for a well-trained and fully equipped army for American defense. He thought "a mobile field Army of 500,000 men, thoroughly trained and fully equipped" would be "sufficient to defend this hemisphere from any foreseeable threat." He proposed changes to make the Army more attractive to volunteers. He favored selective service for one year of duty, but he opposed lengthening the period of service for draftees unless the United States was directly involved in war.[43]

Proponents of draft extension had no difficulty getting the legislation voted favorably out of the Senate Military Affairs Committee. On August 7, after a brief but spirited debate, the Senate approved draft extension forty-five to thirty. Both support and opposition came from all sections of the country, and from both major parties. The greatest opposition came from the Middle West; a majority of senators from the Middle West, Great Plains, Mountain states, and Far West voted against draft extension. The largest support for draft extension came from the South, the Middle Atlantic states, and New England. Outside the interventionist South, the total Senate vote against draft extension exactly equaled the vote for draft extension—twenty-eight to twenty-eight. More than two-thirds of the Democratic senators voting supported draft extension, while nearly two-thirds of the Republicans voting opposed it. Nonetheless, more Democrats than Republicans voted against draft extension; sixteen Democrats, thirteen Republicans, and one Progressive voted nay.[44]

The contest in the House of Representatives was much closer. On August 12 the House approved draft extension by a margin of just 1 vote, 203 to 202. The voting patterns in the House were similar to those in the Senate, but there were differences. Again, the largest vote for draft extension was from the South and the largest vote against was from the Middle West. Party lines were drawn more sharply with most Democrats voting for extension and most Republicans voting against (the Democratic vote was 182 for and 64 against; the Republican vote was 132 against and 21 for). But in the House of Representatives New England congressmen divided their votes equally for and against draft extension (14 to 14), and congressmen from Middle Atlantic states cast a majority against draft extension (56 nay to 42 yea). A substantial majority of all congressmen outside the South opposed draft extension (196 nay, 102 yea). The South provided

101 of the votes needed to adopt draft extension; without the votes of conservative southern Democrats draft extension would have been defeated. The Democratic president could hardly take comfort in the fact that sixty-four members of his own party voted against him on that issue less than four months before the Japanese attack on Pearl Harbor.[45] Extreme interventionists such as Stimson, Knox, Morgenthau, Ickes, and the Fight for Freedom Committee could urge the president to lead more boldly and frankly in interventionist directions, but FDR's political antennae were more sensitively tuned than theirs were. Bolder leadership might have moved the United States to war against the Axis sooner. But that might have been accomplished only after a bitter battle that could have confronted the Axis states with a battered president leading a divided and weakened people; Presidents Lyndon B. Johnson and Richard M. Nixon were to do that a generation later in Vietnam, but that was not Franklin D. Roosevelt's way.

After compromising between what he wanted and what he thought he could get, Roosevelt won his contest with the isolationists on draft extension. And he moved on in internationalist-interventionist directions, both through secret presidential initiatives and openly through Congress. At the very time the Senate and House were deliberating and voting on draft extension, Roosevelt and his top military advisers were meeting secretly at sea in Placentia Bay off Argentia, Newfoundland with Prime Minister Churchill and his top advisers. That conference produced the famous Atlantic Charter for the public record, but its secret deliberations were even more significant as Roosevelt and Churchill planned Anglo-American cooperation against the Axis powers in Europe and the Pacific.[46]

The closeness of his victory on draft extension did not encourage Roosevelt to move more boldly and openly in interventionist directions against isolationist opposition. Despite their defeat, isolationists felt encouraged. The young America First national director, R. Douglas Stuart, Jr., phrased the feelings well when he wrote: "The vote on the draft extension in the House was the most encouraging thing that has happened in many a moon. It turned out perfectly. If the bill had been defeated by one vote, the interventionist press throughout the country would have gone wild condemning Congress for sabotaging national defense. It would have served as an excuse for the President for more executive action toward war. As it turned out, the vote was a sharp rebuff to the Administration and a warning that Congress will not stand for war. The confidence and morale on the part of the members of Congress who share our point of view is infinitely higher than it had been in the past nine months." Stuart may have been whistling in the dark a bit to bolster noninterventionist morale, but there was much truth in what he wrote.[47]

Nazi Germany under Hitler tried to avoid shooting incidents involving American ships in the Atlantic. During the first twenty months of the European war, no ship flying the American flag was attacked or sunk by German submarines or airplanes. Nonetheless, given German efforts to cut Britain's supply lines and American efforts to help assure delivery of aid to Britain, it was virtually inevitable that sooner or later American ships would come under attack in the Battle of the Atlantic and that American lives would be lost. On May 21, 1941, the *Robin Moor*, an American freighter, was torpedoed and sunk in the South Atlantic by a German submarine. The submarine commander ordered the passengers and crew into lifeboats before sinking the ship. There was no loss of life in the incident, but the survivors endured a fearful experience until they were rescued at sea a couple of weeks later.[48]

When the public learned of the sinking, Senator Nye urged the United States to "abandon any assertion of freedom of the seas" and to "adopt a mind-our-own business policy." He said the sinking of the *Robin Moor* was "unfortunate" but was what Americans "might have expected and precisely what our foreign policy has been inviting." America First pointed out that the ship was carrying contraband and feared that it was the "incident" that Roosevelt and the interventionists "were waiting and praying for." They cited a newspaper column by the pro-Roosevelt interventionists, Joseph Alsop and Robert Kintner, in which they wrote that Roosevelt was determined "to force the Germans to fire the first shot." Alsop and Kintner also wrote that "the President and the men around him privately hope the [Atlantic] patrol will produce an incident."[49]

News of the *Robin Moor* reached Roosevelt after he had delivered his major address on May 27; he thought it unwise to deliver another speech so soon after. He did, however, send a message to Congress on June 20 portraying the sinking in the worst possible terms. "The total disregard shown for the most elementary principles of international law and of humanity brands the sinking of the *Robin Moor* as an act of an international outlaw." He saw it as "a first step in assertion of the supreme purpose of the German Reich to seize control of the high seas." The president made it clear that the United States would not yield to such intimidation. The sinking of the *Robin Moor* did not arouse Americans to war fervor, but the president used the incident to reemphasize the evil lawlessness and hostile intentions of Nazi Germany.[50]

Other incidents followed. On August 17 the *Sessa*, an American-owned merchant ship flying the Panamanian flag, was torpedoed near Iceland. One of the casualties was an American. On September 4 the *Greer*, an American destroyer, was missed by two torpedoes fired by a German submarine. The *Steel Seafarer* flying the American flag was bombed in the Red Sea on September 5 with no loss of life. Three other American-owned ships flying the Panamanian flag were torpedoed later in September, 1941.[51]

Those episodes, and particularly the attack on the *Greer*, were the occasion for President Roosevelt's most militant speech to that time, his so-called shoot-on-sight speech on September 11. The idea for that speech was not new. Knox, Stimson, Hopkins, Churchill, and others had been urging the president in more militant directions for months. Late in August Churchill sent a gloomy message to Hopkins expressing concern about "the president's many declarations with regard to the United States being no closer to war and having made no commitments." The prime minister did not know "what will happen if England is fighting alone when 1942 comes." Since Hitler generally kept his submarines east of the twenty-sixth meridian, Churchill feared that Hitler would not "help in any way." Hopkins talked to the president about Churchill's cablegram and told FDR "that not only Churchill but all the members of the [British] Cabinet and all the British people I talked to believed that ultimately we will get into the war on some basis or other and if they ever reached the conclusion that this was not to be the case, that would be a very critical moment in the war and the British appeasers might have some influence on Churchill." In a memo drafted just two days after FDR's shoot-on-sight speech, Hopkins explained that the genesis of the speech went back to the first of July after FDR had initiated his North Atlantic patrol. According to Hopkins, Roosevelt had decided on a full security patrol before the end of July and merely used the *Greer* episode as the occasion for announcing it to the American people. Hopkins, Rosenman, and Hull all shared in drafting the speech. Hull thought it too strong and tried to persuade FDR to soften it, but Hopkins and the other hard-liners prevailed.[52]

In his fireside chat broadcast to the nation on Thursday evening, September 11, President Roosevelt told Americans that a German submarine had fired torpedoes at the clearly marked American destroyer *Greer*. He charged that "the German submarine fired first upon this American destroyer without warning, and with deliberate design to sink her." He called the attack "piracy legally and morally." He also told of the sinking of the *Robin Moor*, the sinking of the *Sessa* flying the flag of Panama, and the bombing of the *Steel Seafarer* in the Red Sea. He explained that the incidents were "not isolated," but were "part of a general plan" by the Nazis "to abolish the freedom of the seas." He charged that the Nazi attack on the *Greer* "was one determined step toward creating a permanent world system based on force, on terror, and on murder." According to Roosevelt, "Normal practices of diplomacy—note writing—are of no possible use in dealing with international outlaws who sink our ships and kill our citizens." He promised, "No matter what it takes, no matter what it costs, we will keep open the line of legitimate commerce in these defensive waters." In one of his more dramatic allusions Roosevelt said: "When you see a rattlesnake poised to strike, you do not wait until he has struck before you crush him. These Nazi submarines and raiders are the rattlesnakes of the Atlantic. They are a menace to the free pathways of the high seas. They are a challenge to our sovereignty." He warned, "From now on, if German or Italian vessels of war enter the waters, the protection of which is necessary for American defense, they do so at their own peril. The orders which I have given as Commander in Chief of the United States Army and Navy are to carry out that policy—at once."[53]

The impact of Roosevelt's speech on public opinion was reduced later in September when the Senate Naval Affairs Committee under the chairmanship of isolationist Democrat David I. Walsh of Massachusetts learned from Chief of Naval Operations Admiral Harold R. Stark that the *Greer*, in cooperation with a Royal Air Force bomber, had been trailing the German submarine for hours before the submarine turned on its pursuer. The submarine loosed its torpedoes at the *Greer* after it had been attacked with depth charges dropped by the British airplane in communication with the *Greer*. The American destroyer also attacked the submarine with depth charges.[54]

On October 17 a German submarine torpedoed the *Kearny*, an American destroyer, with the loss of eleven lives. The *Kearny* was the first United States Navy ship actually hit by German torpedoes, and it was the first ship flying the United States flag on which Americans lost their lives from German action before war was declared. On October 31 a German submarine sank the American destroyer *Reuben James* that was helping escort a convoy. It sank quickly with substantial loss of life. It was the first and only American warship sunk by Germany before war was declared. All of those incidents involving American destroyers in clashes with German submarines occurred more than two years after the European war began. Two of those incidents followed the inauguration of Roosevelt's shoot-on-sight policy.[55]

America isolationists saw the incidents and Roosevelt's shoot-on-sight policy as moves toward involvement in foreign war. The day before the president's fireside chat, America First national headquarters sent letters to all chapter chairmen alerting them to possible themes in the president's talk and outlining actions they should take in response to the speech. The executive committee of the New York chapter of America First called the president's speech "an amazing move to arouse hysteria and plunge us into a foreign war, unwanted by the people, as he knows, and needless for national defense." It called Roosevelt's shoot-on-sight policy "a declaration of war by the President." An America First Research Bureau *Did You Know* release on September 13 charged that the speech proclaimed a shooting war that was not justified, circumvented the spirit of the neutrality and lend-lease legislation, and took the war-making powers away from Congress. It explained that the cargo of the *Robin Moor* was 70 percent contraband, that the *Steel Seafarer* was sunk in the Red Sea "only because President Roosevelt had revoked his earlier proclamation under the Neutrality Act declaring the Red Sea a war zone and forbidding American ships to travel there," and that the *Sessa* was not even flying the American flag when sunk. It concluded that those attacks "resulting in no loss of American lives on any ship operating under the American flag, do not justify American participation in a 'shooting war.' "[56]

On September 14, General Wood announced that an "independent group" of fifty-eight prominent Americans endorsed a statement condemning Roosevelt's policies. The statement charged that the president's shoot-on-sight policy was "supported neither by Congressional sanction nor by the popular will. It is authorized by no statute and undermines the Constitutional provision which gives the war power to Congress alone." Among those endorsing the statement in addition to Wood were historian Charles A. Beard, author and actor Irvin S. Cobb, former governor Philip F. La Follette, Yale international law professor Edwin M. Borchard, Alice Roosevelt Longworth, labor leaders William L. Hutcheson and Kathryn Lewis, Dr. Charles Clayton Morrison of the *Christian Century*, Columbia University international law professor Philip C. Jessup, George N. Peek, Mrs. Burton K. Wheeler, and corporation executive Robert R. Young.[57]

After the attack on the *Kearny* General Wood issued a statement urging Americans to withhold judgment on the incident "until all the facts have been fully and frankly disclosed." John T. Flynn, chairman of the New York America First chapter, asked whether Americans thought their war ships could "hunt the ships of any nation and escape attack." He charged that the United States was "asking for these attacks." He urged Americans to realize that they were "the victims of a conspiracy to hurry them into this war." Senator Nye told an America First audience in New Jersey that "these incidents involving the Greer and the Kearny are incidents very largely of our own making and our own inviting. We cannot order our ships to shoot to destroy the vessels of certain belligerent nations and hope at the same time that the ships of those nations are not going to seek to destroy our ships." On November 1 a meeting in Washington, D.C., of more than two hundred leaders of America First chapters unanimously passed resolutions calling on the president to withdraw American troops from Iceland and to order American naval vessels out of the war zones. They charged Roosevelt with deliberately "misrepresenting the facts of the Greer incident, in order to lend some semblance of legality to his shoot on sight order." They urged an investigation by the Senate Naval Affairs Committee of the circumstances surrounding the sinking of the *Reuben James*.[58]

Roosevelt's last major action to assure delivery of aid across the Atlantic to Britain, and his last major aid-short-of-war proposal actually put to a vote in Congress before Pearl Harbor, was the revision of the Neutrality Act in the fall of 1941. On October 9, the president sent a message asking Congress to revise the neutrality legislation to permit the arming of American merchant ships and to allow them to carry products all the way through war zones to belligerent ports. Though not repealing the whole act, those changes essentially would repeal the "carry" part of cash-and-carry, much as lend-lease had, in effect, bypassed the "cash" part. FDR's move had been preceded by long deliberation both in the White House and in Hull's Department of State, as well as by consultation with Senate and House leaders (not including leading isolationists).[59]

In his message (drafted in the State Department) the president pointed out that conditions had "changed violently since the first American Neutrality Act of 1935." He warned that the United States could not defend itself "in Long Island Sound or in San Francisco Bay. That would be too late." He explained that America would defend itself "wherever such defense becomes necessary under the complex conditions of modern warfare." At the same time he insisted that revision of the Neutrality Act would "not leave the United States any less neutral than we are today, but will make it possible for us to defend the Americas far more successfully, and to give aid far more effectively against the tremendous forces now marching toward conquest of the world." He thought it time for the United States "to stop playing into Hitler's hands, and to unshackle our own." He said that Hitler had "offered a challenge which we as Americans cannot and will not tolerate."[60]

Later in October, in a Navy Day address delivered in Washington and broadcast to the nation, President Roosevelt made his strongest speech before Pearl Harbor. In moving terms he emphasized the alarming German attacks on American ships in the Atlantic, with particular attention to the American destroyer *Kearny* on which eleven seamen had died as the result of submarine attack south of Iceland on October 17. To make his message more personal he listed states that had been home to those dead and wounded young Americans—Illinois, Alabama, California, North Carolina, Ohio, Louisiana, Texas, Pennsylvania, Georgia, Arkansas, New York, and Virginia. He said the purpose of the submarine attack had been "to frighten the American people off the high seas—to force us to make a trembling retreat." Roosevelt told his listeners that he had a secret German map outlining South and Central America "as Hitler proposes to reorganize it." He said he also had a document made by Hitler's government as "a plan to abolish all existing religions" and replace them with "an International Nazi Church." The Nazis would use *Mein Kampf* in place of the Bible, and "in place of the cross of Christ will be put two symbols—the swastika and the naked sword. The god of Blood and Iron will take the place of the God of Love and Mercy." He then denounced "some Americans—not many" who continued "to insist that Hitler's plans need not worry us—that we should not concern ourselves with anything that goes beyond rifle shot of our own shores." Once again he urged revision of the Neutrality Act: "Our American merchant ships must be armed to defend themselves against the rattlesnakes of the sea. Our American merchant ships must be free to carry our American goods into the harbors of our friends. Our American merchant ships must be protected by our American Navy." He closed his oration in martial terms: "Today in the face of this newest and greatest challenge of them all, we Americans have cleared our decks and taken our battle stations. We stand ready in the defense of our Nation and in the faith of our fathers to do what God has given us the power to see as our full duty."[61]

A few years later, Sam Rosenman, who along with Robert Sherwood had helped draft the speech, wrote that by the time he delivered that speech FDR "was convinced that American entry into the war was almost unavoidable." According to Rosenman one of the purposes of the Navy Day speech was "to convince the American people that, despite the propaganda being spread by isolationists and 'America Firsters,' the potential strength of American productive capacity could outmatch the Axis, and that the Allied cause was not hopeless."[62]

Roosevelt used strong language to arouse Americans against Hitler, but isolationists also used strong language to attack what they saw as Roosevelt's efforts to lead the United States to war. As national chairman of America First, General Wood charged that the president was "asking Congress to issue an engraved drowning license to American seamen. It will mean that American ships will be sunk, American lives lost—and that the country will be led into war on a wave of hysteria just as it was in 1917." He contended that "the only reason for the repeal of the Combat Zone prohibition is the war party's need for a series of incendiary incidents." He promised that the America First Committee would "make this the occasion for its most vigorous drive." And it did. Though attacks on America First and on leading isolationists had made them increasingly suspect in the eyes of many Americans, the committee was larger and more efficiently organized by the fall of 1941 than ever before. Its national headquarters in Chicago directed a highly organized and aggressive campaign to defeat the president's efforts to win repeal of the vital provisions of the Neutrality Act.[63]

National and local leaders of America First battled against repeal of the vital provisions of the Neutrality Act as though it were a final step to war. Ever since the enactment of lend-lease, the committee had tried unsuccessfully to move the foreign policy debate away from the issue of aid-short-of-war to the issue of war-or-peace, to the question of whether the United States should or should not declare war and become a full belligerent in the war against the Axis. Most Americans supported the president's efforts to aid Britain against the Axis short-of-war, but at the same time approximately 80 percent opposed a declaration of war against the Axis. Isolationists insisted that those steps short-of-war that Americans approved were, under Roosevelt's leadership, moving the United States closer to involvement in a war that Americans did not approve. In measured public opinion (and in voting patterns in Congress), the isolationists had no real chance to defeat Roosevelt as long as the issue remained aid-short-of-war; their only chance for victory lay in moving away from aid-short-of-war to a focus on the specific question of whether the United States should or should not declare war. But before Pearl Harbor Roosevelt never presented the issue in those terms. He emphasized the evil and danger posed by the Axis (nearly all Americans agreed with him) and urged all-aid-short-of-war to the victims of Axis aggression (most Americans agreed with him), but he never asked for a declaration of war against the Axis (an issue on which 80 percent of Americans and the majority in Congress were opposed).[64]

Many noninterventionists became convinced that they could never defeat Roosevelt and his interventionist foreign policies unless they could shift the debate from aid-short-of-war to the issue of war-or-peace. If they fought revision of the Neutrality Act in the fall of 1941 on an aid-short-of-war basis, the isolationists would lose; it might be their last real chance to shift the debate to the war-peace issue before war became a bloody reality for the United States. Among top America First leaders and advisers who took that view were Hanford MacNider, Samuel B. Pettengill, and John T. Flynn. Pettengill, former Democratic congressman from Indiana, urged General Wood, on behalf of America First, to send an open letter to the president asking him to place the issue of declaring war squarely before Congress for a clear-cut yes or no vote. General Wood and Stuart liked the suggestion, and so did Flynn of the New York chapter.[65]

At an America First national committee meeting in Chicago on October 20, General Wood presented Pettengill's suggestion and expressed his opinion "that such an open letter would tend to crystallize the issue of war or peace and end the subterfuge of the Administration's war policy." In the course of the discussion, at the suggestion of Stuart, the national committee approved the addition of a new principle to the committee's platform. That principle proclaimed: "The Constitution of the United States vests the sole power to declare war in Congress. Until Congress has exercised that power, it is not only the privilege but the duty of every citizen to express to his Representatives his views on the question of peace or war—in order that this grave issue may be decided in accordance with the will of the people and the best traditions of American democracy." And the national committee authorized Wood to send a letter to the president along the lines suggested by Pettengill.[66]

On October 22, while Congress was considering revision of the Neutrality Act, General Wood sent his open letter to President Roosevelt. Drawing heavily on the draft prepared by Pettengill, Wood wrote: "The America First Committee, in the interest of peace, honor and constitutional government, respectfully asks that you cause to be submitted to Congress a resolution for the declaration of a state of war between the United States and the German Reich." He charged: "Each step thus far taken in the international situation has been upon the solemn assurance that it was for the purpose of preserving peace. Actually we have been led to the brink of a devastating war, with inevitable loss of human lives and destruction of our national economy and way of life. This subterfuge must end. We must now squarely face the real issue, war or peace." He promised that America First and other noninterventionists would "oppose with vigor the passage of a war resolution." But he insisted that "the question must be settled now and in the way and by the authority required by the Constitution. If Congress votes for a declaration of war, the constitutional voice of the American people will have spoken and this Committee and all other patriotic Americans will respect that decision. If, on the other hand, Congress, in its wisdom, votes down a declaration of war, the Administration must respect that decision and take no further step toward our involvement."[67]

Many interventionists, including Secretary of War Stimson and Secretary of Interior Ickes, had urged Roosevelt to take the course urged by General Wood—though they believed that the president could successfully rally Congress and the American people to unite behind such a declaration of war. Roosevelt had rejected their urgings, however, and General Wood's letter further convinced him of the wisdom of his course. He never answered the letter, but according to Robert Sherwood's account, Wood's letter strengthened FDR's "conviction that, were he to do this, he would meet with certain and disastrous defeat." Roosevelt continued to use his tried and tested short-of-war formula in battling the isolationist, and they were never able to get the debate squarely on the issue of war or peace—until after the Japanese attack on Pearl Harbor.[68]

Nonetheless, the America First Committee and its allies in Congress fought against revision of the Neutrality Act as though revision were a declaration of war. In a letter to all chapter chairmen, America

First national director R. Douglas Stuart, Jr., wrote: "If the President refuses to put the question honestly before Congress, we will treat the Neutrality repeal for what it is—a war vote. We will fight it as we would fight a declaration of war." He told chapter leaders "that every member of Congress who votes to repeal the Neutrality Law is voting to send American seamen to their death. They must be reminded that the American people will hold them responsible for doing, by subterfuge, what they dare not do directly. The time has come for the people's Representatives to stand up and be counted. From now on the only issue remaining is war and they must vote 'yes' or 'no.' "[69] It was the last major opportunity noninterventionists had before Pearl Harbor to voice and vote their opposition to the president's course.

America First leaders pressed for House and Senate hearings on the proposed changes in the neutrality legislation. They urged prominent noninterventionists to testify against the changes sought by the administration. All over the United States speakers addressed America First meetings and made broadcasts attacking revision of the law. Lindbergh delivered his last two speeches at America First rallies while Congress and the American people were deliberating on revision of the Neutrality Act.[70]

On October 25, America First national headquarters sent an *Emergency Bulletin #1* to all local chapter leaders advising them: "The Crisis is here. The next few days, or weeks at the most, will decide whether we will be plunged into war or remain at peace." In that *Bulletin* Stuart told America First members: "All other appeals we have made to you for help sink into nothingness compared to this appeal. The moment for which we have been preparing for one year has arrived. We are counting on you." The *Bulletin* explained how each chapter should organize its members to assure a maximum flood of letters to the right senators and representatives on the right issues at the right times. Committee headquarters then guided local chapters on where and when to direct their letters to accomplish the best results. They tried not to waste letters or telegrams on those who could not be moved; they concentrated on those who were wavering and might be swayed by their mail. In homes scattered all across the country concerned noninterventionists worked feverishly in their almost desperate efforts to flood Washington with letters and telegrams opposing revision of the Neutrality Act.[71]

Ruth Sarles and others from the America First Research Bureau in Washington helped organize House and Senate opposition to the administration's proposals. They provided relevant data and even wrote speeches when needed. They conferred with Senators Wheeler, Taft, Johnson, Nye, and others in both houses of Congress. On November 1, the committee held a national meeting of chapter leaders in Washington to inform and inspire local leaders. That meeting brought them to the capital, where they could make their voices heard directly to their senators and representatives. In the final days of the battle Stuart and others from the Chicago headquarters went to Washington to help direct the noninterventionist effort. Every honorable thing that could be done to defeat Roosevelt on the issue was done. But that massive, earnest, dramatic noninterventionist effort failed.[72]

Under the leadership of Sol Bloom of New York the House Foreign Affairs Committee held brief hearings on a resolution to permit the arming of American merchant ships. Republican Congressmen Hamilton Fish of New York and George H. Tinkham of Massachusetts, ranking minority members of the committee, walked out in protest against what they saw as gag tactics by the majority. On Monday, October 13, Secretary Hull, Secretary Knox, Secretary Stimson, Chairman of the United States Maritime Commission Admiral Emory S. Land, and Chief of Naval Operations Harold R. Stark testified on behalf of the administration in closed session. After acrimonious controversy in the committee the next day, it heard opposition testimony from three pacifists. It then voted to recommend approval of the administration resolution, and on October 17, by a vote of 259 to 138, it passed in the full House of Representatives.[73]

The Foreign Relations Committee under the chairmanship of Senator Tom Connally of Texas held brief hearings in closed session. Hiram Johnson provided leadership for the opposition in committee, and the opponents met several times in his Senate office to plan their tactics. On October 25, the Foreign Relations Committee voted thirteen to ten to recommend adoption of legislation that would not only authorize arming merchant ships but would also permit those ships to enter conbat areas and belligerent ports.[74] Senate leaders held day-long sessions during the eleven days of debate. Twenty-five senators spoke for the bill and twenty-four against. In the course of his eight-hour address that extended over two days, Democrat Burton K. Wheeler of Montana told the assembled senators, "You men who follow blindly the administration's policy, you men who, under the whip and lash, are going to take this country to war—you are going to take it to hell!" He pleaded with the senators "in the name of Americanism, in the name of the constitutional government, and . . . in the name of the mothers and fathers of this country." Wheeler was "convinced that if the senate takes this step it will be taking a step that the members of the senate will regret the rest of their lives. As God is my judge, I say to the senate, do not do it!" Others spoke with equal passion and earnestness. The weary senators began voting before packed galleries on the evening of November 7. The Senate rejected amendments proposed by the opponents, and then, by a vote of fifty to thirty-seven, approved the revision of the Neutrality Act.[75]

The House spent two days debating the bill as adopted in the Senate. Thirty-eight congressmen spoke for the bill and seventy against. Administration forces in the House faced formidable opposition and had difficulty holding their lines in the face of allegations that the action would be tantamount to a declaration of war. In desperation Speaker of the House Sam Rayburn and House Majority Leader John W. McCormack turned to Roosevelt for help. They asked his opinion on the "effect failure on the part of the House to take favorable action on the Senate amendments would have upon our position in foreign countries and especially in Germany." In a letter to Rayburn and McCormack on November 13, the president wrote that failure to revise the law would "be definitely discouraging" to the British, Chinese, and Russians who were fighting to defend themselves against the aggressors. And he thought failure to revise the legislation would "cause rejoicing in the Axis Nations." He predicted, "Failure would bolster aggressive steps and intentions in Germany, and in the other well-known aggressor Nations under the leadership of Hitler." He thought America's "position in the struggle against aggression would be definitely weakened, not only in Europe and in Asia, but also among our sister Republics in the Americas." Roosevelt contended that it would also "weaken our great effort to produce all we possibly can and as rapidly as we can. Strikes and stoppages of work would become less serious in the mind of the public." At least one congressman believed that Roosevelt's letter made the difference. A few minutes after Rayburn had left the podium to read Roosevelt's letter to the House, it voted 212 to 194 to approve revision of the neutrality legislation. President Roosevelt signed the Neutrality Act of 1941 into law on November 17—less than three weeks before Pearl Harbor. Thenceforth American merchant ships were free to arm and to sail with their cargoes and passengers through the war zones all the way to belligerent ports.[76]

The Neutrality Act of 1941 represented a hard-fought victory by Roosevelt and his followers over the isolationists. When combined with the administration's shoot-on-sight policy, it represented a full-blown no-holds-barred undeclared naval war against Axis forces in the Atlantic in America's efforts to help Britain and the Soviet Union resist and then defeat Nazi Germany and Fascist Italy in Europe. After trying so hard and so often to block the president's moves, the isolationists were terribly discouraged after their defeat in November.

Nonetheless, noninterventionists could find reasons to feel encouraged, and Roosevelt could find cause to pause a bit. More senators and representatives voted against the administration on revision of the Neutrality Act in November than had voted against lend-lease a few months earlier. Noninterventionists gained twenty-nine votes in the House and six votes in the Senate. Twenty-one Republicans voted against revision in the Senate; only six voted for it. Fifteen senators from Roosevelt's own Democratic party voted against him. A shift of ten votes from yea to nay in the House would have defeated the president's move. In the House a majority of congressmen representing districts north of the Mason-Dixon line voted against revision. Those congressmen who voted against the administration represented approximately 50 percent of the American voters. Among representatives of twenty states, a majority of those voting cast their votes against the president's proposal. The representatives from four states cast all their votes against revision in the House—Iowa, North Dakota, South Dakota, and Idaho. Seven states cast all their votes for revision—but all were in the South. Without the South Roosevelt would have been defeated in the House. And the administration even lost the votes of a few southern congressmen. The margin of the Roosevelt administration's victory was much too narrow to encourage any move for a declaration of war. According to public opinion polls, by early November 61 percent of the American people favored revision of the Neutrality Act—but 31 percent opposed.[77]

Robert E. Sherwood, one of Roosevelt's speechwriters, later wrote of that result: "The truth was that, as the world situation became more desperately critical, and as the limitless peril came closer and closer to the United States, isolationist sentiment became ever more strident in expression and aggressive in action, and Roosevelt was relatively powerless to combat it. He had said everything 'short of war' that could be said. He had no more tricks left. The hat from which he had pulled so many rabbits was empty. The president of the United States was now the creature of circumstance which must be shaped not by his own will or his own ingenuity but by the unpredictable determination of his enemies."[78] Secretary of War Henry L. Stimson had long believed that the United States must enter World War II as a full belligerent, that aid-short-of-war would not be sufficient to accomplish the essential defeat of the Axis. He had urged President Roosevelt to explain frankly to Congress and to the American people the seriousness of the international situation. He believed that if the president had turned his marvelous speaking voice and leadership abilities to the task, Congress and the people would have united behind him in voting for war and in supporting that war against the Axis aggressors. But Roosevelt had rejected his advice. Writing in his memoirs after the war, Stimson feared "that the impasse into which America had thought herself in 1941 might have continued indefinitely if that had been the will of the Axis, and if this had happened, the President would have had to shoulder a large share of the blame" because he had failed to put the issue of war squarely and frankly to the American people and to Congress.[79]

But Sherwood was a writer; Stimson had filled high appointive positions in the government. Neither was so skilled or so experienced in politics as Roosevelt. From their rather parochial eastern, urban, interventionist view it was difficult for them to get a truly national perspective. It was easy for them to underestimate or take lightly the continued strength of isolationist opposition. Given their strong interventionist feelings, it was easy for them to believe that Roosevelt overestimated the strength of the opposition. But Roosevelt had a more nearly national perspective and a better feel for the political situation. Furthermore, however much one might prefer candor to indirection, Sherwood and Stimson had underestimated Roosevelt. He had not yet exhausted all options. The options he was exploring had not yet run their full course. And they had overestimated the capacity of the leaders of Axis states to restrain themselves in the face of America's increasingly aggressive efforts to help assure their defeat.

Chapter 30

Political Infighting

By 1941 many Americans feared that Franklin D. Roosevelt was building a dictatorship in the United States—or at least was setting precedents that could lead to dictatorship at the hands of others. By 1941 many other Americans feared that isolationist leaders were Nazi fifth columnists paving the way for fascism in the United States. Neither fear proved justified. But images, suppositions, and myths played their roles in history, even when they did not coincide with realities.

Individuals think and act partly on their expectations (their hopes and their fears) for the future. Those readings of the future normally are based on perceptions of existing circumstances, on patterns mentally projected from the past through the present to some hoped-for (or feared) future, on conceptions of human nature, and on the individual's own temperament and emotional makeup. Given the terrifying Nazi successes in Europe, many in the United States saw the isolationists as either conscious instruments or naïve dupes of Nazi fifth-column subversion in America. Interventionists shared and appealed to those fears in advancing their own foreign policy proposals. Similarly, given the expansion of presidential power under the leadership of Roosevelt as he shaped the New Deal to cope with the depression and later as he shaped foreign policies to cope with Axis challenges, many in the United States worried about the danger of a Roosevelt dictatorship at home. Isolationists shared and appealed to those fears in advancing their noninterventionist views.

Ironically, in 1941 interventionists used arguments in attacking isolationist fifth columnists that were much like those used by Senator Joseph R. McCarthy in attacking liberal internationalists and communist subversion a decade later. And in the early 1970s the eastern urban establishment attacked President Richard M. Nixon, his administration, and his foreign policies in terms much like those that isolationists had used in attacking Roosevelt, his administration, and his foreign policies thirty years earlier.

In 1941 both honest conviction and tactical calculation produced the allegations on both sides in that heated controversy. The issues involved and the possible consequences of alternative policies were so vitally important to the world, to the United States, and to the very lives of individual humans that the debate grew increasingly heated and savage. It was a terrible and terrifying time in world affairs. The survival of independent countries and whole civilizations, including the United States and Western civilization, may have been at stake. Conceivably, totalitarian regimes could conquer the world; political democracy, individual freedom, and national independence could be wiped out. The lives of tens of millions of people were at stake all over the world—and in the United States. Potentially the developments could be as personal as one's next breath, food on the table, or the future of the boy next door. They concerned the kind of society, the kind of lives, that individual Americans might experience daily. The consequences of the foreign policy debate could be personal and vital for every individual.

That debate had gone on for a very long time with ever-mounting intensity. Many of the same individuals (Roosevelt, Wheeler, Johnson, Nye, Fish, Lindbergh, and others) had been slugging away at each other for years. Personalities mixed with politics and mounting emotions to produce as heated a debate as the United States had ever known. Given the violence in comparable contests elsewhere, and in earlier and later debates in the United States, it was surprising (and laudable) that that great debate in the Roosevelt era was largely free of domestic violence. But given the circumstances, it was not surprising that persons on both sides felt, thought, said, and sometimes did nasty and even vicious things in contesting with adversaries.

In those traumatic times political marquis of Queensbury rules did not always prevail. The fighting got rough. Each felt justified in the methods it used. By 1941 the foreign policy debate was a decidedly rugged affair, with few holds barred. Given the terrifying Axis challenges, Roosevelt's charismatic leadership abilities, the power advantages that accrued to the presidential office, the widespread fear of Nazi aggression and oppression, and the intensity of emotions on all sides, isolationists took a terrible beating in that contest. Leading isolationists were scarred for life. Many suffered the destruction of their careers. Their reputations were irreparably damaged because they chose to risk all in battling against the president's foreign policies.[1]

Roosevelt's personal involvement in the infighting focused particularly on a handful of top isolationist leaders whose potential represented serious power challenges or who especially provoked his ire. From his perspective many who wrote, spoke, or voted against him on foreign affairs faded into the ranks of the opposition. Old Arthur Capper, for example, was as isolationist as anyone in the Senate, but FDR felt no great personal animosity against the Kansas Republican. Robert M. La Follette, Jr., of Wisconsin retained Roosevelt's personal respect and political cooperation on domestic issues, even as the two differed sharply on foreign affairs. Hiram Johnson was bitterly critical of Roosevelt, and their earlier political friendship had ended. But FDR may have felt a touch of sadness about the rupture and may have retained traces of his earlier affection for the old warrior. In any event, by 1941 Johnson had faded in health, strength, and vigor. The president had more dangerous opponents to battle.

At the forefront of President Roosevelt's isolationist challengers by 1941 were Colonel Charles A. Lindbergh, Senator Burton K. Wheeler, Senator Gerald P. Nye, and Congressman Hamilton Fish. From Roosevelt's perspective neither Nye of North Dakota nor Fish of New York was sufficiently formidable to constitute any dangerous challenge to his national leadership. But he saw them as troublesome, destructive, and irresponsible; he thought America would be better off if both were retired from political life. By 1941 Burton K. Wheeler was the most able and aggressively effective isolationist leader in the Senate, and a feud raged between the lean Montana Democrat and the urbane patrician in the White House. But it was America's great flying hero, Colonel Charles A. Lindbergh, who posed the most formidable challenge to President Roosevelt's leadership and to his efforts to unite the American people behind his foreign policies.

In the eyes of millions of people Charles A. Lindbergh was the great American hero. He had captured public attention when, as the Lone Eagle in his tiny, single-engine monoplane, *The Spirit of St. Louis*, he had conquered the vast Atlantic in his solo flight from New York to Paris in May, 1927. His tall slender good looks, his modest demeanor, and his sterling character made it easy for Americans to see in him heroic qualities. His marriage in 1929 to the attractive daughter of Dwight Morrow, America's ambassador to Mexico, warmed the hearts of romantics everywhere. The nation's hearts went out to the young couple in 1932 when their first-born son was kidnapped and murdered and when they endured the ordeal of the long trial of the kidnapper. In December, 1935, millions of Americans sympathized when the Lindberghs fled newsmen and crackpots in America and sought temporary refuge first in England and later in France.[2]

Lindbergh had left the University of Wisconsin after only three semesters as an engineering student and never graduated. But he had a keen mind. In 1925 he graduated from Army Air Service pilot training at the top of his class. In the 1930s he teamed with the brilliant Nobel Prize-winning French physician, Dr. Alexis Carrel, in sophisticated scientific experiments and writing. Lindbergh had a searching, probing, experimental mind and the self-discipline, attention to detail, and capacity for sustained concentrated effort that enabled him to convert curiosity into action. His wife's skills as a writer helped him develop his own talents for writing and speaking clearly, simply, and effectively.

Colonel Lindbergh had disliked politics since, as a boy, he had driven for his father's campaign trips in Minnesota. After his flight brought fame, many urged young Lindbergh to seek public office (even the presidency), but he consistently rejected those urgings. He had absolute integrity and was proudly independent (some would call him stubborn, bull-headed, and inflexible). And he had the courage of his convictions. In his battle against American intervention in World War II he proved to have as much courage in public life as he had always had in the skies. In August, 1940, he told a large noninterventionist audience in Chicago, "I prefer to say what I believe, or not to speak at all." Early in 1941 he wrote in his private journal, "I prefer adventure to security, freedom to popularity, and conviction to influence."[3] Such a man was certain to have difficulties in public life.

The aviator's long feud with newsmen, his laudatory reports on German air power, his acceptance of a medal from Goering in 1938, and the beginning of his noninterventionist efforts in 1939 cooled the ardor of many for the Lone Eagle; by 1941 many despised him as much as they had adored him in 1927. His disdain for the political arts and his rigid determination to march to his own drummer contributed to his defeat in his contest with Roosevelt. But Lindbergh retained a purity of image in the eyes of millions of Americans that both enhanced his stature as a noninterventionist leader and helped make him a particularly formidable and worrisome challenge to President Roosevelt and his foreign policies from 1939 through 1941.

May 20, 1940, was the day that William Allen White publicly announced the formation of the Committee to Defend America by Aiding the Allies; it was the day after Colonel Lindbergh's major nationwide broadcast, "The Air Defense of America"; it was a few days before Britain evacuated its forces from Europe at Dunkirk; and it was only a month before France surrendered to Hitler's Germany. On that date President Roosevelt confided to his Secretary of Treasury Henry Morgenthau, Jr., "I am absolutely convinced that Lindbergh is a Nazi." The next day the president wrote Henry L. Stimson, who was soon to join his cabinet as secretary of war, that he was worried "by 'fifth column' activities over here." He wrote, "When I read Lindbergh's speech I felt that it could not have been better put if it had been written by Goebbels himself. What a pity that this youngster has completely abandoned his belief in our form of government and has accepted Nazi methods because apparently they are efficient."[4] Interventionists increasingly used that tactic of identifying isolationists with Nazism to discredit Lindbergh and other noninterventionist opponents of the administration's foreign policies.

On the same day as Roosevelt's letter to Stimson, May 21, 1940, the president authorized the attorney general "to secure information by listening devices direct to the conversation or other communications of persons suspected of subversive activities against the Government of the United States, including suspected spies." Many telegrams received at the White House criticizing the president's defense policies were referred to J. Edgar Hoover, director of the Federal Bureau of Investigation. In May, 1941, correspondence endorsing Lindbergh's opposition to the use of American ships to escort convoys was removed from White House files and "sent to Secret Service."[5]

The White House helped arrange for senators and others to broadcast critical replies to Lindbergh's noninterventionist speeches. It obtained the services of Assistant Secretary of State Adolf A. Berle to help with those replies. For example, Democratic Senator James Byrnes of South Carolina broadcast a vigorous attack on Lindbergh after his radio address of May 19, 1940. The White House got Democratic Senator Key Pittman of Nevada to broadcast "the same sort of beating that JB gave him" after Lindbergh's speech of June 15. Democratic Senator Scott Lucas of Illinois answered Lindbergh's speech of August 4, in Chicago, and Senator Claude Pepper of Florida vehemently denounced the colonel from the Senate floor. Adolf Berle helped former Assistant Secretary of War Louis A. Johnson write the speech that he broadcast in response to Lindbergh's address of October 14, 1940.[6]

President Roosevelt's pugnacious Secretary of Interior Harold L. Ickes began his spirited public attacks on Lindbergh as early as December, 1938. He repeated them often thereafter with increasing ferocity. To keep track of what Lindbergh was saying, Ickes maintained a complete indexed file of all the airman's noninterventionist speeches. In a speech at Columbia University Ickes called Lindbergh a "peripatetic appeaser who would abjectly surrender his sword even before it is demanded." On April 13, 1941, four days before Lindbergh gave his first address as a member of America First, Ickes in a speech accused Lindbergh of being the "No. 1 Nazi fellow traveler" in the United States and "the first American to raise aloft the standard of pro-Naziism." He said the aviator was "the proud possessor of a Nazi decoration which has already been well earned." He described Anne Lindbergh's little book, *The Wave of the Future,* as "the bible of every American Nazi, Fascist, Bundist, and appeaser."[7]

President Roosevelt asked the news commentator Jay Franklin (John F. Carter) to do some research for him on the Civil War Copperheads. Franklin did his work and submitted a fifty-page report to the president on April 22. Copperheads were northerners with prosouthern sympathies who had been critical of Abraham Lincoln and his policies during the Civil War. In his memorandum Franklin compared Colonel Lindbergh to the Civil War General George B. McClellan as similarly "giving the sanction of professional prestige to the doctrines of defeatism." At his press conference three days later (the day after Lindbergh addressed a New York America First rally), newsmen asked Roosevelt why Colonel Lindbergh had not been called into active military service. In his response the president compared Lindbergh to Clement L. Vallandigham, the leading Civil War Copperhead.[8] The allusion delighted most interventionists and infuriated noninterventionists.

The most important response came from Lindbergh himself. In a letter to the president on April 28, 1941, Lindbergh resigned his commission as a colonel in the Army Air Corps Reserve. Since the president, his commander in chief, had "clearly implied" that he was "no longer of use to this country as a reserve officer," and since he had, in effect, questioned Lindbergh's loyalty, character, and motives, the colonel believed that he had "no honorable alternative" to resigning his commission. He took the action "with the utmost regret" because his "relationship with the Air Corps is one of the things that has meant most to me in life." He placed it "second only to my right as a citizen to speak freely to my fellow countrymen, and to discuss with them the issues of war and peace which confront our nation in this crisis." He promised to continue to serve the United States "as a private citizen." Colonel Lindbergh also wrote to Secretary of War Stimson formally resigning his air corps commission. In his private journal Lindbergh reflected on the irony of finding himself "stumping the country with pacifists and . . . resigning as a colonel in the Army Air Corps, when there is no philosophy I disagree with more than that of the pacifist, and nothing I would rather be doing than flying in the Air Corps."[9]

Responses to his resignation were predictable: silence from the White House; denunciations from interventionists; praise from noninterventionists. For example, Senator Robert A. Taft of Ohio wrote Lindbergh congratulating him on his foreign policy stands and criticizing the president's "cowardly" attack on the airman. Some undergraduate students at the University of Southern California formed a Campus Copperhead organization supporting Lindbergh.[10]

On July 14, 1941, in an address in New York, Secretary Ickes again flailed away at Lindbergh. "No one has ever heard Lindbergh utter a word of horror at, or even aversion to, the bloody career that the Nazis are following, nor a word of pity for the innocent men, women and children, who have been deliberately murdered by the nazis in practically every country in Europe." Ickes had "never heard this Knight of the German Eagle denounce Hitler or nazism or Mussolini or fascism." He had not even "heard Lindbergh say a word for democracy itself." As he saw it, "All of Lindbergh's passionate words are to encourage Hitler and to break down the will of his own fellow citizens to resist Hitler and nazism."[11]

Lindbergh saw no advantage in contesting with Ickes, but he tried to assign responsibility for the cabinet member's remarks to the president. On July 16, Lindbergh wrote to Roosevelt concerning Icke's repeated charges that he was connected with a foreign government and the criticism of him for accepting the German medal in 1938. Lindbergh reminded the president that he had received the decoration "in the American Embassy, in the presence of your Ambassador," and "was there at his request in order to assist in creating a better relationship between the American Embassy and the German Government which your Ambassador desired at that time." Lindbergh wrote that if Ickes's statements and implications were false, he had "a right to an apology" from the president's secretary of interior. He insisted that he had "no connection, directly or indirectly, with anyone in Germany or Italy" since he had left Europe in 1939. Lindbergh offered to open his files for the president's investigation and to answer any questions that the president might have about his activities. But he insisted that "unless charges are made and proved," as an American citizen he had "the right to expect truth and justice" from members of the president's cabinet. The only response Lindbergh got from the White House was a memo from Stephen T. Early, the president's secretary, verbally spanking him for releasing his letter to the press before it reached Roosevelt.[12]

Ickes seemed pleased by Lindbergh's letter. He wrote in his diary, "Up to that time I had always admired Lindbergh in one respect. No matter how vigorously he had been attacked personally he had never attempted to answer. He had kept determinedly in the furrow that he was plowing. I had begun to think that no one could get under his skin enough to make him squeal. But at last I had succeeded. I suspect that it was my reference to him as a 'Knight of the German Eagle' that got him." In a reply carried in Frank Knox's *Chicago Daily News*, Ickes wrote, "Neither I nor anyone in this administration ever charged that Mr. Lindbergh had any connection with any foreign government or that he was in communication with any representative of a foreign government. But it is a notorious fact that he has been devoting himself to a cause which, if it should succeed, will be of immeasurable benefit to Hitler." In his article Ickes suggested that Lindbergh could "put himself right by championing the cause of democracy and civilization. He can denounce Hitler and his brutal aggressions. He can cheer on England. He can unite with those who are prepared to defend American institutions."[13] In effect Ickes was saying that Lindbergh could cleanse himself if he would abandon his noninterventionist opposition to Roosevelt's foreign policies and join with Ickes in support of intervention. That Lindbergh would not do. The tone that Ickes (and Roosevelt) had set in attacking Lindbergh increasingly became the general tone of the great debate in the last half of 1941.

At the same time, Lindbergh's criticisms of the Roosevelt administration grew increasingly frequent, bold, and strident during 1941. Lindbergh did not mention Roosevelt by name in any of his speeches during 1939 and 1940. His early allusions to politicians and the administration focused on their relation to the war and intervention. Increasingly during 1941, however, Lindbergh voiced alarm about the president's role in undermining the democratic processes and representative government. He called for "new leadership" and berated "government by subterfuge." He saw President Roosevelt as using dishonest methods to take the United States into war, contrary to the wishes of 80 percent of the American people. And he feared that those methods were creating for the United States the dictatorship that the president professed to be opposing abroad. Lindbergh urged open discussion, more legislative authority in foreign affairs, and limitations on the president's war-making powers.

In an address at an America First meeting in Minneapolis on May 10, 1941, Lindbergh complained that the president asked Americans to fight for the "Four Freedoms," but then he denied them "the freedom to vote on vital issues" and also denied them "freedom of information—the right of a free people to know where they are being led by their government." On May 23 he told an America First audience in Madison Square Garden that in the 1940 presidential campaign Americans were given "just about as much chance" to express their foreign policy views "as the Germans would have been given if Hitler had run against Goering."[14]

In a controversial address in Philadelphia on May 29, Lindbergh called for "new leadership" in the United States. That was the first speech in which he referred to Roosevelt by name. He ridiculed the president's assertion that the safety of America depended upon control of the Cape Verde Islands off the coast of Africa. "Even Hitler never made a statement like that." He charged: "Mr. Roosevelt claims that Hitler desires to dominate the world. But it is Mr. Roosevelt himself who advocates world domination when he says that it is our business to control the wars of Europe and Asia, and that we in America must dominate islands lying off the African coast." In his speech he asked, "Is it not time for us to turn to new policies and to a new leadership?" He called on his listeners to join with the America First Committee to "create a leadership for our nation that places America first."[15]

Critics promptly charged that in calling for "new leadership" Lindbergh was attempting to become the catalyst, "the man on horseback," for a violent fascist overthrow of the American government. For the only time in his noninterventionist speaking career, Lindbergh issued a clarifying statement after that address. In a telegram to the *Baltimore Sun* he explained: "Neither I nor anyone else on the America First Committee advocate proceeding by anything but constitutional methods. It is our opposition who endanger the American Constitution when they object to our freedom of speech and expression. Under the Constitution we have every right to advocate a leadership for this country which is non-interventionist and which places the interests of America first."[16] Many who opposed Lindbergh felt no hesitation, earlier and later, in urging new leadership when a president they disliked was in office. But in the emotional atmosphere before Pearl Harbor they were prepared to put the worst interpretation on anything Lindbergh said.

On August 9 in Cleveland, Lindbergh's speech was "Government by Representation or Subterfuge." It was a direct attack on Roosevelt's tactics. In a key statement he said: "The hypocrisy and subterfuge that surrounds us comes out in every statement of the war party. When we demand that our Government listen to the 80% of the people who oppose war, they shout that we are causing disunity. The same groups who call on us to defend democracy and freedom abroad, demand that we kill democracy and freedom at home by forcing four-fifths of our people into war against their will. The one-fifth who are for war call the four-fifths who are against war the 'fifth column.'" He charged that the interventionists "know that the people of this country will not vote for war, and they therefore plan on involving us through subterfuge." He contended that the interventionists and the administration "plan on creating incidents and situations" to force the United States into war. He insisted that the issue in the United States was "even greater than the issue of war or peace." He saw it as "the issue of whether or not we still have a representative government; whether or not we in the United States of America are still a free people, with the right to decide the fundamental policies of our nation."[17]

On September 11, 1941, at an America First rally in Des Moines, Iowa, Charles A. Lindbergh delivered his most controversial and most damaging address. The purpose of the speech was to place on the record Lindbergh's opinions on which groups were most responsible for pushing the United States into war. He correctly anticipated the uproar his speech would provoke and abuse he would suffer for making it. He entitled the speech, "Who Are the War Agitators?" More than eight thousand people crowded into the Des Moines Coliseum to hear Lindbergh. In his address Lindbergh charged, "The three most important groups who have been pressing this country toward war are the British, the Jewish, and the Roosevelt Administration." He contended that "If any one of these groups—the British, the Jewish, or the Administration—stops agitating for war" there would "be little danger of our involvement." In elaborating on his reference to the Roosevelt administration, Lindbergh charged that it was using "the war to justify the restriction of congressional power, and the assumption of dictatorial procedures."[18]

Then and later most of the attention focused on Lindbergh's reference to the Jews. But that was his only public mention of Jews in any of his speeches. In his treatment of the three major groups of "war agitators," Lindbergh was most critical, least sympathetic, and most persistent in his criticism of the Roosevelt administration.

In Fort Wayne, Indiana, on October 3, in his first address after the Des Moines rally, Lindbergh worried that he might be giving his "last address." He warned "that an Administration which can throw this country into undeclared naval war against the will of our people, and without asking the consent of Congress, can by similar methods prevent freedom of speech among us." Consequently he spoke to his audience as though he were giving his last speech (he did give only one more before Pearl Harbor silenced him). He charged that "not one step the Administration has taken in these last two years was placed honestly before our people as a step toward war." He contended that the administration had "been treating our Congress more and more as the German Reichstag has been treated under the Nazi regime. Congress, like the Reichstag, is not consulted. The issue of war or peace has never been put up to the people nor to its duly elected representatives in Congress because the President and his Administration know that the people would not accept it."[19]

Less than six weeks before Pearl Harbor, in New York's Madison Square Garden, Lindbergh delivered what proved to be his final America First address. In that speech he charged that President Roosevelt and his administration "preach about preserving Democracy and freedom abroad, while they practice Dictatorship and subterfuge at home." In his view, "They used the phrase 'Steps Short of War' to *lead* us to foreign war." He insisted: "The most fundamental issue today is not one of war or peace, but one of integrity. . . . There is no danger to this nation from without. The only danger lies from within." In the last sentence of what was to be his last noninterventionist speech, Lindbergh said, "I appeal to all Americans, no matter what their viewpoint on the war may be, to unite behind the demand for a leadership in Washington that stands squarely upon American traditions—a leadership of integrity instead of subterfuge, of openness instead of secrecy; a leadership that demonstrates its Americanism by taking the American people into its confidence."[20]

Before the Japanese attack on Pearl Harbor on December 7, Lindbergh had agreed to address an America First rally in Boston on December 12. With the coming of war, America First canceled the rally. But Lindbergh had already drafted his speech for that meeting.

Though he never delivered it, it provides a final expression of his views before Pearl Harbor. His intended topic was "What do We Mean by Democracy and Freedom?" He had planned to say "that *democracy* is gone from a nation when its people are no longer informed of the fundamental policies and intentions of their government," and that "*freedom* is a travesty among men who have been forced into war by a President they elected because he promised peace." He wrote: "*Freedom* and *Democracy* cannot long exist without a third quality, a quality called *Integrity*. It is a quality whose absence is alarming in our government today. Without integrity, freedom and democracy will become only politicians' nicknames for an American totalitarian state." In his opinion the word that best described the "danger in America" was not invasion, intervention, Germany, Russia, or Japan; "that word is subterfuge." He insisted: "Subterfuge marked every step we made 'short of war,' and it now marks every step we are making 'short of' a dictatorial system in America. Our nation has been led to war with promises of peace. It is now being led toward dictatorship with promises of democracy."[21]

Lindbergh's long battle against intervention in World War II brought him into personal contact with most leading noninterventionists in and out of Congress. He considered Democratic Senator Burton K. Wheeler of Montana the most able in either house of Congress. Ruth Sarles at the head of the America First Research Bureau in Washington was the committee's liaison with the Senate in 1941. She had close contacts with Senate noninterventionists. Many years later she remembered Wheeler as one of the four most able noninterventionist senators (the others were Robert M. La Follette, Jr. of Wisconsin, Robert A. Taft of Ohio, and George D. Aiken of Vermont). She thought that if anyone could be singled out as *the* noninterventionist leader in the Senate in 1941, that person was Wheeler.[22]

The tall slender Senator Wheeler was bright, quick, and well informed. Despite his break with FDR on court packing in 1937, Wheeler had supported Roosevelt and most of his New Deal, and the president had often consulted him on legislative matters. As a progressive Democrat and a long-time Roosevelt supporter, Wheeler could not lightly be written off as a reactionary Republican anti-New Deal Roosevelt-hater. The well-stocked liquor supply he maintained in his office provided refreshment for those who stopped by to share thoughts, suggestions, and information on legislative tactics or foreign policy. Bailey Stortz, Wheeler's able administrative assistant, knew the legislative ropes. Wheeler had been in the Senate a long time (since 1923) and was a skilled tactician; he did his homework and knew how to get things done. He was an effective speaker and a formidable adversary in debate. He had a sense of humor. He was a fighter with plenty of political courage; he did not back away from battle out of timidity or excess of political caution. He had an up-beat, can-do temperament and style that enabled him to bounce back after reverses, prepared to do battle again another day. Wheeler was his own man, but his feisty wife Lulu, to whom he was deeply devoted, shared his views and encouraged him in his battles against Roosevelt and his foreign policies. No senator was more prominent or active in battling against Roosevelt's foreign policies in 1941 than Burton K. Wheeler. He provided legislative leadership, he orated and debated, and he traveled all over the United States delivering noninterventionist speeches and broadcasts under the auspices of the America First Committee.[23]

Senator Wheeler was a formidable adversary, and Roosevelt knew it. A bitter feud developed between the president and the senator from Montana. Neither of those talented politicians was prepared to pull his punches or back off. The two had set the tone for their contest early in 1941 when Wheeler called lend-lease "the New Deal's triple 'A' foreign policy—it will plow under every fourth American boy," and when Roosevelt responded at a press conference that Wheeler's statement was "the most untruthful," the "most dastardly, unpatriotic thing that has ever been said," and that it was "the rottenest thing that has been said in public life in my generation."[24] Things went on from there!

In his many speeches Wheeler marshaled most of the standard noninterventionist arguments—with special emphases of his own. In April, for example, he told an America First audience in Denver that he disassociated himself "from any 'ism' except patriotic Americanism." He said he had "always opposed dictatorship in any country" and would continue to do so, just as he continued to oppose American involvement in foreign war. He denied charges that he was anti-British. As a bona fide New Dealer he berated Roosevelt for calling in "money changers" and "Wall Street lawyers" to direct interventionist foreign policies. He ridiculed the image reversals that portrayed Willkie, J. P. Morgan, and Thomas Lamont as "liberals," while old progressives such as himself were seen as "Tories, Nazi sympathizers, or anti-Semites" because they opposed involvement in war abroad. He called that "intolerance" and "bigotry." He charged that the Roosevelt administration was doing all it could "to create an incident to excite the American people to war." When the Roosevelt administration called for national unity, Wheeler responded that there would be "an indivisible and enduring unity for peace and for freedom," but that there could "be no unity among the fathers and the mothers to send their sons to watery graves or to foreign battlefields. There will be no unity among the workers, the farmers, and businessmen for repression of traditional and constitutional rights. And there will be no unity for a war that will destroy democracy in America."[25]

Senator Wheeler told an audience in Salt Lake City that "Hitler and Hitlerism" could "never dominate the world so long as America remains a strong democracy," but that America would "cease to be a democracy the minute it actually goes to war." In August he charged that it was "the stupidity and folly and recklessness of American leaders" that had drawn the United States "closer and closer to the European and Asiatic bloodbaths." He insisted that America could save its democracy and freedom by solving its economic and social problems and by building its own military defenses. In a Labor Day speech in Illinois he predicted that labor would lose its rights when America went to war. He was hurt and troubled by attacks on him for his noninterventionist stand, but as he told an audience in California, "There comes a time in a man's life when he has got to stand up for the things that he thinks to be right."[26]

Part of the bitter fighting between Roosevelt and leading isolationists concerned use and control of means for informing and influencing public opinion—including mailing lists, use of the franking privilege, motion pictures, radio, newspapers, and propaganda organs. The use and misuse of those media for transmitting ideas brought charges and countercharges from both sides—sometimes factual, usually emotional, often distorted, and generally overblown. Much of the more vicious infighting originated with private individuals and groups. On the interventionist side those included notably the Fight for Freedom Committee, whose chairman of the executive committee was newsman Ulric Bell, and Friends of Democracy under the Unitarian clergyman the Reverend Leon M. Birkhead. Roosevelt and administration leaders played roles as well. Harry Hopkins, the president's secretary Stephen T. Early, and military aide and secretary to the president, General Edwin M. "Pa" Watson, among others, channeled White House communications and actions on such matters. Among cabinet members, Secretary of Interior Harold L. Ickes willingly and eagerly functioned as a hatchet man for the administration in the battle against the isolationists. He had particularly close relations and communications with leaders of the Fight for Freedom Committee. Often (both then and later) it was impossible to determine with certainty just when, how, and whether Roosevelt was involved, directly or indirectly.[27]

Groups on both sides of the foreign policy debate constructed and used mailing lists to help get their message to the people. The Washington office of America First persuaded noninterventionist congressmen and senators to permit confidential use of their mail for making such mailings lists. They tried to omit those who were critical of noninterventionism or who were pro-German or anti-Semitic. It was sometimes possible to determine or guess where the lists came from or how they had been compiled. There were occasional critical repercussions. Isolationists did not know, however, that at the request of Bell's office Stephen Early authorized typists in the White House mail room to compile lists for Fight for Freedom, Inc. of names and addresses from interventionist postcards sent to the president.[28]

More controversial was use of the franking privilege for mailing literature in the foreign policy debate. Congressmen were permitted legally to send their own speeches and other excerpts from the *Congressional Record* postage-free. It was also legal for bulk packages of franked articles to be sent by a congressman or senator to "one addressee" who could then address and remail them free. Those practices had been used commonly by congressmen of all parties. Administration offices, from the White House on down, also used the franking privilege. There was no legal penalty for legislative misuse, and the practice was so widespread that few in Congress wanted to tamper with the system.[29]

Increasingly in 1941, however, there were allegations that the privilege was being abused. Bell and the Fight for Freedom Committee were particularly aggressive in attacking isolationist misuse of the frank. They charged that anti-Semitic, pro-Nazi, and pro-German groups had sent out mail using franks of Senator Wheeler and other isolationist legislators. Wheeler denied the charge and threatened legal action, but Bell stood his ground and boasted that he had documentary proof. Henry Hoke, a writer and former direct mail advertising man, pressed similar allegations against isolationists.[30]

One much-publicized controversy over use of the frank erupted between Senator Wheeler and Secretary of War Stimson and involved President Roosevelt in the background. On July 24, General George C. Marshall brought Stimson two letters from soldiers complaining that they had received isolationist postcards from Wheeler urging them to write asking Roosevelt to keep America out of war. Believing that Wheeler had circularized American soldiers, Stimson determined to inform the press. Before doing so he telephoned the president. Roosevelt agreed with Stimson and advised him to tell newsmen that Wheeler's action came very close to treason. Stimson was reluctant to put it quite so strongly. But he drafted a statement contending that the mailing would affect discipline and training and would thus impair "defense against the dangers which now confront this country." Stimson charged that Wheeler's action came "very near the line of subversive activities against the United States, if not treason." Roosevelt concurred in Stimson's criticism of Wheeler. It was a major blow at a leading isolationist and his noninterventionist efforts.[31]

On July 28, however, Wheeler took the Senate floor to refute Stimson's charges and to defend his action. He explained that there had been no attempt to circularize men in the armed forces. The words on the cards were from the *Congressional Record*. More than a million of the cards had been sent under Wheeler's frank to a commercial mailing list. Wheeler said that so far as he knew only three of the cards had by chance—not calculated intent—gone to soldiers on active duty. Hiram Johnson and other senators spoke out in defense of Wheeler. Under the circumstances, Secretary Stimson issued a public apology to Wheeler; he thought that was the "manly" thing to do.[32]

Though Wheeler came out of that episode very nearly unscathed, the use of the franking privilege had its unsavory side. On July 29, the German embassy in Washington had informed the German Foreign Ministry in Berlin of the "telling effect" of the million cards sent by Wheeler and of the controversy between Wheeler and Stimson. On July 30, Hans Thomsen, the chargé d'affaires in the German embassy, sent a top secret telegram to Berlin informing the Foreign Ministry that "in recent months the mass dispatch of postcards has proved to be particularly effective as a propaganda action." He explained that "as all of the postcards had the letterhead of the American Congress or of the members of Congress concerned and contained mainly material which was taken from purely American sources and also appeared in one form or other in the official '*Congressional Record*,' our hand was not in any way recognizable."[33]

In September a federal district grand jury in Washington began hearings in an investigation of foreign propaganda in the United States. Sensational articles by investigative reporter Dillard Stokes in the *Washington Post* supplemented the probe. Stokes wrote of strange doings involving some twenty bags of franked envelopes containing isolationist speeches. A House of Representatives truck carried the bags of franked mail from Prescott Dennett's offices of the Make Europe Pay War Debts and Islands for War Debts committees to the offices of Congressman Hamilton Fish. Some of them went into storage, but a dozen were trucked on to the Washington offices of the America First Committee. In making midnight rounds Stokes discovered that some of that franked mail had been burned with trash behind the America First offices. On September 25 a United States marshal seized ten bags of the franked mail at the America First offices for use in the grand jury probe. Charges, countercharges, denials, explanations, and confusion followed. All of it seemed terribly suspicious so far as Fish and America First were concerned. And there were questions about the isolationist legislators whose franks were on the mail involved.[34]

As the grand jury gradually sorted things out, it revealed that George Hill, assistant secretary to Fish, had served as a handyman for a propaganda ring managed by George Sylvester Viereck. Through his contacts with Hill, Viereck had speeches by noninterventionist congressmen and other materials inserted into the *Congressional Record*. Reprints of those and other isolationist pieces then were purchased by Dennett and distributed through his Make Europe Pay War Debts and Islands for War Debts committees. The materials were sent out in franked envelopes or were bundled and sent to various parts of the country where they were then mailed under congressional frank. Those organizations were backed and partially financed by Viereck, who was on the payroll of the German government. Other noninterventionist and pacifist organizations also purchased reprints in franked envelopes through Hill's operation in Fish's offices. Both Hill and Viereck subsequently were convicted and sentenced for their roles in that clandestine arrangement.[35]

The office manager of the Washington chapter of America First denied that it had ordered the bags of franked mail delivered to its offices. Hill's facilities for supplying reprints were known to America First officials. In addition to paying Hill to handle mailings of its war-peace polls, the America First Committee and some of its chapters purchased reprints from Hill. There is no evidence to indicate that America First leaders knew of the ties of Hill with Viereck at the time.[36]

The government did not initiate legal action against any of the congressmen and senators whose franks were used in the arrangement.

Congressman Fish and Senator Nye took the floor for speeches proclaiming their innocence of any wrongdoing and defending their use of the frank. Fish described the episode as an effort to "smear" those who were trying to keep the United States out of the war. In an official report prepared for the Justice Department after the war, attorney O. John Rogge listed Congressmen Stephen A. Day and Hamilton Fish and Senators Rush D. Holt and Ernest Lundeen as legislators who had collaborated with Viereck in the scheme. He listed twenty others (including Senators La Follette, Nye, Reynolds, Shipstead, and Wheeler) as legislators "used" by Viereck, though he found no evidence that any of them "had knowledge of the fact." There is no evidence that they knew of the ties of Hill with Viereck at the time or of the German funds involved.[37]

In a personal letter written in 1947 after he left the Senate, Wheeler defended his use of the frank. He thought it "a perfectly legimate thing" and that the charges were efforts "to smear everyone and anyone" opposed to American involvement in the war. Wheeler wrote: "Every executive branch of the Government from the President on down to every petty bureau and sub-division, have the franking privilege, and they use it to send out tons of propaganda, and the only way it can be contradicted is for members of Congress who are opposed to their views to have the same privilege. The only way to preserve Democracy in this or any other country is to have an informed public opinion, and you cannot have an informed public opinion if your newspapers, your motion pictures, and your radio are carrying on a campaign giving only one side of the picture, and this is particularly so when they are also the views of the executive branches of the Government. Members of Congress who are in opposition to the Administration's views, under those conditions, would have very little, if any opportunity to get their views before any large segment of the population. In the campaign to get this country into war . . . many of the large national and international banking houses were all in favor of the war, as was President Roosevelt, members of his Cabinet, most of the democratic Senators, and most of the newspapers and leading magazines thruout the United States. Only the people were against it. . . . In some states practically all of the newspapers are owned by one corporation, or one group, and a Senator who opposes that corporation, or group of corporations who own or dominate the newspapers, and in some instances the radio as well, could not possibly get his views before the people of this State, were it not for the fact that he had use of the franking privilege."[38] Whatever one concludes on the matter, the franking controversy in 1941 further discredited those who were battling against President Roosevelt's foreign policies.

A proposed Senate investigation of interventionist propaganda in motion pictures and radio broadcasts inflamed emotions and further discredited isolationists. In the 1930s the motion picture industry had produced many antiwar pictures. By 1940–41, however, the industry was overwhelmingly interventionist. The Roosevelt administration and interventionist pressure groups won enthusiastic support in Hollywood. America First, on the other hand, found it almost impossible to get support there and encountered vehement opposition from leading figures in the industry.[39]

In January, 1941, in the midst of the lend-lease debate, Senator Wheeler wrote complaining that motion pictures and newsreels were not giving equal coverage to both sides of the foreign policy debate. He complained of "propaganda for war" that motion picture companies promoted. And he warned that legislation would "have to be enacted regulating the industry in this respect unless the industry itself displays a more impartial attitude." Will Hays, president of the Motion Picture Producers and Distributors of America, replied with a spirited defense of the motion picture industry and denied any "intention to incite to war." Hays forwarded to President Roosevelt copies of the exchange of letters. In February, young R. Douglas Stuart, Jr., of America First wrote that "films that have nothing to do with the European war are now loaded with lies and ideas which bring about an interventionist reaction."[40]

The talented actress Lillian Gish had helped arouse support for World War I. In 1941, however, she was a member of the America First national committee and at various meetings spoke movingly against intervention in the European war. But in August, 1941, she privately told General Wood that because of her active role in America First she had been blacklisted by movie studios in Hollywood and by legitimate theater and had been unable to find employment acting. Her agent finally got her a movie contract offer, but it was made on the condition that she first resign from America First and refrain from stating that reason for her resignation. She needed the work. Consequently (though still opposed to American involvement in World War II), Miss Gish resigned from the committee, gave no more speeches at America First meetings, and never made public the reason for her action.[41]

The proposed Senate investigation of war propaganda in radio and motion pictures was almost entirely a product of noninterventionist efforts. John T. Flynn drafted the resolution, and on August 1 Senator Bennett Champ Clark of Missouri introduced it for himself and Senator Nye. The resolution would have authorized the Senate Committee on Interstate Commerce "or any duly authorized subcommittee" to investigate propaganda in motion pictures and radio broadcasts designed "to influence public sentiment in the direction of participation by the United States in the present European war." On that same day Senator Nye delivered a major radio address in St. Louis on the subject. He charged that motion picture companies had "become the most gigantic engines of propaganda in existence to rouse the war fever in America and plunge this Nation to her destruction." He named the men and companies that he believed dominated the industry. Partly he blamed Hollywood's interventionism on refugees and British actors working there. But he particularly emphasized economic explanations, charging that foreign markets (especially in Britain and the Commonwealth countries) accounted for most of the profits realized from American motion pictures. He also suspected the federal government of encouraging production of interventionist films. War propaganda in movies was particularly "insidious," he said, because viewers expected to be entertained and were not on guard against it.[42]

Wheeler was chairman of the Senate Interstate Commerce Committee, to which the proposed resolution was referred. He appointed the subcommittee to consider the Nye-Clark resolution. That subcommittee was chaired by D. Worth Clark, a Democrat from Idaho who spoke frequently at America First meetings. It included Homer T. Bone, Democrat from Washington; Charles W. Tobey, Republican from New Hampshire; C. Wayland Brooks, Republican from Illinois; and Ernest W. McFarland, Democrat from Arizona. All were active noninterventionists except McFarland. Using funds provided by one of the larger contributors to America First, Flynn directed most of the research for the probe. The America First Committee supported the whole project, which was launched in an atmosphere of much noninterventionist enthusiasm.[43]

The motion picture industry did not go on the defensive in the face of the proposed investigation. Wendell L. Willkie (then an outspoken interventionist) served as its legal counsel, and with enthusiastic backing from the industry and from interventionists he made the hearings more embarrassing for noninterventionists than for the motion picture industry. The probe was promptly subjected to an avalanche of criticism and abuse on the grounds that it and Senator Nye were anti-Semitic. Jews controlled considerably more than half of the motion picture industry, and most of the persons Nye had named in his St. Louis broadcast were Jewish.[44]

Senator Nye, of course, denied the charges, insisting that his only objective was to prevent American intervention in foreign war. He said that the men he had named in his speech did in fact control the motion picture industry; it was their war propaganda he objected to, he said, not their religion. On September 9, Nye elaborated on his views when he testified before Senator Clark's subcommittee. He contended that those charging him with anti-Semitism were doing so "to cover the tracks of those who have been pushing our country on the way to war with their propaganda." He flatly denied that he, Clark, or the investigation were anti-Semitic, and he promised to battle against racial prejudice and anti-Semitism if war brought such prejudice to America. In his testimony he complained that motion pictures portrayed "a lot of glory for war" and exaggerated "the glory of certain peoples engaged in that war." He said the movies were "not revealing the sons of mothers writhing in agony in trench, in mud, on barbed wire, amid scenes of battle or sons of mothers living legless, or lungless, or brainless, or sightless in hospitals."[45]

On October 2, Senator Wheeler told a large audience at an America First rally in Los Angeles that he could not understand how American leaders in the motion picture industry were "willing to pervert their genius from entertainment to war propaganda." He insisted that no one in the Senate wanted to "curb free speech" or "provide censorship," but the legislators did expect the motion picture industry "not to carry on propaganda to try to take American boys to the slaughter pen of Europe and Asia."[46]

Despite their denials and protestations to the contrary, the charges that the probe was anti-Semitic probably encouraged an early adjournment of the hearings in the fall of 1941. They were never renewed. The subcommittee made no report before Pearl Harbor, and on December 18 it recommended that "in the interests of national unity" it would not be desirable to submit a detailed report on its findings.[47] The Nye-Clark resolution and the subcommittee hearings did not change the character of motion pictures, but they did further identify leading isolationists with anti-Semitism in the minds of many Americans.

There was continual tugging and pulling as both sides in the foreign policy debate sought radio time. Each side worried that the other got too much time on the air. In 1938 administration leaders were angered by attacks from radio commentator Boake Carter. They tried to silence him through his sponsor. Roosevelt told Secretary of Labor Frances Perkins that he wished it might be found that Carter was in the country illegally. He had immigrated to the United States from England and was a naturalized citizen. His record was investigated. When Boake Carter's sponsor's contract for his broadcasts ended late in 1938, the White House tried to persuade that company to sponsor the more friendly John Franklin Carter (Jay Franklin) as a commentator. The White House also closely followed the steps that finally ended Father Charles E. Coughlin's inflammatory broadcasts. At the same time the White House had cooperative relations with commentators who supported Roosevelt's foreign policies, including Walter Winchell, a vehement critic of isolationists.[48]

Isolationists complained that most radio commentators were anti-isolationist, thus distorting equal time calculations to the disadvantage of noninterventionists. Isolationists benefited, however, in having Burton K. Wheeler as chairman of the Senate Interstate Commerce Committee. He had good relations with the chairman of the Federal Communications Commission, and broadcast executives could not lightly ignore the senator. Wheeler tried to see to it that the networks and stations did not discriminate against noninterventionists in allocating broadcast time.[49]

During 1941 the America First Committee served as unofficial clearing house for noninterventionist broadcasts, including those not made under America First auspices. It was a difficult task. As Ruth Sarles wrote later, "America First had to scratch and claw at the networks, to cajole and humor, to plead and threaten, in order that it might present a small percentage of the aggregate propaganda of its opponents. America First's problem was acute. The time it weaned away from the networks was frequently given grudgingly and seldom without the admonition: 'Now don't ask again until next month.'"[50]

Roosevelt and interventionists saw the situation differently. In 1941 the president asked the chairman of the FCC to provide him with a report showing how much time the networks were giving America First as compared to the time given those supporting the administration's foreign policies. When that report was not quickly forthcoming, FDR firmly renewed his request. The tabulation he received in November showed a fairly equitable distribution during the first ten months of 1941, but with interventionists getting more broadcast time than isolationists.[51] Almost certainly neither Roosevelt nor the isolationists found the allocation of radio time satisfactory from their differing perspectives.

Roosevelt's standing with the press on foreign policy matters was much stronger than it had been on domestic issues. Colonel Robert R. McCormick's *Chicago Tribune* and the Hearst newspapers headed the list of isolationist newspapers in the United States. They were unrelenting in their attacks on the president and his policies. They were by no means alone. But some of the more prestigious and influential news publications strongly supported the president on foreign affairs. Those included, among others, the *New York Times*, the *New York Herald Tribune*, Frank Knox's *Chicago Daily News*, and Henry Luce's *Time Magazine*. Papers supporting Roosevelt's foreign policies, as often as not, were conservative, Republican, and anti-New Deal on domestic issues. The publications supporting him on foreign affairs were most numerous in the interventionist East and South, but they were by no means limited to those sections. For example, the Gardner Cowles papers in Iowa, the *Des Moines Register* and *Tribune*, were internationalist rather than isolationist in their perspectives. Some newspapers were as biased in their attacks on isolationists as the *Chicago Tribune* was in its attacks on interventionists. They included, among others, *PM*, which began publication in New York in June, 1940, under the editorial direction of Ralph Ingersoll. In a letter to Ingersoll, Roosevelt welcomed the inauguration of the newspaper, just as in 1941 he applauded the founding of Marshall Field's *Chicago Sun* to challenge McCormick's *Tribune* in that heartland city.[52]

Roosevelt was a master at the art of conducting press conferences, though he had an easier task than later presidents who would have to face the unforgiving glare of live television. FDR permitted no direct quotes without explicit permission. He was free to make comments off the record or only for background purposes if he chose (which he often did). And newsmen found it unwise to break his rules. In addition, FDR's warm personality, good humor, timing, sense for the dramatic, and talent for obfuscation usually kept him in command of the situation; newsmen rarely caught him off balance. Generally he was more attracted to writers who urged him to lead boldly than by those who advised caution in pressing his foreign policy moves. In that sense he preferred the outspoken interventionist columnist Dorothy Thompson to an Arthur Krock. The White House courted sympathetic newsmen and cooperated in providing them with "inside" information and guidance, as in 1940 when Joseph Alsop and Robert Kintner wrote their book, *American White Paper*, making the case for FDR's foreign policies.[53]

The most sensational, controversial, and damned newspaper item in the contest between isolationists and the administration was the publication, on December 4, 1941, in the *Chicago Tribune* and *Washington Times-Herald* of secret War Department contingency plans for an American expeditionary force for the military invasion of Hitler's Europe. Isolationists saw the revelation as further evidence of the warlike intentions of the Roosevelt administration and of the huge magnitude of the war effort the plans envisaged; administration leaders and interventionists saw it as further evidence of the treasonous actions of isolationists who would leak such vital information to the world—and to the likely enemy. The White House prepared a statement explaining the plans as only for contingency purposes; "To secure surreptitiously such a study and publish it as a conclusive plan of the United States Government clearly violates the most elemental conception of loyalty, patriotism and good citizenship." Interventionists, administration leaders, the Justice Department, and the FBI scurried about trying to determine who leaked the plans and how. Actually, the same Army Air Force officer who had secretly provided Senator Wheeler with information in June, 1940, had made the contingency plans available to the Montana Democratic senator. Wheeler, in turn, showed them to Chesly Manly, a Washington correspondent for the *Chicago Tribune*, who wrote the article—and stoutly refused to reveal the source for his information.[54]

Both Roosevelt and isolationists followed public opinion polls closely, both filtered their evaluations of polls through their own hopes and observations, and both emphasized those findings that reinforced their different preferences in the foreign policy debate. Roosevelt relied on a wide range of sources in shaping his conceptions of public opinion. Leading pollsters channeled their findings to the White House, as did specialized pollsters. Hadley Cantril from Princeton fed poll results to Mrs. Anna M. Rosenberg for the White House. FDR welcomed polling data, but he did not uncritically let them control his tactical moves.[55]

Throughout 1941 polls consistently showed that a majority of Americans thought it more essential for the United States to help assure defeat of the Axis, even at the risk of war, than it was for the United States to stay out of the war. Polls indicated majority support for each of the aid-short-of-war steps initiated by Roosevelt. Given those patterns, the administration and interventionists pressed for "national unity," urging all Americans to unite behind the president's policies in the face of the Axis menace. That "unity" theme meshed with the interventionist assumption (either explicit or implied) that dissent from the administrations's foreign policies was not really consistent with patriotism or loyalty, and that dissent represented irresponsible partisanship, fifth-column activity, pro-Nazi sympathies, or even treason. Roosevelt did not discourage such attitudes toward noninterventionist dissent, and he did and said much to encourage such attitudes.[56]

Isolationists too followed the polls. They particularly emphasized that some 80 percent of the American people opposed a declaration of war by the United States. In 1941 the America First Committee supported legislation that would have provided for an advisory referendum on whether the United States should or should not declare war; committee leaders were confident that such a referendum would result in an overwhelming vote against war. The committee also financed polls on that question in the congressional districts of Hamilton Fish in New York, Knute Hill in Washington state, Harry Sauthoff in Wisconsin, and Paul Shafer in Michigan. Each of the polls showed exactly what the America First Committee expected it to show—approximately 80 percent opposed to entering the war. The committee considered conducting such a referendum in North Carolina, but Senator Robert R. Reynolds there advised against it because he was convinced it would result in an embarrassing prowar vote.[57]

More than Roosevelt and interventionists, isolationists were skeptical of public opinion poll findings and thought the questions were biased in favor of the administration's policies. In April, Senator Arthur H. Vandenberg wrote to Dr. George Gallup criticizing the choice of some of the questions used in polling. Vandenberg thought Gallup was on "sound ground" when dealing with specific events. He objected, however, to speculative questions, including the question that asked whether Americans favored going to war if there were no other way to defeat Germany and Italy. He thought that question was nebulous and treacherous, "a menace not only to the British who may be misled by it but also to American leadership which may be misled by it."[58]

Early in May, 1941, Senator Nye introduced a resolution calling for an investigation of public opinion polls. In June, he introduced a bill that would have required publications reporting public opinion polls to publish statistics on the number of persons polled and would have required pollsters to keep their raw data for at least two years.[59] Neither of Nye's proposals was approved in the Senate.

In the summer of 1941 the America First Committee provided funds to enable a committee under Robert M. Hutchins, president of the University of Chicago, to conduct an independent public opinion poll. That survey indicated that the public overwhelmingly believed that Congress, rather than the president, should be the source of any action likely to involve the United States in war. It indicated that two-thirds of those with opinions opposed use of American armed forces in bases in Africa, the Azores, or the Cape Verde Islands. Nearly 80 percent opposed American entry into the war as a full belligerent. But approximately two-thirds opposed any offer by the United States to mediate between England and Germany. A clear majority would have been willing to go to war if the Western Hemisphere were attacked.[60]

R. Douglas Stuart, Jr., believed that Americans wanted to stay out of war more than they wanted a British victory over Germany,[61] but his views were not verified by the Hutchins committee poll that America First financed. Until after the Japanese attack on Pearl Harbor, Roosevelt was not able to win national unity behind the administration's foreign policies. Similarly, the America First Committee was never able to focus public attention solely on the simple issue of whether to declare war or not. The possible consequences to the United States of an Axis victory seriously disturbed most Americans. A majority was convinced that Germany had to be defeated even if that required American intervention in the war. Despite noninterventionist efforts, the foreign policy debate in 1941 was conducted largely on the aid-short-of-war grounds chosen by the president—not on the war-or-peace issue the isolationists preferred.

Much of the contest between isolationists and interventionists, even as it involved President Roosevelt, was conducted through private citizens, privately owned facilities, and through nongovernmental organizations—including the America First Committee, Committee to Defend America, Fight for Freedom Committee, Friends of Democracy, and many others. But there were those who wanted the president to establish a government propaganda agency to function powerfully and positively in efforts to rescue American minds away from isolationism. Secretary of Interior Harold L. Ickes was the most persistent advocate in the president's cabinet for the creation of such a government organ.[62]

Ickes had felt a brief flutter of hope for his propaganda scheme in

1938 when the president had appointed the experienced newsman, Lowell Mellett, as director of the National Emergency Council. In 1939 it was abolished, and Roosevelt named Mellett director of a new Office of Government Reports, a part of the executive office of the president. Mellett conducted a low-key informational and coordinating service. He put a premium on building good relations with people in the communications media. He encouraged and helped coordinate programs and activities by internationalist groups. His style was consistent with FDR's early cautious, step-at-a-time approach. Mellett feared that any high-powered government propaganda effort might alienate more than influence and could be counterproductive.[63]

Secretary Ickes had no patience with what he saw as Mellett's cautious, almost timid, approach. For that matter he was impatient with Roosevelt's aid-short-of-war, step-at-a-time approach. He respected the president but became convinced that the United States must enter the war and play its full military role in helping defeat Hitler and the Nazis. He believed that required bold leadership, massive military preparations, and positive ideological preparations as well. Secretary of War Stimson and Secretary of Navy Knox agreed with Ickes, and so did other fervent interventionists inside and outside the government.[64]

Ickes repeatedly tried to prod Roosevelt into a more aggressive and positive propaganda effort. By November, 1940, he had persuaded the president to appoint a cabinet committee (chaired by Ickes, and including Stimson, Knox, and others) to consider what Stimson called "affirmative propaganda." On November 28, Ickes reported for his committee to Roosevelt, "The nation needs adequate defense against subversive propaganda in addition to measures now being taken by the several intelligence services to combat subversive activities." He wrote that "the transcendent importance of the educational effort involved indicates that this agency should be set up and operated by the Government of the United States, but that it should work closely with all voluntary civic organizations having a common purpose." With Mellett's Office of Government Reports probably in mind, Ickes wrote that the new agency should "be kept entirely separate from any other informational effort." His committee believed it could be established without additional legislative authorization or appropriations.[65]

Not until March 3, as the lend-lease battle drew to a close, did FDR finally respond formally to the report Ickes had submitted for his committee on November 28. In his letter on March 3, Roosevelt approved the report "in principle" and asked Ickes to submit names of individuals who might serve as director and as members of the advisory committee.[66] But nothing happened on the matter in the White House—at least not quickly enough for Ickes.

Frustrated and discouraged, Ickes wrote the president again on March 12 that he felt "like a squirrel in a cage" because he had "been getting exactly nowhere" in his efforts to accomplish "an organization to fight German propaganda and to sustain and fortify the morale of our own people." Since his efforts had "not been able to make the wheels go," he asked FDR to relieve him "of any further responsibility in this matter" and put it "in the hands of someone who can make" the necessary progress. But Ickes did not entirely give up his efforts.[67]

At the cabinet meeting on April 17, Stimson, Ickes, Knox, and others helped move the president to action. Stimson introduced the subject, and all agreed something should be done. Extended discussion failed to produce agreement on the person to direct the agency. At the suggestion of Ickes, the president asked Vice-President Henry A. Wallace to serve as acting director until a permanent director was named. Roosevelt suggested that the new agency be named the Office of Civilian Defense. As Stimson recorded it, the new OCD "should encourage home defense but, above all, it should affirmatively stimulate patriotism." Wallace set to work at his task.[68]

Finally, on May 20, 1941, President Roosevelt appointed Mayor Fiorello H. La Guardia of New York City to be the unpaid director of the Office of Civilian Defense. La Guardia was a Republican and had good relations with western progressives. But he was also an outspoken interventionist and had long denounced Hitler and the Nazis in vigorous terms. Early in 1941, as president of the United States Conference of Mayors, La Guardia had submitted to Roosevelt a report on the requirements for defense of city inhabitants in the event of attack. He had a colorful personality, real political skill, and boundless energy.[69]

President Roosevelt's executive order establishing the Office of Civilian Defense directed it "to facilitate constructive civilian participation in the defense program, and to sustain national morale." Roosevelt's conception of the "morale" aspect was made clear when he wrote asking Mellett, Ickes, and Ulric Bell of the Fight for Freedom Committee to confer with La Guardia "in regard to the whole subject of effective publicity to offset the propaganda of the Wheelers, Nyes, and Lindburghs, etc." It was part of the battle against isolationists.[70]

Ickes had not suggested La Guardia for the appointment. He thought the mayor was a good choice for civilian defense, but thought it "a mistake to include morale and counter-propaganda under civilian defense." He doubted whether La Guardia was the right person to head that effort. And La Guardia seemed much too busy to confer in depth with Ickes.[71]

Ickes's misgivings proved justified from his perspective. La Guardia spread his great energies much too thin over too many tasks. Despite his interventionist convictions, he neglected the propaganda, morale, and antiisolationist aspect. Under La Guardia's direction the Office of Civilian Defense did try to improve morale and build support for the administration's policies. Some of those efforts provoked critical responses, as when the OCD sent clergymen an outline for a sermon it suggested they deliver near Armistice Day in November. An editorial in the *Cincinnati Post* claimed that pastors did not object to the proposed sermon's emphases on democracy and freedom of religion; rather, many objected to "the fact that the suggestion comes from a government official." Objections were the stronger because earlier Colonel Early E. W. Duncan, commanding officer of Lowry Field in Colorado, had declared America First headquarters off limits for men under his command and had threatened to make churches off limits whose pastors "preach against true Americanism."[72] Ickes did not necessarily like those steps, but the morale and propaganda efforts by the Office of Civilian Defense were more limited and feeble than Ickes wanted.

The differences on that matter between Roosevelt and Ickes concerned tactics, and perhaps timing; the two did not differ in their attitudes toward isolationists, Hitler, the Nazis, or on the vital necessity for defeating the Axis states. In those troubled times and in that heated contest over foreign policy, neither Roosevelt nor Ickes distinguished clearly between American isolationists on the one hand and Hitler's Nazi agents and sympathizers on the other. And as they faced noninterventionist opposition in 1941, neither FDR nor Ickes gave priority in their scale of values to tolerance, forbearance, or the right to dissent on foreign policy matters.

President Roosevelt was not reticent in trying to use government investigative and legal powers to crush isolationists. On balance, the Justice Department and J. Edgar Hoover's Federal Bureau of Investigation were more restrained in using their resources against isolationists than FDR was. From time to time the FBI received allegations of wrongdoing, foreign connections, or treasonous activities by individual isolationists or isolationist organizations. Often allegations clearly were from cranks and had no factual bases. Hoover acknowledged receipt of allegations and had agents check those that appeared to have any possible substance. He took particular note of them when they came from or were channeled through the White House, the attorney general's office, or members of Congress. The results usually were negative, the charges false, distorted, or providing no bases for legal action.[73]

For example, in 1939 and 1940 the FBI received from various sources allegations concerning foreign connections of Senator Gerald P. Nye. Hoover responded particularly to a letter forwarded from Roosevelt and to a memorandum from Stephen Early, the president's secretary, about Nye and Secretary of War Harry Woodring. As a result, Hoover had FBI agents make a detailed investigation. After the probe Hoover informed Early and the attorney general that "the investigation has failed to develop any substantiation of any of the charges made" against Nye or Woodring.[74] Similar patterns evolved with allegations against other leading isolationists. Charges of misuse of the franking privilege, including those made by Henry Hoke, had some substance and helped lead to the grand jury probe in the fall of 1941 and to subsequent convictions of Viereck, Hill, and others. But despite the many charges of pro-Nazi ties and activities that were directed against Charles A. Lindbergh, the FBI found no grounds for legal actions against him.[75] The dearth of actionable evidence, however, was not what FDR, Ickes, or fervent interventions expected or wanted.

J. Edgar Hoover's FBI received many communications alleging that isolationist organizations were pro-Nazi or subversive, with foreign ties and receiving foreign funds. Such allegations concerning the America First Committee began to reach Hoover soon after it was organized in the fall of 1940, even before the committee began to form local chapters or hold public rallies. Such charges poured in throughout the history of America First and after. The FBI obtained firsthand reports on America First meetings. Some of those reports came from unidentified sources, some from antiisolationist individuals and organizations, some from interventionist newsmen and columnists such as Walter Winchell, some from military intelligence, and others (generally the most balanced and descriptive) from the FBI's own agents.[76]

From time to time isolationists charged the FBI with using wiretaps. In 1940 Roosevelt had authorized the use of wiretaps in terms that could have been directed against isolationists if (like FDR and Ickes) one viewed the isolationists as actual or potential fifth columnists. The State Department's Adolf A. Berle, after long discussion

with Hoover, wrote in his diary that the FBI had "done far less actual
wire tapping than the Treasury, the S.E.C. and several of these agencies." Ickes had, himself, used wire taps in the course of his infighting
within the administration.[77] Hoover was highly sensitive to any criticism of the FBI, and throughout the prewar period he flatly denied
that the FBI used wiretaps on America First offices. Its various reports summarizing its information within the FBI on America First
did not reveal evidence of wire tapping. Indeed, the historian writing
many years after the committee's records were opened for research
may be struck by the skimpiness of the FBI's factual information on
the inside workings of America First, the much erroneous information
it had, the extent to which its files contained undocumented charges
from actively antiisolationist sources, and the skepticism and restraint
that Hoover and the FBI demonstrated in the face of those unsubstantiated allegations.[78]

At the same time, national leaders of America First and leaders of
some local chapters (in Los Angeles, New York, and Washington,
D.C., for example) invited the FBI to examine their files and sought
FBI help in their efforts to cleanse its rolls of any pro-Nazi or subversive elements. Hoover denied that his agents examined America First
rolls, but local agents of the FBI did examine America First files in
Chicago.[79]

Roosevelt prodded the FBI and Justice Department to look into
America First and the affairs of leading isolationists, but he got less
action than he wanted. On February 21, 1941, during the lend-lease
debate, FDR transmitted an America First circular to his secretary,
Stephen Early, with a memorandum asking: "Will you find out from
someone—perhaps F.B.I.—who is paying for this?" Early referred
FDR's memorandum and the circular to Hoover. He responded
promptly with a memorandum dated March 1 that, Hoover wrote,
"not only furnishes the desired information, but provides additional
data concerning the America First Committee." Actually, the eight-
page memorandum provided for the president at that time contained
largely easily available public information (most of it correct) with little detail on the committee's finances. On March 19, Hoover forwarded to General Watson, for the president, a memorandum on the
committee's plans to send senators and congressmen on speaking
tours across the country.[80] From time to time the White House forwarded to Hoover letters that Roosevelt had received from interventionists urging investigation or prosecution of America First and its
leading figures. At the request of Attorney General Francis Biddle, the

FBI provided the Justice Department and the White House with a detailed report on an America First meeting in Los Angeles on October 2 that Senator Wheeler addressed.[81]

On November 17, Roosevelt sent a confidential memorandum to Attorney General Biddle asking him to speak to him "about the possibility of a Grand Jury investigation of the money sources behind the America First Committee." Roosevelt wrote, "It certainly ought to be looked into and I cannot get any action out of Congress."[82] As a result the FBI began preparing an up-to-date summary of what it had in its files on America First. By December 4, the FBI had prepared a twenty-one-page summary memorandum on the America First Committee for the attorney general. It had not, however, made an exhaustive concentrated investigation.[83] And the Justice Department was not yet prepared to undertake a grand jury probe or prosecution of America First.

J. Edgar Hoover, in his capacity as director of the FBI and under the authority of President Roosevelt, also cooperated with British agents and agencies in the United States that shared with Roosevelt and the interventionists in defeating American isolationists. The British Library of Information in New York provided English leaders with impressively full and accurate information on the state of American public and press opinion. It actively helped interventionists, including the Fight for Freedom Committee, in efforts to move public opinion in the direction of aid and involvement on the side of Great Britain's struggle against the Axis states. Similarly, William S. Stephenson and his British Security Co-Ordination in New York, with Roosevelt's assent and Hoover's cooperation, actively helped in the domestic struggle against American isolationists. Stephenson's organization secretly worked to discredit America First, Lindbergh, Fish, and other isolationists.[84]

Chapter 31
Pearl Harbor

In the contest between Roosevelt and the isolationists, East Asia and the Pacific were the "back door to war." Both President Roosevelt and leading opponents of his foreign policies looked primarily to Europe rather than to Asia. Roosevelt saw Hitler and Nazi Germany in Europe as the most dangerous threats to peace, freedom, and security; isolationism took form in opposition to involvement in European wars and alliances. The possibilities of war with Japan seemed less alarming both to interventionists and to isolationists than war in Europe. Though most Americans abhorred Nazi Germany and Fascist Italy, hard line policies toward Japan encountered less opposition than did comparable policies toward the Axis states in Europe.

Moreover, most American actions to check or slow Japanese expansion in Asia and the Pacific were undertaken by executive authority rather than through Congress. Noninterventionists had fewer and less clear-cut opportunities to battle in Congress against Roosevelt's Far East policies than they had in opposing his policies toward the war in Europe. Conceivably lend-lease, draft extension, and revision of neutrality legislation in 1941 might have been couched in terms of the Pacific war—but for the most part they were not. During seventeen months before the Japanese attack on Pearl Harbor the Roosevelt administration did not seek congressional approval for legislation or treaties that would have given noninterventionists opportunities to battle directly against his policies toward the Sino-Japanese war. Not until the closing months of 1941 did most isolationists (or interventionists) direct much attention to the war in Asia. Even then they never fully refocused the foreign policy debate from the Atlantic to the Pacific. Even if they had, by the latter part of 1941 executive decisions (both in Japan and in the United States) had set in motion developments moving the countries toward war that could not readily have been checked by legislative action and were not likely to be reversed by administrative action (in either country).

China remained central to Japanese concerns in East Asia and to differences between the United States and Japan. By 1940 and 1941, however, the Tripartite Pact that bound Japan to Germany and Italy, Japanese expansion into French Indochina, the Russo-German war, hard-line nudgings on Roosevelt from Britain's Churchill, and oil (Japan's need for it and the withholding of it by the United States, Britain, and the Netherlands) combined to make the compound in Asia more complicated and explosive. The Tripartite Pact of September, 1940, made the Rome-Berlin-Tokyo Axis seem more formidable worldwide and increased the alarming possibilities of a two-ocean war for the United States and Britain. The Tripartite Pact and Japan's move into northern Indochina in September, 1940, encouraged the United States to license exports to Japan (including the export of scrap iron). The Russo-German war beginning on June 22, 1941, led Germany to press Japan to strike against the Soviet Union in Asia and made the Soviet Union vulnerable to such a Japanese move. At the same time, the Russo-German war secured Japan's northern flank on the Soviet border and left Japan more free to consider military moves south (or east). Oil became the lubricant that moved the powers onto collision courses.[1]

Oil was of vital concern in Japanese-American relations. Secretary of State Hull and Undersecretary Welles feared that if the United States blocked the flow of oil, it would cause Japan to expand further (particularly to the Dutch East Indies) to obtain essential oil supplies for its war machine. Until the middle of 1941 President Roosevelt shared that concern. More militant interventionists, however, led by Secretary of Interior Ickes, Secretary of Treasury Morgenthau, and Secretary of War Stimson favored banning sale of oil to Japan. Those interventionists had the president's ear in 1941. He continued to be alert to the possibility that stopping oil to Japan might lead that country to expand further into the southwest Pacific and the Dutch East Indies. For example, according to Morgenthau, as late as July 18 Roosevelt gave the cabinet "quite a lecture" warning that if the United States "stopped all oil, it would simply drive the Japanese down to the Dutch East Indies, and it would mean war in the Pacific." But at that same cabinet meeting the president decided to freeze Japanese (and Chinese) assets if Japan took over the rest of Indochina. Japan took Indochina, and the United States froze Japanese assets. That action, along with comparable steps by Great Britain and the

Netherlands, soon stopped the flow of oil to Japan. The loss of access to petroleum supplies might have stopped Japan's war machine if it were prepared to abandon its Greater East Asia Co-Prosperity Sphere and China. But if it persisted in its original goals (and it did), Japan would either have to use diplomatic skills to reopen access to oil supplies, or it would have to expand further (probably into the Dutch East Indies) to gain assured and controlled access to the oil it must have. There were those who predicted each alternative for the Japanese. President Roosevelt heard both sets of arguments and in July decided to freeze Japanese assets.[2]

In mid-August, 1941, President Roosevelt met secretly at sea off Newfoundland with Britain's Prime Minister Churchill. That dramatic meeting produced the eight-point Atlantic Charter outlining Anglo-American goals "after the final destruction of the Nazi tyranny." After the conference, public attention focused on the Atlantic Charter. During their secret deliberations aboard ship, however, Churchill and Roosevelt had concentrated much of their time and attention upon policies toward Japan. Churchill had pressed Roosevelt to warn that further Japanese expansion in the southwest Pacific "might lead to war between the United States and Japan." Roosevelt was not prepared to speak so bluntly, but on his way back to Washington he radioed Secretary Hull directing him to arrange a White House appointment with the Japanese ambassador the day he got back. Fearful of jeopardizing his continuing negotiations with Japan and of provoking war with Japan, Hull persuaded Roosevelt to soften the language Churchill had urged. Roosevelt spoke strongly nonetheless. On the afternoon of August 17, President Roosevelt told Ambassador Nomura that if Japan took "any further steps in pursuance of a policy or program of military domination by force or threat of force of neighboring countries," the United States would "be compelled to take immediately any and all steps which it may deem necessary toward safeguarding the legitimate rights and interests of the United States and American nationals and toward insuring the safety and security of the United States."[3]

Those United States policies toward Japan were consistent with a concise statement of views in a remarkable letter (drafted in the State Department) from President Roosevelt to Francis B. Sayre, the United States high commissioner to the Philippines, dated December 31, 1940: "We of course do not want to be drawn into a war with Japan—we do not want to be drawn into any war anywhere. There is, however, very close connection between the hostilities . . . in the Far East and those . . . in eastern Europe and the Mediterranean. . . . If Japan, moving further southward, should gain possession of the region of the Netherlands East Indies and the Malaya Peninsula, would not the chances of Germany's defeating Great Britain be increased and the chances of England's winning be decreased thereby? I share your view that our strategy should be to render every assistance possible to Great Britain without ourselves entering the war, but would we be rendering every assistance possible to Great Britain were we to give our attention wholly and exclusively to the problems of the immediate defense of the British Isles and of Britain's control of the Atlantic? The British Isles, the British in those Isles, have been able to exist and to defend themselves not only because they have prepared strong local defenses but also because as the heart and the nerve center of the British Empire they have been able to draw upon vast resources for their sustenance and to bring into operation against their enemies economic, military and naval pressures on a world-wide scale. . . .

"The British need assistance along the lines of our generally established policies at many points. . . . Their defense strategy must in the nature of things be global. Our strategy of giving them assistance toward ensuring our own security must envisage both sending of supplies to England and helping to prevent a closing of channels of communication to and from various parts of the world, so that other important sources of supply and other theaters of action will not be denied to the British. We have no intention of being 'sucked into' a war with Japan any more than we have of being 'sucked into' a war with Germany. Whether there will come to us war with either or both of those countries will depend far more upon what they do than upon what we deliberately refrain from doing."[4]

All those considerations in Japanese-American relations were subjects for concerned deliberations in the White House. The differences between the cautious Hull and Welles of the State Department on the one hand and hard-liners such as Ickes, Morgenthau, Stimson, and Knox on the other were not clashes between isolationists and interventionists; they were differences on tactics among administration leaders—all of whom were internationalists or interventionists. None of those matters was presented to Congress for legislative action or advice. During 1941 neither Congress nor the American people (nor the isolationists) played any direct role in shaping or controlling United States policies toward Japan until after the attack on Pearl Harbor on

December 7. The absence of congressional opportunities to pass on policies toward Japan, preoccupation with developments in Europe and the Atlantic, government secrecy, and the general hard-line attitudes of most Americans toward Japan combined in 1941 to weaken isolationist or noninterventionist opposition to Roosevelt's policies toward Japan. Isolationists found it difficult to determine what the president was doing and why, and they found it impossible to block his actions if they discovered or surmised what he was doing.

The secrecy surrounding American policies toward Japan in general and toward the Churchill-Roosevelt talks in particular aroused suspicions and distrust. That secrecy invited flights of imagination. But many of the guesses by isolationist leaders took them closer to the mark than they would have been if they had passively and naïvely accepted the Atlantic Charter as the only significant work of the Churchill-Roosevelt meeting. Isolationist allegations that the Atlantic Charter did not tell the full or most important story of the Roosevelt-Churchill deliberations were correct, even though official secrecy drove them to imperfect guesses about what did occur between the leaders of those two great English-speaking countries.

In October, 1940, R. Douglas Stuart, Jr., national director of the America First Committee, wrote to Senator Wheeler's office in Washington that he thought it "terribly important that we analyze critically our Pacific foreign policy at this time. No one has any comprehension at all of what the score is out there." An America First advertisement in mid-October charged that America was "threatened with self-made 'emergencies' that may involve us in a war with Japan (and instantly thereafter in the European conflict). Nobody even pretends that such a war would be in our own defense. We would have everything to lose. Nothing to gain!"[5]

During 1941 publications of the New York chapter of America First under the chairmanship of John T. Flynn repeatedly charged that American involvement in war in Asia would defend British imperialism—not democracy and freedom. Its publications contended that Britain, France, and the Netherlands had "conquered and exploited" millions in Asia and the Pacific "just as Italy has exploited Ethiopia." That had "nothing to do with either democracy or civilization" and was "certainly not something for which we should fight." The chapter's *America First Bulletin* insisted: "The battle in Asia is Britain's battle—and a battle not for democracy, but to continue her hold on 300,000,000 people in India, millions more in Malay and other territories of Asia, to say nothing of a hundred million in Africa. She is parked there for the gold, the oil, the rubber, the silver, the diamonds, the rich supplies which her capitalists own there—which belong to the peoples of those countries, but which Britain has stolen."[6]

In July, after the United States froze Japanese assets, the executive committee of the New York America First chapter unanimously voted its objections to the United States course. In its official newspaper the chapter deplored the Japanese actions but insisted that the United States had "no business mixing in them," and that involvement was "done not in the interest of democracy or even of our selves but in the interest of Britain's indefensible empire in the East."[7]

On August 11, after the United States had frozen Japanese assets and at the very moment that Roosevelt was conferring at sea secretly with Churchill, the national executive committee of America First under General Wood in Chicago formally approved a resolution opposing American involvement in war with Japan in the Pacific except in case of attack.[8] After the Roosevelt-Churchill meeting and its Atlantic Charter were made public, General Wood said that if there were "no secret agreements beyond the signed declaration," the America First Committee had little objection to the charter. His only objection was the use of the phrase, "after the final destruction of Nazi tyranny," uncertain whether the president had "committed the United States to entrance into the European war to destroy the existing German government" or whether it was "only a wish on the part of Churchill." The following day, August 15, Ruth Sarles in Washington wrote to Stuart in Chicago reporting a different perspective: "The whole Far Eastern situation was thoroughly canvassed by Churchill and Roosevelt and they are ready to take immediate action whenever Japan moves. It does not mean that we would fight if Japan moved into Siam, but we would fight if there were a move toward the Dutch East Indies or Singapore."[9]

On August 19, America First national headquarters released a statement by General Wood complaining "that the English people know more about the meeting of the two leaders than do the American people." According to Wood, "The English people see in the joint declaration assurances on the part of President Roosevelt that America will soon follow up the proposed peace points by active participation in the war." He insisted that Americans were "entitled to know the full facts. Secret agreements made by the President have no place under our Constitution and democratic system. If he has sought personally to commit this nation to war he should advise the American people so that such purported treaty many be considered—and repudiated—by the Senate, in accordance with the Constitution.''[10]

John T. Flynn, at the head of the New York America First chapter, called the Atlantic Charter a "cover-up" and urged Roosevelt and Churchill to "be frank.'' He charged that "their words about all of the peoples in the world naming their own kind of government is meaningless unless it applies to such countries as India, Indo-China, the Dutch Indies, British Malaya, Lithuania, Latvia, Estonia and Finland.'' The America First Research Bureau in Washington produced *Did You Know* studies critically analyzing the Atlantic Charter and implying that secret military arrangements between Roosevelt and Churchill were more important than the charter they had made public.[11]

Isolationist senators advanced similar views. Writing late in February, 1941, Republican Senator Arthur Capper of Kansas favored letting "the Orient stew in its own juice" and giving the Philippines their freedom. He insisted that the United States "had less business in the Far East, in the line of military supremacy and conflict, than we have even in Europe.'' In July, Democratic Senator Burton K. Wheeler of Montana approved the administration's decision to freeze Japanese assets. He thought it would "slow up Japan from an economic standpoint and call their bluff so they will not start anything.'' But he did not want war with Japan. Wheeler believed that if the United States went to war with Japan, it would "be undertaking to preserve the British domination of Asia.'' He described Japan as "one of our best customers and we are one of her best customers. There is no reason why we should not live in peace with her.''[12]

After the Atlantic conference, Republican Senator Hiram Johnson of California wrote his son, "What Churchill and Roosevelt signed was an offensive and defensive alliance, and specifically takes us into the war.'' When FDR denied that the United States had advanced further toward war at the Atlantic meeting, Johnson contended that either Roosevelt was deliberately lying or "in his simplicity, he has been taken to town by Churchill.'' But Johnson did not really believe that Roosevelt had been duped; he was convinced that Roosevelt "knew just what he was doing, and he did it with malice aforethought, and commits us to a fight to the death with the German Reich.'' His reaction was, "God help America.'' Former President Herbert Hoover believed that the Roosevelt administration was doing everything it could "to get us into war through the Japanese back door.''[13]

In an address before an America First meeting in the Bronx, New York, on August 27, Republican Senator Gerald P. Nye of North Dakota ridiculed "the Two Men in a Boat on the bounding waves of the Atlantic" who were "going to disarm the world, except that part of the world which these two men will dominate." He presumed that Britain and the United States would not be able to disarm "because the task is forever to be ours of policing the world, inflicting our ideologies and our wishes upon all the world." He too contended that "much more than the 'eight points' were the subjects of conversation" between Roosevelt and Churchill. Nye quoted Churchill's later radio address to the effect that the president and the prime minister had "jointly pledged their countries to the final destruction of the Nazi tyranny." But even in his critical guessing about what lay behind the facade of the Atlantic Charter, Nye in that speech did not reveal substantial awareness of the significance of the Roosevelt-Churchill meeting for British and American policies toward the war in Asia.[14]

During the closing months of 1941, fruitless negotiations continued between the United States and Japan. As tensions mounted, pressures for firmness in the negotiations grew stronger on both sides. Each side sought fundamental concessions from the other; each offered concessions that failed to come to grips with the heart of the difficulties as the other saw them. Neither gave ground on matters it considered vital, including China and oil. Each saw the other as hostile to its vital interests; neither trusted the good faith or reasonableness of the other. Both braced for the military hostilities that each wanted to avoid but both feared were coming. And secrecy in different ways veiled citizens and legislators of both countries from specific details in the negotiations as the tensions mounted.

In July, 1941, the Japanese government formally determined to establish its Greater East Asia Co-Prosperity Sphere and settle the "China affair"—even if that meant war with the United States. Japanese naval and air forces began preparing secretly for the attack on Pearl Harbor, Hawaii, in the event negotiations should fail. In August Japan proposed a meeting between Prince Fumimaro Konoye and President Roosevelt. Believing that the Japanese premier would not or could not conclude or enforce a satisfactory agreement, Roosevelt and Hull rejected the proposal pending agreement on general principles in advance of such a meeting. In early September the Japanese government formally decided on war with the United States if diplomatic negotiations failed. In October the army and hard-liners strengthened their position in Japan when General Hideki Tojo replaced Konoye as prime minister. In November the Japanese government sent Saburo Kurusu to assist Ambassador Nomuro with the negotiations in Washington.[15]

On October 16, as leadership in the Japanese government shifted from Konoye to Tojo, President Roosevelt canceled his scheduled cabinet meeting and instead met for two hours with Hull, Stimson, Knox, Hopkins, General Marshall, and Admiral Stark to discuss the crisis. As Stimson phrased it in his diary, they faced "the delicate question of diplomatic fencing to be done so as to be sure that Japan was put into the wrong and made the first bad move—overt move." On November 7 President Roosevelt polled his cabinet to determine whether they believed "the people would back us up in case we struck at Japan down there." According to Stimson the cabinet members were "unanimous in feeling the country would support us"—a view that Roosevelt shared. The next day Fiorello La Guardia as director of the Office of Civilian Defense sent letters to all OCD regional directors arguing that there had been "too little emphasis in public discussion on the threat of trouble in the Far East." He thought that situation was "immediate and critical" and urged efforts to correct it. In his own speeches La Guardia promised "to stress the Far Eastern threat with as much vigor" as he could command and urged that same course on others.[16]

On November 20 Ambassador Nomura and Kurusu presented to Secretary Hull a modus vivendi that proved to be Japan's final terms for resolving the diplomatic impasse. Japan proposed that neither government expand further south militarily and that the United States and Japan cooperate to get supplies that each needed in the Netherlands East Indies. Each would restore the commercial relations that had prevailed before the United States had frozen Japanese assets. The United States was to supply oil for Japan. And the United States was not to interfere with relations between Japan and China (that is, the United States was to give Japan a free hand in China).[17]

Roosevelt and Hull considered responding with an alternative modus vivendi. Roosevelt thought it "a fair proposition for the Japanese." In a cable to Churchill, however, he was "not very hopeful" and warned that "we must all be prepared for real trouble, possibly soon." China's Generalissimo Chiang Kai-shek vigorously objected to the modus vivendi. The British, Dutch, and Australian governments had misgivings about it. Churchill cabled Roosevelt asking if it did not give Chiang Kai-shek "a very thin diet." On November 25 Roosevelt met at the White House for an hour and one-half with Hull, Stimson,

Knox, Marshall, and Stark to discuss relations with Japan. According to Stimson's diary, President Roosevelt thought the United States was "likely to be attacked perhaps next Monday, for the Japanese are notorious for making an attack without warning." They discussed the question of how "we should maneuver them into the position of firing the first shot without allowing too much danger to ourselves." Later that day Stimson learned through Magic (America's deciphering of the secret Japanese diplomatic code) that Japan was preparing to move a sizeable expedition of ships and men south. When Roosevelt learned of that the next day, he viewed it as "an evidence of bad faith" on the part of the Japanese.[18]

On November 26 Secretary Hull abandoned the idea for a modus vivendi. Instead, he presented Nomura and Kurusu with American terms that were as unacceptable to Japan as the Japanese proposals had been to the United States. The secretary insisted that Japan endorse Hull's principles of conduct in international affairs. He called on Japan to withdraw all its military forces from China and Indochina. Japan was to support the Nationalist government of China and, in effect, end its commitments to the European Axis. The United States would remove its economic restrictions, conclude a trade treaty, and cooperate with Japan in assuring equality of access to raw materials and markets in Asia. In those proposals Hull wanted to make the American position clear, but he and the other American leaders knew that Japan would reject the terms. As Hull phrased it to Secretary of War Stimson, "I have washed my hands of it and it is now in the hands of you and Knox—the Army and the Navy."[19]

Washington sent war warnings to General Walter Short and Admiral Husband Kimmel in Hawaii and to General Douglas MacArthur in the Philippines. In a memorandum to the president on November 27, General Marshall and Admiral Stark wrote, "If the current negotiations end without agreement, Japan may attack." They pointed out that the Japanese troop movements all seemed to be southward. They thought, "The most essential thing now, from the United States viewpoint, is to gain time."[20]

After conferring with his "War Cabinet" on Friday, November 28, Roosevelt left to spend Thanksgiving in Warm Springs, Georgia. Hull was tired and ill. On December 3, after his return to Washington, FDR told Morgenthau that he thought the Japanese were "doing everything they can to stall until they are ready." He said he was "talking with the English about war plans as to when and where the U.S.A. and Great Britain should strike." On December 6, as tensions mounted, the president sent a message to Emperor Hirohito of Japan seeking his help to try to preserve peace.[21]

Through those mounting tensions noninterventionists floundered ineffectively and somewhat blindly in their efforts to combat the possibility of American involvement in the Asian war. They were handicapped by their lack of precise factual information on Roosevelt's policies toward Japan, on Japan's policies and actions, and on the course of the diplomatic negotiations between the two governments. On November 21 Senator Nye told newsmen that he believed the United States could end the Sino-Japanese war and prevent further hostilities in the Pacific if it were willing to "help Japan save her face" by agreeing to minor concessions for Japan in China. He thought war could be averted by agreeing to the establishment of Japanese air bases at two or three places in China and the resumption of normal trade between the United States and Japan. Nye thought that might be enough to get the Japanese to withdraw their troops from China and to end their war against Chiang Kai-shek. The trouble was, Nye said, "that the Administration doesn't want to settle this thing because it is largely responsible for any war fever that may be felt in this country now." In a letter at the same time Nye wrote that he thought it "probable that if we got into the war it would be through the back door of Japan with Britain negotiating the plays for us."[22]

On December 3 Senator Wheeler told newsmen: "The only time the Administration had intimated that we should go to war with Japan is when the British Empire is threatened. Japan had not threatened us." He repeated his statement made early in the year that the administration's foreign policies might plow under every fourth American boy. As he viewed it, "The only excuse we would have for war with Japan is for the purpose of protecting the British Empire."[23]

On December 5, Stuart at America First national headquarters in Chicago telegraphed Ruth Sarles at the America First Research Bureau in Washington urging her to get members of Congress to broadcast radio speeches opposing involvement in the war in Asia. America First national headquarters was working on a statement it might issue in the near future on the Far East situation. On Saturday, December 6, Sarles wrote Stuart that she had "no clear lead on the Far East situation." She had been trying to arouse interest in the possibility of introducing a resolution in the Senate asking the president to give the Foreign Relations Committee the facts on which his Far East policies were based. She had had no luck in getting congressmen to deliver radio speeches on the Far East, but promised to continue her efforts.

Miss Sarles suggested digging out the old arguments about the military difficulties of fighting a war in Asia. But neither the efforts at America First national headquarters nor those at the committee's Washington offices got much beyond the talking stage by Sunday, December 7, 1941.[24]

America First News published by the Southern California Division of America First on December 5 carried articles on a range of subjects—but none on Japan or the war in Asia. The *America First Bulletin* published by Flynn's New York chapter on December 6 tried to sort through the rumors and concluded: "The Administration, and the Administration alone, will be completely responsible for any breakdown in relations with Japan. The Administration has taken it upon itself to demand actions from Japan that in no way concern the national interests of the United States. None of our territorial possessions are in any way involved." It complained: "Without any authority from the people or Congress, the Administration has threatened Japan with naval and military opposition. It has talked of war without even the faintest suggestion of authorization for such talk from Congress." It doubted that Congress would approve waging war "nine thousand miles from home, to fight for foreign empires in a war that has nothing conceivably to do with our own national interests."[25]

The chapter publication contended that the United States had "never raised a finger for China in all her four years of war until Britain's eastern empire became involved." It maintained that if Congress voted a declaration of war, it would "be plunging the United States into a vast Asiatic conflict for no reason in this world but to save the British and the Dutch empires in Asia." It asked whether Americans were "prepared to send their sons to the battlefields of China, of Indo-China, of Malaya and Burma to tell to the people of Asia how to manage the affairs of Asia, to save India for the British and Java for the Dutch." And it charged that that was "precisely what we may be doing before this year is out" if Roosevelt and Hull were "not restrained."[26]

As the sun brought daylight to Washington, D.C., on the east coast of North America on Sunday morning, December 7, 1941, Hawaii and the Philippines on the western reaches of American territories slumbered under the cover of darkness. Both Japanese and Americans busily decoded the long Japanese reply to Hull's proposal of November 26. When Roosevelt had seen the first parts of that reply the evening before (courtesy of Magic), he had exclaimed, "This means war." The Japanese response was wholly negative. It rejected the American proposal and concluded that it was "impossible to reach an agreement through further negotiations." Both American leaders and Japanese diplomats in Washington realized that the critical moment had arrived, but neither knew what specific form the immediate future might take for Japanese-American relations. The attention of Roosevelt and the other top Americans in Washington focused on the Japanese reply, on the Japanese military movement southward, on the United States course in the event Japan struck militarily (with or without striking American installations), and on the possible reactions of the American people to Japanese (and American) policies and actions in that critical situation.[27]

That morning Stimson and Knox conferred with Hull at length. According to Stimson, Hull was "very certain that the Japs are planning some deviltry" and they all wondered "where the blow will strike." Ambassador Nomura, as directed by his government, arranged an appointment with Hull for 1:00 P.M. to transmit the Japanese reply, but delay in decoding made it necessary for the ambassador to postpone the appointment until 1:45 in the early afternoon. Roosevelt had lunch at his desk in the Oval Room of the White House with Harry Hopkins. At 1:40 P.M. Secretary of Navy Knox telephoned the president to report news that a Japanese air attack was under way on Hawaii in the Pacific. The attack had begun twenty minutes earlier (at 7:50 A.M. Honolulu time) and continued for about an hour and forty-five minutes before the last of the Japanese planes left the flaming, smoking ruins at Pearl Harbor. The president telephoned Hull just as Nomura and Kurusu arrived at the secretary's office at 2:05. He told Hull to receive them coolly without revealing his knowledge of the attack. Hull kept the two diplomats waiting fifteen minutes until he received them at 2:20. He had already read the Japanese reply before they presented it to him. He kept them standing while he went through the motions of reading the document. Then he told them that he had "never seen a document that was more crowded with infamous falsehoods and distortions" and coolly sent them on their way.[28]

Roosevelt also telephoned Stimson with news of the Japanese attack. The secretary of war's "first feeling was of relief that the indecision was over and that a crisis had come in a way which would unite all our people." They had believed that the United States "must fight if the British fought." But they were concerned about the reactions of the American people (and about continued isolationist and noninterventionist agitation) if Japan provoked war with Britain but did not directly strike at American territories and installations. "But now the

Japs have solved the whole thing by attacking us directly in Hawaii."
Stimson believed that a united America had "practically nothing to
fear while the apathy and divisions stirred up by unpatriotic men have
been hitherto very discouraging."[29]

At 3:05 in the afternoon President Roosevelt met with Stimson,
Knox, Hopkins, and others in the first of many dramatic White House
conferences that day.[30] At very nearly that same moment an America
First meeting began at Soldiers and Sailors Memorial Hall in Pittsburgh, Pennsylvania. Some twenty-five hundred people crowded into
the hall. Though he was unable to attend personally, the honorary
chairman of the chapter, former Republican United States Senator
David A. Reed, had issued a statement questioning the necessity and
wisdom of war by the United States against Japan. In his statement
Reed asked, "Is it possible that somebody is scheming to maneuver us
into war in the Pacific in order that we might be more easily pushed
into a greater and more destructive war in Europe and Asia and
Africa?" The program scheduled talks by former state Senator C.
Hale Sipe and Irene Castle McLaughlin, but the main speaker was
Senator Gerald P. Nye.[31]

A few minutes before three o'clock, while they were preparing to
go on the stage, a reporter told them that the White House had announced a Japanese attack on Hawaii and the Philippines. At that
moment Japanese planes actually were in the midst of the last of their
assaults on Hawaii. Nye and the others, however, were skeptical of the
report. Recalling the *Greer* incident, when the first reports were misleading, Nye suspected a hoax or at least exaggeration in the report.
He told the reporter that he would need more reliable information. He
then put the incident out of his mind and, with the others, began the
meeting.

While Sipe was speaking, an army colonel in civilian clothes arose
in the audience to ask whether they knew that Japan had attacked.
Those around him noisily drowned out the colonel, and he was ejected
from the hall. From the speakers platform the disturbance appeared
like others that hecklers had caused at previous meetings. In the hub-
bub the speakers could not hear the colonel's statements and did not
know his identity. Senator Nye began his address shortly before five
o'clock, approximately two hours after the meeting began and an
hour and one-half after the last Japanese planes had left Pearl Harbor. As he was commenting on the role of British propaganda in
American relations with Japan, a reporter laid a note before him that
read: "The Japanese Imperial Government in Tokyo at 4 P.M. an-

nounced a state of war against the United States and Great Britain.''
Nye was taken aback and flustered by the information and was still
not certain whether to believe it or not. He finished the point he was
making at that moment in his speech by citing Sidney Rogerson's English book, *Propaganda in the Next War*, to the effect that the only
way the United States might be brought into another British war
would be through war with Japan. He then told the audience of the attack and quickly closed his remarks and the meeting—still somewhat
doubtful about the truth of the report. That ended the last public
meeting of the America First Committee. News media, both local and
national, made that last meeting seem disgraceful and almost treasonous. But Nye and the others had no apologies. They considered their
noninterventionist efforts both honorable and patriotic in a democracy even up to the very moment they got reliable information that
Japan had brought war to the United States.[32] When newsmen questioned him later, Senator Nye told them, "If Japan attacked, there is
nothing left for Congress to do but declare war." He said that would
not, however, materially change his noninterventionist opinions on
the war in Europe. The *New York Times* quoted Nye as saying that the
attack was "just what Britain had planned for us" and that the United
States had been "doing its utmost to provoke a quarrel with Japan."[33]

Though isolationists had been highly critical of Roosevelt and his
policies, though many believed the administration had provoked
Japan into attacking, and though many were troubled by the unpre-
paredness of American military and naval forces at Pearl Harbor,
they united behind the United States government in opposition to
Japan. On December 7, Charles A. Lindbergh had been spending a
quiet day with his family on the island of Martha's Vineyard off Cape
Cod in Massachusetts. His initial response to news of the attack included a touch of disbelief. Was it really a major attack, or just an exaggerated story by radio commentators? In his journal he wrote that
he was "not surprised that the Japs attacked," believing that the
United States had "been prodding them into war for weeks." He had
expected an attack in the Philippines. He was surprised that the Japanese also struck Pearl Harbor, however, and he was surprised by the
size of the attack and by America's heavy losses. On the Monday
morning after the Japanese attack, Lindbergh telephoned Stuart at
America First headquarters to urge that the meeting he had been
scheduled to address in Boston on December 12 be canceled. He also
called General Wood. Wood's first words to Lindbergh on the telephone were, "Well, he got us in through the back door." Lindbergh

prepared a statement for immediate release to the press through the America First Committee. In his statement he wrote: "We have been stepping closer to war for many months. Now it has come and we must meet it as united Americans regardless of our attitude in the past toward the policy our government has followed. Whether or not that policy has been wise, our country has been attacked by force of arms, and by force of arms we must retaliate. Our own defenses and our own military position have already been neglected too long. We must now turn every effort to building the greatest and most efficient Army, Navy, and Air Force in the world."[34]

Much to his surprise, frail old Senator Hiram Johnson, ranking minority member of the Foreign Relations Committee, was one of the ten congressmen invited to meet with the president, the vice-president, and the cabinet at 9:45 on the evening of Pearl Harbor day. He was the most prominent isolationist present at that somber gathering. (Roosevelt excluded Hamilton Fish, the ranking minority member of the House Foreign Affairs Committee.) Despite their sharp foreign policy differences and though they had not talked with each other for two years, Secretary of Interior Ickes and Senator Johnson, once good friends, exchanged friendly greetings at the White House that evening. Like others, Johnson was shaken by the tragedy at Pearl Harbor, but he thought the "worst part of this Japanese war" was that it would project the United States "very easily into the European war." Writing to his son on December 14, Johnson emphasized that "with our country at war, we want to see it win, and every one of us will do what little we can to promote the cause." He was troubled, however, that with war so many people "believe this means we must assent to everything that is suggested to us by all of those in power; that we must permit ourselves to be deprived of our civil liberties, and must have no minds of our own." He refused to "subscribe to this doctrine." He thought it would not be a long war, but feared that it would "last long enough to demolish our internal economy."[35]

After the Japanese attack Senator Wheeler said that "the only thing to do now is to do our best to lick hell out of them." Former Ambassador Joseph P. Kennedy sent a telegram to the president: "In this great crisis all Americans are with you. Name the Battle Post. I'm yours to command." Former President Hoover pledged his support to the president in the war effort. In personal letters to fellow noninterventionists, however, Hoover wrote that the "continuous putting pins in rattlesnakes finally got this country bitten." He believed that "if Japan had been allowed to go on without these trade restrictions and provocations, she would have collapsed from internal economic reasons alone within a couple of years." He thought history would sustain the wisdom of the noninterventionists and the error of the administration's course.[36]

On December 7, Senator Arthur H. Vandenberg telephoned the White House to inform the president that despite their differences on other matters he pledged his support "without reservation" in the response to Japan. After the declaration of war against Japan on December 8, Vandenberg wrote in his diary that he continued "to believe that a wiser foreign policy could have been followed—although now no one will ever be able to prove it." "Without condoning for an instant the *way* in which Japan precipitated hostilities," Vandenberg wrote that he still thought "we may have *driven* her *needlessly* into hostilities through our dogmatic diplomatic attitudes." But now that the United States was in the war he believed "Nothing matters except VICTORY. The 'arguments' must be postponed."[37]

Senator Capper wrote the president assuring him of his "fullest support and cooperation in steps which may be required to bring the war to a successful conclusion." On December 12, Republican Congressman Fish wrote to President Roosevelt offering his "wholehearted support in helping to achieve final victory." Despite their differences, Fish wrote that "the time for debate and controversy has passed." He asked for an opportunity to discuss with Roosevelt how he could "best help promote unity, uphold your war program, serve my country."[38] Most other prominent prewar noninterventionists, in and out of Congress, similarly pledged their support for the war effort.

On the evening of December 7 the America First national headquarters in Chicago released a statement urging its followers "to give their support to the war effort of this country until the conflict with Japan is brought to a successful conclusion. In this war the America First Committee pledges its aid to the President as commander in chief of the armed forces of the United States." The committee instructed local chapters to postpone all scheduled rallies, and it stopped distribution of noninterventionist literature. The committee's statement, however, deliberately was phrased to leave the door open for possible continued opposition to participation in the European war.[39]

Chapter leaders and noninterventionist congressmen and senators were consulted for their views concerning the committee's course. The overwhelming majority of chapter leaders believed that America First should not dissolve completely. Most recommended that the organization be kept intact for use later on some other public issue. The congressmen and senators consulted advised against a hasty decision. Most of them, including Senators Nye, La Follette, Johnson, and D. Worth Clark and Congressman Karl Mundt, believed the committee should continue in some form. Their views probably were influenced in part by hope for support at the polls. Senator Taft believed the committee should dissolve.[40]

The America First national committee met in Chicago on December 11. A minority of those present believed "some method of adjourning was preferable to complete liquidation." The majority, however, including General Wood and John T. Flynn, favored complete dissolution. They reasoned that the committee had been identified with opposition to participation in the war; continued activity even on different issues would be subject to suspicion and criticism. The majority at that meeting approved the following public statement: "Our principles were right. Had they been followed, war could have been avoided. No good purpose can now be served by considering what might have been, had our objectives been attained. . . . We are at war. Today, though there may be many important subsidiary considerations, the primary objective is . . . victory.

"While the executive branch of the government will take charge of the prosecution of the war, the fundamental rights of American citizens under our Constitution and Bill of Rights must be respected. The long range aims and policies of our country must be determined by the people through Congress. We hope that secret treaties committing America to imperialistic aims or vast burdens in other parts of the world shall be scrupulously avoided to the end that this nation shall become the champion of a just and lasting peace.

"The period of democratic debate on the issue of entering the war is over; the time for military action is here. Therefore, the America First Committee has determined immediately to cease all functions and to dissolve as soon as that can legally be done. And finally, it urges all those who have followed its lead to give their full support to the war effort of the nation, until peace is attained."[41] The committee then undertook the dreary task of dismantling its organization, settling its financial accounts, and gathering its records for posterity. By February, 1942, the process of dissolution was essentially complete, though the America First corporation was not dissolved legally until April 22, to prevent use of the committee's name by other groups.[42]

At noon on Monday, December 8, President Roosevelt solemnly addressed a joint session of Congress. In preparing his speech he had rejected Hull's wishes for a detailed account of the negotiations and events leading to war; he also rejected Lowell Mellett's suggestion that the message state America'a peace aims and thereby make it "more difficult for the Senate later to repudiate an intelligent peace treaty." Instead, his was a short, moving address that he composed without help of his usual speechwriters. It was broadcast nationwide, and countless millions, young and old, listened attentively to his every word. "Yesterday, December 7, 1941—a date which will live in infamy—the United States of America was suddenly and deliberately attacked by the naval and air forces of the Empire of Japan." He promised, "No matter how long it may take us to overcome this premeditated invasion, the American people in their righteous might will win through to absolute victory." He asked Congress to "declare that since the unprovoked and dastardly attack by Japan on Sunday, December seventh, a state of war has existed between the United States and the Japanese Empire."[43]

Both houses of Congress speedily approved a declaration of war on Japan. In the House of Representatives there was just one negative vote (cast by Republican Congresswoman Jeanette Rankin of Montana, who had also voted against war in 1917). Vandenberg made the only speech in the Senate before the vote. Against administration wishes, the Michigan isolationist "felt it was absolutely necessary to establish the reason why our non-interventionists were ready to 'go along'—making it plain that we were not deserting our beliefs, but that we were postponing all further argument over policy until the battle forced upon us by Japan is *won*." He also thought it necessary "in order to better swing the vast anti-war party in the country into unity with this unavoidable decision." When Vandenberg had finished his statement, old Senator Carter Glass, a fervent interventionist, crossed the aisle to shake his hand and thank him for his statement. Others similarly commended Vandenberg. The Senate vote for war with Japan was unanimous with no negative votes. When Germany and Italy declared war on the United States three days later, at the president's request both houses of Congress voted unanimously for war against those two European Axis states.[44]

Over the course of years Franklin D. Roosevelt had been winning his contest with the isolationists. As noninterventionists they were defeated by the Japanese attack on Pearl Harbor and by the decisions of Hitler and Mussolini to war against the United States. The isolationists had taken a severe mauling before Pearl Harbor; they braced for worse after war was declared. Despite wartime unity, Roosevelt never relaxed his determination to crush the isolationists and the foreign policies they represented. For their part, most leading isolationists never confessed error. Despite their support for the war effort, most leading isolationists continued to believe that they had been right before Pearl Harbor, that Roosevelt and his policies had been both unwise and evil, and that history would vindicate them. For example, on December 11, after he had joined with other senators in voting for the declaration of war against Germany and Italy, Senator Vandenberg wrote in his diary: "We 'asked for it' and 'we got it.' The interventionist says today—as the President virtually did in his address to the nation—'See! This proves we were right and that this war was *sure* to involve us.' The non-interventionists says (and I say)—'See! We have insisted from the beginning that this course would lead to war and it has done exactly that.'** Perhaps, in a sense, we are *both* right. But I do not see, on the face of the record, how it can be denied that *we* certainly have been right. . . . I say that when, at long last, Germany turned upon us and declared war against her most aggressive enemy on earth, it is no contribution to 'historical accuracy' (to put it mildly) for us to pretend to say that this war has been '*THRUST UPON US.*' . . . But if this war is worth fighting it is worth accepting for what it is—namely, a belligerent cause which we openly embraced long ago and in which we long since *nominated ourselves* as active participants. The 'thrusting' started two years ago when we repealed the Arms Embargo."[45] And despite their support for the war effort, many prewar isolationists were not prepared to sit idly by while Roosevelt and internationalists shaped America's role in the postwar world once the war was won.

Chapter 32

War and Peace

A few isolationists continued to oppose the war even after Pearl Harbor—but they were the exceptions. Most prewar noninterventionists supported the war effort. Many did so on active duty in the armed forces and in combat. But they did so without abandoning their belief that they had been right before Pearl Harbor. And some were able to serve only over objections from the White House and the Roosevelt administration.

Brigadier General Robert E. Wood, national chairman of America First, had graduated from the United States Military Academy at West Point in 1900 and had served in the army before retiring from active duty in 1919 after World War I. Though sixty-two years old in 1941, Wood was in excellent health and actively sought military combat duty in any capacity. He was denied that privilege. On December 7, 1942, in a private memorandum to Chief of Staff George C. Marshall, President Roosevelt wrote: "I do not think that General R. E. Wood should be put into uniform. He is too old and has, in the past, shown far too great approval of Nazi methods. If General Arnold wishes to continue to use him in a civilian capacity in the supply situation, I have no serious objection." Marshall forwarded FDR's memorandum to General Henry H. Arnold, chief of the Army Air Forces. Consequently, though Wood served as an adviser for Army Ordnance in Chicago, and though he went on worldwide tours for General Arnold advising the air force on supply matters during the war, he did so as a civilian. Roosevelt blocked restoration of his military commission.[1]

R. Douglas Stuart, Jr., founder and national director of America First, held an Army Reserve Officers Training Corps commission in the field artillery reserve. He promptly asked for active duty and early in 1942 was ordered to Fort Sill, Oklahoma. He rose to the rank of army major and served on General Dwight D. Eisenhower's SHAEF staff in England. He was in combat, landing in Europe shortly after D-Day.[2]

Hanford MacNider, Iowa industrialist and national vice-chairman of America First, had been one of America's most decorated military heroes in World War I, awarded medals by France and Italy in addition to the United States. Among his medals was a Purple Heart for wounds suffered in combat. He had been a national commander of the American Legion and had served as assistant secretary of war from 1925 to 1928. After Pearl Harbor, at the age of fifty-two, he again volunteered for military duty. He served as an army combat officer in the southwest Pacific, won promotion to brigadier general, and added more medals to those he had won earlier in World War I— including another Purple Heart.[3]

Major General Thomas S. Hammond, Chicago industrialist and a member of the America First executive committee, headed the Army Ordnance District in Chicago during World War II. Former Governor Philip F. La Follette of Wisconsin, adviser to America First and active opponent of Roosevelt's foreign policies, volunteered for military service after Pearl Harbor, though he was then forty-four years old, married, and the father of three children. He served on the staff of General Douglas MacArthur in the southwest Pacific from October, 1942, until June, 1945, and was a colonel by the end of the war. Republican Senator Henry Cabot Lodge, Jr., of Massachusetts, who had spoken for America First, resigned his Senate position in 1944 at the age of forty-one and served as as army combat officer in Europe. Other younger men active in America First also volunteered for service in the armed forces during World War II, some of them undergoing close scrutiny because of their prewar noninterventionist activities and associations.[4]

Charles A. Lindbergh was nearly forty years old, married, and the father of three living children when the United States entered World War II. He had been a colonel in the Air Corps Reserve until his resignation in April, 1941. Proud of his commission and his flying skills, and devoted to his country, Lindbergh earnestly wanted to serve the United States in the war. And he did so—even in combat. But President Roosevelt and the more fervent interventionists in his cabinet blocked his attempts to regain his air force commission and prevented him from serving as a member of America's armed forces during World War II.

Lindbergh wrote to General Arnold offering his services to the

Army Air Force. The press and others gave the air force and the White House conflicting advice on whether to accept the offer or not. Though some urged "forgive and forget," others vehemently objected to allowing a man they called "a traitor" and a "Nazi" to serve in America's armed forces. One couple wrote, "Our son is in the service and we want no Quislings behind his back."[5]

Several in Roosevelt's cabinet had strong feelings on the matter. As usual, Secretary of Interior Ickes was in the vanguard. He wrote the president vigorously opposing acceptance of Lindbergh's services. Ickes charged that Lindbergh was "a ruthless and conscious fascist, motivated by a hatred for you personally and a contempt for democracy in general." He charged that Lindbergh's actions were "coldly calculated with a view to attaining ultimate power for himself" and that "a military service record" was part of that effort. Ickes warned that it would be "a tragic disservice to American democracy to give one of its bitterest and most ruthless enemies a chance to gain a military record." He urged that Lindbergh "be buried in merciful oblivion." Roosevelt's response was prompt and unequivocal: "What you say about Lindbergh and the potential danger of the man, I agree with wholeheartedly." Without identifying its author, the president sent copies of Ickes's letter to Secretary of War Stimson and Secretary of Navy Knox.[6]

Secretary Knox's response was equally blunt. He wrote to Roosevelt that if it were a navy matter he "would offer Lindbergh an opportunity to enlist as an air cadet, like anybody else would have to do. He has had no training as an officer and ought to earn his commission." Knox's facts were wrong, but his attitude was clear. President Roosevelt endorsed the view and forwarded Knox's memo to Secretary of War Stimson. FDR suggested, "For the time being the matter can be possibly maintained 'under consideration.'"[7]

On January 7, 1942, Lindbergh took the night train to Washington and spent ten days there trying to determine how he might best serve the war effort. It was a discouraging sojourn. He met with Colonel William J. Donovan, who headed the secret Office of Strategic Services throughout World War II, but nothing came of that initiative.[8]

He telephoned General Arnold's office seeking an appointment. The general's aide advised him to make an appointment directly with the secretary of war. Believing that that course had been prearranged, Lindbergh telephoned the War Department and got an appointment with Secretary Stimson. Lindbergh told Stimson that he wanted to be of service in the war effort. He was considering taking some position in the aviation industry, but first wanted to see if he could help in the air force, where he really preferred to serve. Lindbergh confirmed that he still held the opinions he had expressed before Pearl Harbor, but now that the United States was at war he wanted to help in whatever way he might be most effective. Because of Lindbergh's views (Lindbergh thought Stimson held mistaken impressions about them), the secretary of war doubted that Lindbergh would feel the necessary aggressiveness in a "position of command."[9]

Stimson then called in Assistant Secretary of War for Air Robert A. Lovett. Lindbergh felt uncomfortable as Stimson explained to Lovett, in his presence, that because of his "political views" and consequent "lack of aggressiveness" it was inadvisable to place him in a "position of command." Lovett arranged for Lindbergh to meet with him and General Arnold the next day.[10] The discussion was courteous, but the differences proved irreconcilable. Lovett and Arnold thought Lindbergh might not be able to serve "loyally" under the president without repudiating his prewar beliefs. Lindbergh was willing to issue additional statements, but he would not retract his earlier views. He said he had "very little confidence in the President" and would like to see the administration changed, but if he returned to the air force he "would follow the President of the United States as Commander-in-Chief of the Army." That was not sufficient for Lovett and Arnold. Consequently, Lindbergh concluded that, under the circumstances, it would be a mistake for him to return to the air force and that it would be better for him to make his contribution to the war effort through the aviation industry. Lindbergh regretted not being in the air force during the war, but he was "convinced" that the stand he "took on the war was right" and that that would "be realized eventually."[11]

The Roosevelt administration not only blocked Lindbergh's efforts to serve as an air force officer during World War II, it also prevented him from serving as a civilian with various aviation businesses that had government contracts. He had many friends in the aviation industry. Among the companies with which he sought positions were Pan American Airways, United Aircraft Corporation, and Curtiss-Wright. In each instance the corporation would have welcomed Lindbergh's services; in each instance executives checked with the War Department or the White House to determine whether there would be any objections; in each instance there were objections that made it inexpedient for the corporation to employ Lindbergh. None of those businesses felt free to use Lindbergh in their war work in 1942. It seemed that whatever direction he turned, Lindbergh came against a wall. His failures and frustrations produced one of the rare instances when he allowed his spirits to flag and his discouragement to show. He wrote in his personal journal: "I have always believed in the past that every American citizen had the right and the duty to state his opinion in peace and to fight for his country in war. But the Roosevelt Administration seems to think otherwise."[12]

Despite the unwillingness of the Roosevelt administration to use his knowledge and talents in the war effort, Lindbergh found opportunities to serve. And he did so without ever repudiating the stands he had taken on American foreign policies before Pearl Harbor. It was old Henry Ford who provided the first opportunity. A prewar noninterventionist himself, Ford was independent, unconventional, and powerful. He was no more awed by Roosevelt than was Lindbergh. Ford used his company's production facilities for America's war effort, but, like Lindbergh, he did not abandon his personal independence and private convictions in the process. Lindbergh had known Ford since 1927 and had given him a ride in the *Spirit of St. Louis* (Ford's first airplane ride). Though the industrialist was nearly forty years older than the aviator, the two men had developed affection and respect for each other. Both had emerged from rural backgrounds and simpler times in the Middle West, and each retained values rooted in those backgrounds. In their tenacious independence they were kindred spirits; each felt responsibilities toward others, but neither was prepared to sell his genius for the mess of pottage of personal popularity. Both resisted attempts to beat them into conformist molds.[13] Late in 1940 the government contracted for the Ford Motor Company to begin producing Pratt and Whitney aircraft engines at its River Rouge plant. In 1941 the War Department arranged for Ford to produce Consolidated B-24 Liberator four-engine bombers. The company built the huge Willow Run plant for that purpose.[14]

In March, 1942, Ford approached Lindbergh about helping at the Willow Run factory. The War Department had no objections, and that time the White House did not block the arrangement. Ford paid the Lindbergh's moving expenses to Michigan, but the airman did not draw any salary or retainer for his work for the Ford Motor Company during the war. Lindbergh quickly put his technical expertise to work on problems in design, production, and testing of the B-24 bombers and Pratt and Whitney aircraft engines that Ford was building. Lindbergh avoided public comment on the war and foreign affairs. When President Roosevelt visited Willow Run in September, 1942, Lindbergh quietly absented himself.[15]

In 1943 Henry Ford's production of Pratt and Whitney engines, along with Lindbergh's own personal friendships, brought him into consulting and flight-testing projects for the United Aircraft Corporation in Connecticut, in addition to his continuing work for Ford. In that capacity he helped improve the Navy Marine Corsair F4U fighter that used a Pratt and Whitney engine. In April, 1944, Lindbergh went to the Pacific as a technical representative for United Aircraft to study fighters under combat conditions. He was then forty-two years old—middle-aged by usual standards and little less than ancient for a fighter pilot. During a period of nearly five months from April to September, Lindbergh, a civilian, flew fifty combat missions against the Japanese in the South Pacific. Half of those were in Army Air Force twin-engine Lockheed P-38 Lightning fighters, and half were in Marine Corps Vought Corsair F4U single-engine fighters. They included patrol, escort, reconnaissance, strafing, and dive-bombing missions. On some he came under heavy fire from the Japanese. And on July 28, 1944, in a thrilling encounter in which he narrowly missed a head-on crash with his adversary, Lindbergh, flying a P-38, shot down a Japanese plane.[16] Less spectacular, but important for the war effort, while he was in the South Pacific he improved the combat effectiveness of the P-38 by developing procedures that greatly increased the plane's range. Lindbergh also experimented with carrying heavier bomb loads on Corsairs.[17]

Though he performed superbly, both the army and the navy were uneasy about having a civilian, particularly one so famous and controversial, flying in combat. Twice Lindbergh was called to Brisbane, Australia, where he had meetings with General MacArthur. Both army and marine commanders managed to look the other way most of the time with regard to his combat flying. But their uneasiness increased, especially when he went on notably risky missions. In mid-August, General George C. Kennedy, commander of the air force in the South Pacific, finally ordered that he do no more combat flying. By the middle of September he was back in the United States.[18]

His combat was over, but Lindbergh continued to serve America's war effort through United Aircraft and Ford. And in May, 1945, he again traveled abroad. That time he went to Europe as a United Aircraft representative with a naval technical mission to Germany at the close of World War II to study advanced German military airplanes. He was particularly interested in German jet and rocket propulsion. It was his first visit since he had left Europe more that six years before in the spring of 1939. He traveled more than two thousand miles by jeep during some three weeks in American-occupied areas of Germany and Austria. He and others on the technical mission obtained detailed plans of jet engines, helped arrange for shipment of engines to the United States for tests, and aided some Junkers technical experts to move with their families from the Soviet to the American zone. On June 11, while inspecting an underground factory at Nordhausen that had produced the V-1 and V-2 weapons, Lindbergh came on Camp Dora, a Nazi extermination camp. It was a horrifying scene. As he flew back to the United States later, Lindbergh felt no cause to regret his opposition to the beginning of the war or his opposition to American entry into that war. After World War II Lindbergh inconspicuously channeled his energies and talents into air force affairs, Pan American Airways, writing, and activities relating to conservation and ecology. His autobiographical *Spirit of St. Louis* won a Pulitzer Prize in 1954. When Republicans regained the White House, President Dwight D. Eisenhower and Congress in 1954 restored his commission in the Air Force Reserve and promoted him to brigadier general. In 1974 Lindbergh died on the island of Maui in Hawaii at the age of 72.[19]

Even before Pearl Harbor, Americans in and out of government began to think and plan for postwar peace settlements. Roosevelt, isolationists, the American people generally, and millions in other parts of the world gave priority to the immediate task of defeating the Axis, but they also looked ahead to shaping enduring peace after the war had ended. Administration leaders and internationalists wanted to make certain that the United States and the American people did not turn their backs on world responsibilities and international organizations as they had done after World War I. They wanted to make certain that American isolationism did not revive and triumph after World War II as it had after World War I. On the other side, isolationists did not want Roosevelt to use wartime unity as a cover for implementing internationalist solutions for postwar peace settlements. People on all sides pointed to alleged lessons of history (particularly to lessons to be learned from the history of World War I and the Versailles settlement) for guidance on what to do and what not to do after World War II. Those concerns extended all the way from the White House to grass-roots America. Political partisanship intruded, but most on all sides earnestly and honestly groped for the best path to a secure and enduring peace for the United States and the world.[20]

President Roosevelt gave priority to the military requirements for winning the war. He wanted to postpone consideration of peace terms that might divide and weaken the Allies warring against the still powerful and dangerous Axis states. He feared that detailed consideration of postwar peace terms would divide the American people, weaken the war effort, and play into the hands of isolationists. Furthermore, in his usual undoctrinaire way, Roosevelt did not want to get locked into rigid formulas for peace settlements that might make it difficult to adjust flexibly and realistically to practical conditions as he found them at home and abroad when the war ended; he wanted to keep his options open.

Roosevelt favored American membership in an international organization after World War II, much as he had after World War I. He did not, however, have utopian expectations for such a world organization. He favored American membership partly as a way of combating isolationism and isolationists in the United States. He never believed that world organization, by itself, could assure enduring peace. He did not favor or expect an equal role for all states in such an international organization.

Instead, as an undoctrinaire realist Roosevelt assumed that the great powers (those that played the largest roles in defeating the Axis) would have to play dominant roles in any world organization and in preserving peace and security after the war. He saw the great powers (the United States, the Soviet Union, Great Britain, and China) as serving as "Four Policemen" in the postwar period. If the great powers could work together for peace after the war as they were doing to accomplish victory during the war, enduring peace and stability could prevail; if they could not work together effectively after the war, world organization was not likely to be effective. He was alert to the role of power in international affairs and in the maintenance of enduring peace.

Roosevelt shaped his peace views over the course of many years, in countless private conversations, and in hours of private reflection. For example, on September 21, 1943, in a personal letter to George W. Norris of Nebraska, he wrote: "The real problem lies in the methods to be used to attain peace without hate. . . . time is an essential in disseminating the ideals of peace among the very diverse nationalities and national egoes of a vast number of separate peoples who, for one reason or another over a thousand years, have divided themselves into a hundred different forms of hate. . . . That is why I am inclined to believe that we should have a trial or transition period after the fighting stops—we might call it a period of trial and error. . . . I have been visualizing a superimposed—or if you like it, superassumed—obligation

by Russia, China, Britain and ourselves that we will act as sheriffs for
the maintenance of order during the transition period. Such a period
might last two or even three or four years. And, in the meantime,
through the holding of many special conferences the broad ideals
which you and I have in mind might be cleared up."[21]

As early as January, 1940 (nearly two years before Pearl Harbor),
the Department of State had set up a commission under Undersecretary of State Sumner Welles and Ambassador Hugh R. Wilson to plan
policies for the postwar period. It modified and restructured its planning organs from time to time during the war. In August, 1941, the
Roosevelt-Churchill Atlantic Charter was a dramatic signpost pointing toward an enlightened postwar peace settlement.[22]

In October, 1943, Secretary of State Cordell Hull personally traveled to Moscow to meet with Britain's Foreign Secretary Anthony
Eden and the Soviet Union's Foreign Minister Vyacheslav Molotov to
advance wartime planning for postwar peace arrangements. They
agreed to a four-power (including China) declaration calling for unconditional surrender of the Axis powers and for the creation after the
war of "a general international organization, based on the principle of
sovereign equality of all peace-loving states, and open to membership
by all such states, large and small, for the maintenance of international peace and security." That language reflected Hull's perspective
and style. But both Hull and Roosevelt comfortably shared in its antiisolationist connotations.[23]

At the same time, isolationists were not prepared to remain silent
while internationalists worked to shape the kind of peace arrangement
they wanted. In 1942 and 1943, while still supporting the war effort,
isolationists began to speak out on postwar planning. In 1942 former
president Herbert Hoover and Hugh Gibson wrote a thoughtful book,
Problems of a Lasting Peace, that won widespread attention. In a letter to Hoover, Senator Taft of Ohio wrote that "we must look forward to assuming obligations greater than we have ever assumed before in order to reduce the danger of war." But Taft insisted that the
policy "should be determined on the basis of intelligent discussion,
and not forced upon us by the President and a few Utopian thinkers,
whose interest appears to be more in foreign peoples than in the welfare of our own." He wanted no "free trade policy" and opposed any
"international W.P.A."[24]

From December, 1942, onward Senator Nye of North Dakota
spoke on postwar peace settlements. He attacked "interventionists
who have now become globalists." He warned against utopian expec-

tations and urged Americans to be "realistic." He pointed out that the United States could not shape the postwar world in its own image, that America's allies (including the Soviet Union) would have much to say about peace terms, that its allies would be moved by self-interest, that their attitudes would be different from those of the United States, and that the United States ought to look out for its own interests and sovereignty. Nye objected to efforts by internationalists to smear isolationists while those same isolationists were prevented by the war from freely expressing their views.[25]

Though plagued by political reverses and failing health, old George W. Norris of Nebraska was much interested in planning for peace and expressed his views in personal letters. He particularly emphasized the necessity for disarmament if peace were to endure—disarmament of the Axis states and eventually disarmament for all. In April, 1942, he wrote, "If men are deprived of the means of carrying on war by being completely and absolutely disarmed, there will gradually grow up a feeling of trust and friendship which will ultimately bring about, of its own accord, a disarmament which, gradually as it may seem to start with, is necessary in order to pave the way for the universal brotherhood of man." In December, 1942, he wrote that "the peace of the world" would "depend upon Russia, England, the United States, and perhaps China" and that "it would probably be wise to let them frame the treaty without trying to get all the nations of the world at the peace table."[26]

Among the more moderate and politically effective of the prewar noninterventionists in the wartime consideration of postwar peace was Republican Senator Arthur H. Vandenberg of Michigan. After World War II he became a leading architect of bipartisanship and containment in foreign affairs. Even during the war he tried to bridge the gap between the president and Congress in the conduct of the war and on postwar planning in foreign affairs. He tried to find common ground on which Americans could unite in considering postwar policies.[27]

Until 1945, however, Vandenberg functioned in that role without encouragement from President Roosevelt; during his third term as president FDR made little or no direct effort to win Vandenberg's friendship or confidence. Similarly, the Michigan senator undertook his efforts on behalf of postwar planning in foreign affairs without abandoning his continuing political opposition to and personal distrust of Roosevelt. Not until the beginning of FDR's fourth term in 1945, not long before Roosevelt's death, did the two make gestures toward each other that softened their disenchantment with each other a bit. Furthermore, Vandenberg denied that he had become an inter-nationalist, and he never repudiated or apologized for the isolationist or noninterventionist positions he had served so vigorously in the 1930s and before Pearl Harbor. In the middle of 1943 he wrote, "If I have become an 'internationalist' then black is white." He saw him-self as battling against Wendell Willkie and his "One World" ap-proach within the GOP, and against Roosevelt and his New Deal foreign policy nationally. Vandenberg sought common ground in the Republican party, in the Senate, and in the nation that might assure unity for winning the war and for building an enduring peace after the war, while at the same time safeguarding American interests, American sovereignty, and the constitutional authority of the Senate and Congress in foreign affairs. President Roosevelt, interventionists, the Japanese attack, and war combined to bludgeon isolationism into a nearly helpless remnant of its once-great power. Isolationists and isolationism suffered under a near-treasonous public image that made their every word or act suspect during the war. Nonetheless, Vanden-berg, with impeccable credentials as an isolationist, in the course of his continued opposition to FDR and while battling against Willkie's version of internationalism, played a major role in helping build a bipartisan consensus behind foreign policies that salvaged very little of traditional isolationism.[28]

Throughout World War II various leaders and factions maneu-vered for power and position within the Republican party. Isola-tionists and internationalists contested for control of the party, its presidential nomination, and its foreign policy program. Wendell L. Willkie of New York and Governor Harold E. Stassen of Minnesota spoke for doctrinaire internationalism. Governor Thomas E. Dewey of New York had not been an isolationist, but he was sufficiently am-biguous in his foreign policy statements to make both internationalists and isolationists uneasy about him. Old William Allen White of Kan-sas worked patiently and persistently in his efforts to draw Hoover, Landon, Willkie, and other GOP leaders to unite behind a moderate and responsibly internationalist approach to foreign affairs. Arthur H. Vandenberg of Michigan, Robert A. Taft of Ohio, Herbert Hoover of California, and supporters of General Douglas MacArthur were identified with prewar isolationism. Concern for national unity and fear of harmful political effects caused isolationist Republicans to play down isolationist-internationalist differences within the party during the war. They contended that grandstanding efforts by Willkie to commit the GOP to reject isolationism and to embrace bold internationalism would seem like a confession of past error and a repudiation of those Republicans who had espoused isolationism earlier. Such a course, they believed, would play into the hands of President Roosevelt's Democratic party and would hurt many Republicans politically.

Wendell Willkie won a skirmish at a Chicago meeting of the Republican National Committee in April, 1942. The national committee adopted resolutions originally proposed and publicized by Willkie asserting that the United States had an obligation "to assist in the bringing about of understanding, comity and co-operation among the nations of the world in order that our liberty may be preserved and that the blighting and destructive processes of war may not again be forced upon us and upon the free and peace loving peoples of the world." Senator Taft opposed the action. His supporters in the committee watered down Willkie's original proposals, but the press publicized the episode as a victory for Willkie and a Republican repudiation of isolationism and isolationists.[29]

Though Willkie's original resolutions had been softened considerably, Senator Taft feared that "any declaration would be taken as a repudiation of the position of many Republican Congressmen, and would be used against them in the November election by their Democratic opponents." Taft feared they were "heading for a direct fight for control of the Party machinery" and that "it would be fatal to the future of the Party if Willkie and Luce and Dorothy Thompson, together with the wealthy crowd in the east, succeed in their aim." He was convinced that Willkie was wrong if he thought the GOP could win "by being more warlike than Roosevelt." Senator Vandenberg took a different view. He thought it was "all sheer *bunk*" to portray the episode as "the *death* of so-called 'isolationism'" and "a great victory" for Willkie. He thought it was "mere shadow-boxing with platitudes." Vandenberg could agree with the general statement adopted by the national committee and could not see "how *anybody* could disagree with it." He thought Taft had "made a great mistake" in opposing the declaration, thereby giving Willkie "the pretense of a 'victory.'"[30]

That episode was a preview of more extended deliberations in Congress and in the Republican party during 1943. Various legislators in both houses of Congress introduced resolutions pointing to what they hoped would be enduring peace after the war. Initially neither President Roosevelt nor Secretary Hull wanted congressional action on the matter at that time. They feared divisive consequences and were uneasy lest debate on the resolutions revive isolationist opposition.

Nonetheless, Democratic Senator Guy Gillette of Iowa introduced a resolution in February, 1943. A month later Republican Senators Joseph H. Ball of Minnesota and Harold H. Burton of Massachusetts along with Democratic Senators Carl A. Hatch of New Mexico and Lister Hill of Alabama introduced a stronger and more specific resolution. It would have had the president call meetings of the United Nations to form an international organization with authority to administer economic relief and to establish an international police force. The Senate Foreign Relations Committee referred those and other such resolutions to a special subcommittee composed of Senators Tom Connally, Walter George, Alben Barkley, Guy Gillette, Robert La Follette, Jr., Arthur Vandenberg, and Wallace White. None of the members of that subcommittee liked the Ball resolution, the so-called B_2H_2 resolution; they thought it too specific and divisive. All isolationists in and out of Congress disliked it.[31]

Senator Taft feared that the international conferences called for in the B_2H_2 resolution might divide the United Nations and interfere with prosecution of the war. He objected to "the tremendous power given the President" by the resolutions. He wanted to be certain that any agreement for the formation of an international organization be a treaty subject to Senate approval. Senator Wheeler approved international trade and world wide humanitarian efforts, but he opposed giving "some international super-government the authority to carry on these activities." In his opinion "the goal should be instruments of ordered change; not for the enforcement of the status quo." He insisted that "enforcement of peace" was "a contradiction in terms." Senator La Follette battled against the Ball resolution and other resolutions within the subcommittee. In May, 1943, Senator Nye delivered a political address in Chicago in which he tried to arouse Republicans to "come out of their corner swinging and clubbing" against "globalism." He predicted that Americans would "never tolerate any such policing job as globalists seem to contemplate" and warned that "this international policeman isn't going to be the most popular fellow on earth."[32]

Senator Vandenberg wanted to "proceed with extreme prudence lest we *disunite* the *war* effort through a premature attempt in any sort of detail to *unite* the *peace* effort." On July 2, 1943, Vandenberg and Wallace White of Maine introduced the first "all Republican" Senate resolution for postwar peace planning. It called for postwar cooperation to prevent aggression and "to establish permanent peace with justice in a free world." But it also emphasized that that should be done by "sovereign nations" and that it be "by due constitutional process," assuring the Senate's role in any treaty-making process. That proposed resolution was not old-fashioned isolationism, but it was more acceptable to Senate isolationists that the B_2H_2 resolution. Vandenberg contended that his resolution was "at total odds with Mr. Willkie's 'One World.'" He believed his resolution recognized America's "new and unavoidable obligations," but also "speaks up for 'America first.'"[33]

In response to a query from *Life Magazine*, Senator Arthur Capper of Kansas wrote that he was "in favor of international cooperation" and always had been. But he opposed "merging the United States into any form of super-state or union which would place our people, our resources, our country, under international control or the control of any other nation." He could support the Vandenberg-White resolution, but not "the Executive blanket powers to make foreign commitments that are implied in the Ball Burton Hatch Hill resolution."[34]

Former Democratic congressman Samuel B. Pettengill of Indiana, who had been an influential America First adviser, wrote that he was "prepared to go farther" than he "would have gone before Pearl Harbor"; he had no desire to spend the rest of his life "standing at abandoned camp fires." But "if this 'one world' stuff means that we have got to spill our blood from now on to put down every uprising everywhere in the world that does not immediately affect American interests," he "would respectfully decline participating in the negotiations."[35]

On August 26, 1943, Senator Robert A. Taft delivered a major address before the American Bar Association in Chicago summarizing his developing peace views. Like most Americans, Taft favored pursuing the war to complete victory and advocated adequate military defense forces for the United States. He proposed that "after the initial period of relief and reconstruction we must keep out of the internal affairs of other nations, and we must learn to treat with tolerance conditions and ideologies which we may not understand or sympathize with." Taft thought the United States "should attempt again to prevent the occurrence of any war in the world by international action." He advocated a peace settlement providing for "the self-determination of nations." He thought "any effort to impose democracy on the entire world, however, would be impossible and far more likely to cause war than prevent it." And he called for "the revision of the world code of international law, extending it to provide the rules and ideals which shall govern the relations of sovereign nations in times of crisis and with relation to vital national interests."[36]

Taft attacked the alliance arrangement urged by Walter Lippmann in his book, *U.S. Foreign Policy: Shield of the Republic.* He believed alliances were "as likely to fall apart at crucial moments as any defensive plans based on a nation's own armed forces." He thought Lippmann's book might "appeal to the do-gooders who regard it as the manifest destiny of America to confer the benefits of the New Deal on every Hottentot." Taft saw Lippmann's approach as "imperialism" and contended that the United States was "not fitted to a role of imperialism and would fail in any attempt at world domination."[37]

Senator Vandenberg played a central role in compromising Republican foreign policy views at a major Republican meeting at Mackinac Island in Michigan in September, 1943. That conference brought together Republican state governors and national leaders of the party including Vandenberg, Dewey, Taft, and others. Willkie and Stassen on the internationalist extreme were not there; neither were isolationists Hiram Johnson, Gerald Nye, or Hamilton Fish. Senator Vandenberg chaired the Republican Post-War Advisory Council at Mackinac that hammered out a major foreign policy resolution. In his efforts Vandenberg saw himself as "hunting for the middle ground between those extremists at one end of the line who would cheerfully give America away and those extremists at the other end of the line who would attempt a total isolation which has come to be an impossibility." The resolution approved at Mackinac called for "responsible participation by the United States in postwar cooperative organization among sovereign nations to prevent military aggression and to attain permanent peace with organized justice in a free world." At the same time, in shaping the resolution Vandenberg insisted on guarding American sovereignty, rejecting world government, and maintaining the constitutional powers of Congress and the Senate in foreign affairs. Vandenberg's effort at Mackinac won the endorsement of both Senator Taft and Governor Dewey, leading contenders for the GOP presidential nomination in 1944. As Taft phrased it, in adopting the Mackinac resolution the Republican leaders excluded "any international state, as well as extreme isolation." Vandenberg was proud that he had "succeeded in putting forty-nine primadonnas together at Mackinac" and had "discovered the necessary formula." He believed it "an utterly *sound* formula."[38]

Later in September, 1943, the House and Senate renewed consideration of foreign policy resolutions. With the approval of Roosevelt and Hull, on September 21 the House of Representatives approved 360 to 29 a resolution introduced by Democrat J. William Fulbright of Arkansas calling for "the creation of appropriate international machinery with power adequate to establish and to maintain a just and lasting peace, among the nations of the world, and as favoring participation by the United States therein through its constitutional processes." Some thought the resolution too vague, but it clearly pointed away from old-fashioned isolationism. Hamilton Fish of New York was among those who voted for the Fulbright resolution. Most who voted against it were Republicans from the Middle West.[39]

In the Senate, Democrat Tom Connally of Texas, chairman of the Foreign Relations Committee, introduced a compromise resolution that he hoped would win approval. The subcommittee promptly reported Connally's resolution to the Foreign Relations Committee, which then voted twenty to two to recommend its adoption by the Senate. On November 5, 1943, after two weeks of debate, the Senate approved the Connally resolution eighty-five to five. In its final form it called for American participation "in the establishment and maintenance of international authority with power to prevent aggression and to preserve the peace of the world." In deference to Vandenberg and the isolationists, however, it emphasized "free and sovereign nations" and that American adherence should be "only by and with the advice and consent of the Senate of the United States, provided two-thirds of the Senators present concur."[40]

The roles of Senate isolationists in consideration of the Connally resolution dramatized the enfeebled and discredited state to which they had been reduced during World War II. Young Senator La Follette was a member of the subcommittee considering the various resolutions. He opposed both the B_2H_2 and Connally resolutions. He was struck down by pneumonia during the fall of 1943, however, and was reduced to the ineffective expedient of expressing his opposition from his hospital bed and home in Wisconsin. He telegraphed Vandenberg that he thought "a great mistake" was "being made by the committee in its present efforts to commit the United States to a future course in world relationship when the committee and the people of the United States are still in the dark as to the peace table demands and the postwar policies of the other United Nations, including Great Britain, China and Russia." For the final Senate vote La Follette could do no more than make certain that the text of his telegram to Vandenberg

was printed in the *Congressional Record* and that he was paired
against the Connally resolution with a clear indication that he would
have voted against it had he been present.[41]

Most leading isolationists addressed the Senate during the debate
on the Connally resolution. But theirs was a defensive and ineffective
effort. They complained of unfair attacks and smears directed at them
during the war. They denied that they wanted to isolate the United
States or that they were "isolationists" in any literal sense of the
word. Most, in their comments on the Connally resolution, spoke in
"yes, but" terms that were out of tune both with their bolder prewar
isolationism and with the internationalist and collective security connotations the resolution had for the administration and most senators.
Senator Nye, for example, pointed out that any treaty made to implement the resolution should "be made only by and with the advice and
consent of the Senate of the United States, provided two-thirds of the
Senators present concur." He suspected that that paragraph might
"ultimately prove to be the only part of the resolution that has real
and direct meaning and force." Nye defended America First and isolationists; he voiced skepticism about postwar cooperation by America's allies, including Britain and the Soviet Union. But he was "not
ready to close the door to whatever might develop in the way of a
chance to win and enjoy the cooperation of the world." In his remarks
Nye summarized his own recommendations for the peace settlement,
with emphasis on self-determination and antiimperialism. He thought
the United States might eventually "be more definitely and overwhelmingly isolationist in its determination to avoid involvement in
more foreign wars than has ever been true in the past." Others spoke
in similar terms.[42]

But it was old Hiram Johnson of California who provided the
most pathetic symbol for the erosion of isolationist strength. He had
been hospitalized four and one-half months in the middle of 1943. He
returned to his Senate seat to learn that his like-minded colleague on
the Foreign Relations Committee, Robert La Follette, was similarly
absented by hospitalization. On October 13, Johnson telegraphed La
Follette in Wisconsin that he had been "very lonely" until he had
learned that the Wisconsin senator "had voted against the proposed
resolution of the subcommittee." He knew that his defeat on the resolution was "certain." On the day of the final Senate vote, November
5, the old senator, frail and weak, took his feet briefly to explain that
on advice of his doctors and his wife he had refrained from an active
role in the deliberations. He thanked his doctors and his wife, but

took his seat without marshaling for the Senate his reasons for opposing the resolution. Given the old senator's once great vigor, boldness, oratorical powers, and tactical skills, it was a pathetic scene.[43]

Those voting for the Connally resolution included such prewar noninterventionists as Capper, D. Worth Clark, Bennett Champ Clark, Nye, Taft, Vandenberg, and others. The only senators voting against the resolution (in addition to La Follette's pair against it) were three Republicans (Johnson of California, Langer of North Dakota, and Shipstead of Minnesota) and two Democrats (Wheeler of Montana and Reynolds of North Carolina). All were noninterventionists before Pearl Harbor, and all but Reynolds were western progressives on domestic issues.[44]

As the Senate debated the Connally resolution, Irving Brant of the the *Chicago Sun* wrote to President Roosevelt complaining that "the nearer it comes to unanimity the less it will be worth." He thought the "effort to find a formula that would not drive all of the isolationists into opposition" would "make the resolution worthless as an assurance to other governments about American postwar policy." Brant feared that the resolution might be "a political godsend to isolationist senators running for re-election next year. They will vote for it and go before the people on that record, then come back to sabotage the peace." In his opinion, "Any resolution Senator Nye can support must be fatally deficient." In his response Roosevelt wrote that he wondered "how much weight should be attached at this time to any Senate or House Resolution." He contended that he was "paying very little attention to the language of the debate. The affairs of 'mice and men' are becoming less and less affected by verbiage." On November 5, the president wrote to Senator Connally congratulating him on the Senate's action and facetiously asking, "But why, oh, why did you let Nye vote for it?"[45] The overwhelming approval by Congress of the Fulbright and Connally resolutions, just as Hull was shaping and returning to Washington the four-power Moscow Declaration on General Security, encouraged conviction that the isolationists would not prevail, that the Senate would not bar American membership in a world organization, and that the United States would play an active and leading role in preserving peace after the war.

Roosevelt and Hull continued to build on those foundations. Secretary Hull had attempted throughout the war to marshal bipartisan support for a responsible role by the United States in a world organization after the war. In 1944, his final year as secretary of state, he stepped up those efforts. Of particular importance was the formation of a Committee of Eight—eight senators to confer with him and State Department advisers on developing plans for a postwar international organization. That secret committee included four Democrats (Tom Connally of Texas, Alben Barkley of Kentucky, Walter George of Georgia, and Guy Gillette of Iowa), three Republicans (Vandenberg of Michigan, Wallace White of Maine, and Warren Austin of Vermont), and one Progressive (La Follette of Wisconsin). It was not just a token or rubber-stamp group; in its many sessions with Hull its members conducted spirited, thoughtful, responsible discussions. Vandenberg and La Follette resisted committing their committee or the Senate to approval of an international organization without first determining what peace terms would be concluded among the victors after the war. Despite sharp differences among them, the tone in the committee's deliberations was nonpartisan and constructive. Its contributions were evident in the United States positions at the Dumbarton Oaks conference in 1944 and at the United Nations Conference on International Organization in San Francisco that drafted the United Nations Charter in 1945.[46]

That bipartisan, or nonpartisan, approach toward postwar planning for peace continued through the presidential election of 1944. The Democratic party nominated Roosevelt for a fourth term, and the vice-presidential nomination went to Senator Harry S. Truman of Missouri. The party platform pledged "to join with the other United Nations in the establishment of an international organization based on the principle of the sovereign equality of all peace-loving states, open to membership by all such states, large and small, for the prevention of aggression and the maintenance of international peace and security." That organization, the platform asserted, "must be endowed with power to employ armed forces when necessary to prevent aggression and preserve peace." The platform also endorsed, as it had many times before, "an international court of justice" that would include the United States. And it pledged the party's "support to the Atlantic Charter and the Four Freedoms and the application of the principles enunciated therein to the United Nations and other peace-loving nations, large and small."[47]

The Republican party again rejected prewar isolationists and nominated Governor Thomas E. Dewey for president and Governor John W. Bricker of Ohio for vice-president. On foreign affairs the platform closely followed the formula worked out by Vandenberg at the Mackinac conference nearly a year before. The GOP platform sought to accomplish its peace aims "through organized international cooperation and not by joining a World State." It favored "responsible participation by the United States in post-war cooperative organization among sovereign nations to prevent military aggression and to attain permanent peace with organized justice in a free world." The platform promised to "keep the American people informed concerning all agreements with foreign nations" and that treaties and agreements making peace after the war would "be made only by and with the advice and consent of the Senate of the United States provided two-thirds of the Senators present concur." It promised "at all times" to "protect the essential interests and resources of the United States."[48]

By mutual consent the two parties and their candidates largely kept foreign policy issues out of the campaign. The reelection of FDR to a fourth term surprised no one.[49]

With Dumbarton Oaks and the Yalta conferences resolving many details on a world organization, plans went forward for the San Francisco conference to draft the charter for the new world organization. Among the persons President Roosevelt named to the American delegation for the conference was Senator Vandenberg. The Michigan Republican was pleased, but delayed final acceptance until he successfully won assurances from the president that he would be free to speak his own mind at the conference and in the Senate after the conference had completed its deliberations.[50]

Roosevelt's death on April 12, 1945, after his return from Yalta preceded the San Francisco conference. But the new president, Harry S. Truman, did not postpone the conference, and he kept the same persons named earlier by FDR to the American delegation (including Vandenberg).[51]

By the time the completed United Nations Charter finally was submitted to the Senate in July, 1945, the outcome was no longer in doubt. The total effort on behalf of a new international organization to keep the peace and on behalf of American membership in that organization was so overwhelming that it demolished any serious thought of effective opposition. The Mackinac resolution, the Fulbright and Connally resolutions, the four-power Moscow declaration, the organized bipartisan support, the negotiation on detailed matters at Dumbarton Oaks and Yalta, the active educational and propaganda roles by countless individuals and organizations all over the country, the advantages accruing from the war effort against the Axis, the discredited and enfeebled status of isolationism and isolationists—all magnificently orchestrated under the inspiring leadership of President Roosevelt, with dedicated assistance from the ailing old Secretary of

State Hull and from his handsome and energetic successor Edward R. Stettinius, Jr.—combined to make the creation of the United Nations organization and American membership in that organization near certainty.

In the final vote on July 28, 1945, eighty-nine senators voted yea, and only two voted nay. The lone negative votes were cast by progressive Republican Senators Henrik Shipstead of Minnesota and William Langer of North Dakota. Hiram Johnson was on his deathbed. He asked to be paired against the United Nations Charter and would have voted against it if he had had the strength to attend. All other senate isolationists either voted for the United Nations Charter or had been removed by death or defeat at the polls.[52] Isolationism was not completely dead, but its vital signs were just barely evident by the time the United States approved the United Nations Charter. Isolationists and isolationism had taken a beating during World War II from which they never recovered. And there were few who felt any sadness or shed any tears on their behalf.

Chapter 33

End of an Era

In April, 1945, death took Franklin D. Roosevelt, Benito Mussolini, and Adolf Hitler. On April 12, Roosevelt suffered a massive cerebral hemorrhage and died at his cottage in Warm Springs, Georgia. On April 28, the already ousted Mussolini was shot and killed as he tried to flee to Switzerland. Two days later on April 30, Hitler committed suicide in his bunker in the heavily bombed city of Berlin, Germany. But out of the carnage and rubble of that terrible war Franklin D. Roosevelt won his victory even in death. Along with Britain's Winston S. Churchill and the Soviet Union's Joseph Stalin, he had provided leadership for the United Nations allies that crushed the Axis powers. The government of Italy under Marshal Pietro Badoglio had surrendered on September 9, 1943. A thoroughly beaten Germany formally surrendered on V-E Day, May 8, 1945.

Three months later, at 8:15 in the morning of August 6, 1945, a United States Army Air Force B-29 Superfortress four-engine bomber, the *Enola Gay*, dropped an atomic bomb on the city of Hiroshima, Japan. That bomb killed seventy thousand people, injured another seventy thousand, caused the eventual deaths of many more later. It and a second atomic bomb on Nagasaki brought a quick end to the war with Japan. The formal surrender was signed aboard the U.S.S. *Missouri* in Tokyo Bay on V-J Day, September 2, 1945. On the same day that that lone bomber dropped the atomic bomb on Hiroshima, August 6, some seven thousand miles further east at the Bethesda Naval Hospital on the outskirts of Washington, D.C., old Senator Hiram Johnson died. He was nearly seventy-nine. That day had both literal and symbolic significance. It symbolized Roosevelt's triumphs over the last of the Axis states and over the isolationists as well.

During World War II the isolationists were crushed nearly as completely as the Axis powers. The federal government, private individuals and groups, the news media, and voters at the polls shared in destroying them. Other societies in other times had treated and would treat losing factions with more savage physical brutality. But the methods used to destroy isolationists and their values were decisively, even ruthlessly, effective. Their assailants demolished the isolationists in a spirit of triumphant self-righteousness that left no room for compassion, empathy, or sadness—then or later. Not only was the once great power of isolationism shattered, its public image was so tarnished that "isolationist" became (then and later) a smear word used to connote much that was evil and even subversive in America and foreign affairs. (The word had never been of the isolationists's own choosing, and it had never accurately described their views.) In the midst of wartime passions, hatreds, and intolerance, isolationists were identified with Hitler, fascism, totalitarianism, anti-Semitism, and even treason—though in fact most isolationists were no more enamored of alien or totalitarian ideologies than those who assailed them.

The America First Committee had ceased its noninterventionist activities and disbanded after Pearl Harbor. The FBI and the War Department G-2 Military Intelligence Division, however, received reports alleging that the committee or some of its members proposed to go underground and prepare for political action later. Reports that won particular prominence concerned a meeting on December 17, 1941, in the home of Edwin S. Webster, Jr., secretary of the New York America First chapter. Some fifty America First workers had attended, and Charles Lindbergh had spoken informally to the group. Allegations about America First and the meeting in Webster's home were circulated widely by the Reverend Leon Birkhead of Friends of Democracy, Walter Winchell, Drew Pearson, and others through the press, radio, and mails. Reports of the Webster-Lindbergh gathering in New York reached President Roosevelt, Mrs. Roosevelt, Secretary Stimson, and others in the administration.[1]

On February 13, 1942, FBI Director J. Edgar Hoover wrote the White House and Attorney General Francis Biddle about reports of America First plans for future activity and about the gathering in Webster's home. According to Hoover's sources, Lindbergh had told his listeners that America First could "again be a political force" and that "there may be a time soon when the Committee can advocate a negotiated peace." Hoover also provided the White House and the attorney general with a twenty-one-page memorandum on the America First Committee.[2] Lindbergh's personal account of the gathering differed substantially from those accounts reported to the FBI and to the president. According to Lindbergh's journal the party was a combination of an engagement dinner with Webster's fiancée and a farewell dinner for former "street speakers" for America First.[3] Regardless of what had or had not occurred that evening, reports of the gathering helped trigger serious concern about possible future activities by America First.

President Roosevelt was impatient with Attorney General Biddle for being too solicitous about the rights of dissenters and critics of the government. As Biddle phrased it in his memoirs later, Roosevelt "was not much interested . . . in the constitutional right to criticize the government in wartime. He wanted this anti-war talk stopped." FDR persistently prodded his attorney general to take action. Biddle felt the president's coolness and recognized his nudgings.[4]

With the approval of Biddle, on March 16, 1942, Hoover ordered a major nationwide FBI investigation of America First. He directed FBI agents to determine whether the committee was "being kept alive and in operation by individuals and groups who may plan at some time in the future using the organization in a manner detrimental to the internal security of this country." He wrote, "The primary purpose of the inquiries at this time is to ascertain whether the structure set up by the America First Committee is now being used by foreign interests, or by individuals cooperating with foreign interests, in such a manner as to interfere with the national defense effort." He directed the agents to be "discreet," but to give the case "a preferential investigative status." When some agents were slow to report, Hoover firmly pressed them to action. He ordered follow-up inquiries when uncertainties appeared.[5]

FBI special agents in cities all across the country promptly proceeded with their investigations and reported their detailed findings to Hoover in Washington. The reports made clear that the America First national headquarters, regional facilities, and local chapters had in fact disbanded and ceased their noninterventionist activities. The reports provided no evidence that the committee or its leaders were lying low and readying for renewed activity later. Some extremists wanted to continue, and groups such as Gerald L. K. Smith's Committee of 1,000,000 in Detroit, Horace J. Haase's Americans For Peace in New York, and Father Charles E. Coughlin's Social Justice movement sought the support of former America Firsters. Those and other comparable fringe groups were subject to continued investigation and surveillance by the FBI. But the reports from FBI agents across the land provided a remarkably clean bill for the America First Committee, given its loose-knit, heterogeneous, and controversial character.[6]

In addition to the FBI investigation, the Internal Revenue Bureau of the Treasury Department also conducted a meticulous probe of America First. Internal Revenue Bureau agents examined America First financial, membership, and correspondence records in Chicago, New York, Washington, and California. Those agents also studied, page by page, an unofficial typescript history of America First written by Ruth Sarles, former director of the America First Research Bureau in Washington. All that was done without making clear just what they were looking for or why.[7]

In September, 1941, three months before Pearl Harbor, Democratic Congressman Samuel Dickstein of New York had called for an investigation of America First by the House of Representatives Committee on Un-American Activities under the chairmanship of Democratic Congressman Martin Dies of Texas. In urging the probe, Dickstein had charged that America First "was engaged in the business of appeasing the dictators and seeking to organize the American people for fascistic aims." He thought its source of funds "questionable." General Wood promptly wrote Dies welcoming an investigation and promising full cooperation. In November, 1941, the Dies Committee began an investigation of America First and other groups involved in the foreign policy debate. Its agents got masses of information from America First offices in Chicago and Washington. Dies said he wanted to find out how many members of America First also belonged to the German-American Bund and other subversive organizations. He also wanted to determine how strong the influence of Nazis was in the councils of America First and its local chapters. Dies committee agents continued their work after the Japanese attack on Pearl Harbor, but the committee never published a report on the findings of its probe of America First.[8]

The Federal Bureau of Investigation also responded to specific allegations against individual isolationists. For example, on July 16, 1941, the fervently interventionist newspaper columnist Dorothy Thompson had written to J. Edgar Hoover protesting that Senator Wheeler and some of his associates had "been actively participating in a program of abuse and vilification" and a "boycott" of her activities. She wrote that her attorney had advised her that the available evidence indicated "a clear violation of law and an illegal interference" with her work and activities. Thompson believed Wheeler's activities were "part and parcel of what may be fairly termed 'Fifth Column Activities.'" After Pearl Harbor on December 19, her attorney provided the Justice Department and FBI with a fourteen-page "Memorandum of Facts, Law and Exhibits *re* Senator Burton K. Wheeler" making major allegations against the Montana Democrat. It concluded that there had been "a deliberate and malicious conspiracy to undermine American defense and to give aid and succor to a foreign and unfriendly power."[9]

Attorney General Biddle sought the advice of Hoover and Assistant Attorney General Wendell Berge on the allegations. Berge thought only one of the complaints warranted investigation. It concerned an alleged payment of twenty-five thousand dollars to Wheeler by the German consul in San Francisco, Fritz Wiedemann. Hoover reported, however, that the FBI had no information that would confirm the allegation. And the Justice Department found that the individual who had made the allegation to the attorney concerning payment of money to Wheeler had a long record of irresponsibility, dishonesty, and untrustworthiness. Consequently the Justice Department decided not to proceed further with the matter.[10] Other wartime allegations against prominent prewar noninterventionists (generally from interventionist and antiisolationist sources) similarly produced negative or inconclusive findings with insufficient grounds for legal action—even in wartime.

The federal grand jury in Washington, D.C., that had begun its probe of foreign propaganda in the middle of 1941 continued its work after Pearl Harbor. It produced indictments leading to various convictions, including those of George Hill, George Sylvester Viereck, Laura Ingalls, Frank B. Burch, and Ralph Townsend, mainly for failure to register as foreign agents. Ingalls, a colorful aviatrix, had addressed America First meetings; Burch was a sponsor of the Akron, Ohio, chapter of America First; and Townsend had spoken at local meetings of America First. FDR was pleased when the grand jury returned indictments.[11]

On July 21, 1942, with William P. Maloney serving as prosecuting attorney, the grand jury indicted twenty-eight persons for conspiracy to undermine the morale of the armed forces. On January 4, 1943, it produced a superseding indictment. In February, O. John Rogge replaced Maloney as special assistant to the attorney general in charge of the wartime sedition case. He tried to distinguish between loyal dissenters or isolationists on the one hand, and subversive agents of enemy governments on the other. A third and final indictment on

January 4, 1944, charged thirty persons with conspiracy with the German government to undermine the morale of United States armed forces. Among those indicted were Gerald B. Winrod, William Dudley Pelley, Lawrence Dennis, Joseph E. McWilliams, George E. Deatherage, Elizabeth Dilling, Edward James Smythe, and Garland L. Alderman. Most were obscure figures of comparatively little significance or influence. The indictments also listed various publications and organizations that had been used by those indicted to spread their propaganda. The America First Committee was listed as one of those organizations in the first indictment, but not in the third. Only the third indictment was brought to trial.[12]

Though leading isolationists were not indicted, their names were drawn into the unsavory atmosphere of suspicion and distrust that surrounded the sedition indictments and trial. In April, 1942, Townsend asked Senator Nye to write the court on his behalf. He did so. The North Dakota Republican had found Townsend "a loyal and patriotic American citizen." He thought Townsend, like Nye, had only been trying to keep America "free from involvement in the hatreds which were obsessing other parts of the world."[13]

In August, 1942, Charles Lindbergh was subpoenaed to testify for the defense for William Dudley Pelley, head of the fascistic Silver Shirts. Lindbergh had never met Pelley personally and was on the witness stand only twelve minutes. But the episode further identified that leading isolationist in the public mind with seditious elements.[14]

Senators Taft of Ohio, Wheeler of Montana, and Nye were among leading prewar noninterventionists who criticized the grand jury indictments as witch hunts partly aimed against loyal Americans who had criticized the government and its foreign policies before Pearl Harbor. They called on Attorney General Biddle and made their views clearly known to him.[15]

On January 14, 1943, Nye took the floor in the Senate to defend himself against an allegation in the press by columnist Drew Pearson that he had "been active behind the scenes in aiding the appeal of George Sylvester Viereck." Nye called the charge "a deceitful falsehood" and "a lie." He insisted that he had talked with Viereck "only once or twice" and not at all since Pearl Harbor. He conceded that he had "grave doubts about the merit of the charges" against some of those indicted by the grand jury, and he wondered "concerning the issue of personal liberty." He said he held "no brief . . . for anyone guilty of contributing to the undermining of our defense, or undermining the morale of our armed forces," but he thought most of those indicted were "no more guilty than are millions of other Americans who, prior to Pearl Harbor, were giving their voice to their feelings respecting possible involvement in this war." Nye's speech probably accomplished little more than further identify him in the eyes of many Americans with sedition and seditionists.[16]

An FBI agent interviewed General Robert E. Wood concerning his relations with Lawrence Dennis. Wood told the agent that he thought Dennis was "patriotic" and a good citizen. Wood contributed money to help with the legal costs of defending Dennis in the trial.[17]

In November, 1943, Nye took the Senate floor to defend himself against what he called "a spreading of insidious poison by newspapers such as the Communist Daily Worker, PM, the Chicago Sun, the Chicago Daily News, the New York Post, and individuals such as Edgar Mowrer, Dorothy Thompson, Walter Winchell, and other radio and newspaper commentators." He said he detested "fascism and communism with a firmness and conviction as deep as is my love and solicitation for the future of our American form of government."[18]

In June, 1944, when Nye was in the final days of his primary campaign to win renomination for another term in the Senate, news reached him that a defense attorney in the sedition trial had filed an affidavit alleging that he had failed to provide promised evidence for the defense. That news report so infuriated Nye that he scribbled a letter to Attorney General Biddle charging him with bringing the senator "under a cloud of suspicion just five days before" the primary election. He complained that though there were three sedition indictments, the government waited until 1944, an election year, to bring them to trial.[19]

Judge Edward C. Eicher tried to conduct the sedition trial fairly, but he was not able to cope effectively with the antics of defense attorneys. They exhausted his energies, his skills, and his health. The trial dragged on and on. It ended in a mistrial when Judge Eicher died on November 30, 1944. The case was never retried.[20] From whatever perspective, it was an unpleasant and unsavory part of America's participation in World War II. Though none of the leading isolationists was indicted, tried, or convicted in the sedition case, it further besmirched their reputations. The distinctions that Biddle and Rogge tried to make between seditionists and isolationists were badly blurred in the press and in the public eye. Though President Roosevelt at that time was preoccupied with more pressing concerns of winning the war and planning for postwar peace, there is no evidence that he felt any remorse about the damaging effects of the grand jury hearings, the indictments, or the trial upon the reputations of isolationists. The perspectives that he had helped shape earlier and the viewpoints that he made clear to Biddle and others at the top were not on the side of freedom of expression or the right of dissent.

Father Charles E. Coughlin, the outspoken isolationist and anti-Semitic Roman Catholic priest in Royal Oak, Michigan, was not among those indicted during the war. But Attorney General Biddle played a key role in bringing the priest's political and propaganda activities to an end. Biddle explored the possibility of denying *Social Justice* use of the mails, and he considered legal actions. But he worried about divisive consequences. Instead, he worked through the church. He won the help of Leo T. Crowley, chairman of the Federal Deposit Insurance Corporation. Crowley was a Catholic and a friend of President Roosevelt. He agreed to approach Archbishop Edward Mooney of Detroit, under whom Coughlin served. As a result the archbishop told Coughlin that he must stop all political and propaganda activities or be unfrocked. That applied both to publication of *Social Justice* and to radio broadcasts. According to Biddle: "F.D.R. was delighted with the outcome. That was the end of Father Coughlin."[21]

In addition to federal government actions, countless private individuals and groups added their voices, pens, and dollars to the forces that crushed isolationists and isolationism during World War II. Some of those were established organizations and prominent individuals; others were obscure or masked and not clearly identifiable then or later. Many newspaper columnists, editorial writers, and radio commentators slashed away at the isolationists. Walter Winchell, Dorothy Thompson, and Drew Pearson were more virulent than most, but others shared their general perspectives. Despite the prominence of the *Chicago Tribune* and the Hearst newspapers on the anti-Roosevelt side, most leading newspapers, from the *New York Times* and *New York Herald Tribune* on down, shared in discrediting isolationists. More obscure publications did their bit.[22]

Books published during the war further inflamed hatred of isolationists. Among those were *Sabotage! The Secret War against America*, by Michael Sayers and Albert E. Kahn, and *Black Mail* by Henry Hoke. They left little doubt that prominent isolationists were sinister people representing evil and possibly subversive influences in America. Most widely distributed of such wartime books was *Under Cover: My Four Years in the Nazi Underground of America—The Amazing Revelation of How Axis Agents and Our Enemies Within Are Now*

Plotting to Destroy the United States, by John Roy Carlson, the pen name of Avedis Derounian. He used various aliases in his probe, began working for Friends of Democracy in 1940, and for a few months in 1942 was on the payroll of the FBI. Published in 1943, the book sold more than 800,000 copies. By associating prominent isolationists in various ways, often indirect or casual, with pro-Nazis and anti-Semites the book had the effect of giving sinister images to opponents of Roosevelt's foreign policies.[23]

Isolationists tried to defend themselves and fight back, but they were ineffective. Senator Wheeler proposed an investigation of Derounian, but it never materialized. In 1942 William Regnery, formerly on the America First executive committee, provided funds to enable Ruth Sarles to write a history of the America First Committee, but her detailed manuscript was never published.[24] In 1940 John T. Flynn had written a critical book on FDR called *Country Squire in the White House*. With financial help from various isolationists, he investigated sources of attacks on isolationists, and in 1944 he wrote a confidential report, "The Smear Offensive." In his report Flynn described an organized program "to silence all opposition to the foreign policy of the present administration." He charged that "the agencies engaged in this program have organized and carried on a ruthless campaign of vilification and slander deliberately to destroy the reputations of all persons opposing their policies and with a view to intimidating them and any others who might be disposed to follow them." According to Flynn's report, the groups collaborating in the program were the American Communist Party, Friends of Democracy, Inc., the Anti-Defamation League, the Non-Sectarian Anti-Nazi League, and various New Deal agencies. On April 23, 1945, the *Washington Times-Herald* carried an article by Flynn entitled "Uncovering 'Under Cover': The Real Facts about the Smear Book's Odd Author." Early in 1947 the *Chicago Tribune* carried a series of five articles by Flynn entitled "The Smear Terror," developing some of the themes advanced in his earlier 1944 confidential report. In addition, John T. Flynn, William L. Neumann, Harry Elmer Barnes, and others began to write revisionist pamphlets challenging official explanations for the background of the Japanese attack on Pearl Harbor. General Wood, William Regnery, Henry Ford, and other prewar isolationists provided financial help for some of those efforts to fight back.[25] They had little effect, however. They did not significantly damage Roosevelt or his foreign policies. They did not improve the public images of isolationists or isolationism. And they did not prevent isolationists in elective offices from going down to defeat at the hands of voters during and after World War II.

Isolationists held on better than one might have expected in the elections of 1942, the first general elections after Pearl Harbor. The war was not going well for the United States abroad, and wartime planning, production, and controls within the United States had their problems. After weeks of careful deliberation the America First Committee had announced on December 1, 1941, that it would support noninterventionists in the 1942 elections regardless of party affiliations. It began making the changes necessary to comply with legal requirements for that nonpartisan political activity. With the coming of war, the committee stopped its activities and disbanded; it did not function as an organization in the elections of 1942. But there was a residue of political concern that affected individual voters.[26]

By chance fewer isolationist senators faced the voters in 1942 than would face them in 1944 or 1946. Among isolationists no longer in Congress after the elections of 1942 were Republican Congressmen James C. Oliver of Maine and George H. Tinkham of Massachusetts, and Democratic Senator William J. Bulow of South Dakota. But progressive Republican Arthur Capper won reelection to a fifth term in the Senate by a wider vote margin than he had six years before. Senator C. Wayland Brooks won reelection in Illinois, as did Senator Henry Cabot Lodge, Jr., in Massachusetts. And Hamilton Fish won again in FDR's home district, just as he had many times before.[27]

Most shocking was the defeat of 81-year-old independent progressive George W. Norris in Nebraska. Norris had turned away from his earlier isolationism and by 1942 generally identified with Roosevelt's policies on both domestic and foreign affairs. Age was taking its toll on his energies and image. He had already served forty years in Congress—ten in the House and thirty in the Senate. He was weary and seriously considered not running in 1942. But many urged him on, including his friend Franklin Roosevelt. He finally agreed to be an independent candidate again, but did little campaigning. Though Roosevelt warmly endorsed him in 1942, as he had in 1936, the Democratic senatorial candidate and Norris split the pro-Roosevelt vote in 1942. Farmers in Nebraska were unhappy with administration policies.[28]

On election day Norris was soundly beaten by Republican Kenneth S. Wherry, who identified with small business and was critical of the administration's foreign policies. The old man was emotionally shattered by his defeat. He was disappointed that he had lost much of the farm vote. He was troubled and saddened by the virulence of anti-

Roosevelt sentiment. He wrote later that "hate against Roosevelt seems to a great extent to have brought about my defeat for re-election to the Senate." Foreign affairs had not figured prominently in the campaign.[29] Nonetheless, both Roosevelt and foreign affairs affected the results. Roosevelt's conduct of foreign affairs enhanced his strength nationally; it was less helpful in Great Plains states. The same policies that helped make Roosevelt a winner nationally helped make Norris a loser in the farm state of Nebraska. Norris was in tune with FDR and the nation on foreign affairs; but among wheat farmers and cattle growers on Nebraska farms and businessmen on the main streets of small towns in Nebraska, those foreign policy views were less popular. Industry, urbanization, and internationalism were coming to Nebraska as they had to the nation—but not fast enough to save Norris in 1942.

Norris's many friends were deeply saddened by his defeat. Fiorello La Guardia and others raised funds (particularly in the East) to give Norris a sabbatical year in Washington, where he could continue to advise on progressive programs. But Norris saw it as just a "kindness" and turned it down. Roosevelt offered him various positions in his administration. Norris would have liked a place of influence at the peace negotiating table, but declined the other positions offered to him. He struggled to write his autobiography at his home in McCook, Nebraska. His health deteriorated. On August 29, 1944, when Norris suffered his final illness, Roosevelt sent him an affectionate telegram that brought a feeble smile to the old man's face. He died four days later on September 2.[30]

The Democrats retained control in both houses of Congress after the elections of 1942. But the Republicans gained forty-four seats in the House and nine in the Senate.[31] Despite inhibitions imposed by the war and their badly damaged public image, isolationists were not much weaker numerically in Congress after the election than they had been before.

The elections of 1944 served Roosevelt and internationalists much better, however, and further weakened isolationists. The fourth term for FDR was not the controversial issue in 1944 that the third term had been in 1940. Neither Roosevelt nor his Democratic party felt any political need to appease isolationist sentiment in 1944 on either the vice-presidential nomination or the party platform. Though recording his personal preference for Henry A. Wallace, FDR was persuaded that the Iowa Democrat was a political liability. The Democratic convention turned, instead, to Harry S. Truman of Missouri. Like Wallace,

Truman was a midwestern liberal Democrat who had consistently supported the president on both domestic and foreign affairs. He was not an isolationist. The foreign policy plank in the Democratic platform that year called for "the establishment of an international organization based on the principle of the sovereign equality of all peace-loving states, open to membership by all such states, large and small, for the prevention of aggression and the maintenance of international peace and security." It favored "the maintenance of an international court of justice of which the United States shall be a member." It pledged support to the Atlantic Charter and the Four Freedoms. It endorsed the Good Neighbor policy.[32]

The Republican party faced a much more difficult political task in 1944. It had been unable to beat Roosevelt before; the odds against doing so in the midst of war against the Axis were almost impossible, even in the eyes of persons obsessed by hostility to FDR. The party ranged all the way from Wendell Willkie and Governor Harold Stassen on the internationalist extreme to Hamilton Fish and Gerald Nye on the isolationist extreme, with others scattered in between. To accomplish party unity on foreign affairs for such a broad spectrum would be an almost impossible political task. Willkie and others would have handled the problem by quashing the isolationists, but many feared his tactics would divide and further weaken the party. Nye and Fish wanted the GOP to come out boldly against what Nye called "globalists," but they had little voice in party leadership. Indeed, party leaders believed that one of their more essential tasks was to cleanse the GOP of the damaging taint of isolationism. Even unrepentant prewar noninterventionists such as Taft, Hoover, and Vandenberg believed it necessary to free their party from identification with that damaging label and image.[33]

William Allen White of Kansas and Senator Arthur H. Vandenberg of Michigan, in their separate and different ways, were among many Republican leaders who worked to build party unity on foreign policy. White, a moderate internationalist who favored Willkie, and Vandenberg, a prewar noninterventionist who opposed Willkie, differed in their perspectives and tactics. But both tried to find some common ground on foreign affairs on which Republicans could stand while fighting Roosevelt and his New Deal. Neither White nor Vandenberg was a progressive on domestic issues, nor were most others who were working to build common ground within the party on foreign affairs. The old western progressivism that had been so much a part of isolationism in the 1930s was even more absent from those unity efforts than isolationism itself.

White tried to draw former Republican presidential candidates Hoover, Landon, and Willkie together, along with a few Senate and House leaders, to endorse a common foreign policy statement. He never quite accomplished his goal, though personally he believed Hoover, Landon, and Willkie were not all that far apart on fundamentals.[34]

Vandenberg was more hostile to Willkie and more sympathetic to isolationists than was White. In a letter to Thomas W. Lamont on August 4, 1943, Vandenberg worried about "the everlasting recurrence of the 'isolationist' theme" in efforts to build GOP unity. He insisted that he did "not know of *any* 'isolationists' (in the original and literal sense of the word) since Pearl Harbor." He did "not blame the New Dealers for trying to keep this idea alive," but he regretted that "some of our own anti-isolationists continue to bestir the issue just as though nothing had happened since Pearl Harbor." He thought it was "not the so-called 'isolationists' who keep the issue alive, but it is the 'anti-isolationists' who sometimes act as though they were afraid that they might lose their shibboleth." In that same letter, however, Vandenberg wrote that he was "hunting for the middle ground between those extremists at one end of the line who would cheerfully give America away and those extremists at the other end of the line who would attempt total isolation which has come to be an impossibility."[35] Actually, none of the party leaders was trying either to give America away or to accomplish total isolation—but those stereotypes persisted nonetheless.

By negotiating the Mackinac resolution in September, 1943, Vandenberg was more effective and successful in his unity efforts than Willkie, Hoover, Landon, or White. He was tremendously proud of his accomplishment. As outsiders in the process, Willkie, Hoover, Landon, and White were less pleased. But all conceded that the Mackinac resolution that Vandenberg had helped to hammer out at least pointed in the right direction. The result was better than they had expected.[36]

Prominent prewar noninterventionists had no serious chance to win the Republican presidential nomination in 1944 during the war. Vandenberg removed himself from consideration very early. Taft concentrated his political energies on his campaign for reelection to another term in the Senate, on domestic issues, and on support for the nomination of Ohio's Governor John W. Bricker for president.[37] Bricker was as unacceptable to internationalists in the party as Taft would have been. Governor Thomas E. Dewey of New York was not prominently identified with either isolationism or internationalism. On that issue he won neither enthusiastic support nor spirited opposition from either side.

As minorities in American political history had done before and would do again, isolationists during World War II turned to a military hero in their efforts to give strength to their slight chance of defeating Roosevelt and his foreign policies during the war. They turned to General Douglas MacArthur. Key figures in the abortive MacArthur-for-President effort in 1944 included General Wood in Chicago, Senator Vandenberg in Michigan, Major Philip La Follette on MacArthur's staff in the South Pacific, and publisher Frank E. Gannett in upstate New York. Lansing Hoyt in Wisconsin and Joseph P. Savage in Illinois, both of whom had supported the America First Committee earlier, took the initiative for organizing support for MacArthur in their states.[38]

General Wood had known MacArthur when they were both cadets at West Point. Their paths had touched in Panama and in World War I during their military careers. Wood remembered MacArthur as having "an unusually brilliant mind and magnetic personality." He thought MacArthur had "real possibilities as a presidential candidate" and came to believe that he was the only man who could defeat Roosevelt in 1944. When he went on tour for the Army Air Force in the South Pacific, Wood conferred personally with General MacArthur there.[39]

Vandenberg had never personally met or communicated directly with MacArthur. In April, 1943, however, he received a hand-carried cable from General MacArthur thanking the senator for his "attitude of friendship" and expressing "absolute confidence" in the Michigan Republican's "experienced and wise mentorship." As Vandenberg recorded in his diary, " 'Mac' certainly is not 'running away' from *anything*."[40]

Vandenberg wrote that he considered MacArthur "incomparably our most available nominee and incomparably the best qualified man to lead America in the next administration." But he believed that the chance to win the presidential nomination for MacArthur lay in having a deadlock between Willkie and Dewey at the GOP convention. The "only chance" was "as a 'compromise' and not as a 'contender.' " To that end Vandenberg favored a low-key effort ready to make its move when and if the proper moment came. Most of the communications about MacArthur in letters between Vandenberg, Wood, and others were veiled and guarded. They referred to "our candidate" or "our man" without mentioning MacArthur by name. Extant written communications contain little on specific issues; it was the man and his political potential they sought.[41]

The slight chance for any convention deadlock between Willkie and Dewey disappeared with the Republican presidential primary in Wisconsin. Against the advice of Vandenberg and Wood and without the general's permission, Hoyt entered MacArthur's name in the Wisconsin primary. With his political strength fading, Willkie proposed to make a "do or die" effort in the Wisconsin primary. Given Wisconsin's strong isolationism and progressivism in the La Follette tradition, Willkie chose a poor place to make his stand. And so did Hoyt for MacArthur. Dewey won the Wisconsin primary. MacArthur (with a small budget and little organization) came second in total votes and third in the number of delegates. Stassen was next. Willkie was dead last. The Wisconsin primary knocked Willkie out of contention (he died in October before the general election). But in a different way it also eliminated MacArthur. Victory for Dewey and defeat for Willkie eliminated any chance for a convention deadlock on which Vandenberg had placed his hopes for the nomination of MacArthur. MacArthur also did poorly in the Illinois primaries. And when a Nebraska congressman indiscreetly published private correspondence from MacArthur, it became necessary for the general to remove himself from any further consideration for the nomination. As Vandenberg phrased it in a letter to Wood, "And so our great adventure ends!"[42]

Vandenberg was prepared to concede failure for their effort gracefully and throw his support to Dewey in the interests of a strong united GOP effort to unseat Roosevelt. Wood was more reluctant to give up and had more doubts about Dewey. He wrote Landon asking whether a man could be elected governor of New York "without the support of Wall Street interests and of New York's Jewish interests." He worried whether Dewey had given any "pledge" to those interests. He was troubled by Dewey's endorsement of a military alliance between the United States and Britain, and about his statements on Palestine that Wood believed were "directed at the Jewish population in this country." He feared that if Dewey were elected, the United States might "continue Roosevelt's foreign policy." He would have preferred having the Republican party nominate "either a national figure like MacArthur or a man from the Middle West" such as Bricker, Taft, or

Landon. He was "frankly suspicious of any New York candidate." Wood never warmed to Dewey and thought him too close "to the same crowd of New York internationalists which backed Willkie."[43]

At the national convention in Chicago, Dewey won the Republican presidential nomination on the first ballot. The vice-presidential nomination went to Governor Bricker. If General Wood had had his way (which he did not), the platform would have included a "strongly worded" plank on immigration calling for quotas "by race instead of country—the English race, the Scotch race, the Italian race, the Hebrew race, etc." He thought refugees entering the United States "illegally or on temporary certificates" should "be deported at the end of the war." He also favored a plank calling for military demobilization "as rapidly as possible" after the war.[44] But Vandenberg, not Wood, played the central role in shaping language on foreign policy for the platform. He had worked earnestly during the spring of 1944 to win agreement among party leaders for language conforming closely to his "Mackinac idea." According to Vandenberg, "The job was just about done before we ever got to Chicago—and thereafter, it was fairly plain sailing."[45]

In its final form the Republican platform called for prosecuting the war "to total victory against our enemies in full cooperation with the United Nations." It proposed to accomplish the objectives of the war and peace "through organized international cooperation and not by joining a World State." It endorsed "responsible participation by the United States in post-war cooperative organization among sovereign nations to prevent military aggression and to attain permanent peace with organized justice in a free world." It insisted that any peace treaty or agreement "be made only by and with the advice and consent of the Senate of the United States provided two-thirds of the Senators present concur." It endorsed the Good Neighbor policy toward Latin America. It favored a two-term limit for the presidency. And it favored opening Palestine to unrestricted Jewish immigration and land ownership and called for implementation of the Balfour Declaration in Palestine.[46]

Though Roosevelt was skeptical about the effort, Secretary of State Cordell Hull negotiated an agreement with Dewey's foreign policy spokesman, John Foster Dulles, that during the 1944 campaign politics would (in Vandenberg's words) stop "at the water's edge." After three meetings Hull and Dulles issued a joint statement to the press on August 25. In it Hull asserted that the American people considered "the subject of future peace as a nonpartisan subject which must be kept entirely out of politics." Dulles made it clear that Dewey shared that view "on the understanding, however, that it did not preclude full public nonpartisan discussion of the means of attaining a lasting peace." That agreement generally was honored on both sides in the presidential race.[47] But it did not prevent isolationism from being drawn into the campaign.

In his endorsement of the Dumbarton Oaks proposals for an international organization, Dewey may have been trying to free his party and his presidential bid from the stigma of isolationism. At least Assistant Secretary of State Breckinridge Long thought so. He wrote Hull that Dewey "apparently tried to associate himself with our participation in the world organization" and tried "to squeeze every political advantage out of it but still live up to the letter of the agreement."[48]

In a major foreign policy campaign address before a dinner meeting of the Foreign Policy Association in New York on October 21, Roosevelt effectively identified his Republican opposition with isolationism. He reminded his listeners that one of the Republican isolationists who had "killed international cooperation in 1920" after World War I was Senator Hiram Johnson, who would become chairman of the Foreign Relations Committee if the Republicans won control of the Senate. He said that in the years following 1920 "the foreign policy of the Republican Administration was dominated by the heavy hand of isolationism." If the Republicans won in 1944, FDR said, isolationist Gerald Nye would be chairman of the Senate Committee on Appropriations and isolationist Hamilton Fish would chair the House Committee on Rules. Concerning those and others he asked, "Can anyone really suppose that these isolationists have changed their minds about world affairs?" He thought politicians "who embraced the policy of isolationism, and who never raised their forces against it in our days of peril" were not "reliable custodians of the future of America." He conceded that some Republicans were not isolationists (Henry Stimson, for example). And he conceded that some Democrats were isolationists, but he insisted that they were "few and far between" and had "not attained great positions of leadership." He expressed pride that his administration did not "have the support of the isolationist press," specifically "the McCormick-Patterson-Gannett-and-Hearst press."[49]

Dewey was not an isolationist, but one of the burdens he had to carry in his race with Roosevelt was the charge of Republican isolationism. He would have lost to Roosevelt with or without that burden, but FDR made the most of it. With cities providing his greatest strength, Roosevelt easily defeated Dewey on November 7, carrying thirty-six states and winning 432 electoral votes to 99 for Dewey. Dewey was strongest in agricultural states of the Great Plains, Middle West, and upper New England.[50]

Republican Senator Taft of Ohio won reelection by a narrow margin to a second term. He did poorly in urban centers, but the rural voters saved him. A number of prewar isolationists held on to their seats in the House of Representatives, including Dewey Short of Missouri, Karl Mundt of South Dakota, Clare Hoffman and Paul Shafer of Michigan, and William Lemke of North Dakota.[51]

But isolationists took beatings in other Senate and House contests. From FDR's perspective probably the most satisfying isolationist defeat in 1944 ended Republican Hamilton Fish's stay of nearly a quarter of a century as congressman from Roosevelt's home district. Roosevelt and Fish despised each other personally, in addition to their sharp differences on both domestic and foreign policies. Roosevelt had hoped for years for the defeat of Fish. He worked with both Democrats and Republicans inside and outside the district to find the right formula for beating him. In May, 1934, more than a decade before Fish's defeat, Roosevelt wrote the chairman of the Dutchess County Democratic committee suggesting that the party find a popular independent Republican, run him against Fish in the GOP primaries, and run him unopposed in the Democratic primaries. Roosevelt kept that tactic in mind over the years. He also favored redistricting to increase the voting strength of Fish's opponents. In 1944 those determined to oust Fish finally accomplished their objective. August W. Bennett, after losing in the Republican primaries, filed as an independent Republican. He won support against Fish from Republicans Wendell Willkie and Thomas E. Dewey as well as from Democrats. That coalition accomplished the defeat of Fish on November 7. Fish, a colonel in the Officers Reserve Corps, then wrote the president asking for active duty in the army. He assured the president of his "utmost cooperation in winning the war as speedily as possible and in securing a lasting peace." Roosevelt responded that the War Department felt his "call to active duty would not be consistent with its needs."[52]

When the Seventy-ninth Congress began its first session on January 3, 1945, only two of the seven members of the Senate Munitions Investigation Committee of 1934–36 remained. They were Democratic Senator Walter George of Georgia and Republican Senator Arthur Vandenberg of Michigan. Republican Senator W. Warren Barbour had died in office on November 22, 1943. Democrat James P. Pope of Idaho had lost in the 1938 primaries to D. Worth Clark. Clark, in turn, was ousted in the 1944 Democratic primaries by Glen Taylor, after serving only one term in the Senate. Democrat Homer T. Bone of Washington resigned in November, 1944, after Roosevelt had appointed him a judge on the United States Circuit Court of Appeals in San Francisco. Democrat Bennett Champ Clark of Missouri, who had shared with Nye in so many spirited battles against Roosevelt's foreign policies during his two terms in the Senate, suffered defeat in the 1944 Democratic primary. In 1945, after Roosevelt's death, Clark's fellow Missouri Democrat President Harry S. Truman appointed him associate justice of the United States Court of Appeals in the District of Columbia. And Republican Gerald P. Nye of North Dakota, who had been chairman of the Munitions Investigating Committee and one of the most persistent and uncompromising opponents of Roosevelt's foreign policies, went down to defeat at the polls on November 7, 1944.[53]

The tactics used to defeat Nye in North Dakota were similar to those used against Fish in New York. The basic approach was to divide the votes of those who shared Nye's views on public issues and to combine one part with an internationalist vote cutting across party lines in opposition to Nye. The split in the agrarian-oriented isolationist vote was accomplished by political forces within North Dakota— the bitter contest there between Langer and Nye. But interests (and money) from outside the state provided additional input that helped make the difference between victory and defeat for Nye in November.

Nye and Langer shared similar views on both domestic and foreign affairs; both were progressives and both were isolationists. In the 1930s and 1940s, however, they battled against each other for political survival and dominance in North Dakota. By winning support from a mixed bag of Republicans and Democrats who opposed Langer, Nye triumphed in the senatorial election of 1938. But Langer won election to the Senate two years later, and he determined to crush Nye at the first opportunity. In the 1944 Republican primary Langer and his Nonpartisan League threw their support to Usher Burdick in opposition to Nye. That opposition, by itself, would have given Nye a real battle, but there was more.[54]

Willkie Republicans—largely urban, business, and internationalist—supported the candidacy of Fargo attorney Lynn U. Stambaugh. He had been national commander of the American Legion and was expected to win votes from veterans. Many who had voted for Nye in

1938 only because he opposed Langer shifted in 1944 to Stambaugh. In his aggressive campaign Stambaugh denounced the senator's isolationism and charged that Nye "would wrap the United States in a blanket and deny it relationships with any other nation. He hates the British and has contempt for our Allies. He believes the Nazis should be permitted to continue their government of hatred and oppression if they want to. He thinks the United States invited attack by our enemies. Had he succeeded in his efforts to defeat lend-lease, selective service, neutrality revision and other last minute preparedness measures, German and Jap forces might be converging on Bismarck [the capital city of North Dakota] tonight." Those in the Farmers' Union who supported President Roosevelt generally opposed Nye. Substantial opposition to Nye originated outside the state—particularly from internationalists and the East. Nye had won labor support in his earlier campaigns, but in 1944 organized labor actively opposed him, particularly the CIO Political Action Committee. During the campaign the opposition distributed many copies of John Roy Carlson's book, *Under Cover*, in efforts to discredit Nye. The senator's divorce hurt him politically. Nye had little chance for victory if his opponents united behind a single candidate. In the June primary, however, they unintentionally opened the door for his renomination by scattering their support among Burdick, Stambaugh, and the Democratic candidate, John Moses.[55]

Moreover, Nye campaigned aggressively and won substantial support in and out of North Dakota. The Republican state convention endorsed his candidacy. He aroused sympathy by charging that "Willkieites," "New Dealers," Jews, Communists, and eastern newspapers and columnists were out to "get" him. In effect, he asked whether the people of North Dakota were going to choose their own senator or let easterners determine their choice. Like his opponents, however, Nye won support outside the state. Edwin S. Webster, Jr., of New York City, a former member of the America First national committee, helped solicit funds for Nye's campaign. Numerous former America Firsters and isolationists contributed. On June 18, the *Chicago Sunday Tribune* prominently carried a laudatory feature article by Walter Trohan, "Gerald Nye—Man of Courage." That article was distributed widely in North Dakota. In striking contrast to his progressive tone earlier, Nye's speeches in 1944 were distinctly conservative on domestic issues—though they retained their agrarian orientation.[56]

Nye won renomination on June 27, but it was an extremely close contest. Stambaugh ran second (only 972 votes behind Nye).[57]

The campaign before the general elections in the fall was fought as bitterly as the primary had been. One unidentified pamphlet opposing Nye charged, "Consciously or unconsciously, Senator Nye has done a lot for the Nazis and their sympathizers in this country." By 1944 the term "isolationist" had become so derogatory that it hurt Nye even among people who had shared his specific views on foreign policy. To try to protect himself against the damning charge of isolationism, in October, 1944, Nye summarized his foreign policy views in different terms from those he had used earlier. He called for military preparedness, checking aggressor countries, and cooperation with other countries to maintain peace. But he still insisted that "there can be no power given any cooperative international body or force that would let that body or force take our country to war without Constitutional consent."[58]

In a two-man contest with the Democratic candidate, John Moses, Nye might have been reelected on November 7. But Stambaugh ran for the Senate as an independent in the fall, thus splitting the Republican vote between himself and Nye. That obviously pleased (and may have been encouraged by) the Democrats. On September 12, 1944, Nye took the floor in the Senate and charged that, a year before, a former member of the Department of Justice who was "very close to the White House," Joseph B. Keenan, had urged Fay De Witt, a World War I veteran from Minot, North Dakota, to run for senator in the primary against Nye and had promised to finance De Witt's campaign to the extent of $110,000. According to Nye, Senator Langer had introduced Keenan to De Witt. Nye claimed that De Witt was told that if he lost in a three-way race, "he would be taken care of, appointed United States marshal, for instance." When De Witt rejected the offer, he allegedly was told that he was "making a mistake in not accepting the proposition, that there could be a guaranty that some serviceman would be in the race for the United States Senate." Nye introduced statements and affidavits to support his account. Senator Langer then took the floor and denounced "as entirely false the statement that Mr. Joseph B. Keenan ever offered anybody a single dollar to be a candidate against the senior Senator from North Dakota in the coming election." He admitted, however, being at the conversation between Keenan and De Witt.[59] Though they disagreed with Stambaugh's foreign policy views, Langer's followers in the Nonpartisan League backed Stambaugh in their determination to beat Nye. Nye and Stambaugh combined got more votes than Moses, but the Democrat got more votes than either of them individually and was elected.

Stambaugh carried only one county, but he took enough votes away from Nye to help beat the three-term senator. When the Democratic administration then appointed the Republican Stambaugh to the board of the Export-Import Bank in 1945, many interpreted that as his political reward for helping defeat Nye. Moses died soon after taking office, and Governor Fred Aandahl appointed Milton R. Young to fill that Senate seat. Ironically, Young had been Nye's campaign manager in 1944.[60] Senator Young quietly and responsibly served his North Dakota constituents during the generation that he held that office. He was not a doctrinaire internationalist on foreign affairs, but neither did he play the kind of role in foreign affairs that Nye had played (and that Langer would continue to play).

There was fundamental significance in the contrasting patterns of the postwar careers of Gerald P. Nye of North Dakota and Arthur H. Vandenberg of Michigan. On December 19, 1944, his fifty-second birthday, Nye delivered his farewell address to the Senate; it was, in effect, a funeral dirge for his political career and for American isolationism. Three weeks later on January 10, 1945, Vandenberg delivered the most important address of his life before the United States Senate; it was, in effect, a triumphal processional for his emergence as the leading Republican statesman in the Senate for the bipartisan consensus behind America's internationalism, collective security, and containment policies after World War II.

Both Vandenberg and Nye were Republicans. Neither had graduated from college. Both had been newspapermen. Both took their Senate seats initially by appointment. Both had been fervent isolationists. They had cosponsored the resolution calling for Senate investigation of the munitions industry, and both served actively on that investigating committee. Neither repudiated his earlier noninterventionist views or activities. And both supported the war effort after Pearl Harbor. But Nye had operated from an agrarian progressive base in the Great Plains farming state of North Dakota; it had little industrial or urban development. In contrast, Vandenberg was a conservative in the state of Michigan, which included huge heavy industries as well as agriculture; its large cities played major roles in wartime military production for the United States and its allies. Nye was an aggressive crusader for agrarian isolationism against urban-industrial-creditor-eastern internationalism; Vandenberg was more ready to compromise and seek common ground with his adversaries in Michigan, in Washington, and abroad in opposition to the Axis and to the Soviet Union. Nye spoke for an America that was disappearing; Vandenberg increasingly spoke for what was becoming. Vandenberg survived politically and was lauded for his statemanship; Nye had gone down to defeat and was the object of widespread scorn and disdain. It was entirely appropriate that President Roosevelt asked Vandenberg to serve as a member of the American delegation to the United Nations Conference in San Francisco at the same time that Nye's political career ended and his voice on foreign affairs fell silent.

Nye devoted most of his farewell address on December 19 to a discussion of American foreign relations during his two decades in the Senate and to his views on the future. He said that the United States "must prosecute the war to a victorious end, and we must have these allies with us if we are to do it." But he ridiculed the idea that World War II would be "followed by the golden age for America." He feared that within ten or twenty years the United States would "be told that we must go into another European war to keep Russia from seizing control of the world." In Asia, Nye saw "a revived imperialism . . . with the United States held responsible by all Asiatics for having wiped out the one nonwhite empire and having restored all the white, European empires." Senator Nye also predicted: "Our people will be staggering under a debt that may even go beyond the $300,000,000,000 mark. We shall have a standing army that will fill this capital with an officer cast with insatiable appetites for power and that will militarize the whole educational system of our Nation. We shall have the most enormous Navy that ever covered the seas, with all the enormous costs that such a Navy entails. We shall be involved in every quarrel between our partners in this new world order, for they will know how necessary it is for them to be able to count on using our power to win their quarrels, and there will be other quarrels directly between them and us. And when World War No. 3 comes along, as it certainly will as a result of this attempt to divide up Europe and the Near and Middle East between Russia and England, we will be in it from the first day." He said that the only way the United States could keep out of World War III was: "By minding our own business. By keeping out of these entangling alliances. By developing our own markets here in this hemisphere and devoting our strength honestly and solely to the defense of our own territory." Appropriately, he cited Charles A. Beard's book, *The Open Door at Home*, to support his contention that "it is quite possible for us to find, in our own domestic market and in the trade which we can easily develop on friendly terms with our neighbors in this hemisphere, all the prosperity we need for our American people." He did not repudiate or apologize for any part of his career in the Senate. He closed his oration with an expression of "faith in the good purpose and patriotic spirit of the plain people of America and in what I have come to know, during 20 years, to be the purpose and spirit of the Senate." His address got little attention. The *New York Times* buried it in a half-column on page 16 and in a short editorial concluded that the only "good effect" of the talk was to "prove to the complete satisfaction of the voters of North Dakota how right they were when they rejected him in the last election." Nye made a futile effort to regain a seat in the Senate in 1946. He died in Washington at the age of seventy-eight in 1971. By that time one of his sons had been seriously wounded in combat in Vietnam. His youngest son was serving as an air force pilot in Southeast Asia. And at the moment the former isolationist senator died, the United States was pressing on with its unpopular war in Vietnam that ended with defeat after his death.[61]

Vandenberg's address on January 10, 1945, got a much different reception. He labored hard in its preparation and considered it of major import. The press and the public pointed to the address as Senator Vandenberg's repudiation of his earlier isolationism and the announcement of his sudden endorsement of internationalism. Except for the drama of the presentation, however, there was little abrupt about it. He did say that the "oceans have ceased to be moats which automatically protect our ramparts," but he did not explicitly mention isolationism or repudiate his prewar noninterventionist efforts. In his address Senator Vandenberg included many attitudes that he had been emphasing for years, including concern for guarding America's self-interests, supporting American military power, and taking a critical and distrustful view of the Soviet Union's role (and England's) in world affairs. Furthermore, in his speech the Michigan Senator advanced ideas that he had been developing all during World War II, including the need for national and allied unity in defeating the Axis and in planning the peace. He criticized President Roosevelt for not candidly reasserting America's postwar objectives in the terms outlined long before in the Atlantic Charter.[62] Like Roosevelt, Vandenberg was moving with the currents in Michigan, in the United States, and in the Western world; he was on his way to the pinnacle of his career. In contrast, Nye was beaten, rejected, and (with his foreign policy views) cast on the political junk heap.

The political careers of other leading Senate isolationists outlasted Roosevelt and continued on after his death on April 12, 1945. But in most cases they did so largely because their six-year terms prevented voters and internationalists from ousting them sooner. Each successive election after the war removed more of the prewar isolationists from public office.

In the elections of 1946 the Republicans won control of both houses of Congress for the first time since Herbert Hoover was president. Vandenberg won reelection to another term in the Senate, and as ranking Republican he became chairman of the Foreign Relations Committee in the Eightieth Congress, beginning in 1947.[63]

Other prewar noninterventionists, however, fell by the wayside in 1946. Democrat David I. Walsh of Massachusetts lost in November to Republican Henry Cabot Lodge, Jr. Both had been noninterventionists before Pearl Harbor, but Lodge had resigned his Senate seat to serve in the army in the Mediterranean and European theaters before returning to run against Walsh after the war. He was an attractive personality who successfully put his isolationist past behind him and identified with the internationalist wing of his party after the war.[64]

Two of the three Republicans who had opposed Senate approval of the United Nations Charter in 1945 were gone when the Eightieth Congress began its sessions. Hiram Johnson had been too ill to vote but had been paired against the United Nations Charter. He died on August 6, 1945, the year before his fifth term in the Senate would have ended. California Governor Earl Warren appointed William F. Knowland to fill the vacancy, and in 1946 Knowland won election to a full term. Unrepentant isolationist William Langer of North Dakota won reelection in 1946 to a second term in the Senate without either repudiating or compromising his agrarian radical, antieastern, anticolonial isolationism. From 1953 until 1959 he served on the Foreign Relations Committee but had little influence on its course. He was very nearly alone on many issues, domestic and foreign. That does not seem to have troubled him greatly so long as his North Dakota constituents were content with him. He was still in the Senate when he died in 1959. Minnesota's Henrik Shipstead, along with Langer, had voted against Senate approval of the United Nations Charter. He was defeated in the Republican primary in 1946 in his bid for a fifth term. He died in 1960.[65]

In 1946 Young Bob La Follette lost to Joseph R. McCarthy in the Republican primary in Wisconsin. Many variables accounted for his defeat, including overconfidence, opposition from regular Republicans on the right and from labor and the CIO Political Action Committee on the left, McCarthy's aggressive campaign, and La Follette's failure to give his campaign the time and energy it required. After it was all over, La Follette and many of his supporters believed that opposition from Communists and Communist-led labor unions contributed to his defeat. La Follette's isolationist image hurt him. The candidate for the Democratic nomination charged that "La Follette spent five years before the war voting for Hitler." McCarthy's margin of victory was only five thousand votes, but it ended the career of that able progressive and prewar noninterventionist. Seven years later, in 1953, La Follette committed suicide.[66] His brother Philip La Follette, former governor of Wisconsin, returned after World War II from military service on General MacArthur's staff in the South Pacific. He engaged in some political activity, particularly trying to win the GOP presidential nomination for MacArthur. But he never again ran for political office.[67]

Further west in Montana, Burton K. Wheeler, after twenty-four years in the Senate, was defeated in the Democratic primary in his bid for a fifth term. He had won by a huge margin in 1940 and allowed too little time for campaigning in 1946. He quickly sensed that he was in difficulty when he felt the unfamiliar coolness and remoteness of the audiences he addressed. Despite his long record as a progressive, for the first time in his political career he faced formidable opposition from the Farmers' Union and labor unions. Initially he had begun his political career by battling the Anaconda Copper Mining Company in Montana, but in 1946 he was accused of being a "company man." Though Wheeler's campaign did not lack money, his opponent benefited from contributions from outside Montana from liberal, labor, and internationalist sources in the urban Northeast. Like La Follette, Wheeler believed that Communist-controlled unions played energetic roles in his opposition; detailed reports in FBI files confirm his belief that Communists had targeted him for defeat. And, of course, Wheeler's isolationist reputation hurt him.[68]

Though he might have lost anyway, the most spectacular blow against Wheeler during the primary campaign was the publication of a book entitled *The Plot against America: Senator Wheeler and the Forces behind Him*. Written by David George Kin, the pen name for David George Plotkin of New York City, the book was a vicious 394-page diatribe. For example, it referred to the "Benedict Arnold like Wheeler" who was "the saboteur of the People's War Against Hitler." It charged that "the Nazi-fascist Wheeler" was "the tool of Wall Street-in-America." It contended that Wheeler "had dreams of becoming an American Quisling, Hitler's handyman, after Big Business in Wall Street and Big Business in Berlin had made a deal to divide the world between them." Wheeler asked the Senate Campaign Investigating Committee to investigate the background and character of the book. When it reported on February 1, 1947, the Senate committee called the book "one of the vilest, most contemptible, and obscene pieces of so-called literature ever to be published concerning a man in public office in the United States." But by that time the damage was done. Wheeler lost by a margin of six thousand votes in the Democratic primary. His opponent, in turn, lost to the Republican candidate, Zales Ecton, in the general election. After one term Ecton was defeated in his bid for reelection in 1952 by Democrat Mike Mansfield, who was to have a long and distinguished career in the Senate. Wheeler never again ran for public office. Instead, he practiced law in Washington in partnership with one of his sons. He died there in 1975 at the age of 92.[69]

The Eightieth Congress, which assembled in the Capitol on January 3, 1947, was the first elected after the death of Roosevelt. It had Republican majorities in both houses, but most of Roosevelt's old isolationist adversaries were gone. Of the leading prewar Senate noninterventionists, Brooks, Capper, Edwin Johnson, Langer, Lodge, McCarran, Taft, Tobey, Vandenberg, and White remained. Vandenberg and Lodge had successfully identified with leadership of Senate internationalists. Brooks was defeated in 1948. Old age and growing opposition led Capper to decide against running for reelection in 1948. He died in 1951 at the age of eighty-six.[70] Younger senators and representatives elected after Pearl Harbor would take nationalist or so-called neoisolationist positions on foreign affairs. But prickly old William Langer was more nearly alone on public issues than he would have been if he had been in the Senate a decade earlier.[71] Death had taken President Roosevelt on April 12, 1945. But even in death he had triumphed decisively over his isolationist adversaries.

Continuity and change are constants in human history. Neither isolationism nor the socioeconomic-emotional bases for isolationist perspectives entirely disappeared. Remnants of rural and small-town America survived, as did foreign policy projections of that America. As long as they lived, old isolationists continued to believe that history would vindicate them and would demonstrate the wisdom of their guidance on foreign affairs (and the accuracy of their charges against Roosevelt). Critics of American involvement in Vietnam thirty years later (many of them Democratic urban liberal internationalists) resurrected arguments that isolationists had used earlier.[72] But the socioeconomic bases for those older unilateralist and noninterventionist policies had eroded. A way of life and a mode of thinking were fading from the American scene.

Franklin D. Roosevelt was more nearly in tune with what the United States and the world were becoming. Science and technology, industry and finance, urbanization, modern transportation and communication systems, and the terrible destructiveness of military weapons in the nuclear age swept away most of the bases for isolationism during the century that followed Roosevelt's birth. If he had lived on, Roosevelt would have disliked many of the developments in the United States, in foreign affairs, and in the world during the second half of the twentieth century. But he would have moved with the increasingly dominant urban forces as they projected into a vastly enlarged and expanded multilateral role for the United States in world affairs.

Notes

Chapter 1

1 An expanded version of the remainder of this chapter was published earlier in Wayne S. Cole, "Franklin D. Roosevelt and the Isolationists, 1932-1945," in *Proceedings of the Conference on War and Diplomacy, 1976,* ed. David H. White (Charleston, S.C.: The Citadel, 1976), pp. 1-11.

2 The first three volumes of Professor Frank Freidel's biography of Roosevelt are invaluable for an understanding of background influences and experiences during Roosevelt's early years: *Franklin D. Roosevelt: The Apprenticeship; Franklin D. Roosevelt: The Ordeal; Franklin D. Roosevelt: The Triumph* (Boston: Little, Brown and Company, 1952-56). For a scholarly study of FDR and foreign affairs, see Robert Dallek, *Franklin D. Roosevelt and American Foreign Policy, 1932-45* (New York: Oxford University Press, 1979).

3 Philip La Follette, *Adventure in Politics: The Memoirs of Philip La Follette,* pp. 179-80.

4 Henry A. Wallace Diary, February 13, 1940.

5 The best scholarly historical definition of isolationism is in Albert K. Weinberg, "The Historical Meaning of the American Doctrine of Isolation," *American Political Science Review* 34 (1940): 539-47. For scholarly studies that focus more directly on isolationism in the Roosevelt era, see Selig Adler, *The Isolationist Impulse: Its Twentieth-Century Reaction* (London and New York: Abelard-Schuman Limited, 1957); Wayne S. Cole, "A Tale of Two Isolationists—Told Three Wars Later," *The Society for Historians of American Foreign Relations Newsletter* 5 (March 1974): 2-16; and Manfred Jonas, *Isolationism in America, 1935-1941* (Ithaca, N.Y.: Cornell University Press, 1966). See also Raymond A. Esthus, "Isolationism and World Power," *Diplomatic History* 2 (Spring 1978): 117-29.

6 Among many accounts analyzing sources of support for isolationism, see Bernard Fensterwald, Jr., "The Anatomy of American 'Isola-

tionism' and Expansionism," *Journal of Conflict Resolution* 2 (June 1958): 111–39; Samuel Lubell, "Who Votes Isolationist and Why," *Harper's Magazine,* April 1951, pp. 29–36; Leroy N. Rieselbach, *The Roots of Isolationism: Congressional Voting and Presidential Leadership in Foreign Policy* (Indianapolis: Bobbs-Merrill Comapny, 1966); and Ralph H. Smuckler, "The Region of Isolationism," *American Political Science Review* 47 (June 1953): 386–401.

7 For a scholarly history on FDR and the progressives, see Ronald L. Feinman, *Twilight of Progressivism: The Western Republicans and the New Deal* (Baltimore, Md.: Johns Hopkins University Press, 1981).

8 Hadley Cantril and Mildred Strunk, eds. *Public Opinion, 1935–1936* (Princeton, N.J.: Princeton University Press, 1951), pp. 966–78.

Chapter 2

1 Burton K. Wheeler, with Paul F. Healy, *Yankee From the West: The Candid, Turbulent Life Story of the Yankee-born U.S. Senator from Montana;* and Richard T. Ruetten, "Senator Burton K. Wheeler and Insurgency in the 1920's," in *The American West: A Reorientation,* ed. Gene M. Gressley (Laramie: University of Wyoming Publications, 1966), pp. 111–31.

2 Interview with Burton K. Wheeler, Washington, D.C., October 23, 1969.

3 Ibid.; Wheeler, *Yankee From the West,* pp. 294–95.

4 Wheeler, *Yankee From the West,* pp. 295–96; Wheeler to Oswald Garrison Villard, April 29, 1930, Oswald Garrison Villard Papers.

5 Franklin D. Roosevelt, *F.D.R.: His Personal Letters, 1928–1945,* 1:129–30.

6 Wheeler to Villard, January 9, 1932, Villard Papers.

7 Wheeler, *Yankee From the West,* p. 285.

8 Ibid., p. 297; interview with Wheeler, October 23, 1969.

9 The definitive biography is Richard Lowitt, *George W. Norris: Making of a Progressive, 1861–1912* (Syracuse, N.Y.: Syracuse University Press, 1963); *George W. Norris: Persistence of a Progressive, 1913–1933* (Urbana: University of Illinois Press, 1971); and *George W. Norris: Triumph of a Progressive, 1933–1944* (Urbana: University of Illinois Press, 1978). See also George W. Norris, *Fighting Liberal: The Autobiography of George W. Norris.*

10 George W. Norris to Edward J. Jeffries, March 23, 1931, Norris to Arthur G. Wray, February 4, 1932, George W. Norris Papers.

11 Norris to Jeffries, March 23, 1931, Norris to Wray, February 4, 1932, Norris Papers.

12 Norris to Franklin D. Roosevelt, December 28, 1928, Roosevelt to Norris, January 6, 1930, June 30, 1931, Norris to Wray, February 4,

1932, and clipping from *Philadelphia Record,* May 6, 1932, Norris Papers.

13 Norris to John Haynes Holmes, May 10, 1932, May 21, 1932, Norris Papers.

14 Hiram Johnson to Hiram Johnson, Jr., and Archibald M. Johnson, January 18, 1932, January 23, 1932, Hiram W. Johnson Papers.

15 Johnson to Hiram Johnson, Jr., and Archibald M. Johnson, May 1, 1932, Johnson Papers.

16 Wayne S. Cole, *Senator Gerald P. Nye and American Foreign Relations* (Minneapolis: University of Minnesota Press, 1962); *New York World,* June 16, 1931; *New York Times,* March 28, 1932, p. 2; *North Dakota Progressive* (Bismarck), July 5, 1932.

17 William Randolph Hearst to E. D. Coblentz, January 21, 1932, Johnson Papers.

18 Franklin D. Roosevelt, *Looking Forward* (New York: John Day Company, 1933), pp. 254–56.

19 Norman H. Davis to Frank L. Polk, Norman H. Davis Papers; William E. Dodd to Cyrus S. Eaton, June 7, 1932, William E. Dodd Papers.

20 Cordell Hull, *The Memoirs of Cordell Hull,* 1:150–53; Kirk H. Porter and Donald Bruce Johnson, comps., *National Party Platforms, 1840–1956* (Urbana: University of Illinois Press, 1956), pp. 331–33, 339–51.

21 Sir R. Lindsay to Sir John Simon, July 21, 1932, Foreign Office 414/270, pp. 19–20, British Foreign Office Records.

22 Mimeographed press release, Columbia Broadcasting System, Washington, D.C., June 14, 1932, Arthur Capper Papers; interview with Charles A. Lindbergh, Washington, D.C., June 7, 1972.

23 *Devils Lake* (N.D.) *Journal,* October 25, 1932, October 31, 1932, November 2, 1932; interview with Gerald P. Nye, Chevy Chase, Maryland, July 27, 1959; James Couzens to John Carson, September 22, 1932, Couzens to F. A. Fischer, October 5, 1932, James Couzens Papers; William E. Borah to Alfred J. Dunn, October 3, 1932, William E. Borah Papers.

24 *New York Times,* September 26, 1932; *Washington Post,* October 25, 1932; George W. Norris to Homer T. Bone, October 1, 1932, George W. Norris Papers.

25 Johnson to Hiram Johnson, Jr., July 9, 1932, Johnson Papers; Johnson to Charles L. McNary, October 7, 1932, Charles L. McNary Papers; night letter to Johnson from seventy newsmen, October 11, 1932, Johnson to E. P. Clark and others, October 12, 1932, Franklin D. Roosevelt Papers, President's Personal File 1134; Johnson to Cutting, October 18, 1932, Bronson M. Cutting Papers.

26 Amos R. E. Pinchot to Charles Hallinan, September 20, 1932, Pinchot to David K. Niles, September 23, 1932, Amos R. E. Pinchot Papers.

27 Daniel C. Roper to William E. Dodd, August 29, 1932, Dodd Papers.

28 Francis B. Sayre to Franklin D. Roosevelt, October 13, 1932, Francis B. Sayre Papers.
29 D. G. Osborne to Sir John Simon, October 27, 1932, Foreign Office 414/270, pp. 62–63, British Foreign Office Records.

Chapter 3

1 Johnson to Hiram Johnson, Jr., January 15, 1933, Johnson Papers.
2 Clipping from *McCook* (Nebr.) *Gazette,* November 18, 1932, Norris Papers; interview with Burton K. Wheeler, October 23, 1969; Burton K. Wheeler, with Paul F. Healy, *Yankee from the West: The Candid, Turbulent Life Story of the Yankee-born U.S. Senator from Montana,* p. 298.
3 Johnson to Hiram Johnson, Jr., December 18, 1932, Johnson Papers.
4 Johnson to Hiram Johnson, Jr., January 22, 1933, Johnson Papers.
5 Clipping from *Baltimore Sun,* February 1, 1928, Etienne de P. Bujac to Edgar F. Puryear, October 24, 1928, Bronson M. Cutting Papers; *Time Magazine,* May 20, 1935, pp. 14–15; Robert M. La Follette, Jr., to Phil La Follette, January 20, 1933, La Follette Family Papers.
6 Robert La Follette to Philip La Follette, January 20, 1933, La Follette Family Papers.
7 Patrick J. Maney, *"Young Bob" La Follette: A Biography of Robert M. La Follette, Jr., 1895–1953* (Columbia and London: University of Missouri Press, 1978); Philip La Follette, *Adventure in Politics: The Memoirs of Philip La Follette;* Alan Edmond Kent, "Portrait in Isolationism: The La Follettes and Foreign Policy" (Ph.D. diss., University of Wisconsin, 1956).
8 La Follette, *Adventure in Politics,* pp. 184–203.
9 Robert La Follette to Philip La Follette, January 20, 1933, La Follette Family Papers.
10 Ibid., January 20, 24, 1933.
11 Ibid., January 24, 1933.
12 Night cable Robert La Follette to Philip La Follette, February 21, March 1, 6, 1933, Robert La Follette to Fola and Mid La Follette, February 24, 1933, Robert La Follette to Roosevelt, March 6, 1933, La Follette Family Papers.
13 La Follette, *Adventure in Politics,* pp. 204–7; memorandum [by Philip La Follette], Washington, D.C., March 20, 1933, La Follette Family Papers.
14 Johnson to Charles K. McClatchy, February 26, 1933, Johnson Papers.
15 Johnson to Hiram Johnson, Jr., January 22, 1933, Johnson Papers.
16 Johnson to Charles K. McClatchy, February 26, 1933, Johnson Papers.
17 Norris to Joseph T. Robinson, November 16, 1932, Norris Papers.

18 Harold L. Ickes to Robert M. La Follette, Jr., January 24, 1933, La
Follette to Ickes, January 27, 30, 1933, February 6, 1933, La Follette
Family Papers; John P. Robertson to David K. Niles, January 24,
1933, Norris Papers; Johnson to Ickes, December 14, 1932, Johnson
Papers.

Chapter 4

1 Johnson to Hiram Johnson, Jr., January 29, 1933, February 12, 1933,
Johnson papers; clipping from *Pittsburgh Sun-Telegraph,* February 22,
1933, Gerald P. Nye Papers; Vandenberg to Ernest Kanzler, March 7,
1933, Arthur H. Vandenberg Papers.
2 Johnson to Hiram Johnson, Jr., March 5, 12, 19, 1933, Johnson
Papers.
3 Ibid., April 1, 16, 1933, Johnson Papers.
4 Ibid., June 4, 16, 1933, Johnson Papers.
5 Norris to Carl F. Marsh, April 8, 1933, Norris Papers.
6 Franklin D. Roosevelt, *The Public Papers and Addresses of Franklin
D. Roosevelt,* 2:122–29; *Congressional Record,* 73d Congress, 1st sess.,
1933, 77:2339–41, 2808–2809, 3474–75, 3600, 3764; [John P.
Robertson] to John G. Maher, June 3, 1933, Norris Papers.
7 Patrick J. Maney, *"Young Bob" La Follette: A Biography of Robert
M. La Follette, Jr., 1895–1953* (Columbia and London: University of
Missouri Press, 1978), pp. 65–66, 114–16; La Follette to Alfred T.
Rogers, April 20, 1933, La Follette Family Papers; La Follette to Fola
and George Middleton, April 3, 1933, La Follette Family Papers.
8 *Congressional Record,* 73d Congress, 1st sess., 1933, 77:937, 995, 1013,
1042, 1102; Robert M. La Follette, Jr., to Thomas M. Duncan, March
17, 1933, La Follette to Philip La Follette, April 13, 1933, La Follette
Family Papers; Maney, *"Young Bob" La Follette,* pp. 114–16.
9 Robert La Follette to Fola and George Middleton, April 3, 1933, La
Follette Family Papers.
10 *New York Times,* June 27, 1933, p. 12; Melvin D. Hildreth to Donald
R. Richberg, April 1, 1935, Donald R. Richberg Papers; Charles A.
Beard and G. H. E. Smith, *The Open Door at Home: A Trial Philosophy of National Interest* (New York: Macmillan Co., 1934).
11 Borah to Hunter Woodson, May 1, 1933, Borah to George L. Record,
June 19, 1933, Borah Papers.
12 *Congressional Record,* 73d Congress, 1st sess., 1933, 77:4373, 5162–65,
5247, 5424–25, 5834–39, 5861.
13 Hugh S. Johnson, *The Blue Eagle from Egg to Earth* (Garden City,
N.Y.: Doubleday & Co., 1935).
14 *New York Times,* November 26, 1933, p. 27; clipping from *St. Louis
Post-Dispatch,* November 25, 1933, Nye Papers.

15 Roosevelt, *Public Papers and Addresses,* 2:550–54.
16 Borah to Pat Harrison, January 20, 1934, Borah Papers; *Congressional Record,* 73d Congress, 2d sess., 1934, 78:1442–44.
17 Johnson, *Blue Eagle,* pp. 271–302; R. C. Lindsay to Sir John Simon, January 31, 1934, Foreign Office 414/272, p. 120, British Foreign Office Records.
18 Roosevelt, *Public Papers and Addresses,* 3:136–38; interview with Gerald P. Nye, Chevy Chase, Maryland, July 20, 1959.
19 Roosevelt, *Public Papers and Addresses,* 3:137–38; Johnson, *Blue Eagle,* pp. 272–74; Sir R. Lindsay to Sir John Simon, May 24, 1934, Foreign Office 414/272, pp. 249–50, British Foreign Office Records; Arthur M. Schlesinger, Jr., *The Coming of the New Deal* (Boston: Houghton Mifflin Co., 1959), pp. 132–35.
20 *Congressional Record,* 73d Congress, 2d sess., 1934, 78:9234–35.
21 Borah to E. W. Hamman, October 7, 1934, Borah Papers.
22 Roosevelt to Johnson, July 2, 1934, Johnson to Roosevelt, September 24, 1934, Roosevelt to Johnson, September 25, 1934, President's Personal File 702, Roosevelt Papers; *Congressional Record,* 74th Congress, 1st sess., 1935, 79:1905–1906.
23 Johnson to Hiram Johnson, Jr., April 16, 1933, Johnson Papers; *Congressional Record,* 73d Congress, 1st sess., 1933, 77:3118, 1429, 1557–59, 1630, 1730–32, 1830–35, 1970–73, 2311, 2392–94.
24 *Congressional Record,* 73d Congress, 1st sess., 1933, 77:1637.
25 Wheeler, *Yankee From the West,* pp. 302–4; *Congressional Record,* 73d Congress, 1st sess., 1933, 77:1821–30.
26 *Congressional Record,* 73d Congress, 1st sess., 1933, 77:1830–35, 1842; Raymond Moley, *After Seven Years* (Lincoln: University of Nebraska Press, 1971), pp. 156–58.
27 Moley, *After Seven Years,* pp. 158–61; *Congressional Record,* 73d Congress, 1st sess., 1933, 77:2216–17, 2170–71, 2234, 2409–10, 2551–52.
28 *Congressional Record,* 73d Congress, 1st sess., 1933, 77:2562, 2815, 3066, 3078–79, 3116–24, 3499.
29 *Progressive,* September 2, 1933, p. 2.
30 Text of radio address over WIBW by Capper, May 23, 1933, and letter, Capper to Stanley Resor, June 17, 1933, Capper Papers.

Chapter 5

1 Raymond Moley, *After Seven Years,* p. 207.
2 Ibid., p. 196.
3 Ibid.; Elliot A. Rosen, *Hoover, Roosevelt, and the Brains Trust: From Depression to New Deal* (New York: Columbia University Press, 1977), pp. 118–50.

4 Herbert Hoover, *The Memoirs of Herbert Hoover: The Great Depression, 1929–1941*, pp. 178–91; Franklin D. Roosevelt, *The Public Papers and Addresses of Franklin D. Roosevelt*, 1:867–84; Henry L. Stimson and McGeorge Bundy, *On Active Service in Peace and War*, pp. 288–96.

5 Roosevelt, *Public Papers and Addresses*, 1:867–84; Moley, *After Seven Years*, pp. 67–79, 84–101.

6 Moley, *After Seven Years*, pp. 90–108, 111–15.

7 Ibid., 79–82, 113–16.

8 Ibid., 104–5; U.S., Department of State, *Foreign Relations of the United States: Diplomatic Papers, 1933*, 1:465–71.

9 Moley, *After Seven Years*, pp. 163–65, 197; Department of State, *Foreign Relations, 1933*, 1:472–73.

10 Department of State, *Foreign Relations, 1933*, 1:489–509; Moley, *After Seven Years*, pp. 199–207; Cordell Hull, *The Memoirs of Cordell Hull*, 1:246–48.

11 Moley, *After Seven Years*, pp. 217–18; Hull, *Memoirs of Cordell Hull*, 1:249; Henry L. Stimson to Herbert Hoover, July 31, 1933, Post-Presidential Individual File, Herbert Hoover Papers; Harold L. Ickes diary, January 18, 1938.

12 Edgar B. Nixon, ed., *Franklin D. Roosevelt and Foreign Affairs*, 1:133; Jonathan Bourne, Jr., to Roosevelt, May 15, 1933, Official File 17, Roosevelt Papers; telegram Johnson to Hiram Johnson, Jr., May 21, 1933, Johnson to Archibald M. and Hiram W. Johnson, Jr., May 26, 1933, Johnson Papers; Harold L. Ickes, *The Secret Diary of Harold L. Ickes*, vol. 1, *The First Thousand Days, 1933–1936*, pp. 42–45.

13 Johnson to Archibald and Hiram Johnson, Jr., May 26, 1933, Johnson Papers.

14 Phil La Follette to Robert La Follette, June 1, 1933, La Follette Family Papers; Johnson to Hiram Johnson, Jr., June 4, 1933, Johnson Papers.

15 Johnson to Hiram Johnson, Jr., June 4, 1933, Johnson Papers; Couzens to Merlin Wiley, July 26, 1932, Roosevelt to Couzens, May 30, 1933, Couzens Papers; Harry Barnard, *Independent Man: The Life of Senator James Couzens* (New York: Charles Scribner's Sons, 1958).

16 Moley, *After Seven Years*, pp. 218–19; Hull, *Memoirs of Cordell Hull*, 1:249–50; Department of State, *Foreign Relations, 1933*, 1:620–27.

17 Hull, *Memoirs of Cordell Hull*, 1:250–53.

18 Ibid.; Orville H. Bullitt, ed., *For the President Personal and Secret: Correspondence between Franklin D. Roosevelt and William C. Bullitt*, pp. 34–35; Department of State, *Foreign Relations, 1933*, 1:633–34.

19 Moley, *After Seven Years*, pp. 208–10, 406–14.

20 Hull, *Memoirs of Cordell Hull*, 1:249.

21 Ibid., 1:256–57; Department of State, *Foreign Relations, 1933*, 1:636–40; Moley, *After Seven Years*, pp. 226–27.

22 Hull, *Memoirs of Cordell Hull,* 1:253-59; Department of State, *Foreign Relations, 1933,* 1:640-55.

23 Department of State, *Foreign Relations, 1933,* 1:640-41; Hull, *Memoirs of Cordell Hull,* 1:258-59; Nixon, *Roosevelt and Foreign Affairs,* 1:235-39; P. A. London News Agency Press Release, June 19, 1933, Couzens Papers.

24 Nixon, *Roosevelt and Foreign Affairs,* 1:240-43; Moley, *After Seven Years,* pp. 231-44; Hull, *Memoirs of Cordell Hull,* 1:259-60.

25 Moley, *After Seven Years,* pp. 244-50, 415-18; Department of State, *Foreign Relations, 1933,* 1:665-66; Nixon, *Roosevelt and Foreign Affairs,* 1:248-50.

26 Department of State, *Foreign Relations, 1933,* 1:667-68; Moley, *After Seven Years,* pp. 250-53; Nixon, *Roosevelt and Foreign Affairs,* 1:263-64.

27 Moley, *After Seven Years,* pp. 252-56; Department of State, *Foreign Relations, 1933,* 1:669-670; Nixon, *Roosevelt and Foreign Affairs,* 1:264-66.

28 Department of State, *Foreign Relations, 1933,* 1:673-74; Nixon, *Roosevelt and Foreign Affairs,* 1:268-70.

29 Moley, *After Seven Years,* pp. 260-66; Hull, *Memoirs of Cordell Hull,* 1:262-63; Department of State, *Foreign Relations, 1933,* 1:683-84; Nixon, *Roosevelt and Foreign Affairs,* 1:271.

30 Hull, *Memoirs of Cordell Hull,* 1:262-67.

31 Telegram, Bingham to acting secretary of state, July 4, 1933, President's Secretary's File, London Economic Conference, Roosevelt Papers; Department of State, *Foreign Relations, 1933,* 1:680; Hull, *Memoirs of Cordell Hull,* 1:266.

32 Moley, *After Seven Years,* pp. 266-67.

33 Ibid., pp. 270-72.

34 Ibid., pp. 274-80.

35 Department of State, *Foreign Relations, 1933,* 1:698, 734; MacDonald to Hull, July 5, 1933, Hull to MacDonald, July 11, 1933, Hull to Roosevelt, July 12, 1933, President's Secretary's File, London Economic Conference, Roosevelt Papers; cablegram, Hull to Roosevelt, July 11, 1933, Cordell Hull Papers.

36 Jay Pierrepont Moffat diary, July 5, 1933; Moley, *After Seven Years,* p. 271.

Chapter 6

1 There is no full published biography of Davis. This sketch of him is based largely on research in the Norman H. Davis Papers.

2 Davis to Roosevelt, April 17, 1928, Davis Papers.

3 Among many general accounts on disarmament, see Merze Tate, *The*

United States and Armaments (Cambridge, Mass.: Harvard University Press, 1948); Robert H. Ferrell, *American Diplomacy in the Great Depression* (New Haven, Conn.: Yale University Press, 1957), pp. 87–105, 194–214.

4 Davis to Walter Lippmann, August 22, 1932, Davis to Hugh Gibson, December 31, 1932, Davis Papers; Roosevelt to Marvin McIntyre, March 9, 1933, Official File 29, Roosevelt Papers.

5 Edgar B. Nixon, ed., *Franklin D. Roosevelt and Foreign Affairs,* 1:124–28; Department of State, *Foreign Relations of the United States, 1933,* 1:140–45; Franklin D. Roosevelt, *The Public Papers and Addresses of Franklin D. Roosevelt,* 2:185–93.

6 Roosevelt, *Public Papers and Addresses,* 2:193–201; Department of State, *Foreign Relations, 1933,* 1:147–54, 159–65; Nixon, *Roosevelt and Foreign Affairs,* 1:128 n, 136–61; Box 1, Official File 404, Roosevelt Papers.

7 Department of State, *Foreign Relations, 1933,* 1:89–116, 124–26, 150–59; Nixon, *Roosevelt and Foreign Affairs,* 1:56–58.

8 Department of State, *Foreign Relations, 1933,* 1:113–16, 124–26.

9 Ibid., 1:91–97, 106–8, 113–16, 124–26, 150.

10 Capper to Stimson, February 18, 1932, Roosevelt to Capper, March 22, 1933, Capper Papers.

11 Moffat diary, December 21, 1932, January 5, 9, 10, 11, 15, 1933, February 9, 15, 1933; Department of State, *Foreign Relations, 1933,* 1:358–59; Joseph C. Green to Hugh R. Gibson, March 13, 1933, Hugh R. Wilson Papers; Borah to Bon O. Adams, March 7, 1933, Borah Papers.

12 Green to Gibson, March 13, 1933, Wilson Papers; Department of State, *Foreign Relations, 1933,* 1:364; Capper to Roosevelt, March 17, 1933, Roosevelt to Capper, March 22, 1933, Official File 178, Roosevelt Papers; Hull to Capper, March 27, 1933, Capper Papers.

13 Moffat diary, March 20, 22, 1933; Green to Hugh R. Wilson, April 12, 1933, Wilson Papers.

14 Moffat diary, March 22, 27, 28, 1933; Borah press release, March 22, 1933, Borah Papers; Sam D. McReynolds to Morton D. Hull, April 1, 1933, "Final Vote H. J. Res. 93," n.d., H. J. Res. 93, 73d Congress, Papers Supporting House Bills and Resolutions, Record Group 233, National Archives; *Congressional Record,* 73d Congress, 1st sess., 1933, 77:1850.

15 Department of State, *Foreign Relations, 1933,* 1:365–67.

16 Department of State, *Foreign Relations, 1933,* 1:369–78.

17 Green to Wilson, June 3, 1933, Wilson Papers; Johnson to Moore, May 5, 25, 1933, Johnson Papers.

18 Johnson to Moore, May 25, 1933, Johnson Papers.

19 Green to Wilson, June 3, 1933, Wilson Papers; McReynolds to Manley O. Hudson, May 27, 1933, McReynolds to Sol Bloom, May 27, 1933,

Bloom to McReynolds, May 29, 1933, H. J. Res. 93, 73d Congress, Papers Supporting House Bills and Resolutions, Record Group 233, National Archives.

20 Green to Wilson, June 3, 1933, Wilson Papers; Moffat diary, January 2, 1934; Cordell Hull, *The Memoirs of Cordell Hull,* 1:229–30; Department of State, *Foreign Relations, 1933,* 1:378; Hull to Roosevelt, May 27, 1933, Official File 404, Roosevelt Papers.

21 Wilson to Green, June 18, 1933, Green to Wilson, June 29, 1933, Wilson Papers.

22 Moffat to Hull and Phillips, January 23, 1934, Moffat Papers.

23 Nixon, *Roosevelt and Foreign Affairs,* 1:610–13; Davis to Moffat, January 26, 1934, Davis Papers.

24 William Phillips diary, February 16, 1934; Moffat diary, February 28, 1934; Green to Gibson, April 13, 1934, Wilson Papers.

25 Nixon, *Roosevelt and Foreign Affairs,* 2:227–29; Department of State, *Foreign Relations, 1933,* 1:303–4. On this subject, see Stephen E. Pelz, *Race to Pearl Harbor: The Failure of the Second London Naval Conference and the Onset of World War II* (Cambridge: Harvard University Press, 1974).

26 Department of State, *Foreign Relations, 1934,* 1:405–25; Department of State, *Papers Relating to the Foreign Relations of the United States: Japan, 1931–1941,* 1:249–76.

27 Franklin D. Roosevelt, *F.D.R.: His Personal Letters,* 1:544–46; Department of State, *Foreign Relations: Japan,* 1:284–97; Department of State, *Foreign Relations, 1936,* 1:22–101.

28 Davis to Ray Atherton, February 15, 1935, Davis Papers.

29 *Congressional Record,* 73d Congress, 2d sess., 1934, 78:3782; United States Senate, *Hearings before the Special Committee Investigating the Munitions Industry,* 9:2161.

30 Moffat diary, November 28, 29, 30, 1934; Green to Hull, December 1, 1934, File Number 811.113 Senate Investigation/164, Record Group 59, Department of State Records; Hull to Nye, February 8, 1935, and enclosed copy of item from *Osaka Mainichi,* December 23, 1934, Nye Papers; *Hearings before Committee Investigating the Munitions Industry,* 36:12033.

31 *Congressional Record,* 74th Congress, 2d sess., 1936, 80:6801–2.

32 Hull, *Memoirs of Cordell Hull,* 1:455–56.

33 Davis to Jay Allen, April 15, 1938, Davis Papers.

Chapter 7

1 Henry L. Stimson and McGeorge Bundy, *On Active Service in Peace and War,* pp. 213–18.

2. Among the many accounts on the war debts controversy, see Harold
   G. Moulton and Leo Pasvolsky, *War Debts and World Prosperity*
   (Washington: Brookings Institution, 1932); Benjamin H. Williams,
   Economic Foreign Policy of the United States (New York and London:
   McGraw-Hill Book Co., 1929), pp. 217–42; Robert H. Ferrell,
   American Diplomacy in the Great Depression (New Haven, Conn.:
   Yale University Press, 1957), pp. 106–19.
3. Herbert Hoover, *The Memoirs of Herbert Hoover: The Great
   Depression, 1929–1941,* pp. 171–91; Stimson and Bundy, *On Active
   Service,* pp. 211–19, 288–96; Franklin D. Roosevelt, *The Public Papers
   and Addresses of Franklin D. Roosevelt,* 1:867–84; Raymond Moley,
   After Seven Years, pp. 67–79; Moffat diary, November 23, 1932.
4. Moley, *After Seven Years,* pp. 90–108; Edgar B. Nixon, ed., *Franklin
   D. Roosevelt and Foreign Affairs,* 1:13 n.
5. Roosevelt, *Public Papers and Addresses,* 1:867–71, 877–84; Hoover,
   Memoirs of Herbert Hoover: The Great Depression, pp. 185–91;
   Moley, *After Seven Years,* pp. 84–101, 405; Nixon, *Roosevelt and
   Foreign Affairs,* 1:1–17.
6. Nixon, *Roosevelt and Foreign Affairs,* 1:8–13; Department of State,
   Foreign Relations of the United States, 1933, 1:471; Moley, *After
   Seven Years,* pp. 199–207.
7. Moley, *After Seven Years,* p. 197; Department of State, *Foreign
   Relations, 1933,* 1:472–73, 490–509, 621; Hull, *Memoirs of Cordell
   Hull,* 1:250, 256.
8. Roosevelt, *Public Papers and Addresses,* 2:242–44, 3:275–83; Nixon,
   Roosevelt and Foreign Affairs, 1:126–34, 207–11, 228–35.
9. This account is based largely on research in the Hiram W. Johnson
   Papers, especially his so-called diary letters written regularly to his son.
   See also Spencer C. Olin, Jr., *California's Prodigal Sons: Hiram
   Johnson and the Progressives, 1911–1917* (Berkeley: University of
   California Press, 1968).
10. *Congressional Record,* 72d Congress, 1st sess., 1932, 75:6052–62;
    Johnson to Archibald and Hiram Johnson, Jr., January 18, March 21,
    1932, Johnson Papers.
11. Johnson to Archibald and Hiram Johnson, Jr., April 17, 1932, day
    letter Johnson to Farley, November 14, 1932, Johnson Papers.
12. Johnson to Hiram Johnson, Jr., January 7, 1933, Johnson Papers.
13. Ibid., January 7, 22, 1933, Johnson Papers; *Congressional Record,* 72d
    Congress, 2d sess., 1933, 76:1268–79.
14. *Congressional Record,* 72d Congress, 2d sess., 1933, 76:1284–94.
15. Stimson and Bundy, *On Active Service,* p. 217; Johnson to Hiram
    Johnson, Jr., January 7, 1933, Johnson Papers.
16. Johnson to Hiram Johnson, Jr., February 4, 1933, Johnson to Charles
    K. McClatchy, February 12, 1933, Johnson Papers.

17 Memorandum listing dates in progress of S. 682, n.d., Johnson to Archibald and Hiram Johnson, Jr., June 16, 1933, Johnson Papers.
18 Johnson to Hiram Johnson, Jr., April 23, Louis M. Howe to Johnson, June 27, 1933, Roosevelt to Johnson, July 31, 1933, Johnson Papers; Johnson to Marvin H. McIntyre, January 11, 1934, and enclosed print of S. 682, Official File 212, Johnson to McIntyre, January 12, 1934, Official File 126, Roosevelt Papers; memorandum for Hull [from R. Walton Moore], January 19, 1934, Moore to Robinson, January 27, 1934, R. Walton Moore Papers.
19 Johnson to Hiram Johnson, Jr., February 4, 1934, Johnson Papers.
20 Ibid., Johnson to Roosevelt, January 29, 1934, Johnson Papers; Nixon, *Roosevelt and Foreign Affairs*, 1:615–16; Department of State, *Foreign Relations, 1934*, 1:525–26.
21 *Congressional Record*, 73d Congress, 2d sess., 1934, 78:1822–24.
22 Johnson to Byrns, February 3, 1934, Johnson to Moore, February 3, 1934, Johnson Papers.
23 Moore to Johnson, March 1, 7, 1934, Johnson to Moore, March 5, 1934, Johnson Papers; Moore to Hackworth, March 10, 1934, Moore Papers; Moore to Roosevelt, March 12, 1934, Official File 212, Roosevelt Papers; Johnson to McReynolds, March 16, 1934, Johnson Papers.
24 *Congressional Record*, 73d Congress, 2d sess., 1934, 78:6048–57.
25 Moore to Phillips, March 21, 1934, Moore Papers; Lindsay to Sir John Simon, March 14, 1934, Foreign Office 414/272, pp. 160–61, British Foreign Office Records.
26 Department of State, *Foreign Relations, 1934*, 1:527; Nixon, *Roosevelt and Foreign Affairs*, 2:26–27; Johnson to Hiram Johnson, Jr. May 13, 19, 1934, Johnson Papers.
27 Moffat diary, April 25, 1934; Phillips diary, April 27, 1934; memorandum for the president [from Moore], May 5, 1934, Moore Papers; Department of State, *Foreign Relations, 1934*, 1:528–42.
28 Nixon, *Roosevelt and Foreign Affairs*, 2:91–94, 126–34.

Chapter 8

1 Franklin D. Roosevelt, *F.D.R.: His Personal Letters*, 1:58; Franklin D. Roosevelt, *The Public Papers and Addresses of Franklin D. Roosevelt*, 1:155–57.
2 Cordell Hull, *The Memoirs of Cordell Hull*, 1:352; Kirk H. Porter and Donald Bruce Johnson, comps., *National Party Platforms, 1840–1956* (Urbana: University of Illinois Press, 1956), p. 331; Roosevelt, *Public Papers and Addresses*, 1:656–57.
3 Raymond Moley, *After Seven Years*, pp. 47–51.

4 Roosevelt, *Public Papers and Addresses,* 1:724–25, 761–69, 834–36, 853.

5 Edgar B. Nixon, ed., *Franklin D. Roosevelt and Foreign Affairs,* 1:19.

6 Julius W. Pratt, *Cordell Hull, 1933–44,* ed. Robert H. Ferrell, 2 vols., The American Secretaries of State and Their Diplomacy, vols. 13, 14 (New York: Cooper Square Publishers, Inc., 1964), 1:1–12, 107–112; Hull, *Memoirs of Cordell Hull,* 1:3–163, 352–53; William R. Allen, "Cordell Hull and the Defense of the Trade Agreements Program, 1934–1940," in *Isolation and Security,* ed. Alexander De Conde (Durham, N.C.: Duke University Press, 1957), pp. 107–32.

7 Moley, *After Seven Years,* pp. 111–15; Tom Connally, *My Name is Tom Connally,* pp. 200–02, 208; Sir R. Lindsay to Viscount Halifax, August 16, 1938, Foreign Office 414/275, p. 17, British Foreign Office Records.

8 Gilbert C. Fite, *George N. Peek and the Fight for Farm Parity* (Norman: University of Oklahoma Press, 1954); George N. Peek, with Samuel Crowther, *Why Quit Our Own.*

9 Peek and Crowther, *Why Quit Our Own,* pp. 12–23, 49–156; J. Samuel Walker, *Henry A. Wallace and American Foreign Policy* (Westport, Conn.: Greenwood Press, 1976), pp. 36, 44.

10 Peek and Crowther, *Why Quit Our Own,* pp. 22–27; Hull, *Memoirs of Cordell Hull,* 1:353–57, 370–71; Phillips diary, December 4, 11, 12, 1933, January 2, 1934, February 27, 1934, March 23, 1934; Nixon, ed., *Roosevelt and Foreign Affairs,* 1:482–86, 519–21, 2:32.

11 Hull, *Memoirs of Cordell Hull,* 1:353–57; Peek and Crowther, *Why Quit Our Own,* pp. 23–30, 196–200; Roosevelt, *Public Papers and Addresses,* 3:113–16.

12 Hull, *Memoirs of Cordell Hull,* 1:357; Peek and Crowther, *Why Quit Our Own,* pp. 200–209; *Congressional Record,* 73d Congress, 2d sess., 1934, 78:5808.

13 Johnson to Hiram Johnson, Jr., March 3, 1934, Johnson to Charles K. McClatchy, March 11, 1934, Johnson to Hiram Johnson, Jr., April 15, 1934, June 2, 1934, Johnson Papers; Borah to George F. Bauer, May 1, 1934, Borah Papers; Capper to William Allen White, June 1, 1934, William Allen White Papers.

14 *Congressional Record,* 73d Congress, 2d sess., 1934, 78:10363, 10395.

15 Hull, *Memoirs of Cordell Hull,* 1:357.

16 Ibid., 1:358–72; Peek and Crowther, *Why Quit Our Own,* pp. 234–78; Nixon, ed., *Roosevelt and Foreign Affairs,* 2:274.

17 Peek and Crowther, *Why Quit Our Own,* pp. 331–35; Hull, *Memoirs of Cordell Hull,* 1:371–74; Phillips diary, December 13, 1934; Moffat diary, December 14, 1934.

18 Hull, *Memoirs of Cordell Hull,* 1:374; Moffat diary, December 14, 1934.

19 Phillips diary, February 14, 1935, May 6, 17, 1935; Harold L. Ickes, *The Secret Diary of Harold L. Ickes,* 1:360.
20 Nixon, ed., *Roosevelt and Foreign Affairs,* 2:561–63; Roosevelt, *F.D.R.: His Personal Letters,* 1:494–96.
21 Roosevelt, *F.D.R.: His Personal Letters,* 1:493–94; Nixon, ed., *Roosevelt and Foreign Affairs,* 2:580, 590.
22 Peek and Crowther, *Why Quit Our Own,* pp. 279–96; Stimson to Hoover, November 26, 1935, Post-Presidential Individual File, Hoover Papers; Coudert to Roosevelt, November 21, 1935, President's Personal File 269, Roosevelt Papers; Borah to R. H. Young, March 7, 1933, Borah Papers; McNary to W. T. Vinton, April 30, 1938, McNary Papers.
23 Peek and Crowther, *Why Quit Our Own,* pp. 35–38.
24 Roosevelt, *F.D.R.: His Personal Letters,* 1:520–22.
25 Ibid., 1:518–20.
26 Nixon, ed., *Roosevelt and Foreign Affairs,* 3:92–94, 119–20.
27 Wayne S. Cole, *America First: The Battle against Intervention, 1940–1941* (Madison: University of Wisconsin Press, 1953), pp. 22, 78.
28 James D. Mooney to Hull, June 6, 1934, Norman Davis to Hull, April 10, 1935, Thomas W. Lamont to Hull, May 3, 1935, Cordell Hull Papers; *Congressional Record,* 75th Congress, 1st sess., 1937, 81:1501, 1510–13, 1545–48, 1590–92, 1594–98, 1612.
29 *Congressional Record,* 75th Congress, 1st sess., 1937, 81:1064–65, 1593–94, 1612, 2025.
30 Roosevelt to Mellett, January 23, 1939, Lowell Mellett Papers; Roosevelt to Farley, March 29, 1939, President's Secretary's File, Post Office Department folder, Hull to Roosevelt, December 4, 1939, President's Secretary's File, Cordell Hull, 1939–41, 1943 folder, Roosevelt Papers; Hull to McNary, December 16, 1939, McNary Papers.
31 Francis B. Sayre to William Phillips, April 12, 1937, Francis B. Sayre Papers; telegram Sir R. Lindsay to Viscount Halifax, October 8, 1938, Foreign Office 414/275, pp. 32–33, British Foreign Office Records; Wood to Henry A. Wallace, March 8, 1939, Harry Hopkins Papers; McNary to F. R. Marshall, January 19, 1939, McNary to W. J. Bethl, January 21, 1939, McNary to Fred W. Clemens, November 7, 1939, McNary Papers.
32 *Congressional Record,* 76th Congress, 3d sess., 1940, 86:1936.
33 Pittman to Henry F. Grady, November 24, 1939, Pittman to Lee Ellsworth, January 9, 1940, Key Pittman Papers.
34 Pittman to Edwin C. Johnson, March 7, 1940, Pittman Papers; Lothian to Halifax, April 4, 1940, Foreign Office 371/24250, pp. 503–4, Lothian to Halifax, April 9, 1940, Foreign Office 371/24234, p. 26, British Foreign Office Records; *Congressional Record,* 76th Congress, 3d sess., 1940, 86:4105.

35 *Congressional Record,* 76th Congress, 3d sess., 1940, 86:4105. My thinking on the evolving patterns in the Reciprocal Trade Program has benefited greatly from conversations with Dr. Thomas R. Wessel and from his excellent thesis on the subject ("Agriculture and the Reciprocal Trade Agreements Act, 1934-1937" [M.A. thesis, University of Maryland, 1968]).

Chapter 9

1 Franklin D. Roosevelt, *F.D.R.: His Personal Letters,* 1:141-42; *Griggs County Sentinel-Courier* (Cooperstown, North Dakota), September 18, 1919, October 9, 1919, November 13, 1919, December 4, 1919; Thomas C. Kennedy, *Charles A. Beard and American Foreign Policy* (Gainesville: University Presses of Florida, 1975), pp. 36, 40-42; Selig Adler, *The Isolationist Impulse: Its Twentieth-Century Reaction* (London and New York: Abelard-Schuman Ltd., 1957), pp. 188-202, 227-37.
2 Ralph Stone, *The Irreconcilables: The Fight against the League of Nations* (Lexington: University Press of Kentucky, 1970); Kirk H. Porter and Donald Bruce Johnson, comps., *National Party Platforms, 1840-1956* (Urbana: University of Illinois Press, 1956), pp. 331-70.
3 Edgar B. Nixon, ed., *Franklin D. Roosevelt and Foreign Affairs,* 1:23-24; Franklin D. Roosevelt, *Looking Forward* (New York: John Day Company, 1933), pp. 254-55.
4 Moffat diary, August 18, 1932, August 17, 1933.
5 Department of State, *Foreign Relations of the United States, 1933,* 1:156
6 Moffat diary, August 17, 1933, September 21, 1933; Hull to Norman H. Davis, September 20, 1933, Hull Papers.
7 Nixon, ed., *Roosevelt and Foreign Affairs,* 1:457-58; McIntyre to Nichols, November 12, 1933, Official File 184A, Roosevelt Papers.
8 Nixon, ed., *Roosevelt and Foreign Affairs,* 1:558-64.
9 Borah to Arthur Deerin Call, December 19, 1933, Borah Papers; Couzens to A. L. Bleazby, April 11, 1934, Couzens Papers; Phillips to McIntyre, April 13, 1935, Roosevelt to Hull, April 15, 1935, Official File 184, Roosevelt Papers.
10 Green to Norman Davis, October 26, 1935, Davis Papers; James Dunn to J. Pierrepont Moffat, November 20, 1935, Moffat Papers; Cordell Hull, *The Memoirs of Cordell Hull,* 1:426-42.
11 *New York Times,* October 27, 1935, p. 34; clipping from *Washington Herald,* November 6, 1935, Henrik Shipstead Papers; Arthur H. Vandenberg, "The Neutrality Controversy," *Congressional Digest* 15 (January 1936): 20; Johnson to Hiram Johnson, Jr., March 22, 1936, Johnson Papers.

12 Nixon, ed., *Roosevelt and Foreign Affairs*, 3:424.

13 Borah to Robert R. Reed, November 9, 1937, Borah Papers; Norris to Freda Kirchwey, March 19, 1938, Norris Papers.

14 A. A. Berle, Jr., to Roosevelt, April 2, 1940, Roosevelt to Woolley, April 4, 1940, Official File 184A, Roosevelt Papers.

15 Lindsay to Sir John Simon, January 24, 1935, Foreign Office 414/272, p. 114.

16 Porter and Johnson, comp., *National Party Platforms*, pp. 251, 260; *Congressional Record*, 69th Congress, 1st sess., 1926, 67: 2795–2825; Hull, *Memoirs of Cordell Hull*, 1:387–88.

17 Hull, *Memoirs of Cordell Hull*, 1:387–88; Thomas J. Walsh to Esther E. Lape, June 9, 1932, Walsh-Erickson Papers.

18 Johnson to Hiram W. Johnson, Jr., April 1, 1933, Johnson Papers; D. Y. Thomas to Esther E. Lape, May 7, 1933, Official File 202A, Roosevelt Papers.

19 Hull, *Memoirs of Cordell Hull*, 1:388; Phillips diary, December 11, 1933, December 28, 1934; Moffat diary, December 14, 1933, September 14, 1934; Tom Connally, *My Name Is Tom Connally*, p. 210; Johnson to George W. Pepper, March 19, 24, 1934, Johnson to Hiram W. Johnson, Jr., December 22, 1934, Johnson Papers.

20 Department of State, *Foreign Relations, 1935*, 1:384–85; Nixon, ed., *Roosevelt and Foreign Affairs*, 2:335–43; Hull, *Memoirs of Cordell Hull*, 1:388.

21 Hull, *Memoirs of Cordell Hull*, 1:388; Department of State, *Foreign Relations, 1935*, 1:385–88; Nixon, ed., *Roosevelt and Foreign Affairs*, 2:346–49.

22 Nixon, ed., *Roosevelt and Foreign Affairs*, 2:353–57, 363–64; Phillips diary, January 9, 1935; Josiah W. Bailey to Josephus Daniels, January 21, 1935, Josiah W. Bailey Papers.

23 Johnson to Hiram W. Johnson, Jr., December 22, 1934, January 31, 1935; Phillips diary, January 16, 1935; *Congressional Record*, 74th Congress, 1st sess., 1935, 79:479–90.

24 *Congressional Record*, 74th Congress, 1st sess. 1935, 79:563–78, 636–41, 695–703, 771–77, 873–76.

25 Ibid., 79:892–94, 964–66, 977, 1142; Department of State, *Foreign Relations, 1935*, 1:387–88.

26 *Congressional Record*, 74th Congress, 1st sess., 1935, 79:893–94, 1142–43, 1146–47; Lindsay to Simon, January 24, 1935, Foreign Office 414/272, pp. 113–14, British Foreign Office Records; Connally, *My Name Is Tom Connally*, p. 211.

27 Johnson to Hiram W. Johnson, Jr., January 31, 1935, Johnson Papers.

28 Ibid.; Lindsay to Simon, February 1, 1935, Foreign Office 414/272, pp. 120–21, British Foreign Office Records.

29 Johnson to Hiram W. Johnson, Jr., January 31, 1935, Johnson
Papers; Phillips diary, January 29, 1935.
30 *Congressional Record*, 74th Congress, 1st sess., 1935, 79:1146–47;
Phillips diary, January 29, 1935.
31 Johnson to Hiram W. Johnson, Jr., January 31, 1935, Johnson
Papers; Connally, *My Name Is Tom Connally,* p. 211; telegram Borah
to Coughlin, January 30, 1935, Borah to Hearst, January 30, 1935,
Borah to Robert L. Burger, March 20, 1937, Borah Papers; Lindsay to
Simon, February 1, 1935, Foreign Office 414/272, p. 121, British
Foreign Office Records; Moore to William E. Dodd, June 10, 1935,
Dodd Papers; Roosevelt, *F.D.R.: His Personal Letters,* 1:451–52.
32 Phillips diary, January 30, 1935; Hull, *Memoirs of Cordell Hull,* 1:389;
Dodd to Robinson, January 30, 1935, Dodd Papers; Stimson to Roose-
velt, February 2, 1935, President's Personal File 20, Roosevelt Papers.
33 Phillips diary, January 31, 1935, February 1, 1935; Harold L. Ickes,
The Secret Diary of Harold L. Ickes, 1:287; Roosevelt, *F.D.R.: His
Personal Letters,* 1:449–51; Roosevelt to Philip C. Jessup, February 2,
1935, Official File 202, Roosevelt Papers; Nixon, ed., *Roosevelt and
Foreign Affairs,* 2:387, 397–98.
34 Tugwell diary, February 2, 1935, John Franklin Carter, "Memorandum
of Conversation at Dr. Tugwell's House, Evening of February 1,
1935," February 2, 1935, memorandum by Paul Appleby, n.d.,
Rexford G. Tugwell Papers.
35 Carter, "Memorandum of Conversation," February 2, 1935, Tugwell
Papers.
36 Microfilm of Franklin D. Roosevelt's press conferences, January 31,
1941, Roosevelt Papers; Tugwell diary, February 3, 1941, Tugwell
Papers.
37 Carter, "Memorandum of Conversation," February 2, 1935, Tugwell
Papers.
38 Johnson to Hiram W. Johnson, Jr., February 10, 1935, Johnson
Papers; Hull, *Memoirs of Cordell Hull,* 1:389.

Chapter 10

1 For data on Father Coughlin and on his relations with the Roosevelt
administration, see Official File 306, Roosevelt Papers; Charles J. Tull,
Father Coughlin and the New Deal (Syracuse, N.Y.: Syracuse
University Press, 1965); and Geoffrey S. Smith, *To Save a Nation:
American Countersubversives, the New Deal, and the Coming of World
War II* (New York: Basic Books, Inc., 1973), pp. 11–52, 122–38.
2 Franklin D. Roosevelt, *F.D.R.: His Personal Letters,* 1:387–88; Van-
denberg entries on January 26, 27, 1934, scrapbook 6, Vandenberg

Papers; *Congressional Record,* 73d Congress, 2d sess., 1934, 78:1464–65.

3 Franklin D. Roosevelt, *The Public Papers and Addresses of Franklin D. Roosevelt,* 3:253–56; *Congressional Record,* 73d Congress, 2d sess., 1934, 78:10135, 11060.

4 Among many accounts on the silver issue, see Henry Morgenthau, Jr., *From the Morgenthau Diaries,* vol. 1, *Years of Crisis, 1928–1938,* pp. 183–228; Arthur M. Schlesinger, Jr., *The Age of Roosevelt: The Coming of the New Deal* (Boston: Houghton Mifflin Co., 1959), pp. 248–52; Fred L. Israel, *Nevada's Key Pittman* (Lincoln: University of Nebraska Press, 1963), pp. 75–95, 100–120.

5 Roosevelt to Edward M. House, November 27, 1934, President's Personal File 222, Roosevelt Papers; *Congressional Record,* 74th Congress, 1st sess., 1935, 79:2014–28.

6 *Congressional Record,* 74th Congress, 1st sess., 1935, 79:4073–76, 4147–52, 4160–66, 4183, 4289, 4348–64; Philip La Follette to Robert M. La Follette, Jr., February 8, 1935, President's Personal File 6659, Roosevelt Papers.

7 *Congressional Record,* 74th Congress, 1st sess., 1935, 79:942, 4366, 5150–51, 5135, 5464; Johnson to Hiram W. Johnson, Jr., April 7, 1935, Johnson Papers.

8 *Congressional Record,* 73d Congress, 2d sess., 1934, 78:12046; Ibid., 74th Congress, 1st sess., 1935, 79:7681, 9731, 10259, 10300, 10719.

9 *Congressional Record,* 74th Congress, 1st sess., 1935, 79:6068–70, 9272–73, 9425–27, 9532–35, 9650, 12759–60, 12793–94, 13993.

10 Roosevelt, *Public Papers and Addresses,* 3:29–40; Robert M. La Follette, Jr., memorandum on Saint Lawrence Waterway Treaty, August 12, 1932, La Follette Family Papers; resolution of Board of Directors of New Jersey State Chamber of Commerce, December 12, 1932, telegram James M. Curley and Richard Parkhurst to Borah, December 13, 1932, Borah Papers; Vandenberg to Roosevelt, April 6, 1933, Vandenberg Papers; *Congressional Record,* 73d Congress, 1st sess., 1933, 77:2348–64, 2412–14, 4971–74, 5398, 5403–5404; Robert F. Wagner to H. E. Flack, May 15, 1933, Robert F. Wagner Papers; Edgar B. Nixon, ed., *Franklin D. Roosevelt and Foreign Affairs,* 1:144–46, 165, 199–201, 213.

11 Roosevelt, *Public Papers and Addresses,* 2:314.

12 Ibid., 3:29–40; Nixon, ed., *Roosevelt and Foreign Affairs,* 1:583–85; McIntyre to Pittman, January 11, 1934, and enclosed undated note from Roosevelt to Pittman, Pittman Papers; *Congressional Record,* 73d Congress, 2d sess., 1934, 78:531–42, 789–814.

13 Lindsay to Simon, February 9, 1934, Foreign Office 414/272, pp. 127–29, British Foreign Office Records; *Congressional Record,* 73d Congress, 2d sess., 1934, 78:915–27, 1656–78, 1757–72, 1821–22, 1829–35, 2410–13, 3980–96, 4063–71, 4231–36, 4423–24; Nixon, ed.,

Roosevelt and Foreign Affairs, 1:596-99; Pittman to Louis Howe, March 10, 1934, President's Secretary's File, Saint Lawrence Waterway folder, Roosevelt Papers; Vandenberg to Henry J. Allen, January 29, 1934, Vandenberg Papers; Phillips diary, February 16, 1934.

14 *Congressional Record,* 73d Congress, 2d sess., 1934, 78:4475; Lindsay to Simon, March 22, 1934, Foreign Office 414/272, pp. 175-77, British Foreign Office Records.

15 Nixon, ed., *Roosevelt and Foreign Affairs,* 2:393-97, 572-73.

16 Burton K. Wheeler, *Yankee From the West: The Candid, Turbulent Life Story of the Yankee-born U.S. Senator from Montana,* pp. 306-8; Max Freedman, annot., *Roosevelt and Frankfurter: Their Correspondence, 1928-1945,* pp. 269-72; Harold L. Ickes, *The Secret Diary of Harold L. Ickes,* vol. 1, *The First Thousand Days,* pp. 363-64; Raymond Moley, *After Seven Years,* pp. 302-4.

17 Wheeler, *Yankee From the West,* pp. 306-9; *Congressional Record,* 74th Congress, 1st sess., 1935, 79:8374-75, 8383-8408, 8491, 8682-90, 8931.

18 Moley, *After Seven Years,* pp. 303-4; Wheeler, *Yankee From the West,* pp. 308-12; *Congressional Record,* 74th Congress, 1st sess., 1935, 79:9040-65.

19 Wheeler, *Yankee From the West,* pp. 312-13; Moley, *After Seven Years,* pp. 315-16, 316 n; *Congressional Record,* 74th Congress, 1st sess., 1935, 79:10639-40, 14470-73, 14626-27.

20 Moley, *After Seven Years,* pp. 308-14; *New York Times,* June 22, 1935, pp. 1, 2.

21 Wood to Roosevelt, July 18, 1935, Wood to McIntyre, August 8, 1935, President's Personal File 1365, White House statement, August 15, 1935, President's Personal File 62, Roosevelt Papers.

Chapter 11

1 Portions of this chapter, much revised and expanded here, were published earlier in Wayne S. Cole, *Senator Gerald P. Nye and American Foreign Relations* (Minneapolis: University of Minnesota Press, 1962), pp. 65-96. The most detailed history of the munitions investigation is John E. Wiltz, *In Search of Peace: The Senate Munitions Inquiry, 1934-36* (Baton Rouge: Louisiana State University Press, 1963).

2 Dorothy Detzer, *Appointment on the Hill,* pp. 151-57; clipping *Chicago American,* January 6, 1936, Nye Papers. Nye believed that in her book Dorothy Detzer "was taking much more credit unto herself and others for the conception of the investigation and the legislative steps to bring it about" than she really deserved (draft of letter, Nye to the author [December, 1962]).

3 Cole, *Senator Gerald P. Nye,* pp. 17–65; Nye to the author, March 11, 1960; conversations with Mrs. Gerald P. Nye, Chevy Chase, Maryland, August 7, 8, 1959; Walter Trohan, "Gerald Nye—Man of Courage," *Chicago Tribune,* June 18, 1944, Graphic Section, p. 1. The author had many personal conversations and interviews with the former Senator Nye between 1956 and 1971 and heard him deliver four or five lectures.

4 Memorandum by Joseph C. Green, January 18, 1934, File Number 811.113 Senate Investigation/1, Department of State Records, Record Group 59.

5 *Congressional Record,* 73d Congress, 2d sess., 1934, 78:2153; Detzer, *Appointment on the Hill,* pp. 157–58.

6 Detzer, *Appointment on the Hill,* pp. 159–60; Moffat diary, February 15, 1934, Moffat to Phillips, February 14, 1934, Moffat Papers; *Congressional Record,* 73d Congress, 2d sess., 1934, 78:4228–29.

7 "Arms and Men," *Fortune,* March 1934, p. 53; H. C. Englebrecht and F. C. Hanighen, *Merchants of Death: A Study of the International Armament Industry* (New York: Dodd, Mead & Company, 1934); Detzer, *Appointment on the Hill,* pp. 159–61; various letters in Official File 178, Roosevelt papers.

8 *Congressional Record,* 73d Congress, 2d sess., 1934, 78:6472–75, 6484–85; Detzer, *Appointment on the Hill,* pp. 161–63.

9 *Congressional Record,* 73d Congress, 2d sess., 1934, 78:4229, 6485.

10 Interview with Gerald P. Nye, Washington, D.C., July 20, 1959; Homer T. Bone to the author, September 24, 1959; Cordell Hull, *The Memoirs of Cordell Hull,* 1:398.

11 Hull, *Memoirs of Cordell Hull,* 1:400; Hull to Nye, April 27, 1934, File Number 811.113 Senate Investigation/7, Department of State Records, Record Group 59.

12 *Congressional Record,* 73d Congress, 2d sess., 1934, 78:9095; Hull, *Memoirs of Cordell Hull,* 1:400; Department of State, *Foreign Relations of the United States, 1934,* 1:427–28; Hull to Nye, May 18, 1934, File Number 862.248/61, Department of State Records, Record Group 59.

13 Clippings from *Grand Forks* (N.D.) *Herald,* May 22, 1934, *Washington Post,* September 23, 1934, Nye Papers; Raushenbush to Nye, August 10, 1934, Records of the Special Committee Investigating the Munitions Industry, General Subject File, Record Group 46; *News-Week,* June 2, 1934, p. 10; *Congressional Record,* 74th Congress, 1st sess., 1935, 79:444–45, 10131–43; Detzer, *Appointment on the Hill,* pp. 164–68.

14 Minutes of meeting of Senate Committee Investigating the Munitions Industry, June 1, 1934, Executive File, Record Group 46; Moffat diary, June 8, 1934; Morgenthau to Roosevelt, June 12, 1934, L. W. Douglas to attorney general, June 12, 1934, Homer Cummings to Hull, June 13, 1934, Official File 178, Roosevelt Papers.

15 U.S., Senate, *Hearings before the Special Committee Investigating the Munitions Industry,* 73d Congress, 2d sess., parts 1–39 (part 40, published in 1943, consists of an index of the hearings and reports).

16 MacArthur to Nye, August 8, 1934, General Subject File, Munitions Investigating Committee Records, Record Group 46.

17 Department of State, *Foreign Relations, 1934,* 1:429–30; Phillips diary, September 10, 12, 1934; Moffat diary, September 10, 1934, memorandum by Moffat, September 8, 1934, Moffat Papers.

18 Moffat diary, September 7, 10, 14, 1934; Welles to Hull, September 5, 7, 1934, Hull Papers; Department of State, *Foreign Relations, 1934,* 1:428–36, 438–48.

19 Jay Pierrepont Moffat, *The Moffat Papers: Selections from the Diplomatic Journals of Jay Pierrepont Moffat, 1919–1943,* pp. 113–14; Department of State, *Foreign Relations, 1934,* 1:437–38.

20 Moffat, *The Moffat Papers,* pp. 114–15; *Washington Evening Star,* September 14, 1934.

21 The Nye Papers at the Herbert Hoover Presidential Library, West Branch, Iowa, have the complete file of correspondence on Senator Nye's speaking engagements from 1936 through 1941 inclusive, with some items from earlier and later years. It also contains the full texts of many of those speeches and the hand-written notes and outlines for many others. This author also heard Nye deliver four or five lectures in the senator's later years. For examples, see Gerald P. Nye, "Should Governments Exercise Direct Control of Munitions Industries," *Congressional Digest,* 13 (November 1934): 266–70; Gerald P. Nye, "Munitions" (address given before Empire Club of Canada in Toronto, November 15, 1934).

22 Department of State, *Foreign Relations, 1934,* 1:191–93.

23 Moffat to Hugh R. Wilson, October 3, 1934, Moffat Papers.

24 Edgar B. Nixon, ed., *Franklin D. Roosevelt and Foreign Affairs,* 2:311–14.

25 *News-Week,* December 22, 1934, pp. 3–4; Memorandum by Joseph C. Green, December 26, 1934, File Number 811.113 Senate Investigation/185, Department of State Records, Record Group 59; numerous letters to the president in Official File 178, Roosevelt Papers; Bernard M. Baruch, *Baruch: The Public Years,* pp. 267–68.

26 Brent Dow Allinson, "Senator Nye Sums Up," *Christian Century,* January 16, 1935, pp. 80–81; *Congressional Record,* 74th Congress, 1st sess., 1935, 79:460.

27 Department of State, *Foreign Relations, 1935,* 1:316. The enclosed undated, unsigned, seven-page memorandum is not printed in this volume, but is in the Roosevelt Papers.

28 Department of State, *Foreign Relations, 1935,* 1:318–19.

29 Ibid., 1:363–64; clipping from *Washington Post,* March 20, 1935, Nye Papers.

30 Nixon, ed., *Roosevelt and Foreign Affairs,* 2:448; Hull, *Memoirs of Cordell Hull,* 1:402.

31 Department of State, *Foreign Relations, 1935,* 1:360–73; William C. Potter to Hull, March 5, 1935, Nye to Hull, March 6, 1935, Hull to Nye, March 15, 1935, Hull to Potter, March 9, 1935, memorandum of conversation between Hull and Lindsay, March 14, 1935, memorandum Green to Hull, March 20, 1935, File Number 811.113 Senate Investigation/214, 215, 216, 226, 237A, 247, Department of State Records, Record Group 59; minutes of meetings of Senate Committee Investigating the Munitions Industry, March 22, 1935, Executive File, Record Group 46; Hull, *Memoirs of Cordell Hull,* 1:401–2.

32 Nixon, ed., *Roosevelt and Foreign Affairs,* 2:470–76; Department of State, *Foreign Relations, 1935,* 1:331–39, 370–71; Hull, *Memoirs of Cordell Hull,* 1:403.

33 Memorandum Green to Hull, March 20, 1935, File Number 811.113 Senate Investigation/226; Department of State, *Foreign Relations, 1935,* 1:370–71.

34 Nye to Hull, August 13, 1935, memorandum by Joseph C. Green, August 14, 1935, Hull to Nye, August 15, 1935, January 6, 1936, File Number 811.113 Senate Investigation/285, 288, 371, Department of State Records, Record Group 59; minutes of meeting of Senate Committee Investigating the Munitions Industry, August 14, 1935, Executive File, Record Group 46.

35 Franklin D. Roosevelt, *F.D.R.: His Personal Letters,* 1:506–7.

36 Green to Moffat, January 9, 1936, Moffat Papers.

37 U.S., Senate, *Hearings before the Special Committee Investigating the Munitions Industry,* part 28, pp. 8509–13; Hull, *Memoirs of Cordell Hull,* 1:403.

38 *Congressional Record,* 74th Congress, 2d sess., 1936, 80:501–13, 562–79; Tom Connally, *My Name Is Tom Connally,* p. 214.

39 *Congressional Record,* 74th Congress, 2d sess., 1936, 80:572–73; Leffingwell to Glass, May 3, 1935, Glass to Leffingwell, May 6, 1935, Carter Glass Papers.

40 Hull, *Memoirs of Cordell Hull,* 1:403–4; memorandum by Green, January 18, 1936, File Number 811.113 Senate Investigation/384, Department of State Records, Record Group 59; U.S., Senate, *Hearings before the Special Committee Investigating the Munitions Industry,* part 28, pp. 8633–34; Johnson to Hiram Johnson, Jr., January 18, 1936, Johnson papers; Norris to Richard J. Hunt, January 22, 1936, Norris Papers; Green to Moffat, April 22, 1936, Moffat Papers.

41 *Congressional Record,* 74th Congress, 1st sess., 1935, 79:4726–27.

42 U.S., Senate, Special Committee on Investigation of the Munitions Industry, *Munitions Industry,* Senate Report 944, parts 1–7.

43 U.S., Senate, Special Committee on Investigation of the Munitions Industry, *Munitions Industry: Preliminary Report on Naval Shipbuilding,* Senate Report 944, part 1. See particularly pp. 1–11, 147.

44 U.S., Senate, Special Committee on Investigation of the Munitions Industry, *Munitions Industry: Preliminary Report on Wartime Taxation and Price Control,* Senate Report 944, part 2, 74th Congress, 1st session, particularly pp. 3–7; U.S., Senate, Special Committee to Investigate the Munitions Industry, *To Prevent Profiteering in War,* Senate Report No. 577, 74th Congress, 1st session.

45 U.S., Senate, Special Committee on Investigation of the Munitions Industry, *Munitions Industry: Report on Activities and Sales of Munitions Companies,* Senate Report 944, part 3, particularly pp. 3–12; U.S., Senate, Special Committee on Investigation of the Munitions Industry, *Munitions Industry: Report on Existing Legislation,* Senate Report 944, part 5, particularly pp. 1–9, 58.

46 U.S., Senate, Special Committee on Investigation of the Munitions Industry, *Munitions Industry: Supplemental Report on the Adequacy of Existing Legislation,* Senate Report 944, part 6, particularly pp. 1–7.

47 U.S., Senate, Special Committee on Investigation of the Munitions Industry, *Munitions Industry: Report on Government Manufacture of Munitions,* Senate Report 944, part 7, particularly pp. 121–23.

48 Green to Moffat, April 22, 1936, Moffat Papers; *Congressional Record,* 74th Congress, 1st sess., 1935, 79:14535–36; Detzer, *Appointment on the Hill,* p. 171.

49 Raushenbush to Nye, February 8, 1935, General Subject File, Munitions Investigating Committee Records; *Congressional Record,* 74th Congress, 1st sess., 1935, 79:14535, 2d sess., 1936, 80:656, 75th Congress, 1st sess., 1937, 81:674–75, 3d sess., 1938, 83:5824; Nye to Raushenbush, June 17, 1936, clippings *Washington Evening Star,* February 27, 1936, April 3, 1936, *New York Times,* April 20, 1938, Nye Papers.

50 *Congressional Record,* 75th Congress, 1st sess., 1937, 81:5408; Hadley Cantril, and Mildred Strunk, eds., *Public Opinion, 1935–1946* (Princeton, N.J.: Princeton University Press, 1951), p. 491; clipping *Baltimore Sun,* February 22, 1937, David I. Walsh to Nye, August 18, 1937, and enclosing copy of letter from A. B. Cook, August 17, 1937, Nye Papers; Department of State, *Foreign Relations, 1935,* 1:318–19.

51 See chapter 12.

52 Hull, *Memoirs of Cordell Hull,* 1:404; Connally, *My Name Is Tom Connally,* pp. 211–14.

53 Vandenberg diary entry, March 3 [1937], Scrapbook #9, Vandenberg Papers; *Congressional Record,* 78th Congress, 2d sess., 1944, 90:9686.

Chapter 12

1 Portions of this chapter, much revised and expanded here, were published earlier in Wayne S. Cole, *Senator Gerald P. Nye and American Foreign Relations* (Minneapolis: University of Minnesota

Press, 1962), pp. 97–111. The best and the most detailed scholarly history of the neutrality legislation is Robert A. Divine, *The Illusion of Neutrality* (Chicago: University of Chicago Press, 1962).

2 Wayne S. Cole, "Senator Key Pittman and American Neutrality Policies, 1933–1940," *Mississippi Valley Historical Review* 46 (March 1960): 644–62. For a detailed critical biography, see Fred L. Israel, *Nevada's Key Pittman* (Lincoln: University of Nebraska Press, 1963).

3 Moffat diary, January 10, April 14–16, 1934, Walter H. Mallory to Moffat, December 8, 20, 1933, Moffat to Mallory, December 26, 1933, Dulles to Moffat, March 16, 1934, Moffat to Dulles, March 19, 1934, Moffat Papers; "Proposed Group on Neutrality Policy," December 11, 1933, House Foreign Affairs Committee Records, Record Group 233; Borchard to Moore, January 31, 1934, Borah Papers; Davis to Roosevelt, February 23, 1934, Hull Papers; Moore to Warren, March 21, 1934, Moore to Borchard, March 27, 1934, Moore to Warren, March 27, 1934, Mallory to Moore, March 31, 1934, Moore to Mallory, April 2, 1934, Moore Papers.

4 Memo H.S.C. to Moffat, Hackworth, Phillips, and Moore, April 14, 1934, Moffat Papers; Moffat diary, April 17, 1934; Phillips diary, June 1, 7, 1934, September 24, 1934; Warren to Moore, July 27, 1934, August 1, 1934, Moore to Warren, August 4, 1934, "A Memorandum on Some Problems Arising in the Maintenance and Enforcement of the Neutrality of the United States," August 1934, "Neutrality," by R.W.M., August 21, 1934, Moore Papers; Moore to Roosevelt, August 27, 1934, Official File 1561, Roosevelt Papers.

5 Roosevelt to Hull, September 25, 1934, Official File 1561, Roosevelt Papers; Phillips diary, November 17, 1934, December 12, 14, 1934, January 4, 9, 1935; Moore memorandum, December 20, 1934, and Neutrality 1934 folder, Moore Papers.

6 Moffat to Phillips, December 4, 1934, Moffat Papers; Phillips diary, December 12, 14, 1934; "Memorandum Regarding Neutrality" from Davis to Hull, [January 18, 1935], Davis and Hull Papers.

7 Moore to Hull, February 8, 1935, Moore Papers; Moffat diary, December 15 and 16, 1934.

8 U.S., Senate, *Hearings before the Special Committee Investigating the Munitions Industry*, part 1, pp. 1–2.

9 Department of State, *Foreign Relations of the United States, 1934,* 1:449–88; *Congressional Record,* 74th Congress, 1st sess., 1935, 79:461; Department of State, *Foreign Relations, 1935,* 1:316–18; Green to Nye, February 23, 1935, Administrative Files, Munitions Investigating Committee Records, Record Group 46.

10 Cordell Hull, *The Memoirs of Cordell Hull,* 1:405; Department of State, *Foreign Relations, 1935,* 1:318–23.

11 Hull, *Memoirs of Cordell Hull,* 1:405; Department of State, *Foreign Relations, 1935,* 1:363–64; "Memorandum of Conversation" by Green,

March 27, 1935, File Number 811.113 Senate Investigation/242, Department of State Records, Record Group 59.

12 *New York Times,* March 31, 1935, p. 26; Borah to Borchard, April 1, 1935, Borah Papers; Johnson to Moore, April 14, 1935, Johnson Papers.

13 Department of State, *Foreign Relations, 1935,* 1:323–25, 328–29; *Congressional Record,* 74th Congress, 1st sess., 1935, 79:4726.

14 Printed copies of S.J. Res. 99, 100, 120, and S. 2998, Nye Papers.

15 Department of State, *Foreign Relations, 1935,* 1:330–39; Pittman to Hull, April 10, 1935, Senate Committee on Foreign Relations Records, Record Group 46; Phillips diary, June 27, 1935; Green to Davis, July 8, 1935, Davis Papers.

16 Hull to Nye, June 18, 1935, Hull to James P. Pope, June 18, 1935, Nye Papers; Department of State, *Foreign Relations, 1935,* 1:333–35, 336–39, 341; memorandum by Green, June 28, 1935, File Number 811.04418/55, Department of State Records, Record Group 59.

17 Raushenbush to William T. Stone, June 26, 1935, Neutrality File, Munitions Investigating Committee Records, Record Group 46; Phillips diary, June 27, 1935; Hull, *Memoirs of Cordell Hull,* 1:410.

18 Clark and Nye to Pittman, July 3, 1935 with enclosed memorandum, Neutrality File, Munitions Investigating Committee Records, Record Group 46.

19 Hull, *Memoirs of Cordell Hull,* 1:410; Phillips to Hull, June 28, 1935, memo by Phillips, July 3, 1935, File Number 811.04418/55, Department of State Records, Record Group 59; Department of State, *Foreign Relations, 1935,* 1:342; Green to Davis, July 8, 19, 1935, Davis Papers; Raushenbush to Lawrence Brown, July 10, 1935, telegram Raushenbush to Stone, July 10, 1935, Neutrality File, Munitions Investigating Committee Records, Record Group 46; Pittman to Hull, July 17, 1935, Senate Foreign Relations Committee Records, Record Group 46.

20 Raushenbush to Stone, July 11, 16, 1935, Neutrality File, Munitions Investigating Committee Records, Record Group 46; Green to Davis, August 2, 1935, Davis Papers.

21 Hull, *Memoirs of Cordell Hull,* 1:411; Department of State, *Foreign Relations, 1935,* 1:345–50; Phillips diary, August 8, 1935; Green to Davis, August 14, 15, 16, 1935, Davis Papers; memoranda by Moore, August 16, 17, 1935, Moore Papers.

22 Nye to Pittman, August 18, 1935, Senate Foreign Relations Committee Records, Record Group 46; mimeographed press release, August 19, 1935, Nye Papers.

23 Edgar B. Nixon, ed., *Franklin D. Roosevelt and Foreign Affairs,* 2:605–10; Green to Davis, August 19, 1935 and enclosures, Davis Papers.

24 "File—Neutrality," August 19, [1935], Neutrality File, Munitions

Investigating Committee Records, Record Group 46; Johnson to John Bassett Moore, August 30, 1935, Johnson to Borchard, September 24, 1935, Johnson Papers; Green to Moffat, October 12, 1935, Moffat Papers.

25 Telegram Raushenbush to Stone, August 20, 1935, Neutrality File, Munitions Investigating Committee Records, Record Group 46; *New York Times,* August 21, 1935, p. 1; clipping *New York Post,* August 21, 1935, Nye Papers; *Congressional Record,* 74th Congress, 1st sess., 1935, 79:13775–93.

26 *Congressional Record,* 74th Congress, 1st sess., 1935, 79:13951–56; Green to Moffat, October 12, 1935, Moffat Papers.

27 Nixon, ed., *Roosevelt and Foreign Affairs,* 2:634–37; White House memorandum, August 16, 1935, Official File 1561, Roosevelt Papers.

28 Green to Moffat, October 12, 1935, Moffat Papers; Green to Davis, August 21, 23, 1935, Davis Papers.

29 Green to Davis, August 22, 1935, Davis Papers; Hull to Stimson, August 22, 1935, Hull Papers.

30 Green to Davis, August 23, 1935, Davis Papers; Green to Moffat, October 12, 1935, Moffat Papers.

31 Green to Davis, August 23, 1935, Davis Papers; Green to Moffat, October 12, 1935, Moffat Papers.

32 *Congressional Record,* 74th Congress, 1st sess., 1935, 79:14283, 14430–34.

33 Tom Connally, *My Name Is Tom Connally,* pp. 220–21; Nixon, ed., *Roosevelt and Foreign Affairs,* 2:623; Franklin D. Roosevelt, *F.D.R.: His Personal Letters,* 1:504–5.

34 Department of State, *Foreign Relations, 1935,* 1:350–52; Nixon, ed., *Roosevelt and Foreign Affairs,* 2:630–32; Green to Davis, September 4, 1935, Davis Papers.

35 Nixon, ed., *Roosevelt and Foreign Affairs,* 2:631–33; Hull, *Memoirs of Cordell Hull,* 1:415; Green to Davis, September 4, 1935, Davis Papers.

36 Print of S.J. Res. 173, Nye Papers; *Congressional Record,* 74th Congress, 1st sess., 1935, 79:14535; Department of State, *Foreign Relations, 1935,* 1:350–52.

37 Confidential print of D. G. Osborne to Sir Samuel Hoare, September 5, 1935, Foreign Office 414/272, pp. 52–54, British Foreign Office Records.

38 Dunn to Moffat, November 20, 1935, Moffat Papers.

39 Hull, *Memoirs of Cordell Hull,* 1:427–41; Green to Hugh R. Wilson, October 8, 1935, Wilson Papers; Nixon, ed., *Roosevelt and Foreign Affairs,* 3:94–95, 121.

40 Norris to Richard Manthey, October 14, 1935, Norris Papers; telegram Nye to Hull, October 16, 1935, File Number 711.00111 Armament Control/202, Department of State Records, Record Group 59; *New York Times,* October 27, 1935, p. 34; Davis to Arthur Sweetser,

October 16, 1935, Davis Papers; Nixon, ed., *Roosevelt and Foreign Affairs*, 3:87–88.

41 Department of State, *Foreign Relations, 1935,* 1:826–33; Roosevelt, *F.D.R.: His Personal Letters,* 1:529–30.

42 Hull, *Memoirs of Cordell Hull,* 1:460–63; Nixon, ed., *Roosevelt and Foreign Affairs,* 3:152–56; Green to Moffat, November 25, 1935, Moffat Papers.

43 Raushenbush to Nye, November 23, 1935, undated radiogram Raushenbush to Nye, radiogram Nye to Raushenbush, December 10, 1935, Administrative File, Munitions Investigating Committee Records, Record Group 46; *Congressional Record,* 74th Congress, 2d sess., 1936, 80:47; clipping *Washington Post,* January 6, 1936, Nye Papers; Hull, *Memoirs of Cordell Hull,* 1:463–65.

44 Green to Moffat, January 9, 1936, Moffat Papers; C. W. Y[ost] to Green, January 8, 1936, File Number 811.04418/110, Department of State Records, Record Group 59; Hull, *Memoirs of Cordell Hull,* 1:461–64.

45 Connally, *My Name Is Tom Connally,* pp. 221–22; Johnson to Moore, January 2, 8, 10, 24, 1936, Borchard to Johnson, January 6, 13, 1936, Johnson to Hiram Johnson, Jr., January 18, 25, 28, 1936, February 2, 1936, February 16, 1936, Johnson to Borchard, February 21, 1936, Johnson Papers; Borah to J. David Stern, November 26, 1935, Borah Papers.

46 Pittman to Raymond Moley, February 5, 1936, Senate Foreign Relations Committee Records, Record Group 46; Hull, *Memoirs of Cordell Hull,* 1:465–66; Connally, *My Name Is Tom Connally,* p. 222; clipping *Washington Post,* February 12, 1936, Nye Papers.

47 Clippings *New York Times,* February 14, 1936, *Baltimore Sun,* February 14, 1936, Nye Papers.

48 Clipping *Washington Star,* February 14, 1936, Nye Papers; Nixon, ed., *Roosevelt and Foreign Affairs,* 3:195–96; *Congressional Record,* 74th Congress, 2d sess., 1936, 80:2253.

49 *Congressional Record,* 74th Congress, 2d sess., 1936, 80:2291–2306; clipping *Washington Herald,* February 19, 1936, Nye Papers.

50 Clipping *New York Times,* February 19, 1936, Nye Papers; Hull, *Memoirs of Cordell Hull,* 1:465–67.

Chapter 13

1 Mimeographed "Statement by Secretary Roper on the Accident to the Transcontinental and Western Air, Inc., at Atlanta, Missouri, May 6, 1935," June 14, 1935, and enclosed "Report of the Accident Board of the Bureau of Air Commerce, Department of Commerce," June 5, 1935, Cutting Papers.

2 Cutting to H. Phelps Putnam, March 21, 1934, July 7, 19, 1934, October 13, 1934, February 7, 1935, April 18, 1935, J. D. Atwood to Daniel C. Roper, April 5, 1934, Cutting to Borah, September 29, 1934, Cutting to Johnson, October 22, 1934, Boake Carter to Hamilton Murray, December 20, 1934, and enclosed transcript of broadcast December 14, 1934, clippings from *Washington Post,* May 7, 1934, *Kansas City Times,* May 7, 1935, *Time Magazine,* May 20, 1935, pp. 14–15, Cutting Papers; Ickes diary, December 17, 1934, pp. 730–31, April 13, 1935, p. 929, February 29, 1936, pp. 1416–17; Harold L. Ickes, *The Secret Diary of Harold L. Ickes,* vol. 1, *The First Thousand Days,* pp. 358–59.

3 Norris to Roosevelt, January 19, 1934, Roosevelt to Norris, January 24, 1934, Norris to Cutting, June 25, 1934, clipping *Washington Post,* November 23, 1934, Norris Papers; Johnson to Edgar F. Puryear, October 27, 1934, Johnson to Cutting, November 16, 1934, Cutting Papers; Ickes diary, December 17, 1934, pp. 730–31, April 13, 1935, p. 929, February 29, 1936, pp. 1416–17; Johnson to Hiram Johnson, Jr., December 22, 1934, May 13, 1935, Johnson Papers; Ickes, *Secret Diary of Harold L. Ickes,* 1:358–59.

4 Henry A. Wallace diary, January 26, 1935; White to Ickes, February 7, 1935, Ickes to White, February 16, 1935, Ickes Papers; Ickes, *Secret Diary of Harold L. Ickes,* 1:313.

5 Max Freedman, annot., *Roosevelt and Frankfurter: Their Correspondence, 1928–1945,* pp. 269–71; Ickes, *Secret Diary of Harold L. Ickes,* 1:363–64.

6 Clipping *New York Sun,* May 20, 1935, Norris Papers.

7 *New York Times,* June 22, 1935, pp. 1–2.

8 Roosevelt to House, March 10, 1935, President's Personal File 222, Roosevelt Papers; Patrick J. Maney, *"Young Bob" La Follette: A Biography of Robert M. La Follette, Jr., 1895–1953* (Columbia and London: University of Missouri Press, 1978), pp. 144–45; Hoover to Henry P. Fletcher, August 25, 1934, Henry P. Fletcher Papers; undated clippings in Shipstead Papers; Franklin D. Roosevelt, *F.D.R.: His Personal Letters, 1928–1945,* 1:618–19.

9 The outstanding biography of Long is T. Harry Williams, *Huey Long* (New York: Alfred A. Knopf, 1970). On Coughlin, see Charles J. Tull, *Father Coughlin and the New Deal* (Syracuse, N.Y.: Syracuse University Press, 1965). See also David H. Bennett, *Demagogues in the Depression: American Radicals and the Union Party* (New Brunswick, N.J.: Rutgers University Press, 1969). Relevant manuscripts are in Official File 306, Official File 1403, Roosevelt Papers.

10 Burton K. Wheeler, *Yankee From the West: The Candid, Turbulent Life Story of the Yankee-born U.S. Senator from Montana,* pp. 280–91; interview with Burton K. Wheeler, Washington, D.C., October 23, 1969.

11 Frank Freidel, *Franklin D. Roosevelt: The Triumph* (Boston: Little, Brown and Co., 1956), p. 331; James A. Farley, *Behind the Ballots: The Personal History of a Politician*, pp. 249–50.

12 White to Ickes, February 7, 1935, Ickes to White, February 16, 1935, Ickes Papers.

13 Roosevelt, *F.D.R.: His Personal Letters,* 1:452–54; Edgar B. Nixon, ed., *Franklin D. Roosevelt and Foreign Affairs,* 2:437.

14 Johnson to Hiram Johnson, Jr., April 19, 1935, Johnson Papers; Ickes, *Secret Diary of Harold L. Ickes,* 1:363.

15 *New York Times,* July 7, 1935, pp, 1, 21. For a scholarly biography of Lemke, see Edward C. Blackorby, *Prairie Rebel: The Public Life of William Lemke* (Lincoln: University of Nebraska Press, 1963).

16 Capper to Charles F. Scott, January 11, 1935, Capper Papers; clipping *Washington Daily News,* March 9, 1934, Nye Papers; *New York Times,* December 14, 1934, pp. 1, 2, March 24, 1935, p. 32, June 9, 1935, p. 3; interview with Gerald P. Nye, Washington, D.C., July 20, 1959.

17 Biographical and political studies of Borah include Claudius O. Johnson, *Borah of Idaho* (Seattle: University of Washington Press, 1936); Marian McKenna, *Borah* (Ann Arbor: University of Michigan Press, 1961); and LeRoy Ashby, *The Spearless Leader: Senator William E. Borah and the Progressive Movement in the 1920's* (Urbana: University of Ilinois Press, 1972).

18 John P. Robertson to Richard Neuberger, November 7, 1935, Norris Papers; Philip La Follette, *Adventure in Politics: The Memoirs of Philip La Follette,* p. 22.

19 A general scholarly study of Borah and foreign affairs is Robert James Maddox, *William E. Borah and American Foreign Policy* (Baton Rouge: Louisiana State University Press, 1969).

20 Memo of telephone call from Judge Will Cummings, March 14 [1935], memo Roosevelt to McIntyre, March 20, 1935, President's Personal File 2358, Roosevelt Papers; Roosevelt, *F.D.R.: His Personal Letters,* 1:468.

21 Walter Lippmann, "Borah versus Roosevelt," reprint from *Congressional Record,* April 18, 1936, Borah Papers.

22 Borah to Jess B. Hawley, May 19, 1936, Borah Papers.

23 Cora Rubin to Lemuel E. Oldham, February 3, 1936, Fish to N. H. Davis, February 15, 1936, Borah Papers; Fish to Fiorello H. La Guardia, December 27, 1935, Fiorello H. La Guardia Papers; Fish to Amos R. E. Pinchot, December 27, 1935, Fish to Pinchot, January 22, 1936, Amos R. E. Pinchot Papers; clipping *McKenzie County* (N.D.) *Farmer,* January 2, 1936, Nye Papers.

24 Borah to Arthur G. Shoup, March 30, 1936, Bachmann to J. M. Inman, April 10, 1936, Bachmann to Oliver O. Haga, April 16, 1936, Borah to Axel F. Gergdahl, April 17, 1936, Borah to Henry L.

Stoddard, May 19, 1936, and undated tabulation of votes cast in primaries for presidential candidates, Borah Papers; Taft to N. Henry Gellert, May 21, 1936, Robert A. Taft Papers; William E. Marsh to Frank Knox, April 16, 1936, Frank Knox Papers.

25 William Allen White to Borah, July 7, 1936, White to Nicholas M. Butler, September 9, 1936, White Papers; Kirk H. Porter and Donald Bruce Johnson, comps., *National Party Platforms: 1840–1956* (Urbana: University of Illinois Press, 1956), p. 368.

26 Porter and Johnson, comps., *National Party Platforms,* pp. 368–69; White to Butler, September 9, 1936, White Papers; Robertson to Neuberger, March 27, 1936, Norris Papers; clipping *Devils Lake* (N.D.) *Journal,* June 13, 1936, Nye Papers; *New York Times,* June 13, 1936, p. 9; Phillips diary, August 12, 1936.

27 Cordell Hull, *The Memoirs of Cordell Hull,* 1:485–86; Porter and Johnson, comps., *National Party Platforms,* p. 363; Norris to Wagner, June 12, 1936, Norris Papers; Edgar B. Nixon, ed., *Franklin D. Roosevelt and Foreign Affairs,* 3:326–29; Ickes, *Secret Diary of Harold L. Ickes,* 1:620–24.

28 Ickes, *Secret Diary of Harold L. Ickes,* 1:655–59, 661–62; Ickes diary, August 10, 1936.

29 Eichelberger to Roosevelt, August 12, 1936, President's Personal File 3833, Roosevelt Papers.

30 Nixon, ed., *Roosevelt and Foreign Affairs,* 3:377–84; Phillips diary, August 10, 13, 14, 1936.

31 Ickes, *Secret Diary of Harold L. Ickes,* 1:662–65; telegram Nye to Roosevelt, August 17, 1936, telegram Roosevelt to Nye, August 17, 1936, telegram Ambrose O'Connell to McIntyre, August 20, 1936, President's Personal File 1614, Roosevelt Papers; interview with Gerald P. Nye, August 4, 1959. For Nye's reaction to FDR's speech, see telegram, Nye to United Press, August 16, 1936, Moore Papers.

32 Frankin D. Roosevelt, *The Public Papers and Addresses of Franklin D. Roosevelt,* 5:293–339; telegram McIntyre to Wheeler, Murray, Frazier, and Nye, August 21, 1936, President's Personal File 723, Roosevelt Papers.

33 Clipping *Fargo* (N.D.) *Forum,* September 6, 1936, Nye Papers; *New York Times,* October 2, 1936, p. 9; telegram Ickes to Nye, October 30, 1936, Ickes Papers; Ickes, *Secret Diary of Harold L. Ickes,* 1:698, 2:10; Wayne S. Cole, *Senator Gerald P. Nye and American Foreign Relations* (Minneapolis: University of Minnesota Press, 1962), pp. 133–40.

34 Homer E. Socolofsky, *Arthur Capper: Publisher, Politician, and Philanthropist* (Lawrence: University of Kansas Press, 1962), pp. 176–78.

35 Will Durant to McIntyre, June 26, 1936, Farley to Durant, July 24, 1936, Orr Chapman to Harllee Branch, July 1, 1936, Branch to Roosevelt, July 7, 1936, President's Personal File 2358, Roosevelt Papers;

Landon to Borah, August 3, 1936, telegram Fred A. Seaton to Carl A. Rott, October 31, 1936, William Hutchinson to Landon, November 10, 1936, Landon to Hutchinson, November 28, 1936, Alf M. Landon Papers; Pinchot to W. P. Eno, August 3, 1936, Gannett to Pinchot October 17, 1936, Pinchot to Borah, October 20, 1936, Pinchot Papers; Roosevelt, *F.D.R.: His Personal Letters,* 1:660–61.

36 Arthur H. Vandenberg, "The Republican Indictment," *Fortune,* October 1936, pp. 110–13, 178, 183–84; *Time,* October 26, 1936, pp. 18–19.

37 Hoover to Fletcher, August 25, 1934, Post-Presidential Individual File, Hoover Papers; Nixon, ed., *Roosevelt and Foreign Affairs,* 3:12–14; Johnson to Borchard, October 3, 1935, Roosevelt to Johnson, November 4, 1935, Roosevelt to secretary of treasury, November 16, 1935, memo to Senator Johnson, May 28, 1936, Roosevelt to Buchanan, May 28, 1936, Johnson Papers.

38 Johnson to Hiram Johnson, Jr., May 9, 1936, telegram M. Connor to John Francis Neylan, June 23, 1936, Johnson to Hiram Johnson, Jr., August 26, 1936, September 6, 1936, Johnson to Edward G. Lowry, September 8, 1936, Johnson Papers.

39 Johnson to Hiram Johnson, Jr., September 6, 1936, October 5, 1936, Johnson Papers.

40 Ickes, *Secret Diary of Harold L. Ickes,* 1:693, 697–98; Roosevelt, *F.D.R.: His Personal Letters,* 1:622–23; Johnson to Hiram Johnson, Jr., October 24, 1936, Johnson Papers.

41 Ickes, *Secret Diary of Harold L. Ickes,* 1:616–17; interview with Alf M. Landon, Topeka, Kansas, July 29, 1966; Orr Chapman to Harllee Branch, July 1, 1936, President's Personal File 2358, Roosevelt Papers; Landon to Borah, August 3, 1936, telegram Seaton to Rott, October 31, 1936, Hutchinson to Landon, November 10, 1936, Landon to Hutchinson, November 28, 1936, White to Landon, November 14, 1936, Landon to White, December 17, 1936, Landon Papers; Gannett to Borah, September 4, 1936, Borah Papers; Pinchot to Roberts, October 10, 1936, telegram Gannett to Borah, October 13, 1936, Gannett to Pinchot, October 17, 1936, Pinchot to Borah, October 20, 1936, Pinchot Papers.

42 Interview with Landon, July 29, 1966; Stimson to Moffat, November 17, 1936, Moffat Papers.

43 George Wolfskill, *The Revolt of the Conservatives: A History of the American Liberty League, 1934–1940* (Boston: Houghton Mifflin Company, 1962) is an excellent scholarly study of the Liberty League. It does not, however, explicitly emphasize either the internationalist orientation of the league's leadership or the related point that it drew its greatest support from the urban Northeast and won little following in rural and small-town America in the West.

44 Interview with Landon, July 29, 1966; telegram White to Armstrong,

October 19, 1936, telegram Armstrong to White, October 19, 1936,
White to Armstrong, November 2, 11, 1936, telegram White to
Landon, October 20, 1936, White to Landon, October 22, 1936, White
Papers; Vandenberg to Landon, July 30, 1936, Landon to Vandenberg,
August 3, 1936, Warburg to Landon, August 28, 1936, Landon to
Warburg, September 8, 1936, Landon Papers; Kellogg to Castle,
September 26, 1936, Castle to Kellogg, September 30, 1936, October 6,
1936, William R. Castle Papers; Landon to Raymond Clapper, October
25, 1941, Raymond Clapper Papers; confidential print of V. A. L.
Mallet to Mr. Eden, August 31, 1936, Foreign Office 414/273,
pp. 60–62, British Foreign Office Records. An excellent scholarly
biography of Landon is Donald R. McCoy, *Landon of Kansas*
(Lincoln: University of Nebraska Press, 1966).

45 Norris to Norman Baker, January 16, 1936, Roosevelt to Norris,
September 19, 1936, Norris to Henry J. Baker, September 22, 1936,
Roosevelt to Norris, November 14, 1936, Norris Papers; Roosevelt to
Norris, November 22, 1935, mimeographed address by Roosevelt to
Nebraskans, October 10, 1936, President's Personal File 880, Roosevelt
Papers; Roosevelt, *F.D.R.: His Personal Letters,* 1:618–19; Ickes,
Secret Diary of Harold L. Ickes, 1:683.

46 John P. Robertson to Melvin D. Hildreth, October 25, 1935, Robertson
to H. C. Shober, July 10, 1936, Norris to Conference of Progressives,
September 11, 1936, Frank P. Walsh to Norris, September 30, 1936,
Norris Papers; Ickes, *Secret Diary of Harold L. Ickes,* 1:532, 543–44,
655; telegram Robert La Follette to Roosevelt, September 11, 1936,
telegram Roosevelt to La Follette, September 28, 1936, October 15,
1936, La Follette to Roosevelt, October 20, 1936, President's Personal
File 1792, telegram Philip F. La Follette to Roosevelt, October 19, 29,
1936, Roosevelt to La Follette, October 26, 1936, President's Personal
File 6659, Jesse S. Raphael to Harry Slattery, September 29, 1936,
President's Personal File 1820, Roosevelt to Wheeler, October 23,
1936, Wheeler to Roosevelt, October 24, 1936, Roosevelt to Wheeler,
October 26, 1936, President's Personal File 723, Roosevelt Papers;
Robert La Follette to Maurice P. Davison, September 22, 1936, La
Follette to Fola La Follette, October 13, 1936, La Follette Family
Papers; Roosevelt, *F.D.R: His Personal Letters,* 1:616; interview with
Burton K. Wheeler, Washington, D.C., October 23, 1969; text of radio
address by Henrik Shipstead, October 20, 1936, Roosevelt to Shipstead,
November 4, 1936, President's Personal File 2863, Roosevelt Papers;
clipping *Labor,* November 3, 1936, Shipstead Papers; Harry Barnard,
Independent Man: The Life of Senator James Couzens (New York:
Charles Scribner's Sons, 1958), pp. 304–21.

47 Farley to Roosevelt, November 2, 1936, President's Secretary's File,
Post Office Department folder, Roosevelt Papers; Farley memo-

randum, November 1, 1936, James A. Farley Papers; Samuel Lubell, *The Future of American Politics,* 2d ed., rev. (New York: Doubleday and Company, 1956), pp. 44–54; Edgar Eugene Robinson, *They Voted For Roosevelt: The Presidential Vote, 1932–1944* (Stanford, Calif.: Stanford University Press, 1947), pp. 8–9, 20–21; Walter Johnson, *1600 Pennsylvania Avenue: Presidents and the People, 1929–1959* (Boston: Little, Brown and Company, 1960), pp. 91–92; Earle D. Ross, *Iowa Agriculture: An Historical Survey* (Iowa City: State Historical Society of Iowa, 1951), p. 176.

48 Johnson to Hiram W. Johnson, Jr., November 10, 1936, Johnson Papers.

Chapter 14

1 The definitive scholarly history of the court-packing controversy is likely to be the forthcoming book by Professor William E. Leuchtenburg of Columbia University. George W. Norris to Roosevelt, February 1, 1935, Norris to Francis J. Heney, May 6, 1936, George W. Norris Papers; Roosevelt to Joseph M. Patterson, November 9, 1936, President's Personal File 245, Franklin D. Roosevelt Papers. For FDR's own account of the background of his decision, see Roosevelt to Frankfurter, February 9, 1937, Felix Frankfurter Papers.

2 Stimson to Roosevelt, June 4, 1935, President's Personal File 20, Roosevelt Papers.

3 Arthur H. Vandenberg, "Should Congress Be Empowered to Override Supreme Court Decisions?—Negative," *Congressional Digest,* December, 1935, pp. 303, 305, 307; Arthur H. Vandenberg, "A Layman Looks at the Supreme Court," *Vital Speeches of the Day,* March 9, 1936, pp. 368–70.

4 Franklin D. Roosevelt, *The Public Papers and Addresses of Franklin D. Roosevelt,* 6:xlvii–lxxii, 51–66.

5 Ibid., pp. 35–50, 74–78, 113–33.

6 Arthur H. Vandenberg "Diary," February 6 [1937], Arthur H. Vandenberg Papers; Alf M. Landon to John Lambert, February 24, 1937, Alf M. Landon Papers.

7 Burton K. Wheeler, *Yankee from the West: The Candid, Turbulent Life Story of the Yankee-born U.S. Senator from Montana,* pp. 322–23.

8 Ibid., pp. 319–22; interview with Burton K. Wheeler, Washington, D.C., October 23, 1969; William Gibbs McAdoo to Clifford C. Anglim, February 10, 1937, William Gibbs McAdoo Papers; Harold L. Ickes, *The Secret Diary of Harold L. Ickes,* vol. 2, *The Inside Struggle, 1936–1939,* p. 69.

9 Vandenberg diary, February 18 [1937], Vandenberg Papers; interview with Gerald P. Nye, Washington, D.C., July 20, 1959; interview with Burton K. Wheeler, Washington, D.C., October 23, 1969.

10 *Congressional Record,* 75th Congress, 1st sess., 1937, Appendix, 81:311–14.

11 Interview with Nye, July 20, 1959; telegram A. F. Whitney to Nye, February 24, 1937, Daniel J. Tobin to Nye, February 26, 1937, Gerald P. Nye Papers; Ickes, *Secret Diary of Harold L. Ickes,* 2:125, 129, 135.

12 Vandenberg diary, March 2 [1937], Vandenberg to Harvey Campbell, March 13, 1937, Vandenberg Papers.

13 Wheeler, *Yankee from the West,* p. 325.

14 Ibid., pp. 327–30; J. R. to Roosevelt, February 19, 1937, President's Secretary's File, Supreme Court, 1935–42 folder, Roosevelt Papers.

15 Wheeler, *Yankee from the West,* pp. 330–33; James A. Farley, *Jim Farley's Story: The Roosevelt Years,* p. 78.

16 Raymond Moley, *After Seven Years,* pp. 357, 424–34; Homer Cummings to Roosevelt, February 15, 1937, President's Personal File 743, Elmer Graham to Roosevelt, June 30, 1937, Official File 1770, Roosevelt Papers.

17 Ickes, *Secret Diary of Harold L. Ickes,* 2:69–70, 139; Johnson to Moley, March 13, 1937, Johnson to Hiram Johnson, Jr., March 15, 1937, Johnson to John Francis Neylan, March 26, 1937, Johnson to Hiram Johnson, Jr., April 16, 1937, Hiram W. Johnson Papers.

18 Capper to Amos R. E. Pinchot, February 16, 1937, Amos R. E. Pinchot Papers; Capper to Matt I. Sullivan, March 19, 1937, Rush D. Holt to Matt I. Sullivan, March 22, 1937, Johnson Papers; clippings *Minneapolis Journal,* January 10, 1937, *New York Times,* May 12, 1937, Henrik Shipstead Papers; Taft to Alfred R. Whitman, March 4, 1937, Robert A. Taft Papers.

19 Norris to Roosevelt, February 1, 1935, Norris to Jessie Cales, January 11, 1936, Norris to James H. Le Gates, March 28, 1936, Norris to Francis J. Heney, May 6, 1936, Norris to William Hirth, November 20, 1936, Norris to J. B. S. Hardman, March 5, 1937, Norris to Dr. G. E. Peters, April 14, 1937, Norris to Lewis C. Westwood, April 14, 1937, Norris to Weeb Rice, May 12, 1937, Norris to J. Victor Romigh, June 5, 1937, John P. Robertson to Kenneth F. Reed, August 2, 1937, Norris Papers; Norris to Wiliam Allen White, February 27, 1937, William Allen White Papers.

20 Wheeler to Pinchot, May 28, 1937, Pinchot Papers; Vandenberg diary, May 18 [1937], Vandenberg Papers; Farley, *Jim Farley's Story,* pp. 81–83; Tom Connally, *My Name Is Tom Connally,* pp. 190–91.

21 Farley, *Jim Farley's Story,* pp. 86–91; Wheeler, *Yankee from the West,* pp. 336–38; Alben W. Barkley, *That Reminds Me—,* pp. 153–54; Connally, *My Name Is Tom Connally,* pp. 188–92.

22 Roosevelt to Barkley, July 15, 1937, President's Secretary's File,

Supreme Court, 1935-42 folder, Roosevelt Papers; Barkley, *That Reminds Me—,* pp. 154-56; Farley, *Jim Farley's Story,* pp. 87-93; Press Release [July 1937], David I. Walsh Papers.

23 *Congressional Record,* 75th Congress, 1st sess., 1937, 81:7381.

24 Ickes, *Secret Diary of Harold L. Ickes,* 2:165, 182; Harold L. Ickes Diary, August 4, 1937, p. 2238, Harold L. Ickes Papers.

25 Johnson to Hiram Johnson, Jr., August 14, 1937, Johnson Papers; Ickes, *Secret Diary of Harold L. Ickes,* 2:190-91; *Congressional Record,* 75th Congress, 1st sess., 1937, 81:9103.

26 Roosevelt, *Public Papers and Addresses,* 6:376-413; Wheeler, *Yankee from the West,* pp. 341-46; Farley, *Jim Farley's Story,* pp. 95-97, 120-50.

27 Connally, *My Name Is Tom Connally,* pp. 194-95.

28 Roosevelt, *Public Papers and Addresses,* 7:179-92; *Congressional Record,* 75th Congress, 3d sess., 1938, 83:4204, 5123. For a detailed scholarly history of this subject, see Richard Polenberg, *Reorganizing Roosevelt's Government: The Controversy over Executive Reorganization, 1936-1939* (Cambridge: Harvard University Press, 1966).

29 *Congressional Record,* 75th Congress, 3d sess., 1938, 83:3645, 4204, 5123; press release, "Statement of Hon. David I. Walsh on the Reorganization Bill," March 23, 1938, Walsh Papers; Johnson to Hiram Johnson, Jr., March 26, 1938, Johnson Papers.

Chapter 15

1 Among the scholarly histories of the Spanish civil war, see Hugh Thomas, *The Spanish Civil War* (London: Eyre & Spottiswoode Ltd., 1961). Among scholarly studies of United States policies toward the Spanish civil war, see Allen Guttman, *The Wound in the Heart: America and the Spanish Civil War* (New York: Free Press, 1962); F. Jay Taylor, *The United States and the Spanish Civil War, 1936-1939* (New York: Bookman Associates, 1956); and Richard P. Traina, *American Diplomacy and the Spanish Civil War, 1936-1939* (Bloomington: Indiana University Press, 1968). The American ambassador's account is Claude G. Bowers, *My Mission to Spain* (New York: Simon and Schuster, 1954).

2 Department of State, *Foreign Relations of the United States: Diplomatic Papers, 1936,* 2:437-78; Cordell Hull, *The Memoirs of Cordell Hull,* 1:475-85.

3 Edgar B. Nixon, ed., *Franklin D. Roosevelt and Foreign Affairs,* 3:565-66, 592-93. Moore served as acting secretary of state in December, 1936, and the first part of January, 1937, while Hull was in South America attending the Inter-American Conference in Buenos Aires.

4 Hull, *Memoirs of Cordell Hull,* 1:490; Department of State, *Foreign Relations, 1936,* 2:618–20; Moore to Roosevelt, January 5, 1937, President's Secretary's File, Neutrality folder, Roosevelt Papers.

5 Nixon, ed., *Roosevelt and Foreign Affairs,* 3:562–65.

6 Department of State, *Foreign Relations, 1936,* 2:623–24; Borah press release, December 29, 1936, William E. Borah Papers.

7 Hull, *Memoirs of Cordell Hull,* 1:490; James A. White to Marvin H. McIntyre, December 30, 1936, R. Walton Moore Papers; Nixon, ed., *Roosevelt and Foreign Affairs,* 3:567 n.

8 Memorandum by K from White, January 6, 1937, Official File 1561, Roosevelt Papers; *Congressional Record,* 75th Congress, 1st sess., 1937, 81:73–75; Nixon, ed., *Roosevelt and Foreign Affairs,* 3:376; Nye to Moore, December 30, 1936, Green to Moore, December 31, 1936, Moore to Nye, January 5, 1937, File Number 711.00111 Registration Licenses/317, Record Group 59, Department of State Records.

9 *Congressional Record,* 75th Congress, 1st sess., 1937, 81:76–79.

10 Ibid., 81:77–80, 98–99.

11 Ibid., 81:75.

12 Hull, *Memoirs of Cordell Hull,* 1:491; clipping *Washington Herald,* January 7, 1937, Nye Papers.

13 Department of State, *Foreign Relations of the United States: Diplomatic Papers, 1937,* 1:215–72; Nixon, ed., *Roosevelt and Foreign Affairs,* 3:395–400, 414–20, 427–31, 435–39, 464–69; Bowers to William E. Dodd, September 10, 1936, William E. Dodd Papers; Bowers to Pittman, June 26, 1937, Senate Foreign Relations Committee Papers, Record Group 46; Bowers to Arthur Capper, September 29, 1937, Arthur Capper Papers; Bowers to Roosevelt, October 11, 1937, President's Secretary's File, Spain folder, Roosevelt Papers.

14 *Congressional Record,* 75th Congress, 1st sess., 1937, 81:2737, 2805, 3315–17; Pittman to Hull, April 10, 1937, Hull to Pittman, April 20, 1937, File Number 811.04418/254, Record Group 59, Department of State Records.

15 *Congressional Record,* 75th Congress, 1st sess., 1937, 81:2865; print of S.J. Res. 120, 75th Congress, Record Group 46, Papers Supporting Senate Bills and Resolutions.

16 Hull to Pittman, May 4, 1937, unsigned memo on S.J. Res. 120, 75th Congress, Record Group 46, Papers Supporting Senate Bills and Resolutions.

17 On Nye, see Wayne S. Cole, *Senator Gerald P. Nye and American Foreign Relations* (Minneapolis: University of Minnesota Press, 1962). On Thomas, see W. A. Swanberg, *Norman Thomas: The Last Idealist* (New York: Scribner's, 1976).

18 Thomas to Roosevelt, June 9, 1937, President's Personal File 4840, Roosevelt Papers.

19 Roosevelt to McIntyre, June 16, 1937, President's Personal File 4840, Roosevelt to Hull, June 29, 1937, Official File 1561, Roosevelt Papers; Department of State, *Foreign Relations, 1937,* 1:344-57; Nye to Pittman, April 14, 1938, S.J. Res. 120, 75th Congress, Record Group 46, Papers Supporting Senate Bills and Resolutions; Pittman to Nye, April 19, 1938, Pittman to Hull, April 19, 1938, Sumner Welles to Pittman, April 23, 1938, File Number 811.04418/305, Record Group 59, Department of State Records.

20 Sayre to Davis, November 24, 1936, Norman H. Davis papers; Hull, *Memoirs of Cordell Hull,* 1:506-8.

21 U.S., Senate, Special Committee on Investigation of the Munitions Industry, *Munitions Industry: Report on Existing Legislation,* and *Supplemental Report on the Adequacy of Existing Legislation,* Senate Report 944, parts 5 and 6, particularly pp. 1-9 of each report and p. 58 of part 5.

22 Hull, *Memoirs of Cordell Hull,* 1:508.

23 *Congressional Record,* 75th Congress, 1st sess., 1937, 81:337; Pittman to Hull, January 22, 1937, S.J. Res. 51, 75th Congress, Record Group 46, Papers Supporting Senate Bills and Resolutions; Moore to Hull, January 25, 1937, Moore Papers.

24 *Congressional Record,* 75th Congress, 1st sess., 1937, 81:611; Jack Alexander, "Missouri Dark Mule," *Saturday Evening Post,* October 8, 1938, pp. 5-7, 32-37; "Sharpshooters into Arms Trade," *Literary Digest,* January 18, 1936, p. 33; Ralph Coghlan, "Missouri—a Threat and a Promise," *Nation,* November 2, 1932, pp. 422-24.

25 Johnson to Hiram W. Johnson, Jr., February 6, 1937, Johnson to John Bassett Moore, February 20, 1937, Johnson Papers; transcript of meeting of Senate Foreign Relations Committee, February 13, 1937, Senate Foreign Relations Committee Papers, Record Group 46; Moore to Roosevelt, February 15, 1937, Official File 1561, Roosevelt Papers.

26 Clipping *Washington Post,* February 27, 1937, Nye Papers; *Congressional Record,* 75th Congress, 1st sess., 1937, 81:1798-1807; Moore to Roosevelt, March 4, 1937, Official File 1561, Roosevelt Papers; Johnson to Hiram W. Johnson, Jr., March 7, 1937, Johnson Papers.

27 Hull, *Memoirs of Cordell Hull,* 1:508-9; McReynolds to Sam J. McAllester, March 24, 1937, H.J. Res. 242, 75th Congress, Record Group 233, Papers Supporting House Bills and Resolutions; Franklin D. Roosevelt, *F.D.R.: His Personal Letters, 1928-1945,* 1:673-74.

28 *Congressional Record,* 75th Congress, 1st sess., 1937, 81:3954-56; clipping *Washington Post,* April 29, 1937, Nye Papers.

29 *Congressional Record,* 75th Congress, 1st sess., 1937, 81:3962; Hull to Roosevelt, April 30, 1937, President's Secretary's File, Neutrality folder, Roosevelt Papers; clipping *Washington Post,* May 2, 1937, Nye Papers.

30 Hull, *Memoirs of Cordell Hull,* 1:507–9; clipping *Washington Post,* May 2, 1937, Nye Papers; *Congressional Record,* 75th Congress, 1st sess., 1937, 81:4264; Welles to Pittman, May 27, 1937, S. 2370, 75th Congress, Record Group 46, Papers Supporting Senate Bills and Resolutions; *Congressional Digest,* October 1939, p. 230.

31 Nye to Lippmann, April 26, 1939, Nye Papers.

32 Hadley Cantril and Mildred Strunk, eds., *Public Opinion, 1935–1946* (Princeton, N.J.: Princeton University Press, 1951), pp. 807–8; Lewis B. Schwellenbach to George E. Flood, March 19, 1938, Lewis B. Schwellenbach Papers; Nye to William F. Montavon, April 29, 1938, and enclosed statement by Nye, Nye Papers; Harold L. Ickes, *The Secret Diary of Harold L. Ickes,* vol. 2, *The Inside Struggle, 1936–1939,* pp. 377–78, 380, 388–90; Joseph P. Lash, *Eleanor and Franklin* (New York: W. W. Norton & Company, 1971), pp. 568–70. For a sample of the mail received, see boxes 631 through 640 in Borah Papers.

33 *Congressional Record,* 75th Congress, 3d sess., 1938, 83:6030.

34 Interviews with Gerald P. Nye, Chevy Chase, Maryland, August 17, 21, 1959.

35 J. Pierrepont Moffat diary, May 2, 3, 4, 5, 6, 9, 10, 11, 1938; Moore to Hull, May 5, 1938, Moore Papers.

36 Department of State, *Foreign Relations of the United States: Diplomatic Papers, 1938,* 1:194–95; Moffat diary, May 5, 1938.

37 Moffat diary, May 13, 1938; clipping *New York Sun,* May 14, 1938, Nye Papers; Theodore Francis Green to William Armstrong, June 8, 1938, Green to Thomas F. Kelley, February 10, 1939, Theodore Francis Green Papers.

38 Gerald P. Nye, "America's Interest in Spain" (mimeographed copy of address over a Blue Network of NBC, May 20, 1938), Nye Papers; Borah to Eugene Davidson, April 21, 1938, Borah Papers.

39 Roosevelt, *F.D.R.: His Personal Letters,* 2:832–33.

40 Borah to Ignatius W. Cox, January 13, 1939, Borah Papers; *Congressional Record,* 76th Congress, 1st sess., 1939, 84:742–43; Norris to Richard W. Hogue, February 14, 1939, Norris Papers.

41 Ickes, *Secret Diary of Harold L. Ickes,* 2:569–70.

Chapter 16

1 The best scholarly history of United States policies during the early phases of the Sino-Japanese war is Dorothy Borg, *The United States and the Far Eastern Crisis of 1933–1938* (Cambridge: Harvard University Press, 1964). On Grew, see Waldo Heinrichs, Jr., *American Ambassador: Joseph C. Grew and the Development of the United States Diplomatic Tradition* (Boston: Little, Brown and Co., 1966);

Joseph C. Grew, *Ten Years in Japan* (New York: Simon and Schuster, 1944); and Joseph C. Grew, *Turbulent Era: A Diplomatic Record of Forty Years, 1904–1945* (Boston: Houghton Mifflin Co., 1952). For Johnson, see Russell D. Buhite, *Nelson T. Johnson and American Policy toward China, 1925–1941* (East Lansing: Michigan State University Press, 1968). See also Dorothy Borg and Shumpei Okamoto, eds., *Pearl Harbor as History: Japanese-American Relations, 1931–1941* (New York: Columbia University Press, 1973).

2 Cordell Hull, *The Memoirs of Cordell Hull*, 1:556–58; Franklin D. Roosevelt, *F.D.R.: His Personal Letters, 1928–1945*, 2:873; Borg, *United States and Far Eastern Crisis*, pp. 334–54.

3 Department of State, *Papers Relating to the Foreign Relations of the United States: Japan, 1931–1941*, 1:325–26; Hull, *Memoirs of Cordell Hull*, 1:535–37.

4 *New York Times*, July 30, 1937, p. 1; Key Pittman, "Neutrality," *Vital Speeches of the Day*, September 1, 1937, pp. 700–702; Borah to Mrs. Thomas E. Kinney, November 18, 1937, Borah Papers.

5 *Congressional Record*, 75th Congress, 1st sess., 1937, 81:2187; *New York Times*, August 15, 1937, p. 1.

6 Hull, *Memoirs of Cordell Hull*, 1:544–45.

7 Eichelberger to M. H. McIntyre, July 17, 1937, Eichelberger to Roosevelt, July 17, 1937, and enclosed memorandum, President's Personal File 3833, Sterrett to Roosevelt, September 18, 1937, Roosevelt to Sterrett, October 7, 1937, President's Personal File 2080, Roosevelt Papers; Clark M. Eichelberger, *Organizing for Peace: A Personal History of the Founding of the United Nations*, pp. 226–34.

8 Harold L. Ickes, *The Secret Diary of Harold L. Ickes*, vol. 2, *The Inside Struggle, 1936–1939*, pp. 213–14, 221–22.

9 Hull, *Memoirs of Cordell Hull*, 1:545.

10 Franklin D. Roosevelt, *The Public Papers and Addresses of Franklin D. Roosevelt*, 6:406–11; Department of State, *Foreign Relations of United States: Japan, 1931–1941*, 1:379–83.

11 Roosevelt, *Public Papers and Addresses*, 6:414, 422–25; Roosevelt, *F.D.R.: His Personal Letters*, 1:719.

12 For a thoughtful analysis of Roosevelt's speech and reactions, see Dorothy Borg, *United States and Far Eastern Crisis*, pp. 369–98, and her earlier article, "Notes on Roosevelt's 'Quarantine' Speech," *Political Science Quarterly* 72 (September 1957): 405–33.

13 Borchard to Borah, October 6, 1937, Borah to Samuel E. Newman, October 7, 1937, Borah Papers; *New York Times*, October 8, 1937, p. 2; Landon to William Hard, October 11, 1937, Landon Papers.

14 Telegram Johnson to Raymond Moley, October 11, 1937, Johnson to Hiram Johnson, Jr., February 12, 1938, Johnson to Borchard, June 20, 1938, Johnson Papers; Castle to Landon, October 20, 1937, Landon Papers.

15 Hull, *Memoirs of Cordell Hull,* 1:545; Moffat diary, October 5, 1937.
16 Telegram Villard to Marvin H. McIntyre, October 6, 1937, President's Personal File 2178, Jessup to Roosevelt, October 6, 1937, President's Personal File 200B, Roosevelt Papers.
17 Knox to George Messersmith, October 6, 1937, Frank Knox Papers; *New York Times,* October 7, 1937, p. 1; telegram Eichelberger to McIntyre, October 9, 1937, President's Personal File 3833, Roosevelt Papers; confidential print Anthony Eden to V. A. L. Mallet, October 7, 1937, Foreign Office 414/274, p. 35, British Foreign Office Records.
18 Moffat diary, October 8, 1937.
19 Sumner Welles, *The Time for Decision,* pp. 64–67; Department of State, *Foreign Relations of the United States, 1937,* 1:665–70; Hull, *Memoirs of Cordell Hull,* 1:546–49; Adolf A. Berle, *Navigating the Rapids, 1918–1971: From the Papers of Adolf A. Berle,* pp. 140–43; telegrams Sir R. Lindsay to Foreign Office, January 11, 1938, Foreign Office 371/21526, British Foreign Office Records; and Mary Jo Tudor, "President Roosevelt's Peace Moves in Europe: September, 1937 to May, 1939" (M.A. thesis, University of Maryland, 1967), pp. 8–13.
20 John McVickar Haight, Jr., "Franklin D. Roosevelt and a Naval Quarantine of Japan," *Pacific Historical Review* 40 (1971): 203–20; Ickes, *Secret Diary of Harold L. Ickes,* 2:274–75.
21 Haight, "Roosevelt and Naval Quarantine of Japan," pp. 221–26; Welles, *Time for Decision,* pp. 66–69; Department of State, *Foreign Relations of the United States: Diplomatic Papers, 1938,* 1:115–32; Anthony Eden, *Facing the Dictators* (Boston: Houghton Mifflin Company, 1962), pp. 624–53; A. Cadogan to Anthony Eden, January 13, 1938, Foreign Office to Sir R. Lindsay, January 13, 1938, Eden to Chamberlain, January 17, 1938, Foreign Office to Sir R. Lindsay, January 21, 1938, Lindsay to Foreign Office, February 9, 1938, February 12, 1938, February 25, 1938, Foreign Office to Lindsay, March 11, 1938, Lindsay to Foreign Office, March 12, 1938, Foreign Office 371/21526, pp. 19–131; Tudor, "Roosevelt's Peace Moves," pp. 13–29.
22 Department of State, *Foreign Relations, 1937,* 4:1–83; Borg, *United States and Far Eastern Crisis,* pp. 399–441.
23 Department of State, *Foreign Relations, 1937,* 4:83–236, but see especially pp. 84–86, 112–13, 119–20, 124–25, 134, 145–47, 152–55, 160–62, 175–77, 212–14, 221–24, 233–36; Department of State, *Foreign Relations: Japan, 1931–1941,* 1:404–22; Hull, *Memoirs of Cordell Hull,* 1:550–56; Hugh R. Wilson to Joseph C. Grew, October 18, 1937, Hugh R. Wilson Papers; Moffat diary, October 28, 1937; Norman H. Davis to Grace Ellet, December 27, 1937, Davis Papers.
24 Department of State, *Foreign Relations: Japan, 1931–1941,* 1:517–63; Department of State, *Foreign Relations, 1937,* 4:485–520. For a

scholarly history of the *Panay* incident and its aftermath, see Manny T. Koginos, *The Panay Incident: Prelude to War* (Lafayette, Ind.: Purdue University Studies, 1967).

25 *New York Times,* December 14, 1937, p. 23; Borah to William W. Allen, December 17, 1937, Borah Papers.

Chapter 17

1 Cordell Hull, *The Memoirs of Cordell Hull,* 1:564; Sir R. Lindsay to Foreign Office, January 10, 1938, Foreign Office 371/22525, p. 344, British Foreign Office Records.

2 Merle Curti, *Peace or War: The American Struggle, 1636-1936* (New York: W. W. Norton and Co., 1936), p. 281; Bruce L. Larson, *Lindbergh of Minnesota: A Political Biography* (New York: Harcourt Brace Jovanovich, Inc., 1973), p. 201; Kirk H. Porter and Donald Bruce Johnson, comps., *National Party Platforms, 1840-1956* (Urbana: University of Illinois Press, 1956), pp. 250, 255, 256.

3 Among the scholarly histories of the Ludlow amendment are Ernest C. Bolt, Jr., *Ballots before Bullets: The War Referendum Approach to Peace in America, 1914-1941* (Charlottesville: University Press of Virginia, 1977), pp. 152-85; Walter R. Griffin, "Louis Ludlow and the War Referendum Crusade, 1935-1941," *Indiana Magazine of History* 64 (December 1968): 267-88; Manny T. Koginos, *The Panay Incident: Prelude to War* (Lafayette, Ind.: Purdue University Studies, 1967), pp. 80-97. For a vivid expression of Ludlow's admiration for Thomas Jefferson, see L. L. Ludlow, "The Vision of Jefferson," *Vital Speeches of the Day,* May 15, 1940, pp. 479-80.

4 Frear to Roosevelt, January 6, 1934, Frear to "My dear Sir," January 8, 1934, Norris Papers; Bolt, *Ballots before Bullets,* pp. 143-51; Griffin, "Louis Ludlow," pp. 272-73.

5 Ludlow to "My dear Friend," n.d., Fiorello H. La Guardia Papers; Ludlow to "Dear Friend and Colleague," April 6, 1937, H.J. Res. 199, 75th Congress, Record Group 233, Papers Supporting House Bills and Resolutions; Griffin, "Louis Ludlow," pp. 274-75.

6 *Congressional Record,* 73d Congress, 2d sess., 1934, 78:6898, 75th Congress, 3d sess., 1938, 83:2410-11.

7 Frederick J. Libby, *To End War: The Story of the National Council for Prevention of War* (Nyack, New York: Fellowship Publications, 1969), pp. 80, 113-15, 146-48, 150; Clark M. Eichelberger, *Organizing for Peace: A Personal History of the Founding of the United Nations,* pp. 60-68; Bolt, *Ballots before Bullets,* pp. 166-67; Joseph P. Lash, *Eleanor and Franklin* (New York: W. W. Norton & Co., 1971), pp. 555-65; Robert Edwin Bowers, "The American Peace Movement,

1933–41'' (Ph.D. diss., University of Wisconsin, 1949), pp. iv, 342–43; interview with Mrs. Ruth Sarles Benedict, Bethesda, Maryland, December 28, 1978.

8 Ludlow to Roosevelt, September 11, 1937, Roosevelt to Ludlow, September 16, 1937, Official File 150-C, Roosevelt Papers.

9 Griffin, "Louis Ludlow," p. 276; "Vote 'X' for War," *Newsweek,* December 27, 1937, p. 13.

10 Senator Arthur Capper, "Pro—Should a War Referendum Amendment Be Added to the Constitution?," *Congressional Digest,* February 1938, pp. 43–44.

11 Ludlow press release, December 22, 1937, Official File 3084, Roosevelt Papers.

12 Fourteen church leaders, "Pro—Should a War Referendum Amendment Be Added to the Constitution?," *Congressional Digest,* February 1938, p. 52.

13 Telegram Landon to Roosevelt, December 20, 1937, President's Personal File 3855, Roosevelt Papers.

14 Knox to Mrs. Annie Knox, December 19, 1937, Knox Papers.

15 Henry L. Stimson and McGeorge Bundy, *On Active Service in Peace and War,* p. 313; "War Referendum: Should the People Be Allowed to Vote on Whether We Fight Abroad?," *Literary Digest,* January 1, 1938, p. 7; "Con—Should a War Referendum Amendment Be Added to the Constitution?," *Congressional Digest,* February 1938, p. 64.

16 Press reaction is summarized in Koginos, *Panay Incident,* pp. 87–92.

17 Hull, *Memoirs of Cordell Hull,* 1:563–64.

18 Ibid.; Hull to McReynolds, January 8, 1938, File Number 711.0011 War Referendum/6A, Record Group 59, Department of State Records; *Newsweek,* December 27, 1937, p. 13.

19 James A. Farley, *Jim Farley's Story: The Roosevelt Years,* pp. 117–18.

20 Ibid., p. 118; Farley to Roosevelt, January 10, 1938, and enclosed memorandum on *"Ludlow Resolution,"* January 10, 1938, President's Secretary's File, Post Office Department Farley folder, Roosevelt Papers.

21 *Congressional Record,* 75th Congress, 3d sess., 1938, 83:276–77.

22 Ibid., 83:277.

23 Ibid., 83:282–83.

24 Ibid.; memorandum on Ludlow Resolution, January 10, 1938, enclosed with Farley to Roosevelt, January 10, 1938, President's Secretary's File, Post Office Department Farley folder, Roosevelt Papers; Roosevelt to Hull, January 25, 1938, and enclosed tabulation of vote by states, Cordell Hull Papers; Farley, *Jim Farley's Story,* p. 118.

25 *Congressional Record,* 75th Congress, 3d sess., 1938, 83:2410–11, 5573, 76th Congress, 2d sess., 1939, 85:999–1000, 77th Congress, 1st sess., 1941, 87:2610; Ludlow to Henrik Shipstead, April 5, 1940, Shipstead Papers; *New York Times,* December 11, 1940, p. 19; Wayne S. Cole,

America First: The Battle against Intervention, 1940–1941 (Madison: University of Wisconsin Press, 1953), pp. 56–61.

26 This paragraph is based on the author's tabulations and calculations from the vote listed in *Congressional Record,* 75th Congress, 3d sess., 1938, 83:282–83.

27 Franklin D. Roosevelt, *F.D.R.: His Personal Letters, 1928–1945,* 2:750–52.

Chapter 18

1 Harold L. Ickes, *The Secret Diary of Harold L. Ickes,* vol. 2, *The Inside Struggle, 1936–1939,* pp. 246, 255–63, 278–79; James A. Farley, *Jim Farley's Story: The Roosevelt Years,* pp. 108–17.

2 Roosevelt to Sweet, November 10, 1937, President's Personal File 1524, Roosevelt Papers.

3 Edgar B. Nixon, ed., *Franklin D. Roosevelt and Foreign Affairs,* 1:370; Samuel Eliot Morison, *The Two-Ocean War: A Short History of the United States Navy in the Second World War* (Boston: Little, Brown and Co., 1963), pp. 20–25; Waldo H. Heinrichs, Jr., "The Role of the United States Navy," in *Pearl Harbor as History: Japanese-American Relations, 1931–1941,* ed. Dorothy Borg and Shumpei Okamoto (New York: Columbia University Press, 1973), pp. 199, 207–16.

4 Ickes, *Secret Diary of Harold L. Ickes,* 2:268–69; Franklin D. Roosevelt, *The Public Papers and Addresses of Franklin D. Roosevelt,* 6:554–55, 7:1, 19.

5 Roosevelt, *Public Papers and Addresses,* 7:68–71.

6 *Congressional Record,* 73d Congress, 2d sess., 1934, 78:3812–14.

7 P.M. [Moffat] to Hull, February 21, 1934, Hull to Roosevelt, n.d., Official File 404A, Roosevelt Papers.

8 Clipping *New York Times,* March 23, 1937, Nye Papers.

9 Clipping *New York Herald-Tribune,* January 1, 1938, Norris to Earl Constantine, December 31, 1937, Norris Papers.

10 Norris to Borchard, January 4, 1938, Norris Papers.

11 *New York Times,* December 30, 1937, p. 8; *Congressional Record,* 75th Congress, 3d sess., 1938, 83:6135.

12 *Congressional Record,* 75th Congress, 3d sess., 1938, 83: *Appendix,* pp. 238–39.

13 Ibid., 83:5571, 5827; Nye to Borah, Brown, Bulow, Capper, Clark, Davis, Donahey, Frazier, Hitchcock, Johnson, King, La Follette, Pope, Shipstead, Thomas, Vandenberg, and Wheeler, April 23, 1938, Capper Papers.

14 Johnson to Hiram Johnson, Jr., January 29, 1938, Johnson Papers; *Congressional Record,* 75th Congress, 3d sess., 1938, 83:1263.

15 *Congressional Record,* 75th Congress, 3d sess., 1938, 83:1325–28.

16 Ibid., 83:1621–22.

17 Ibid., 83:1764–65; Johnson to Hiram Johnson, Jr., February 12, 1938, Johnson Papers.

18 Cordell Hull, *The Memoirs of Cordell Hull,* 1:574.

19 Ibid., 1:575.

20 *Congressional Record,* 75th Congress, 3d sess., 1938, 83:3767–68, 6135, 7124.

Chapter 19

1 The standard biography of Chamberlain is Keith G. Feiling, *The Life of Neville Chamberlain* (London: Macmillan, 1946). Biographies of Hitler include Alan Bullock, *Hitler: A Study in Tyranny,* rev. ed. (New York: Harper, 1964); and John Toland, *Adolf Hitler* (Garden City, New York: Doubleday & Co., 1976). Scholarly studies of the Munich crisis include John W. Wheeler-Bennett, *Munich: Prologue to Tragedy* (New York: Macmillan Co., 1948); Keith Eubank, *Munich* (Norman: University of Oklahoma Press, 1963); and Telford Taylor, *Munich: The Price of Peace* (Garden City, N.Y.: Doubleday & Co., 1979).

2 Biographies of Kennedy include David E. Koskoff, *Joseph P. Kennedy: A Life and Times* (Englewood Cliffs, N.J.: Prentice-Hall, 1974), and Richard J. Whalen, *The Founding Father: The Story of Joseph P. Kennedy* (New York: New American Library, 1964). See also Michael R. Beschloss, *Kennedy and Roosevelt: The Uneasy Alliance* (New York: W. W. Norton & Co., 1980).

3 Franklin D. Roosevelt, *F.D.R.: His Personal Letters, 1928–1945,* 2:743–44; Moffat diary, January 27, 1938; Koskoff, *Kennedy,* pp. 114–22; Richardson Dougall and Mary Patricia Chapman, *United States Chiefs of Mission, 1778–1973* (Washington, D.C.: Department of State, 1973), p. 160.

4 Lord Arthur Riverdale to Thomas J. Watson, March 24, 1938, George E. Harding to M. H. McIntyre, June 21, 1938, Official File 3060, Franklin Mott Gunther to Roosevelt, April 19, 1938, President's Secretary's File, Department of State 1938 folder, Roosevelt Papers.

5 Kennedy to Roosevelt, March 11, 1938, Hull Papers.

6 Sir Ronald Lindsay to Foreign Office, March 12, 1938, F.O. 371/22526, p. 19, British Foreign Office Records.

7 Moffat diary, March 12, 1938; Hull to Roosevelt, March 13, 1938, Hull Papers; Hull to Roosevelt, March 14, 1938, telegram Hull to Kennedy, March 14, 1938, Official File 3060, Roosevelt Papers.

8 Moffat diary, March 15, 1938; Cordell Hull, *The Memoirs of Cordell Hull,* 1:576.

9 Borah to Mrs. D. F. Bacon, March 21, 1938, Borah to William Hirth,

April 20, 1938, Kennedy to Borah, April 28, 1938, Borah Papers.

10 Many of the telegrams, letters, and reports from America's diplomats in Europe during those crises are included in Department of State, *Foreign Relations of the United States: Diplomatic Papers, 1938,* 1:384–739. For Bullitt's correspondence with Roosevelt, see Orville H. Bullitt, ed., *For the President, Personal and Secret: Correspondence between Franklin D. Roosevelt and William C. Bullitt,* pp. 245–303. Adolf A. Berle, Jr., diary, February 16, 21, 1938, Berle to Hull and Welles, March 16, 1938, Berle diary; Moffat diary, January 27, 1938, February 9, 1939, December 8, 1939.

11 Lindbergh's account of his early years is Charles A. Lindbergh, *Boyhood on the Upper Mississippi: A Reminiscent Letter.* His autobiographies covering his life through his flight to Paris in 1927 are *"We,"* and *The Spirit of St. Louis,* for which he was awarded a Pulitzer Prize. His wife traces her life up to the time of their marriage in *Bring Me a Unicorn: Diaries and Letters of Anne Morrow Lindbergh, 1922–1928.* Among the better of the several biographies of Lindbergh are Walter S. Ross, *The Last Hero: Charles A. Lindbergh* (New York: Harper & Row, 1964, 1965, 1968); and Kenneth S. Davis, *The Hero: Charles A. Lindbergh and the American Dream* (Garden City, New York: Doubleday & Co., 1959). Neither author had access to Lindbergh or his papers. Wayne S. Cole, *Charles A. Lindbergh and the Battle against American Intervention in World War II* (New York and London: Harcourt Brace Jovanovich, 1974) focuses particularly on Lindbergh's career from 1936 to 1945 and is based on research in the Lindbergh papers as well as on personal interviews with General Lindbergh.

12 Those years are treated movingly in Anne Morrow Lindbergh, *Hour of Gold, Hour of Lead: Diaries and Letters of Anne Morrow Lindbergh, 1929–1932,* and *Locked Rooms and Open Doors: Diaries and Letters of Anne Morrow Lindbergh, 1933–1935.*

13 Those years are treated in Charles A. Lindbergh, *The Wartime Journals of Charles A. Lindbergh,* pp. 3–111; *The Flower and the Nettle: Diaries and Letters of Anne Morrow Lindbergh, 1936–1939;* Colonel Truman Smith, manuscript, "Air Intelligence Activities: Office of the Military Attache, American Embassy, Berlin, Germany, August 1935–April 1939 with Special Reference to the Services of Colonel Charles A. Lindbergh, Air Corps (Res.)," 1956; and Cole, *Charles A. Lindbergh,* pp. 25–46. For the initial exchange of letters between Smith and Lindbergh, see Smith to Lindbergh, May 25, 1936, Lindbergh to Smith, June 5, 1936, Charles A. Lindbergh Papers.

14 Lindbergh expressed those views in countless letters and conversations. For two among many possible examples, see Lindbergh to Colonel Raymond Lee, September 13, 1938, and Lindbergh to R. H. Brand, September 17, 1938, Lindbergh Papers.

15 Lindbergh, *Wartime Journals,* pp. 26–32; *Flower and the Nettle,* pp. 254–92; and invitations and letters of acceptance in Lindbergh Papers.

16 Lindbergh, *Wartime Journals,* pp. 33–69; *Flower and the Nettle,* pp. 295–401; Lindbergh to Colonel Lee, September 13, 1938, Lindbergh Papers.

17 Lindbergh, *Wartime Journals,* pp. 69–70.

18 E. L. Woodward and Rohan Butler, eds., *Documents on British Foreign Policy, 1919–1939,* 3d ser., 2:310–12, 452–54; Department of State, *Foreign Relations, 1938,* 1:70; Lindbergh, *Flower and the Nettle,* p. 407; Lindbergh to Colonel Lee, September 13, 1938, and many other letters in Lindbergh Papers.

19 Lindbergh, *Wartime Journals,* pp. 71–73; *Flower and the Nettle,* pp. 407–10; Hull, *Memoirs of Cordell Hull,* 1:590.

20 Department of State, *Foreign Relations, 1938,* 1:72–73. Lindbergh's complete letter to Kennedy, dated September 22, 1938, is in the Lindbergh Papers.

21 Lindbergh, *Wartime Journals,* pp. 72–79; Sir John Slessor, *The Central Blue: Recollections and Reflections,* pp. 218–22.

22 Hull, *Memoirs of Cordell Hull,* 1:586–87.

23 Roosevelt, *Public Papers and Addresses,* 7:491–94.

24 Berle diary, September 1, 1938, pp. 67–68; Henry Morgenthau, Jr., *From the Morgenthau Diaries,* vol. 1, *Years of Crisis, 1928–1938,* p. 518; Roosevelt, *F.D.R.: His Personal Letters,* 2:809; Roosevelt to Hull, September 1, 1938, President's Secretary's File, Cordell Hull, 1938 folder, Roosevelt Papers; Whalen, *Founding Father,* pp. 230–32.

25 Roosevelt to Phillips, September 15, 1938, President's Secretary's File, Italy, 1933–38 folder, Roosevelt Papers; Hull, *Memoirs of Cordell Hull,* 1:591, 595–96.

26 Department of State, *Foreign Relations, 1938,* 1:509–12, 615–18; Bullitt, ed., *For the President,* pp. 279–80, 285; Hull, *Memoirs of Cordell Hull,* 1:590–93.

27 Kennedy to Roosevelt, n.d., with attached four-page excerpt from Lindbergh letter, Roosevelt to chief of staff and chief of naval operations, February 10, 1938, William D. Leahy to Roosevelt, February 14, 1938, Malin Craig to Colonel Edwin M. Watson, February 11, 1938, President's Secretary's File, Navy, Roosevelt Papers.

28 Lindbergh to Land, September 12, 1938, Emory Scott Land Papers. At the top of the first page of this eight-page letter is written: "Noted by The President and Col. McIntyre—9/27—v.v."

29 Roosevelt, *Public Papers and Addresses,* 7:531–32; Department of State, *Foreign Relations, 1938,* 1:657–58.

30 Department of State, *Foreign Relations, 1938,* 1:661–64, 669–73; Roosevelt, *Public Papers and Addresses,* 7:532–35.

31 Department of State, *Foreign Relations, 1938,* 1:675–80, 684–85; Roosevelt, *Public Papers and Addresses,* 7:535–37.
32 Department of State, *Foreign Relations, 1938,* 1:688–89, 691–94, 697–704.
33 Ibid.
34 For examples, see ibid., 1:70–71, 493–95, 500–501, 509–12; Bullitt, ed., *For the President,* pp. 256–58, 261–64, 268.
35 Roosevelt, *F.D.R.: His Personal Letters,* 2:816–17, 824–26.
36 Lindbergh, *Wartime Journals,* pp. 79–93, 116; Bullitt, ed., *For the President,* pp. 297–303; [Charles A. Lindbergh], "Canadian Plan," October 7, 1938, Lindbergh to Jean Monnet, October 7, 1938, Lindbergh Papers.
37 Lindbergh, *Wartime Journals,* pp. 94–111; *Flower and the Nettle,* pp. 425–40; Cole, *Charles A. Lindbergh,* pp. 39–43.
38 Cole, *Charles A. Lindbergh,* pp. 44–45, 59–61; Lindbergh, *Wartime Journals,* pp. 84–87, 110–12, 120, 125–32, 139–42; *Flower and the Nettle,* pp. 434–36, 439, 450, 453, 456; Hugh Wilson diary, October 25, 1938, Wilson Papers; Lindbergh to Alexis Carrel, November 28, December 10, 1938, Lindbergh Papers; Truman Smith, "Air Intelligence Activities," pp. 111–16; Bullitt, ed., *For the President,* pp. 312–15.
39 Lindbergh, *Wartime Journals,* pp. 175–258; interview with Charles A. Lindbergh, Washington, D.C., June 7, 1972.
40 Hull, *Memoirs of Cordell Hull,* 1:596; Koskoff, *Kennedy,* pp. 158–60; Claire Dundt to Roosevelt, October 23, 1938, Marcelle Schubert and Janet Dinkelapiel to Roosevelt, October 28, 1938, Official File 3060, Roosevelt Papers; Knox to Hull, October 25, 1938, Hull Papers.
41 Koskoff, *Kennedy,* pp. 161–62; Bruce Rogers to Kennedy, November 27, 1938, Rogers to Roosevelt, November 27, 1938, Official File 3060, Roosevelt Papers.
42 Minutes by J. V. Perowne, September 4, 1939, F.O. 371/22816, p. 25, Foreign Office to marquess of Lothian, October 3, 1939, F.O. 371/22827, p. 162, minutes of T. North Whitehead, January 25, 1940, F.O. 371/24251, p. 54, minutes by J. V. Perowne and T. Balfour, January 29, 1940, F.O. 371/24248, minutes by J. V. Perowne, August 22, 1940, F.O. 371/24251, p. 77, British Foreign Office Records; Henry Morgenthau, Jr. Presidential Diaries, October 3, 1939.
43 Kennedy to Roosevelt, July 20, 1939, Hull Papers; Kennedy to Roosevelt, September 10, 1939, President's Secretary's File, Kennedy 1939 folder, Kennedy to Roosevelt, November 3, 1939, President's Secretary's File, Great Britain Kennedy 1939 folder, and other letters in Roosevelt Papers; minutes by T. North Whitehead, January 25, 1940, F.O. 371/24251, p. 54, C. A. Warner to Balfour, March 3, 1940, F.O. 371/24251, p. 63, British Foreign Office Records; Kennedy to Robert E. Wood, December 11, 1940, Robert E. Wood Papers.

Chapter 20

1 James A. Farley, *Jim Farley's Story: The Roosevelt Years,* pp. 120–50; James C. Cobb, "The Big Boy Has Scared the Lard out of Them," *Research Studies* 43 (June 1975): 123–26.

2 Hoover to John W. Bricker, June 21, 1937, August 24, 1937, Post-Presidential Individual file, Herbert Hoover Papers; Landon to John G. Townsend, Jr., October 6, 1937, Landon to Harold B. Johnson, October 26, 1937, Landon Papers; William R. Castle to Landon, November 6, 1937, Landon to Castle, November 15, 1937, William R. Castle Papers; *New York Times,* May 6, 1937, p. 20; clipping *Washington Star,* May 4, 1937, Nye Papers; Vandenberg, "The Truth about the Coalition Manifesto," Scrapbook #10, Vandenberg Papers; Arthur H. Vandenberg, "'United We Stand—,'" *Saturday Evening Post,* April 30, 1938, pp. 25, 79–81.

3 Philip La Follette, *Adventure in Politics: The Memoirs of Philip La Follette,* pp. 246–55; Patrick J. Maney, *"Young Bob" La Follette: A Biography of Robert M. La Follette, Jr., 1895–1953* (Columbia and London: University of Missouri Press, 1978), pp. 203–6.

4 Adolf A. Berle, *Navigating the Rapids, 1918–1971: From the Papers of Adolf A. Berle,* pp. 173–74.

5 La Follette, *Adventure in Politics,* pp. 253–56; Maney, *"Young Bob" La Follette,* pp. 205–9; Berle, *Navigating the Rapids,* pp. 174–76; Harold L. Ickes, *The Secret Diary of Harold L. Ickes,* vol. 2, *The Inside Struggle, 1936–1939,* pp. 379–80, 385, 393–95.

6 For Taft's election, see James T. Patterson, *Mr. Republican: A Biography of Robert A. Taft* (Boston: Houghton Mifflin Company, 1972), pp. 160–70. On Nye's contest with Langer, see Wayne S. Cole, *Senator Gerald P. Nye and American Foreign Relations* (Minneapolis: University of Minnesota Press, 1962), pp. 145–49.

7 Farley, *Jim Farley's Story,* p. 148.

8 Those valuable letters to Farley from every state in the union are in Official File 300, 1938, Roosevelt Papers. The most thoughtful scholarly analysis of the foreign policy implications of the elections of 1938 is Charles J. Errico, "The New Deal, Internationalism, and the New American Consensus, 1938–1940," *Maryland Historian* 9 (Spring 1978): 17–31.

9 Farley, *Jim Farley's Story,* pp. 148–49; Ickes, *Secret Diary of Harold L. Ickes,* 2:498–501; Roosevelt to Farley, December 2, 1938, President's Secretary's File, Post Office Department—James A. Farley folder, Roosevelt Papers.

10 White to Raymond Robins, November 22, 1938, White Papers.

11 Franklin D. Roosevelt, *The Public Papers and Addresses of Franklin D. Roosevelt,* 8:1–12.

Chapter 21

1 Transcript of Hearings on National Defense before United States
Committee on Military Affairs, Washington, D.C., January 27, 1939,
President's Secretary's File, U.S. Senate, Roosevelt Papers; J. Cuny,
"Douglas DB-7s in French Service," *A.A.H.S. Journal*, Spring 1968,
pp. 1–15; Kenneth G. Munson, *Aircraft of World War Two* (Garden
City, New York: Doubleday and Company, 1962), pp. 62–63; Franklin
D. Roosevelt, *The Public Papers and Addresses of Franklin D.
Roosevelt*, 8:3.

2 Confidential print of telegram Lindsay to Halifax, September 12, 1938,
F.O. 414/275, p. 26, British Foreign Office Records.

3 Lindsay to Foreign Office, September 19, 1938, F.O. 371/21527,
pp. 22–23, British Foreign Office Records.

4 Ibid., pp. 25–26. Earlier that same day Roosevelt had tried out those
thoughts in a conversation with Secretary of Treasury Henry Morgenthau, Jr. (Henry Morgenthau, Jr., *From the Morgenthau Diaries*,
vol. 1, *Years of Crisis, 1928–1938*, p. 519).

5 Lindsay to Foreign Office, September 21, 1938, Foreign Office to
Lindsay, September 23, 1938, F.O. 371/21527, pp. 27–28, British
Foreign Office Records.

6 Harold L. Ickes, *The Secret Diary of Harold L. Ickes*, vol. 2, *The
Inside Struggle, 1936–1939*, pp. 472–74.

7 Arthur Murray, "Note of Certain Conversations between President
Franklin D. Roosevelt and Colonel Hon. Arthur Murray during
Colonel and Mrs Murray's Stay with the President at Hyde Park on the
Hudson, October 16th to 24th, 1938," PREM 1/367, British Foreign
Office Records; Franklin D. Roosevelt, *F.D.R.: His Personal Letters*,
1:198, 715–16, 2:757–58, 781–82.

8 Unsigned and undated note, probably from Syers to Chamberlain,
Murray to Syers, December 11, 1938, Murray to Chamberlain,
February 1, 1939, and note by N.C. at top of Murray's note of his
conversation with Roosevelt, PREM 1/367, British Foreign Office
Records.

9 Orville Bullitt, ed., *For the President, Personal and Secret:
Correspondence between Franklin D. Roosevelt and William C. Bullitt*,
pp. 297–303; Charles A. Lindbergh, *The Wartime Journals of Charles
A. Lindbergh*, pp. 79–93. For a scholarly history of American aid to
France, see John McVickar Haight, Jr., *American Aid to France,
1938–1940* (New York: Atheneum, 1970).

10 Bullitt, ed., *For the President*, p. 302; Lindbergh to Bullitt, October 26,
1938, Lindbergh to Arnold, November 2, 1938, Lindbergh Papers.

11 Confidential print of V. A. L. Mallet to Halifax, December 15, 1938,
F.O. 414/275, pp. 70–72, British Foreign Office Records.

12 Department of State, *Foreign Relations, 1938,* 2:297–314; Henry Morgenthau, Jr., *From the Morgenthau Diaries,* vol. 2, *Years of Urgency, 1938–1941,* pp. 64–71; transcript of Hearings on National Defense before United States Committee on Military Affairs, Washington, D.C., January 27, 1939, President's Secretary's File, U.S. Senate, Roosevelt Papers.

13 *New York Times,* January 11, 1939, pp. 1, 13; confidential print of Mallet to Sir John Simon, January 11, 1939, Mallet to Halifax, January 20, 1939, F.O. 414/276, pp. 5–6, 24, British Foreign Office Records; David E. Koskoff, *Joseph P. Kennedy: A Life and Times* (Englewood Cliffs, N.J.: Prentice-Hall, 1974), p. 183.

14 Roosevelt, *Public Papers and Addresses,* 8:70–74.

15 *Congressional Directory,* 76th Congress, 1st sess., 1939, p. 181.

16 Transcript of Hearings on National Defense before United States Committee on Military Affairs, Washington, D.C., January 27, 1939, President's Secretary's File, U.S. Senate, Roosevelt Papers; Morgenthau, *Years of Urgency,* pp. 71–72; H. H. Arnold, *Global Mission,* pp. 184–86.

17 *New York Times,* January 28, 1939, p. 1; transcript of Hearings on National Defense before United States Committee on Military Affairs, Washington, D.C., January 27, 1939, President's Secretary's File, U.S. Senate, Roosevelt Papers.

18 Morgenthau Presidential Diaries, January 31, 1939; transcript, "Conference with the Senate Military Affairs Committee, Executive Offices of the White House, January 31, 1939, 12.45 P.M.," p. 3, President's Personal File 1-P, Roosevelt Papers.

19 Transcript, "Conference with the Senate Military Affairs Committee, Executive Offices of the White House, January 31, 1939, 12.45 P.M.," pp. 1–5, President's Personal File 1-P, Roosevelt Papers.

20 Ibid., pp. 5–7.

21 Ibid., pp. 7–11.

22 Ibid., pp. 12–14.

23 Ibid., pp. 14–24.

24 Undated eleven-page memorandum in Senator Nye's handwriting in envelope with Nye's frank labeled "President & Military Affairs Com," Nye Papers.

25 *Congressional Record,* 76th Congress, 1st sess., 1939, 84:1010–14.

26 Interviews with Gerald P. Nye in Washington, D.C., August 27, 1956, August 26, 1958, and in Chevy Chase, Maryland, July 29, 1959; clipping *New York Sun,* February 18, 1939, Nye Papers.

27 Microfilm of Franklin D. Roosevelt's press conferences, February 3, 1939, Roosevelt Papers; Roosevelt, *Public Papers and Addresses,* 8:110–15.

28 Early to Hennings, February 3, 1939, and attached text of address, President's Personal File 5807, Roosevelt Papers.
29 Johnson to Hiram W. Johnson, Jr., February 11, 1939, February 19, 1939, Johnson to Frank P. Doherty, February 11, 1939, Johnson Papers.
30 Microfilm of Franklin D. Roosevelt's press conferences, February 17, 1939, Roosevelt Papers.
31 Interviews with Gerald P. Nye in Washington, D.C., August 27, 1956, August 26, 1958, and in Chevy Chase, Maryland, July 29, 1959.

Chapter 22

1 The best scholarly history of the revision of the neutrality legislation is Robert A. Divine, *The Illusion of Neutrality* (Chicago: University of Chicago Press, 1962), pp. 229–335.
2 Moffat diary, October 18, 1938, November 7, 1938; Green H. Hackworth, Joseph C. Green, and Carlton Savage, *"Proposed Changes in Neutrality Act of May 1, 1937,"* October 28, 1938, Berle Papers; Pittman to Moore, October 13, 1938, Senate Foreign Relations Committee Papers, Record Group 46.
3 Franklin D. Roosevelt, *The Public Papers and Addresses of Franklin D. Roosevelt,* 8:3–4; Cordell Hull, *The Memoirs of Cordell Hull,* 1:613.
4 Mallet to Foreign Office, January 27, 1939, F.O. 371/22962, pp. 67–68, British Foreign Office Records.
5 Moore to Roosevelt, March 18, 1939, File Number 811.04418/375A, Joseph C. Green to acting secretary, March 21, 1939, File Number 811.04418/365, Department of State Records, Record Group 59; Hull, *Memoirs of Cordell Hull,* 1:612–14; Committee on Foreign Relations print, *Text of Legislation Relating to Neutrality, Peace, and Our Foreign Policy Pending in the Committee on Foreign Relations, United States Senate* (Washington: U.S. Government Printing Office, 1939), pp. 1–16.
6 Franklin D. Roosevelt, *F.D.R.: His Personal Letters,* 2:873; Committee on Foreign Relations print, *Text of Legislation Relating to Neutrality,* pp. 27–32; Hull, *Memoirs of Cordell Hull,* 1:613.
7 Committee on Foreign Relations print, *Text of Legislation Relating to Neutrality,* pp. 17–25; *Congressional Record,* 76th Congress, 1st sess., 1939, *Appendix,* 84:1317–18.
8 For a full and clear statement of Nye's understanding of Roosevelt's foreign policy views, see *Congressional Record,* 76th Congress, 2d sess., 1939, 85:360–83.

9 Unsigned three-page memorandum, March 30, 1939, Senate Foreign
   Relations Committee Papers, Record Group 46; Henry L. Stimson
   diary, #29; Moffat diary, April 5, 1939.
10 Johnson to Philip B. Johnson, April 9, 1939, Johnson to Hiram W.
   Johnson, Jr., April 22, 1939, Johnson Papers.
11 Form letter from La Follette, May 1939, La Follette Family Papers.
12 Hull, *Memoirs of Cordell Hull,* 1:642–43; Moffat diary, May 3, 1939.
13 Moffat diary, May 8, 1939; Berle diary, May 8, 1939, p. 106; Johnson
   to John Bassett Moore, May 12, 1939, Johnson Papers; Hull, *Memoirs
   of Cordell Hull,* 1:643; confidential print Sir R. Lindsay to Viscount
   Halifax, May 23, 1939, F.O. 414/276, p. 95, British Foreign Office
   Records.
14 Hull, *Memoirs of Cordell Hull,* 1:643; Sol Bloom, *The Autobiography
   of Sol Bloom,* pp. 227–35; confidential print Lindsay to Halifax, May
   23, 1939, F.O. 414/276, p. 96.
15 Hull, *Memoirs of Cordell Hull,* 1:644–45; memorandum by Carlton
   Savage, May 27, 1939, memorandum Hull to Roosevelt, May 26, 1939,
   File Number 811.04418/434A, Department of State Records, Record
   Group 59; Department of State Press Release No. 216, May 27, 1939,
   Official File 1561, Roosevelt Papers.
16 Memo from E. M. W. [Watson] to Roosevelt, June 13, 1939, and
   attached report from Moore, Official File 1561, Roosevelt Papers;
   confidential print Lindsay to Halifax, June 16, 1939, July 2, 1939,
   F.O. 414/276, pp. 1, 108–9, British Foreign Office Records;
   Morgenthau presidential diary, June 30, 1939, pp. 154–56.
17 Hull, *Memoirs of Cordell Hull,* 1:645–46; Bloom, *Autobiography of
   Sol Bloom,* p. 235; *Congressional Record,* 76th Congress, 1st sess.,
   1939, 84:8511–14; Adolf A. Berle, *Navigating the Rapids, 1918–1971:
   From the Papers of Adolf A. Berle,* p. 231.
18 Morgenthau presidential diary, June 30, 1939, pp. 156–57; Roosevelt,
   F.D.R.: His Personal Letters, 2:899–900; Harold Ickes, *The Secret
   Diary of Harold L. Ickes,* vol. 2, *The Inside Struggle, 1936–1939,*
   p. 676; Roosevelt to Caroline O'Day, July 1, 1939, President's Personal File 2557, Roosevelt Papers.
19 Hull, *Memoirs of Cordell Hull,* 1:646–47; press release statement by
   secretary of state, July 1, 1939, Berle Papers.
20 Nye, Clark, La Follette, and Johnson to "Dear Senator," July 6, 1939,
   Series C, La Follette Family Papers; clipping from *Philadelphia
   Record,* July 7, 1939, Nye Papers; Johnson to Hiram W. Johnson, Jr.,
   July 8, 1939, Johnson Papers.
21 Clipping *Washington Times-Herald,* July 12, 1939, Nye Papers; confidential print Lindsay to Halifax, July 14, 1939, F.O. 414/276,
   pp. 23–25, British Foreign Office Records; Tom Connally, *My Name Is*

Tom Connally, p. 227; "Senate Committee on Foreign Relations Neutrality Vote," n.d., Senate Foreign Relations Committee Papers, Record Group 46; Johnson to Hiram W. Johnson, Jr., July 16, 1939, Johnson Papers.

22 Department of State, *Foreign Relations of the United States, 1939,* 1:662–70; Hull, *Memoirs of Cordell Hull,* 1:647–53.

23 Hull, *Memoirs of Cordell Hull,* 1:648–53; Roosevelt, *Public Papers and Addresses,* 8:381–87. The accounts by participants at the White House meeting on July 18 vary considerably in detail. They do not even agree on who was present at the meeting. The standard accounts as written in most history books emphasize the roles of Borah and Garner more than most of those written by participants. The account in this chapter is based on those accounts by Roosevelt, Hull, Barkley, Austin, and Connally. Connally claimed to have been at the meeting, though none of the other accounts name him as a participant. See Roosevelt, *Public Papers and Addresses,* 8:390–93; Hull, *Memoirs of Cordell Hull,* 1:649–51; Alben Barkley, *That Reminds Me—,* pp. 260–61; "The Failure of Neutrality Revision in Mid-Summer, 1939: Warren R. Austin's Memorandum of the White House Conference of July 18," submitted by George T. Mazuzan, *Vermont History* 42 (Summer 1974): 239–44; Connally, *My Name Is Tom Connally,* pp. 227–28.

24 Hull, *Memoirs of Cordell Hull,* 1:649–51.

25 Geoffrey Parsons to Mrs. Helen Rogers Reid, January 4, 1940, Series D. Reid Family Papers; *Week* (London), October 5, 1938, Lindbergh Papers.

26 Roosevelt, *Public Papers and Addresses,* 8:390–93; "Warren R. Austin's Memorandum of the White House Conference," *Vermont History* 42:239–44.

27 Roosevelt, *Public Papers and Addresses,* 8:387–88; Borah to John Haynes Holmes, July 19, 1939, Borah Papers; Hull, *Memoirs of Cordell Hull,* 1:653.

28 Stephen T. Early diary, September 1, 1939, Stephen T. Early Papers; Moffat diary, September 1, 1939; Roosevelt, *Public Papers and Addresses,* 8:455–57; Morgenthau presidential diary, September 1, 1939, p. 272; Department of State, *Foreign Relations, 1939,* 1:541–42.

29 Roosevelt, *Public Papers and Addresses,* 8:460–64.

30 Ickes, *Secret Diary of Harold L. Ickes,* 2:709–15; Lord Lothian to Foreign Office, September 4, 1939, F.O. 371/22816, p. 15, British Foreign Office Records; Lothian to Halifax, September 5, 1939, F.O. 800/324, pp. 48–50, Lord Halifax Papers; Department of State, *Foreign Relations, 1939,* 1:685–93; Roosevelt, *Public Papers and Addresses,* 8:464–78.

610 Notes to pages 321-26

31 Roosevelt, *Public Papers and Addresses,* 8:510; memorandum Early to
Roosevelt, September 7, 1939, telegram Roosevelt to the vice-president
and ten others, September 13, 1939, Official File 1561, Roosevelt
Papers; Early diary, September 7, 1939, September 13, 1939, Early
Papers.

32 William E. Borah, "Retain the Arms Embargo," *Vital Speeches of the
Day,* October 1, 1939, pp. 741-43; Roosevelt, *F.D.R.: His Personal
Letters,* 2:921.

33 Transcript, "Conference of the President with Democratic and
Republican Leaders Preceding the Opening of a Special Session of the
Congress, Executive Offices of the White House, September 20, 1939,
3.05 P.M.," Official File 1561, Roosevelt Papers. Those attending the
meeting were Roosevelt, Early, Garner, McCormack, Hull, Barkley,
McNary, Pittman, Byrnes, Austin, Minton, Rayburn, Martin, Mapes,
Bloom, Landon, and Knox.

34 Ibid., pp. 1-3, 58-61.

35 Ibid., pp. 10, 48-49, 56.

36 Ibid., pp. 10-55.

37 Ibid., pp. 62-70.

38 Roosevelt, *Public Papers and Addresses,* 8:512-22.

39 Hull, *Memoirs of Cordell Hull,* 1:694-95; Pittman to Charles F. Boss,
Jr., September 25, 1939, Senate Foreign Relations Committee Papers,
Record Group 46; card from Senate Committee on Foreign Relations to
Theodore Green, September 28, 1939, Green Papers; La Follette to
Rachel La Follette, September 25, 1939, La Follette Family Papers;
Roosevelt, *Public Papers and Addresses,* 8:524.

40 *Congressional Record,* 76th Congress, 2d sess., 1939, 85:52-69; Hull
Memoirs of Cordell Hull, 1:694-95.

41 *Congressional Digest,* October 1939, pp. 244-46; *Congressional
Record,* 76th Congress, 2d sess., 1939, *Appendix,* 85:76-77;
Congressional Record, 76th Congress, 2d sess., 1939, 85:490-92.

42 Memorandum Matthew F. McGuire to Roosevelt, September 21, 1939,
President's Secretary's File, Neutrality folder, Roosevelt Papers;
Moffat diary, September 23 and 24, 1939; *Congressional Record,* 76th
Congress, 2d sess., 1939, *Appendix,* 85:506; Barbour to William Allen
White, November 3, 1939, White Papers.

43 George W. Norris, "American Neutrality," *Vital Speeches of the Day,*
November 1, 1939, pp. 62-64; clipping *Washington Post,* October 4,
1939, Norris Papers; Norris to Paul F. Good, October 12, 1939, Norris
Papers.

44 Telegram Roosevelt to Borah, July 7, 1938, President's Personal File
2358, Roosevelt Papers; Cora Rubin to Harry F. Klinefelter, July 28,
1938, telegram Borah to International News Service, September 1,
1939, Borah Papers.

45 Clipping *Washington Times-Herald,* September 12, 1939, Nye Papers; lists of senators attending meetings in Johnson's office on October 2, 3, 6, 13, 16, 24, Johnson Papers; La Follette to Rachel La Follette, September 23, 24, 1939, La Follette Family Papers; Vandenberg diary, October 27, 1939, Vandenberg Papers.

46 Johnson to Hiram W. Johnson, Jr., September 24, 1939, Johnson Papers; La Follette to Rachel La Follette, September 23, 30, 1939, La Follette Family Papers.

47 La Follette to Rachel La Follette, September 24, 1939, La Follette Family Papers; telegram Gerald W. Movius to Associated Press, September 13, 1939, Nye to Mrs. Bennett Champ Clark, January 14, 1941, Nye Papers; Vandenberg to Howard C. Lawrence, October 7, 1939, Vandenberg diary, October 27, 1939, Vandenberg Papers; Johnson to Clark and La Follette, October 14, 1939, Johnson Papers.

48 Borah to Jess Hawley, October 31, 1939, Borah Papers; Johnson to Hiram W. Johnson, Jr., September 24, 1939, Johnson Papers.

49 R. Walton Moore to Early, September 21, 1939, Official File 1561, Roosevelt Papers; Borchrd to Nye, September 25, 1939, Nye Papers.

50 Bennett Champ Clark, "Con—Should the Congress Amend the Present Neutrality Law?," *Congressional Digest,* October 1939, p. 249; clipping *Chicago Daily Times,* September 15, 1939, Nye Papers; *Congressional Record,* 76th Congress, 2d sess., 1939, *Appendix,* 85:562-63.

51 Vandenberg diary, September 15, 1939, Vandenberg Papers.

52 Charles A. Lindbergh, *The Wartime Journals of Charles A. Lindbergh,* pp. 248-76; C. B. Allen, "The Facts about Lindbergh," *Saturday Evening Post,* December 28, 1940, p. 12; C. B. Allen, "The Day F.D.R. Tried to Bribe Lindbergh," *Pathway,* November 1970, pp. 7-8; Charles A. Lindbergh, "What America's Decision Should Be," *Vital Speeches of the Day,* November 1, 1939, pp. 57-59; interview with Charles A. Lindbergh, Washington, D.C., June 7, 1972; Wayne S. Cole, *Charles A. Lindbergh and the Battle against American Intervention in World War II* (New York and London: Harcourt Brace Jovanovich, 1974), pp. 70-75, 91-92.

53 Confidential print Lothian to Halifax, January 9, 1940, and enclosed "Report on the Debate in Congress on the Neutrality Bill," January 9, 1940, F.O. 414/277, pp. 17-25, British Foreign Office Records; "Gallup and Fortune Polls," *Public Opinion Quarterly* 4 (1940): 105-12; memorandum by Joseph C. Green, September 19, 1939, File Number 811.04418/696, Department of State Records, Record Group 59; clipping *Devils Lake* (N.D.) *Journal,* September 25, 1939, Nye Papers; James W. Wadsworth to F. M. O'Connell, October 11, 1939, Wadsworth Family Papers; Vandenberg diary, October 27, 1939, Vandenberg Papers.

54 *Congressional Record,* 76th Congress, 2d sess., 1939, 85:233-37, 1024-25.

55 Ibid., 85:1344–45, 1353–56, 1389; Roosevelt, *Public Papers and Addresses,* 8:559–64.
56 Chamberlain to Roosevelt, November 8, 1939, Roosevelt to Sir Alan Lascelles, November 13, 1939, President's Secretary's File, Great Britain 1939 folder, Roosevelt Papers.
57 Comments of Hon. David I. Walsh on passage of neutrality bill, Washington, D.C., October 27, 1939, Walsh Papers; Vandenberg diary, October 27, 1939, Vandenberg Papers; Borah to August Rosqvist, October 30, 1939, Borah to Jess Hawley, October 31, 1939, Borah Papers.

Chapter 23

1   Henry A. Wallace diary, February 18, 1940, Henry A. Wallace Papers.
2   Franklin D. Roosevelt, *F.D.R.: His Personal Letters, 1928–1945,* 1:571, 638.
3   Ibid., 1:733–34.
4   Richard N. Current, "Hamilton Fish: Crusading Isolationist," in *Public Men in and out of Office,* ed. J. T. Salter (Chapel Hill: University of North Carolina Press, 1946), pp. 210–24; *Current Biography* 2 (1941): 278–80; "Hamilton Fish of New York," *Social Justice,* March 17, 1941, pp. 11–12.
5   Hamilton Fish, *FDR: The Other Side of the Coin: How We Were Tricked into World War II,* pp. 79–91. Department of State records on the Fish mission are in File Number 811.0312 Fish, Hamilton/1ff. I am indebted to Mr. Terrance P. Walbert for bringing this file and its location to my attention.
6   Fish, *FDR,* pp. 92–99.
7   Roosevelt, *F.D.R.: Personal Letters,* 2:951.
8   Fish, *FDR,* pp. 100–14.
9   Davis to Roosevelt, October 11, 1939, Verne Marshall Papers. Copies of this letter and the letter from Davis to Roosevelt, October 12, 1939, are also in the Post-Presidential Individual File, Hoover Papers. See also memorandum of conversation between Roosevelt, Davis, and Berle, September 15, 1939, Berle diary. An account of this whole Davis episode was also related in an interview by the author with Verne Marshall, Cedar Rapids, Iowa, December 19, 1948.
10 Memorandum of conversation between Roosevelt, Davis, and Berle, September 15, 1939, Berle diary.
11 Roosevelt to Berle, September 15, 1939, Berle to Roosevelt, September 18, 25, 1939, Berle Papers.
12 Davis to Roosevelt, October 11, 1939, Marshall Papers; memorandum by Berle of conversation between Davis, Walter A. Jones, Moffat, and Berle, October 12, 1939, Berle diary.

13 Davis to Roosevelt, October 11, 1939, Marshall Papers. For another account of the Davis mission with a different emphasis, see O. John Rogge, *The Official German Report,* pp. 238–58.

14 Davis to Roosevelt, October 11, 1939, Marshall Papers.

15 Ibid.

16 Memorandum by Berle of conversation between Davis, Jones, Moffat, and Berle, October 12, 1939, Berle diary; Moffat to Berle, October 12, 1939, Moffat diaries; Davis to Roosevelt, October 12, 1939, Marshall Papers.

17 Berle diary, October 6, 1939, memorandum by Berle of conversation between Davis, Jones, Moffat, and Berle, October 12, 1939, Berle diary, October 16, 1939.

18 Roosevelt, *F.D.R.: Personal Letters,* 2:935–36, 938–39; Early diary, October 14, 1939, Early Papers.

19 *New York Times,* October 8, 1939, p. 39; Thomas to Roosevelt, October 8, 1939, President's Personal File 4840, radiogram Villard to Roosevelt, October 20, 1939, President's Personal File 2178, Roosevelt Papers; memorandum by Berle of conversation between Lewis and Berle, October 23, 1939, Berle diary, Berle diary, February 27, 1940.

20 Interview with Verne Marshall, Cedar Rapids, Iowa, December 19, 1948; Davis to Hoover, October 18, 1940, and enclosed letters, Post-Presidential Individual File, Hoover Papers; Marshall to Raymond Moley, November 11, 1940, Marshall to D. M. Linnard, January 21, 1941, Marshall to Alf M. Landon, January 25, 1941, Marshall to Hamilton Fish, February 21, 1941, Marshall to B. B. Hickenlooper, December 16, 1945, Marshall to Karl E. Mundt, December 23, 1948, Marshall to Charles C. Tansill, April 11, 1951, Marshall Papers. The account in William Stevenson, *A Man Called Intrepid: The Secret War* (New York and London: Harcourt Brace Jovanovich, 1976), pp. 294–95, implies that the British Security Coordination under William Stephenson was responsible for the death of Davis.

21 Telegram Lothian to Halifax, February 2, 1940, F.O. 800/324, pp. 137–39, Halifax Papers.

22 Department of State, *Foreign Relations of the United States: Diplomatic Papers, 1940,* 1:1–4.

23 Cordell Hull, *The Memoirs of Cordell Hull,* 1:737–38; Orville H. Bullitt, ed., *For the President, Personal and Secret: Correspondence between Franklin D. Roosevelt and William C. Bullitt,* pp. 403–5.

24 Wilson diary, February 12, 1940, Wilson Papers.

25 Minute from C. A. Warner to Mr. Balfour, March 3, 1940, F.O. 371/24251, p. 63, British Foreign Office Records.

26 Benjamin Welles, with the assistance of Dr. William M. Franklin, is presently writing a biography of his father based on research in his personal and official papers and records.

27 Department of State, *Foreign Relations, 1940,* 1:4.

28 For an excellent scholarly study of the Welles mission, see Stanley E. Hilton, "The Welles Mission to Europe, February–March 1940: Illusion or Realism?," *Journal of American History* 58 (June 1971): 93–120. Welles report on his mission is in Department of State, *Foreign Relations, 1940,* 1:21–117. See also Sumner Welles, *The Time for Decision,* pp. 73–147.

29 Robert E. Sherwood, *Roosevelt and Hopkins: An Intimate History,* pp. 49–50, 126.

30 Franklin D. Roosevelt, *The Public Papers and Addresses of Franklin D. Roosevelt,* 9:102–4.

31 Ibid., 9:111–12.

32 Ibid., 9:634–39.

33 *Washington Post,* December 31, 1940, p. 1; *Vital Speeches of the Day,* January 15, 1941, pp. 203–5; clipping *New York Post,* January 11, 1941, America First Committee Papers; *Vital Speeches of the Day,* June 1, 1941, pp. 489–91.

34 Telegram Wheeler to Roosevelt, September 2, 1943, President's Personal File 723, Roosevelt Papers.

35 *Chicago Tribune,* December 12, 1940, p. 1; *New York Times,* December 12, 1940, p. 18, December 14, 1940, p. 10; Wood to Howard, December 14, 1940, Wood Papers; clipping *Chicago Sunday Times,* February 2, 1941, mimeographed text of address by Wood over MBS, "Our Foreign Policy Today," July 7, 1941, America First Papers.

36 Lindbergh statement read before Senate Committee on Foreign Relations, February 6, 1941, Lindbergh address at America First rally in New York, April 23, 1941, Lindbergh to Wood, October 27, 1941, Lindbergh to John T. Flynn, January 6, 1942, Lindbergh to Paul Palmer, July 6, 1942, Lindbergh Papers.

37 Mimeographed address by Nye, "No Further without War," broadcast over NBC, May 3, 1941, clipping *San Francisco Chronicle,* June 25, 1941, *A.F.C. Bulletin* (New York), May 31, 1941, June 7, 1941, America First Papers; Bowles to Hoover, November 28, 1941, Post-Presidential Individual File, Hoover Papers.

38 Wayne S. Cole, *America First: The Battle against Intervention, 1940–1941* (Madison: University of Wisconsin Press, 1953), pp. 38–39, 42–43; Frederick J. Libby to Lindbergh, July 29, 1941, America First Papers.

39 Clipping *Chicago Daily News,* January 31, 1941, America First Papers.

Chapter 24

1 *Congressional Record,* 75th Congress, 1st sess., 1937, 81:8585–86. The recollections were voiced by many in North Dakota and elsewhere when

the author was doing research for a book on Nye more than twenty years after the Senate speech quoted here.

2 Norris to Alice P. Fong, January 8, 1938, Norris Papers.

3 Print of Senate Resolution 166 attached to Hull to Pittman, July 21, 1939, File Number 711.942/174, Department of State Records, Record Group 59.

4 On independent iron and steel producers, see F. C. Dezendorf, Jr., to Tom Connally, June 19, 1936, File Number 811.6511/30, Department of State Records, Record Group 59; and Roger L. Wensley to Eugene J. Keogh, May 8, 1937, House of Representatives Committee on Foreign Affairs Records, Record Group 233. On cotton export interests, see George Sealy to Marvin McIntyre, May 22, 1939, President's Personal File 6692, Roosevelt Papers; and telegram William D. Felder to Pittman, December 16, 1939, Senate Foreign Relations Committee Records, Record Group 46. For various perspectives on sanctions against Japan advanced in and to the Department of State and diplomatic service in 1939, see Department of State, *Foreign Relations of the United States, 1939,* 3:475–558.

5 Roosevelt to Hull, May 17, 1937, Kopplemann to Roosevelt, May 22, 1937, unsigned White House memorandum, May 24, 1937, "Memorandum Concerning Proposed Scrap Steel Embargo," [by Donald R. Richberg], May 25, 1937, Official File 342, Roosevelt Papers; Hull to Lister Hill, May 18, 1937, Claude A. Swanson to Hill, June 16, 1937, Malin Craig to Hill, June 25, 1937, H.R. 6278, 75th Congress, Papers Supporting House Bills and Resolutions, Record Group 233.

6 For a history of the pressure group, see Donald J. Friedman, *The Road From Isolation: The Campaign of the American Committee for Non-participation in Japanese Aggression, 1938–1941* (Cambridge, Mass.: East Asian Research Center, Harvard University, 1968).

7 For a biography of Pittman, see Fred L. Israel, *Nevada's Key Pittman* (Lincoln: University of Nebraska Press, 1963). See also Wayne S. Cole, "Senator Key Pittman and American Neutrality Policies, 1933–1940," *Mississippi Valley Historical Review* 46 (March 1960): 644–62.

8 Franklin D. Roosevelt, *F.D.R.: His Personal Letters, 1928–1945,* 2:873; Price to Pittman, March 28, 1939, Hull Papers; Carlton Savage to Hull, April 20, 1939, File Number 811.04418/394, Department of State Records, Record Group 59; Pittman to Stimson, April 30, 1939, Senate Foreign Relations Committee Records, Record Group 46.

9 Sam D. McReynolds to Hull, January 31, 1939, and enclosed print of H.R. 3419 introduced on January 30, 1939, Hull to McReynolds, February 13, 1939, File Number 894.24/589, Department of State Records, Record Group 59.

10 Price to Pittman, April 12, 1939, Senate Foreign Relations Committee Records, Record Group 46; print of S.J. Res. 123, 76th Congress, April 27, 1939 and July 11, 1939, Papers Supporting Senate Bills and

Resolutions, Record Group 46; print of S.J. Res. 143, 76th Congress, June 1, 1939, Schwellenbach Papers.

11 Hull to Pittman, July 21, 1939, S.J. Res. 123, 76th Congress, Papers Supporting Senate Bills and Resolutions, Record Group 46.

12 On Vandenberg's career and personality, see Arthur H. Vandenberg, *The Private Papers of Senator Vandenberg;* C. David Tompkins, *Senator Arthur H. Vandenberg: The Evolution of a Modern Republican, 1884-1945* (Lansing: Michigan State University Press, 1970); Ray Tucker, "Marked Man," *Collier's,* March 9, 1935, pp. 26, 38; *News-Week,* February 22, 1936, pp. 29-30; *Time,* October 2, 1939, pp. 13-17; Jonathan Mitchell, "Vandenberg: Heroes' Child," *New Republic,* April 8, 1940, pp. 461-63.

13 For example, see Vandenberg to Albert F. May, Jr., February 2, 1940, Vandenberg Papers.

14 Print of S. Res. 166, July 18, 1939, File Number 711.942/174, Department of State Records, Record Group 59.

15 Hull to Pittman, July 21, 1939, File Number 711.942/174, Department of State Records, Record Group 59; R. Walton Moore to William C. Bullitt, July 25, 1939, Moore Papers; Cordell Hull, *The Memoirs of Cordell Hull,* 1:636-37.

16 Castle to Vandenberg, July 30, 1939, Vandenberg Papers.

17 Vandenberg to Castle, August 1, 1939, Vandenberg Papers.

18 Department of State, *Foreign Relations, 1939,* 3:568-69; Vandenberg to Hull, August 17, 1939, Vandenberg Papers.

19 Department of State, *Foreign Relations, 1939,* 3:573-76, 578-80.

20 "American Policy in the Far East: Lippmann-Vandenberg Controversy," over initials of M.M.H. [prepared by Miss R. Bacon of Far Eastern Affairs, Department of State], February 9, 1940, File Number 711.942/573, Department of State Records, Record Group 59.

21 Vandenberg to Drew Pearson, March 12, 1940, Vandenberg Papers.

22 Price to Pittman, October 30, 1939, November 1, 1939, Senate Foreign Relations Committee Records, Record Group 46; Price to Green, November 1, 1939, Green Papers.

23 Telegram Price to Pittman, November 7, 1939, telegram Pittman to Stimson, November 9, 1939, Stimson to Pittman, November 20, 1939, and enclosed "Confidential Notes on Luncheon Given by the Hon. Henry L. Stimson on November 9, 1939, at the Lunch Club, 63 Wall Street," telegram Pittman to Vincent Sheehan, January 24, 1940, Pittman to Raymond Leslie Buell, February 1, 1940, Senate Foreign Relations Committee Records, Record Group 46; *New York Times,* November 26, 1939, p. 1.

24 Department of State, *Foreign Relations: Japan, 1931-1941,* 1:595-96, 2:202-10; Department of State, *Foreign Relations, 1938,* 3:618.

25 Moore to Hull, May 8, 13, 1940, Moore Papers.

26 *Congressional Record,* 76th Congress, 3d sess., 1940, 86:6860–62.
27 Ibid., 86:7843, 7933–35. Eighty senators voted yea. Among the sixteen absent and not voting were Senators Clark of Missouri, Frazier, Lundeen, McCarran, and Nye.
28 Ibid., 86:8899–8903, 8984.
29 Department of State, *Foreign Relations: Japan, 1931–1941,* 2:211–22.
30 Henry Morgenthau, *From the Morgenthau Diaries,* vol. 2, *Years of Urgency, 1938–1941,* pp. 348–55; Ickes to Roosevelt, October 17, 1940, President's Secretary's File, Interior—Ickes, 1940 folder, Roosevelt Papers; Stimson diary, #30, July 19, 26, 1940, September 19, 1940; Morgenthau presidential diaries, August 16, 1940.
31 Department of State, *Foreign Relations: Japan, 1931–1941,* 2:222–29; memorandum from Eleanor Roosevelt to Roosevelt, November 12, 1940, Roosevelt to Eleanor Roosevelt, November 13, 1940, President's Secretary's File, Eleanor Roosevelt folder, Roosevelt Papers; Roosevelt, *F.D.R.: Personal Letters,* 2:1077.

Chapter 25

1 This general interpretive theme is advanced in different terms in Irwin F. Gellman, "The New Deal's Use of Nazism in Latin America," in *Perspectives in American Diplomacy: Essays on Europe, Latin America, China, and the Cold War,* ed. Jules Davids (New York: Arno Press, 1976), pp. 178–207. I gratefully acknowledge with much thanks Dr. Gellman's contributions to my thinking on the Latin American aspect of the subject, both in the chapter cited above and in many thoughtful conversations. See also Alton Frye, *Nazi Germany and the American Hemisphere, 1933–1941* (New Haven, Conn., and London: Yale University Press, 1967), and Gerald K. Haines, "Under the Eagle's Wing: The Franklin Roosevelt Administration Forges an American Hemisphere," *Diplomatic History* 1 (Fall 1977): 373–88.
2 On the history of the Monroe Doctrine, see Dexter Perkins, *A History of the Monroe Doctrine* (Boston: Little, Brown & Company, 1955) and Perkins's other books and articles on the subject.
3 *Congressional Record,* 70th Congress, 1st sess., 1928, 69:933–34; Norris to J. Nevin Sayre, February 4, 1928, Norris to W. G. Lewis, March 27, 1928, Norris Papers; Borah to Ramón Grau San Martín, October 6, 1933, Borah Papers.
4 Borah to Edwin M. Borchard, February 6, 1935, Hull to Key Pittman, February 12, 1935, Borah to Harvey O. Yoder, March 14, 1935, Borah to J. B. Malone, September 19, 1935, Borah Papers.
5 Johnson to Hiram W. Johnson, Jr., March 21, 1932, Johnson Papers; Albert F. Coyle to Cutting, July 14, 1934, January 19, 1935, Bronson

M. Cutting Papers; Coyle to Oscar E. Erickson and Oscar J. Butten-
dahl, May 20, 1936, Nye Papers; *Congressional Record,* 74th Cong.,
2d sess., 1936, 80:10058; Nye to Hull, August 17, 1939, Livesey
memorandum, August 22, 1939, File Number 832.51/1561, Department
of State Records, Record Group 59.

6 The best scholarly history of Roosevelt's policies toward Latin
America, based on extensive research, is Irwin F. Gellman, *Good
Neighbor Diplomacy: United States Policies in Latin America,
1933-1945* (Baltimore, Md.: Johns Hopkins University Press, 1979).

7 Department of State, *Foreign Relations of the United States, 1936,*
5:3-34; Edgar B. Nixon, ed., *Franklin D. Roosevelt and Foreign
Affairs,* 3:516-21; Cordell Hull, *The Memoirs of Cordell Hull,*
1:493-503; Sumner Welles, *Time for Decision,* pp. 204-8; Laurence
Duggan, *The Americas: The Search for Hemisphere Security* (New
York: Henry Holt and Company, 1949), pp. 71-72.

8 Department of State, *Foreign Relations, 1938,* 5:1-88; Hull, *Memoirs
of Cordell Hull,* 1:601-11; Landon to William Allen White, November
18, 1938, White Papers; Adolf A. Berle, *Navigating the Rapids,
1918-1971: From the Papers of Adolf A. Berle,* pp. 191-93; Duggan,
The Americas, p. 73; Welles, *Time for Decision,* pp. 208-9.

9 Department of State, *Foreign Relations, 1939,* 5:15-41; Welles, *Time
for Decision,* pp. 210-14; Hull, *Memoirs of Cordell Hull,* 1:688-91;
Duggan, *The Americas,* pp. 82-83.

10 Hull, *Memoirs of Cordell Hull,* 1:813-30; Duggan, *The Americas,*
pp. 83-84; Welles, *Time for Decision,* pp. 214-16; Berle, *Navigating
the Rapids,* pp. 328-31.

Chapter 26

1 Winston S. Churchill, *The Second World War,* vol. 2, *Their Finest
Hour,* p. 118.

2 Hadley Cantril and Mildred Strunk, eds., *Public Opinion,
1935-1946* (Princeton, N.J.: Princeton University Press, 1951),
pp. 970-76.

3 Ibid., pp. 973-76.

4 Walter Johnson, *William Allen White's America* (New York: Henry
Holt and Company, 1947); White to Walter W. Liggett, April 9, 1932,
White to Lewis Gannett, April 18, 1932, White to Marguerita Villard,
April 30, 1932, White to Mrs. C. M. Anderson, June 24, 1932, White
to Clyde Reed, November 7, 1932, White to Harold Ickes, May 23,
1933, White to Allan Nevins, May 24, 1934, White to Judson King,
August 30, 1940, William Allen White Papers.

5 White "To Whom It May Concern," March 17, 1932, Clark M. Eichelberger to White, March 28, 1932, telegram James T. Shotwell to

White, September 27, 1939, White to Frank Knox, October 23, 1939, Hull to White, October 31, 1939, White to Hull, November 6, 1939, Roosevelt to White, November 8, 1939, William Allen White Papers; Clark M. Eichelberger, *Organizing for Peace: A Personal History of the Founding of the United Nations* (New York: Harper & Row, 1977), pp. 106–11.

6 Roosevelt to White, December 14, 1939, President's Personal File 1196, Roosevelt Papers; Franklin D. Roosevelt, *F.D.R.: His Personal Letters, 1928–1945,* 2:967–68.

7 White to Sherwood, December 27, 1939, Roosevelt to White, January 23, 1940, William Allen White Papers; White to Roosevelt, December 22, 1939, President's Personal File 1196, Roosevelt Papers.

8 Rexford G. Tugwell diary, February 6, [1940], Rexford G. Tugwell Papers.

9 For a sympathetic scholarly history of the White Committee by a historian who was a member of the organization, see Walter Johnson, *The Battle against Isolation* (Chicago: University of Chicago Press, 1944). See also Eichelberger, *Organizing for Peace,* pp. 119–45; Margaret Olson to White, December 9, 1940, F. R. Coudert to White, December 14, 1940, William Allen White Papers; materials dated April 15, 1941 and May 1, 1941, Official File 4230, Roosevelt Papers.

10 For biographies of Stimson, see Elting E. Morison, *Turmoil and Tradition: A Study of the Life and Times of Henry L. Stimson* (Boston: Houghton Mifflin Company, 1960); and Richard N. Current, *Secretary Stimson: A Study in Statecraft* (New Brunswick, N.J.: Rutgers University Press, 1954). For Stimson's memoirs, see Henry L. Stimson and McGeorge Bundy, *On Active Service in Peace and War.* On Knox, see Steven M. Mark, "An American Interventionist: Frank Knox and United States Foreign Relations" (Ph.D. diss., University of Maryland, 1977).

11 Stimson and Bundy, *On Active Service,* pp. 297–305, 310–24; Roosevelt, *F.D.R.: Personal Letters,* 1:320–21, 2:1041–42; Max Freedman, annot., *Roosevelt and Frankfurter: Their Correspondence, 1928–1945,* pp. 521–30; Morgenthau presidential diaries, April 18, 29, May 13, 14, June 3, 1940; Stimson diary, May 8, June 25, 1940; Stimson to Roosevelt, June 1, 1940, President's Personal File 20, press release, June 20, 1940, Official File 2315, Roosevelt Papers; Stimson to Hoover, June 19, 1940, Post-Presidential Individual file, Hoover Papers.

12 Knox to Mrs. Annie Knox, June 25, 1934, Knox to Hull, October 12, 1937, Knox Papers; Knox to Hull, December 15, 1937, Hull Papers; Knox to William Allen White, September 25, 29, 1939, October 18, 1939, Landon to White, October 3, 1939, White Papers; Ickes to Roosevelt, September 18, 1939, President's Secretary's File, Interior Department—Ickes, 1937–1939 folder, Knox to Roosevelt, October 4,

1939, Official File 1561, telegram Stephen Early to Roosevelt, October 6, 1939, President's Personal File 4083, Roosevelt Papers; Harold L. Ickes, *The Secret Diary of Harold L. Ickes,* vol. 3, *The Lowering Clouds, 1939–1941,* pp. 12, 21, 23–24.

13 [Frank Knox], "Memorandum of Conversation with President Roosevelt on December 10, 1939, at the White House," December 12, 1939, Knox Papers; Knox to Roosevelt, December 15, 1939, Roosevelt to Knox, December 29, 1939, President's Secretary's File, Frank Knox, 1940–41 folder, Roosevelt Papers; Roosevelt, *F.D.R.: Personal Letters,* 2:975–77.

14 Knox to Roosevelt, January 17, 1940, March 22, 1940, May 18, 21, 27, 1940, President's Secretary's File, Frank Knox, 1940–41 folder, Knox to Roosevelt, June 7, 1940, President's Personal File 6691, press release, June 20, 1940, Official File 2315, Roosevelt Papers; Knox to Mrs. Knox, January 28, 1940, June 15, 1940, Knox Papers; Knox to White, May 28, 1940, William Allen White Papers.

15 White to Claude Pepper, July 8, 1940, William Allen White Papers; *Congressional Record,* 76th Congress, 3d sess., 1940, 86:9341, 9411–12.

16 For a detailed history of the destroyer deal, see Philip Goodhart, *Fifty Ships That Saved the World: The Foundation of the Anglo-American Alliance* (Garden City, N.Y.: Doubleday and Company, 1965).

17 Francis L. Loewenheim, Harold D. Langley, and Manfred Jonas, eds., *Roosevelt and Churchill: Their Secret Wartime Correspondence,* pp. 94–95; Department of State, *Foreign Relations of the United States, 1940,* 3:49–50; Roosevelt, *F.D.R.: Personal Letters,* 2:1036; Hull, *Memoirs of Cordell Hull,* 1:831–32.

18 Telegram for Prime Minister to Governments of Canada, Australia, New Zealand, and the Union of South Africa, June 7, 1940, F.O. 371/24239, British Foreign Office Records; Loewenheim, Langley, and Jonas, eds., *Roosevelt and Churchill,* p. 106; George R. I. to Roosevelt, June 26, 1940, President's Secretary's File, King and Queen folder, Roosevelt Papers; Cordell Hull, *The Memoirs of Cordell Hull,* 1:831–41; Johnson, *Battle against Isolation,* pp. 98–117; Mark Lincoln Chadwin, *The Hawks of World War II* (Chapel Hill: University of North Carolina Press, 1968), pp. 74–108.

19 Department of State, *Foreign Relations, 1940,* 3:58–59.

20 Ibid., 3:61–67; Harold D. Smith to Roosevelt, March 20, 1940, Official File 212, Roosevelt Papers.

21 Department of State, *Foreign Relations, 1940,* 3:58–71; telegram White to Roosevelt, August 11, 1940, President's Personal File 1196, Roosevelt Papers.

22 Robert H. Jackson to Knox, August 17, 1940, H.R.S. [Stark] to Roosevelt, August 21, 1940, September 3, 1940, President's Secretary's File, Corres. on 50 Destroyers & Naval Bases folder, Roosevelt Papers.

23 Hull, *Memoirs of Cordell Hull,* 1:834–43; Ben V. Cohen to Marguerite

Le Hand, August 12, 1940, and enclosure, Jackson to Roosevelt, August 27, 1940, Hull to Roosevelt, August 31, 1940, and enclosures, Roosevelt to Hull, September 2, 1940, President's Secretary's File, Corres. on 50 Destroyers & Naval Bases folder, Roosevelt Papers; Department of State, *Foreign Relations, 1940,* 3:73–75; Stimson diary, September 7, 1940.

24 Churchill, *Their Finest Hour,* pp. 403–4.

25 Vandenberg to George W. Welsh, August 19, 1940, Vandenberg Papers.

26 Walsh to Roosevelt, August 19, 1940, Walsh Papers; Roosevelt, *F.D.R.: Personal Letters,* 2:1056–58.

27 *New York Times,* August 26, 1940, p. 8.

28 Henry Cabot Lodge, Jr., *"The Drift toward War"* (Chicago: America First Committee, September 25, 1940), in America First Committee Papers.

29 Early to Roosevelt, August 16, 1940, Early Papers; Stimson and Bundy, *On Active Service,* p. 356.

30 Robert E. Sherwood, *Roosevelt and Hopkins: An Intimate Biography,* pp. 156–57; *Who's Who in America, 1940–1941,* p. 580; Clark to Roosevelt, September 13, 1933, December 1, [1934], May 21, 1940, President's Personal File 1958, Roosevelt Papers.

31 Clark to Roosevelt, May 16, 21, 1940, Roosevelt to Clark, May 18, 1940, President's Personal File 1958, Roosevelt Papers; Roosevelt, *F.D.R.: Personal Letters,* 2:1026.

32 Harry [S. Hooker] to Marguerite Le Hand, May 23, 1940, President's Personal File 482, Roosevelt Papers; telegram Clark to Fiorello La Guardia, June 5, 1940, La Guardia Papers; Wadsworth to W. G. Robinson, August 22, 1945, Wadsworth Family Papers.

33 Wadsworth to La Guardia, July 18, 1940, La Guardia Papers; Wadsworth to Wendell L. Willkie, July 24, 1940, Wadsworth Papers; Franklin D. Roosevelt, *The Public Papers and Addresses of Franklin D. Roosevelt,* 9:295, 317–22, 337–40; Stimson and Bundy, *On Active Service,* pp. 345–47; Charles Joseph Errico, "Foreign Affairs and the Presidential Election of 1940," (Ph.D. diss., University of Maryland, 1973), pp. 239, 256–58; Cantril and Strunk, eds., *Public Opinion, 1935–1946,* pp. 458–62.

34 John Nevin Sayre to Oswald Garrison Villard, August 9, 1940, Villard to Sayre, August 10, 1940, Oswald Garrison Villard Papers; Robert A. Taft to Wendell L. Willkie, August 13, 1940, Taft Papers; La Follette to "Dearest Ones," August 13, 1940, La Follette Family Papers.

35 Norris to G. A. Moon, July 23, 1940, John P. Robertson to Everett T. Winter, September 5, 1940, Norris Papers.

36 Norman Thomas to Roosevelt, July 24, 1940, August 5, 1940, August 15, 1940, Roosevelt to Thomas, July 31, 1940, August 12, 1940, August 19, 1940, President's Personal File 4840, Roosevelt Papers.

37 Vic Donahey to Roosevelt, August 1, 1940, Roosevelt to Donahey, August 3, 1940, Roosevelt to Barkley, August 3, 1940, Official File 1413, Roosevelt Papers.

38 La Follette to "Dear Friend," August 1940, La Follette to "Dear Ones," August 9, 1940, La Follette Family Papers; Taft to Willkie, August 13, 1940, Taft Papers; Walsh to Robert Norton, August 29, 1940, Walsh Papers.

39 *Congressional Record,* 76th Congress, 3d sess., 1940, 86:10819, 10807.

40 Burton K. Wheeler, "Marching down the Road to War," *Vital Speeches of the Day,* September 1, 1940, pp. 689–92; Johnson to Hiram W. Johnson, Jr., September 1, 1940, Johnson Papers.

41 *Congressional Record,* 76th Congress, 3d sess., 1940, 86:11748–49; Stimson diary, September 9, 1940.

42 *Congressional Record,* 76th Congress, 3d sess., 1940, 86:11142, 11754–55, 12160–61, 12227, 12290. For a poignant expression of Nye's growing awareness of and reaction to those changing images, see ibid., 86:10804–8.

43 Ibid., 86:12156–60.

44 For a detailed history of the America First Committee based on the records of the organization, see Wayne S. Cole, *America First: The Battle against Intervention, 1940–1941* (Madison: University of Wisconsin Press, 1953).

45 Ibid., pp. 10–14; R. Douglas Stuart, Jr. to the author, February 16, 1948, August 31, 1950; Kingman Brewster, Jr., to the author, March 28, 1948; *Chicago Tribune,* September 5, 1940, p. 3. Among the students active in Stuart's group at Yale were Kingman Brewster, Jr., later president of Yale University and United States ambassador to Great Britain; Potter Stewart, later associate justice of the United States Supreme Court; R. Sargent Shriver, Jr., later director of the Peace Corps, United States ambassador to France, and Democratic candidate for vice-president of the United States; and Gerald R. Ford, later president of the United States.

46 For a scholarly article on General Wood, see Justus D. Doenecke, "General Robert E. Wood: The Evolution of a Conservative," *Journal of the Illinois State Historical Society* 71 (August 1978): 162–75. See also *Current Biography* 2 (May 1941):88–90; "General Robert E. Wood, President," *Fortune* 17 (May 1938): 104–10; Wood to Roosevelt, February 24, 1934, October 24, 1934, President's Personal File 1365, Roosevelt Papers; Wood to Borah, May 19, 1936, Borah Papers; interviews with R. Douglas Stuart, Jr., San Francisco, California, April 6, 1949, May 6, 1949.

47 *Future: The Magazine for Young Men,* March 1941, p. 6; Wood to Isaac A. Pennypacker, July 15, 1941, Katrina McCormick to Page Hufty, August 4, 1941, America First Papers; interview with Stuart,

April 6, 1949; interview with Harry C. Schnibbe, Denver, Colorado, June 21, 1949.
48 Cole, *America First,* pp. 19–23.
49 Ibid., pp. 31–33; Files of Contributors of Larger Amounts, F. H. Camphausen to Miss Matz, December 11, 1941, America First Audit Reports, July 29, 1940 to February 7, 1942, and list of small contributors, America First Papers. The America First Papers also include financial statements of various local chapters.
50 Cole, *America First,* pp. 26–31; Wayne S. Cole, "America First and the South, 1940–1941," *Journal of Southern History* 22 (February 1956): 36–47.
51 *Chicago Tribune,* September 5, 1940, p. 3.
52 Stuart to Mrs. Burton K. Wheeler, August 13, 1940, clipping *Chicago Tribune,* November 13, 1940, America First Papers.

Chapter 27

1 For scholarly histories of the role of foreign policy issues in the presidential election of 1940, see Robert A. Divine, *Foreign Policy and U.S. Presidential Elections, 1940–1948* (New York: New Viewpoints, 1974), pp. 3–89; and Charles Joseph Errico, "Foreign Affairs and the Presidential Election of 1940" (Ph.D. diss., University of Maryland, 1973).
2 Morgenthau presidential diaries, January 24, 1940, p. 420.
3 Henry Breckinridge to Frederick R. Coudert, July 20, 1939, Henry Breckinridge Papers.
4 Morgenthau presidential diaries, January 24, 1940, pp. 419–20.
5 Ickes to Anna Boettiger, June 1, 1949, Ickes Papers; Eleanor Roosevelt, *This I Remember,* p. 213; Cordell Hull, *The Memoirs of Cordell Hull,* 1:855–58; Robert E. Sherwood, *Roosevelt and Hopkins: An Intimate History,* pp. 93–95; James A. Farley, *Jim Farley's Story: The Roosevelt Years,* pp. 153–56, 224; Samuel I. Rosenman, *Working with Roosevelt,* pp. 200–203; Harold L. Ickes, *The Secret Diary of Harold L. Ickes,* vol. 3, *The Lowering Clouds, 1939–1941,* pp. 108, 232.
6 Knox to Alf M. Landon, November 17, 1937, Landon Papers; Pinchot to Wheeler, January 5, 1938, Pinchot Papers; Landon to Henry P. Fletcher, June 10, 1938, Henry P. Fletcher Papers; Burton K. Wheeler, *Yankee from the West: The Candid, Turbulent Life Story of the Yankee-born U.S. Senator from Montana,* p. 354; Berle diary, June 26, 1939.
7 Wheeler, *Yankee from the West,* pp. 358–60; Wheeler to Oswald Garrison Villard, July 17, 1939, Villard Papers; Lothian to Halifax,

February 12, 1940, F.O. 371/24233, British Foreigh Office Records; Lauchlin Currie to Roosevelt, February 21, 1940, President's Secretary's File, U.S. Senate, 1940 folder, Roosevelt Papers.

8 Wheeler, *Yankee from the West,* pp. 362–63; Burton K. Wheeler to the author, April 2, 1957; Cohen to Frankfurter, October 27, 1941, Felix Frankfurter Papers.

9 Wheeler, *Yankee from the West,* pp. 17–18, 347–51, 353–58.

10 Rosenman, *Working with Roosevelt,* p. 430; Ickes, *Secret Diary of Harold L. Ickes,* 3:108, 254; Wheeler, *Yankee from the West,* pp. 361–63; Berle diary, June 26, 1939; Farley, *Jim Farley's Story,* pp. 162, 203, 224.

11 Wheeler, *Yankee from the West,* pp. 18–20; Wheeler to the author, April 2, 1957.

12 Wheeler, *Yankee from the West,* pp. 20–21.

13 Ibid., p. 21; Wheeler to author, April 2, 1957.

14 Farley to Francis B. Sayre, June 19, 1940, Francis B. Sayre Papers; Hull, *Memoirs of Cordell Hull,* 1:858–60; Morgenthau presidential diaries, June 28, 1940, p. 598; [Cordell Hull], "Memo of Conversation," July 3, 1940, Hull Papers.

15 Clipping *Washington Post,* July 12, 1939, President's Personal File 880, Roosevelt Papers; Norris to Pepper, August 28, 1939, Norris to Ickes, September 8, 1939, Norris Papers.

16 Johnson to Hiram W. Johnson, Jr., April 20, 1940, Johnson Papers.

17 *New York Times,* February 22, 1940, p. 17, June 22, 1940, p. 6; *Congressional Record,* 76th Congress, 3d sess., 1940, 86:8790–98.

18 Hadley Cantril and Mildred Strunk, eds., *Public Opinion, 1935–1946* (Princeton, N.J.: Princeton University Press, 1951), pp. 601–10; Wayne S. Cole, *Senator Gerald P. Nye and American Foreign Relations* (Minneapolis: University of Minnesota Press, 1962), pp. 171–72; James T. Patterson, *Mr. Republican: A Biography of Robert A. Taft* (Boston: Houghton Mifflin Company, 1972), pp. 205–22; Vandenberg to Fred L. Woodworth, July 17, 1939, Vandenberg diary, January 28, [1940], Vandenberg Papers; Emil Hurja to Theodore Francis Green, June 1, 1939, Green Papers; MacNider to Lane Goodell, April 25, 1940, Hanford MacNider Papers; *New York Times,* January 10, 1940, p. 1, April 1, 1940, p. 2.

19 Donald Bruce Johnson, *The Republican Party and Wendell Willkie* (Urbana: University of Illinois Press, 1960), pp. 1–73; Errico, "Foreign Affairs and the Presidential Election of 1940," pp. 54–67; Landon to Harold B. Johnson, November 24, 1939, Landon to W. W. Waymack, May 31, 1940, Landon Papers; Gardner Cowles, Jr. to White, May 3, 1940, William Allen White Papers.

20 Lothian to Halifax, June 30, 1940, F.O. 371/24234, British Foreign Office Records; Kirk H. Porter and Donald Bruce Johnson, comps.,

National Party Platforms, 1840–1956 (Urbana: University of Illinois Press, 1956), pp. 389–90.

21 *"Inside Stuff—Real History,"* n.d., Scrapbook #12, Vandenberg diary; Arthur H. Vandenberg, *The Private Papers of Senator Vandenberg,* pp. 5–6.

22 Johnson, *Republican Party and Wendell Wilkie,* pp. 87–108; Errico, "Foreign Affairs and the Presidential Election of 1940," pp. 91–105; White to Landon, July 5, 1940, William Allen White Papers; Taft to Horace D. Taft, July 6, 1940, Taft Papers; Landon to W. A. Sheaffer, July 14, 1940, Landon Papers; Joe Martin, *My First Fifty Years in Politics,* pp. 153–61.

23 Sherwood, *Roosevelt and Hopkins,* pp. 173–79; Farley, *Jim Farley's Story,* pp. 259–88; Alben W. Barkley, *That Reminds Me—,* pp. 183–87; Ickes, *Secret Diary of Harold L. Ickes,* 3:237–56; Wheeler, *Yankee from the West,* pp. 364–66; Errico, "Foreign Affairs and the Presidential Election of 1940," pp. 153–60; Franklin D. Roosevelt, *The Public Papers and Addresses of Franklin D. Roosevelt,* 9:292.

24 Wheeler, *Yankee from the West,* pp. 22–24; Hull, *Memoirs of Cordell Hull,* 1:862; Rosenman, *Working with Roosevelt,* pp. 211–12; Wheeler to author, April 2, 1957; Porter and Johnson, comps., *National Party Platforms,* p. 382; James F. Byrnes to Roosevelt, March 28, 1944, Samuel I. Rosenman Papers.

25 Porter and Johnson, comps., *National Party Platforms,* pp. 382–83; Hull, *Memoirs of Cordell Hull,* 1:862; Byrnes to Roosevelt, March 28, 1944, Rosenman Papers; Wheeler to author, April 2, 1957; Ickes, *Secret Diary of Harold L. Ickes,* 3:254.

26 J. Samuel Walker, *Henry A. Wallace and American Foreign Policy* (Westport, Conn.: Greenwood Press, 1976), especially pp. 72–73; Rosenman, *Working with Roosevelt,* pp. 213–19; Grace Tully, *F.D.R.: My Boss,* pp. 238–39; Farley, *Jim Farley's Story,* pp. 299–306; Eleanor Roosevelt, *This I Remember,* pp. 214–20; Ickes, *Secret Diary of Harold L. Ickes,* 3:257–62.

27 Stimson diary, August 20, 1940, p. 3.

28 Johnson to Hiram W. Johnson, Jr., August 30, 1940, Johnson Papers; Lothian to Halifax, August 29, 1940, F.O. 800/324, Halifax Papers.

29 Johnson, *Republican Party and Wendell Willkie,* pp. 148–53; Errico, "Foreign Affairs and the Presidential Election of 1940," pp. 314–48.

30 *Hearings before the Committee on Foreign Relations, United States Senate,* 77th Congress, 1st sess., 1941, on S. 275, p. 905.

31 Franklin D. Roosevelt, *The Public Papers and Addresses of Franklin D. Roosevelt,* 9:293–558, especially pp. 293–303, 311–13.

32 Ibid., 9:301–2.

33 Rosenman, *Working with Roosevelt,* pp. 1–12, 222–55; Sherwood, *Roosevelt and Hopkins,* pp. 183–201, 212–19; Berle diary, October 29, 1940.

34 Roosevelt, *Public Papers and Addresses,* 9:415.
35 Ibid., 9:459–67; John P. Marinaro to Edward J. Flynn, September 24, 1940, Flynn to Marguerite Le Hand, September 26, 1940, President's Personal File 1820, Roosevelt Papers.
36 Allen to Roosevelt, October 19, 1940, Roosevelt to Allen, October 22, 1940, President's Secretary's File 7112, Roosevelt Papers.
37 Roosevelt, *Public Papers and Addresses,* 9:485–95; Rosenman, *Working with Roosevelt,* pp. 236–38.
38 Roosevelt, *Public Papers and Addresses,* 9:495–98.
39 Ibid., 9:499–510; Sherwood, *Roosevelt and Hopkins,* pp. 189–90; Rosenman, *Working with Roosevelt,* pp. 238–41.
40 Sherwood, *Roosevelt and Hopkins,* pp. 191–92; Rosenman, *Working with Roosevelt,* pp. 242–44; Roosevelt, *Public Papers and Addresses,* 9:514–24.
41 Roosevelt, *Public Papers and Addresses,* 9:544–53.
42 Norris to Howard Y. Williams, September 20, 1940, Norris to Edward R. Burke, September 30, 1940, Maria Heinemann to John P. Robertson, October 8, 1940, Cannell to E. G. Moan, November 5, 1940, Norris to Rice Lardner, July 20, 1940, Norris Papers; Cudahy to Edwin Watson, September 28, 1940, Watson to Cudahy, October 4, 1940, President's Personal File 1193, telegrams H. W. Nichols to Stephen Early, October 29, 1940, Egerton Shore to Early, October 29, 1940, Official File 3060, Roosevelt to Bennett Champ Clark, November 25, 1940, President's Personal File 4658, Roosevelt Papers; Patrick J. Maney, *"Young Bob" La Follette: A Biography of Robert M. La Follette, Jr., 1895–1953* (Columbia and London: University of Missouri Press, 1978), pp. 241–44; David E. Koskoff, *Joseph P. Kennedy: A Life and Times* (Englewood Cliffs, N.J.: Prentice-Hall, 1974), pp. 229–31, 296–99.
43 Wheeler to Amos R. E. Pinchot, October 11, 1940, Pinchot Papers; Wheeler, *Yankee from the West,* p. 26.
44 Clipping *Minneapolis Star Journal,* August 1, 1940, Shipstead Papers.
45 Roosevelt, *Public Papers and Addresses,* 9:322–23; Johnson to Hiram W. Johnson, Jr., August 4, 1940, Johnson to Robert E. Girvin, August 4, 1940, Johnson to Hiram W. Johnson, Jr., November 2, 1940, November 9, 1940, Johnson Papers.
46 Cole, *Senator Gerald P. Nye,* pp. 173–75; Edward C. Blackorby, *Prairie Rebel: The Public Life of William Lemke* (Lincoln: University of Nebraska Press, 1963), pp. 243–55; Gerald P. Nye, "No Third Term, No War" (mimeographed text of address over Mutual Broadcasting System, Chicago, November 2, 1940), Nye Papers.
47 Walsh to Philip J. Philbin, October 7, 1940, Walsh Papers; Sherwood, *Roosevelt and Hopkins,* pp. 192–93; Johnson, *Republican Party and Wendell Willkie,* pp. 153–55.

48 Wayne S. Cole, *Charles A. Lindbergh and the Battle against American Intervention in World War II* (New York and London: Harcourt Brace Jovanovich, 1974), pp. 106-11; Charles A. Lindbergh, *The Wartime Journals of Charles A. Lindbergh,* pp. 413-14; list of Lindbergh's addresses and the final drafts of those addresses, Lindbergh Papers.

49 Wayne S. Cole, *America First: The Battle against Intervention, 1940-1941* (Madison: University of Wisconsin Press, 1953), pp. 26, 167-75; Stuart to Wood, August 14, 1940, Wood to Latham R. Reed, October 23, 1940, Stuart to Sidney Hertzberg, October 28, 1940, Minutes of America First Board of Directors, November 1, 1940, Clay Judson to Stuart, November 2, 1940, America First Papers; Stuart to Walsh, November 2, 1940, Walsh Papers.

50 Bureau of the Census with the Social Science Research Council, *Historical Statistics of the United States: Colonial Times to 1957* (Washington: U.S. Government Printing Office, 1960), pp. 682-86; Wilfred E. Binkley, *America Political Parties: Their Natural History* (New York: Alfred A. Knopf, 1947), pp. 382-86; Samuel Lubell, *The Future of American Politics,* 2d ed. rev. (Garden City, New York: Doubleday Anchor Books, 1956), pp. 54-60.

51 *Congressional Directory,* 77th Congress, 1st sess., 1941, pp. iii, 157, 159, 163; Wheeler, *Yankee from the West,* p. 26; Wheeler to Alben W. Barkley, November 7, 1940, Alben W. Barkley Papers. Based on the author's tabulation of foreign policy roll call votes during FDR's first two terms in office, no senator voted isolationist more consistently than Lynn J. Frazier from 1933 to 1941.

Chapter 28

1 For a detailed scholarly history of the background and enactment of lend-lease, see Warren F. Kimball, *The Most Unsordid Act: Lend-Lease, 1939-1941* (Baltimore, Md.: Johns Hopkins Press, 1969). Winston S. Churchill, *The Second World War,* vol. 2, *Their Finest Hour,* pp. 558-67; Francis L. Loewenheim, Harold D. Langley, and Manfred Jonas, eds., *Roosevelt and Churchill: Their Secret Wartime Correspondence,* pp. 122-26.

2 Churchill, *Their Finest Hour,* pp. 567-68; Robert E. Sherwood, *Roosevelt and Hopkins: An Intimate History,* pp. 222-25; Franklin D. Roosevelt, *The Public Papers and Addresses of Franklin D. Roosevelt,* 9:604-13; Ickes to Roosevelt, August 2, 1940, President's Secretary's File, Correspondence on 50 Destroyers and Naval Bases Folder, Franklin D. Roosevelt Papers.

3 Lowell Mellett to Roosevelt, December 30, 1940, Lowell Mellett Papers; Roosevelt, *Public Papers and Addresses,* 9:633-44.

4 Roosevelt, *Public Papers and Addresses,* 9:638-39; Samuel I. Rosenman, *Working with Roosevelt,* p. 262.
5 Roosevelt, *Public Papers and Addresses,* 9:639-44.
6 Ibid., 9:663-70.
7 Ibid., 9:668-70.
8 Ibid., 9:672.
9 Henry Morgenthau presidential diaries, December 31, 1940; Cordell Hull, *The Memoirs of Cordell Hull,* 2:919-25; Henry Morgenthau, Jr., *From the Morgenthau Diaries,* vol. 2, *Years of Urgency, 1938-1941,* pp. 210-17.
10 Sol Bloom, *The Autobiography of Sol Bloom,* pp. 240-42; Roosevelt, *Public Papers and Addresses,* 9:674; Franklin D. Roosevelt, *F.D.R.: His Personal Letters, 1928-1945,* 2:1107, 1114; Arthur H. Vandenberg to Walter F. George, January 15, 1941, Arthur H. Vandenberg Papers; Hadley Cantril and Mildred Strunk, eds., *Public Opinion, 1935-1946* (Princeton, N.J.: Princeton University Press, 1951), pp. 409-10.
11 Minutes of Board of Directors Meeting, America First Committee, December 27, 1940, America First Committee Papers; *New York Times,* December 29, 1940, p. 12, January 12, 1941, p. 7; *Chicago Tribune,* December 31, 1940, p. 1, January 12, 1941, p. 2; Wayne S. Cole, *America First: The Battle against Intervention, 1940-1941* (Madison: University of Wisconsin Press, 1953), pp. 43-49; memos to Mr. Forster, January 15, 1941 through March 10, 1941, Official File 4193, Roosevelt Papers.
12 Johnson to Hiram W. Johnson, Jr., January 11, 1941, Hiram W. Johnson Papers; John T. Flynn, Herbert Agar, Josh Lee, and Burton K. Wheeler, *Should Congress Adopt the Lend-Lease Program?* (Washington: Pamphlet of the American Forum of the Air, January 12, 1941), p. 9; Roosevelt, *Public Papers and Addresses,* 9:711-12.
13 Telegram Fish to Herbert Hoover, January 14, 1941, Post-Presidential Individual File, Herbert Hoover Papers; *New York Times,* January 15, 1941, p. 1; *Hearings before the Committee on Foreign Affairs, House of Representatives,* 77th Congress, 1st sess., on H.R. 1776, 25:350-61, 481-99.
14 *House Hearings,* H.R. 1776, 25:371-435; Charles A. Lindbergh statement read before House Foreign Affairs Committee, January 23, 1941, Charles A. Lindbergh Papers; Wayne S. Cole, *Charles A. Lindbergh and the Battle against American Intervention in World War II* (New York: Harcourt Brace Jovanovich, 1974), pp. 25-93.
15 Lindbergh statement read before House Committee, January 23, 1941, Lindbergh Papers.
16 Ibid.; *House Hearings,* H.R. 1776, 25:376-77.
17 *House Hearings,* H.R. 1776, 25:378-435.
18 Johnson to Hiram W. Johnson, Jr., February 2, 1941, Johnson

Papers; Henry L. Stimson diary, January 29, 1941; *New York Times,* February 1, 1941, p. 6.

19 Johnson to Hiram W. Johnson, Jr., February 2, 9, 1941, Johnson Papers.

20 Ibid., February 2, 9, 1941, Johnson Papers.

21 *Hearings before the Committee on Foreign Relations, United States Senate,* 77th Congress, 1st sess., on S. 275, 1941, 78:307–13, 341–98.

22 Ibid., 78:490–550; Charles A. Lindbergh statement read before Senate Foreign Relations Committee, February 6, 1941, Lindbergh Papers; *New York Times,* February 7, 1941, pp. 1–6.

23 *Congressional Record,* 77th Congress, 1st sess., 1941, 87:815.

24 Tom Connally, *My Name Is Tom Connally,* p. 244; Ruth Sarles, "A Story of America First" [Chicago, 1942], pp. 25/157–33/165. I did research in this manuscript history in the copy loaned to me in 1979 by the author, Mrs. Ruth Sarles Benedict. Another copy has been added to the America First Committee Papers since I researched that collection.

25 *Congressional Record,* 77th Congress, 1st sess., 1941, 87:1108–21, 1363–70, 1735, 2082–96.

26 Clipping *Austin Herald,* February 25, 1941, Henrik Shipstead Papers; Johnson to Hiram W. Johnson, Jr., March 2, 9, 1941, Johnson Papers; Robert A. Taft to Alben W. Barkley, January 31, 1941, mimeographed press release, February 8, 1941, Robert A. Taft Papers; Stimson diary, March 1, 2, 1941; Arthur H. Vandenberg diary, March 8, 1941, Vandenberg Papers.

27 Cole, *America First,* pp. 43–50; Walter Johnson, *The Battle against Isolation* (Chicago: University of Chicago Press, 1944), pp. 206–10; Clark M. Eichelberger, *Organizing for Peace: A Personal History of the Founding of the United Nations,* pp. 153–55; Frederick J. Libby, *To End War: The Story of the National Council for Prevention of War,* pp. 162–64.

28 *Congressional Record,* 77th Congress, 1st sess., 1941, 87:2097.

29 Ibid., 87:2097–98, 2509.

30 Cordell Hull, *The Memoirs of Cordell Hull,* 2:925; Roosevelt, *Public Papers and Addresses,* 10:63.

Chapter 29

1 Francis L. Loewenheim, Harold D. Langley, and Manfred Jonas, eds., *Roosevelt and Churchill: Their Secret Wartime Correspondence,* pp. 126–27; Winston S. Churchill, *The Second World War,* vol. 2, *Their Finest Hour,* pp. 588–99.

2 For a scholarly study of the Battle of the Atlantic, see Thomas A. Bailey and Paul B. Ryan, *Hitler vs. Roosevelt: The Undeclared Naval*

War (New York: Free Press, 1979). My thinking also benefited from a thoughtful, well-researched paper by William B. Bader, "Congress and the 'War Powers': Roosevelt's 'Little' War," presented at a colloquium at the Woodrow Wilson International Center for Scholars, Washington, D.C., on October 26, 1977.

3 *United States Maritime Commission* Statement Showing Vessels Approved for Transfer to Foreign Ownership and/or Registry October 26, 1938 to October 25, 1939, Neutrality folder, President's Secretary's File, Roosevelt Papers; Adolf A. Berle diary, October 31, 1939; Hull to Land, November 6, 8, 1939, Cordell Hull Papers; Jay Pierrepont Moffat diary, November 7, 1939, Jay Pierrepont Moffat Papers; Roosevelt to William Allen White, November 13, 1939, William Allen White Papers; clipping *Bismarck* (N.D.) *Tribune,* November 13, 1939, Gerald P. Nye Papers; Franklin D. Roosevelt, *F.D.R.: His Personal Letters, 1928–1945,* 2:1213–15.

4 Wheeler, La Follette, Clark, Shipstead, Reed, and Bulow to "Dear Colleague," March 29, 1941, Ruth Sarles, "Story of America First," pp. 5/186–6/187, 2/608–3/609, America First Papers.

5 Sarles, "Story of America First," p. 3/609, Sarles to Kendrick Lee, April 20, 21, 1941, America First Papers; *Congressional Record,* 77th Congress, 1st sess., 1941, 87:3374.

6 Sarles, "Story of America First," pp. 5/186–6/187, 3/609–5/611, America First Committee Bulletins, #177, 177-A, April 2, 1941, #192, April 10, 1941, America First Committee, *Convoy: A Funeral Train* (Chicago, n.d.), America First Papers; clipping *Chicago Herald-American,* April 12, 1941, Nye Papers; Wayne S. Cole, *America First: The Battle against Intervention, 1940–1941* (Madison: University of Wisconsin Press, 1953), pp. 155–56. Daily tabulations of letters, cards, and petitions received at the White House favoring or opposing convoys are on memos for Mr. Forster in Official File 4193, Roosevelt Papers.

7 Stimson diary, December 19, 1940, March 24, April 10, 1941; Morgenthau presidential diary, April 2, 1941; Robert E. Sherwood, *Roosevelt and Hopkins: An Intimate History,* pp. 291–92; Loewenheim, Langley, and Jonas, eds., *Roosevelt and Churchill,* pp. 137–38; Winston S. Churchill, *The Second World War,* vol. 3, *The Grand Alliance,* pp. 139–46.

8 Franklin D. Roosevelt, *The Public Papers and Addresses of Franklin D. Roosevelt,* 10:132–38.

9 C. H[ull] to Roosevelt, April 29, 1941, and FDR's "OK" written on it, Cordell Hull 1939–41, 1943 folder, President's Secretary's File, Roosevelt Papers; Hull to George, April 29, 1941, Hull Papers; Sarles to Lee, May 4, 1941, Sarles, "Story of America First," p. 13/194, America First Papers.

10 Sarles to Lee, May 11, 18, 1941, telegram Stuart to Lindbergh, May 13, 1941, day letter Wood to Tobey, May 13, 1941, telegram Tobey to Wood, May 15, 1941, America First Papers; Stimson diary, April 22, 1941.

11 Henry L. Stimson and McGeorge Bundy, *On Active Service in Peace and War,* pp. 367-76; Henry Morgenthau, Jr., *From the Morgenthau Diaries,* vol. 2, *Years of Urgency, 1938-1941,* pp. 251-54; Ickes to Roosevelt, April 28, 1941, Harold L. Ickes Papers; Sherwood, *Roosevelt and Hopkins,* p. 293.

12 Walter Johnson, *The Battle against Isolation* (Chicago: University of Chicago Press, 1944), pp. 179-205; Clark M. Eichelberger, *Organizing for Peace: A Personal History of the Founding of the United Nations,* pp. 144-50; Mark Lincoln Chadwin, *The Hawks of World War II* (Chapel Hill: University of North Carolina Press, 1968), especially pp. 43-73, 159-231. The generalization about the Fight for Freedom Committee's relations with Ickes was based on my examination of the Ickes Papers in 1974. The generalization on the contrasting styles of Fight for Freedom and the Committee to Defend America was based on my research in the records of those two organizations in the Princeton University Library in 1971.

13 Morgenthau presidential diaries, May 17, 1941; Stimson diary, May 23, 1941.

14 Ickes to Roosevelt, April 28, 1941, Ickes Papers; Morison to Roosevelt, May 1, 1941, President's Personal File 5713, Lamont to Roosevelt, May 19, 1941, President's Personal File 1820, Bullitt to Roosevelt, May 21, 1941, President's Personal File 1124, Stimson to Roosevelt, May 24, 1941, President's Personal File 1820, Conant to Roosevelt, May 20, 1941, and enclosed copy of excerpts from address, President's Personal File 91, Roosevelt Papers; Stevenson to Lowell Mellett, May 5, 1941, Mellett Papers; Max Freedman, annot., *Roosevelt and Frankfurter: Their Correspondence, 1928-1945,* pp. 599-601; Sherwood, *Roosevelt and Hopkins,* pp. 292-93.

15 Hopkins to Miss Tully, May 15, 1941, and attached four-page memorandum headed "For publication in London May 11, 1941 Copy of Article for the Sunday Express by Raymond Gram Swing," President's Personal File 1820, Roosevelt Papers.

16 Sherwood, *Roosevelt and Hopkins,* pp. 292-98; Samuel I. Rosenman, *Working with Roosevelt,* pp. 278-84; Freedman, annot., *Roosevelt and Frankfurter,* pp. 600-601; Stimson diary, May 20, 23, 24, 25, 27, 1941.

17 Franklin D. Roosevelt, *The Public Papers and Addresses of Franklin D. Roosevelt,* 10:181-85.

18 Ibid., 10:185-88.

19 Ibid., 19:188-90.

20 Ibid., 10:190-91.

21 Ibid., 10:193–94.
22 Sherwood, *Roosevelt and Hopkins,* p. 298; Hadley Cantril to Mrs. Anna M. Rosenberg, June 16, 1941, Princeton Public Opinion Poll, 1941, 1944 folder, President's Secretary's File, Roosevelt Papers.
23 *"Statement Issued by General Wood"* attached to America First Committee Bulletin #287, May 28, 1941, Lillian Gish to Stuart, June 4, 1941, "Statement Issued by General R. E. Wood Speaking for the National Executive Committee of the America First Committee," May 28, 1941, Wood to Ray F. Moseley, May 29, 1941, Sarles, "Story of America First," p. 6/612, America First Papers; Wheeler to "Dear Sir," n.d., La Follette Family Papers.
24 Roosevelt, *Public Papers and Addresses,* 10:255–64; Sherwood, *Roosevelt and Hopkins,* pp. 290–91; Loewenheim, Langley, and Jonas, eds., *Roosevelt and Churchill,* pp. 143–44.
25 W. D. H[assett] to Roosevelt, July 3, 1941, Navy Department 1941, 1943 folder, President's Secretary's File, Roosevelt Papers; Ulric Bell to Carter Glass, July 9, 1941, Carter Glass Papers; Harold L. Ickes, *The Secret Diary of Harold L. Ickes,* vol. 3, *The Lowering Clouds, 1939–1941,* pp. 563, 571.
26 News release from New York America First Committee chapter, July 7, 1941, America First Research Bureau, *Did You Know* (Washington, July 9, 1941), p. 4, *Shield America* (Kansas City, Mo.), November 11, 1941, p. 1, America First Papers; Hoover to Taft, July 14, 1941, Taft to Hoover, July 16, 1941, Taft Papers.
27 Churchill, *Grand Alliance,* pp. 369–73; Cordell Hull, *The Memoirs of Cordell Hull,* 2:973; Roosevelt to Oursler, June 25, 1941, President's Personal File 2993, Roosevelt Papers; Roosevelt, *F.D.R.: His Personal Letters,* 2:1201–2; Raymond H. Dawson, *The Decision to Aid Russia, 1941* (Chapel Hill: University of North Carolina Press, 1959), especially pp. 65–179.
28 Minutes of America First Board of Directors Meeting, Chicago, June 23, 1941, Sarles, "Story of America First," p. 7/613, America First Papers; Capper to C. C. Isely, June 24, 1941, Arthur Capper Papers; Johnson to Hiram W. Johnson, Jr., June 24, 1941, Johnson Papers; Herbert Hoover, *A Call to American Reason* (Chicago, June 29, 1941), p. 11.
29 Mimeographed press release, July 1, 1941 of "Radio Speech of Representative Hamilton Fish over the Blue Network of the National Broadcasting Co., Monday Evening, June 30, 1941, at 6:45 P.M. (E.S.T.)," America First Papers; final draft of Lindbergh address read at America First Committee meeting in San Francisco, California, July 1, 1941, Lindbergh Papers; *Newsweek,* July 7, 1941, p. 12.
30 *Daily Worker* (New York), December 26, 1940, p. 5, January 12, 1941, p. 2, May 24, 1941, p. 6, June 23, 1941, p. 1; Samuel Walker, "Communists and Isolationism: The American Peace Mobilization, 1940–1941," *Maryland Historian* 4 (Spring 1973): 1–12.

31 Dawson, *Decision to Aid Russia, 1941,* pp. 217–94.
32 Stimson and Bundy, *On Active Service,* pp. 376–78; Roosevelt to C. A. Dykstra, January 11, 1941, Official File 1413, Roosevelt Papers.
33 Stimson diary, July 11, 21, 1941; Tugwell diary, July 12, 1941, Rexford Guy Tugwell Papers; Burton K. Wheeler to R. E. Wood, July 17, 1941, America First Papers; George W. Marshall to Roosevelt, July 16, 1941, F. H. La Guardia to Roosevelt, July 17, 1941, Official File 1413, Roosevelt Papers.
34 Wood to Robert R. Reynolds, July 17, 1941, Stuart to John T. Flynn, July 31, 1941, Wood to Morris Burns Stanley, March 31, 1943, America First Papers.
35 America First Committee Bulletin #389, July 7, 1941, and enclosed press release, America First Papers. See also *Chicago Tribune,* July 5, 1941, p. 1.
36 America First Committee Bulletin #444, July 28, 1941, Flynn to Page Hufty, July 30, 1941, Stuart to Flynn, July 31, 1941, America First Papers.
37 Harry C. Schnibbe to Arthur A. Brooks, Jr., July 22, 1941, Donald S. MacKay to Senate Military Affairs Committee, July 15, 1941, John S. Broeksmit, Jr. to Douglas Dobson, July 19, 1941, minutes of Executive Board of Boston America First Committee Chapter, August 5, 1941, Helen Lamont to Reynolds, July 25, 1941, *America First Bulletin* (New York), July 26, 1941, pp. 1–4, Flynn to Hufty, July 30, 1941, America First Papers.
38 America First Research Bureau, *Did You Know, #9,* July 15, 1941, pp. 1–3, #10, July 17, 1941, pp. 1–3, #11, July 17, 1941, pp. 1–5, America First Papers.
39 Ibid., #12, July 24, 1941, pp. 1–4, America First Papers.
40 *America First Bulletin* (New York), July 26, 1941, p. 4, America First Papers.
41 Marshall to Roosevelt, July 16, 1941, Patterson to Roosevelt, July 17, 1941, Official File 1413, Roosevelt Papers; Stimson diary, July 11, 21, 1941; Roosevelt, *Public Papers and Addresses,* 10:272–77.
42 Nye to J. Austin White, July 31, 1941, Nye Papers.
43 Stimson and Bundy, *On Active Service,* p. 377; telegram Hammond to Reynolds, July 18, 1941, telegram Stuart to Wheeler, July 18, 1941, America First Papers; *Hearings before the Committee on Military Affairs, United States Senate,* 77th Congress, 1st sess., 1941, S.J. Res. 92 and 93, pp. 207–8.
44 *Congressional Record,* 77th Congress, 1st sess., 1941, 87:6881. The generalizations and figures in this paragraph are based on the author's tabulations using the Senate vote on S.J. Res. 95 as listed in the *Congressional Record.*
45 Ibid., 87:7074–75. The generalizations and tabulations are by the author based on the House vote on S.J. Res. 95 as listed in the *Congressional Record.*

46 For a detailed scholarly history of that conference, see Theodore A. Wilson, *The First Summit: Roosevelt and Churchill at Placentia Bay, 1941* (Boston: Houghton Mifflin Company, 1969).

47 Stuart to Chester Bowles, August 14, 1941, America First Papers.

48 Bailey and Ryan, *Hitler vs. Roosevelt*, pp. 138–43. Among the better studies of Hitler's Nazi German policies toward the United States in the Atlantic, see Hans L. Trefousse, *Germany and American Neutrality, 1939–1941* (New York: Bookman Associates, 1951); James V. Compton, *The Swastika and the Eagle: Hitler, the United States, and the Origins of World War II* (Boston: Houghton Mifflin Company, 1967); and Alton Frye, *Nazi Germany and the American Hemisphere, 1933–1941* (New Haven, Conn., and London: Yale University Press, 1967).

49 Clipping *Cincinnati Times-Star,* June 16, 1941, America First Research Bureau, *Did You Know, #1,* June 18, 1941, pp. 1–3, *#2,* June 21, 1941, pp. 1–3, *#22,* September 13, 1941, pp. 1–5, *#24,* September 23, 1941, pp. 1–4, *America First Bulletin* (New York), June 21, 1941, p. 1, clipping *Chicago Times,* June 4, 1941, Stuart to all chapter chairmen, June 4, 1941, America First Papers; clipping *Killdeer* (N.D.) *Herald,* June 19, 1941, Nye Papers.

50 Roosevelt, *Public Papers and Addresses,* 10:227–30.

51 Bailey and Ryan, *Hitler vs. Roosevelt,* pp. 168–81, 188–92; *New York Times,* October 18, 1941, p. 3.

52 Memorandum for Hopkins of paraphrase of London's telegram No. 3979, August 29, [1941], memorandum by Hopkins, September 2, 1941, memorandum by Hopkins September 13, 1941, Harry L. Hopkins Papers; Sherwood, *Roosevelt and Hopkins,* pp. 370–72; Rosenman, *Working with Roosevelt,* pp. 290–92.

53 Roosevelt, *Public Papers and Addresses,* 10:384–92.

54 Bailey and Ryan, *Hitler vs. Roosevelt,* pp. 168–83; Roosevelt to Stark, September 18, 1941, Navy Dept., 1941 folder, Knox to J. M. Patterson, n.d., Frank Knox 1940–41 folder, President's Secretay's File, Roosevelt Papers.

55 Bailey and Ryan, *Hitler vs. Roosevelt,* pp. 196–98, 204–7.

56 Page Hufty "To All Chapter Chairmen," September 10, 1941, America First Research Bureau, *Did You Know, #22,* September 13, 1941, pp. 1–5, America First Papers; *New York Times,* September 13, 1941, p. 3.

57 *New York Times,* September 15, 1941, p. 2; news release from R. E. Wood, September 15, 1941, America First Papers.

58 News release of statement by Wood, October 17, 1941, America First Committee news release, Washington, D.C., November 2, 1941, America First Papers; *New York Times,* October 18, 1941, p. 3; *Washington Post,* October 18, 1941, p. 4.

59 Roosevelt, *Public Papers and Addresses,* 10:406–13; Hull, *Memoirs of Cordell Hull,* 2:943, 1046–48; Sherwood, *Roosevelt and Hopkins,* pp. 379–80; Connally, *My Name Is Tom Connally,* pp. 245–46.

60 Roosevelt, *Public Papers and Addresses,* 10:406–11.
61 Ibid., 10:438–44.
62 Ibid., 10:444–45.
63 America First Research Bureau, *Did You Know, #*28, October 25, 1941, pp. 32–33; *Chicago Tribune,* October 10, 1941, p. 11; Cole, *America First,* pp. 162–66.
64 Cole, *America First,* pp. 51–67.
65 MacNider to Wood, September 20, 1941, Stuart to Jay C. Hormel, September 19, 1941, Pettengill to Wood, October 9, 1941, and enclosed draft for open letter to the president, teletype message Flynn to Wood and Stuart, October 20, 1941, America First Papers.
66 Minutes of America First national committee meeting, October 20, 1941, America First Papers.
67 Wood open letter to the president, October 22, 1941, America First Papers; *Chicago Tribune,* October 23, 1941, p. 1.
68 Stimson and Bundy, *On Active Service,* pp. 364–76; Ickes to Roosevelt, June 23, 1941, Ickes Papers; Sidney Homer, Jr. to Roosevelt, September 10, 1941, Official File 463-C, Roosevelt Papers; Sherwood, *Roosevelt and Hopkins,* p. 382.
69 Stuart "To All Chapter Chairmen," October 22, 1941, America First Papers.
70 Telegram Stuart to Flynn, October 13, 1941, telegram Flynn to Sol Bloom, October 13, 1941, Hufty to Richard A. Moore, Stuart, October 18, 1941, teletype Flynn to Wood, October 20, 1941, telegram Wood to Connally, October 20, 1941, America First Papers; Stuart to Villard, October 16, 1941, Oswald Garrison Villard Papers; Cole, *America First,* pp. 162–66; Wayne S. Cole, *Charles A. Lindbergh and the Battle against American Intervention in World War II* (New York and London: Harcourt Brace Jovanovich, 1974), pp. 191–92, 202–3.
71 America First Committee, *Emergency Bulletin #1* (Chicago, October 25, 1941), night letter Hufty to America First chapters in St. Louis, Springfield, and Kansas City, October 27, 1941, night letter Hufty to America First chapters in Albuquerque and Encino, New Mexico, October 27, 1941, Mrs. Amy P. Hurt to Stuart, November 15, 1941, Frank C. Ward to America First headquarters, November 17, 1941, America First Papers.
72 Sarles, "Story of America First," pp. 16/254–36/274, book wire Stuart to America First national committee members, October 29, 1941, Lee Swanson to Willard E. Fraser, November 13, 1941, Wood to John L. Wheeler, December 18, 1941, Sarles to Wood, November 14, 1941, America First Papers; *Chicago Tribune,* October 31, 1941, p. 10; Cole, *America First,* pp. 162–66.
73 Sarles, "Story of America First," pp. 10/248–15/253, America First Papers; Stimson diary, October 13, 1941; Hull, *Memoirs of Cordell Hull,* 2:1048–49.

74 Sarles, "Story of America First," pp. 16/254–21/259, America First Papers; Johnson to Hiram W. Johnson, Jr., October 26, 1941, Johnson Papers; Hull, *Memoirs of Cordell Hull,* 2:1048–49.

75 Sarles, "Story of America First," pp. 18/256–30/268, clipping *Chicago Tribune,* datelined November 6, 1941, America First Papers; *Congressional Record,* 77th Congress, 1st sess., 1941, 87:8305–14, 8680.

76 Sarles, "Story of America First," pp. 31/269–36/274, telegram Stuart to Frank C. Ward, November 12, 1941, book wire H. C. Schnibbe to all America First chapters, November 12, 1941, America First Papers; Sam Rayburn and John W. McCormack to Roosevelt, November 12, 1941, Roosevelt to Rayburn and McCormack, November 13, 1941, Frank W. Boykin to Edwin M. Watson, November 13, 1941, Official File 1561, Roosevelt Papers; Roosevelt, *Public Papers and Addresses,* 10:487–90; *Congressional Record,* 77th Congress, 1st sess., 1941, 87:8890–91.

77 *Congressional Record,* 77th Congress, 1st sess., 1941, 87:8680, 8891; Sarles, "Story of America First," pp. 36/274–41/279, undated America First news release, telegram Stuart to E. J. Ryan, November 7, 1941, form letter Wood to all members and friends of America First, November 13, 1941, America First Committee Bulletin, #687, November 14, 1941, and unidentified memo, America First Papers; Johnson to Hiram W. Johnson, Jr., November 8, 1941, Johnson Papers; W. D. H[assett] to Roosevelt, November 1, 1941, President's Personal File 8101, Roosevelt Papers; *Public Opinion Quarterly* 6 (Spring 1942): 162.

78 Sherwood, *Roosevelt and Hopkins,* pp. 382–83.

79 Stimson and Bundy, *On Active Service,* pp. 371–76.

Chapter 30

1 For a well-researched scholarly article on the general subject treated in this chapter, see Richard W. Steele, "Franklin D. Roosevelt and His Foreign Policy Critics," *Political Science Quarterly* 94 (Spring 1979): 15–32. For a criticism of Steele's article and an apologia for Roosevelt and his methods see, in the same issue, Arthur M. Schlesinger, Jr., "A Comment on 'Roosevelt and His Foreign Policy Critics,'" *Political Science Quarterly* 94 (Spring 1979): 33–35.

2 Wayne S. Cole, *Charles A. Lindbergh and the Battle against American Intervention in World War II* (New York and London: Harcourt Brace Jovanovich, 1974), pp. 17–24. This author had various conversations, both in person and via telephone, with Lindbergh in 1972–74, exchanged many letters with him, and researched Lindbergh's personal papers in Yale University Library, New Haven, Connecticut. For Lindbergh's autobiographical accounts, see Charles A. Lindbergh,

"We"; The Spirit of St. Louis; The Wartime Journals of Charles A. Lindbergh; Autobiography of Values. For his wife's personal accounts, see Anne Morrow Lindbergh, North to the Orient; Listen! the Wind; Bring Me a Unicorn: Diaries and Letters of Anne Morrow Lindbergh, 1922–1928; Hour of Gold, Hour of Lead: Diaries and Letters of Anne Morrow Lindbergh, 1929–1932; Locked Rooms and Open Doors: Diaries and Letters of Anne Morrow Lindbergh, 1933–1935; The Flower and the Nettle: Diaries and Letters of Anne Morrow Lindbergh, 1936–1939; War Within and Without: Diaries and Letters of Anne Morrow Lindbergh, 1939–1944.

3 Final draft of address Lindbergh read at Chicago rally, August 4, 1940, Lindbergh Papers; Lindbergh, Wartime Journals, p. 452.

4 Henry Morgenthau, Jr., presidential diaries, May 20, 1940, p. 563; Roosevelt to Stimson, May 21, 1940, Stimson Papers. This paragraph and the pages that immediately follow on Lindbergh are drawn, in somewhat revised form, from Cole, Charles A. Lindbergh, pp. 128–34.

5 Confidential memorandum Roosevelt to attorney general, May 21, 1940, President's Secretary's File, Justice Department—Robert Jackson folder, unsigned memorandum, May 31, 1940, Official File 463-C, file memo, May 6, 1941, Official File 4193, Roosevelt Papers.

6 New York Times, May 23, 1940, pp. 1, 17, June 17, 1940, p. 5, August 6, 1940, pp. 1, 6, October 17, 1940, p. 10; undated memorandum for Mr. Early, and enclosed undated shorthand memo on White House letterhead, Early Papers; telegram G. W. Johnstone to Key Pittman, June 16, 1940, Pittman Papers; W. D. H[assett] to Early, October 12, 1940, Early Papers; Adolf A. Berle, Navigating the Rapids, 1918–1971: From the Papers of Adolf A. Berle, pp. 343–44; Berle diary, October 17, 1940, Berle Papers.

7 New York Times, December 18, 1940, p. 30; Chicago Tribune, April 14, 1941, p. 11.

8 John F. Carter to Miss Le Hand, April 22, 1941, and enclosed "Memorandum on the 'Copperhead' Government," President's Personal File 1820, Roosevelt Papers; microfilm of Roosevelt's Press Conferences, April 25, 1941, roll 9, pp. 293–94; Chicago Tribune, April 26, 1941, p. 2.

9 Lindbergh to Roosevelt, April 28, 1941, Official File 92, Roosevelt Papers; Lindbergh to Stimson, April 28, 1941, Lindbergh Papers; Lindbergh, Wartime Journals, pp. 478–80.

10 Robert A. Taft to Lindbergh, April 30, 1941, Lindbergh Papers; Chicago Tribune, June 5, 1941, p. 1.

11 Mimeographed address by Harold L. Ickes, "France Forever," given at Manhattan Center, New York City, July 14, 1941, Lindbergh Papers.

12 Lindbergh to Roosevelt, July 16, 1941, Early to Lindbergh, July 19, 1941, President's Personal File 1080, Roosevelt Papers; Lindbergh, Wartime Journals, p. 518.

13 Harold L. Ickes, *The Secret Diary of Harold L. Ickes,* vol. 3, *The Lowering Clouds, 1939–1941,* pp. 581–82; *Chicago Daily News,* July 25, 1941, p. 4.

14 Final drafts of addresses Lindbergh read at America First rallies in Minneapolis, Minnesota, May 10, 1941, and in New York City, May 23, 1941, Lindbergh Papers. These two paragraphs and the pages that immediately follow on Lindbergh are drawn, in somewhat revised form, from Cole, *Charles A. Lindbergh,* pp. 186, 189–92.

15 Final draft of address Lindbergh read at America First rally in Philadelphia, Pennsylvania, May 29, 1941, Lindbergh Papers.

16 Telegram Lindbergh to *Baltimore Sun,* n.d., Lindbergh Papers; *America First Bulletin* (New York), June 14, 1941, pp. 1, 3, America First Papers.

17 Lindbergh, "Government by Representation or by Subterfuge?," final draft read at meeting in Cleveland, August 9, 1941, Lindbergh Papers.

18 Lindbergh, *Wartime Journals,* pp. 536–38; *Des Moines Register,* September 12, 1941, p. 1; Lindbergh, "Who Are the War Agitators?," final typed draft, September 11, 1941, Lindbergh Papers. For a more detailed account of the Lindbergh speech, including its background, contents, and aftermath see Cole, *Charles A. Lindbergh,* pp. 157–92.

19 Lindbergh, "A Heritage at Stake," final draft read at meeting in Fort Wayne, Indiana, October 3, 1941, Lindbergh Papers.

20 Lindbergh, "Facing the Record and the Facts," final draft read at meeting in Madison Square Garden, New York, October 30, 1941, Lindbergh Papers.

21 Lindbergh, "What Do We Mean by Democracy and Freedom?," preliminary draft of speech that Lindbergh was to have read at Boston America First rally, December 12, 1941, Lindbergh Papers. The meeting was canceled after the Pearl Harbor attack.

22 Interview with Charles A. Lindbergh, Washington, D.C., June 7, 1972; interviews with Mrs. Ruth Sarles Benedict, Bethesda, Maryland, December 28, 1978, and Oxford, Maryland, May 28, 1980.

23 Interviews with Mrs. Ruth Sarles Benedict, December 28, 1978, and May 28, 1980; interview with Burton K. Wheeler, Washington, D.C., October 23, 1969. Wheeler's autobiography is Burton K. Wheeler, *Yankee from the West: The Candid, Turbulent Life Story of the Yankee-born U.S. Senator from Montana.* On November 11, 1967 the present author attended a dinner party and small social gathering in the Nye home in Chevy Chase, Maryland, at which both former Senator Burton K. Wheeler and former Senator Gerald P. Nye were present and reminisced about their years together in the Senate and in America First.

24 John T. Flynn, Herbert Agar, Josh Lee, and Burton K. Wheeler, *Should Congress Adopt the Lend-Lease Program?* (Pamphlet of the

American Forum of the Air, Washington, January 12, 1941), p. 9;
Franklin D. Roosevelt, *The Public Papers and Addresses of Franklin
D. Roosevelt,* 9:711–12.

25 Mimeographed text of speech delivered by Senator Wheeler at Denver
Municipal Auditorium, April 16, 1941, America First Papers.

26 *Chicago Tribune,* April 17, 1941, p. 2; *Washington Post,* September 2,
1941, p. 4; text of address by Senator Wheeler, Lucas, Illinois, August
28, 1941, mimeographed text of address by Senator Wheeler, Oklahoma City, August 29, 1941, and clipping from *Los Angeles Examiner,*
October 3, 1941, America First Papers.

27 On the Fight for Freedom Committee, see Mark Lincoln Chadwin, *The
Hawks of World War II* (Chapel Hill: University of North Carolina
Press, 1968). The generalization on Ickes's relations with leaders of
Fight for Freedom, Inc. is based on research in the Ickes Papers. The
author has also researched the papers of Fight for Freedom, Inc. at
Princeton University. See also Berle, *Navigating the Rapids,* p. 258.

28 R. Douglas Stuart, Jr. to Edward Cooper, January 6, 1941, Cooper to
Stuart, January 21, 1941, L. W. Feader to John L. Wheeler, February
14, 1941, Katrina McCormick to Robert L. Bliss, March 17, 1941,
April 8, 1941, May 19, 1941, Bliss to McCormick, April 11, 1941,
McCormick to Robert La Follette, July 17, 1941, La Follette to
McCormick, July 24, 1941, McCormick to Page Hufty, August 1,
1941, Schnibbe to Arthur A. Brooks, Jr., August 2, 1941, America
First Papers; McCormick to Nye, June 30, 1941, Nye to McCormick,
July 3, 1941, Nye Papers; memo to Early, May 27, 1941, with response
by SE at the bottom, and file memo, June 4, 1941, Official File 4461,
Roosevelt Papers.

29 Transcript of Laws Relating to the Franking Privilege of Members of
Congress, Post Office Department, Washington, D.C; Ramsey S. Black
to Nye, July 24, 1941, Nye Papers; Henry Hoke, *War in The Mails*
(New York, 1941), America First Papers.

30 Telegram Wheeler to Ulric Bell, June 17, 1941, telegram Bell to
Wheeler, June 21, 1941, RMC to Bell, [June 20, 1941], L. M. Birkhead
To Whom It May Concern, June 20, 1941, Fight for Freedom Commit-
tee Papers; Bell to Early, July 10, 1941, and enclosed press release,
Early to Bell, July 11, 1941, Official File 4461, Roosevelt Papers;
Hoke, *War in The Mails,* America First Papers.

31 Stimson diary, July 24, 1941; Henry L. Stimson and McGeorge Bundy,
On Active Service in Peace and War, p. 378; R. B. Lord to Edwin M.
Watson, July 24, 1941, Official File 463-C, Roosevelt Papers.

32 *Congressional Record,* 77th Congress, 1st sess., 1941, 87:6332–44;
Stimson diary, July 28, 29, 1941; Stimson and Bundy, *On Active
Service,* p. 378.

33 *Documents on German Foreign Policy, 1918-1945,* series D, 13:234,
234 n.

34 *Washington Post,* September 25, 1941, p. 1, September 26, 1941,
   pp. 1–2, September 27, 1941, pp. 1, 7, September 28, 1941, pp. 1, 12,
   September 29, 1941, p. 1, September 30, 1941, p. 4, October 9, 1941,
   p. 6, October 11, 1941, p. 4, October 12, 1941, p. 6, October 24, 1941,
   pp. 1, 17, October 25, 1941, p. 4; interview with Mrs. Ruth Sarles
   Benedict, May 28, 1980.
35 *Washington Post,* October 14, 1941, p. 1; *Newsweek,* October 20,
   1941, pp. 21–22; *Time,* March 2, 1942, p. 14; Michael Sayers and
   Albert E. Kahn, *Sabotage! The Secret War against America* (New
   York: Harper & Brothers, 1942), pp. 187–89.
36 *Washington Post,* October 11, 1941, p. 4; Hugh W. Fisher to Stuart,
   March 16, 1941, Stuart to Fisher, March 17, 1941, Sarles to Robert L.
   Bliss, April 27, 1941, Fisher to Clay Pugh, June 19, 1941, Richard A.
   Moore to Hamilton Fish, October 27, 1941, America First Papers;
   interview with Mrs. Ruth Sarles Benedict, May 28, 1980.
37 *Congressional Record,* 77th Congress, 1st sess., 1941, 87:7576–81,
   pt. 8:8207; O. John Rogge, *The Official German Report,* pp. 152–72.
38 Letter Burton K. Wheeler to author, October 20, 1947.
39 Wayne S. Cole, *America First: The Battle against Intervention,*
   1940–41 (Madison: University of Wisconsin Press, 1953), pp. 140,
   248; Chadwin, *Hawks of World War II,* p. 216; Walter Johnson, *The*
   Battle against Isolation (Chicago: University of Chicago Press, 1944),
   p. 153.
40 Will H. Hays to Roosevelt, January 17, 1941, and enclosed mimeographed copies of Wheeler to Hays, January 13, 1941 and Hays to
   Wheeler, January 14, 1941, Roosevelt to Hays, January 22, 1941,
   President's Personal File 1945, Roosevelt Papers; Stuart to James
   Simpson, Jr., February 19, 1941, America First Papers.
41 Wood to Gish, March 31, 1941, confidential memorandum dictated by
   Richard A. Moore, August 28, 1941, pencil note by Stuart on memo
   from F.H.C. to Stuart, September 9, 1941, clipping *Chicago Daily*
   News, September 10, 1941, America First Papers.
42 Nye to Clark, August 1, 1941, Papers Supporting Senate Bills and
   Resolutions, 77th Congress, S. Res. 152, Record Group 46; *Congres-*
   sional Record, 77th Congress, 1st sess., 1941, 87:6565; Gerald P. Nye,
   Our Madness Increases as Our Emergency Shrinks (Washington:
   Government Printing Office, 1941); Gerald P. Nye, "War Propaganda
   —Our Madness Increases as Our Emergency Shrinks," *Vital Speeches*
   of the Day, September 15, 1941, pp. 720–23.
43 Wheeler to D. Worth Clark, August 5, 1941, Flynn to Wheeler, August
   6, 1941, Bennett Champ Clark to A. W. Wells, August 12, 1941,
   Papers Supporting Senate Bills and Resolutions, 77th Congress, S. Res.
   152, Record Group 46; Wood to John L. Wheeler, August 11, 1941,
   America First Papers; Cole, *America First,* pp. 140–41.

44 Memorandum of conversation between Frank Knox and Ulric Bell, August 25, 1941, telegram Stephen Early to Bell, August 27, 1941, mimeographed form letter from Bell, August 29, 1941, and attached statement to Congress, September 8, 1941, Fight for Freedom Committee Papers; Lowell Mellett to Roosevelt, August 27, 1941, Mellett Papers; Chadwin, *Hawks of World War II,* pp. 216-19.

45 Nye to Wiliam Stern, August 29, 1941, copy of statement by Nye before Interstate Commerce Subcommittee, September 9, 1941, Nye Papers; *Congressional Record,* 77th Congress, 1st sess., 1941, 87:7627-30.

46 Clipping *Los Angeles Examiner,* October 3, 1941, America First Papers.

47 Sarles to Hufty, October 3, 1941, America First Papers; Bennett Champ Clark to C. E. Lay, November 22, 1941, D. Worth Clark to Wheeler, December 18, 1941, Papers Supporting Senate Bills and Resolutions, 77th Congress, S. Res. 152, Record Group 46.

48 M. H. M[cIntyre] to Early, November 27, 1937, Early to Roosevelt, November 5, 1938, July 8, 1940, September 26, 1940, Early Papers; Moffat diary, January 26, 1938; Franc C. Page to Colby M. Chester, March 18, 1938, Page to Hull, March 21, 1938, Joseph E. Davies to Hull, March 28, 1938, Hull Papers; Ickes diary, February 6, 1938, Ickes to Bennett L. Williams, November 27, 1940, Ickes Papers; Harold L. Ickes, *The Secret Diary of Harold L. Ickes,* vol. 2, *The Inside Struggle, 1936-1939,* p. 313; Berle, *Navigating the Rapids,* pp. 259, 288, 298-99; Boake Carter to Hiram Johnson, March 17, 1938, Johnson Papers; Berle diary, October 10, 1940.

49 *Des Moines Register,* March 6, 1941, p. 8; Stuart to Page Hufty, March 27, 1941, Stuart to William B. Benton, July 2, 1941, Stuart to Sarles, July 3, 1941, America First Committee Bulletin #516, August 25, 1941, America First Papers; Early to Roosevelt, July 3, 1941, Early Papers; Wheeler, *Yankee from the West,* pp. 421-24.

50 Bertha Tallman to Fred Burdick, August 11, 1941, Sarles, "Story of America First," p. 37/112.

51 Roosevelt to James Lawrence Fly, October 30, 1941, Paul Porter to Hassett, [November 12, 1941], and attached report on network coverage of foreign policy speeches, Official File 3575, Roosevelt Papers. According to the report, from January 1 to October 31, 1941 the national networks carried sixty-three hours and thirty-two minutes of isolationist programs and seventy-two hours and fifty-six minutes of interventionist programs.

52 The generalizations in this paragraph are based on the Roosevelt correspondence with and about newsmen, on research in numerous newspapers and clipping files from all parts of the country, and on research in the papers of various newspaper people and writers,

including the Reid Family Papers, Eric Sevareid Papers, Raymond Clapper Papers, Elmer Davis Papers, and William Allen White Papers. See, particularly, Robert E. Sherwood, *Roosevelt and Hopkins: An Intimate History,* p. 165; Early to Roosevelt, July 23, 1940, Ingersoll to Early, April 1, 1940, Roosevelt to Ingersoll, May 21, 1940, Ingersoll to Roosevelt, May 28, 1940, President's Personal File 6646, L. B. Sherman, Jr., to Roosevelt, September 16, 1941, memorandum Roosevelt to Early, n.d., Early to Sherman, September 20, 1941, President's Personal File 426, Roosevelt to Marshall Field III, November 12, 1941, President's Personal File 7859, Roosevelt Papers.

53 Microfilm of Roosevelt's Press Conferences; Roosevelt to James W. Gerard, July 29, 1939, President's Personal File 897, Krock to Roosevelt, May 1, 1939, Early to Krock, May 8, 1939, memorandum by Roosevelt, May 4, 1942, President's Personal File 675, Roosevelt to Dorothy Thompson, July 8, 1940, November 27, 1944, President's Personal File 6650, Joseph W. Alsop, Jr., to Eleanor Roosevelt, September 29, 1939, Early to Grace Tully, October 5, 1939, Alsop to Early, n.d., Early to Roosevelt, March 25, 1940, telegram Early to Roosevelt, April 23, 1940, Kintner to William Hassett, May 14, 1940, June 6, 1940, President's Personal File 300, Roosevelt Papers.

54 Wheeler, *Yankee from the West,* pp. 32–36; Walter Trohan, *Political Animals: Memoirs of a Sentimental Cynic,* pp. 169–72; Ickes, *Secret Diary of Harold L. Ickes,* 3:659–60; Stimson and Bundy, *On Active Service,* p. 393; General Albert C. Wedemeyer, *Wedemeyer Reports!,* pp. 15–43; Ruth Sarles to R. Douglas Stuart, Jr., December 6, 1941, Ruth Sarles diary, November 28, [1941], Ruth Sarles Benedict Papers; Henry W. Hobson and Ulric Bell to Roosevelt, December 5, 1941, Official File 4461, press release statement by the president, December 5, 1941, President's Secretary's File, War Department 1940–41, 1944 folder, Roosevelt Papers; Francis Biddle notes on cabinet meetings, December 5, 1941, [Biddle] memorandum, December 6, 1941, Francis Biddle Papers.

55 Sherwood, *Roosevelt and Hopkins,* p. 105; Roosevelt to Mellett, August 12, 1940, President's Personal File 4721, letters exchanged between Hadley Cantril and Mrs. Anna M. Rosenberg in 1941 and enclosed public opinion polls, President's Personal File 1820, various items in President's Secretary's File, Princeton Public Opinion Poll, 1941, 1944 folder, Roosevelt to Gallup, October 2, 1942, President's Personal File 4721, Roosevelt Papers; Mellett to Roosevelt, October 20, 1941, and enclosure, Mellett Papers.

56 For examples, see John Franklin Carter to Roosevelt, January 28, 1941, Roosevelt to Carter, February 3, 1941, President's Personal File 5325, Roosevelt to Mrs. Emmons Blaine, February 3, 1941, President's

Personal File 3981, Roosevelt Papers; memorandum, "Division for American Unity," by Harold B. Hoskins, Mellett Papers.

57 Cole, *America First,* pp. 51-60.

58 Vandenberg to Gallup, April 28, 1941, Vandenberg Papers.

59 *Congressional Record,* 77th Congress, 1st sess., 1941, 87:3606, 5865-66.

60 Samuel E. Gill, "American Public Opinion regarding the European War June 28-July 3, 1941" (mimeographed report on the results of the Hutchins committee survey, New York, 1941), Gill to Robert M. Hutchins, July 1, 1941, Stuart to Mrs. Bennett Champ Clark, July 19, 1941, America First Papers.

61 Stuart to Chester Bowles, April 29, 1941, America First Papers.

62 For a well-researched scholarly article on this subject, see Richard W. Steele, "Preparing the Public for War: Efforts to Establish a National Propaganda Agency, 1940-41," *American Historical Review* 85 (October 1970): 1640-53.

63 Ickes, *Secret Diary of Harold L. Ickes,* 2:375; Roosevelt to Mellett, July 1, 1939, Mellett to Roosevelt, October 29, 1940, December 13, 1940, December 20, 1940, March 17, 1941, May 5, 1941, Mellett Papers.

64 Ickes to Rexford G. Tugwell, April 24, 1941, Ickes to Roosevelt, April 28, 1941, Ickes Papers; Stimson diary, April 9, 1941, April 21, 1941, April 22, 1941, May 9, 1941, May 12, 1941, July 3, 1941; Stimson to Roosevelt, May 24, 1941, President's Personal File 1820, Roosevelt Papers; Stimson and Bundy, *On Active Service,* pp. 364-76.

65 Ickes, *Secret Diary of Harold L. Ickes,* 3:368, 395-96; Ickes to Roosevelt, September 11, 1939, President's Secretary's File, Interior Department—Ickes, 1937-1939 folder, Roosevelt Papers; Ickes to Roosevelt, November 28, 1940, Ickes Papers; Stimson diary, November 13, 1940.

66 Roosevelt to Ickes, March 3, 1941, Ickes to Roosevelt, March 6, 1941, Ickes Papers.

67 Ickes to Roosevelt, March 12, 1941, Ickes Papers.

68 Stimson diary, April 17, 1941, and memorandum on cabinet meeting of April 17; Ickes, *Secret Diary of Harold L. Ickes,* 3:483-84; memorandum from ld to Watson, April 19, 1941, Official File 4422, Roosevelt Papers; Ickes to Roosevelt, April 30, 1941, Ickes Papers.

69 Roosevelt to Fiorello H. La Guardia, May 20, 1941, Roosevelt Executive Order Establishing Office of Civilian Defense, May 20, 1941, Official File 4422, La Guardia to Roosevelt, January 31, 1941, Official File 1892, Roosevelt Papers. For a scholarly biography of La Guardia, see Arthur Mann, *La Guardia,* 2 vols. (Philadelphia: J. B. Lippincott, 1959-65).

70 Roosevelt Executive Order Establishing Office of Civilian Defense, May 20, 1941, Official File 4422, Roosevelt to Mellett, May 19, 1941, President's Personal File 2409, Roosevelt Papers.

71 Ickes to Roosevelt, May 22, 1941, Ickes to Pope, June 5, 1941, Ickes Papers; Ickes, *Secret Diary of Harold L. Ickes,* 3:518–19.

72 Pope to Ickes, May 26, 1941, June 2, 1941, Ickes to Pope, June 5, 1941, Ickes to Roosevelt, September 17, 1941, Ickes Papers; press release of address by La Guardia, June 17, 1941, La Guardia to "My dear Colleague," June 27, 1941, Fiorello H. La Guardia Papers; C. D. Jackson to Mellett, memorandum, "Division for American Unity," by Harold B. Hoskins, July 28, 1941, Mellett Papers; John Q. Schisler to Roosevelt, November 13, 1941 and attached undated clipping from *Cincinnati Post,* telegram Andrew T. Thompson to Roosevelt, November 18, 1941, Official File 4422, Roosevelt Papers; clipping from *Chicago Daily News,* November 6, 1941, America First Papers; Sherman Miles to J. Edgar Hoover, December 19, 1941, and attached memorandum on America First Committee from War Department, Military Intelligence Division, G-2, declassified by U.S. Army Intelligence and Security Command, Fort George G. Meade, Maryland.

73 Under the Freedom of Information Act the Federal Bureau of Investigation in 1977, 1978, and 1979 made available to me copies of more than ten thousand FBI documents relating to a dozen leading isolationists and to three isolationist organizations. The Criminal Division of the Department of Justice, Army Intelligence, Naval Investigative Service, and the Department of State also made documents available for my use. The Central Intelligence Agency declined to release any documents presumed to be in their custody for my use.

74 R. B. Hood to J. Edgar Hoover, October 10, 1939, January 11, 1940, James M. Witherow to Hoover, January 31, 1940, February 24, 1940, July 13, 1940, O. John Rogge to Hoover, May 7, 1940, G. A. More to Roosevelt, April 29, 1940, memorandum dated July 8, 1940, J. Edgar Hoover to Matthew F. McGuire, Federal Bureau of Investigation Records; clipping *Washington Post,* July 11, 1940, Nye Papers.

75 J. K. Mumford to D. M. Ladd, August 21, 1942, and attached twenty-four page memorandum on Lindbergh with four-page index, FBI Records.

76 Based on examination of approximately five thousand copies of documents on America First in FBI files and from Military Intelligence Division, G-2.

77 Confidential memorandum Roosevelt to attorney general, May 21, 1940, President's Secretary's File, Justice Department—Robert Jackson folder, Roosevelt Papers; Berle diary, March 22, 1940; Morgenthau presidential diaries, June 25, 1940, p. 593. The entry in the Berle diary at Roosevelt Library is fuller than the one in Berle, *Navigating the Rapids,* p. 297.

78 Hoover to Edward T. Austin, October 17, 1941, Hoover to Robert E. Wood, October 17, 1941, FBI Records. For FBI reports summarizing their information on America First, see those dated January 29, 1941, March 1, 1941, August 29, 1941, and December 4, 1941, FBI Records.

79 T. S. Hammond to W. S. Deveraux, January 17, 1941, Robert L. Bliss to FBI, Chicago, March 13, 1941, Devereaux to Bliss, March 27, 1941, R. G. Danner to Mrs. Erma Russell Tweed, May 22, 1941, Stuart to Wood, June 6, 1941, Stuart to Janet A. Fairbank, June 6, 1941, Hammond to Major J. M. Patterson, November 7, 1941, America First Papers; memorandum of telephone call from Mrs. Bennett Champ Clark to FBI, September 27, 1941, D. M. Ladd to Hoover, September 27, 1941, Edwin S. Webster, Jr. to Hoover, March 28, 1941, FBI Records.

80 Roosevelt to Early, February 21, 1941, Early to Hoover, February 21, 1941 and enclosure, Hoover to K. R. McIntire, February 26, 1941, Hoover to Early, March 1, 1941 and attached eight-page memorandum on America First Committee, Hoover to Edwin Watson, March 19, 1941, Hoover to attorney general, March 19, 1941, and attached memorandum dated March 19, 1941, FBI Records.

81 Letters to Roosevelt urging investigation or prosecution of America First or its leaders are sprinkled all through the FBI Records on America First. See also D. M. Ladd to Hoover, September 27, 1941, R. B. Hood to Hoover, October 3, 1941, Hoover to attorney general, October 8, 1941, FBI Records.

82 Roosevelt to attorney general, November 17, 1941, President's Secretary's File, Justice Department 1938–1944 folder, Roosevelt Papers.

83 D. M. Ladd to Hoover, December 4, 1941, and attached twenty-one-page memorandum Hoover for attorney general, December 4, 1941, FBI Records.

84 Chadwin, *Hawks of World War II,* pp. 138–39, 186–87, 245; H. Montgomery Hyde, *Room 3603: The Story of the British Intelligence Center in New York during World War II* (New York: Farrar, Straus and Co., 1962), pp. 2–5, 26–27, 72–74; A. A. Berle to Sumner Welles, September 27, 1941, Berle diary, Berle Papers.

Chapter 31

1 Among scholarly histories of Japanese-American relations in 1941, see Herbert Feis, *The Road to Pearl Harbor: The Coming of the War between the United States and Japan* (Princeton, N.J.: Princeton University Press, 1950); and Dorothy Borg and Shumpei Okamoto, eds., *Pearl Harbor as History: Japanese-American Relations, 1931–1941* (New York: Columbia University Press, 1973). The best and most detailed scholarly history of the attack on Pearl Harbor is Gordon W.

Prange, *At Dawn We Slept: The Untold Story of Pearl Harbor* (New York: McGraw-Hill Book Co., 1981).

2 Stimson diary, July 19, July 26, September 19, November 29, 1940, February 11, 1941; Morgenthau presidential diaries, August 16, 1940, July 18, 1941; Harold L. Ickes to Roosevelt, October 17, 1940, June 25, 1941, President's Secretary's File, Interior—Ickes folders, Roosevelt Papers; Roosevelt to Eleanor Roosevelt, November 13, 1940, President's Secretary's File, Eleanor Roosevelt folder, Roosevelt Papers; Feis, *Road to Pearl Harbor,* pp. 157–60, 242–52; Jonathan G. Utley, "Upstairs, Downstairs at Foggy Bottom: Oil Exports and Japan, 1940–41," *Prologue* 8 (1976): 26–28.

3 For a scholarly history of the Atlantic conference, see Theodore A. Wilson, *The First Summit: Roosevelt and Churchill at Placentia Bay, 1941* (Boston: Houghton Mifflin, 1969). See also Robert E. Sherwood, *Roosevelt and Hopkins: An Intimate History,* pp. 350–64; Winston S. Churchill, *The Second World War,* vol. 3, *The Grand Alliance,* pp. 419–50; Cordell Hull, *The Memoirs of Cordell Hull,* 2:1017–20; Department of State, *Papers Relating to the Foreign Relations of the United States: Japan, 1931–1941,* 2:556–59.

4 Roosevelt to Sayre, December 31, 1940, Francis B. Sayre Papers.

5 Stuart to Edward Cooper, October 5, 1940, and clippings from *St. Louis Post-Dispatch,* October 15, 27, 1940, America First Papers.

6 *America First Bulletin* (New York), June 21, 1941, p. 2, August 16, 1941, p. 3, America First Papers.

7 Ibid., August 2, 1941, pp. 1–2, America First Papers.

8 Minutes of America First Board of Directors Meeting, Chicago, August 11, 1941, America First Papers.

9 News release statement by General R. E. Wood, August 14, 1941, America First Papers; Sarles to Stuart, August 15, 1941, Benedict Papers.

10 News release from Richard A. Moore, August 19, 1941, America First Papers.

11 *America First Bulletin,* August 23, 1941, p. 2, America First Committee Research Bureau, *Did You Know,* #19, August 23, 1941, #20, August 23, 1941, #21A, September 2, 1941, #21B, September 2, 1941, America First Papers.

12 Capper to F. J. Hall, February 26, 1941, Capper Papers; *Chicago Tribune,* July 27, 1941, p. 3, August 29, 1941, p. 7.

13 Johnson to Hiram W. Johnson, Jr., August 17, 1941, Johnson Papers; Hoover to William R. Castle, September 4, 1941, William R. Castle Papers.

14 News release by New York America First committee of text of Senator Nye speech, "Two Men in a Boat," Breinlinger's Park, the Bronx, delivered August 27, 1941, America First Papers.

15 Feis, *Road to Pearl Harbor,* pp. 215–17, 251–54, 264–87; Department of State, *Foreign Relations: Japan, 1931–1941,* 2:554–743.

16 Stimson diary, October 16, November 7, 1941; La Guardia to Colonel Franklin D'Olier, November 8, 1941, Murray W. Stand to La Guardia, March 4, 1942, La Guardia Papers; Biddle notes on cabinet meeting, November 7, 1941, Biddle Papers.

17 Department of State, *Foreign Relations: Japan, 1931–1941,* 2:753–56.

18 Franklin D. Roosevelt, *F.D.R.: His Personal Letters, 1928–1945,* 2:1245–47; Churchill, *The Grand Alliance,* pp. 595–97; Hull, *Memoirs of Cordell Hull,* 2:1069–82; Stimson diary, November 25, 26, 1941; Stimson to Roosevelt, November 25, 1941, President's Secretary's File, War Department—Henry L. Stimson folder, Roosevelt Papers.

19 Hull, *Memoirs of Cordell Hull,* 2:1081–86; Department of State, *Foreign Relations: Japan, 1931–1941,* 2:764–70; Stimson diary, November 26, 27, 1941.

20 Hull, *Memoirs of Cordell Hull,* 2:1087–88; Stimson diary, November 27, 1941; radiogram Marshall to Short, November 27, 1941, Hull Papers; Roosevelt, *F.D.R.: His Personal Letters,* 2:1247–48; Marshall and Stark to Roosevelt, November 27, 1941, President's Secretary's File, Navy Dept., 1941, 1943 folder, Roosevelt Papers.

21 Stimson diary, November 28, 1941; Morgenthau presidential diaries, December 1, 3, 1941; Department of State, *Foreign Relations: Japan, 1931–1941,* 2:784–86.

22 *New York Times,* November 21, 1941, p. 5; Nye to Millard C. Dorntge, November 22, 1941, Nye Papers.

23 *Washington Post,* December 4, 1941, p. 12; *America First Bulletin,* December 6, 1941, p. 4, America First Papers.

24 Telegram Stuart to Sarles, December 5, 1941, [Stuart] to Robert Harriss, December 5, 1941, Sarles to Stuart, December 6, 1941, America First Papers.

25 *America First News* (Los Angeles), December 5, 1941, *America First Bulletin* (New York), December 6, 1941, pp. 1–2, America First Papers.

26 *America First Bulletin,* December 6, 1941, p. 3, America First Papers.

27 Sherwood, *Roosevelt and Hopkins,* pp. 424–29; Department of State, *Foreign Relations: Japan, 1931–1941,* 2:787–92.

28 Stimson diary, December 7, 1941; Sherwood, *Roosevelt and Hopkins,* pp. 430–31; Hull, *Memoirs of Cordell Hull,* 2:1095–96; Department of State, *Foreign Relations: Japan, 1931–1941,* 2:786–92.

29 Stimson diary, December 7, 1941; Henry L. Stimson and McGeorge Bundy, *On Active Service in Peace and War,* p. 393.

30 The president's appointments Sunday, December 7, 1941, Hopkins Papers.

31 Gordon to Nye, December 1, 2, 1941, Sipe to Nye, December 9, 1941, Nye Papers; news release from Pittsburgh America First Committee,

n.d., America First Papers. The telegram that General Wood had sent to be read at the Pittsburgh rally did not mention Japan or the developments in Asia or the Pacific (telegram Wood to Gordon, December 6, 1941, to be delivered December 7, 1941, at 2:30 P.M., America First Papers).

32 Gordon to Nye, December 9, 1941, undated account of Pittsburgh America First meeting in Nye's handwriting apparently written about December 9 or 10, Nye to Gordon, January 7, 1942, clippings from *Pittsburgh Press* and *Pittsburgh Sun Telegraph,* December 8, 1941, Nye Papers; M. E. Armbruster to Page Hufty, December 11, 1941, and attached undated clipping from *Pittsburgh Press,* America First Papers; interview with Gerald P. Nye, Washington, D.C., July 20, 1959. In a letter from Sipe to Nye, December 9, 1941, however, and a detailed memorandum that the former senator Nye typed on July 3, 1969, late in his life, they contend that they had known nothing of the attack before they went on the stage. Nye based his 1969 memorandum on the Sipe letter and on his recollections at that time as well as the recollections of Mrs. Nye, who was at his side before, during, and after the meeting. In 1969, however, Nye did recall that while Irene Castle McLaughlin was speaking, he was "summoned into the wing off the platform by a reporter and shown a dispatch decling [sic] the White House had announced an attack by the Japanes [sic] upon Pearl Harbor. It concerned me of course, but I was driven to wonder what possible lesser incident might have been the cause for the dispatch. Remembering how, only a few weeks earlier, our American resolve to stay out of the pending war in Europe had been shaken by the news of a German submarine, without provocation, attacking our Destroyer Greer out in the Atlantic, this while we were presumably practicing neutrality, I recalled how it was several days before we learned that the Greer had actually been hunting and chasing the submarine for hours. Naturally I was inclined to discount the seriousness of the Pearl Harbor dispatch I was being shown, and indicated my absence of grave concern in the absence of more information to the reporter, and went back to my chair on the platform. Not until an hour or so later, while I was bringing my address to its conclusion, did I have what was, at once, alarming and confirming report of the seriousness of the hour" (Sipe to Nye, December 9, 1941, Nye "To Whomsoever May be Concerned," July 3, 1969, Nye Papers).

33 Clipping *Pittsburgh Press,* December 8, 1941, Nye Papers; *New York Times,* December 8, 1941, p. 6.

34 Charles A. Lindbergh, *The Wartime Journals of Charles A. Lindbergh,* pp. 560–61; telegram Lindbergh to Stuart, December 8, 1941, Lindbergh Papers; *New York Times,* December 9, 1941, p. 44.

35 President's appointments Sunday, December 7, 1941, Hopkins Papers; Johnson to Theodore Roche, December 9, 1941, Johnson to Hiram W.

Johnson, Jr., December 13, 1941, Johnson Papers; Harold L. Ickes,
*The Secret Diary of Harold L. Ickes, vol. 3, The Lowering Clouds,
1939–1941,* p. 666; Sherwood, *Roosevelt and Hopkins,* pp. 432–33.

36 *Washington Post,* December 8, 1941, p. 1; telegram Kennedy to Roose-
velt, December 7, 1941, President's Personal File 207, Roosevelt
Papers; Hoover to Robert A. Taft, December 8, 1941, Taft Papers;
Hoover to William R. Castle, December 8, 1941, Castle Papers.

37 Vandenberg diary, December 8, 1941, Scrapbook #14, Vandenberg
Papers.

38 Capper to Roosevelt, December 9, 1941, President's Personal File 7332,
Fish to Roosevelt, Decmber 12, 1941, President's Personal File 4744,
Roosevelt Papers.

39 *Chicago Tribune,* December 8, 1941, p. 14; book wire Stuart to all
chapter chairmen, December 8, 1941, teletype message Stuart and
Moore to R. L. Bliss, December 8, 1941, teletype message Stuart to
Flynn, December 8, 1941, Stuart to F. H. Camphausen, December 8,
1941, William S. Foulis to Samuel B. Pettengill, December 8, 1941,
America First Papers.

40 Form letter Stuart "To All Chapter Chairmen," December 8, 1941,
Sarles to Stuart, December 10, 1941, E. R. Essig to Stuart, December
11, 1941, J. W. Blodgett, Jr., to Stuart, December 10, 1941, Isabel
French to Stuart, December 10, 1941, America First Papers. A memo
in the folder on this subject said that seventy-three of the eighty-two
responses from chapters favored adjournment. Only nine voted for
dissolution.

41 Minutes of Special Meeting of America First National Committee,
Chicago, December 11, 1941, E. S. Webster, Jr., to Wood, December
18, 1941, Wood to O. A. Case, December 15, 1941, Wood to E. R.
Essig, December 31, 1941, Stuart to Paul Cotton, December 18, 1941,
minutes of Adjourned Special Meeting of America First National
Committee, Chicago, January 29, 1942, America First Papers; *Chicago
Tribune,* December 12, 1941, p. 16. The final committee statement was
based on a draft submitted by Clay Judson. Because the vote for
dissolution on December 11, 1941, was less than a majority of the total
national committee, the final official vote for dissolution was not made
until January 29, 1942.

42 Stuart to all chapter chairmen, December 11, 16, 1941, Flynn to Wood,
December 22, 1941, J. L. Wheeler to J. L. Fallon, January 7, 1942,
Stuart to J. W. Blodgett, Jr., January 7, 1942, J. R. Boldt, Jr., to
H. C. Schnibbe, December 28, 1941, W. H. Regnery to America First
Committee, January 12, 1942, J. L. Fallon to Robert Vietig, February
3, 1942, and Chapter Dissolution Files, America First Papers; E. J.
Barrett to the author, July 12, 1949; interview with General Robert E.
Wood, Chicago, December 23, 1947.

43 Ickes, *Secret Diary of Harold L. Ickes,* 3:664; Mellett to Roosevelt,

December 8, 1941, Mellett Papers; Department of State, *Foreign Relations: Japan, 1931–1942,* 2:793–95.
44 Vandenberg diary, December 8, 11, 1941, Scrapbook #14, Vandenberg Papers.
45 Ibid., December 11, 1941, Scrapbook #14, Vandenberg Papers.

Chapter 32

1 Private memorandum Roosevelt to Chief of Staff [Marshall], December 7, 1942, Marshall to Arnold, n.d., H. H. Arnold Papers. I am grateful to Dr. Joseph L. Strange for bringing these two items to my attention and for making copies available to me. See also Wood to William J. Donovan, February 20, 1942, Wood to Frank A. Calhoun, April 1, 1942, Robert E. Wood Papers; Wood to Lindbergh, September 26, 1944, Lindbergh Papers; interview with General Robert E. Wood, Chicago, Illinois, December 23, 1947; Forrest C. Pogue, *George C. Marshall: Organizer of Victory* (New York: Viking Press, 1973), p. 120; H. H. Arnold, *Global Mission,* pp. 189, 359; *Who's Who in America, 1948–1949,* p. 2735.
2 F. H. Camphausen to B. K. Leach, January 14, 1942, James L. Fallon to Vera Sessler, Feburary 4, 1942, America First Papers; interview with R. Douglas Stuart, Jr., San Francisco, California, April 6, 1949.
3 Wood to Philip La Follette, December 10, 1942, Wood Papers; *Des Moines Sunday Register,* August 31, 1958, p. 7-G; *Washington Post,* February 18, 1968, p. D10; *Who's Who in America, 1948–1949,* p. 1556.
4 *Who's Who in America, 1948–1949,* p. 1024; Philip La Follette, *Adventure in Politics: The Memoirs of Philip La Follette,* pp. 266–71; *Who's Who in America, 1958–1959,* p. 1687; Henry Cabot Lodge, *The Storm Has Many Eyes: A Personal Narrative,* pp. 57–59; John B. Gordon to undersecretary of war and to undersecretary of navy, December 10, 1941, Arthur A. Brooks, Jr. to James Fallon, January 8, 1942, America First Papers; J. D. Holtzermann to Lindbergh, April 4, 1942, Lindbergh Papers; Roosevelt to Stimson, May 18, 1942, Stimson to Roosevelt, May 21, 1942, President's Secretary's File, War Department—Henry L. Stimson folder, Roosevelt Papers; interview with Harry C. Schnibbe, Denver, Colorado, June 21, 1949.
5 This account of Lindbergh's war record is drawn, in slightly revised form, from my earlier account, Wayne S. Cole, *Charles A. Lindbergh and the Battle against American Intervention in World War II* (New York and London: Harcourt Brace Jovanovich, 1974), pp. 218–28. Charles A. Lindbergh, *The Wartime Journals of Charles A. Lindbergh,* pp. 566–72; Lindbergh to Philip R. Love, January 30, 1942, Lindbergh Papers; Lindbergh to Arnold, December 20, 1941, Arnold, "Memo-

randum of Record,'' December 30, 1941, Arnold Papers. For various letters advising on whether to allow Lindbergh to serve or not, see Lindbergh folders, Arnold Papers, and Official File 92, Roosevelt Papers.

6 Ickes to Roosevelt, December 30, 1941, Roosevelt to Ickes, December 30, 1941, President's Secretary's File, Interior: Harold Ickes, 1941 folder, Roosevelt Papers; Stephen Early to Knox, December 31, 1941 and enclosure, Early Papers; Early to Stimson, December 31, 1941 and enclosure, Stimson Papers.

7 Knox to Roosevelt, January 1, 1942, Roosevelt to Stimson, January 12, 1942, President's Secretary's File, War Department—Henry L. Stimson folder, Roosevelt Papers.

8 Lindbergh, *Wartime Journals,* pp. 573-74.

9 Ibid., pp. 576-80; Stimson diary, January 12, 1942, Stimson to Roosevelt, January 13, 1942, Stimson Papers; Lindbergh to Love, January 30, 1942, Lindbergh Papers.

10 Lindbergh, *Wartime Journals,* p. 581; Stimson diary, January 12, 1942, Stimson to Roosevelt, January 13, 1942, Stimson Papers; Lindbergh to Love, January 30, 1942, Lindbergh Papers.

11 Stimson to Roosevelt, January 13, 1942, Stimson Papers; Lindbergh to Love, January 30, 1942, Lindbergh Papers; Lindbergh, *Wartime Journals,* pp. 581-84.

12 Lindbergh, *Wartime Journals,* pp. 584-600; Lindbergh to Love, January 30, 1942, Lindbergh Papers; Anne Morrow Lindbergh, *War Within and Without: Diaries and Letters of Anne Morrow Lindbergh, 1939-1944,* p. 247.

13 Lindbergh, *Wartime Journals,* pp. 300, 362-65, 375-77, 534, 608, 629. See also Reynold M. Wik, *Henry Ford and Grass-Roots America* (Ann Arbor: University of Michigan Press, 1972).

14 *New York Times,* May 29, 1940, p. 9; Stimson to Roosevelt, March 4, 1942, President's Secretary's File, War Department—Henry L. Stimson folder, Roosevelt Papers; Lindbergh, *Wartime Journals,* pp. 553 n, 732-33.

15 Lindbergh, *Wartime Journals,* pp. 603, 607-10, 621, 675-76, 699, 716-17, 735-36, 750-54; Lindbergh to Amos R. E. Pinchot, December 5, 1942, Russell Gnau to Lindbergh, March 27, 1942, Lindbergh Papers; telephone conversation with General Lindbergh, November 6, 1973.

16 Lindbergh, *Wartime Journals,* pp. 750, 769-924, especially pp. 887-89, 912; interview with General Lindbergh, Darien, Connecticut, June 13, 1972.

17 Lindbergh, *Wartime Journals,* pp. 864-65, 872-76, 911, 916-22; interview with General Lindbergh, Washington, D.C., May 17, 1973; letter Lindbergh to author, March 11, 1974.

18 Lindbergh, *Wartime Journals,* pp. 818, 870-74, 884, 904-13, 916-27.

19 Ibid., pp. 930–98; copy of draft turned over to *Chicago Tribune,* July 25, 1945, Lindbergh Papers; telephone conversations with General Lindbergh, July 4, 1973, and November 6, 1973; interview with General Lindbergh, Washington, D.C., May 17, 1973; *Washington Post,* August 27, 1974, pp. A1, C3; Cole, *Charles A. Lindbergh,* pp. 231–34; Tom D. Crouch, ed., *Charles A. Lindbergh: An American Life* (Washington, D.C.: National Air and Space Museum, Smithsonian Institution, 1977), pp. 45–47, 71–80. See also his posthumous volume, Charles A. Lindbergh, *Autobiography of Values,* pp. 195–236.

20 For a scholarly history of wartime activities leading to the formation of the United Nations at the close of World War II, see Robert A. Divine, *Second Chance: The Triumph of Internationalism in America during World War II* (New York: Atheneum, 1967).

21 Roosevelt to Norris, September 21, 1943, George W. Norris Papers. See also Clark M. Eichelberger, *Organizing for Peace: A Personal History of the Founding of the United Nations,* pp. 236–48. For a statement of FDR's peace views in 1923 or 1924, see [Franklin D. Roosevelt], "A Plan to Preserve World Peace—Offered for 'The American Peace Award,'" n.d. [1923 or 1924], Personal File, Roosevelt Papers. That document is printed in full in Eleanor Roosevelt, *This I Remember,* pp. 353–66.

22 Cordell Hull, *The Memoirs of Cordell Hull,* 2:1626–39; Lowell Mellett to Roosevelt, December 8, 1941, Mellett Papers; Roosevelt to Eichelberger, April 30, 1942, Roosevelt to McIntyre, May 25, 1942, file memo, May 27, 1942, President's Personal File 3833, Roosevelt Papers; Eichelberger, *Organizing for Peace,* pp. 236–48.

23 Hull, *Memoirs of Cordell Hull,* 2:1292–1307; Eichelberger, *Organizing for Peace,* pp. 220–21.

24 Herbert Hoover and Hugh Gibson, *The Problems of Lasting Peace* (Garden City, New York: Doubleday, Doran and Co., 1942); Taft to Hoover, July 14, 1942, Taft Papers.

25 *Congressional Record,* 77th Congress, 2d sess., 1942, 88:A4189–91; ibid., 78th Congress, 1st sess., 1943, 89:A2553–56; Nye to Alexander H. Uhl, January 28, 1943 and enclosed interview, Nye Papers.

26 Norris to William Allen White, April 21, 1942, Norris to Mrs. Mildred Riorden Blake, December 8, 1942, Norris Papers.

27 Vandenberg to Roosevelt, December 15, 1941, Vandenberg to Henry Hazlitt, February 20, 1942, Vandenberg Papers.

28 Arthur H. Vandenberg, *The Private Papers of Senator Vandenberg,* pp. 21–219, especially pp. 69, 75–76, 92, 128, 139–40, 146–55.

29 Ibid., pp. 29–31.

30 Ibid., p. 30; Vandenberg diary, April 21, 1942, Scrapbook #14, Vandenberg Papers; Taft to Hulbert Taft, April 27, 1942, Taft Papers.

31 Vandenberg, *Private Papers,* pp. 37–53; Hull, *Memoirs of Cordell*

Hull, 2:1259-63; Tom Connally, *My Name Is Tom Connally,* pp. 263-64.

32 Mimeographed text of radio addresses by Robert A. Taft and Burton K. Wheeler, Washington, April 7, 1942, Taft Papers; La Follette to Philip F. La Follette, March 23, 1943, April 12, 1943, La Follette Family Papers; *Congressional Record,* 78th Congress, 1st sess., 1943, 89:A2553-56.

33 Vandenberg to Melvin Marcus, April 23, 1943, Vandenberg to Henry K. Dehaan, July 8, 1943, Vandenberg Papers; Vandenberg, *Private Papers,* pp. 53-54; Wendell L. Willkie, *One World.*

34 Telegram Capper to Roger Butterfield, August 23, 1943, Capper Papers.

35 Pettengill to Vandenberg, August 18, 1943, Vandenberg Papers.

36 Robert A. Taft, *American Foreign Policy* (n.p., n.d.), Taft Papers. I am grateful to Professor James T. Patterson for bringing the importance of this address to my attention.

37 Ibid.

38 Vandenberg, *Private Papers,* pp. 55-60; Taft to Arthur Krock, September 16, 1943, Taft Papers; Dewey to Vandenberg, September 16, 1943, Vandenberg to Henry R. Luce, September 24, 1943, Vandenberg Papers.

39 *Congressional Record,* 78th Congress, 1st sess., 1943, 89:7662, 7728-29.

40 Connally, *My Name Is Tom Connally,* pp. 263-64; Vandenberg, *Private Papers,* pp. 61-65; *Congressional Record,* 78th Congress, 1st sess., 1943, 89:9221-22.

41 Telegram La Follette to Vandenberg, October 6, 12, 1943, La Follette Family Papers; *Congressional Record,* 78th Congress, 1st sess., 1943, 89:8666, 9221.

42 *Congressional Record,* 78th Congress, 1st sess., 1943, 89:8886-95, 9082-91, 9095-9103, 9105-6, 9175-83.

43 Ibid., 89:9210-11; telegrams Johnson to La Follette, September 30, 1943, October 13, 1943, La Follette Family Papers; Johnson to Hiram W. Johnson, Jr., October 14, 1943, Johnson Papers.

44 *Congressional Record,* 78th Congress, 1st sess., 1943, 89:9221-22.

45 Brant to Roosevelt, October 27, 1943, Roosevelt to Brant, October 29, 1943, President's Personal File 7859, Roosevelt Papers; Roosevelt, *F.D.R.: His Personal Letters,* 2:1467.

46 Vandenberg, *Private Papers,* pp. 90-125; Hull, *Memoirs of Cordell Hull,* 2:1656-85.

47 Kirk H. Porter and Donald Bruce Johnson, comps., *National Party Platforms, 1840-1956* (Urbana: University of Illinois Press, 1956), p. 403.

48 Ibid., pp. 407-8; Vandenberg, *Private Papers,* pp. 86-89.

49 Vandenberg, *Private Papers,* pp. 111–13, 123–25.
50 Ibid., pp. 139–40, 146–59.
51 Ibid., pp. 165–69.
52 Ibid., pp. 218–19; *Congressional Record,* 79th Congress, 1st sess., 1945, 91:8188–90.

Chapter 33

1 Military Intelligence Division, G-2 Reports, January 3, 17, 31, February 6, 9, 1942, transmitted to J. Edgar Hoover, D. M. Ladd to Hoover, January 29, February 13, 1942, FBI Records; J. P. Warburg to John J. McCloy, January 9, 1942 and attached "Report on Two Meetings of the Nucleus of America First, One of Which Was Attended by Charles Lindbergh," December 19, 1941, memorandum by McCloy, January 12, 1942, Stimson Papers; Rosalie M. Gordon to Lindbergh, January 22, 1942, and clippings from *New York World-Telegram,* January 9, 1942, *PM,* January 9, 1942, *New York Post,* January 9, 1942, Lindbergh Papers; telegram Mrs. Frank R. Fuller to Roosevelt, January 12, 1942, Laura Hayes Fuller to Mrs. Roosevelt, January 12, 1942, Roosevelt to secretary of war and General Arnold, January 20, 1942, John W. Martyn to General Watson, January 26, 1942, Official File 92, Roosevelt Papers.
2 Hoover to Watson, February 13, 1942 and attached 21-page memorandum on America First Committee, February 13, 1942, FBI Records. These items are also in Official File 10-B, Roosevelt Papers.
3 Charles A. Lindbergh, *The Wartime Journals of Charles A. Lindbergh,* pp. 568–69, 597–600.
4 Francies Biddle, *In Brief Authority,* pp. 237–38.
5 Memorandum Hoover to special agents in charge in 57 cities and to top FBI officials, March 16, 1942, telegram Hoover to all SACs, May 11, 1942, FBI Records.
6 This paragraph is based on the dozens of reports to Hoover from FBI special agents in charge in cities all across the United States in 1942 and early 1943 on America First, on Smith's Committee of 1,000,000, on Haase's Americans for Peace, and on other individuals and groups, in FBI Records. See also Biddle to Roosevelt, June 2, 1943, President's Secretary's File, Justice Department—Francis Biddle folder, Roosevelt Papers. The FBI records available to me, however, did not include any final report by Hoover to Roosevelt or to Biddle based on those many SAC FBI reports to Hoover in 1942 and 1943.
7 J. K. Mumford to Mr. Ladd, October 16, 1942, FBI Records; Robert E. Wood to Ruth Benedict, October 1, 1943 and attached undated letter Clay Judson to Wood, Wood to Charles S. Bell, October 15, 1943, Wood to Benedict, December 7, 1943, Benedict to Wood, Decem-

ber 13, 1943, Benedict Papers; interview with Mrs. Ruth Sarles Benedict, Oxford, Maryland, May 28, 1980.

8 *Chicago Tribune,* September 3, 1941, p. 1, November 13, 1941, p. 1, November 14, 1941, p. 2; *Washington Post,* December 5, 1941, pp. 1, 4; Wood to Dies, September 5, 1941, November 13, 1941, Dies to Wood, December 1, 1941, Stuart to Wood, December 3, 1941, Harry J. Pfaltzgraff to Stuart, January 3, 1942, Sarles, "Story of America First," pp. 4/328–5/329, America First Papers; Sarles to Wood, June 25, 1942, Benedict Papers.

9 Thompson to Hoover, July 16, 1941, Louis Nizer to Wendell Berge, December 19, 1941, and attached "Memorandum of Facts, Law and Exhibits Re Senator Burton K. Wheeler" by Nizer, Thompson to Hoover, December 24, 1941, Thompson to Berge, December 24, 1941, FBI Records.

10 Berge to Hoover, January 17, 1942, February 9, 1942, Berge to Biddle, February 9, 1942, Hoover to Berge, February 28, 1942, March 4, 1942, FBI Records; James M. McInerney to Berge, January 31, 1942, Criminal Division, Department of Justice Records, Washington, D.C.; Biddle to Berge and Hoover, December 31, 1941, Berge to Biddle, January 3, 1942, February 9, 1942, Office of Attorney General Records, Washington, D.C.

11 Biddle, *In Brief Authority,* pp. 235–38; Wayne S. Cole, *America First: The Battle against Intervention, 1940–1941* (Madison: University of Wisconsin Press, 1953), pp. 121–25.

12 Biddle, *In Brief Authority,* pp. 238–43; *New York Times,* July 24, 1942, pp. 1, 8, January 5, 1943, pp. 1, 12, December 1, 1944, p. 16; O. John Rogge, *The Official German Report,* pp. 173–218; Henry Hoke, *It's a Secret* (New York: Reynal & Hitchcock, 1946), pp. 47–51.

13 Townsend to Nye, April 6, 1942, Nye to Joseph Y. Reeves, April 11, 1942, Nye Papers.

14 Press release, Indianapolis, Indiana, August 4, 1942, Lindbergh Papers; Lindbergh, *Wartime Journals,* pp. 683–89.

15 Biddle, *In Brief Authority,* pp. 238–40; L. B. Nichols to Tolson, August 17, 1942 and attached clipping from *Washington Times-Herald,* August 17, 1942, FBI Records; *Congressional Record,* 78th Congress, 1st sess., 1943, 89:168–69; Nye to Biddle [June 22, 1944], Nye Papers.

16 *Congressional Record,* 78th Congress, 1st sess., 1943, 89:167–69.

17 Wood to Dennis, January 19, 1943, June 5, 1944, Wood Papers.

18 *Congressional Record,* 78th Congress, 1st sess., 1943, 89:10133–34.

19 Nye to Biddle and attached clipping from *Grand Forks* (N.D.) *Herald,* June 22, 1944, Nye Papers; *New York Times,* July 26, 1944, p. 20.

20 Biddle, *In Brief Authority,* pp. 241–43; *New York Times,* December 1, 1944, p. 16; James Rowe to Biddle, September 25, 1944, Herbert Wechsler memorandum for the attorney general, June 16, 1945, Biddle Papers.

21 Biddle, *In Brief Authority,* pp. 243–48; Post Office Department Information Service Press Release, April 15, 1942, Coughlin to Biddle, April 20, 1942, Biddle notes on cabinet meetings, May 1, 7, 1942, [Biddle] memorandum, May 4, 1942, Biddle Papers.
22 The FBI records include many copies and clippings of such material.
23 Michael Sayers and Albert E. Kahn, *Sabotage! The Secret War against America* (New York: Harper & Brothers, 1942); Henry Hoke, *Black Mail* (New York: Book Service, Inc., 1944); John Roy Carlson, *Under Cover: My Four Years in the Nazi Underworld of America—The Amazing Revelation of How Axis Agents and Our Enemies Within Are Now Plotting to Destroy the United States;* Hoover to Wheeler, November 18, 1943, FBI Records; *Chicago Tribune,* January 15, 1947, pp. 1, 8; *New Yorker,* July 26, 1947, p. 30, August 2, 1947, pp. 35–36; John Roy Carlson, "Inside the America First Movement," *American Mercury,* January 1942, pp. 7–25; John T. Flynn, "The Smear Offensive: A Report" [1944], Wood Papers; mimeographed press release text of Gerald P. Nye broadcast, April 18, 1944, Nye Papers.
24 Wheeler to Hoover, November 16, 1943, FBI Records; F. H. Camphausen to Ruth Sarles, January 12, 1942, R. Douglas Stuart, Jr., to Sarles, January 12, 1942, Regnery to Sarles, May 21, 1942, Sarles to Wood, October 6, 1942, Regnery to Sarles, March 2, 1943, Sarles, "A Story of America First" [1942], Benedict Papers; interview with Mrs. Ruth Sarles Benedict, Oxford, Maryland, May 28, 1980.
25 John T. Flynn, *Country Squire in the White House* (New York: Doubleday, Doran and Co., 1940); Flynn to Wood, April 7, 1944, Wood to Flynn, April 12, 1944, Flynn, "The Smear Offensive: A Report" [1944], Wood Papers; *Washington Times-Herald,* April 23, 1944; *Chicago Tribune,* January 12, 13, 14, 15, 16, 1947; John T. Flynn, *The Truth about Pearl Harbor* (New York: John T. Flynn, 1944); John T. Flynn, *The Final Secret of Pearl Harbor* (New York: John T. Flynn, 1945); William L. Neumann, *The Genesis of Pearl Harbor* (Philadelphia: Pacifist Research Bureau, 1945); Harry Elmer Barnes, *The Struggle against the Historical Blackout* (privately printed, 1947); Wood to Lindbergh, January 21, 1944, Lindbergh to Barnes, November 30, 1944, December 30, 1944, April 7, 1945, Lindbergh Papers.
26 Cole, *America First,* pp. 178–88; interview with Harry C. Schnibbe, Denver, Colorado, June 21, 1949. For a thoughtful letter pointing to some of the variables and issues affecting the elections of 1942, see Robert M. La Follette, Jr., to Philip F. La Follette, November 10, 1942, La Follette Family Papers.
27 *Congressional Directory,* 78th Congress, 1st sess., January 1943, pp. III, 9–174; Homer E. Socolofsky, *Arthur Capper: Publisher, Politician, and Philanthropist* (Lawrence: University of Kansas Press, 1962), pp. 202–5; Sarles to Flynn, May 8, 1942, Benedict Papers.

28 Norris to Charles C. Moore, March 13, 1941, Roosevelt to Norris, July 6, 1942, Norris to Mrs. Charles G. Miller, July 23, 1942, Norris Papers; David K. Niles to Grace Tully, June 26, 1941, mimeographed press release, October 20, 1942, Roosevelt to Norris, October 22, 1942, President's Personal File 880, Roosevelt Papers. For a detailed scholarly account of Norris and the election of 1942, see Richard Lowitt, *George W. Norris: The Triumph of a Progressive, 1933-1944* (Urbana: University of Illinois Press, 1978), pp. 419-33.

29 Norris to Marvin Jones, November 5, 1942, Norris to Larry K. Boehme, April 5, 1944, Norris Papers; Johnson to Hiram W. Johnson, Jr., November 29, 1942, Johnson Papers.

30 James Loeb, Jr., to Norris, December 22, 1942, La Guardia to Norris, December 26, 1942, La Guardia to Dubinsky, January 8, 1943, La Guardia Papers; David E. Lilienthal to Marvin McIntyre, December 22, 1942, Official File 292, Roosevelt to Norris, August 23, 1943, Norris to Hull, September 7, 1943, Norris to Roosevelt, September 7, 1943, telegram Roosevelt to Norris, August 29, 1944, Mrs. Norris to Roosevelt, September 21, 1944, President's Personal File 880, Roosevelt Papers; Roosevelt to Norris, May 8, 1943, July 24, 1943, Norris to Roosevelt, May 14, 1943, Norris to Nathan Robertson, September 23, 1941, Norris to Stephen S. Wise, November 15, 1943, Norris to J. P. Robertson, March 7, 1944, Norris to Sherman Minton, March 15, 1944, Norris Papers; Lowitt, *George W. Norris,* p. 468.

31 Henry A. Wallace, *The Price of Vision: The Diary of Henry A. Wallace, 1942-1946,* p. 129 n.

32 Ibid., pp. 361-71; J. Samuel Walker, *Henry A. Wallace and American Foreign Policy* (Westport, Conn.: Greenwood Press, 1976), pp. 111-13; Biddle, *In Brief Authority,* pp. 355-58; Alben W. Barkley, *That Reminds Me—,* pp. 188-91; Kirk H. Porter and Donald Bruce Johnson, comps., *National Party Platforms, 1840-1956* (Urbana: University of Illinois Press, 1956), pp. 402-4.

33 William Allen White to Warren R. Austin, March 18, 1943, White to Harrison Spangler, April 6, 1943, White to Hoover, June 1, 1943, White Papers; Vandenberg to Thomas W. Lamont, August 4, 1943, Vandenberg Papers; Taft to Hoover, September 23, 1943, John D. M. Hamilton to Hoover, July 26, 1943, Post-Presidential Individual File, Hoover Papers; *Congressional Record,* 78th Congress, 1st sess., 1943, 89:A2553-56.

34 White to Landon, July 15, 1942, White to Hoover, July 17, 1942, White to Capper, March 18, 1943, White to Spangler, April 6, 1943, White to Capper, May 17, 1943, White to Lamont, May 17, 1943, White to Spangler, September 13, 1943, White Papers.

35 Vandenberg to Lamont, August 4, 1943, Vandenberg Papers.

36 White to Hoover, September 13, 1943, Willkie to White, September 19, 1943, White Papers; Landon to Hoover, September 15, 1943, Hoover

to Landon, September 20, 1943, Hoover to Bricker, October 1, 1943, Post-Presidential Individual File, Hoover Papers.

37 Press release text of letter Taft to Bert Long, December 4, 1942, Taft to John A. Tholmer, September 29, 1943, Taft Papers. For a scholarly study of Taft and the election of 1944, see James T. Patterson, *Mr. Republican: A Biography of Robert A. Taft* (Boston: Houghton Mifflin Co., 1972), pp. 268–84.

38 Vandenberg, *Private Papers,* pp. 75–86; Wood to Vandenberg, October 5, 1943, Vandenberg Papers.

39 Wood to Philip La Follette, December 10, 1942, Wood Papers; Wood to Vandenberg, June 24, 1943, November 6, 1943, Vandenberg Papers.

40 Vandenberg, *Private Papers,* pp. 77–78.

41 Vandenberg to Joseph P. Savage, July 2, 1943, Vandenberg to General C. A. Willoughby, August 17, 1943, Vandenberg to Wood, February 11, 1944, Vandenberg Papers.

42 Vandenberg, *Private Papers,* pp. 83–86; Vandenberg to Wood, February 11, 1944, Vandenberg to Savage, February 24, 1944, Wood to Vandenberg, April 7, 13, 1944, Vandenberg to Wood, April 10, 15, May 1, 1944, Vandenberg Papers; Wood to Mrs. Philip F. La Follette, March 22, 1944, Wood to Robert Harriss, April 7, 1944, Wood Papers; Donald Bruce Johnson, *The Republican Party and Wendell Willkie* (Urbana: University of Illinois Press, 1960), pp. 272–80.

43 Vandenberg to Wood, April 10, 1944, Wood to Vandenberg, April 13, 1944, Vandenberg Papers; Wood to Landon, April 10, 1944, Wood to William Benton, May 12, 1944, Wood Papers.

44 Wood to Spangler, April 19, 1944, Taft Papers.

45 Vandenberg to Charles A. Easton, March 8, 1944, May 22, 1944, Vandenberg to Dewey, May 10, 1944, Dulles to Vandenberg, June 12, 1944, Vandenberg to Dulles, June 14, 1944, Vandenberg diary, June 26–29, 1944, Vandenberg Papers; Vandenberg, *Private Papers,* pp. 86–88.

46 Porter and Johnson, comps., *National Party Platforms,* pp. 407–13.

47 Cordell Hull, *The Memoirs of Cordell Hull,* 2:1689–94; Vandenberg, *Private Papers,* pp. 111–13.

48 Breckinridge Long to Hull, October 19, 1944, Breckinridge Long Papers.

49 Franklin D. Roosevelt, *The Public Papers and Addresses of Franklin D. Roosevelt,* 13:345–49.

50 Wilfred E. Binkley, *American Political Parties: Their Natural History,* 2d ed. (New York: Alfred A. Knopf, 1947), pp. 388–95; U.S., Bureau of the Census, *Historical Statistics of the United States: Colonial Times to 1957* (Washington: U.S. Government Printing Office, 1960), pp. 682–86.

51 *Congressional Directory,* 79th Congress, 1st sess., February 1945, pp. III, 9–156. For Taft's campaign and reelection, see Patterson, *Mr. Republican,* pp. 272–83.

52 Franklin D. Roosevelt, *F.D.R.: His Personal Letters, 1928–1945,* 1:402–3; William D. Hassett, *Off the Record with F.D.R., 1942–1945* (New Brunswick, N.J.: Rutgers University Press, 1958), pp. 51, 80, 86–87, 94, 130, 132, 135, 291–92; Jonathan Daniels, *White House Witness, 1942–1945* (Garden City, New York: Doubleday & Co., 1975), p. 45; Fish to Roosevelt, December 23, 1944, Roosevelt to Stimson, December 28, 1944, Stimson to Roosevelt, January 5, 1945, Roosevelt to Fish, January 5, 1945, President's Personal File 4744, Roosevelt Papers.

53 *Congressional Directory,* 79th Congress, 1st sess., February 1945, pp. III, 20, 23, 50, 59, 69, 90, 126, 147–48, 446; *Congressional Directory,* 80th Congress, 1st sess., January 1947, pp. 449–50; George Fort Milton to Ralph Coghlan, August 3, 1944, George Fort Milton Papers; Bennett Champ Clark to Oswald Garrison Villard, November 9, 1944, Villard Papers; Allen Drury, *A Senate Journal, 1943–1945* (New York: McGraw-Hill Book Co., 1963), pp. 129, 284.

54 For a detailed account of Nye's political battles, see Wayne S. Cole, *Senator Gerald P. Nye and American Foreign Relations* (Minneapolis: University of Minnesota Press, 1962), pp. 145–49, 212–16, 219–21. On Langer, see Glenn H. Smith, *Langer of North Dakota: A Study in Isolationism, 1940–1959* (New York: Garland Publishing Inc., 1979), pp. 33–41.

55 Cole, *Senator Gerald P. Nye,* pp. 212–13; clippings *Fargo* (N.D.) *Forum,* January 2, 1944, May 28, 1944, June 17, 1944, *Chicago Sun,* May 18, 1944, *Time,* June 19, 1944, press release text of radio address by Nye, April 18, 1944, Nye Papers; interviews with Gerald P. Nye, Washington, D.C., July 20, 1959, J. C. Goll, Bismarck, North Dakota, March 5, 1960, Math Dahl, Bismarck, North Dakota, March 1, 1960; D. K. N[iles] to Grace Tully, March 9, 1944, Official File 300, Roosevelt Papers; *Congressional Record,* 78th Congress, 2d sess., 1944, 90:A1965.

56 Clippings *Minot* (N.D.) *Daily News,* January 10, 1944, *Fargo* (N.D.) *Forum,* March 19, 1944, *Chicago Tribune,* June 18, 1944, Webster to Nye, November 3, 1943, Nye to Webster, November 8, 29, 1943, Nye to Howard A. Smith, December 18, 1943, Gerald W. Movius to editor of *Grand Forks* (N.D.) *Herald,* January 21, 1944, press release text of radio addresses by Nye, April 18, May 24, 1944, P. L. Foss to Nye, June 27, 1944, Nye Papers; Webster to Lindbergh, October 8, 1943 and attached undated mimeographed form letter from Webster, Lindbergh Papers.

57 Thomas Hall, Secretary of State, *Compilation of Election Returns: National and State, 1930–1944* ([Bismarck, N.D.], 1945); clipping *Fargo* (N.D.) *Forum,* July 2, 1944, Nye Papers.

58 *Which Way North Dakota* (n.p., n.d.), Nye Papers. For Nye's campaign statement on foreign policy, see print of radio address by Nye, October 18, 1944, Nye Papers. This author interviewed and visited with many people in Bismarck, North Dakota in March 1960 who knew Nye or had voted for or against him in 1944.

59 Nye to Villard, September 6, 1944, Villard Papers; Edmund Waterman to James E. Murray, October 10, 1944, Murray to Edwin M. Watson, October 20, 1944, Official File 366-A, Roosevelt Papers; Drury, *Senate Journal,* pp. 265–68; *Congressional Record,* 78th Congress, 2d sess., 1944, 90:7669–76.

60 Clippings *Bismarck* (N.D.) *Tribune,* August 28, 1944, September 5, 1944, *Fargo* (N.D.) *Forum,* September 1, 1944, Loren R. Gajewski to Nye, November 10, 1944, Josephine Efteland to Nye, November 9, 1944, Nye to Milton Young, November 14, 1944, Nye to Fred Aandahl, November 21, 1944, Nye Papers; Hall, *Compilation of Election Returns;* interviews with Gerald P. Nye, Washington, D.C., July 20, 1959, J. C. Goll, Bismarck, North Dakota, March 5, 1960, and Math Dahl, Bismarck, North Dakota, March 1, 1960; Fred G. Aandahl to the author, September 15, 1961; Stambaugh entry in *Who's Who in America, 1958–1959,* p. 2623.

61 *Congressional Record,* 78th Congress, 2d sess., 1944, 90:9683–89; *New York Times,* December 20, 1944, p. 16, December 21, 1944, p. 20; Gerald P. Nye's last public address, University of Maryland, College Park, Maryland, March 29, 1971; interview with Gerald P. Nye, College Park, Maryland, March 29, 1971; clipping *Washington Evening Star,* July 19, 1971; Marguerite Nye to author, December 10, 1971.

62 *Congressional Record,* 79th Congress, 1st sess., 1945, 91:164–67; Vandenberg, *Private Papers,* pp. 126–45.

63 Vandenberg, *Private Papers,* pp. 304–19.

64 Lodge, *Storm Has Many Eyes,* pp. 56–61; Walsh to A. A. D. Rahn, May 14, 1946, Walsh to John J. Hagarty, November 12, 1946, George F. Booth to Walsh, November 26, 1946, David I. Walsh Papers; *Congressional Directory,* 80th Congress, 1st sess., February 1947, p. 50. In his book Lodge covered his prewar noninterventionist position in one brief, apologetic paragraph that emphasized his support for military preparedness.

65 *Congressional Directory,* 80th Congress, 1st sess., February 1947, pp. III, 9, 58, 95; Smith, *Langer of North Dakota,* pp. 39–41, 66–67; *Des Moines Tribune,* November 9, 1959, p. 3, June 27, 1960, p. 18. For a scholarly study of Shipstead's life and public career, see Sister

Mary René Lorentz, "Henrik Shipstead: Minnesota Independent, 1923–1946" (Ph.D. diss., Catholic University of America, 1963).

66 Patrick J. Maney, *"Young Bob" La Follette: A Biography of Robert M. La Follette, Jr., 1895–1953* (Columbia and London: University of Missouri Press, 1978), pp. 287–304, 310–14.

67 Philip La Follette, *Adventure in Politics: The Memoirs of Philip La Follette,* pp. 268–84.

68 Burton K. Wheeler, *Yankee from the West: The Candid, Turbulent Life Story of the Yankee-Born U.S. Senator from Montana,* pp. 400–410; *New York Times,* April 26, 1946, p. 15; Burton K. Wheeler to the author, April 10, 1957; FBI reports, Butte, Montana, November 5, 1945, and June 14, 1946, FBI Records.

69 David George Kin, *The Plot Against America: Senator Wheeler and the Forces behind Him* (Missoula, Mont.: John E. Kennedy, Publishers, 1946), especially pp. 8, 302–5, 341; *New York Times,* February 2, 1947, p. 38; Wheeler to author, April 10, 1957; Wheeler, *Yankee from the West,* pp. 408–13; interview with Burton K. Wheeler, Washington, D.C., October 23, 1969; *Washington Post,* January 8, 1975, p. C6; E. A. Tamm to J. Edgar Hoover, April 12, 1946 and attached item, Tamm to Hoover, May 29, 1946 and attached memorandum on David George Kin, May 22, 1946, FBI Records.

70 *Congressional Directory,* 80th Congress, 1st sess., February 1947, pp. III, 9–174; Socolofsky, *Arthur Capper,* pp. 211–14, 224.

71 For scholarly histories on nationalists and so-called isolationists after World War II, see Justus D. Doenecke, *Not to the Swift: The Old Isolationists in the Cold War Era* (Lewisburg, Pa.: Bucknell University Press, 1979); Joan Lee Bryniarski, "Against the Tide: Senate Opposition to the Intenationalist Foreign Policy of Presidents Franklin D. Roosevelt and Harry S. Truman, 1943–1949" (Ph.D. diss., University of Maryland, 1972); David R. Kepley, "Challenges to Bipartisanship: Senate Republicans and American Foreign Policy, 1948–1952" (Ph.D. diss., University of Maryland, 1979).

72 For some of the many accounts noting similarities and differences between critics of the Vietnam war and noninterventionists before World War II, see Thomas G. Paterson, "Isolationism Revisited," *Nation,* September 1, 1969, pp. 166–69; Selig Adler, "The Ghost of Isolationism," *Foreign Service Journal,* November 1969, pp. 34–37; and Wayne S. Cole, "A Tale of Two Isolationists—Told Three Wars Later," *Society for Historians of American Foreign Relations Newsletter* 5 (March 1974): 2–16.

Selected Bibliography

This book is based largely on research in original primary sources—manuscript, oral, and printed. This selected bibliography lists only the primary sources helpful for this study. Scholarly secondary accounts of special importance have been cited in the notes. They may be supplemented from the following historiographical and bibliographical aids:

Burns, Richard Dean, ed. *Guide to American Foreign Relations since 1700.* Santa Barbara, Calif.: ABC Clio, 1983.

Cole, Wayne S. "American Entry into World War II: A Historiographical Appraisal." *Mississippi Valley Historical Review* 43 (March 1957): 595–617.

Doenecke, Justus D. "Beyond Polemics: An Historiographical Reappraisal of American Entry into World War II." *History Teacher* 12 (February 1979): 217–51.

Doenecke, Justus D. *The Literature of Isolationism: A Guide to Noninterventionist Scholarship, 1930–1972.* Colorado Springs, Colo.: Ralph Myles, Publisher, 1972.

Haines, Gerald K. and Walker, J. Samuel, eds. *American Foreign Relations: A Historiographical Review.* Westport, Conn.: Greenwood Press, 1981.

Stewart, William J., comp. and annot. (with the assistance of Jeanne Schauble). *The Era of Franklin D. Roosevelt: A Selected Bibliography of Periodical, Essay, and Dissertation Literature, 1945–1971.* Hyde Park, N.Y.: Franklin D. Roosevelt Library, 1974.

Manuscript Collections

Ackerman, Carl W., Papers. Library of Congress, Washington, D.C.

Alsop, Joseph W., and Alsop, Stewart J. O., Papers. Library of Congress, Washington, D.C.

America First Committee Papers. Hoover Library on War, Revolution and Peace, Stanford, Calif.

Arnold, Henry H., Papers. Library of Congress, Washington, D.C.

Bailey, Josiah W., Papers. William R. Perkins Library, Duke University, Durham, N.C.

Balderston, John L., Papers. Library of Congress, Washington, D.C.

Barkley, Alben W., Papers. Margaret I. King Library, University of Kentucky, Lexington, Ky.

Benedict, Ruth Sarles, Papers. Oxford, Md.

Berle, Adolf A., Papers and Diary. Franklin D. Roosevelt Library, Hyde Park, N.Y.

Biddle, Francis, Papers. Franklin D. Roosevelt Library, Hyde Park, N.Y.

Bixby, Harold M., Papers. Library of Congress, Washington, D.C.

Borah, William E., Papers. Library of Congress, Washington, D.C.

Breckinridge, Henry, Papers. Library of Congress, Washington, D.C.

British Foreign Office Papers. Public Record Office, London, England.

Burton, Harold H., Papers. Library of Congress, Washington, D.C.

Capper, Arthur, Papers. Kansas State Historical Society, Topeka, Kans.

Carr, Wilbur J., Papers. Library of Congress, Washington, D.C.

Castle, William R. Papers. Herbert Hoover Presidential Library, West Branch, Iowa.

Clapper, Raymond, Papers. Library of Congress, Washington, D.C.

Committee to Defend America Papers. Princeton University Library, Princeton, N.J.

Connally, Tom, Papers. Library of Congress, Washington, D.C.

Couzens, James, Papers. Library of Congress, Washington, D.C.

Creel, George, Papers. Library of Congress, Washington, D.C.

Cutting, Bronson M., Papers. Library of Congress, Washington, D.C.

Davis, Elmer, Papers. Library of Congress, Washington, D.C.

Davis, Norman H., Papers. Library of Congress, Washington, D.C.

Dern, George H., Papers. Library of Congress, Washington, D.C.

Dodd, William E., Papers. Library of Congress, Washington, D.C.

Early, Stephen T., Papers. Franklin D. Roosevelt Library, Hyde Park, N.Y.

Farley, James A., Papers. Library of Congress, Washington, D.C.

Fight for Freedom Committee Papers. Princeton University Library, Princeton, N.J.

Fletcher, Henry P., Papers. Library of Congress, Washington, D.C.

Flynn, John T., Papers. University of Oregon Library, Eugene, Oreg.

Frankfurter, Felix, Papers. Library of Congress, Washington, D.C.

Glass, Carter, Papers. University of Virginia Library, Charlottesville, Va.

Green, Theodore Francis, Papers. Library of Congress, Washington, D.C.

Halifax, Lord, Papers. Public Record Office, London, England.

Holmes, John Haynes, Papers. Library of Congress, Washington, D.C.
Hoover, Herbert, Papers. Herbert Hoover Presidential Library, West
Branch, Iowa.
Hopkins, Harry, Papers. Franklin D. Roosevelt Library, Hyde Park, N.Y.
Hull, Cordell, Papers. Library of Congress, Washington, D.C.
Ickes, Harold L., Papers and Diary. Library of Congress, Washington,
D.C.
Johnson, Hiram, Papers. Bancroft Library, University of California,
Berkeley, Calif.
Knox, Frank, Papers. Library of Congress, Washington, D.C.
La Follette Family Papers. Library of Congress, Washington, D.C.
La Follette, Philip F., Papers. State Historical Society of Wisconsin,
Madison, Wis.
La Guardia, Fiorello H., Papers. Municipal Archives and Records Center,
New York Public Library, New York, N.Y.
Land, Emory Scott, Papers. Library of Congress, Washington, D.C.
Landon, Alf M., Papers. Kansas State Historical Society, Topeka, Kans.
Lewis, James Hamilton, Papers. Library of Congress, Washington, D.C.
Lindbergh, Charles A., Papers. Sterling Memorial Library, Yale
University, New Haven, Conn.
Long, Breckinridge, Papers. Library of Congress, Washington, D.C.
McAdoo, William Gibbs, Papers. Library of Congress, Washington, D.C.
McNary, Charles L., Papers. Library of Congress, Washington, D.C.
MacNider, Hanford, Papers. Herbert Hoover Presidential Library, West
Branch, Iowa.
Marshall, Verne, Papers. Herbert Hoover Presidential Library, West
Branch, Iowa.
Mellett, Lowell, Papers. Franklin D. Roosevelt Library, Hyde Park, N.Y.
Mills, Ogden L., Papers. Library of Congress, Washington, D.C.
Milton, George Fort, Papers. Library of Congress, Washington, D.C.
Moffat, Jay Pierrepont, Papers and Diary. Houghton Library, Harvard
University, Cambridge, Mass.
Moore, R. Walton, Papers. Franklin D. Roosevelt Library, Hyde Park,
N.Y.
Morgenthau, Henry, Jr., Presidential Diaries. Franklin D. Roosevelt
Library, Hyde Park, N.Y.
Norris, George W., Papers. Library of Congress, Washington, D.C.
Nye, Gerald P., Papers. Herbert Hoover Presidential Library, West
Branch, Iowa.
Phillips, William, Papers and Diary. Houghton Library, Harvard
University, Cambridge, Mass.
Pinchot, Amos R. E., Papers. Library of Congress, Washington, D.C.
Pittman, Key, Papers. Library of Congress, Washington, D.C.

Rainey, Henry T., Papers. Library of Congress, Washington, D.C.

Reid Family Papers. Library of Congress, Washington, D.C.

Richberg, Donald R., Papers. Library of Congress, Washington, D.C.

Roosevelt, Franklin D., Papers. Franklin D. Roosevelt Library, Hyde Park, N.Y.

Rosenman, Samuel I., Papers. Franklin D. Roosevelt Library, Hyde Park, N.Y.

Sayre, Francis B., Papers. Library of Congress, Washington, D.C.

Schwellenbach, Lewis, Papers. Library of Congress, Washington, D.C.

Sevareid, Eric, Papers. Library of Congress, Washington, D.C.

Shipstead, Henrik, Papers. Minnesota Historical Society, Saint Paul, Minn.

Shouse, Jouett, Papers. Margaret I. King Library, University of Kentucky, Lexington, Ky.

Smith, Truman, "Air Intelligence Activities: Office of the Military Attache, American Embassy, Berlin, Germany, August 1935—April 1939 with Special Reference to the Services of Colonel Charles A. Lindbergh, Air Corps (Res.)." Sterling Memorial Library, Yale University, New Haven, Conn.

Stimson, Henry L., Papers and Diary. Sterling Memorial Library, Yale University, New Haven, Conn.

Stuart, R. Douglas, Jr., Papers. San Francisco, Calif.

Taft, Robert A., Papers. Library of Congress, Washington, D.C.

Tansill, Charles C., Papers. Herbert Hoover Presidential Library, West Branch, Iowa.

Thomas, Elbert D., Papers. Franklin D. Roosevelt Library, Hyde Park, N.Y.

Trohan, Walter, Papers. Herbert Hoover Presidential Library, West Branch, Iowa.

Tugwell, Rexford G., Papers. Franklin D. Roosevelt Library, Hyde Park, N.Y.

Tydings, Millard E., Papers. Theodore R. McKeldin Library, University of Maryland, College Park, Md.

U.S., Congress, House of Representatives Committee on Foreign Affairs Papers. National Archives, Washington, D.C.

U.S., Congress, House of Representatives Papers Supporting Bills and Resolutions. National Archives, Washington, D.C.

U.S., Congress, Senate Committee on Foreign Relations Papers. National Archives, Washington, D.C.

U.S., Congress, Senate Papers Supporting Bills and Resolutions. National Archives, Washington, D.C.

U.S., Congress, Senate Special Committee Investigating the Munitions Industry Records. National Archives, Washington, D.C.

U.S., Federal Bureau of Investigation Papers. J. Edgar Hoover Building, Washington, D.C.

U.S., Justice, Department of, Papers. Department of Justice, Washington, D.C.

U.S., State, Department of, Records. National Archives, Washington, D.C.

Vandenberg, Arthur H., Papers. Bentley Library, University of Michigan, Ann Arbor, Mich.

Villard, Oswald Garrison, Papers. Houghton Library, Harvard University, Cambridge, Mass.

Wadsworth Family Papers. Library of Congress, Washington, D.C.

Wagner, Robert F., Papers. Georgetown University Library, Washington, D.C.

Wallace, Henry A., Papers. Library of Congress, Washington, D.C.

Wallace, Henry A., Papers and Diary. University of Iowa Libraries, Iowa City, Iowa.

Walsh, David I., Papers. Dinand Library, College of the Holy Cross, Worcester, Mass.

Walsh-Erickson Papers. Library of Congress, Washington, D.C.

White, Wallace H., Papers. Library of Congress, Washington, D.C.

White, William Allen, Papers. Library of Congress, Washington, D.C.

Wilson, Hugh R., Papers. Herbert Hoover Presidential Library, West Branch, Iowa.

Wood, Robert E., Papers. Herbert Hoover Presidential Library, West Branch, Iowa.

Interviews

Bannister, Robert J., Des Moines, Iowa, September 15, 1947.

Benedict, Ruth Sarles, Bethesda, Kensington, and Oxford, Md., several interviews and conversations, 1978–80.

Bie, Christian and Karen, Hyde Park, N.Y., July 25, 1958.

Brundage, Avery, Chicago, Ill., December 18, 1948.

La Follette, Philip F., Madison, Wis., January 16, 1948.

Landon, Alf M., Topeka, Kans., July 27, 29, 1966.

Lindbergh, Charles A., Washington, D.C., Darien, Conn., and New York, N.Y., four personal conversations and twenty-one telephone conversations, 1972–74.

Marshall, Verne, Cedar Rapids, Iowa, December 19, 1948.

Nye, Gerald P., Washington, D.C., and Chevy Chase, Silver Spring, and College Park, Md., many conversations and interviews between 1956 and 1971.

Owen, John S., Washington, D.C., April 7, 1973.
Parkinson, Hugh R., San Francisco, Calif., May 13, 1949.
Schnibbe, Harry C., Denver, Colo., June 21, 1949.
Stuart, R. Douglas, Jr., San Francisco, Calif., April 6, 1949, May 6, 1949, and June 17, 1949.
Van Hyning, Mrs. Lyrl Clark, Chicago, Ill., December 18, 1948.
Wheeler, Burton K., Washington, D.C., October 23, 1969.
Wood, Robert E., Chicago, Ill., December 23, 1947, and August 11, 1949.

Government Documents

GERMANY

Documents on German Foreign Policy, 1918-1945. Series D. 13 vols. Washington: Government Printing Office, 1957-64.

UNITED KINGDOM

Woodward, E. L., and Butler, Rohan, eds. *Documents on British Foreign Policy, 1919-1939.* 3d ser. 10 vols. London: HMSO, 1949-61.

UNITED STATES

Congressional Record, 1926-45.
U.S., Congress, House, Committee on Foreign Affairs. *Hearings before Committee on Foreign Affairs,* 77th Congress, 1st sess., 1941.
U.S., Congress, House, Special Committee on Un-American Activities. *Nazi Activities.* Section 1 of *Report on the Axis Front Movement in the United States,* which is part 7 of Appendix to *Investigation of Un-American Propaganda Activities in the United States,* 78th Congress, 1st sess., 1943.
U.S., Congress, Senate, Committee on Foreign Relations. *Hearings before Committee on Foreign Relations.* 77th Congress, 1st sess., 1941.
U.S., Congress, Senate, Committee on Military Affairs. *Hearings before Committee on Military Affairs,* 77th Congress, 1st sess., 1941.
U.S., Congress, Senate, Special Committee on Investigation of the Munitions Industry. *Hearings before the Special Committee Investigating the Munitions Industry.* 40 parts. 73d Congress, 2d sess., 1934-43.
U.S., Congress, Senate, Special Committee on Investigation of the Munitions Industry. *Munitions Industry.* 7 parts. Senate Report 944, 74th Congress, 1st sess., 1935-36.
U.S., Department of State. *Foreign Relations of the United States, 1931-1945.* Washington: Government Printing Office, 1946-70.

Published Letters, Journals, and Memoirs

Arnold, H. H. *Global Mission.* New York: Harper & Brothers, 1949.

Barkley, Alben W. *That Reminds Me—.* Garden City, N.Y.: Doubleday & Co., 1954.

Baruch, Bernard M. *Baruch: The Public Years.* New York: Holt, Rinehart and Winston, 1960.

Berle, Adolf A. *Navigating the Rapids, 1918–1971: From the Papers of Adolf A. Berle.* Edited by Beatrice Bishop Berle and Travis Beal Jacobs. New York: Harcourt Brace Jovanovich, 1973.

Biddle, Francis. *In Brief Authority.* Garden City, N.Y.: Doubleday & Co., 1962.

Bloom, Sol. *The Autobiography of Sol Bloom.* New York: G. P. Putnam's Sons, 1948.

Bullitt, Orville H., ed. *For the President, Personal and Secret: Correspondence between Franklin D. Roosevelt and William C. Bullitt.* Boston: Houghton Mifflin Co., 1972.

Carlson, John Roy. *Under Cover: My Four Years in the Nazi Underworld of America—The Amazing Revelation of How Axis Agents and Our Enemies Within Are Now Plotting to Destroy the United States.* Cleveland, Ohio, and New York: World Publishing Co., 1943.

Celler, Emanuel. *You Never Leave Brooklyn: The Autobiography of Emanuel Celler.* New York: John Day Co., 1953.

Churchill, Winston S. *The Second World War.* 6 vols. Boston: Houghton Mifflin Co., 1948–53.

Connally, Tom (as told to Alfred Steinberg). *My Name Is Tom Connally.* New York: Thomas Y. Crowell Co., 1954.

Daniels, Jonathan. *White House Witness, 1942–1945.* Garden City, N.Y.: Doubleday & Co., 1975.

Detzer, Dorothy. *Appointment on the Hill.* New York: Henry Holt and Co., 1948.

Drury, Allen. *A Senate Journal, 1943–1945.* New York: McGraw-Hill Book Co., 1963.

Eichelberger, Clark M. *Organizing for Peace: A Personal History of the Founding of the United Nations.* New York: Harper & Row, 1977.

Farley, James A. *Behind the Ballots: The Personal History of a Politician.* New York: Harcourt, Brace and Co., 1938.

––––––. *Jim Farley's Story: The Roosevelt Years.* New York: McGraw-Hill Book Co., 1948.

Feis, Herbert. *1933: Characters in Crisis.* Boston: Little, Brown and Co., 1966.

Fields, Alonzo. *My Twenty-one Years in the White House.* New York: Crest Book, 1960, 1961.

Fish, Hamilton. *FDR, The Other Side of the Coin: How We Were Tricked into World War II*. New York: Vantage Press, 1962.

Freedman, Max, annot. *Roosevelt and Frankfurter: Their Correspondence, 1928-1945*. Boston: Little, Brown and Co., 1967.

Hassett, William D. *Off the Record with F.D.R., 1942-1945*. New Brunswick, N.J.: Rutgers University Press, 1958.

Hoover, Herbert. *The Memoirs of Herbert Hoover: The Great Depression, 1929-1941*. New York: Macmillan Co., 1952.

Hull, Cordell. *The Memoirs of Cordell Hull*. 2 vols. New York: Macmillan Co., 1948.

Ickes, Harold L. *The Secret Diary of Harold L. Ickes*. 3 vols. New York: Simon and Schuster, 1953-54.

Johnson, Hugh. *The Blue Eagle from Egg to Earth*. Garden City, N.Y.: Doubleday & Co., 1935.

Kin, David George. *The Plot Against America: Senator Wheeler and the Forces behind Him*. Missoula, Mont.: John E. Kennedy, Publishers, 1946.

La Follette, Philip. *Adventure in Politics: The Memoirs of Philip La Follette*. Edited by Donald Young. New York: Holt, Rinehart and Winston, 1970.

Libby, Frederick J. *To End War: The Story of the National Council for Prevention of War*. Nyack, N.Y.: Fellowship Publications, 1969.

Lindbergh, Anne Morrow. *Diaries and Letters of Anne Morrow Lindbergh, 1922-1944*. 5 vols. New York: Harcourt Brace Jovanovich, 1972-80.

_____. *Listen! the Wind*. New York: Harcourt, Brace and Co., 1938.

_____. *North to the Orient*. New York: Harcourt, Brace and Co., 1935.

_____. *The Wave of the Future: A Confession of Faith*. New York: Harcourt, Brace and Co., 1940.

Lindbergh, Charles A. *Autobiography of Values*. New York: Harcourt Brace Jovanovich, 1976, 1977, 1978.

_____. *Boyhood on the Upper Mississippi: A Reminiscent Letter*. Saint Paul: Minnesota Historical Society, 1972.

_____. *Of Flight and Life*. New York: Charles Scribner's Sons, 1948.

_____. *The Spirit of St. Louis*. New York: Charles Scribner's Sons, 1953.

_____. *The Wartime Journals of Charles A. Lindbergh*. New York: Harcourt Brace Jovanovich, 1970.

_____. *We*. New York and London: G. P. Putnam's Sons, 1927.

Lodge, Henry Cabot. *The Storm Has Many Eyes: A Personal Narrative*. New York: W. W. Norton & Co., 1973.

Loewenheim, Francis L.; Langley, Harold D.; and Jonas, Manfred, eds. *Roosevelt and Churchill: Their Secret Wartime Correspondence*. New York: E. P. Dutton & Co., 1975.

Long, Breckinridge. *The War Diary of Breckinridge Long.* Edited by Fred L. Israel. Lincoln: University of Nebraska Press, 1966.

Martin, Joe (as told to Robert J. Donovan). *My First Fifty Years in Politics.* New York: McGraw-Hill Book Co., 1960.

Moffat, Jay Pierrepont. *The Moffat Papers: Selections from the Diplomatic Journals of Jay Pierrepont Moffat, 1919–1943.* Edited by Nancy Harrison Hooker. Cambridge, Mass.: Harvard University Press, 1956.

Moley, Raymond. *After Seven Years.* New York: Harper & Brothers, 1939.

Morgenthau, Henry, Jr. *From the Morgenthau Diaries.* 3 vols. By John Morton Blum. Boston: Houghton Mifflin Co., 1959–67.

Nicolson, Harold. *Harold Nicolson: Diaries and Letters, 1930–1939.* Edited by Nigel Nicolson. New York: Atheneum, 1966.

Nixon, Edgar B., ed. *Franklin D. Roosevelt and Foreign Affairs.* 3 vols. Cambridge, Mass.: Harvard University Press, Belknap Press, 1969.

Norris, George W. *Fighting Liberal: The Autobiography of George W. Norris.* New York: Macmillan Co., 1945.

Peek, George N. (with Samuel Crowther). *Why Quit Our Own.* New York: D. Van Nostrand Co., 1936.

Perkins, Frances. *The Roosevelt I Knew.* New York: Viking Press, 1946.

Rogge, O. John. *The Official German Report.* New York: Thomas Yoseloff, 1961.

Roosevelt, Eleanor. *This I Remember.* New York: Harper & Brothers, 1949.

Roosevelt, Franklin D. *F.D.R.: His Personal Letters, 1928–1945.* Edited by Elliott Roosevelt and Joseph P. Lash. 2 vols. New York: Duell, Sloan and Pearce, 1950.

_____. *The Public Papers and Addresses of Franklin D. Roosevelt.* Edited by Samuel I. Rosenman. 13 vols. New York: Random House and Harper & Brothers, 1938–50.

Roosevelt, James, and Shalett, Sidney. *Affectionately, F.D.R.* London: George G. Harrap & Co., 1960.

Rosenman, Samuel I. *Working With Roosevelt.* New York: Harper & Brothers, 1952.

Sherwood, Robert E. *Roosevelt and Hopkins: An Intimate History.* New York: Harper & Brothers, 1948.

Slessor, John. *The Central Blue: Recollections and Reflections.* London: Cassell and Co., 1957.

Stettinius, Edward R., Jr. *The Diaries of Edward R. Stettinius, Jr., 1943–1946.* Edited by Thomas M. Campbell and George C. Herring. New York: New Viewpoints, 1975.

Stimson, Henry L., and Bundy, McGeorge. *On Active Service in Peace and War.* New York: Harper & Brothers, 1947, 1948.

Trohan, Walter. *Political Animals: Memoirs of a Sentimental Cynic.* Garden City, New York: Doubleday & Co., 1975.

Tully, Grace. *F.D.R.: My Boss.* New York: Charles Scribner's Sons, 1949.

Vandenberg, Arthur H. *The Private Papers of Senator Vandenberg.* Edited by Arthur H. Vandenberg, Jr., and Joe Alex Morris. Boston: Houghton Mifflin Co., 1952.

Wallace, Henry A. *The Price of Vision: The Diary of Henry A. Wallace, 1942-1946.* Edited by John Morton Blum. Boston: Houghton Mifflin Co., 1973.

Wedemeyer, Albert C. *Wedemeyer Reports!* New York: Henry Holt and Co., 1958.

Welles, Sumner. *The Time for Decision.* New York: Harper & Brothers, 1944.

Wheeler, Burton K. (with Paul F. Healy). *Yankee from the West: The Candid, Turbulent Life Story of the Yankee-born U.S. Senator from Montana.* Garden City, N.Y.: Doubleday & Co., 1962.

Willkie, Wendell L. *One World.* New York: Simon and Schuster, 1943.

Index

Aandahl, Fred, 550
Acheson, Dean, 61, 373
Agrarian influences, 1, 3–4; decline of, 207, 555–56; and Dewey, 546; and isolationism, 14, 46–47, 128–29, 555–56; and McNary, 392; and munitions investigation, 142, 146–47; and naval preparedness, 266; and neutrality legislation, 185; and Norris, 538–39; and Nye, 143–44, 547, 550; and Peek, 99–100, 105–6; and progressive isolationists, 35–38; and reciprocity bills, 102–10; and Roosevelt, 3–4; and Saint Lawrence Seaway, 135; and trade, 95; and war debts, 82. *See also* Rural America; Small-town America
Agricultural Adjustment Act (AAA), 47–52, 211
Agricultural Adjustment Administration (AAA), 100, 130
Aid-short-of war, 11–12; beginnings of, 297–302; evaluation of, 298–99; and Lindbergh, 419, 466; and Republican platform, 391–92; Roosevelt's policies on, 304–8, 320, 370–74, 409–22, 427, 430, 454–55
Aiken, George D., 467
Air power: and battle of Britain,

10; Bullitt analyses of, 302–3; and European war, 319; isolationist views on, 7; Lindbergh analyses of, 281–82, 285, 416–17, 419; Roosevelt views on, 149, 302, 305–6, 412; and Wheeler's views, 387–88
Alderman, Garland L., 534
Allen, Robert S., 399
Alliances: opposed by isolationists, 7, 24, 118, 199, 271–72, 522, 543, 551
Alsop, Joseph, 442, 479
America First Committee, 12, 481; beginnings of, 379–82; investigations of, 12, 485–87, 530–32, 534; and Japan, 492, 498–99, 502–3; leaders and speakers for, 108, 344–45, 379–81, 390, 468–69, 474; mailing lists of, 470; opposition to, 427–28, 472, 487; after Pearl Harbor, 501–2, 504–5, 530, 537, 548, 648 n. 32; policies and actions of, 261, 381, 403–4, 410, 414–21, 425–26, 431–32, 434–39, 442, 445–46, 448–52, 475–76, 480–81, 538; and radio broadcasts, 477
American Committee for Non-Participation in Japanese Aggression, 348–49, 353
American Labor Party, 419

D